The Psychoanalytic Study
of the Child

VOLUME XXIII

The Psychoanalytic Study

of the Child

VOLUME XXIII

INTERNATIONAL UNIVERSITIES PRESS, INC.
New York   New York

CONTENTS

I

Problems of Psychopathology and Therapy

II

Contributions to Psychoanalytic Theory

III

Aspects of Normal and Pathological Development

IV

Clinical Contributions

V

Psychoanalysis and Jurisprudence

WILLIE HOFFER, M.D., PH.D.

Since Willie Hoffer's untimely death in 1967, appreciations of him as a person and of his work have been expressed on several occasions and are finding their way into print in our journals. What is described most frequently are his positive therapeutic approach to his analytic patients, his untiring efficiency as editor of the *International Journal*, his objective and conciliatory attitude to his colleagues, and his never-failing readiness to help, support and serve his friends. What is left for this Annual to emphasize, in addition to these traits, is the unique role he played in laying the foundations for a sound and well-planned approach to and study of children of all ages.

Willie Hoffer had an early initiation into the study of children in 1919 in Vienna. As friend and follower of Siegfried Bernfeld, he became his helpmate in a first experiment to apply psychoanalytic principles to education, i.e., to establish and run Kinderheim Baumgarten, a residential home for orphaned Jewish children and adolescents who were running wild as victims of the First World War. The disheartening experiences with this difficult venture, which turned Bernfeld into a skeptic, left Hoffer with intriguing problems and queries, many of which came nearer to be answered when August Aichhorn and his work with the "wayward youth" of the times entered the orbit of the Vienna Psycho-Analytical Society. From then onward, in many fascinating discussions, Hoffer maintained a position between Bernfeld's speculatively, highly theoretical attitude and Aichhorn's more down-to-earth, practical and positive approach to psychoanalytic education.

In the '20s and '30s, our group of Vienna child analysts made its

7

first tentative gestures toward influencing the educational system
of the City—attempts, though, which were confined to occasional
lecturing to diverse audiences of teachers. It is very much to Hoffer's
credit that he assessed such activities as inadequate and, therefore,
futile. In his judgment, effective psychoanalytic training for all those
who dealt with children had to be planned as carefully as the training of analytic candidates was already planned in the courses of the
official psychoanalytic Institutes. True, the paedagogues' need for
basic knowledge was somewhat different, normal psychoanalytic child
psychology taking precedence over psychopathology. Equally true,
a personal analysis, desirable as it may be for educators, is by no
means as indispensable for them as it is for the future analyst. What
Hoffer considered as essential, however, was the setting up of a systematic study plan devised for carefully selected students whose
stable attendance was assured for a number of years. Integrated in-
struction was accompanied by seminars in which the teachers' case
material was discussed, a procedure that enabled the lecturers to
supervise carefully the practical application of every bit of theoretical knowledge. Willie Hoffer thus became the creator of the Vienna
Psychoanalytic Training Course for Educators. Graduates of this
course are spread all over the Western world, several of them holding positions of considerable influence.

It was a logical further step for Hoffer soon afterward to assume
the editorship of the *Zeitschift für psychoanalytische Pädagogik*. Under his direction this journal offered to child analysts, analytically
trained teachers and nursery school teachers a welcome opportunity
to describe their problems and to publish their findings.

When during the Second World War the Hampstead Nurseries
came into being in London, Hoffer found himself once more drawn
into the problems and intricacies of child development. What he
found there was a new version of the Kinderheim Baumgarten of
his remote past, this time offering material from the first weeks and
months of life onward, in a wide range from strict normality to the
severest pathology. Fortunately for him, this time he could indulge
freely in observing, filming, and discussing the phenomena, with no
administrative worries attached to the task as they had been previously. Some of his most important concepts on early child develop-

ment, such as the "hand-mouth coordination" and the "silent trauma," can be traced back to this experience.[1]

Willie Hoffer belongs to a small, select group of analysts for whom the reconstructive data gained in the analyses of adults blend harmoniously with the observational data gained in the direct contact with young children—a useful combination which adds up to a true psychoanalytic study of the child.

ANNA FREUD

APPENDIX

1922

Ein Knabenbund in einer Schulgemeinde. In: *Vom Gemeinschaftsleben der Jugend,* ed. S. Bernfeld. Leipzig: Internationaler Psychoanalytischer Verlag, pp. 76-144.

1924

Phantasiespiele der Kinder und ihre Beziehung zur dichterischen Produktivität. Vienna: Internationaler Psychoanalytischer Verlag.

1926

Über die männliche Latenz und ihre spezifische Erkrankung. *Int. Z. Psa.,* 12:391-399.

1931

Der Onaniekampf im Tagebuch des Jugendlichen. *Z. psa. Päd.,* 5:35-38.

Kind und Märchen. *Z. psa. Päd.,* 5:107-111.

1932

Das Archaische im Spiel. *Z. psa. Päd.,* 6:230-238.

Der ärztliche Berater. *Z. psa. Päd.,* 6:496-504.

1935

Einleitung einer Kinderanalyse. *Z. psa. Päd.,* 9:271-292.

[1] For a list of Hoffer's most important publications on child development, see the Appendix.

1940

Analyse einer postencephalitischen Geistesstörung. *Int. Z. Psa.,* 25:264-286.

1945

Psychoanalytic Education. *This Annual,* 1:293-307.

1946

Diaries of Adolescent Schizophrenics (Hebephrenics). *This Annual,* 2:293-312.

1949

Mouth, Hand and Ego-Integration. *This Annual,* 3/4:49-56.
Deceiving the Deceiver. In: *Searchlights on Delinquency,* ed. K. R.
   Eissler. New York: International Universities Press, pp. 150-155.

1950

Development of the Body Ego. *This Annual,* 5:18-24.
Oral Aggressiveness and Ego Development. *Int. J. Psa.,* 31:156-160.
Three Psychological Criteria for the Termination of Treatment.
   Int. J. Psa., 31:194-195.

1952

The Mutual Influences in the Development of Ego and Id: Earliest
   Stages. *This Annual,* 7:31-41.

1954

Defensive Process and Defensive Organization: Their Place in
   Psycho-Analytic Technique. *Int. J. Psa.,* 35:194-198.

1955

Psychoanalysis: Practical and Research Aspects. Baltimore: Williams
   & Wilkins.

1956

Transference and Transference Neurosis. *Int. J. Psa.,* 37:377-379.

1965

Siegfried Bernfeld and "Jerubbaal." *Year Book X of the Leo Baeck Institute* (London), pp. 150-167.

1967

Bemerkungen zur Abwehrlehre. In: *Hoofdstukken uit de hedendaagse psychoanalyse,* ed. P. J. van der Leeuw, E. C. M. Frijling-Schreuder, & P. C. Kuiper. Arnhem: van Loghum Slaterus, pp. 20-30. [English: Notes on the Theory of Defense. *This Annual,* 23:178-188, 1968.]

I

PROBLEMS OF PSYCHOPATHOLOGY
AND THERAPY

THE PHALLIC WOMAN
The Ubiquitous Fantasy in Perversions

ROBERT C. BAK, M.D. (New York)

In his Freud Anniversary Lecture (1966), the late W. Hoffer made the cogent observation that the acquisition of new knowledge, or the development of new points of view, usually occurs at the cost of losing some ground previously gained. Agreeing with Hoffer, I believe that some of our basic assumptions in clinical psychoanalysis have been relegated to the background as we have focused either on advances in theory or on new areas of research. I am referring here to the integration of the theory of aggression, to the studies of ego functions and maturation, to the researches in child development, separation and individuation, primary identifications and early trauma—briefly, to all the advances in our knowledge that emphasize the first two years of life, the preoedipal period, and the prephallic phase of development.

The work of Hartmann (1964) and his collaborators (1949) on the maturational sequences of autonomous ego functions and the development of their more or less independent functioning from the drives has enriched our view of regression, as did Greenacre's description of the faulty integration of perceptual ego apparatuses with libidinal phases (1952, 1953).

Observations of the overexcitation of the aggressive drive in infancy and its deleterious influence on all libidinal phases called attention to aggressive conflicts and the defenses used against them, e.g., the substitution of sexual, i.e., perverse, solutions via regression to safeguard the object (Bak, 1956).

The emphasis on the role of pregenital factors, especially orality (Gillespie, 1940, 1952), and our increased understanding of separation-individuation processes (Mahler, 1963) may all have contributed to a shift of emphasis and to a lesser appreciation of the central

15

significance of the castration complex and the phallic phase. I believe
this was a rather general trend, which was also clearly reflected in
my earlier papers on this subject (1953, 1965).

The clarifications in these areas were also invaluable for our understanding of sexual pathology because they contributed to our insight into the disturbances that influence the phallic phase and enhance the intensity of the castration anxiety. Further, they pointed to
the avenues of regression and the modes of defenses preordained by
early identifications. I believe, though, that no precursors of the
castration complex can diminish the importance of the phallic phase.
In Freud's words, *"the significance of the castration complex can only
be rightly appreciated if its origin in the phase of phallic primacy is
also taken into account"* (1923b, p. 144).

In attempting to integrate the interplay of castration anxiety, the
aggressive conflict, and the early identifications in the dynamics of
perversions, I stated at the Geneva Congress in 1955: "Common to
all perversions is the dramatized denial of castration," and: "Perverse symptoms are regressive adaptations of the ego to secure gratification without destroying the object and endangering the self which
is identified with the object" (Bak, 1956). I now add, more specifically, that in all perversions the dramatized or ritualized denial of
castration is acted out through the regressive revival of the fantasy
of the maternal or female phallus. This primal fantasy constitutes the
psychological core of the bisexual identification. In relation to the
castration complex, Freud repeatedly emphasized the universality
of this fantasy in the male, which is abandoned only reluctantly in
the course of normal development. I believe that this fantasy becomes reinvested and is ubiquitous in perversions in the male and
that it probably plays a similar, though not identical, role in the
sexual pathology of the female. The central *defensive* position consists in the regressive alterations that this fantasy undergoes in the
various developmental phases, as well as the search for, and the symbolic materialization of, the female phallus. Perversions are acted out
in various, more or less dominant forms, through identification with
the phallic mother, with objects that can be fantasied, or, following a
narcissistic split, through projection.

If one considers the main defensive position in the perversions to be the reinvestment of the fantasy of the phallic woman, fetishism is the basic perversion. Indeed, quite recently Hornstra (1967) described the penis as the principal fetish of homosexuals. But fetishism, whether it exists "as a mere hint" (Freud, 1940a, p. 203) or in its fully developed form in which the use of an inanimate object is an absolute condition for gratification, is germane to the phallic phase. Although multiple perversions are more frequent than isolated ones (Kraepelin; quoted by Greenacre, 1955), fetishism or fetishistic aspects appear both in association with other perverse tendencies or as isolated phenomena. Multiple fixations may account for the variety of perverse manifestations. Sachs (1923) and Glover (1923) point to layers of perverse symptoms, and while in many cases there is a multiplicity, there are others in which one form may be dominant and exclusive. Homosexuality becomes overt, even if only sporadically. Greenacre (1955) believes that the various perverse forms are probably a consequence of early traumatizations that precede the traumata in the phallic phase and result in an "enormous stimulation of aggression . . . [which] tends to make for some confluence of discharge routes, or at least the ready availability of alternate routes" (p. 189). The extent to which early traumata can be implicated in the causation and development of perversions will be discussed below.

CASE REPORTS

In what follows, while drawing on my entire case material, I shall present only some clinical vignettes and two cases in somewhat greater detail.

A relevant example is the case of fetishism to which Freud referred in "Splitting of the Ego in the Process of Defence" (1940b). As a small boy, under the impact of the castration threat, the patient developed a masturbation fantasy in which he was a gingerbread man being pursued and eaten by an oriental potentate. He later developed a fetish involving the female body, which substituted for the missing female phallus. In this case, severe gastrointestinal disorders in the first year of life may have contributed to the orality accounting for the regressive emergence of the gingerbread man fantasy, as well as to the anality that led to passive solutions. The overstimulation through the life-endangering gastrointestinal disorder left behind the oral and anal fixation points, increased aggression, and the primary identification; in addition, all three factors may have acted synergistically toward intensifying genital excitement and masturbation and thus provoked traumatization from the outside world. Until late in life, the patient's object choice was dominated by the need to find the uninjured phallic female, in terms of Fenichel's "girl-penis" equation (1936), and his potency was supported by sadistic fantasies. Further analysis enabled him to make a felicitous object choice and mature adaptation.

Case 1

Another case illustrates how multiple fixations contribute to the regressive solution of oedipal guilt. This patient was a self-flagellant from eight to nine years of age. As a young man he developed a masochistic type of homosexuality. This pattern was changed to heterosexual practices with the addition of patent-leather boot and belt fetishism—he was being beaten by women possessing these characteristics. His moral masochism found expression in his need to be cheated and exploited by business associates.

This patient's history combined several significant factors. He was subjected to painful experiences as a consequence of a birth injury that required orthopedic procedures. He had a twin sister who was healthier, stronger, and much more active. Her presence led to early sexual overstimulation, which set the stage for masochistic solutions, heightened bisexuality conflicts, increased feminine identifications, and intensified castration anxiety. He reached the phallic phase, probably quite early, as testified to by the fetishes and the perverse rituals which he used in an attempt to integrate several developmental fixations. The outbreaks of perverse activities were triggered by the severe oedipal guilt that resulted from a long series of futile rebellions and the wish to surpass an outstanding father. The overwhelming guilt remained unsatisfied by the constant failure of these attempts, the patient seeking additional punishment through the routes of preoedipal fixations.

In both cases, the defense was organized around the phallic phase and varied representations of the phallic woman.

Case 2

The conviction of the existence of a female phallus can be sustained well into adult years.

A young man in his middle twenties came for treatment because he was afraid to end his four-year engagement and to marry. He felt insecure about his capacity to perform the sexual act. Until that time he had had intercourse a few times: in *darkness,* or furtively without being undressed. As an adult he had not been confronted with the nude female body.

The patient's main erotic interest was focused on the female breasts. His conditions for sexual arousal were: *big breasts, sticking out, nipples pointed upward.* The flattening of the breasts in the supine position already aroused his anxiety. He also had a preference for women with heavy piano legs. Other fetishistic interests included brassieres, lace panties, and corsets. One of the most highly charged erotic impulses was the wish to grab the breast with force and plop it *out from behind the brassiere.* The same mechanism can be surmised behind his exhibitionistic impulse to press his erect penis against passengers in the subway. "Even though nothing is seen— there is the acknowledgment." Without denying the vagina, he maintained the belief that women also have penises, somewhat smaller, shorter, and thinner. Later, when during the treatment he experimented with intercourse and looked at the female organs, he returned with the report that *he did actually see* the woman's penis and the therapist was mistaken in contradicting him. Subsequently he bought a flashlight to examine the female organs. Repeated evidence of the absence of the penis in women slowly demolished his *conscious* conviction.

His masturbation practices centered on his nipples, which were highly sensitive and which he scratched with nail files, sometimes to bleeding. The smell of his mother's clothes excited him, and he went through an intense transvestite phase that passed. He keenly remembered being deprived of physical closeness to his mother because of her illness and many scenes in which he was curious about her body and breasts; he frequently saw her in bed, but from a respectable distance, and was often admonished not to come too close to her lest she be disturbed. These exposures, coupled with the prohibition against touching, stimulated prehensile vision (Greenacre, 1953) and led to strong scoptophilia. He watched his two sisters in the bathroom through the keyhole and later, in puberty, he watched them undress in a bathhouse. His conclusion was that the hair covered up the penis; it was to be found behind the pubic hair. A series of anal-exhibitionistic dreams, of being seated on the toilet in public, indicated earlier scenes of discovery.

The patient's parents both suffered from heart conditions and had nightly attacks of cardiac asthma. In the child's mind, the heavy breathing of the mother and the doctor's visits at night became confused with the primal scene and led to sadistic fantasies of intercourse. These constituted the core of his childhood neurosis: pavor nocturnus and nightmares. Furthermore, from early childhood on, beginning at the age of four or five years, the patient suffered from inflammation of the middle ear, frequently required punctures of the ear drum, and often experienced intense pain. This became one of the important sources of castration anxiety and a factor that contributed to his feminine identification in which he confused his illness with his mother's.

The patient's personality was characterized by "niceness," and his overt behavior seemed devoid of aggressiveness. In his development the turn to passivity followed the hostile oedipal rivalry and the fantasies of yanking his father's penis off or crushing it. These, together with the later death wishes, constituted the basis of his severe unconscious feeling of guilt and his fear of retaliation.

As a result of the treatment he prospered, married, and for the next twelve years of marriage maintained his genital potency. An exacerbation of his symptomatology occurred when his wife had a unilateral mastectomy. Thus it seems that his potency was largely predicated on the breast-penis equation.

The patient seemed to have escaped overt homosexuality, but strong passive homosexual attitudes to impressive father figures persisted. The fetishistic and transvestite phases clearly demonstrate the revival and impersonation of the phallic woman, predominantly the mother and the sisters. The role of separation and castration anxiety in this symptomatology has been amply discussed (Fenichel, 1945; Bak, 1953; Greenacre, 1953).

There is an inherent and obvious link between fetishism and

homosexuality, on the one hand, and voyeurism and exhibitionism, on the other. Active and passive aims alternate according to the reality situations, which influence the potential for and the actual content of identifications. They can also be condensed or delegated to the sexual partner. The narcissistic split and the ego syntonicity of one or the other aim have been discussed in "Aggression and Perversion" (Bak, 1956). The male exhibitionist is identified with the mother's "uncertain" sexual identity—"penis or no penis"—and the viewer's shock induced by the sudden sight of the penis represents a reversal in that the originally traumatic perception of not seeing the penis is undone.

In this case, the fantasy was acted out in a more subtle form, namely, the phallus, though remaining *hidden*, was recognized by a woman.

Case 3

An exhibitionist sought treatment only after a mild coronary followed by an anxiety state. He had lived a rather retiring life in order to defend himself against acting out, though he had had some rather close calls with the law. The "uncertainty" of the genital image played an important role in the patient's impulse to touch the genitals of little children, male or female, and to ask, "What have you got there?" The perversion to exhibit had a counterpart in his strong homosexual impulses to be masturbated by an older man. These impulses also appeared in projection and represented the core of the paranoid substructure (see Glover, 1923).

Case 4

Another patient, an obsessional neurotic, was not at all disturbed by his lack of genital potency. It was well rationalized as a measure to prevent further pregnancies in his wife. He felt an intense aversion to the female organ and had abstained from sexual intercourse for the last six years. Instead, they engaged in various oral activities in the course of which they told obscene stories to each other; the really gratifying masturbation fantasies were restricted to images of phalluses. He had a preference for fancy underpants (polka dots and stripes in various colors), and several times in his life he had exhibited in company. The penis had to be limp, not erect. The voyeuristic impulses manifested themselves mainly in the wish to watch others in intercourse, and particularly in the desire to follow a woman into the bathroom and put his hand under her genitals. He practiced this with his wife and occasionally he acted it out with strangers by suddenly entering bathrooms that were not locked. In his childhood the male members of his family had been free about their excretory functions, while his mother had carefully locked the door. The identification with the phallic mother in exhibitionism and the search for the female phallus in voyeurism are commonplace.

A transvestite patient (see case 5 below) denied ever having had the idea of a maternal phallus since he was so many times exposed to the "big black patch" of his mother's pubic hair. Yet, when he noticed his receding hairline and became worried about it, he "dreamed of having long black silky hair like my mother." He remembered his mother combing her long hair and tightening it into a sleek flat hairdo with a "bun" or "rat" at the back of the head. He was particularly fascinated by changes in which the long locks of hair could be hidden and disappear and then be let out again from behind the bun.

The element of "being hidden but there" is an important constituent of the origin and vicissitudes of the primary fantasy.

Theoretical Implications

Freud assumed that the male child takes the maternal phallus for granted. He frequently referred to this belief and described the various thought constructs which the child erects when he is confronted with the painful perception of the lack of the penis. According to Freud (1927), it is precisely this perception that furnishes the dynamic power to the castration anxiety.

Imre Hermann (1949) questions the validity of this assumption and maintains that the little boy fabricates, quasi confabulates, the mother's penis in a way similar to eidetic phenomena. He assumes that the child lying in bed with his mother also notices the differences in smell, in the bulk of the lower parts of the body, and *has* the knowledge that the mother lacks the penis. Hermann supports his argument by stressing that the child has access to animal observations, especially urination, and he quotes the relevant material from Little Hans, especially the *"bigness* of the mother's widdler" (Freud, 1909).

Contrary to this argument, however, one is impressed by the fact that in most male domestic animals, especially dogs and horses, the penis is hidden. The genitals can be thrust forward and come into sight, but they also disappear by retraction. The observation of differences in urination (just as in the case of Little Hans) easily remains inconclusive, particularly if one keeps in mind that there are different ways of urination and that the child himself can urinate in both sitting and standing positions. The road of regression to anality is paved by earlier observations of female members on the toilet and by smelling their fecal odors, experiences that reinforce fantasies of identity by means of respiratory identification.

According to Hermann (1949), the fabrication, the quasi-self-deception, is derived from the gigantic image of the mother's genital. (This aspect was present in both cases described in my paper on fetishism [1953] as well as in case 2.) Hermann maintains that this gigantic image of the mother's genital accounts for the fetishistic predilection for oversized legs and hips as well as for the origin and function of obscenity by means of which the "gross," "thick," and "crude" words reawaken the illusion and safety of the phallic mother. The rather widespread use of obscenities in connection with the sexual act is a further indication of the universality and the survival of the primal fantasy.

The assumption that this universal primal fantasy is reinvested at puberty is made very plausible by the frequency of such early adolescent practices as hiding the penis between the thighs and the attempts at autofellatio. Moreover, there are cases in which a perversion, such as tranvestism or the choice of transvestite sexual objects, becomes overt in middle age; such cases again confirm that the fantasy had lain dormant in the id and became reinvested under the impact of fresh traumata, which invariably constituted a severe castration threat. The survival of the primal fantasy can also be recognized in the various forepleasure activities which not only gratify pregenital zonal pleasures but in which the primal fantasy fleetingly re-emerges and is relived in the sexual act. In the course of normal development, the *value* of the missing maternal phallus is displaced onto other parts of the female body, especially the breasts, nates, and legs.

Eissler (1958) recently pointed out that the fetishist does not deny the lack of a penis in women but considers it a reversible state. We know that Freud (1940b) assumed that fetishists maintain two contradictory sets of ideas which lead to a "splitting of the ego." I have abandoned this concept in regard to both normal development and pathology. I believe that Freud, Hermann, and several other investigators overrated the child's actual knowledge of women having no penis. It seems more accurate to assume that due to the equivocal perceptions and the lack of intimate knowledge of the female genital, the child's ego suspends the decision about the presence or absence of the penis and leaves it "uncertain," defensively mistrusting his own perception, neither denying nor accepting it. The ego, rather than incurring a split, attempts a tentative synthesis by upholding an "uncertainty" as a "maybe." This "uncertainty" concerning the genital area frequently plays a role in perverse fantasies, as it did in the first patient (described in my paper on fetishism [1953]) who, with his lower part obscured, danced in front of his father.

In Freud's case of fetishism to which I referred earlier, the fantasies depicted one strong aggressive woman tormenting another gentle girl and forcing her to have intercourse. It is emphasized that in the fantasy it remains "uncertain" which of the women possesses the penis. I found supporting evidence in a late note of Freud's dated June 16 [1938]: "It is interesting that in connection with early experiences, as contrasted with later experiences, all the various reactions to them survive, of course including contradictory ones. *Instead of a decision, which would have been the outcome later.* Explanation: weakness of the power of synthesis, retention of the characteristic of the primary processes" (Freud, 1941, p. 299).

I would like to think that Freud would not have objected to my proposition of "uncertainty" instead of a "split in the ego." My own clinical material confirms the presence of such fantasies in fetishists, but I consider them to be elaborations of and variations on the theme of "uncertainty." One of my patients (see Bak, 1953) had the fantasy that his mother had a gigantic detachable phallus which she gave or lent to his older brother. This was a major determinant of his choice of homosexual objects.

Case 5

The following case report illustrates the organizing role of early trauma.

The patient was a transvestite, who had been combating these urges since the age of thirteen or fourteen. The compulsion to dress up in female clothing, especially to put on his sister's garments, appeared after a separation from her. Prior to her departure to college, there had been considerable physical intimacy between them which stopped only at sexual intercourse. Their sex play in bed, however, had consisted mainly in flattening out her breasts. The masturbatory fantasies that he evolved after her departure were characterized chiefly by *undoing the separation from the sister.* Wearing her clothing, he fantasied himself as her roommate going out on dates. He preferred to put on dresses in which she had been admired and photographed by the father. The house was full of photographs of his sister, whereas only one of his pictures was displayed. Later, transvestism was acted out; he took pictures of himself dressed up, invented elaborate mechanisms to take the picture, and then, more boldly, went to photographers to have his picture taken as a woman. The irresistible impulse to take pictures of himself contained an element of enraged jealous rivalry.

The heightened significance of the visual image could also be traced to scoptophilic experiences in which he watched his mother dressing and undressing in front of the mirror. In the transvestite rituals even the angle of the mother's mirror fixed to a wardrobe door had to be reproduced exactly. I was informed that this practice is not infrequent among transvestites.

Dressing up and undressing in front of a mirror dominated his practices for a long time. The penis was bandaged and very forcefully tied backward, and the testes pushed back into the inguinal canal. Such episodes were followed by intense castration anxiety— he feared that the shaft was broken, that the penis had become crooked, that the spermal duct was torn and he would be sterile. The urge to appear in female clothing in public became stronger and more irresistible.

Several factors probably contributed to this development. Behind the surface of a positive climate and transference, the patient harbored vengeful feelings and the wish to frustrate the analyst, to render him as powerless and incompetent as the father, feelings which provoked a sense of guilt and the wish to be discovered and punished. But, above all, this irrepressible urge of transvestites to pass in public as a woman is a fulfillment, a proof in the outside world, in *reality,* of the existence of the female phallus. On the one hand, it is an attempt to rid the ego of the anxiety engendered by the "uncertainty"; on the other, the main thrill of the experience that must be repeated again and again lies in the achievement of unity and fusion with the phallic mother and sister. These fused self and object representations are built on early and later recollections. For a long time the patient did *search* in the outside world for the realization of such an image. This ideal girl, with all the specifications, *had* to exist; she had to be found. "It exists." Needless to say, he was continuously disappointed. This type of search for the perfect (not castrated-phallic object) is all too familiar.

The recent development of surgical techniques to change the sex of individuals influenced the further course of his treatment. The patient actually succeeded in finding a working team of physicians, psychologists, and surgeons who by means of hormonal and surgical interventions brought his fantasy of transformation close to reality. The identification with the a-phallic mother seemed to have become more and more prominent. Parallel with this malignant development was the patient's continued growth and his increasing success in his profession and other fields of endeavor. Victory, i.e., victory over the father, was wrought with guilt; and even though two of his major activities followed those of his father, he could permit himself to surpass his father only by simultaneously engaging in self-destructive behavior. In the field of sport, he accepted victory only if he could accuse himself of cheating, thus undoing his triumph.

The self-destructive activities may have served multiple functions (Waelder, 1930)—to assuage the guilty aggressions (especially surpassing the father and humiliating him, denigrating him as the mother had done) and to stop the extraordinarily strong castration anxiety by regression to the negative oedipus complex. It may be, however, that the pivotal satisfaction in the contemplated self-mutilation lay in the fulfillment of *the omnipotent wish to change sex and achieve certainty.*

Case 6

A young woman, whose symptomatology was essentially obsessional neurotic, was for years preoccupied with the wish to be changed into a man; she wanted to be operated upon and have male organs transplanted. Before she developed this near-delusional idea, she suffered from beating fantasies and passed through a short phase of homosexuality. Freud (1919) commented on the frequency of this fantasy in women, a fantasy which is usually accompanied by the abandonment of femininity in their development. The coexistence of the illusory penis or secret phallus and masochism in women is well established in clinical experience (see also Rado, 1933).

In male masochism, the reinvestment of the phallic mother may be abandoned in the regressive process (as it was in one of my cases), and give rise to fantasies of being slaughtered, hung in a butcher shop, canned and eaten.

Freud's fetishist (1940b) in his childhood went through a long phase of masturbation fantasies in which he was pursued and eaten by an oriental potentate. The fetishism, in his case, *represents progress,* in that a later developmental phase (i.e., the phallic), less dangerous to self-preservation, was reached and strongly cathected.

In my patient (case 5) the unrealizable fantasy of "the impossible"—the mother possessing the phallus—was realized with a negative prefix in the "transformation." The mother was "castrated."

I shall now summarize the traumatic influences in this patient's early childhood. He was frequently in bed with both parents, enjoying intimate physical contact with them. He remembered his mother's thin, silky long hair, her body curves, and her silky lingerie; he recalled feeling his father's belly and the pleasure of the confused sensations deriving from the two bodies.

These tactile exposures that oversensitized and erotized the entire body surface were later augmented by the visual overexposures, particularly those in which he watched his mother change her dresses.

The patient's older sister reacted to the brother with violent and unusually intense penis envy. She completely abandoned all girlish

activities, dressed as a cowboy, carried toy pistols, and, putting some
object into her pants, walked around saying she had a penis. She
undressed the patient, who was then about three and a half years old,
pushed his penis inside, saying, "Now you are a girl." This particular game was covered by infantile amnesia. He learned about it only
in young adulthood, when his sister told him about it in response to
his confession of his transvestite wishes. Prior to this knowledge it
appeared in anxiety situations as an obsessive impulse to cry out:
"I'm a girl." The seduction and early patterning of his sexual
activity resulted in a very strong fixation and conscious love for
her; however, after her revelation of their childhood history and
her reminiscing, his suffering changed his love into an inexorable
hatred. His confession of transvestism was his declaration of the
extent of his love that was not understood. In the course of treatment he had one homosexual episode; the only emotion he experienced was during a strong embrace. As youngsters he and his
sister had practiced such embraces, from which the mother had to
tear them forcibly apart.

Discussion

Clinical Remarks

The clinical case material reconfirms the finding that multiple
perverse manifestations frequently occur in the same individual.
They can be present concurrently or manifest themselves separately
in different life phases. Puberty, quite obviously, is the phase during
which perverse practices most frequently begin to emerge, but the
loss of sexual potency in advancing age may also precipitate the
appearance of perversions.

The clinical syndromes showed a preponderance of obsessional
symptoms, impulsive character structures, and borderline personalities. My material did not confirm a close relationship between perversion and psychosis, though in some cases the two coexist (Bak,
1965).

Dynamics

Castration anxiety and its phase specificity to the phallic phase
play the central role in perversion. Conspicuous traumatic experi-

ences do not necessarily occur in the phallic phase or relate specifically to castration, but it is the phallic phase in which the child
has to deal more or less directly with the varied fantasies concerning
the security and loss of his genital. The oedipal rivalry invariably
appears and furthers the retaliative fantasies by reviving earlier
observations (of the female genital), castration threats, and projected aggression, and the ego is thus confronted with the need to
deal with the reality of penislessness. In this struggle a part of
reality—though it is not lost—is changed into "uncertainty" by the
reinvestment of the fantasy of the phallic mother. This "uncertainty" helps maintain an oscillatory identification with either parent, prevents the clear demarcation of the two sexes that would
lead to "certainty" of sexual identity, and sustains a bisexual position by fused self representations. The bisexual identifications may
have forerunners in earlier primary identifications and defective
separation-individuation processes that promote the narcissistic split
in perversions. In the fluctuation between active and passive aims,
the change from subject to object, introjection and projection of
drive contents are facilitated. The more dominant aspect of the perversion is the more ego syntonic; however, what predominates is
also determined by whether the ego allies itself with the aggressive
drive or with the preservation of the object. In the dramatized
perverse rituals both partners usually set out to prove the existence
of the female phallus. The aims are threefold:

1. The ego resorts to this regressive adaptation in order to
achieve instinctual gratification. The ego yields to the pressure of
the id demands. The id is indifferent to the form of gratification,
though heterosexual genital potency is not blocked to the same
degree in all cases. In the sexual gratification, not only the libidinal
and aggressive tension is being discharged (a primary aim of the id),
but previous ego states are relived and a reunion with the incestuous
objects takes place. This leads to the second aim.

2. Perverse rituals serve the function of undoing separation. The
increased dependence on parents (Payne, 1939) is inadequate to
express the adhesiveness of the attachment to the mother or her
substitute. The early difficulties in separating from the mother—
though they are common enough in the neuroses as well—manifest

themselves in tenacious clinging and prolonged attachment to transitional objects.

In sadomasochistic perversions, especially those in which the object is immobilized and tied down with ropes, this stubborn clinging and the fear of the object's moving away may be additional important factors (Bak, 1956).

These intense relationships and exaggerated physical intimacies between mother and child may persist until puberty. There is a great sensitivity to being left alone, not to say abandoned. Separations not infrequently initiate and trigger the emergence of perversion. It seems that separation, even in adulthood, is tantamount to object loss, but the loss of an object that is cathected with highly ambivalent strivings. The rage in reaction to abandonment often remains unconscious, so that one can assume that the disappearance of the object is unconsciously equated with its destruction.

3. The defensive use of the perverse symptoms (in conjunction with the defenses against castration) accomplishes the solution of the aggressive conflict. Freud (1923a) mentioned the transformation of aggressive impulses into libidinal gratification, of active destruction into passively being loved, a change that is achieved by shifts in displaceable energy, and he assumed that similar mechanisms are at work in the development of certain types of homosexuality. One of the blocks to genital potency is that the phallic activity is overaggressivized, and this can no longer be discharged in the sexual act, as could be seen most convincingly in case 2. When the patient became sexually potent, he complained about the intrusion of such thoughts as: "What if I bashed her head against the wall." In case 5, on the other hand, the ego used the traumatic fixation in the defensive process for the solution of the aggressive conflict. The defensive process utilizes the displaceable energies, distributing them between the two drives and thus increasing the libidinal investment of fused representations, while the change from object to subject is predicated upon the specific traumata and the preceding fused identifications.

Trauma

The search for the causes of the increased sensitivity to castration anxiety led several authors to the exploration of the preoedipal and prephallic era. Gillespie (1952) emphasized the oral fixations as the main predisposing factor. I have emphasized the disturbances in the early mother-child relationship which increase separation anxiety and clinging and may actually threaten survival (Bak, 1953). Greenacre (1953) attempted to separate the disturbances in the first eighteen months of life and those which occur in the phallic period. She put particular emphasis on the various accidental illnesses, such as acute fever and skin conditions, which may induce physical sensations of sudden fluctuations in body size and leave the body image poorly defined (i.e., "uncertain"). Greenacre's findings relate to "hard-core" fetishists, and her hypothesis is supported clinically by those fetishists who choose hard, resistant, indestructible objects, which frequently reinforce (but also cover) body parts.

While the possibility of an early traumatic origin of body image "uncertainty" cannot be excluded, it seems more likely that the "uncertainty" of the body image is a later regressive phenomenon that derives from the "uncertainty" of the perception of the phallic-nonphallic mother and extends to the entire body surface. This uncertainty of body image may also be a factor in masochism (Bak, 1956), in which case the search for *feelings* and the reality of *pain* could be explained as an attempt to demarcate the body boundaries.

Greenacre emphasized several lasting influences of early traumata: the overstimulation of aggression leads in the undifferentiated phase to an increase in primary masochism, which could be considered the basis of several subsequent perversions. The traumata need not be particularly conspicuous; they may range from unspecific and incidental events, such as overstimulation in the preoedipal phases, to more specific traumata in the phallic phase. The early traumata (during the first eighteen months) may not have a direct causal connection with the perverse symptoms, but may account for the coincidental borderline and psychotic disturbances, which are based in part on primary identification and passive masochistic solutions. They explain, to some extent, the alternations between psychotic pictures and the acting out of perversion.

Glover (1933) tends to see a dynamic interrelation between the two states and postulates transitional states. I am inclined to see them as variations of different types of defense against different types of threats originating in different libidinal phases, though they are predominantly dependent upon the nature of the aggressive conflict. I believe that early traumata promote primary identifications and the clinging overattachment to the mother. If the traumata are severe, they disrupt the development of ego functions, as a consequence of which the later dedifferentiation is more or less irreversible. The early traumata probably contribute to the considerable overstimulation of aggression, which influences not only all the later libidinal phases, but establishes discharge patterns before they can be brought under the control of the ego. The early traumata may well account for the various ego dysfunctions which manifest themselves later in malignant psychotic pictures. Early ego distortions usually involve and distort the sexual development. A combination of psychotic states and perversions is therefore by no means rare.

While we may attach etiological significance to the traumata in the ego disorders (without discounting constitutional factors), we cannot do so in the perversions. A general significance of early traumata and ego defects is not borne out by the many cases of fixed perversions, especially male and female homosexuality, in which there is no appreciable defect in the psychic structure (either ego or superego). Moreover, these persons are capable of forming stable object relations, though, of course, of a narcissistic type.

The Oedipal Conflict

The underlying preoedipal identification with the mother does not seem to prevent the development of a marked oedipal rivalry. This is due in part to an efflorescence of sadism which is carried over: the preoedipal aggression originally directed against the breast is later transferred to fantasies of violent attacks on the paternal phallus. Such fantasies as attacking the father's penis, stealing it, crushing it, cutting it off, or humiliating and ridiculing, belittling and degrading the father, are frequent and invariably lead to feelings of unconscious guilt and fear of retaliation, although the death wishes against the father may remain conscious.

One frequently encounters a triangular constellation in which the mother's seduction takes a specific form. The boy is made to feel that he is not only preferred, but closer to the mother through a bond of identity. The father is made an outsider, a stranger, a *quantité négligeable*. In several instances the patients were close to the realization of incest and had substantial reasons to imagine that the renunciation had been up to them. This threat of incest and the fantasies of identity with the mother mobilize the negative oedipus complex and point the way to the ego's reinvestment of the feminine attitude and the passivity used defensively.

This form of development, i.e., the oscillatory sexual identity, acts as a hindrance to the formation of a stable superego, which owes its core to the father identification. The so-called "step" in the ego (Freud, 1923a) may be made, but may not reach a sufficient degree of autonomous functioning. Moral directives and ideals may be strongly invested and maintained, but a strict "truth-" or "reality"-orientedness is often lacking. An all-pervasive "uncertainty" and a relativization of values may develop. It seems to me that the idealization of the parents, or the identification with their superegos, plays a secondary role in superego development compared to that of the acceptance of the sex differences and the possibility of castration. The compromise formation in the "uncertain" acceptance that I have described in perversions prevents the stable structuralization of the superego. According to Hermann (1929), one of the indications of the development of a "true" superego vs. a "pseudo" superego is the quasi-hallucinatory screen memory in which a body injury is clearly recalled—an unmistakable acknowledgment of the possibility of castration.

Specific Determinants

With regard to etiology, it is intriguing to speculate on constitutional predisposition, i.e., the genetic factors that may facilitate or even determine primary identifications. A similar role may be played by inborn deficiencies of the ego apparatuses.

Among the developmental factors, I shall refer only to a few. The protracted anal intimacies between mother and child (see, e.g., case I [Bak, 1953]) not only pattern the perverse ritual, but together with the mother's hostile attitude to genitality prevent stable reaction formations against anality and thus promote the outbreak of overt homosexuality. The negative of this development is the "homosexual manqué" in whom the anal reaction formations block the path to homosexuality (A. Freud, 1965).

Visual and tactile overstimulation as a result of protracted exposures seems to have a determining influence on transvestism, exhibitionism, and fetishism. Direct restrictions of motility and uncertainties of body boundaries, whether original or regressive, may lead to masochistic maneuvers that utilize pain for the demarcation of the body.

A hitherto unnoticed but impressive clinical connection between perversion and musical talent (among my cases of perversion, there were four musicians and one musically talented man) was discovered by Hermann (1963), who assumes that acoustic and *vibrational* experiences play an important role in the development of perversion. One of his patients, a musician, had strong painful reactions to dissonance in early childhood. This may lead to the search for identities (homosexual) or for vibrational sensations that are elaborated into being torn apart (masochism). By postulating a possible connection between the acoustic and musical functions of the temporal lobe, Hermann seeks a general and perhaps more neurological approach to the perversions. In support of his thesis, he points to data demonstrating changes in sexual behavior in animals with temporal lobe lesions. While one need not adopt Hermann's neurological approach, one could certainly find clinical evidence of the importance of early acoustic and vibrational experiences.

Acting Out

Acting out is inherent in the perverse character and, *per definitionem,* in the integrated perversions. There nevertheless remains the question, at least in some instances, why action in the outside world becomes uncontrollable. For long periods of time, the masturbatory satisfaction suffices, but at some point participation of the external world and its affirmation become imperative, even at considerable risks. In my estimation, the search for punishment and the denial of the consequences of the act ("the getting away with it"), though present, are peripheral in the motivation.

1. *The aggressive conflict involves reality* much more than the libidinal one and requires not only far more extensive defense activities on the part of the ego but also the denial by action in the outside world.

2. The aggressive conflict can scarcely be separated from the intensified anxiety that stems in part from superego demands, but,

more decisively, from the fear of retaliation from the side of reality —a generalized castration fear.

The orgastic experience—which does not necessarily require *action,* according to a hypothesis developed by Eissler (1958)—serves as an ego function "to ascertain an incontrovertible truth." It is an affirmative function of the orgasm that "the ego succeeds in giving reality a structure that conforms to the unconscious representation" (p. 241).

I agree with Glover (1923) that perversions arise when infantile anxieties are reanimated and that they represent one way of dealing with the crisis through overlibidinization; moreover, that in some respect perversions help *patch over flaws in the development of the reality sense,* the core of which we consider the denial of sex differences. This may refer to some defensive advantage of a perverse solution versus a psychotic or even a neurotic one. Thus, the overlibidinization may *prevent further regression in the ego;* or, in the process of emerging from extensive object loss, it may help reinvest part objects and even further more highly developed narcissistic object relationships.

The need for acting out, however, derives its strength from the *orgastic affirmation of the truth of the primal fantasy,* on the one hand, and by the participation of the outside world, on the other. By actually engaging *dramatis personae,* the fantasy becomes indisputable reality.

BIBLIOGRAPHY

Bak, R. C. (1953), Fetishism. *J. Amer. Psa. Assn.,* 1:285-298.
—— (1956), Aggression and Perversion. In: *Perversions: Psychodynamics and Therapy,* ed. S. Lorand. New York: Random House, pp. 231-240.
—— (1965), Comments on Object Relations in Schizophrenia. New York Psychoanalytic Society Abraham A. Brill Lecture, November 24, 1964. Abstract in: *Psa. Quart.,* 34:473-475.
Eissler, K. R. (1958), Notes on Problems of Technique in the Psychoanalytic Treatment of Adolescents. *This Annual,* 13:223-254.
Fenichel, O. (1936), The Symbolic Equation: Girl=Penis. *The Collected Papers of Otto Fenichel,* 2:3-18. New York: Norton, 1954.
—— (1945), *The Psychoanalytic Theory of Neurosis.* New York: Norton.
Freud, A. (1965), *Normality and Pathology in Childhood.* New York: International Universities Press.
Freud, S. (1909), Analysis of a Phobia in a Five-Year-Old Boy. *Standard Edition,* 10:3-149. London: Hogarth Press, 1955.

—— (1919), 'A Child Is Being Beaten.' *Standard Edition*, 17:175-204. London: Hogarth Press, 1955.

—— (1923a), The Ego and the Id. *Standard Edition*, 19:3-66. London: Hogarth Press, 1961.

—— (1923b), The Infantile Genital Organization. *Standard Edition*, 19:141-145. London: Hogarth Press, 1961.

—— (1927), Fetishism. *Standard Edition*, 21:149-157. London: Hogarth Press, 1961.

—— (1940a), An Outline of Psycho-Analysis. *Standard Edition*, 23:141-207. London: Hogarth Press, 1964.

—— (1940b), Splitting of the Ego in the Process of Defence. *Standard Edition*, 23:271-278. London: Hogarth Press, 1964.

—— (1941), Findings, Ideas, Problems. *Standard Edition*, 23:299-300. London: Hogarth Press, 1964.

Gillespie, W. H. (1940), A Contribution to the Study of Fetishism. *Int. J. Psa.*, 21:401-415.

—— (1952), Notes on the Analysis of Sexual Perversions. *Int. J. Psa.*, 33:397-402.

Glover, E. (1923), The Relation of Perversion-Formation to the Development of Reality-Sense. *Int. J. Psa.*, 14:486-504.

—— (1964), Aggression and Sadomasochism. In: *The Pathology and Treatment of Sexual Deviation*, ed. I. Rozen. London & New York: Oxford University Press, pp. 149-153.

Greenacre, P. (1952), *Trauma, Growth, and Personality*. New York: Norton.

—— (1953), Certain Relationships between Fetishism and the Faulty Development of the Body Image. *This Annual*, 8:79-98.

—— (1955), Further Considerations regarding Fetishism. *This Annual*, 10:187-194.

Hartmann, H. (1964), *Essays on Ego Psychology*. New York: International Universities Press.

—— Kris, E., & Loewenstein, R. M. (1949), Notes on the Theory of Aggression. *This Annual*, 3/4:9-36.

Hermann, I. (1929), Die Zwangsneurose und ein historisches Moment in der Über-Ich-Bildung. *Int. Z. Psa.*, 15:471-480.

—— (1949), The Giant Mother, the Phallic Mother, Obscenity. *Psa. Rev.*, 36:302-307.

—— (1963), Nemi perverzio és Zeneiség [Sexual Perversion and Musicality]. *Magyar Pschologiai Szemle*, 20(1):138.

Hoffer, W. (1966), Infant Observations and Concepts Relating to Infancy. Freud Anniversary Lecture, The New York Psychoanalytic Institute, given on April 12.

Hornstra, L. (1967), Homosexuality. *Int. J. Psa.*, 48:394-402.

Mahler, M. S. (1963), Thoughts about Development and Individuation. *This Annual*, 18:307-324.

Payne, S. M. (1939), The Fetishist and His Ego. In: *The Psychoanalytic Reader*, ed. R. Fliess. New York: International Universities Press, 1948, pp. 41-51.

Rado, S. (1933), Fear of Castration in Women. *Psa. Quart.*, 2:425-475.

Sachs, H. (1923), Zur Genese der Perversionen. *Int. Z. Psa.*, 9:172-182.

Waelder, R. (1930), The Principle of Multiple Function. *Psa. Quart.*, 5:45-62, 1936.

INDICATIONS AND CONTRAINDICATIONS
FOR CHILD ANALYSIS

ANNA FREUD, LL.D., Sc.D. (London)

In a paper on "Indications for Child Analysis," written and published in 1945, I made the attempt "to find indications for the therapeutic use of child analysis not so much in the neurotic manifestations themselves as in the bearing of these manifestations on the maturation process within the individual child" (p. 148f.). Thereby I shifted the emphasis from the purely clinical and pathological features of a case to its developmental aspects, with the clear intention to let the latter be decisive for either the recommendation for or the recommendation against analysis. It seems to me the proper time to re-examine this precept, after more than twenty years of its use in private as well as in clinic practice.

I. The Infantile Neuroses

We have all learned to recognize as obstacles to personality growth of an individual child the *conflicts* raging between the different agencies of his internal structure, i.e., processes which consume the energy at the disposal of the person instead of leaving it available for the various tasks of life; unsuitable *defenses* against drive activity which cripple the efficiency of the ego and restrict its sphere of influence; *anxieties* which at their height create an inner atmosphere unfavorable for the smooth unfolding of important ego functions; *fixations* of large quantities of libido on early developmental stages which impoverish further psychosexual advance; *regressive moves* in the area of either drives or ego which undo development; severe *repression of aggression* which limits any kind of productive activity.

This paper was presented at the third annual scientific meeting of The American Association for Child Psychoanalysis, Inc., New Haven, Conn., on April 21, 1968.

We have also learned to classify all these manifestations as internal ones. Rooted in the child's previous history, they exert their influence over his present and future life and prevent any inner equilibrium as thoroughly as they prevent adaptation to the demands of external reality. What they represent for us in their combination with each other is the essence of the infantile neurosis, i.e., the pathological state which has shown itself as eminently amenable to analytic therapy. It is in cases of this kind that we have no hesitation to declare that treatment by child analysis is clearly indicated. Only a therapy devised to reach into the extreme depth of the psychic apparatus and to revive experiences of the remote past can be expected to alter the quality of the defenses, to undo regressions, and, generally, to alter the balance of forces within the structure of the personality.

II. Developmental Problems and Disturbances

Our recommendations for analytic treatment become much more hesitant when we are confronted with cases of another kind which, though showing some resemblance to the first-named category, differ from it in important respects. Similar to the infantile neuroses, their pathology is based on conflicts which are lodged internally; dissimilar to them, these conflicts do not exert their influence from the past but are acute and ongoing, i.e., caused by the pressures of the developmental phase through which the child is passing at the time. Children with such developmental disorders may seem affected as severely as those who suffer from a circumscribed neurosis. They are brought for diagnosis usually at the peak of the phase, i.e., at the time when their suffering is most intense.

We might arrive more easily at a decision for analytic treatment in these instances if we were not mindful of the lessons learned from corresponding clinical pictures in the life of adults. As it is expressed most forcibly in "Analysis Terminable and Interminable" (1937): "the work of analysis proceeds best if the patient's pathogenic experiences belong to the past, so that his ego can stand at a distance from them. In states of acute crisis analysis is to all intents and purposes unusable. The ego's whole interest is taken up by the painful reality and it withholds itself from analysis, which is attempting

to go below the surface and uncover the influences of the past"
(p. 232).

As analysts of adults we have learned to respect such reservations.
Taught by repeated failures, most of us now hesitate to take patients
into treatment while they are engaged in ongoing and exciting love
affairs, precarious and upsetting as their course may be; or immediately after major frustrations before the individual's own ego has
found time to absorb their impact; or after object loss by death
during the period of acute mourning; or before impending examinations, great as the fear of them may be; or when the individual
is confronted by acute physical threats such as blindness or cancer
and has to come to terms with the danger of disablement or death.

As analysts of children we have to admit that most of the developmental problems of childhood closely resemble these adult situations
of crisis. The oedipus complex itself is, after all, the prototype of an
upsetting love affair, complete with hopes, expectations, jealousies,
rivalries, and inevitable frustrations. What a young child goes
through at the birth of a sibling is essentially not very different from
experiences of bereavement in later life since it is felt as loss of the
mother or, at least, loss of faith in the mother's love. The heightened
ambivalence of the anal-sadistic phase, coupled with the projections
of aggression, threatens the child with the destruction of his love
objects as well as with injury and destruction at the hands of the
love objects. The increase of castration anxiety which occurs normally with the onset of the phallic phase is experienced by many
boys as a threat of permanent disablement. Finally, the process of
development itself has the character of an exciting venture which,
to speak with Greenson (1967), "may drain a patient's motivation
[for analysis] or deplete his energies" (p. 55).

Faced with the necessity to decide for or against treatment of
these cases, the child analyst finds himself torn between conflicting
opinions. On the one hand, he knows that such difficulties are
ubiquitous, inevitable, and, in fact, part of life itself. Since they are
phase-bound, they are by definition potentially transitory and, with
any luck, will be outgrown when further maturational advances intervene. Meanwhile it is a legitimate task for the child's ego to deal
with them and the legitimate duty of the parents to support the child
in his endeavors.

On the other hand, this is not the whole story. There is also sufficient analytic evidence to show that a child's ego may adopt unsuitable solutions and that these may remain permanent throughout life. Moreover, not all parents support their children in sensible endeavors. Many mishandle their offspring during these critical periods and deal more than clumsily with whatever oral, anal, phallic or aggressive problems succeed each other and complicate their lives.

It is for these reasons that many analytic observers are convinced that during the whole period of development many children are in danger and that, where actual crises develop, only analytic help, applied without delay, will be effective in avoiding crippling solutions and thereby serve a truly preventive aim.

In the diagnostic conferences of our Clinic a recommendation for or against treatment of such cases is not arrived at without all the positive and negative possibilities being aired in all directions. The decision arrived at after lengthy discussion is most often not unanimous. Usually a minority opinion advocates waiting and watching for the ego's spontaneous compromises, while the majority verdict recommends immediate analytic treatment to avoid lasting harm being done to the child's further chance of normal growth.

III. Environmental Interferences with Development

Difficult as the afore-mentioned decisions for and against analysis are, they dwindle to nothing when we compare them with the quandary of the child analyst who is faced with the multitude of children who are, quite obviously, victims of the external circumstances of their lives. It may be a confusing factor for their assessment that, in their case as well, damage is also located in their structure. But, in contrast to Group I and Group II, damage is not self-inflicted as a result of internal strife, but is caused and maintained by active, ongoing influences lodged in the environment. These influences can be of two kinds: either negative in the sense that they disregard and therefore frustrate important developmental needs of the child; or negative in the sense that they directly and forcefully act in opposition to the normal direction of development itself. In both instances the child victim is in need of therapeutic help. But in neither case is the type of help clearly indicated, nor the therapist's role in the process clearly circumscribed.

Frustration of Developmental Needs and Its Consequences

Under normal family conditions a young child's developmental needs are provided for almost automatically by the "expectable environment" (Hartmann, 1939). It is only when the environment fails the child and his needs are disregarded that the whole complex interaction between requirement and fulfillment reveals itself in detail.

That every single aspect of the child's personality is affected adversely unless definite sources of supply and support are made available to him has been proved beyond doubt by analytic work carried out with the children of severely disturbed parents, concentration camp and institutional children, orphaned children, handicapped children, etc. Not only does every infant have definite needs stemming from his unformed and unstructured state, but these needs also change and vary with ongoing development. At every stage of his growth the child needs help from definite environmental attitudes and suffers harm if this help is not forthcoming.

To remind ourselves of a few examples only:

The sufficiency of primary narcissism, and consequently the individual's later self-esteem, seems to depend on the mother's undisturbed emotional attachment to her small infant.

Pleasure in motor activity as well as later grace of movement seem to be based on the fulfillment of the infant's need to be touched and cuddled, i.e., on the satisfaction of his skin erotism. Here the mother has to play an active part in libidinizing the various parts of the child's body.

Object relationships do not mature into object constancy unless the child's first loved figures remain stable.

Archaic fears are not overcome unless the mother fulfills her role as the child's auxiliary ego.

The cognitive functions of the child's ego do not mature unless appropriate stimulation is offered at the appropriate periods. Unstimulated or understimulated children appear as mentally retarded.

Excessive defense activity leading to inhibition of function is

avoided only where the environment shows tolerance toward the
child's drive activity.

The ego's supremacy over the id requires as a precondition the
right measure of parental guidance toward impulse control.

A boy's phallic strivings need the mother's pride and pleasure in
his masculinity as their counterpart. Similarly, a girl's turn to femininity may be stopped unless it is met by her father's interested
oedipal response.

Work with the blind has provided us with valuable proof how the
absence of a single channel of communication between the child and
his environment not only affects the development of his object relationships, and consequently his identifications, but how damage
spreads from the libidinal area to the ego functions until, in the last
resort, one unfulfilled need (for visual contact and stimulation) distorts the entire process of development.

In clinical practice, the referral of such cases seems to outnumber
those of the two first-named groups. A more exact appraisal of the
proportion between them is complicated by the fact that these multiple developmental faults[1] represent a fertile breeding ground for
neurotic problems which proliferate on it to the extent that in the
final diagnosis the latter more or less obscure the former. It is a further complicating factor that, regarding these disorders, the parents
are much more motivated for seeking therapy than they are in other
instances. They may remain completely oblivious of or indifferent
to a child's suffering from internal conflicts about his death wishes,
his aggression, his masturbation fantasies; of his anxieties, phobic
withdrawals, inhibitions or compulsions. But they become vocal and
insistent in their demands for a cure if the child's immature object
relations make him difficult to live with; if his intellectual backward-
ness affects his school performance; or if his lack of impulse control
brings him into conflict with the law.

From the aspect of indication or contraindication for child
analysis, basic developmental defects pose considerable problems.
Therapeutic help, in answer to the parents' or the school's request,
can hardly be refused since the difficulties caused by the child's abnormality are of an urgent nature. Nevertheless, once embarked on

---

[1] See M. Balint (1958) on "basic faults."

therapy, the child analyst feels doubtful of his aim and competence. He is face to face with the so far unanswered question whether and how far the neglect of developmental needs can be undone by treatment.

True to his analytic training, the therapist's efforts will be directed toward reviving the original harmful events. Since these have determined the direction and distortions of development, he will find that their impact cannot be eliminated and that his successes are confined to alleviating the child's responses to their aftereffects. This means that he may have to be content to deal analytically with the neurotic superstructure which does not cause, merely overlays, the basic damage to the personality.

Therapists who are not willing to restrict themselves to this limited field may find two other avenues of approach, neither of them truly analytic. They may turn the treatment situation itself into an improved version of the child's initial environment and within this framework aim at the belated fulfillment of the neglected developmental needs. As a form of "corrective emotional" (i.e., developmental) "experience" this may be successful, especially with the very young when the original frustration of needs and their later fulfillment are not too far apart in time.

Or, as a form of family psychiatry, therapists may feel that their main work lies with the parents rather than with the child and that developmental harm, whether past or present, is undone best by the very people who have caused it initially. In this instance, therapeutic success or failure depends on three factors: on the extent to which the attitudes and personalities of the parents are normal enough to be open to change; on the extent to which the originally environmental factors have been internalized by the child and have become influences working from within; and on the unknown extent to which major developmental trends prove to be irreversible once they have been established.

For the therapeutic concerns of the child analyst it is vital to distinguish in his assessments between the neurotic and developmental disorders, in which the child's ego plays the central pathogenic role, and the "deficiency illnesses," i.e., the pathological distortions which can be traced back to the lack of some external agent that is an essential requirement for normal growth. By relieving pressure on the immature ego and by improving its spontaneous solutions, child analysis has therapeutic chances which are almost unlimited in the former cases. In contrast, with the latter, therapy works merely on the fringes, while underneath the child's stunted personality remains unchanged. At the worst, the benefit is not on the side of the patient at all but on that of the analyst, who from the treatment of such cases gains valuable insights into the conditions of growth and thereby acquires new weapons for carrying on the fight for safeguarding the best interests of children and, in general, for the prevention of mental illness.

Environmental Obstacles to Development

Our difficulties increase further with another category of cases in which the environmental or parental obstacles to development meet head on with some of the major internal complexes, impulses, anxieties, and fantasies of the child and intensify or fixate the latter beyond any chance of their being outgrown, overcome, or brought under ego control in the normal manner. Examples of this kind are also numerous.

We know, for instance, that there is an early phase in life, before the boundaries between self and object world are established, when the infant in his own feeling "merges" with the mother and to all intents and purposes lives in symbiotic unity with her. Normally, this phase is followed by the child's wish to establish his personal independence and identity, i.e., by the "separation-individuation phase."[2] But we may well ask ourselves how separation and the establishment of a separate identity can be expected to take place in a child for whom merging is not only his but the mother's admitted need, i.e., when the latter declares openly that she feels at one with her by then five-year-old son, as if they were both an "amorphous mass" (as happened in one of our Clinic cases).

In the analysis of adults as well as children it is one of our tasks to disentangle the real personality of the parents from the projections and fantastic additions with which their image is overlaid in the child's mind so that they are turned into frightening and threatening figures. This may make us forget that not all the threats which

---

[2] According to Margaret Mahler (1963).

emanate from the parental figures are products of the child's fantasy. From our clinical experience, we can quote a number of cases where a mother actually dreads to be left alone with the child since she feels compelling urges to throw the child out of the window, down the staircase, or to put poison in his food.

The wish to see the parents' naked bodies is, as we know, an integral part of infantile sexuality and, if not too severely checked, one that develops easily into the sublimated derivatives of wishing to know, to investigate, to explore the unknown. Nevertheless, its fate is different in cases where the child's sexual curiosity coincides with open exhibitionistic tendencies on the part of the parents. We have had dealings with a mother who gave way to the urge to display her genital parts to her growing boys; with a father who had to be warned off taking his small daughter to the lavatory to have her watch him urinate and at times hold his penis. Other parents are prompted by the same urge to allow their children to be present in the parental bedroom as witnesses to the parents' sex play.[3]

According to the common infantile sexual theories, parental intercourse is understood as an act of violent aggression with potential harm inflicted on either one or on both partners; impregnation, as the result of oral intake; birth, as anal output, etc. Normally, these theories change to correspond with ongoing phase development until, finally, the true facts are established and accepted by the adolescent on the basis of his maturing genitality. This advance does not happen where the pregenital meaning of the events is reinforced by the parents' actual fights or by openly displayed perverse behavior. Similarly, it is extremely unlikely that a child will outgrow his or her oedipal fantasies in situations where father or mother, either consciously or unconsciously, elevate the child into a substitute sexual partner or commit real acts of seduction with him.[4]

Where the parents themselves are innocent of such interference with development, fate may do the damage in their stead. Handicapped children such as the blind, the physically deformed, those mutilated by operations do not have the same chance as the physi-

3 Dr. J. Rosen, a member of the Hampstead Child-Therapy Clinic, is at present studying our records and preparing a detailed investigation listing the effects of such parental complicity with the child's scoptophilia.

4 See the case of a little girl, treated and described for the Hampstead Clinic by M. Mason.

cally normal ones to overcome their castration complex. Children who are orphaned early in life have greater difficulty than others in dealing with their death wishes which they believe to be all-powerful.[5]

Individuals whose childhood proceeds under the influences of such experiences have a much reduced chance of growing up normally. The appeal for help which is implicit in their precarious circumstances is too strong to be dismissed lightly and often brings them into treatment.[6] But this does not by any means imply that child analysis is indicated for them as the treatment of choice and that its technical tools are found to be potent enough to counteract the ongoing upsetting influences. As I have said before, child analysis is most clearly indicated where the patient's fears, fights, crises, and conflicts are the product of his inner world and can be solved or dissolved into nothing by tracing their roots into the unconscious, by enlightenment, insight, and interpretation. Where the threat, the attacker or the seducer are real people, the therapeutic situation changes altogether. It is only understandable that the chances of successful therapy are reduced most in cases where the pathogenic influences are embodied in the parents themselves, i.e., in the very people who are expected to safeguard the child's mental health and whenever this is endangered, to help him to regain it.

BIBLIOGRAPHY

Balint, M. (1958), The Three Areas of the Mind. *Int. J. Psycho-Anal.,* 39:328-340.
Freud, A. (1945), Indications for Child Analysis. *This Annual,* 1:127-149.
Freud, S. (1937), Analysis Terminable and Interminable. *Standard Edition,* 23:209-253. London: Hogarth Press, 1964.
Greenson, R. R. (1967), *The Technique and Practice of Psychoanalysis.* New York: International Universities Press.
Hartmann, H. (1939), *Ego Psychology and the Problem of Adaptation.* New York: International Universities Press, 1958.
Mahler, M. S. (1963), *Thoughts about Development and Individuation. This Annual,* 18:307-324.

[5] As an example of a physically handicapped child, see J. Novick's analytic study of a boy with clubfoot, a patient of the Hampstead Clinic.
[6] In fact, many cases of this kind are being analyzed at present in the Hampstead Clinic.

PERVERSIONS

General Considerations Regarding Their Genetic and Dynamic Background

PHYLLIS GREENACRE, M.D. (New York)

This paper will attempt to summarize ideas concerning the nature of perversions, especially emphasizing the genetic and dynamic aspects. The multiplicity of the forms and the varied intensities in which perversions appear may be confusing in efforts to understand their essential character. Drawing on a fairly wide range of clinical pictures from those cases which seem but slightly deviant from the normal to those extreme forms of perversion which may startle by their bizarre characteristics, the attention of the investigator must first focus on relatively pronounced cases in which perverse development is clear and definite.

I shall refer first to fetishism, which next to homosexuality is seen more frequently in patients under treatment than the other more florid perversions. Patients rarely seek treatment because of it, however, and, as Freud (1927) remarked, many patients regard their practice as abnormal but not as a symptom. It is uncovered—or rather, comes under scrutiny—in the course of working with other disturbances. In a review of the literature (1953) I found that in only one case was fetishism reported as a presenting symptom (Romm, 1949), and then it was due to the rebellion of the wife, who was obliged to participate in the fetishistic ritual which drove the patient to treatment.

While the careful study of a very few cases is of the utmost importance and furnishes the best foundation for clinical psycho-

This paper is an expanded version of my discussion of Robert Bak's paper, "The Phallic Woman: The Ubiquitous Fantasy in Perversions," read at the meeting of the New York Psychoanalytic Society on February 27, 1968.

analytic research, it is nevertheless difficult to accumulate sufficient experience on which to base broader generalizations. A few years ago I undertook to supplement my own experience by combing the literature for clinical reports both as to the appearance of fetishism and the history of the fetishist. These were naturally uneven and would hardly do for a statistical survey. My ideas about fetishism were based on this material as well as on the cases of the few patients with whom I worked analytically. I have previously (1951, 1955, 1960a) reported cases in which fetishistic symptoms were intermittent, not severe, and not so clearly attached to sexual practices.

Fetishism generally appears as a distortion of sexual behavior in which there is the obligatory use of some nongenital object as part of the sexual act and without which gratification cannot be obtained. The fetish usually must possess qualities representing, in only slightly concealed form, body parts and body attributes. Articles of leather such as shoes, gloves, thongs; articles of clothing closely associated with the body, such as underwear; braids of hair and wigs—these all have the common fetishistic properties. Furthermore, the fetish must be something that is visible, tangible, inanimate, invested with body odors, and not easily destructible. In less severe cases, these requirements are not so stringent and an actual part of the body may be used as a fetishistic support, e.g., focusing by vision or touch on the neck, the ear, the breast or the ankle of the partner in fact or in memory; or fantasies of greater or lesser complexity may do fetishistic service in intercourse and sometimes even in masturbation.

In certain instances there may be predilections for special forms of foreplay or the introduction of unusual ritualistic elements. These appear as uniquely valued mementoes containing some rudiments from the infantile period. Such cases merge into normal variations of the sexual relationship and cannot be considered true fetishism, since the fetish is not so rigidly and compulsively demanded, nor is its absence so crippling. One of the questions which presents itself here is: "Why is it necessary that the fetish be represented in so concrete a form? Why must it be visible, tangible, durable, smellable, and completely at the disposal of the fetishist? Why will not imagination do as well?" I shall return to this question later. From a phenomenological point of view, fetishism as well as many of the other forms of perversion would appear to be disturbances in sexual development. Our

more recent studies of early ego development would indicate that the
fundamental disturbance is in this area, and that the defectively developed ego uses the pressures of the maturing libidinal phases for its
own purposes in characteristic ways because of the extreme and persistent narcissistic needs.

But let us look at what happens in the actual fetishistic performance. It is clear that the fetishist's sense of his own genital body
identity is not firmly established and that he needs the fetish to
bolster his uncertain masculinity—a fact especially apparent in the
performance of the sexual act. The existence of an unusually severe
castration complex is evident in many different ways, and is associated with two opposing views of the female genitals. These either
are conceived of as degraded, dirty—and mutilated (essentially anal);
or there is a latent illusion of the female possessing a penis. This illusion may be manifest, but is more often preconscious and is betrayed
in various slips, dreams, and special attitudes. This lacuna in the
reality sense may be severe or only slight; and it may be, but is not
always, obligatorily associated with other appreciable disturbances
of reality perception. In many cases, the perception is unusually keen
and bright when it is not directed at the genital area, and has a
quality that is suggestive of the brightness of the screen memory. The
fetishist does not really believe that the female has a phallus, since
his generally good perception, under the cloak of common sense,
would tell him otherwise.

In fetishism, and probably in most perversions, there is a prolongation of the introjective-projective stage in which there is an incomplete separation of the "I" from the "other" and an oscillation
between the two. This is associated with a more than usually strong
capacity for primary identification. This capacity persists, however,
in a lesser degree in all human beings and may be activated in
crowds, where communication may be through touch, vision, and
bodily contact with or without verbal participation. Because of the
active persistence of primary identification to an unusual degree, the
fetishist feels castrated when he is directly confronted with the female
genital area. The fetish then serves to concretize the female phallus
for him. He can incorporate it through vision, touch, and smell, and
appropriate it as his own, thereby salvaging his potency.

The severity of the castration complex in fetishists had long been recognized and was clearly enunciated by Freud (1927) when he referred to the fetish as a substitute for the maternal phallus which the little boy had believed in and could not relinquish. He described the fetish as "a token of triumph over the threat of castration and a protection against it" (p. 154). In his paper on the splitting of the ego in the defensive process, Freud (1940) again took up the subject of fetishism and saw this defensive splitting as accounting for the capacity of the fetishist to maintain two opposing images of the female genitals. He still saw the castration complex as originating in the phallic phase as he had described it in 1923. He thought then that the boy child assumed that all other human beings and inanimate objects as well had phallic equipment like himself; that the boy undoubtedly perceived the distinction between men and women but had no occasion to connect it with the genitals; and he said very frankly that the girl's early development was unknown to him. Freud had previously (1905) postulated a constitutional debility, "an executive weakness of the sexual apparatus," which had been especially affected by some trauma of childhood; the specific nature of the trauma in turn determined the special character of the fetish. Abraham (1910) also emphasized a constitutional weakness. By 1939, Sylvia Payne referred to constitutional weakness of the *ego*.

But our observations have been extended and our ideas both about the castration complex and the ego have been changed somewhat since the 1923-1938 period.[1] Here I would value the pertinent work done on the theories of aggression; the studies of ego maturation and function; the observations of the course of and interferences with separation and individuation; the scrutiny of the stages of object relationship; and, not insignificantly, the revived interest in the body image, the early body ego, the self representation, and problems of identity. I would think that all of these have value in understanding and enlarging our vision of the importance of and variations in the phallic phase with its intimate relationship with the oedipus complex. They furnish specific insight into the differences

---

[1] E. Glover (1933) published a paper on "The Relation of Perversion-Formation to the Development of Reality-Sense" in which he mentions that perversions help to patch over flaws in the developing reality sense. Fenichel (1930), Balint (1935), Gillespie (1940, 1952), Hermann (1949), Wulff (1946), and Wilson (1948) emphasized some disturbances in the ego and the persistence of the introjection-projection mechanisms. Gillespie further emphasized the basic orality and the important role of aggression.

and complexities of the infantile organization which already exists as the child enters this phase.

It is now a common observation that fear of castration in boys and penis envy in girls occur earlier than used to be thought—i.e., well before the phallic phase, quite commonly about the age of two. The late Ernst Kris used to remark that some fear of castration is built into the very body structure since the male genitals look as though they could readily be rubbed or pulled off. I also recall that at a meeting in Stockbridge in 1950, Anna Freud commented that observations of young children in wartime nurseries had shown the early appearance of penis envy so clearly as to force revision of earlier conceptions that it only arose with the phallic phase (A. Freud, 1951). But I believe that this early castration fear has a different quality from that of its later form as it reaches the phallic phase and is under the pressure and pull of the oedipal conflict.

In the earlier years, these problems are much more involved with body narcissism in the investment of the own body parts as possessions. I have thought that toward the end of the second year there was regularly some enhancement of genital sensitivity (phallic or clitoral) that occurred simultaneously with the increasing maturation of the body sphincters; it also was associated with an upsurge of general body exhilaration and sensory responsiveness that accompany the gaining of the upright position and walking. The penis may then be seen from more angles and positions than before, and the increased interest in urination gives it an added stimulation and importance as a body part. While the early phallic awareness and sensitivity seem not to be comparable in compelling force with the libidinal pressure of the phallic period, these two periods (in the second and fourth years) appear to have some implicit relationship. In both, the child shows not only an increase in spontaneous exhilaration, but also a very marked sensitivity to body traumas and the definite appearance of or increase in fear of castration.

It seems that the "castration" fear of the anal period is not always merely a fear of giving up the stool as a part of the body, but is one of losing the phallus as well, with which the stool is so intimately associated in body area and in form. But after a time the stool becomes a *thing* which can be disposed of, and at the same time the phallus as a separate organ gains enhanced sensual value with the maturation of the phallic phase. The greater frequency of erections at this time may also significantly increase the importance of the phallus both as it is felt and as it is observed. This increases the fear of its loss. When there has been repeated use of enemas, the anal and phallic periods may not be so clearly demarcated one from the other; then not only the fear of castration but also the fear of disintegration and death arises (Brodsky, 1959), due sometimes to the confusion of the explosive enema discharge with the genital orgasm.

It is exactly the peculiar quality of the castration complex that comes into florescence and completion in the phallic phase—rather than originating in it, as Freud postulated in 1923—and of the uniquely sharp guilt of the oepidal period which differentiate the perversions from the neuroses. The extremeness of the castration fear and of the oedipal guilt in the perverse patient is commensurate with the special vehemence and quality of the oedipal hostility. While the outlines of the more regular problems of the phallic phase and the oedipus complex *appear* to be etched in uncommonly heavily, closer examination indicates that this is due to the attenuation of the object relationship, with a corresponding increase in the narcissistically driven aggressive components. Envy, spite, possessiveness, and derogation of one or both parents may play a larger part than is true in the healthier object-related jealousy, which permits the boy a freer postoedipal identification with the father. The oedipal period is altogether more complicated than in the neuroses. I believe that we can understand the situation better if we examine the vicissitudes of the pregenital development.

First of all, it should be emphasized that few analysts see a great many fetishists in the course of practice. This is in contrast to the at present rather high proportion of patients who show defects and distortions of early ego development and generally are referred to as "borderline cases." Since fetishists also show somewhat comparable problems of ego development, the determining elements which make the difference may be of some importance.

In my experience then, there generally seems to be a definite disturbance of development in the first two years of life affecting and undermining the orderly progression of the work of separation and individuation. A failure of satisfactory maternal care, the mother either depriving or overwhelming the infant, makes a fertile ground for the later development of perverse tendencies, but this failure by itself does not offer conditions for the specific perverse content. It means that there is a prolongation of the uncertainty about the "I" and the "other," and that there already exists a situation conducive to continued oscillation in relationships. These conditions also tend to make for an impairment or slowing of object relationship and consequently for a greater retention of primary aggression and an increase in secondary aggression by frustration.

But awareness of the anatomical differences between the sexes begins about this time, and toward the end of this period larval forms of penis envy and of castration fear definitely begin to emerge. In recent years we have had many opportunities for direct observation of the early perceptions and interests of both boy and girl infants; it is therefore natural to make some revision of earlier impressions that are not borne out by actual observations.

We know now that visual focusing occurs much earlier than we used to think (Spitz, 1965) and that the effect of the discovery of the anatomical differences depends not only on its timing, but on the frequency of exposure to the opposite sex and on the situations which surround the repeated observations. In this early period two sets of conditions seem especially to predispose the young child to confusion about the anatomical differences—to such an extent as to impair his perceptions of his own body, particularly of the genitals, and thus to interfere with the development of a firm body image in this area. The first of these is the situation in which the boy child is early and repetitively exposed to the sight of the female genitals, and the second is the occurrence at this time of any severe and real body trauma either to himself or to someone with whom he is closely associated. Here my experience has led me to a conclusion quite different from those expressed by Bak (1968). He believes that the boy child has but little opportunity to see the female genital area and that as a consequence the child's ideas about this remain vague and uncertain.

If the child is not actually exposed to the sight of the female genitals early in his life, then Freud's 1923 postulation may be fulfilled and the boy supposes that all others are like himself in the possession of the phallus. But it seems that except in conditions of extreme isolation there is usually some occasion for awareness of the

anatomical genital differences between men and women and between
boys and girls long before the age of four. These conditions exist in
families in which the parents frequently appear nude before the
child, but even more in situations in which there are two children
of opposite sex, either twins or only a year or two apart in age, who
are constantly cared for together, daily bathed and dressed together.
If early exposure is thus repeated and almost constant, both an interest in and a confusion about the genitals may develop.

These conditions predispose to confusion even in children whose
separation and individuation have not been seriously interfered with.
This is due to the fact that while the genitals take second place in
relation to the face, fingers, and toes as a focus of attention, they are
somewhat like the face in showing recognizable differences from person to person. Further, although the child cannot see his own face,
by the age of two he has usually been shown it repeatedly in a mirror
and has begun to be familiar with it as *his,* although the mirror also
raises a question of "I" and the "other" in *young* children. In the
case of his genitals he can see them as well as touch them, but he
cannot see them nearly as clearly as he can see the genital parts of
the "other," whether child or adult. For the boy there actually is
some discrepancy between the image obtained from looking down at
the genitals and that of seeing them directly reflected in the mirror.
This is sometimes disconcerting. One patient said that when in childhood he masturbated in front of a mirror with a fantasy that he was
being watched, he always felt that the mirror image was not the
correct one, but was extra large. This problem of the mirror is exploited in *Through the Looking Glass,* whose author had a special
interest in photographing prepuberty girls.

After he has learned to stand and to walk, the boy has a new
visual relationship with his own genitals, but even then it is not so
clear as his vision of the "other's." Conditions which affect individuation in such a way that they interfere with the attainment of
separation will naturally intensify this genital confusion and make
for a continued oscillation and a need to check repeatedly—in the
boy taking the form, "What belongs to me? Does or doesn't she have
it too?" I think that at this period children under stress regress to the
feeling-thought of the mother's breast not only as a direct comfort
but as a substitute to offset the seemingly castrated state of the

mother. This may be a component in the orality mentioned especially by Gillespie (1940, 1952), which often appears as an important
characteristic of the fetishist, and the interest in the breast in foreplay may be reassuring to the man with a castration anxiety that is
at least moderately severe but does not reach such a state as to demand a fetish. It is certainly also related to the common fetishistic
transitional object, which clearly bridges the gap between the "I"
and the "other" (Winnicott, 1953). Its softness, its smelliness, the
insistence on its individual identity, and the need to have it near the
face for a good soporific effect—these qualities betray its closeness to
the maternal breast. Occasionally this early fetish continues on into
a later form, but more frequently it is given up spontaneously with
the phallic-oedipal period. It seems to be about as frequent in girl
as in boy babies (N. Spiegel, 1967).

Freud's early emphasis on the boy's needful insistence on the
phallus of the mother has led to its being given the central place in
the dynamics of fetishism or even in all perversions (Bak, 1968). Since
it is almost ubiquitous anyway, being a consequence of the discovery
of the anatomical differences between the sexes, it requires some degree of predisposition to give it much force. It persists with different
degrees of intensity and in multiple forms in dreams, fantasies, and
various neurotic symptoms. It is especially strong and persistent in
many perverse conditions and clearly attains a compelling importance in fetishism. But this stern obligatory need to believe in the
phallic mother must be preceded by disturbances in the first two
years of life which drastically affect the progress of separation and
individuation (Mahler, 1968), and in consequence interfere with the
developing object relationship and the orderly progress of the libidinal phases.

Further, it has seemed that traumas played an important and
specific role in cases of pronounced fetishism, transvestism, and related perversions. I was first impressed by the fact that these patients
had suffered characteristic traumas at the ages of two and four, and
had thought that these were the cause of the disturbance. But study
of the early years in other conditions brought the conclusion that under any circumstances, these two periods, the second and fourth years,
were times of special sensitivity to body injuries. It was probably the
phase which made the effect of any body injury so important in chil-

dren who were already unusually uncertain about their bodies and especially their genital equipment. Furthermore, the injury which had such a specific and strong effect was one involving bleeding and mutilation. Particularly an injury occurring in the second year— even if it was to the mother or someone else, e.g., a pet—had as much or more effect than an injury to the child himself. At this age children are more often exposed to seeing bloody injuries than one might think. It is by no means rare that children see menstrual bleeding, accidents, and miscarriages. We know that direct injury to the child in the fourth year may produce serious shock and collapse, and this is a time at which operations should be avoided unless they are imperative.

I return now to the question why there must be such a concrete representation of the phallus. We know that in cases in which the trauma is less severe, fantasies may play a useful role, especially if they reach a semi-concretization through frequently being acted out in bizarre ritualistic fashions. But if an actual trauma has been witnessed or directly experienced, the shock may have been such as to interfere with reality testing. Then the second or third looks at the damaged area, which are necessary to establish or correct the first fleeting impression of the damage, become intolerable because they risk reinstating the sense of overwhelming panic as it was originally experienced. The denial of the actually witnessed injury can be met only by the use of a tangible, visible, smellable, and nondestructible part, which is the fetish. As in the case of most defenses, however, the fetish often contains direct or symbolic relics of the originally overwhelming situation.

Not much has been said thus far of the role and patterns of aggression in the perversions and specifically in cases of fetishism. The various manifestations of aggression and the defenses set up to hold it in check deserve considerably more study. Certainly, there is an increase in sadomasochistic behavior in all perversions and a tendency to show rather pointless anger to relieve anxiety, anger which is obviously displaced and serves a discharge function rather than one of effecting a remedy. Where there has been actual trauma of some proportion, the aggression seems to be deflected in a somewhat diffuse paranoid way; and in cases where the injury sustained was shockingly severe, the aggression becomes bound or frozen in a way that suggests a physiological grounding of it with an accompanying alteration in the quality of conscious perceptions. Haziness and a need to deny the experience may follow, sometimes preceded by an excessive clarity but with feelings of derealization. In any event, displacement occurs with a scattering of elements of the experience in various ways. In some cases, especially where there was a large component of primitive aggression dating from the first months of life and associated with a history of early abandonment and/or later exploitative overwhelmment, there were extreme rages which, at least in one instance, were followed by accident proneness and a variety of changing polymorphous perverse behavior. In others in which there were severe disturbances in the anal period so that anal and phallic phases were not well differentiated, rage also occurred, sometimes definitely associated with genital arousal.

During latency, when sexual interest persists but is more than ordinarily under the influence of aggressive drives (especially when there has been a rather inadequate resolution of the oedipus complex), there seems to be a fairly normal outcropping of fetishism (in the form of lucky stones and special adornments), in both boys and girls, and some tendency to abortive forms of transvestism, especially in the uncertain period of prepuberty. I think here also of the childhood game popular at parties for children in the latency years; the game in which a child is blindfolded, whirled around until he is dizzy, and then directed to pin the tail on a picture of a donkey. Is not this play representative of the bewilderment about where the appendage belongs?

If I were to attempt a formula describing the development of perversions (such as fetishism, transvestism, voyeurism, and exhibitionism), I would say that due to early disturbances in the mother-infant relationship there is a severe impairment of object relationships which combines with a specifically determined weakness of the body and self images, especially involving the genitals. This becomes most significant during the phallic and oedipal periods when castration anxiety is extraordinarily acute, due to the quality of the aggression aroused at these times. The maturing sexual drives are distorted in the interest of bolstering the body image. There is then a vicious circle of recurring castration panic for which the fetish or the ritualized behavior serve almost literally as a stopgap permitting the semblance of a more nearly adequate sexual performance or relationship. This may have more narcissistic than object-related value.

In earlier experiences with cases of fetishism, I was inclined to emphasize the multiplicity of perverse structures in the single individual, and thought that they were always part of a polymorphous perverse organization, usually in the setting of an unstable or even psychopathic character. Further experience has led me to modify this somewhat, as I have seen perverse development in relatively good character structures, especially in some creative people. Moreover, a perversion in well-defended isolation not infrequently is seen in clergymen and teachers. The difference probably depends partly on the nature of the superego development. There seems to be considerable variability in the degree of polymorphous perverse development in psychopathic characters and in criminals. These people, of whatever type, do not often come to an analyst and one must search biographies, novels as well as scientific literature and the annals of crime to get reports. I have thought more recently, especially after working on the impostor, that it might be possible to understand different varieties of perverse characters by combining the study of early distortions of ego development with an investigation of the characters of the parents and the parental relationship, in order to explore their effect on the general concepts of masculinity and femininity which the child develops throughout the entire preoedipal period; and, more significantly, to illuminate the considerable contribution that these parental character traits make to the postoedipal part of the superego formation and the development of ego ideals.

To return to the subject of the role of aggression in perversions: it is clear that anger may be used as a discharge to lessen anxiety or tension; and, conversely, intense aggression may be aroused without the child having the ability for immediate discharge. These conditions favor sadomasochistic tendencies, which are characteristic of all perversions. But there are other states in which sadomasochistic practices form the central content of the perversion. Here the sadism may be the chief surface manifestation and the masochism may be experienced through identification with the victim. It seems then that the sadist and his victim are often one and the same person, i.e., different aspects of the self image in the unconscious of the aggressor. In certain cases one may also see quite clearly that the masochist attracts and elicits the sadism as though to complete himself in this way. This may be somewhat similar to the way in which some trans-vestites represent both parents in themselves and play out the different parental roles with different parts of their own bodies. In addition, the lives of many sadists show how consistently they have been driven to flirt with danger and self-destruction, as though their real aim was death or isolation from life through prolonged incarceration. But here we cross over into the field of those perversions which appear as criminal acts and also come upon the question of the incidence of other perversions among criminals.

This is a difficult field for the analyst, for it is one in which there really is no chance to analyze the patients. The only contributions that psychoanalysis can make are based on deductions derived from the psychoanalytic treatment of less severe cases and on the study of the rare biographical accounts of individual criminals. In recent years, perhaps due in part to the growing concern with problems of violence in a world which is simultaneously contracting in some ways and unbelievably expanding in others, and influenced by whatever depth of psychological insight analysis has lent, a few writers have invested their talents in giving us rather comprehensive studies of individual criminals and their crimes. What has impressed me is the indication of severe disturbances from the very first year of life. It is also evident that very often this is part of a disrupted family life which provides little chance for healing and which must also be viewed against a wider social background (whether of community or family society) tending to stimulate and to perpetuate the dominance of sadomasochistic developments.

Whether we look at this first year of life as the period of early individuation or categorize it in terms of libido as the oral phase, we do know that it is the time in which colossal realignments of biological forces are beginning to be made. The primordial aggressive life force is prenatally in the service of bodily differentiation and enormous growth which can occur because of the fetus's parasitic position. If there is postnatally a severe degree of interference with the contact with the mother (in the autistic and early individuation periods described by Mahler), then there must develop a kind of "phase hunger" for clinging by touch, mouth, and vision, one involving much more biological aggressive pressure and, conversely, more suffering in its deprivation than would be true under more favorable conditions. It is also evident that such interference between mother and infant is apt to be part of a disturbed family life, due to actual separation from the mother by illness or death or as part of an intrafamily chaotic condition. Whatever its causes, too frequently it means a multiplication of bad conditions with exposure to too much inappropriate stimulation and too much neglect. One must further remember that in this earliest period of life there is little differentiation between subject and object—and between primary sadism and primary masochism.

It has seemed to me that this is the nucleus of the most severe criminal perversions expressed in violence: that true and full genital pleasure rarely develops. Genitality may be abandoned altogether in favor of narcissistically driven aggressive orgies. Or it may continue a wavering and uncertain course with homosexual and other perverse patchwork to sustain its phantom quality, which may also be expressed in a symbolic, displaced, and inverted way through the use of weapons for violence. Strong oral drives may be seen directly or in disguised forms in the devouring quality of the general aggression. The grandiose "love" is the love of conquest, with a vision of world-wide notoriety or worldwide domination, a desire that to some extent is further determined by the contribution of the preadolescent years.

In this discussion of crime as a form of perversion, I lay myself open to the criticism that I am applying analytic concepts to cases of patients whom I have not seen and who cannot be analyzed. I must accept this; but I would hope sometime to present from biographies of criminals the material which seems to me significant. I also find some support in Freud's discussion in "The Economic Problem of Masochism" (1924). After stating his view that sexual excitation occurs as an accessory effect of a series of internal processes as soon as the intensity of these exceeds certain quantitative limits, he continues that nothing very important takes place in the organism without contributing a component to the excitation of the sexual instinct. He thought, further, that the sympathetic excitation of physical pain and distress would be an infantile physiological mechanism which would cease to operate later on. It would reach a varying degree of development in different sexual constitutions but would in any case provide the physiological foundation on which the structure of erotogenic masochism is subsequently erected in the mind. Later in the same paper Freud states, "If one is prepared to overlook a little inexactitude, it may be said that the death instinct which is operative in the organism—the primal sadism—is identical with masochism" (p. 164).

I would have only two relatively slight modifications of this statement: first, physical pain and distress in infancy are associated with aroused aggression, which is relieved in part through physiological discharges and in part by contact with the mother. But when there is no relief through relation with a maternal object or her representative, the effect is paralyzing. Secondly, it is my belief that aggression has a normal (nonhostile) nonobject-related source in the enormous pressure of growth prenatally, and that this continues at a high but diminishing rate in the first months of life (Greenacre, 1960b). It cannot be considered hostile and truly sadistic until there is at least some small margin of object relatedness. (Without that the infant dies from intercurrent physical illness.) If, however, that margin of object relatedness is very much diminished or so interfered with that it seems lacking, then the primary masochism and the primary sadism approach being the same.

BIBLIOGRAPHY

Abraham, K. (1910), Remarks on the Psycho-Analysis of a Case of Foot and Corset Fetishism. *Selected Papers on Psycho-Analysis.* London: Hogarth Press, 1927, pp. 125-136.

Bak, R. C. (1953), Fetishism. *J. Amer. Psa. Assn.,* 1:285-298.

—— (1968), The Phallic Woman: The Ubiquitous Fantasy in Perversions. *This Annual,* 23:15-36.

Balint, M. (1935), A Contribution to Fetishism. *Int. J. Psa.,* 16:481-483.

Brodsky, B. (1959), The Self-Representation, Anality, and the Fear of Dying. *J. Amer. Psa. Assn.,* 7:95-108.

Fenichel, O. (1930), The Psychology of Transvestitism. *Int. J. Psa.,* 11:211-227.

Freud, A. (1951), Observations on Child Development. *This Annual,* 6:18-30.

Freud, S. (1905), Three Essays on the Theory of Sexuality. *Standard Edition,* 7:125-243. London: Hogarth Press, 1953.

—— (1923), The Infantile Genital Organization. *Standard Edition,* 19:141-145. London: Hogarth Press, 1961.

—— (1924), The Economic Problem of Masochism. *Standard Edition,* 19:159-170. London: Hogarth Press, 1961.

—— (1927), Fetishism. *Standard Edition,* 21:149-157. London: Hogarth Press, 1961.

—— (1940), Splitting of the Ego in the Process of Defence. *Standard Edition,* 23:271-278. London: Hogarth Press, 1964.

Gillespie, W. H. (1940), A Contribution to the Study of Fetishism. *Int. J. Psa.,* 21:401-415.

—— (1952), Notes on the Analysis of Sexual Perversions. *Int. J. Psa.*, 33:397-402.

Glover, E. (1933), The Relation of Perversion-Formation to the Development of Reality-Sense. *Int. J. Psa.*, 14:486-504.

Glover, J. (1927), Notes on an Unusual Form of Perversion. *Int. J. Psa.*, 8:10-24.

Greenacre, P. (1951), Respiratory Incorporation and the Phallic Phase. *This Annual,* 6:180-205.

—— (1953), Certain Relationships between Fetishism and the Faulty Development of the Body Image. *This Annual,* 8:79-98.

—— (1955), Further Considerations regarding Fetishism. *This Annual,* 10:187-195.

—— (1960a), Further Notes on Fetishism. *This Annual,* 15:191-207.

—— (1960b), Considerations regarding the Parent-Infant Relationship. *Int. J. Psa.,* 41:571-584.

—— (1960c), Regression and Fixation. *J. Amer. Psa. Assn.,* 8:703-723.

Hermann, I. (1949), The Giant Mother, the Phallic Mother, Obscenity. *Psa. Rev.,* 36:302-307.

Mahler, M. S. (1968), *On Human Symbiosis and the Vicissitudes of Individuation.* New York: International Universities Press.

Payne, S. M. (1939), Some Observations on the Ego Development of the Fetishist. *Int. J. Psa.,* 20:161-170.

Romm, M. (1949), Some Dynamics in Fetishism. *Psa. Quart.,* 18:137-153.

Spiegel, N. T. (1967), An Infantile Fetish and Its Persistence into Young Womanhood. *This Annual,* 22:402-425.

Spitz, R. A. (1965), *The First Year of Life.* New York: International Universities Press.

Wilson, G. W. (1948), A Further Contribution to the Study of Olfactory Repression with Particular Reference to Transvestitism. *Psa. Quart.,* 17:322-339.

Winnicott, D. W. (1953), Transitional Objects and Transitional Phenomena. *Int. J. Psa.,* 34:89-97.

Wulff, M. (1946), Fetishism and Object Choice in Early Childhood. *Psa. Quart.,* 15:450-471.

THEORETICAL AND CLINICAL NOTES ON THE INTERACTION OF SOME RELEVANT VARIABLES IN THE PRODUCTION OF NEUROTIC DISTURBANCES

ALEX HOLDER, Ph.D. (London)

The general theme chosen for discussion at the conference which gave rise to the present paper was that of the interaction of external and internal factors in producing illness. As I thought about this intricate topic it seemed essential to me to clarify, in the first place, some questions of terminology. While there can be little disagreement on what constitutes the range of external factors (real experiences) which impinge on the mental apparatus, the meaning of the term "internal" appears to be much more ambiguous and calls for elucidation and clarification. It seems to me that it can be conceptualized in at least three different ways. In the first place it encompasses one of the polarities in the dichotomy between nature and nurture. In this sense it would refer to what has been denoted by such terms as "innate," "constitutional," "dispositional" or "hereditary," and our topic would then largely be concerned with similar considerations as those in John Benjamin's paper on "The Innate and the Experiential in Development" (1961). A second possibility of conceptualizing "internal" is in terms of the demands of the instinctual drives, thus juxtaposing such demands with those arising from the outside world and studying the outcome—whether adaptive or maladaptive—of conflicts between what can essentially be reduced to a contrast between the dynamic forces of the pleasure principle on the one hand and the reality principle on the other. This con-

This paper was read at a study weekend of the Association of Child Psychotherapists in London, in March, 1967, and subsequently at the Hampstead Child-Therapy Clinic.

The present paper has, in part, been financed by the National Institute of Mental Health, Grant MH-05683-0405.

ceptualization of "internal" differs from the first one only insofar as
it takes into account the developmental vicissitudes of instinctual
drives as a consequence of maturational and defensive processes.

Both of these conceptualizations, though legitimate, present us
with a number of difficulties and drawbacks, at least insofar as we
restrict ourselves to drawing conclusions from our analytic experience with neurotic children. Usually we see these children after they
have been exposed to a multitude of life experiences over a number
of years so that any evaluation of the contribution of innate factors
to their pathology must remain highly speculative. It is for this reason that one accepts studies of this kind with a good deal of skepti-
cism, such as, for instance, the paper by Alpert, Neubauer, and Weil
on "Unusual Variations in Drive Endowment" (1956) in which the
authors have attempted to draw conclusions with regard to the various drive endowments of three children, on the basis of their respective histories, the characteristics of their parents and grandparents,
and therapeutic and observational data on the three children who
were referred at the ages of three years in two cases and four and a
half years in the third. Although I am in full agreement with the
authors' general assumption that "initial variations in quantity, balance, and distribution of drives are found in greater or lesser degree
in all children and have significant bearing on development—on the
coloring of infantile neurosis, character disorder, as well as on deeper
pathology," it seems doubtful whether one can retrospectively draw
valid conclusions with regard to the specificity of such endowments
in any particular child. As Provence and Lipton (1962) have shown,
the assessment of such factors of endowment presents difficulties even
when attempted soon after birth. As they point out, "there are differences in biological endowment; normal infants differ from each
other at birth in ways that can be recognized and described, though
the nature and significance of these differences is by no means fully
documented or understood."

The clinical material which will be presented in this paper will
therefore largely bypass any speculative conclusions about the contributions of innate variables to the pathologies to be described. Nor
shall I restrict my definition of "internal" to the instinctual drives
and their demands for work on the mental apparatus since this view

is inclined to disregard the vital importance of the ego as an executive agency which mediates between psychic and material reality.

I have in this way already given some indication of the way in which I propose to conceptualize the term "internal" for the purpose of this paper, and I would like to spell this out in somewhat greater detail. Let me clarify at the outset that when I speak of "internal and external factors" I have in mind content rather than processes, and that I am studying the interaction of content impinging on the mental apparatus from the external world—i.e., actual or material experiences—with mental content. "Internal" then applies to any content which is capable of, or actually has, a mental representation. This definition takes account of the constantly ongoing process of internalization through which actual experiences become an integral part of what we call "internal" through their registration in the form of memory traces and grouping of ideas (microstructures) on which the ego can draw for its adaptive purposes unless their availability has been restricted through defensive processes. Perhaps the most familiar example of a special type of such internalization is the gradual organization and structuralization of the superego whose introjects are largely based on identifications with parental demands and expectations which acquire a special status of authority within the mental economy.

Thus what is endopsychic becomes a rapidly increasing and constantly enriched world from the time onward when, very early in life, the infant acquires the capacity to distinguish between internal and external. Freud considered "this step forward" in his paper on "Negation" (1925) where he reminds us that all internal "presentations originate from perceptions and are repetitions of them. Thus originally the mere existence of a presentation was a guarantee of the reality of what was presented. The antithesis between subjective and objective does not exist from the first. It only comes into being from the fact that thinking possesses the capacity to bring before the mind once more something that has once been perceived, by reproducing it as a presentation without the external object having still to be there." What is not explicit in this passage, but is so in many others in Freud's works, is the fact that presentations in the ego arise not only from external perceptions but from internal ones as well, the latter including instinctual drive representations in the form of wishes, fantasies, thoughts, affect representations, etc. It is therefore useful to consider the representational world within the ego as the organization or microstructure within which much of the interaction between various mental contents—ideational, affective, and perceptual—takes place, both at a conscious and, predominantly so, at an unconscious level.

On the basis of these considerations, it becomes apparent that the task of studying the interaction of internal and external factors involves the consideration of three variables and not only two, these variables being (1) the instinctual drives; (2) the ego (under which, for purposes of simplification and with good justification, I also include the superego); and (3) the multitude of experiences impinging on the mental apparatus from without. It is at once apparent that, from a developmental point of view, the interaction of these variables becomes increasingly more complex and with it the retrospective attempts to disentangle the contributions from each of them in any particular clinical picture. Not only is the quantity of any contribution important, but even more crucial is the timing, that is, the period in an infant's or child's life when any particular interaction takes place. Among the vast literature which deals with this aspect I should like to refer especially to the many detailed studies dealing with the adverse effects on further development of very early experiences of maternal deprivation, effects which are very different from those brought about if similar deprivations occur at a later stage of a child's maturation and development (Provence and Lipton, 1962; Bowlby, 1961; Winnicott, 1962; Spitz, 1965; Ritvo et al., 1963). Bowlby (1961), in this respect, has referred to certain "critical phases in the development of modes of regulating conflict," the knowledge of which, he feels, would give us important clues for the understanding of the etiology of neuroses. But so far we know very little about such critical phases or the specific features relevant in any of them, at least as far as human beings are concerned. We can, of course, study the effects of, say, maternal deprivation in general terms, and it is possible that such studies will eventually provide us with the necessary data to define such critical phases. But in contrast to workers like Provence and Lipton who, in their careful longitudinal study of *Infants in Institutions* (1962), were able to assess the various variables more accurately through observing them from birth onward, our work with disturbed children of advanced ages makes it at times not only difficult to elicit definite information as regards the timing of certain adverse influences but even more difficult, if not impossible, to make any valid assessments of the state of the drive and ego organizations at the crucial time in the child's past when the interaction took place. Samuel Ritvo and his co-workers (1963) have drawn our attention to a further difficulty which must be taken into account, namely, the fact that certain constitutionally determined disturbances may manifest themselves only as a function of maturational processes, i.e., they may appear only after months or years.

A consideration of some basic assumptions in connection with the variables which I have enumerated will highlight the complexity of the factors involved. Let us start with the experiential variable since, in many ways, it seems the most straightforward and usually permits a fairly accurate assessment. Within its range falls any external event—if we now restrict ourselves to the problem of psychopathology—that may have an adverse effect on the mental development of any individual. Although it is obvious that the relationships of objects, particularly the mother, to the growing individual constitute the most important external influence, we must not overlook the potential pathological effects of less object-related experiences, such as accidents or similar traumatogenic events. Although we are often in a good position with regard to the details of an experience to which a particular child was subjected, we are still faced with the much more difficult task of assessing the effects which it had on his mental life. I am here thinking, for instance, of a nine-year-old boy patient who, at the age of five, had, within a period of three weeks, some nine episodes of sudden collapse, without the loss of consciousness, but with transitory periods of being unable to speak. Although he usually recovered from these episodes by the following day, this did not occur after the last attack, which at first left him unable to speak and with the right side of the mouth not moving. He was hospitalized for some three weeks and subjected to a series of neurological and other examinations. His speech slowly returned, but there remained some weakness on his right side which was severe enough for him to have to change from being right-handed to becoming left-handed. Without going into the diagnostic assessment of these attacks here, what needs emphasizing in this context is how difficult it is to evaluate the impact that these experiences must have had on this boy. Although he has been in treatment now for nearly a year, it is still impossible to say what these experiences some four years ago meant to him and how they have affected his mental equilibrium specifically.

We have to consider a further difficulty in the assessment of the impact that the experiential variable has on an individual, especially if we are thinking of the early postnatal period. The difficulty arises from the fact that the mental life and attitudes of the person caring for the infant—usually the mother—form an essential and crucial aspect, and as far as the infant is concerned, must be considered a part of the experiential variable. The subtle cues which the infant receives as a reflection of the mother's unconscious attitude toward him exercise a more profound effect on his mental development than do the actual ministrations in terms of feeding, bodily care, etc. What makes it difficult to assess this factor in the analysis of a child is that where it relates to the earliest period of absolute dependence there is no possibility of it entering the transference. But it is precisely during this period that the mother's unconscious attitude has its most profound repercussions on the growing individual.

With regard to the second variable, that of the instinctual drives, matters would be simplified considerably if we could assume that the instinctual drive organization constitutes an innate given which changes only in accordance with predetermined maturational criteria of differentiation, predominance, and organization. Such a view is indeed implied in many of Freud's formulations, extending throughout his life. Thus we can still read in one of his last works, the *Outline* (1940), that the id "contains everything that is inherited, that is present at birth, that is laid down in the constitution—above all, therefore, the instincts, which originate from the somatic organization and which find a first psychical expression here [in the id] in forms unknown to us." However, more recent work suggests that even the instinctual drives allow for modifications to a certain extent, changes which are determined by experiential rather than predetermined maturational factors. Here we find ourselves in agreement with Benjamin (1961) who has stated his views in this respect in the following terms: "If one accepts . . . Freud's own position as regards the psychological nature of instinctual drives, their nonidentity with their somatic sources; if the unconscious *wish* aspect of the drive is emphasized, as it repeatedly was by Freud, in contrast to needs (tissue states) on the biological level; then it follows . . . that the immutability and permanence of instinctual drives, also repeatedly emphasized by Freud, cannot be taken too literally; that one must think of changes in drive organization not only in terms of maturation and differentiation but also in terms of learning as co-determined by experience; that no instinctual drive is completely determined by innate variables or constants alone . . . one comes to the conclusion that drive theory as well as the theory of ego development demand consideration of both the innate and the experiential, and their interaction" (p. 26 f.). Certain defense mechanisms, in particular reaction formations, or sublimatory activities do indeed suggest permanent alterations with regard to the quality and/or quantity of certain drive impulses. Such considerations draw our attention to the fact that, when taking the instinctual drive variable into account, we must guard ourselves against a possible oversimplification and falsification of data by clinging too narrowly to the well-defined and established maturational development of instinctual drives alone.

There might be some justification in treating the sexual and the aggressive drive components as separate variables, as we indeed often do in clinical and theoretical considerations. However, it seems to me that such a division introduces a certain degree of artificiality inasmuch as we never find manifestations of either of these basic drives in pure culture but rather such which reflect varying degrees of fusion or defusion of these drives.

Turning now to the third variable, the ego, the main question is whether we regard its development and structuralization as a function of the mutual influences from the sides of the instinctual drives and the external world alone, or whether we assign to the ego a relative independence from these other sources and ascribe to it a certain degree of autonomy. That I am inclined to take the latter view is obvious from considering the ego as a separate variable. In this I follow the views expressed by authors who have given prominence to ego-psychological considerations, such as Hartmann, Rapaport, and many others. They have argued that the development and organization of the ego not only is based on experiential factors but is codetermined and much influenced by innate factors, i.e., autonomous ego roots. Rapaport (1960) formulates this assumption in the following way: "While originally all structures were considered to be related to drive and conflict [between drive demands and those emanating from the external world], it is now assumed that . . . their function is not primarily dependent on drives: thus they are termed *ego apparatuses of primary autonomy* . . . the apparatuses of primary autonomy are only relatively autonomous from drive and conflict. But their autonomy does imply *first,* that drives only trigger their function and do not determine their course; *second,* that they can and do function even when they do not serve the gratification of a specific drive." Similar considerations apply to the so-called *structures of secondary autonomy* which are based on functional changes through which they "become means of action and adaptation in the service of the ego." Both they and the structures of primary autonomy are assumed to have neutral energies at their disposal. For our present considerations, the structures of primary autonomy are of more crucial importance since they imply—in contrast to the structures of secondary autonomy which are acquired—the existence of inborn and organized ego nuclei.

These brief theoretical considerations seemed necessary in order to delineate my own point of view as well as to emphasize the complexities we are faced with in trying to assess the interaction of internal and external factors in the production of neurotic disturbances. In any such assessment we are forced to make a number of assumptions with regard to any of the three variables described, assumptions which are neither verifiable qualitatively beyond a certain point, nor measurable quantitatively. If, with regard to each of the three variables, we assume a hypothetical norm at any given developmental point on the one hand, and deviations from this norm along a continuum in both directions, we arrive at eight basic patterns of possible interaction between these variables, ranging from a hypothetical state of "normality" (however one would define this with regard to each variable) at one end to gross deviations from the norm within each variable at the other end. The former pattern would have reference to a healthy, normal, nonneurotic individual, while the latter would suggest a disturbance of the most serious nature. The variations between these two extremes are, of course, innumerable and are a reflection of the fact that no two clinical pictures are alike even though there may be many similarities between them.

With this theoretical framework in mind, I would now like to discuss some relevant features of two cases, a boy whom I shall call Johnny, and a girl called Susan. Their pathologies are quite different and thus, too, is the interaction between the different variables, both endopsychic and external.

I shall start with Johnny because our scant knowledge of his early history at once highlights the difficulties of our task. Johnny, like his brother two years before him, was born by Caesarian section. According to his mother, he cried for the first two months of his life, but she had no idea why he did so. If we add to this her account of her great difficulties in breast feeding him and discontinuing it after four months, we may be justified in concluding that something was amiss in the mother-child relationship from the very beginning. Although we learned at the time of Johnny's referral—he was then seven and a half years old—that his mother was suffering from depressive episodes and crying fits, we would probably never have known that her own neurotic disturbance began to manifest itself when she was expecting Johnny and that her state of depression worsened after his birth, had it not been for some information supplied by her own therapist with whom she had sought help some eighteen months before Johnny's own referral. We also knew that Johnny's mother was twice hospitalized for a week when he was a baby, but more precise information with regard to these and further separations for convalescing purposes was not available. Johnny's analysis, in particular his intense transference reactions to holiday breaks throughout his long treatment, gave ample confirmation of the profoundly disturbing and disrupting effects of his early experiences with his mother. And if we take into account the mother's depression, we are, I think, justified in assuming that Johnny not only was subjected to physical separations from his mother in early infancy but was at other times also confronted by a mother figure who was emotionally withdrawn from him and on whom he could not reliably depend. We have to remind ourselves in this context that for the developing child the mother's psychic life constitutes an important aspect of the child's external world. This is particularly crucial during the first phase of an infant's life when his healthy growth is absolutely dependent on the mother's capacity to sense and adapt to her infant's needs. In Winnicott's (1960) terminology we might say that Johnny was deprived of a "good-enough mother" who would have been able to meet his needs at the very beginning of his life, i.e., during the "holding phase" of "absolute dependence" when such a figure is of paramount importance. In Johnny's later disturbance and in many features which emerged in the course of his analysis, one could detect what Winnicott refers to as "false self-defence," which he sees as one of the possible vicissitudes of infants who have missed good-enough mothering in the early stages and which he characterizes in the following way: "The use of defences, especially that of a successful false self, enables many children to seem to give good promise, but eventually a breakdown reveals the fact of the true self's absence from the scene." Throughout his analysis Johnny remained in constant search of his true self which, until the very last, he had difficulties in finding or recognizing. At school he was often accused of not being himself, a reproach which he earned himself by his perpetual need to be like others. It seemed at times as if he had a very shaky foundation within himself to build upon, that is, as far as his self representation was concerned. He was often uncertain which one of the many different selves he presented toward the outside world was his true self.

Johnny's neurotic disturbance (including a number of psychosomatic symptoms, suicidal ideas, fears and aggressive behavior) was superimposed on an ego organization which was disturbed and distorted from the very beginnings. Furthermore, on the basis of what we know about Johnny's early history and mothering, we might be inclined to conclude that the effects of Johnny's earliest experiences were the most crucial factor for his later disturbance. In this way we would put considerable weight on the side of the experiential variable. And there can certainly be no doubt that the impact of the kind of experiences to which Johnny must have been subjected is correspondingly more profound the earlier in life they occur. But even if we accept all this, we are still left with the important question why Johnny did not develop into a much more disturbed boy, for instance, with borderline features. I think the answer to this question is twofold. On the one hand, it seems likely that Johnny did receive—even though only intermittently—a certain degree of "good-enough mothering" which helped him in his early attempts at integration. On the other hand, we have to assume that these auxiliary ego supports from the outside were met by and interacted with an essentially healthy and strong ego nucleus in terms of an innate potential. In taking this line of thought, I depart from the views expressed by authors like Winnicott which imply that there is no ego to begin with—as Winnicott puts it: "the start is when the ego starts," which, for him, is not at birth—and who put the main emphasis with regard to ego growth on external factors, in particular on the earliest mother-child interaction. Rather, I am following the thinking and arguments of Hartmann and others who see the origins of the ego as something more than a "developmental by-product of the influence of reality on instinctual drives," namely, as a psychic structure which has "a partly independent origin" and in the development of which an autonomous factor plays an important part (Hartmann, 1950). This is also in accordance with thoughts which Freud expressed in some of his later works. For instance, in "Analysis Terminable and Interminable" (1937), he speaks of "the existence and importance of original, innate distinguishing characteristics of the ego . . . each ego is endowed from the first with individual dispositions and trends." Freud continues his argument by referring to the notion that phylogenetic acquisitions become part of ontogenetic inheritance, thus affecting ego nuclei as much as the instinctual drives since the two, originally, were one during the undifferentiated phase. And even though the ego does not exist in any organized or structured form from the beginning, "the lines of development, trends and reactions which it will later exhibit are already laid down for it."

The importance of these theoretical considerations for our clinical data and their evaluation is that, in Johnny's case, autonomous ego factors seemed to play a crucial part from an early stage onward in the ego's defense—albeit in primitive forms—against instinctual tendencies and against reality, the latter being of particular importance in view of his early experiences. It was most revealing to witness, at the end of Johnny's analysis—in the course of which he had developed into a young adolescent—that the prospect of the final separation from me revived what could only be regarded as very early and primitive defensive reaction patterns. Although on the surface they looked like being of an oral-destructive quality, genetically their significance seemed to lie much more in primitive efforts to preserve and hold on to the object by means of incorporation. I am here using incorporation not in the sense of an instinctual process but rather as one belonging to the ego, although originally, no doubt, it was modeled on and much closer to the instinctually determined incorporative mode. It would be rewarding to take this as the starting point for some comments on the early interactions between the two variables of the instinctual drives and the ego, but this would lead too far away from my actual topic.

Rather, I now turn to another aspect of Johnny's pathology where, in both our clinical and theoretical assessment, we are on somewhat firmer ground than with the early, preverbal experiences discussed previously. From the very beginning of his analysis, Johnny was a restless, often hyperactive child. Since during the first years of his analysis he communicated predominantly by means of play activities (accompanied, of course, by verbal comments) these features were perhaps less striking than after he had decided to make use of the couch when he had matured into a young adolescent. There were few prolonged periods when he could lie on the couch in a relaxed manner. More typical was a frequent turning and tossing about which fulfilled a tension-reducing function. But it was often difficult to know whether these forms of a more general restlessness served the discharge of predominantly libidinal or aggressive tension states, although the content of preceding, subsequent, and concomitant verbalizations provided significant clues with regard to the dynamic forces underlying his restlessness. At other times, his pounding or kicking the couch or the adjoining wall with his feet or fists was far less ambiguous in its significance.

Except for the very beginning of his analysis, Johnny's verbal communications were always very direct and open, and he had no difficulties in giving expression to wishes and fantasies which were often most crude and primitive. In addition, those which were accompanied by a motor discharge of one kind or another were always striking by their combination or side-by-side existence—without any apparent conflict—of sexual wishes on the one hand and aggressive, destructive wishes on the other. Even as an adolescent, Johnny showed this remarkable coexistence of the two primary instinctual drives within one and the same fantasy, a state of affairs which might surprise us less if we met it in a very young child in the midst of his conflicts around ambivalence. Johnny's intercourse fantasies, for instance, were of the most sadistic quality imaginable, including mutilating and killing wishes, and although there were increasing indications in the course of his analysis that such fantasies produced feelings of guilt—which were reflected in strong self-punitive tendencies and depressed states—there could remain little doubt that Johnny's ego had never been able to become strong and coherent enough to master the pressures from the side of the instinctual drives in more adaptive ways.

I have already indicated that the experiences during Johnny's earliest infancy did not foster the development of a well-functioning ego organization, that already at the beginning of his life he had to cope with experiences which put a heavy strain on his total mental functioning. But that was not all. Throughout his childhood, he was subjected to what can only be termed cumulative seductive experiences within his home environment. Not only did he share a room with his older brother until well into latency where the two boys constantly engaged in highly sexualized and aggressivized games, but he was also confronted by very disturbed and seductive parents. His father in particular found his own satisfaction in playing overexciting and overstimulating games with his children, parading in the nude in front of them or still taking baths together with them when Johnny was well into latency. Such overstimulation from the side of the father was not restricted to the physical sphere but also extended to his verbal communications. His sexual jokes in the form of riddles, etc., seemed to be of a similar crudeness as Johnny's own fantasies which emerged during treatment.

Apart from these cumulative seductive experiences an event took place when Johnny was about six years old. This event, as his treatment showed, was of traumatogenic significance. His parents, in a disastrously misguided attempt at sexual enlightenment, decided that the best way to prevent Johnny from having any fears or misconceptions about the female genital was to let him have a close look at one, and so Johnny's mother one day confronted him with her genital at close range, explaining all the details to him. Johnny has never been quite able to recover from the shock of this perception.

At times one got the impression that the image of his mother's genital haunts him like a bad dream.

These few illustrations of one aspect of external reality which Johnny had to cope with throughout his childhood give some picture of the pathogenic influences in Johnny's early life. Without any doubt, there were others as well. If we now look at this from the point of view of the interaction between internal and external forces, it will become clear how essential it is to consider not only two variables in this context but rather three, i.e., external reality, the ego, and the instinctual drives.

Johnny's developing ego—deviant as it must already have been as a result of the impact of his very earliest experiences—was subsequently set the almost impossible task of gaining control over instinctual wishes and fantasies connected with them. These not only were permitted copious gratification in reality but were constantly and directly stimulated from the side of the external world. Under more normal circumstances, the influences of the external world and the child's identifications with and introjections of its demands act as powerful reinforcements of the ego's endeavor to establish control over the pressures from the instinctual drives. In Johnny's case, however, the interplay of the various dynamic forces was quite different. Many of his instinctual wishes found reinforcement in the attitudes of those who exercised the most crucial influences on him during his early formative years. As a consequence of this pathogenic interaction of dynamic forces, the flooding of the ego by conflicting wishes and fantasies not only became a threat which could be dealt with quickly and effectively by defensive measures, but often became internal reality in terms of the ego's representational world, necessitating fresh defensive measures over and over again. Rather than being able to build up a stable and automatically functioning defensive organization which could operate with a minimal expenditure of mental energy, Johnny was forced to expand so much energy for defensive purposes that his ego conveyed a distinct impression of impoverishment as far as its general functioning was concerned.

Notwithstanding the fact and importance of Johnny's earliest experiences and the harmful effects which they must have had on the beginnings of his ego structuralization, there is no doubt in my mind that Johnny's later seductive and overstimulating experiences and their interaction with his developing ego organization were of crucial significance in the production of the neurotic disturbance which eventually brought him into treatment.

I would now like to discuss some features of Johnny's pathology which are relevant in this context, as well as some of his coping mechanisms connected with them.

The effects of the interaction between internal and external forces during Johnny's childhood had profound repercussions in the realm of his object relationships. One could see this reflected in the transference in the frequent and prolonged periods of pronounced sexualization, at first both on a physical and verbal level and later, after his move to the couch, predominantly restricted to the verbal sphere. Johnny's outpourings of crude sexual and aggressive fantasies seemed at times to assume the symbolic significance of a shared sexual experience. His lack of control over the intrusion of id content into his ego—fostered as this had been by the childhood experiences he was subjected to—was reflected in all his object relationships. Those to boys were severely interfered with by underlying, but often quite conscious, homosexual or destructive wishes and fantasies. While his actual relationships to boys as well as girls were characterized by pronounced sadomasochistic features, his fantasy relationships to one and the same girl could fluctuate, within a few days, from a most urgent desire to go out with that girl and have sexual intercourse with her to sadistic wishes of plunging a compass into her breasts, ripping her genitals apart or killing her. Many of the fantasies about girls reflected Johnny's unresolved ambivalent feelings toward his mother, while, in addition to this, a clear link could be shown up between his destructive wishes with regard to the female genital and the traumatic experience he had been subjected to by his mother.

Furthermore, Johnny suffered from a severe learning disturbance, his learning being seriously handicapped by the constant intrusion of sexual and aggressive fantasies or by way of the sexual symbolism with which he immediately invested a good deal of what he had to learn.

He was suffering from a murderer phobia at the time of his referral, a phobia which, for a prolonged period of time during his treatment, spread considerably with the development of persecutory fears of people following him in the street, intent on attacking and killing him. I cannot here go into the homosexual implications of these fantasies but have to restrict myself to their origin and the significance in terms of internal and external forces. The analysis of Johnny's murderer phobia showed that it was primarily based on a projection of his aggressive wishes against his father, wishes which had been made all the more conflictive when they acquired their full dynamic force during the oedipal phase because they clashed with the ideational and affective representations of his father in his role of a seductive and libidinally overgratifying object. Here one could see how preceding experiential factors contributed toward making a normal developmental conflict (the oedipus complex) into a much more acute phenomenon which Johnny could not master without developing symptoms. In addition to this, it became evident, following the working through of his projections, that a strong aggressive component had become an integral part of his superego introjects, the effects of which could be seen in pronounced self-punitive tendencies. In view of the unconscious links between success and the removal of the oedipal rival, it was not surprising to find that such self-punitive manifestations revealed themselves particularly strongly after successes and achievements on Johnny's part. To give but one example: his entry into puberty was accompanied by the return of heavy wheezing attacks, a symptom which had considerably lessened in intensity and frequency since the early part of his analysis. Its pronounced return at a time when he had physically matured into a potential rival of his father on a genital level highlighted the self-punitive significance of this overdetermined symptom. Johnny himself experienced these wheezing attacks as a punishment for his ability to produce semen.

Before leaving Johnny I would like to mention one further aspect of his pathology because it illustrates the difficulties we are faced with in studying the interaction between external and internal factors. One of the most intricate problems presented by Johnny was his bisexual conflict, with frequent oscillations, throughout his analysis, between masculine and feminine tendencies. If we think of Freud's concept of the complemental series, we have to ask ourselves, in Johnny's case as well as in many others, whether we ought to assume a strong constitutionally given potential toward conflict, in which case a minimal experiential contribution would be sufficient to tilt the balance one way or another; or whether Johnny's endowment was such that, under more normal experiential circumstances, he would have developed in the direction of a less conflictive masculine and heterosexual position. If we accept the first hypothesis, we would put the weight in the assessment of later conflicts in this area on internal factors and practically disregard the contributions from experiential sources. Adopting the second hypothesis would place the emphasis on the influence of external factors in the creation of internalized conflicts with regard to sexual identity. Ritvo and his co-workers (1963) have, among others, emphasized the importance of the environment in fostering or limiting the actuality of existing potentials. They state: "The influence of the environment on the predisposition or equipment must be considered an important factor for the development of the child. As Kris pointed out in emphasizing some of the extreme possibilities, the environmental influence may reinforce the predisposition or it may act in the opposite direction. The child will have different personality characteristics and adaptations if his predispositions are reinforced than if they are mitigated" (p. 142). There are two considerations which make me believe that the second hypothesis applies in Johnny's case. In the first place we have to think of the seductive and sexualized relationships which, throughout his childhood, he had with two male figures, his father and brother, and that in his relationship to his older and extremely dominant brother, Johnny was constantly pushed into a passive, submissive position. Secondly, we can see confirmation from Johnny's analysis itself in the fact that his bisexual conflict became amenable to interpretations and working through, which eventually led to a clear ascendancy of masculine and heterosexual strivings, while his homosexual tendencies became increasingly conflictive and ego dystonic.

Johnny is a most complex case to which I cannot do full justice in singling out a few aspects which seem relevant to my present topic. Nevertheless, I would now like to turn to my second example, the case of Susan, whose pathology is perhaps less intricate than that of Johnny so that we find ourselves on firmer ground with regard to the evaluation of the interaction of the three variables.

Susan was referred to treatment at the age of six. She and her family—which included a younger brother and sister—were known to our well-baby clinic from the time of the birth of Susan's brother, when Susan was twenty-one months old. Thus we had a fairly good continuous picture of the mother-child interaction, at least from the age of two onward. Susan's preceding history suggests that she received an adequate amount of good mothering during the earliest stages of complete dependence, and apart from transitory sleep disturbances in early childhood there were no indications of neurotic development. It seems important to note that at the time of her brother's birth and the separation from her mother which this involved, Susan showed progressive rather than the more generally expected regressive steps: she made a spurt forward in her speech development and she began feeding herself. We can see in this a first indication of the strength and control of her ego, and of the extent to which her ego was capable of coping with such a painful and frustrating situation, without showing any external signs of distress.

The well-baby clinic's outstanding impression of the mother-child interaction was that, although Susan's mother was devoted and well-intentioned, she demonstrated a striking lack of empathy with Susan's instinctual needs. Rather, she was imposing her own will and expectations on Susan who, perhaps surprisingly, complied with these demands without any sign of protest. The extent of Susan's control and compliance was indeed extraordinary. She did everything her mother asked of her, showed no aggression or jealousy toward her brother or anger with her mother, not even on the many occasions on which Susan's mother denied her the sweets routinely offered after each examination. For Susan's mother, this excessive self-control in her child was something positive, an ideal state of affairs. In terms of the interaction between the three variables we might say that the external world presented Susan with well-defined expectations and demands concerning the gratification of instinctual wishes as well as the need to inhibit certain reactions of protest. Susan effectively identified with these parental expectations, thus developing internalized controls which became structured both in terms of ideal selves and superego introjects. Taking into account the parents' critical and adverse reaction to all forms of instinctual manifestations and particularly those connected with oral and anal drive impulses, it became a question of mental economics whether and how long Susan

would be able to retain such an excessive control over the pressures
of the instinctual drives without showing signs of a disturbance.

At the time of her referral, the writing was clearly on the wall.
She had developed what amounted to a mild form of school phobia,
the dynamics of which turned out to lie in her repressed but extremely strong death wishes against her mother and the resultant
anxieties aroused by any separation from her. A severe conflict between her superego demands and some of her libidinal and aggressive
wishes which threatened to break through was reflected in her inability to tolerate praise and affection from her parents. What upset
Susan's parents most of all was that she had become provocative,
particularly at mealtimes, when she infuriated them by spitting and
dropping food, knocking things over, tipping her chair, pulling faces,
etc. Susan's parents showed considerable insight in seeing this development largely as a consequence of their having put too much
pressure on Susan from early onward in an attempt to turn her into
their image of what an ideal child should be like.

At the beginning of treatment Susan presented herself as an
almost obsessionally controlled child, extremely anxious over the
possibility of making a wrong step and do something of which I
might disapprove. Two things became very clear during this initial
phase, namely, the restrictions which her obsessional controls imposed upon her ego in terms of its range of activities and freedom of
functioning in general, and the impression of severe impoverishment
which Susan conveyed as a consequence of the large quantities of
energy which she constantly had to invest for the upkeep of her
defenses.

The loosening of these defenses through the analytic process soon
brought about a complete change in this initial picture, with instinctual manifestations breaking through more and more frequently and
with greater intensity, not, of course, without at first arousing tremendous anxieties in Susan and leading to the transference of her
phobic reactions, as a consequence of which treatment was in jeop-
ardy for some time. However, with the help of restrictions imposed
on the extent to which Susan could gratify certain of her anally colored provocative and exhibitionistic wishes, her anxieties could be
restricted sufficiently to allow her ego to tolerate and master them.

Susan's treatment was facilitated by the circumstance that she

developed something which corresponded very much to what we
term transference neurosis in adult analysis. Hence the majority of
her conflicts became focused within the transference and thus were
accessible to interpretation and working through. This work suggested that her ability for perfect self-control—her parents' ideal
with which she had identified—came to grief when her hostile wishes
against her mother received a powerful reinforcement at the time
she moved into the oedipal phase. Until then it seemed that Susan
had managed to keep these death wishes under successful repression,
together with the development of obsessional controls which were
facilitated by a strong fixation at the anal level. In this, one could see
all the ingredients of the later development of an obsessional neurosis. The fact that Susan was able to find more adaptive solutions to
her conflicts and progress into latency after a comparatively short
analysis is not only a reflection of the basically very healthy state of
her ego but also an indication that her maladaptive solutions were
not yet fully structuralized and therefore comparatively easy to
change.

It seems to me that Susan's case provides a good illustration of
the fact that throughout childhood the interplay between the various dynamic forces, the three variables, changes continuously as a
function of maturational processes. It is the latter which may make
an essential contribution to throwing an apparently well-functioning apparatus out of gear. This is what seems to have happened in
Susan's case. She had developed a very sound and well-functioning
ego structure which initially enabled her to comply with what were
essentially pathogenic demands made upon her from the side of the
external world. There can be little doubt that a child with a weaker
ego and a stronger instinctual drive endowment than Susan's would
have been unable to cope with such excessive demands for self-
control and would probably have developed signs of a neurotic
disturbance at a much earlier age. Susan, however, showed a remarkable capacity, from an early age onward, to identify with and
introject unreasonable parental demands and expectations and in
this way to establish effective internal controls over the pressures
of her instinctual drives. As I indicated previously, these controls
became severely threatened when, with her libidinal progression
into the phallic-oedipal phase, certain conflicts gained in magnitude

through increased instinctual pressures. In particular, the strength of her positive oedipal wishes—which she transferred in all their intensity—concomitantly gave fresh impetus to her aggressive wishes directed against her mother, wishes which had until then been fairly effectively kept in check. It was a sign of her acceptance of these hostile wishes against her mother and of her wish to take her place as her father's partner when Susan, after about a year of analysis, was able to dramatize a story in which her real, good, ideal mother was dead, while she had to live together with her beloved father and a horrible, nagging stepmother who eventually disappeared, leaving Susan alone together with her father.

If we compare the pictures presented by Johnny and Susan, we can single out a number of important differences. In contrast to Johnny, Susan's ego had—if we may put it in this way—a good and favorable start, its early organization and structuralization being allowed to progress unimpeded by adverse experiences. While both of Susan's parents (as well as her siblings) are essentially healthy, devoted, and well-intentioned people, Johnny's mother and father, as well as his brother, are severely disturbed people. While the depression of Johnny's mother constituted the most serious experiential contribution to Johnny's later disturbance at the very beginning of his life, his subsequent interaction with his father's and brother's pathologies became a further important pathogenic factor on the side of the external world. In contrast to this, the pathogenic influences to which Susan was subjected were comparatively slight, and, above all, they seem to have assumed significance only at a time when a considerable structuralization of her ego had taken place, when she had progressed well beyond the stage of absolute dependence. All this is reflected in the fact that Susan's analysis lasted less than two years and that she has since then maintained a most satisfactory adjustment to reality, while Johnny's analysis lasted for nearly seven years, with his adjustment at the end of it still remaining rather precariously balanced.

I would like to add a few concluding remarks. It seems to me that it is easier to make theoretical assumptions with regard to the interaction between endopsychic and environmental forces than it is to tease out, in clinical practice, the precise contributions from each variable and the results this produced. Of course, we can study

the result in the present, i.e., in the clinical picture presented by a
patient. But how much and in what ways each of the variables has
contributed in the past to produce the present picture is a much
more difficult task. This task is essentially one of reconstruction
which, when it forms an integral part of the analytic process, can
provide us, via the transference, with invaluable data regarding the
interaction of the three variables and the causal connections between them on various levels. This has been shown by Kris (1956)
in his paper on "The Recovery of Childhood Memories in Psychoanalysis." But then again we have to be aware of the limitations
imposed in this respect, as far as reconstructive work pertaining
to the first phase of childhood is concerned. As Winnicott (1960) has
pointed out, reconstruction in analysis cannot penetrate to an individual's first phase of life—what he calls the "holding phase"—
since it "cannot appear in the transference because of the patient's
lack of knowledge of the maternal care, either in its good or in its
failing aspects, as it existed in the original infantile setting." The
one certainty which comes to our help in our assessments is the fact
that the further back we penetrate into childhood in our attempts
to disentangle the contributions from the side of the various variables, the more importance we have to ascribe to the powerful influence of the external world on the child's maturing and developing internal world. Anna Freud (1965) states: "In treatment, especially the very young reveal the extent to which they are dominated
by the object world, i.e., how much of their behavior and pathology
is determined by environmental influences." But at the same time
Anna Freud warns us not to restrict the pathogenic agents to external factors alone or to take their interaction with internal ones
lightly. She continues: "Every psychoanalytic investigation shows
that pathogenic factors are operative on both sides, and once they
are intertwined, pathology becomes ingrained in the structure of
the personality and is removed only by therapeutic measures which
effect the structure . . . child analysts have to remember that the
detrimental external factors which crowd their view achieve their
pathological significance by way of interaction with the innate disposition and acquired, internalized libidinal and ego attitudes."
Here, in her reference to external factors, to the innate disposition,
and to the acquired, internalized libidinal and ego attitudes, Anna

Freud distinguishes the three variables that I have taken as my starting point. If this paper has brought up more problems and difficulties than it has answered questions and uncertainties, this is as much due to the intricate nature of our topic as to the lack of fundamental and verifiable knowledge about the earliest modes of mental functioning.

BIBLIOGRAPHY

Alpert, A., Neubauer P. B., & Weil, A. P. (1956), Unusual Variations in Drive Endowment. *This Annual,* 11:125-163.
Benjamin, J. D. (1961), The Innate and the Experiential in Development. In: *Lectures in Experimental Psychiatry,* ed. H. W. Brosin. Pittsburgh: University of Pittsburgh Press, pp. 19-42.
Bowlby, J. (1961), The Theories of Psychological Development in Children. In: *Psychosomatic Aspects of Paediatrics,* ed. R. Mackeith & J. Sandler. London: Pergamon Press, pp. 54-66.
Freud, A. (1965), *Normality and Pathology in Childhood.* New York: International Universities Press.
Freud, S. (1925), Negation. *Standard Edition,* 19:235-239. London: Hogarth Press, 1961.
—— (1937), Analysis Terminable and Interminable. *Standard Edition,* 23:209-253. London: Hogarth Press, 1964.
—— (1940 [1938]), An Outline of Psycho-Analysis. *Standard Edition,* 23:141-207. London: Hogarth Press, 1964.
Hartmann, H. (1950), Comments on the Psychoanalytic Theory of the Ego. *Essays on Ego Psychology.* New York: International Universities Press, 1964, pp. 113-141.
Kris, E. (1956), The Recovery of Childhood Memories in Psychoanalysis. *This Annual,* 11:54-88.
Provence, S. & Lipton, R. C. (1962), *Infants in Institutions.* New York: International Universities Press.
Rapaport, D. (1960), *The Structure of Psychoanalytic Theory* [*Psychological Issues,* Monogr. 6]. New York: International Universities Press.
Ritvo, S., McCollum, A. T., Omwake, E., Provence, S., & Solnit, A. J. (1963), Some Relations of Constitution, Environment, and Personality as Observed in a Longitudinal Study of Child Development. In: *Modern Perspectives in Child Development,* ed. A. J. Solnit & S. Provence. New York: International Universities Press, pp. 107-143.
Spitz, R. A. (1965), *The First Year of Life.* New York: International Universities Press.
Winnicott, D. W. (1960), The Theory of the Parent-Infant Relationship. *The Maturational Processes and the Facilitating Environment.* New York: International Universities Press, 1965, pp. 37-55.
—— (1962), Ego Integration in Child Development. *The Maturational Processes and the Facilitating Environment.* New York: International Universities Press, 1965, pp. 56-63.

THE PSYCHOANALYTIC TREATMENT OF NARCISSISTIC PERSONALITY DISORDERS

Outline of a Systematic Approach

HEINZ KOHUT, M.D. (Chicago)

INTRODUCTORY CONSIDERATIONS

The classification of the transferencelike structures mobilized during the analysis of narcissistic personalities presented here is based on previous conceptualizations (Kohut, 1966) of which only the following brief summary can be given. It was suggested that the child's original narcissistic balance, the perfection of his primary narcissism, is disturbed by the unavoidable shortcomings of maternal care, but that the child attempts to save the original experience of perfection by assigning it on the one hand to a grandiose and exhibitionistic image of the self: the *grandiose self*,[1] and, on the other hand, to an admired you: the *idealized parent imago*. The central mechanisms which these two basic narcissistic configurations employ in order to preserve a part of the original experience are, of course, antithetical. Yet they coexist from the beginning and their individual and largely

---

This essay sets forth the principal lines of thought pursued in a longer study of certain aspects of the analysis of narcissistic personalities. Apart from minor changes, it was given in the present form as the Third Freud Anniversary Lecture of the Psychoanalytic Association of New York on May 20, 1968. A much briefer preview of the same topic was presented at the Second Pan-American Congress in Buenos Aires on August 2, 1966.

Many areas which in the present essay could only be touched upon will be taken up in greater detail in the forthcoming larger study on the same topic; and some important aspects of the problem had to be omitted altogether within the present confines. Remarks referring to incompleteness of discussion or to outright omission, which are encountered throughout the paper, usually indicate topics (including references to the work of others) which will be taken up in the longer study.

[1] The tautological term "narcissistic self" employed in the previous essay (1966) is now replaced by the term *grandiose self*.

independent lines of development are open to separate scrutiny. At this moment it can only be pointed out that, under optimum developmental conditions, the exhibitionism and grandiosity of the archaic grandiose self are gradually tamed, and that the whole structure ultimately becomes integrated into the adult personality and supplies the instinctual fuel for our ego-syntonic ambitions and purposes, for the enjoyment of our activities, and for important aspects of our self-esteem. And, under similarly favorable circumstances, the idealized parent imago, too, becomes integrated into the adult personality. Introjected as our idealized superego, it becomes an important component of our psychic organization by holding up to us the guiding leadership of its ideals. If the child, however, suffers severe narcissistic traumata, then the grandiose self does not merge into the relevant ego content but is retained in its unaltered form and strives for the fulfillment of its archaic aims. And if the child experiences traumatic disappointments in the admired adult, then the idealized parent imago, too, is retained in its unaltered form, is not transformed into tension-regulating psychic structure but remains an archaic, transitional object that is required for the maintenance of narcissistic homeostasis.

Severe regressions, whether occurring spontaneously or during therapy, may lead to the activation of unstable, prepsychological fragments of the mind-body-self and its functions which belong to the stage of *autoerotism* (cf. Nagera, 1964). The pathognomonically specific, transferencelike, therapeutically salutary conditions, however, on which I am focusing, are based on the activation of psychologically elaborated, cohesive configurations which enter into stable amalgamations with the *narcissistically* perceived psychic representation of the analyst. The relative stability of this narcissistic transference-amalgamation, however, is the prerequisite for the performance of the analytic task in the pathogenic narcissistic areas of the personality.

THE NARCISSISTIC TRANSFERENCES

I shall now examine the two narcissistic transferences delimited in accordance with the previously given conceptualizations: the therapeutic activation of the idealized parent imago for which the term *idealizing transference* will be employed, and the activation of the grandiose self which will be called the *mirror transference*.

Therapeutic Activation of the Idealized Parent Imago: The Idealizing Transference

The *idealizing transference* is the therapeutic revival of the early state in which the psyche saves a part of the lost experience of global narcissistic perfection by assigning it to an archaic (transitional) object, the idealized parent imago. Since all bliss and power now reside in the idealized object, the child feels empty and powerless when he is separated from it and he attempts, therefore, to maintain a continuous union with it.

Idealization, whether it is directed at a dimly perceived archaic mother-breast or at the clearly recognized oedipal parent, belongs genetically and dynamically in a narcissistic context. The idealizing cathexes, however, although retaining their narcissistic character, become increasingly neutralized and aim-inhibited. It is especially in the most advanced stages of their early development that the idealizations (which now coexist with powerful object-instinctual cathexes) exert their strongest and most important influence on the phase-appropriate internalization processes. At the end of the oedipal period, for example, the internalization of object-cathected aspects of the parental imago accounts for the contents (i.e., the commands and prohibitions) and functions (i.e., praise, scolding, punishment) of the superego; the internalization of the narcissistic aspects, however, for the exalted position of these contents and functions. It is from the narcissistic instinctual component of their cathexes that the aura of absolute perfection of the values and standards of the superego and of the omniscience and might of the whole structure are derived. That stream of narcissism, however, which is subsumed under the term idealized parent imago remains vulnerable throughout its whole early development, i.e., from the stage of the incipient, archaic idealized object (which is still almost merged with the self) to the time of the massive reinternalization of the idealized aspect of the imago of the oedipal parent (who is already firmly established as separate from the self). The period of greatest vulnerability ends when an idealized nuclear superego has been formed, since the capacity for the idealization of his central values and standards which the child thus acquires exerts a lasting beneficial influence on the psychic economy in the narcissistic sectors of the personality.

The beginning of latency, however, may be considered as still belonging to the oedipal phase. It constitutes the last of the several periods of greatest danger in early childhood during which the psyche is especially susceptible to traumatization because after a spurt of development a new balance of psychological forces is only insecurely established. If we apply this *principle of the vulnerability of new structures* to the superego at the beginning of latency and, in particular, to the newly established idealization of its values and standards and of its rewarding and punishing functions, it will not surprise us to learn from clinical experience that a severe disappointment in the idealized oedipal object, even at the beginning of latency, may yet undo a precariously established idealization of the superego, may recathect the imago of the idealized object, and thus lead to a renewed insistence on finding an external object of perfection.

Under optimal circumstances the child experiences gradual disappointment in the idealized object—or, expressed differently: the child's evaluation of the idealized object becomes increasingly realistic—which leads to a withdrawal of the narcissistic idealizing cathexes from the object imago and to their gradual (or more massive but phase-appropriate) internalization, i.e., to the acquisition of permanent psychological structures which continue, endopsychically, the functions which had previously been fulfilled by the idealized object. If the child's relationship to the idealized object is, however, severely disturbed, e.g., if he suffers a traumatic (intense and sudden, or not phase-appropriate) disappointment in it, then the child does not acquire the needed internal structure, but his psyche remains fixated on an archaic object imago, and the personality will later, and throughout life, be dependent on certain objects in what seems to be an intense form of object hunger. The intensity of the search for and of the dependency on these objects is due to the fact that they are striven for as a substitute for missing segments of the psychic structure. These objects are not loved for their attributes, and their actions are only dimly recognized; they are needed in order to replace the functions of a segment of the mental apparatus which had not been established in childhood.

The structural defects which are the result of early disturbances in the relationship with the idealized object cannot be discussed within the confines of this essay. The following clinical illustration will instead focus on the effect of later traumatic disappointments, up to and including early latency.

Mr. A., a tall, asthenic man in his late twenties, was a chemist in a pharmaceutical firm. Although he entered analysis with the complaint that he felt sexually stimulated by men, it soon became apparent that his homosexual preoccupations constituted only one of the several indications of an underlying broad personality defect. More important were periods of feeling depressed (with an associated drop in his work capacity); and, as a trigger to the preceding disturbance, a specific vulnerability of his self-esteem, manifested by his sensitivity to criticism, or simply to the absence of praise, from the people whom he experienced as his elders or superiors. Thus, although he was a man of considerable intelligence who performed his tasks with skill and creative ability, he was forever in search of approval: from the head of the research laboratory where he was employed, from a number of senior colleagues, and from the fathers of the girls whom he dated. He was sensitively aware of these men and of their opinion of him. So long as he felt that they approved of him, he experienced himself as whole, acceptable, and capable; and was then indeed able to do well in his work and to be creative and successful. At slight signs of disapproval of him, however, or of lack of understanding for him, he would become depressed, would tend to become first enraged and then cold, haughty, and isolated, and his creativeness deteriorated.

The cohesive transference permitted the gradual reconstruction of a certain genetically decisive pattern. Repeatedly, throughout his childhood, the patient had felt abruptly disappointed in the power of his father just when he had (re-)established him as a figure of protective strength and efficiency. As is frequent, the first memories which the patient supplied subsequent to the transference activations of the crucial pattern referred to a comparatively late period. The family had come to the United States when the patient was nine and the father, who had been prosperous in Europe, was unable to repeat his earlier successes in this country. Time and again, however, the father shared his newest plans with his son and stirred the child's fantasies and expectations; but time and again he sold out in panic when the occurrence of unforeseen events and his lack of familiarity with the American scene combined to block his purposes. Although these memories had always been conscious, the patient had not previously appreciated the intensity of the contrast between the phase of great trust in the father, who was most confidence-inspiring while he was forging his plans, and the subsequent disappointment.

Most prominent among the patient's relevant recollections of earlier occurrences of the idealization-disappointment sequence were those of two events which affected the family fortunes decisively when the patient was six and eight years old respectively. The father who, during the patient's early childhood, had been a virile and handsome man had owned a small but flourishing industry. Judging by many indications and memories, father and son had been very close emotionally and the son had admired his father greatly. Suddenly, when the patient was six, German armies invaded the country, and the family, which was Jewish, fled. Although the father had initially reacted with helplessness and panic, he had later been able to re-establish his business, though on a much reduced scale, but, as a consequence of the German invasion of the country to which they had escaped (the patient was eight at that time), everything was again lost and the family had to flee once more.

The patient's memories implicated the beginning of latency as the period when the structural defect was incurred. There is no doubt, however, that earlier experiences, related to his pathological mother, had sensitized him and accounted for the severity of the later acquired structural defect.

Described in metapsychological terms, his defect was the insufficient idealization of the superego and, concomitantly, a recathexis of the idealized parent imago of the late preoedipal and the oedipal stages. The symptomatic result of this defect was circumscribed yet profound. Since the patient had suffered a traumatic disappointment in the narcissistically invested aspects of the father imago, his superego did not possess the requisite exalted status and was thus unable to raise the patient's self-esteem. In view of the fact, however, that the patient had not felt equally deprived of those aspects of the father imago that were invested with object-instinctual cathexes, his superego was relatively intact with regard to those of its contents and functions that were built up as the heir to the object-instinctual dimensions of the oedipal father relationship. His nuclear goals and standards were indeed those of his cultural background transmitted by his father; what he lacked was the ability to feel more than a fleeting sense of satisfaction when living up to his standards or reaching his goals. Only through the confirmatory approval of external admired figures was he able to obtain a sense of heightened self-esteem. In the transference he seemed thus insatiable in two demands that he directed toward the idealized analyst: that the analyst share the patient's values, goals, and standards (and thus imbue them with significance through their idealization); and that the analyst confirm through the expression of a warm glow of pleasure and participation that the patient had lived up to his values and standards and had successfully worked toward a goal. Without the analyst's expression of his empathic comprehension of these needs, the patient's values and goals seemed trite and uninspiring to him and his successes were meaningless and left him feeling depressed and empty.

The Genesis of the Pathogenic Fixation on the Idealized Parent Imago

As can be regularly ascertained, the essential genetic trauma is grounded in the parents' own narcissistic fixations, and the parents' narcissistic needs contribute decisively to the child's remaining enmeshed within the narcissistic web of the parents' personality until, for example, the sudden recognition of the shortcomings of the parent, or the child's sudden desperate recognition of how far out of step his own emotional development has become, confronts him with the insuperable task of achieving the wholesale internalization of a chronic narcissistic relationship. The complexity of the pathogenic interplay between parent and child, and the varieties of its forms, defy a comprehensive description. Yet in a properly conducted analysis, the crucial pattern will often emerge with great clarity.

Mr. B., for example, established a narcissistic transference in which the analyst's presence increased and solidified his self-esteem and thus, secondarily, improved his ego functioning and efficiency.[2] To any impending disruption of this beneficial deployment of narcissistic cathexes, he responded with rage, and with a decathexis of the narcissistically invested analyst, and a hypercathexis of his grandiose self, manifested by cold and imperious behavior. But, finally (after the analyst had gone away, for example), he reached a comparatively stable balance: he withdrew to lonely intellectual activities which, although pursued with less creativity than before, provided him with a sense of self-sufficiency. In his words, he "rowed out alone to the middle of the lake and looked at the moon." When, however, the possibility of re-establishing the relationship to the narcissistically invested object offered itself, he reacted with the same rage that he had experienced when the transference—to use his own significant analogy—had become "unplugged." At first I thought that the reaction was nonspecific, consisting of yet unexpressed rage about the analyst's leaving, and of anger at having to give up a new-found protective balance. These explanations were, however, incomplete since the patient was in fact by his reactions describing an important sequence of early events. The patient's mother had been intensely enmeshed with him, and had supervised and controlled him in a most stringent fashion. His exact feeding time, for example, and in later childhood, his eating time, was determined by a mechanical timer—reminiscent of the devices which Schreber's father employed with his children (Niederland, 1959)—and thus the child felt that he had no mind of his own and that his mother was continuing to perform his mental functions long beyond the time when such maternal activities, carried out empathically, are indeed phase-appropriate and required. Under the impact of the anxious recognition of the inappropriateness of this relationship, he would in later childhood withdraw to his room to think his own thoughts, uninfluenced by her interference. When he had just begun to achieve some reliance on this minimum of autonomous functioning, his mother had a buzzer installed. From then on, she would interrupt his attempts of internal separation from her whenever he wanted to be alone. The buzzer summoned him more compellingly (because the mechanical device was experienced as akin to an endopsychic

[2] The episode described here concerns a patient who was treated by a colleague (a woman) in regular consultation with the author.

communication) than would have her voice or knocking. No wonder, then, that he reacted with rage to the return of the analyst after he had "rowed to the center of the lake to look at the moon."

The Process of Working Through and Some Other Clinical Problems in the Idealizing Transference

Little need be said concerning the beginning of the analysis. Although there may be severe resistances, especially those motivated by apprehensions about the extinction of individuality due to the wish to merge into the idealized object, the pathognomonic regression will establish itself spontaneously if the analyst does not interfere by premature transference interpretations. The working-through phase of the analysis can, however, begin only after the pathognomonic idealizing transference has been firmly established. It is set into motion by the fact that the instinctual equilibrium which the analysand aims to maintain is sooner or later disturbed. In the undisturbed transference the patient feels powerful, good, and capable. Anything, however, that deprives him of the idealized analyst creates a disturbance of his self-esteem: he feels powerless and worthless, and if his ego is not assisted by interpretations concerning the loss of the idealized parent imago, the patient may turn to archaic precursors of the idealized parent imago or may abandon it altogether and regress further to reactively mobilized archaic stages of the grandiose self. The retreat to archaic idealizations may manifest itself in the form of vague, impersonal, trancelike religious feelings; the hypercathexis of archaic forms of the grandiose self and of the (autoerotic) body self will produce the syndrome of emotional coldness, tendency toward affectation in speech and behavior, shame propensity, and hypochondria.

Although such temporary cathectic shifts toward the archaic stages of the idealized parent imago and of the grandiose self are common occurrences in the analysis of narcissistic personalities, they may be precipitated by seemingly minute narcissistic injuries the discovery of which may put the analyst's empathy and clinical acumen to a severe test.

The essence, however, of the curative process in the idealizing transference can be epitomized in a few comparatively simple principles. A working-through process is set in motion in which the repressed narcissistic strivings with which the archaic object is invested are admitted into consciousness. Although the ego and superego resistances with which we are familiar from the analysis of the transference neuroses also do occur here, and although there are in addition specific ego resistances (motivated by anxiety concerning hypomanic overstimulation) which oppose the mobilization of the idealizing cathexes, the major part of the working-through process concerns the loss of the narcissistically experienced object. If the repeated interpretations of the meaning of separations from the analyst on the level of the idealizing narcissistic libido are given with correct empathy for the analysand's feelings—in particular for what appears to be his lack of emotions, i.e., his coldness and retreat, e.g., in response to separations—then there will gradually emerge a host of meaningful memories which concern the dynamic prototypes of the present experience. The patient will recall lonely hours during his childhood in which he attempted to overcome a feeling of fragmentation, hypochondria, and deadness which was due to the separation from the idealized parent. And he will remember, and gratefully understand, how he tried to substitute for the idealized parent imago and its functions by creating erotized replacements and through the frantic hypercathexis of the grandiose self: how he rubbed his face against the rough floor in the basement, looked at the mother's photograph, went through her drawers and smelled her underwear; and how he turned to the performance of grandiose athletic feats in which flying fantasies were being enacted by the child, in order to reassure himself. Adult analogues in the analysis (during the weekend, for example) are intense voyeuristic preoccupations, the impulse to shoplift, and recklessly speedy drives in the car. Childhood memories and deepening understanding of the analogous transference experiences converge in giving assistance to the patient's ego, and the formerly automatic reactions become gradually more aim-inhibited.

The ego acquires increasing tolerance for the analyst's absence and for the analyst's occasional failure to achieve a correct empathic understanding. The patient learns that the idealizing libido need not be immediately withdrawn from the idealized imago and that the painful and dangerous regressive shifts of the narcissistic cathexes can be prevented. Concomitant with the increase of the ability to maintain a part of the idealizing investment despite the separation, there is also an enhancement of internalization, i.e., the analysand's psychic organization acquires the capacity to perform some of the functions previously performed by the idealized object.

Therapeutic Activation of the Grandiose Self: The Mirror Transference

Analogous to the idealized object in the idealizing transference, it is the grandiose self which is reactivated in the transferencelike condition referred to as the *mirror transference*.

The mirror transference constitutes the therapeutic revival of the developmental stage in which the child attempts to retain a part of the original, all-embracing narcissism by concentrating perfection and power upon a grandiose self and by assigning all imperfections to the outside.

The mirror transference occurs in three forms which relate to specific stages of development of the grandiose self:

1. An archaic form in which the self-experience of the analysand includes the analyst; it will be referred to as *merger through the extension of the grandiose self*.

2. A less archaic form in which the patient assumes that the analyst is like him or that the analyst's psychological makeup is similar to his; it will be called the *alter-ego transference* or *twinship*.

3. A still less archaic form in which the analyst is experienced as a separate person who, however, has significance to the patient only within the framework of the needs generated by his therapeutically reactivated grandiose self. Here the term *mirror transference* is most accurate and will again be employed. In this narrower sense the mirror transference is the reinstatement of the phase in which the gleam in the mother's eye, which mirrors the child's exhibitionistic display, and other forms of maternal participation in the child's narcissistic enjoyment confirm the child's self-esteem and, by a gradually increasing selectivity of these responses, begin to channel it into realistic directions. If the development of the grandiose self is traumatically disturbed, however, then this psychic structure may become cut off from further integrative participation in the development of the personality. Insecurely repressed in an archaic form, it is, on the one hand, removed from further external influence; yet, on

the other hand, continues to disturb realistic adaptation by its recurrent intrusions into the ego. In the mirror transference, however, it may become cohesively remobilized, and a new road to its gradual modification is opened.

The central activity in the clinical process during the mirror transference concerns the raising to consciousness of the patient's infantile fantasies of exhibitionistic grandeur. In view of the strong resistances which oppose this process and the intensive efforts required in overcoming them, it may at times be disappointing for the analyst to behold the apparently trivial fantasy which the patient has ultimately brought into the light of day.

True, at times even the content of the fantasy permits an empathic understanding of the shame and hypochondria, and of the anxiety which the patient experiences: shame, because the revelation is at times still accompanied by the discharge of unneutralized exhibitionistic libido; and anxiety because the grandiosity isolates the analysand and threatens him with permanent object loss.

Patient C., for example, told the following dream during a period when he was looking forward to being publicly honored: "The question was raised of finding a successor for me. I thought: How about God?" The dream was partly the result of the attempt to soften the grandiosity through humor; yet it aroused excitement and anxiety, and led, against renewed resistances, to the recall of childhood fantasies in which he had felt that he was God.

In many instances, however, the nuclear grandiosity is only hinted at. Patient D., for example, recalled with intense shame and resistance that as a child he used to imagine that he was running the streetcars in the city. The fantasy appeared harmless enough; but the shame and resistance became more understandable when the patient explained that he was operating the streetcars via a "thought control" which emanated from his head, above the clouds.

Although the content of the grandiose fantasy cannot be further discussed here, it is important to clarify the role of the mirror transference which enables its emergence. As indicated before, the patient's major resistances are motivated by his attempt to escape from the uneasy elation alternating with fear of permanent object loss, painful self-consciousness, shame-tension, and hypochondria which is due to the dedifferentiating intrusions of grandiose fantasies and narcissistic-exhibitionistic libido into the ego. The transference, however, functions as a specific therapeutic buffer. In the mirror transference, in the narrower sense, the patient is able to mobilize his grandiose fantasies and exhibitionism on the basis of the hope that the therapist's empathic participation and emotional response will not allow the narcissistic tensions to reach excessively painful or dangerous levels. In the twinship and the merger, the analogous protection is provided by the long-term deployment of the narcissistic cathexes upon the therapist, who now is the carrier of the patient's infantile greatness and exhibitionism.

Later, especially with the aid of the very last clinical example referred to in this presentation, some of the specific, concrete clinical steps by which the mobilized infantile narcissistic demands gradually become tamed and neutralized will be demonstrated. Here, however, the general significance of the mirror transference in the context of therapy will be examined.

The rational aims of therapy could not, by themselves, persuade the vulnerable ego of the narcissistically fixated analysand to forego denial and acting out and to face and to examine the needs and claims of the archaic grandiose self. In order to actuate, and to maintain in motion, the painful process which leads to the confrontation of the grandiose fantasies with a realistic conception of the self, and to the realization that life offers only limited possibilities for the gratification of the narcissistic-exhibitionistic wishes, a mirror transference must be established. If it does not develop, the patient's grandiosity remains concentrated upon the grandiose self, the ego's defensive position remains rigid, and ego expansion cannot take place.

The mirror transference rests on the therapeutic reactivation of the grandiose self. That the analyst can be enlisted in the support of this structure is an expression of the fact that the formation of a cohesive grandiose self was indeed achieved during childhood; the listening, perceiving, and echoing-mirroring presence of the analyst now reinforces the psychological forces which maintain the cohesiveness of the self-image, archaic and (by adult standards) unrealistic though it may be. Analogous to the therapeutically invaluable, controlled, temporary swings toward the disintegration of the idealizing parent imago when the idealizing transference is disturbed, we may

encounter as a consequence of a disturbance of the mirror transference the temporary fragmentation of the narcissistically cathected,
cohesive (body-mind) self and a temporary concentration of the narcissistic cathexes on isolated body parts, isolated mental functions,
and isolated actions, which are then experienced as dangerously
disconnected from a crumbling self. As is the case in the idealizing
transference, these temporary disturbances of the transference equilibrium occupy in the analysis of narcissistic personalities a central
position of strategic importance which corresponds to the place of
the structural conflict in the ordinary transference neuroses; and
their analysis tends to elicit the deepest insights and leads to the
most solid accretions of psychic structure.

The following constitutes an especially instructive illustration of
such a temporary regressive fragmentation of the therapeutically activated grandiose self.

Mr. E. was a graduate student whose psychopathology and personality structure will not be discussed except to say that he sought
relief from painful narcissistic tension states by a number of perverse means in which the inconstancy of his objects and sexual goals
were indicative of the fact that he could trust no source of satisfaction. This brief report concerns a weekend during an early phase
of the long analysis when the patient was already beginning to realize
that separations from the analyst[3] upset his psychic equilibrium, but
when he did not yet understand the specific nature of the support
which the analysis provided. During earlier weekend separations a
vaguely perceived inner threat had driven him to dangerous voyeuristic activities in public toilets during which he achieved a feeling of
merger with the man at whom he gazed. This time, however, he was
able, through an act of artistic sublimation, not only to spare himself
the aforementioned cruder means of protection against the threatened dissolution of the self, but also to explain the nature of the
reassurance he was receiving from the analyst. During this weekend,
the patient painted a picture of the analyst. The key to the understanding of this artistic production lay in the fact that in it the
analyst had neither eyes nor nose—the place of these sensory organs
was taken by the analysand. On the basis of this evidence and of addi-

[3] This analysis was carried out by a senior student at the Chicago Institute for
Psychoanalysis under regular supervision by the author.

tional corroborative material, the conclusion could be reached that a decisive support to the maintenance of the patient's narcissistically cathected self image was supplied by the analyst's perception of him. The patient felt whole when he thought that he was acceptingly looked at by an object that substituted for an insufficiently developed endopsychic function: the analyst provided a replacement for the lacking narcissistic cathexis of the self.

Some General Therapeutic Considerations Concerning the Mirror Transference

The analysand's demands for attention, admiration, and for a variety of other forms of mirroring and echoing responses to the mobilized grandiose self, which fill the mirror transference in the narrow sense of this term, do not usually constitute great cognitive problems for the analyst, although he may have to mobilize much subtle understanding to keep pace with the patient's defensive denials of his demands or with the retreat from them when the immediate empathic response to them is not forthcoming. Here it is of decisive importance that the analyst comprehend and acknowledge the phase-appropriateness of the demands of the grandiose self and that he grasp the fact that for a long time it is a mistake to emphasize to the patient that his demands are unrealistic. If the analyst demonstrates to the patient that the narcissistic needs are appropriate within the context of the total early phase that is being revived in the transference and that they have to be expressed, then the patient will gradually reveal the urges and fantasies of the grandiose self, and the slow process is thus initiated that leads to the integration of the grandiose self into the realistic structure of the ego and to an adaptively useful transformation of its energies.

The empathic comprehension of the reactivation of the earlier developmental stages (the alter-ego transference or twinship; the merger with the analyst through the extension of the grandiose self) is, however, not achieved easily. It is, for example, usually difficult for the analyst to hold fast to the realization that the meagerness of object-related imagery with regard to current and past figures as well as with regard to the analyst himself is the appropriate manifestation of an archaic narcissistic relationship. A frequent misunderstanding of the mirror transference in general and of the therapeutic activation of the most archaic stages of the grandiose self in particular thus consists in its being mistaken for the outgrowth of a widespread resistance against the establishment of an object-instinctual transference. And many analyses of narcissistic personality disorders are either short-circuited at this point (leading to a brief analysis of subsidiary sectors of the personality in which ordinary transferences do occur while the principal disturbance, which is narcissistic, remains untouched) or are forced into a mistaken and unprofitable direction against diffuse, nonspecific, and chronic ego resistances of the analysand.

If the establishment of a mirror transference is, however, not prevented, the gradual mobilization of the repressed grandiose self will take place and a number of specific, pathognomonic, and therapeutically valuable resistances will be set in motion. The principal end of the working-through processes in the idealizing transference is the internalization of the idealized object which leads to the strengthening of the matrix of the ego and to the strengthening of the patient's ideals; the principal end of the working-through processes in the mirror transference is the transformation of the grandiose self which results in a firming of the ego's potential for action (through the increasing realism of the ambitions of the personality) and in increasingly realistic self-esteem.

An important question posed by the analysis of narcissistic personalities, especially in the area of the grandiose self, concerns the degree of therapeutic activity which needs to be employed by the analyst. In applying Aichhorn's technique with juvenile delinquents (1936), for example, the analyst offers himself actively to the patient as a replica of his grandiose self, in a relationship which resembles the twinship (or alter-ego) variant of a mirror transference (see also A. Freud's illuminating summary [1951]). A delinquent's capacity to attach himself to the analyst in admiration indicates, however, that an idealized parent imago and the deep wish to form an idealizing transference are (preconsciously) present, but, in consequence of early disappointments, they are denied and hidden. It was Aichhorn's special understanding for the delinquent that led him to offer himself first as a mirror image of the delinquent's grandiose self. He was thus able to initiate a veiled mobilization of idealizing cathexes toward an idealized object without yet disturbing the necessary protection of the defensively created grandiose self and its activities. Once a bond is established, however, a gradual shift from the omnipotence of the grandiose self to the more deeply longed-for omnipotence of an idealized object (and the requisite therapeutic dependence on it) can be achieved.

In the analytic treatment of the ordinary cases of narcissistic personality disturbance, however, the active encouragement of idealization is not desirable. It leads to the establishment of a tenacious transference bondage, bringing about the formation of a cover of massive identification and hampering the gradual alteration of the existing narcissistic structures. But a spontaneously occurring therapeutic mobilization of the idealized parent imago or of the grandiose self is indeed to be welcomed and must not be interfered with.

There are two antithetical pitfalls concerning the form of the interpretations which focus on the narcissistic transferences: the analyst's readiness to moralize about the patient's narcissism; and his tendency toward abstractness of the relevant interpretations.

The triad of value judgments, moralizing, and therapeutic activism in which the analyst steps beyond the basic analytic attitude to become the patient's leader and teacher is most likely to occur when the psychopathology under scrutiny is not understood metapsychologically. Under these circumstances the analyst can hardly be blamed when he tends to abandon the ineffective analytic armamentarium and instead offers himself to the patient as an object to identify with in order to achieve therapeutic changes. If lack of success in areas that are not yet understood metapsychologically is tolerated, however, without the abandonment of analytic means, then the occurrence of new analytic insights is not prevented and scientific progress can be made.

Where metapsychological understanding is not entirely lacking but is incomplete, analysts tend to supplement their interpretations with suggestive pressure and the weight of the personality of the therapist becomes of greater importance. There are thus certain analysts who are said to be exceptionally gifted in the analysis of "borderline" cases and anecdotes about their therapeutic activities become widely known in analytic circles. But just as the surgeon, in the heroic era of surgery, was a charismatically gifted individual who performed great feats of courage and skill, while the modern surgeon tends to be a calm, well-trained craftsman, so also with the analyst. As our knowledge about the narcissistic disorders increases, their treatment becomes the work of analysts who do not employ any special charisma of their personalities but restrict themselves to the use of the tools that provide rational success: interpretations and reconstructions. There are, of course, moments when a forceful statement is indicated as a final move in persuading the patient that the gratifications obtained from the unmodified narcissistic fantasies are spurious. A skillful analyst of an older generation, for example, as asserted by local psychoanalytic lore, would make his point at a strategic juncture by silently handing over a crown and scepter to his unsuspecting analysand instead of confronting him with yet another verbal interpretation. In general, however, the psychoanalytic process is most enhanced if we trust the spontaneous synthetic functions of the patient's ego to integrate the narcissistic configurations gradually, in an atmosphere of analytic-empathic acceptance, instead of driving the analysand toward an imitation of the analyst's scornful rejection of the analysand's lack of realism.

The second danger, namely, that interpretations regarding the narcissistic transference might become too abstract, can be much diminished if we avoid falling victim to the widespread confusion between object relations and object love. We must bear in mind that our interpretations about the idealizing transference and the mirror transference are statements about an intense object relationship, despite the fact that the object is invested with narcissistic cathexes, and that we are explaining to the analysand how his very narcissism leads him to a heightened sensitivity about certain specific aspects and actions of the object, the analyst, whom he experiences in a narcissistic mode.

If the analyst's interpretations are noncondemnatory; if he can clarify to the patient in concrete terms the significance and the meaning of his (often acted-out) messages, of his seemingly irrational hypersensitivity, and of the back-and-forth flow of the cathexis of the narcissistic positions; and especially, if he can demonstrate to the patient that these archaic attitudes are comprehensible, adaptive, and valuable within the context of the total state of personality development of which they form a part—then the mature segment of the ego will not turn away from the grandiosity of the archaic

self or from the awesome features of the overestimated, narcissistically experienced object. Over and over again, in small, psychologically manageable portions, the ego will deal with the disappointment at having to recognize that the claims of the grandiose self are
unrealistic. And, in response to this experience, it will either mourn-
fully withdraw a part of the narcissistic investment from the archaic
image of the self, or it will, with the aid of newly acquired structure,
neutralize the associated narcissistic energies or channel them into
aim-inhibited pursuits. And over and over again, in small, psychologically manageable portions, the ego will deal with the disappointment at having to recognize that the idealized object is unavailable
or imperfect. And, in response to this experience, it will withdraw
a part of the idealizing investment from the object and strengthen
the corresponding internal structures. In short, if the ego learns
first to accept the presence of the mobilized narcissistic structures,
it will gradually integrate them into its own realm, and the analyst
will witness the establishment of ego dominance and ego autonomy
in the narcissistic sector of the personality.

REACTIONS OF THE ANALYST

Reactions of the Analyst during the Mobilization of the Patient's Idealized Parent Imago in the Idealizing Transference

Some time ago I was consulted by a colleague concerning a stalemate which seemed to have been present from the beginning of the
analysis and to have persisted through two years of work. Since the
patient, a shallow, promiscuous woman, showed a serious disturbance
of her ability to establish meaningful object relationships and presented a history of severe childhood traumata, I tended initially to
agree with the analyst that the extent of the narcissistic fixations
prevented the establishment of that minimum of transferences without which analysis cannot proceed. Still, I asked the analyst for an
account of the early sessions, with particular attention to activities on
his part which the patient might have experienced as a rebuff.
Among the earliest transference manifestations several dreams of
this Catholic patient had contained the figure of an inspired, ide-
alistic priest. While these early dreams had remained uninterpreted,
the analyst remembered—clearly against resistance—that he had

subsequently indicated that he was not a Catholic. He had justified this move by her supposed need to be acquainted with a minimum of the actual situation since in his view the patient's hold on reality was tenuous. This event must have been very significant for the patient. We later understood that, as an initial, tentative transference step, she had reinstated an attitude of idealizing religious devotion from the beginning of adolescence, an attitude which in turn had been the revival of awe and admiration from childhood. These earliest idealizations, as we could conclude later, had been a refuge from bizarre tensions and fantasies caused by traumatic stimulations and frustrations from the side of her pathological parents. The analyst's misguided remark, however, that he was not a Catholic— i.e., not an idealized good and healthy version of the patient—constituted a rebuff for her and led to the stalemate, which the analyst, with the aid of a number of consultations concerning this patient and his response to her, was later largely able to break.

I am focusing neither on the transference nor on the effect of the analyst's mistake on the analysis, but on the elucidation of a countertransference symptom. A combination of circumstances, among them the fact that I observed other, similar incidents, allows me to offer the following explanation with a high degree of conviction. An analytically unwarranted rejection of a patient's idealizing attitudes is usually motivated by a defensive fending off of narcissistic tensions, experienced as embarrassment and leading even to hypochondriacal preoccupations, which are generated in the analyst when repressed fantasies of his grandiose self become stimulated by the patient's idealization.

Are these reactions of the analyst in the main motivated by current stress, or are they related to the dangerous mobilization of specific repressed unconscious constellations?

In a letter to Binswanger, Freud (1913) expressed himself as follows about the problem of countertransference: "What is given to the patient," Freud said, must be "consciously allotted, and then more or less of it as the need may arise. Occasionally a great deal...." And later Freud set down the crucial maxim: "To give someone too little because one loves him too much is being unjust to the patient and a technical error."

If a patient's incestuous object-libidinal demands elicit an intense unconscious response in the analyst, he may become overly technical vis-à-vis the patient's wishes or will not even recognize them—at any rate, his ego will not have the freedom to choose the response required by the analysis. A parallel situation may arise in the analysis of a narcissistic personality disturbance when the remobilization of the idealized parent imago prompts the analysand to see the analyst as the embodiment of idealized perfection. If the analyst has not come to terms with his own grandiose self, he may respond to the idealization with an intense stimulation of his unconscious grandiose fantasies and an intensification of defenses which bring about his rejection of the patient's idealizing transference. If the analyst's defensive attitude becomes chronic, the establishment of a workable idealizing transference is interfered with and the analytic process is blocked.

It makes little difference whether the rejection of the patient's idealization is blunt, which is rare; or subtle (as in the instance reported), which is common; or, which is most frequent, almost concealed by correct, but prematurely given, genetic or dynamic interpretations (such as the analyst's quickly calling the patient's attention to idealized figures in his past or pointing out hostile impulses which supposedly underlie the idealizing ones). The rejection may express itself through no more than a slight overobjectivity of the analyst's attitude; or it may reveal itself in the tendency to disparage the narcissistic idealization in a humorous and kindly way. And finally, it is even deleterious to emphasize the patient's assets at a time when he attempts the idealizing expansion of the ingrained narcissistic positions and feels insignificant by comparison with the therapist—appealing though it might seem when the analyst expresses respect for his patient. In short, during those phases of the analysis of narcissistic personalities when an idealizing transference begins to germinate, there is only one correct analytic attitude: to accept the admiration.

Reactions of the Analyst during the Therapeutic Mobilization of the Patient's Grandiose Self in the Mirror Transference

The mirror transference occurs in different forms which expose the analyst to different emotional tasks. In the mirror transference in the narrower sense the patient reacts to the ebb and flow of the analyst's empathy with, and response to, his narcissistic needs, and the presence of the analyst is thus acknowledged. Even these circumstances, however, may elicit reactions in the analyst which interfere with the therapeutic reactivation of the grandiose self since the analyst's own narcissistic needs may make him intolerant of a situation in which he is reduced to the role of mirror for the patient's infantile narcissism. In the twinship (alter-ego) and merger varieties of the remobilization of the grandiose self, however, the analyst is deprived of even the minimum of narcissistic gratification: the patient's acknowledgment of his separate existence. While in the mirror transference the analyst may become incapable of comprehending the patient's narcissistic needs and of responding to them, the most common dangers in the twinship or merger are his boredom, his lack of emotional involvement with the patient, and his precarious maintenance of attention. A theoretical discussion of these failures must, however, be omitted here. On the one hand, it would require an examination of the psychology of attention in the absence of stimulation by object cathexes; on the other hand, one would have to study certain aspects of the vulnerability of empathy in analysts which are genetically related to the fact that a specific empathic sensitivity, acquired in an early narcissistic relationship, often contributes decisively to the motivation for becoming an analyst. Instead of a theoretical discussion, however, the attempt will be made to illuminate the subject matter with the aid of a clinical example.

Miss F., age twenty-five, had sought analysis because of diffuse dissatisfactions. Despite the fact that she was active in her profession and had numerous social contacts, she was not intimate with anyone, and felt different from other people and isolated. She had a series of love relationships but had rejected marriage because she knew that such a step would be a sham. She was subject to sudden changes in her mood with an associated uncertainty about the reality of her feelings and thoughts. In metapsychological terms the disturbance was due to a faulty integration of the grandiose self which led to swings between states of anxious excitement and elation over a secret "preciousness" which made her vastly better than anyone else (during times when the ego came close to giving way to the hypercathected grandiose self) and states of emotional depletion (when the ego used all its strength to wall itself off from the un-realistic, grandiose substructure). Genetically, the fact that the mother had been depressed during several periods early in the child's life had prevented the gradual integration of the narcissistic-ex-hibitionistic cathexes of the grandiose self. During decisive periods of her childhood the girl's presence and activities had not called forth maternal pleasure and approval. On the contrary, whenever she tried to speak about herself, the mother deflected, imperceptibly, the focus of attention to her own depressive self-preoccupations, and thus the child was deprived of that optimal maternal acceptance which transforms crude exhibitionism and grandiosity into adaptably useful self-esteem and self-enjoyment.

During extended phases of the analysis, beginning at a time when I did not yet understand the patient's psychopathology, the follow-ing progression of events frequently occurred during analytic ses-sions. The patient would arrive in a friendly mood, settle down quietly, and begin to communicate her thoughts and feelings: about current topics; the transference; and insights concerning the connec-tion between present and past, and between transferences upon the analyst and analogous strivings toward others. In brief, the first part of the sessions had the appearance of a well-moving self-analysis when the analyst is, indeed, little else than an interested observer who holds himself in readiness for the next wave of resistances. The stage in question lasted much longer, however, than the periods of self-analysis encountered in other analyses. I noted, furthermore, that I was not able to maintain the attitude of interested attention which normally establishes itself effortlessly and spontaneously when one listens to an analysand's work of free associations during periods of relatively unimpeded self-analysis. And, finally, after a prolonged period of ignorance and misunderstanding during which I was inclined to argue with the patient about the correctness of my inter-pretations and to suspect the presence of stubborn, hidden resist-ances, I came to the crucial recognition that the patient demanded a specific response to her communications, and that she completely rejected any other. Unlike the analysand during periods of genuine self-analysis, the patient could not tolerate the analyst's silence, but, at approximately the mid-point of the sessions, she would suddenly get violently angry at me for being silent. (The archaic nature of her need, it may be added, was betrayed by the suddenness with which it appeared—like the sudden transition from satiation to hunger or from hunger to satiation in very young children.) I gradually learned, however, that she would immediately become calm and content when I, at these moments, simply summarized or repeated what she had in essence already said (such as, "You are again struggling to free yourself from becoming embroiled in your mother's suspiciousness against men." Or, "You have worked your way through to the understanding that the fantasies about the visiting Englishman are reflections of fantasies about me"). But if I went beyond what the patient herself had already said or discovered, even by a single step only (such as: "The fantasies about the visiting foreigner are reflections of fantasies about me and, in addition, I think that they are a revival of the dangerous stimulation to which you felt exposed by your father's fantasy-stories about you"), she would again get violently angry (regardless of the fact that what I had added might be known to her, too), and would furiously accuse me, in a tense, high-pitched voice, of undermining her, that with my remark I had destroyed everything she had built up, and that I was wrecking the analysis.

Certain convictions can only be acquired firsthand and I am thus not able to demonstrate in detail the correctness of the following conclusions. During this phase of the analysis the patient had begun to remobilize an archaic, intensely cathected image of the self which had heretofore been kept in repression. Concomitant with the remobilization of the grandiose self, on which she had remained fixated, there also arose the renewed need for an archaic object that would be nothing more than the embodiment of a psychological function which the patient's psyche could not yet perform for itself: to respond empathically to her narcissistic display and to provide her with narcissistic sustenance through approval, mirroring, and echoing. The patient thus attempted, with the aid of my confirming, mirroring presence, to integrate a hypercathected archaic self into the rest of her personality. This process began at this stage with a cautious reinstatement of a sense of the reality of her thoughts and feelings; it later moved gradually toward the transformation of her intense exhibitionistic needs into an ego-syntonic sense of her own value and an enjoyment of her activities.

Due to the fact that I was at that time not sufficiently alert to the pitfalls of such transference demands, many of my interventions interfered with the work of structure formation. But I know that the obstacles that opposed my understanding lay not only in the cognitive area; and I can affirm, without transgressing the rules of decorum and without indulging in the kind of immodest self-revelation which ultimately hides more than it admits, that there were specific hindrances in my own personality which stood in my way. There was a residual insistence, related to deep and old fixation points, on seeing myself in the narcissistic center of the stage; and, although I had of course for a long time struggled with the relevant childhood delusions and thought that I had, on the whole, achieved dominance over them, I was not up to the extreme demands posed by the conceptually unaided confrontation with the reactivated grandiose self of my patient. Thus I refused to entertain the possibility that I was not an object for the patient, not an amalgam with the patient's childhood loves and hatreds, but only, as I reluctantly came to see, an impersonal function, without significance except insofar as it related to the kingdom of her own remobilized narcissistic grandeur and exhibitionism. For a long time I insisted, therefore, that the patient's reproaches related to specific transference fantasies and wishes on the oedipal level—but I could make no headway in this direction. It was ultimately, I believe, the high-pitched tone of her voice which expressed such utter conviction of being right—the conviction of a very young child; a pent-up, heretofore unexpressed conviction—which led me on the right track. I recognized that, whenever I did more (or less) than to provide simple approval or confirmation in response to the patient's reports of her own discoveries, I became for her the depressive mother who deflected the narcissistic cathexes from the child upon herself, or who did not provide the needed narcissistic echo.

The clinical situation described in the foregoing pages and, especially, the analyst's therapeutic responses to it require further elucidation.

At first hearing I might seem to be stating that, in instances of this type, the analyst must indulge a transference wish of the analysand; specifically, that the patient had not received the necessary emotional echo or approval from the depressive mother, and that the analyst must now give it to her in order to provide a "corrective emotional experience" (Alexander, French, et al., 1946).

There are indeed patients for whom this type of indulgence is not only a temporary tactical requirement during certain stressful phases of analysis but who cannot ever undertake the steps which lead to that increased ego dominance over the childhood wish which is the specific aim of psychoanalytic work. And there is, furthermore, no doubt that, occasionally, the indulgence of an important childhood wish—especially if it is provided with an air of conviction and in a therapeutic atmosphere that carries a quasi-religious, magical connotation of the efficacy of love—can have lasting beneficial effects with regard to the relief of symptoms and behavioral change in the patient.

The analytic process in analyzable cases, however, as in the one described in the present clinical vignette, develops in a different way. Although, for tactical reasons, the analyst might in such instances transitorily have to provide what one might call a *reluctant compliance with the childhood wish,* the true analytic aim is not indulgence but mastery based on insight, achieved in a setting of (tolerable) analytic abstinence. The recognition of the specific childhood demand was only the beginning of the working-through process concerning the grandiose self. It was followed by the recall of clusters of analogous memories concerning her mother's entering a phase of depressive self-preoccupation during later periods of the patient's life. Finally, a central set of poignant memories, upon which a series of earlier and later ones seemed to be telescoped, referred specifically to episodes when she came home from kindergarten and early elementary school. At such times she would rush home as fast as she could, joyfully anticipating telling her mother about her successes in school. She recalled then how her mother opened the door, but, instead of the mother's face lighting up, her expression remained blank; and how, when the patient began talking about school and play and about her achievements and successes of the preceding hours, the mother appeared to listen and participate, but imperceptibly the topic of the conversation shifted and the mother began to talk about herself, her headache and her tiredness and her other physical self-preoccupations. All that the patient could directly recall about her own reactions was that she felt suddenly drained of energy and empty; she was for a long time unable to remember feeling any rage at her mother on such occasions. It was only after a prolonged period of working through that she could gradually establish connections between the rage which she experienced against me, when I did not understand her demands, and feelings she had experienced as a child.

This phase was then followed by a slow, shame-provoking, and anxious revelation of her persistent infantile grandiosity and exhibitionism; the working through accomplished during this period led ultimately to increased ego dominance over the old grandiosity and exhibitionism, and thus to greater self-confidence and to other favorable transformations of her narcissism in this segment of her personality.

CONCLUDING REMARKS

The foregoing examination must, in its entirety, be considered a summarizing preview of a broader study; no retrospective survey of the findings and opinions that have been presented will, therefore, be given. It must be stressed, however, that there are some important aspects of the subject matter which either could only be mentioned briefly or had to be disregarded altogether.

Thus, as mentioned initially, it was necessary to omit almost all references to the work of others, such as, for example, the significant contributions by H. Hartmann (1953), K. R. Eissler (1953), E. Jacobson (1964), and A. Reich (1960); furthermore, it was not possible to compare the approach toward our subject matter taken in the present study with that chosen by such important authors as Federn (1952) on the one hand and Mahler (1952) on the other; and, finally, still within the same context, it was not possible to discuss the work of Melanie Klein and her school which often appears to be concerned with disorders that are related to those scrutinized in this essay.

No attempt was made to define and delimit the area of psychopathology with which this study is dealing; the question of the appropriateness of the use of the term transference in the present context could not be taken up; the discussion of the role of aggression had to be bypassed; the recurrent traumatic states in which the focus of the analysis shifts temporarily to the near-exclusive consideration of the overburdenedness of the psyche could not be illuminated; many other difficulties, therapeutic limitations and failures were not considered; and, most regrettably, it was not possible to demonstrate the specific wholesome changes that occur as the result of the transformation of the narcissistic structures and of their energies. In all: it was the aim of this contribution to give the outline of a systematic approach to the psychoanalytic treatment of narcissistic personalities; a thorough scrutiny of the subject could not be undertaken.

BIBLIOGRAPHY

Aichhorn, A. (1936), The Narcissistic Transference of the "Juvenile Impostor." In: *Delinquency and Child Guidance,* ed. O. Fleischmann, P. Kramer, & H. Ross. New York: International Universities Press, 1964, pp. 174-191.

Alexander, F., French, T. M., et al. (1946), *Psychoanalytic Therapy: Principles and Application.* New York: Ronald Press.

Eissler, K. R. (1953), Notes upon the Emotionality of a Schizophrenic Patient and Its Relation to Problems of Technique. *This Annual,* 8:199-251.

Federn, P. (1952), *Ego Psychology and the Psychoses,* ed. E. Weiss. New York: Basic Books.

Freud, A. (1951), Obituary: August Aichhorn. *Int. J. Psa.,* 32:51-56.

Freud, S. (1913), Letter to Ludwig Binswanger of February 20, 1913. In: Binswanger, L. *Erinnerungen an Sigmund Freud.* Bern: Francke Verlag, 1956, p. 65.

Hartmann, H. (1953), Contribution to the Metapsychology of Schizophrenia. *This Annual,* 8:177-198.

Jacobson, E. (1964), *The Self and the Object World.* New York: International Universities Press.

Kohut, H. (1966), Forms and Transformations of Narcissism. *J. Amer. Psa. Assn.,* 14:243-272.

Mahler, M. S. (1952), On Child Psychosis and Schizophrenia: Autistic and Symbiotic Infantile Psychoses. *This Annual,* 7:286-305.

Nagera, H. (1964), Autoerotism, Autoerotic Activities, and Ego Development. *This Annual,* 19:240-255.

Niederland, W. G. (1959), Schreber: Father and Son. *Psa. Quart.,* 28:151-169.

Reich, A. (1960), Pathologic Forms of Self-esteem Regulation. *This Annual,* 15:215-232.

THE BODY IMAGE, THE FUNCTION OF MASTURBATION, AND ADOLESCENCE

Problems of the Ownership of the Body

MOSES LAUFER, Ph.D. (London)

The ideas I wish to examine in this paper are based on observations made during the treatment of disturbed adolescents. Although the clinical material that I shall present is related to the pathology of these adolescents, it is normal adolescence which I am trying to understand. I shall examine (1) the role that masturbation and masturbation fantasies play in enabling the adolescent to establish the primacy of genitality; and (2) the internal factors which determine whether or not the adolescent will succeed in changing the image of his body so that this image will include his mature genitals as functioning organs.

I have often been faced with the need to decide whether some of the behavior or fantasies which adolescents reported was part of normal adolescence or whether these contained the core of their pathology. Some adolescents reported masturbation fantasies which sounded very regressive in nature, but they did not seem to interfere seriously with their social and sexual adaptation. Other ado-

The author is a member of the Hampstead Child-Therapy Clinic, which is at present maintained by The Field Foundation, Inc., New York; The Anna Freud Foundation, New York; The Grant Foundation, Inc., New York; The Estate of Flora Haas, New York; The Walter E. Meyer Research Institute of Law, New York; The National Institute of Mental Health, Bethesda, Maryland; The Old Dominion Foundation, New York; The Psychoanalytic Research and Development Fund, Inc., New York; The Taconic Foundation, Inc., New York.

Director, Centre for the Study of Adolescence/Brent Consultation Centre. The Centre for the Study of Adolescence is supported by The Grant Foundation, Inc., New York. The Brent Consultation Centre, a walk-in consultation service for adolescents, is under the auspices of the Education Department, London Borough of Brent. Honorary staff member, University College Hospital, Department of Psychological Medicine, London.

Part of this paper was presented to the British Psycho-Analytical Society, July, 1968.

lescents seemed to present a much more organized picture, but they nevertheless felt that they had reached a deadlock in their development. They experienced their masturbation or masturbation fantasies as repeated proofs that something was badly wrong with them (and their assessments were very often right).

Such differences in the extent and quality of the anxiety experienced by adolescents over masturbation and masturbation fantasies made me think that I might be observing the pathological side of something that serves a very important function in normal adolescence, namely, the function of helping the ego reorganize itself around the supremacy of genitality (which at the same time means the successful repression of pregenital wishes). In the cases to be presented, the deadlock which these adolescents felt they had reached seemed to represent their awareness that they were unable to use masturbation or masturbation fantasies as something equivalent to "trial action." Not only was genitality dangerous to these adolescents, but the prephallic fantasies (even though these were ego alien) offered such satisfaction that they severely hindered development. The very nature of these regressive fantasies prevented their use as "trial action" for adult sexual behavior.

In each of the cases, certain preoedipal experiences had distorted the oedipal solution in such a way that genitality would inevitably be disrupted—and this distortion was, in adolescence, then fought out within themselves around the question of the "ownership of the body." One crucial factor seems to be whether the adolescent can affectively experience his mature body as belonging to himself or whether he reacts to it as if it still belonged to his mother who first cared for it. These adolescents felt that in masturbation and in the accompanying fantasies they were reliving a real experience, and that this included the satisfaction of regressive wishes. They were unable to break with this pattern and felt they had no control over their bodies. They regarded their bodies either as their enemies or as something quite separate from the rest of themselves. In their need to create the feeling that their bodies were either nonexistent or free of danger, they resorted to various means—suicide attempts, taking drugs, overeating. These adolescents experienced masturbation (referred to by Freud as the "primary addiction") or the masturbation fantasies as something equivalent to a failure in repression or as the vehicle for the satisfaction of something perverse and shameful. In the cases to be reported, not one of the adolescents was able to use masturbation and the fantasies as a constructive step furthering development to adulthood, such as in establishing hetero-sexual object relationships or the primacy of the genitals.

In the first part of this paper I shall briefly review the literature related to (1) the body image, and (2) masturbation. The second part contains the clinical material, which is followed by a discussion of some of my ideas about the relationship between masturbation, the body image, and adolescence as a developmental stage.

REVIEW OF LITERATURE

The Body Image

Although a number of authors have reported observations which are related to the development of the body image (Bak, 1939; Bon-nard, 1958; Eissler, 1958; Federn, 1952; Jacobson, 1964; Peto, 1959; Schilder, 1935), I shall confine my remarks to those contributions that contain either detailed clinical observations or pertinent theo-retical formulations.

In these writings two main points are relevant to my topic: (1) that the body and the relationship to one's own body are central factors in determining the development of the mental apparatus; and (2) that there seems to be a close link between the body image and the development of ego functions, in particular perception and reality testing. However, there is considerable variation in the evalu-ation of which factor is most important in determining the mental image that the person has of his own body.

In *The Ego and the Id* (1923), Freud states:

A person's own body, and above all its surface, is a place from which both external and internal perceptions may spring. It is *seen* like any other object, but to the *touch* it yields two kinds of sensations, one of which may be equivalent to an internal per-ception [p. 25]. The ego is first and foremost a bodily ego; it is not merely a surface entity, but is itself the projection of a surface [p. 26]. I.e. the ego is ultimately derived from bodily sensations, chiefly from those springing from the surface of the body. It may thus be regarded as a mental projection of the surface of the body, besides . . . representing the superficies of the mental apparatus [p. 26, n. added in 1927].

In his detailed discussion of Freud's ideas relating to the role of the body in ego development, Hoffer (1950) distinguished between the infant's sight of his body and his reaction to touching his body. "Coming in touch with its own body elicits two sensations of the same quality and these lead to the distinction between the self and the not-self, between body and what subsequently becomes environment. In consequence this factor contributes to the processes of structural differentiation. Delimitation between the self-body and the outer world, the world where the objects are found, is thus initiated" (p. 19).

Both Greenacre and Mahler have consistently examined the development of the body image, and Winnicott (1953) reported some observations that seem especially relevant to the problem I defined earlier as "ownership of the body." Mahler (1963) summarized one of her main hypotheses as follows:

> . . . normal separation-individuation is the first crucial prerequisite for the development and maintenance of the "sense of identity." . . . I have suggested that the feeling of identity may be defined as the cohesive cathexis of our securely individuated and differentiated self-image, and that its beginnings may be traced back to the first two years of life, at which time the child gradually emerges, that is to say, "hatches" from the symbiotic common membrane. . . . In conceptualizing the genesis of the eventual "sense of identity," I tend to regard demarcation of the body image from the image of the object, the mother, as the core of the process [p. 309].

Peter Blos (1967) applied this idea of Mahler's to adolescence, which he describes as "the second individuation process, the first one having been completed toward the end of the third year of life with the attainment of object constancy. . . . What is in infancy a 'hatching from the symbiotic membrane to become an individuated toddler' (Mahler, 1963), becomes in adolescence the shedding of family dependencies, the loosening of infantile object ties in order to become a member of society at large or, simply, of the adult world" (p. 163).

Winnicott (1953), studying the first not-me possession, is much more explicit about this process, linking these first body-mother-transitional object experiences with the development of the ego, and especially with the development of reality testing and sublimation. He states:

> There is no possibility whatever for an infant to proceed from the pleasure-principle to the reality principle or towards and beyond primary identification . . . unless there is a good enough mother. The good enough 'mother' . . . is one who makes active adaptation to the infant's needs, an active adaptation that gradually lessens, according to the infant's growing ability to account for failure of adaptation and to tolerate the results of frustration. . . . The mother, at the beginning, by almost 100 per cent. adaptation affords the infant the opportunity for the *illusion* that her breast is part of the infant. It is, as it were, under magical control. The same can be said in terms of infant care in general, in the quiet times between excitements. Omnipotence is nearly a fact of experience. The mother's eventual task is gradually to disillusion the infant, but she has no hope of success unless at first she has been able to give sufficient opportunity for illusion [p. 94f.].
>
> [In a paper on adolescence (1961) he links what is described as "this essential phase of infancy" with what occurs in adolescence:] The adolescent is essentially an isolate. It is from a position of isolation that a beginning is made which may result in relationships between individuals, and eventually in socialization. In this respect the adolescent is repeating an essential phase of infancy, for the infant is an isolate, at least until he or she has repudiated the not-me, and has become set up as a separated-off individual, one that can form relationships with objects that are external to the self and outside the area of omnipotent control [p. 81].

Although Winnicott's remarks refer back to the experience of infancy, I think that the role of the mother in encouraging adaptation remains crucial throughout the preoedipal period. During this entire period the child relies on the mother to frustrate his wish for her constantly to care for and stimulate his body (see Brunswick, 1940). When there has been a failure in this area of the mother-child relationship, one can later observe the adolescent's inability to experience the mature body as belonging to himself. The original failure determines the manner in which the oedipal conflict is solved, and this is again repeated in relation to the change in the image of the body in adolescence.

Greenacre's observations and conclusions have been especially helpful to me in understanding the body-image changes during adolescence; for this reason I shall report her views in some detail. In her paper on the faulty development of the body image in cases of fetishism (1953), she states:

> Our body image develops largely from endogenous sensations, from contacts with the outer world (of which feeling one part of the body with another is a peculiar condensation) and from seeing our own bodies [p. 91].
>
> [She elaborated on this point in a later paper (1958):] The body areas which are then [after the development and maintenance of speech] most significant in comparing and contrasting and establishing individual recognition of the body self, and that of others, are the *face* and the *genitals*. While some response to the mother's or nurse's face occurs very early, there can be no comparison of this with the own face until relatively late. . . . They are obviously of basic importance in the sense of identity. At the same time they are the areas which are least easily visible to the individual himself. . . . [These factors have a different influence on the quality of the child's experience in different stages of his development.] What I have emphasized so far in regard to the early incorporation of the body, and especially the genital parts of another person, proceeds mostly through the combined agency of touch and vision and is largely a "build-up" of the body image according to the body surface, i.e., with stress on body exterior rather than a real internalized incorporation through the mouth. . . . [During the second half of the second year], however, and especially during the third year, the gradual increase in genital feelings—clitoral and phallic—give endogenous sensations and pressures from within a kind of sensory peg which combines locally with the body imagery produced by visual and tactile appreciation of the own genitals and those of the others. With the gradual intensification of these endogenous phallic sensations, this part of the body assumes greater importance [p. 616f.].
>
> [She summarizes part of her thesis as follows:] It would seem to me that identity, although generally having a stable core both in body and psychic structure and functioning, is nonetheless subject to various changes and nodal points of development, roughly following stages of body and maturational achievement

with their accompanying and emotional problems. Consequently, no sense of adult functional identity can be completed until after adolescence is well past and assimilated [p. 626].

The relevance of the conclusions reached by the authors to whom I have referred lies in the different kind of emphasis they place not only on the ingredients of body-image formation, but on the extent to which developmental stages participate in the formation of the body image. As a summary of the various conclusions presented by these authors, the following points can be listed: (1) the central role of the body in early ego development; (2) the importance of pre-oedipal experiences in the development of the body image; (3) the body image as a unity; (4) the demarcation of body "boundaries," which are determined partly by inner sensation and partly by the relationship to the outside, that is, the mother; (5) the role of the mother in creating the first relationship to the outside world (Winnicott), and then the quality of the phallic-oedipal experiences in the development of the body image (Greenacre); (6) the role of incorporation and identification; (7) the change in the body image with the change in phallic-clitoral sensations (Greenacre).

Masturbation

For purposes of this paper, I shall limit my remarks to those psychoanalytic writings which have special bearing on the topic of this paper.

In the *Three Essays* (1905) Freud begins the chapter on "The Transformations of Puberty" by stating: "With the arrival of puberty, changes set in which are destined to give infantile sexual life its final, normal shape" (p. 207). Further on in this chapter, he states,

This last pleasure [which is associated to the discharge of "the sexual substances"] is the highest in intensity, and its mechanism differs from that of the earlier pleasure [the mechanism of fore-pleasure]. It is brought about entirely by discharge: it is wholly a pleasure of satisfaction and with it the tension of the libido is for the time being extinguished [p. 210]. Puberty, which brings about so great an accession of libido in boys, is marked in girls by a fresh wave of *repression,* in which it is precisely clitoridal sexuality that is affected" [p. 220].

[In a footnote dated 1915, Freud remarks:] The problem of

why the sense of guilt of neurotics is, as Bleuler [1913] recently recognized, regularly attached to the memory of some masturbatory activity, usually at puberty, still awaits an exhaustive analytic explanation. [Added 1920]: The most general and most important factor concerned must no doubt be that masturbation represents the executive agency of the whole of infantile sexuality and is, therefore, able to take over the sense of guilt attaching to it [p. 189].

[In his contributions to the 1912 discussion on masturbation, Freud remarked:] And do not forget that masturbation is not to be equated with sexual activity in general: it is sexual activity subjected to certain limiting conditions. Thus it also remains possible that it is precisely these peculiarities of masturbatory activity which are the vehicles of its pathogenic effects [p. 251].

Anna Freud (1949) called attention to the fact that the

child's struggle against masturbation is directed on the one hand against the content of the fantasy, which as a result may disappear from consciousness, on the other hand against the bodily act itself. . . . The inner prohibition may concern the use of the hands in stimulating the genitalia. . . . Or the prohibition may be directed against the place of stimulation (penis, clitoris) so that the masturbatory activity becomes displaced to another part of the body. . . . In certain cases, on the other hand, this struggle against masturbation is abnormally successful. The ego then, and usually under the influence of castration-anxiety, inhibits even the occasional, relieving, masturbatory outbursts. As a result, the masturbation-fantasy is deprived of all bodily outlet, the libidinal and aggressive energy attached to it is completely blocked and dammed up, and eventually is displaced with full force from the realm of sex-life into the realm of ego-activities. Masturbation-fantasies are then acted out in dealings with the external world, which become, thereby, sexualized, distorted and maladjusted [p. 203f.].

K. R. Eissler (1958) noted: "Clinical experience has demonstrated that a delayed onset of masturbation or even its total absence (unless there is an early onset of heterosexual intercourse) during adolescence is generally a bad prognostic sign. Therefore, masturbation is an indispensable part of healthy adolescence. However, adolescent masturbation favors the evolution and integration of perverted fantasies" (p. 243). Although Eissler's statement is correct in a general sense, I think it is crucial to distinguish here between the male and the female adolescent because normally girls react differently to masturbation and its renunciation. This is described by Lampl-de Groot (1950) as follows:

For the development of sound femininity the gradual renunciation or reduction of masturbation during latency, at least in our present civilization, seems to be most favorable. A mild relapse during puberty with preference of introitus or vagina may serve the transition to adulthood. However, in many cases there is little or no masturbation at all in puberty. This may be an escape from the . . . [sadomasochistic] fantasies, originating in the masculinity complex, or it may also be caused by guilt feelings and anxiety and thus have a neurotic basis. But it may also be a preparation for the healthy submission to adult sexual life during which normal vaginal orgasm is experienced for the first time and the remainders of the infantile fantasies are adjusted to adulthood and thus enter the realistic world of the woman, in family life, and in other social or professional tasks [p. 173].

Jacobson (1964) has similar views:

The most incisive and upsetting experiences are the boy's first ejaculations and the onset of menstruation in the girl. We are familiar with the child's ambivalent reactions to these major events. Since the boy's first ejaculations commonly lead him to masturbation, they revive his castration fears and evoke guilt conflicts of such intensity that frequently the pleasure of becoming a man is overshadowed or smothered by long-lasting fears of this step. The beginning of menstruation in the girl arouses different but potentially even more dangerous conflicts, since genital bleeding is bound to reanimate the infantile belief in her castration . . . menstrual pain, discomfort, and fear of touching the bleeding genitals commonly prevent the young girl from masturbating, at least during the period. In adolescent girls, therefore, we rarely find *conscious* masturbation conflicts of such severity as in boys. The punitive aspects of their monthly bleedings tend in any event to absorb their guilt feelings [p. 162f.].

In addition to the points referred to above, several observations made by other authors (Blos, Deutsch, Geleerd, Harley, Spiegel) are relevant to this paper: (1) Masturbation during adolescence contains a new dimension that is especially important to the person; that is, sexual feelings and fantasies are now experienced within the context of possessing mature genitals. (2) Perverse fantasies, if present, can be repressed and possibly remain unconscious; or masturbation can be used as a vehicle for their satisfaction. (3) Normally, in adolescence, masturbation seems to fulfill an important function in encouraging certain changes in the mental apparatus (see Francis, 1968).

CASE REPORTS

I shall introduce the clinical material with an observation. The first psychotic-type behavior or "breakdown" frequently occurs soon after puberty has been reached. When we then look at the adolescent's history more closely, we generally detect signs of earlier pathology, but the actual "break" usually comes only with the onset of puberty. A psychoanalytic colleague recently told me that a number of the adolescents admitted to the acute admissions ward of the mental hospital where he works "broke down" following their first emission or soon after the beginning of menstruation.[1] When these patients are asked about their immediate fear or panic, they tend to explain it on the basis of their "confusion"; or they say that certain feelings drove them mad; and, sometimes more specifically, that they either wished intercourse with the parent of the opposite sex or they became terrified by the thought that they would kill one of their parents.

This observation is certainly an extreme of what normally occurs in the minds of many adolescents. However, in the adolescents who do break down we can observe the failure in the defense organization that would normally keep the oedipal and preoedipal fantasies or wishes under repression, a failure that leads to the adolescent's ego suddenly being overwhelmed. We are able to explain some of these manifestations as indications of the ego's inability to deal with the quantitative and qualitative changes in the instinctual demands taking place at puberty; as a result what is normally an unconscious fantasy may now become either a conscious thought or, worse still, an action. If the "break" is not totally psychotic, the adolescent will

[1] See also Helene Deutsch (1968), who emphasizes the traumatic effect of the first ejaculation.

become terrified, and his behavior will portray a combination of confusion and fear.

I begin with the rather extreme example of a "breakdown" following the onset of puberty because of its relevance to the body-image formation and its clinical interest. I believe that in such cases a combination of several factors is at work—a dissociation from one's physically mature body; a sudden collapse of the oedipal identifications; a failure of the defenses against the oedipal aggression, which suddenly becomes available in such huge quantities that the adolescent is literally overwhelmed by it. The guilt inherent in this process may help explain some of the adolescent suicides and even attempted suicides. As will be shown in the case reports, a breakdown that manifests itself in the form of suicide or attempted suicide is an aggressive attack on the internalized parent and at the same time is an attack on the person's own body, which at that moment *is experienced as separate from the rest of oneself and as not belonging to oneself.* For some of these adolescents, dying means *killing the body but not necessarily killing the mind.*

I am now treating two adolescent patients (one male and one female) who both made suicide attempts. In tracing their histories and the development of the relationship to their bodies, a central feature is the extent to which they dissociated their minds from their bodies and from the sensations arising in their bodies. They both felt that they must not have feelings; and both viewed the internalized mother as the person who was responsible for the control of their feelings. The mother-child relationship had been disrupted in the preoedipal period, distorting the child's relationship to himself and to objects, and determining fixation points that endangered future development. But the crucial factor in the disruption of the mother-child relationship was the manner in which it distorted ego development by the identifications made at this time (Ritvo and Solnit, 1958) and by the distortions of the body ego—these are the factors which then determine how the child's ego will cope with the oedipal conflict. When this faulty oedipal solution is again tested in puberty in the context of physical maturity, the adolescent experiences his body and body sensations as foreign and dangerous to his whole functioning. The two adolescents referred to both felt as though their mothers were giving them permission to experience feelings;

but they also felt that she could withdraw this permission at any time, and then the body and its sensations had to be disowned.

Another patient of mine, who finally did kill herself, used to talk of her body as that "filthy, ugly, horrible mass which is attached to me." In early adolescence, following the onset of menstruation and the growth of large breasts (the size of her breasts was very important to her—no matter what she did or how she dressed she could not hide them), she had her first "breakdown" in the form of taking to bed for a period of three months. At that time her body was "tired," but she felt that masturbation had confirmed that she was horrible. While she was in bed her mother took over the care of her body— something the patient encouraged and wanted to perpetuate. In her recollection one of the "lovely things" about staying in bed was that she could just lie there and think—she did not feel anything, her body was being looked after by her mother. Later in adolescence she formed a lesbian relationship, which was satisfactory as long as she could feel that this relationship was a "meeting of two minds" while her body was "available" to the other girl. She could never accept the fact that the enormous guilt she felt had anything to do with her recent behavior—she had to continue to keep the body and its sensations separate from her mind (see case 2 below).

When these patients described their masturbatory activities after puberty, it became clear that masturbation represented a perpetual demand by the body to feel something that they attempted to deny in the first place. It seems that, in their experience, the fantasies which accompanied masturbation confirmed their worthlessness or their abnormality, and the pleasure or satisfaction which they derived from masturbation was wrong and should be eliminated or destroyed in some way. While they seemed to be aware of an ongoing internal battle, they could not alter their attitudes to their bodies or to the sensations coming from their bodies. Put a different way, masturbation and the accompanying fantasies were never experienced as "trial actions"—instead the masturbation carried into consciousness the distorted oedipal fantasies which encouraged further regression. For this reason, their masturbation and the fantasies had to be experienced as ego alien.

The material of the adolescents who tried to reject their bodies or the body sensations contained a repetitive theme: masturbation, or even a pleasurable feeling in their genitals, either was a confrontation with their abnormality or represented their being forced by some unknown or uncontrollable power to give up an earlier state of equilibrium. It was as if puberty had suddenly changed the body into an enemy. Yet, in every instance in which the period before adolescence was worshiped or longed for, it turned out that the patient's suffering during latency had been severe. The difference in his experience of childhood and adolescence was that in childhood he could find some means of avoiding the stress, whereas in adolescence the reality of having a physically mature body forced him to fight his body and body feelings.

The following case material is intended to show why these adolescents were unable to reach genitality, and how the preoedipal fixations had distorted the relationship to their own bodies. In each one of these cases, the masturbatory activities and the accompanying fantasies disclosed that these adolescents had reached an intrapsychic deadlock. The deadlock was proof that the adolescent process itself was severely handicapped by the need to perpetuate the separation of body sensations from the image of themselves as sexually mature.

Case 1

Alan was referred to me at the age of eighteen following a suicidal attempt. He had an outstanding academic record and is now a university student. Six months prior to referral, a friend invited him to a party at Christmas. Alan reluctantly accepted. At the party he met a number of people, but he could not allow himself to dance with one girl who he thought was attractive. When he got home, he was miserable and angry. He felt there must be things in life other than girls, parties or sex. When he awoke the next morning, he decided to kill himself, without thinking too much about it. He swallowed a poisonous substance, which he had obtained from the laboratory where he had worked. "I kept it just in case I needed it."

One central theme in his treatment was the question whether it is right to do something actively to bring about an emission. When he had a nocturnal emission, he felt that it had nothing to do with him, whereas to masturbate would mean that he had decided to ejaculate. Throughout latency and early adolescence he refused to recognize that his body had any needs at all—it was as if eating, sleeping, and defecating where habits or were equivalent to reflex actions. One just did them. When he had the first nocturnal emission, he was furious with his body for tricking him into producing semen. In early adolescence he tried to masturbate, but he did not feel anything in his penis. Although this worried him, it also relieved him because it proved that "the body is the body, and it's got nothing to do with me."

Alan was the only child of very unhappy parents. He remembered his father as a withdrawn, depressed, and ignorant man. According to Alan, he and his father had almost nothing to do with each other. This was very similar to his mother's attitude toward his father. The parents had had separate bedrooms for as long as Alan could remember. He and his mother spent all their time together, while the father lived what seemed to be a totally separate existence. Until very recently, Alan often went to the theatre or cinema or on a Sunday outing with his mother, while the father stayed at home in his room.

Among the many intimacies and bodily routines between Alan and his mother in childhood, one seemed to be especially significant: the mother had regularly wiped Alan's anus after defecation. He insisted that she do this until there was no sign of feces on the paper. But suddenly, around the age of seven or eight, he refused to let anybody else do this and undertook it himself, sometimes spending ten minutes wiping himself and using about a half a roll of paper. Various recollections of his latency indicate that this was the central theme of his primal scene fantasy, i.e., that one partner does something via the anus to the other partner. This fantasy also contained his fear of anal penetration and his wish for it. There was great confusion in his mind about the proper roles of the male and the female, with a belief that it might be the woman (with the phallus) who does this to the man (the weak and castrated father).

This fantasy also contained his hatred of the mother, of whom he was still frightened. At this point in his adolescence, he felt very tied to her, even though he sometimes imagined that if he let himself go he could kill her.

The suicide attempt, then, can be understood in this context. He remembered that after he had come home from the party, he had wondered what it might be like to have intercourse with one of the girls he had met. He was convinced that he would never succeed.

He was frightened that he would completely lose control—as if it might turn out to be catastrophic for him. He thought he would have to do something drastic to succeed—and suicide seemed to him to be the answer. In treatment we have been able to establish that the suicide would simultaneously have served a number of purposes —it would have enabled him to destroy and rid himself of the hated internalized mother; and it would have done away with his weak and ineffectual body. But he never thought it would mean *his* death—it meant only the death of his body. Prior to his suicide attempt he had occasionally speculated whether something could be done about his body, and he had had the fantasy that if he killed his body, he might become alive again with a new and properly functioning body.

Case 2

Susan, a brilliant student, came to analysis after she had broken down at the university. The tutors had been worried that she might kill herself. She was hospitalized for a period, and sought treatment soon after she graduated with distinction. She was twenty-one when treatment began. After fifteen months the treatment was discontinued when funds were stopped. Three months later she committed suicide.

Throughout her life, Susan had been considered a brilliant person, and her mother had always insisted that Susan's mind be developed. To Susan, her mind made her much better than her younger brother. Yet, while she saw no advantage in being a man, to be a female was abhorrent and made her worthless. In early adolescence, she masturbated a great deal with the fantasy that either a man or another woman made love to her, but this would be done through some kind of anal penetration. During masturbation she would feel wild, crazy, and wonderful—all at the same time. At times she masturbated anally, or crouched down as if she was defecating. She would then always feel terrible and often hoped that she would die.

As mentioned earlier in the paper, in early adolescence she took to bed for three months, during which time her mother took care of her. In a lesbian relationship which she established when she was seventeen, she and the other girl would hold each other or kiss or masturbate one another. At that time Susan believed it might be possible to live happily with this girl. When this girl started a relationship with a boy, Susan was distressed to the point of considering suicide.

As a child, and even during her adolescence, Susan was convinced that her body was not quite complete, a conviction clearly related to her fantasy of possessing a penis. In adolescence, however, it took the form that she could not allow boys to come close to her. She could not bear the reality of having a vagina—this would be equivalent to giving up any hope that she could in some way alter her body. She was convinced that her mother had done something to her body, and that if she renounced sexual feelings, she might be allowed to have a complete body. Sexual feelings were a "demand and a curse on me," because they jeopardized the defense against the hatred of the mother for giving her such a useless and incomplete body.

Susan's mother thought of her as being much better than her brother—she had an outstanding mind, she could create with her mind, and she did not have to be like other children. She was something "special," which for Susan meant that she must not be occupied by sexual thoughts or wishes. During her adolescence, the body-mind split was strengthened very much by the need to keep her perverse masturbation fantasies separate from her mind—it was as if she was not responsible for these fantasies, even though the guilt she experienced was enormous. At the same time, this body-mind split helped temporarily in her defense against the extreme aggression directed at the mother. But this precarious balance was upset when she reached puberty and now, for the first time, her perverse masturbation fantasies became conscious. Masturbation then took on the meaning of confirming that her body was dirty and worthless, while at the same time gratifying in fantasy her perverse wishes. Moreover, it was equivalent to a failure in her ability to keep repressed the wish to destroy her body, which also meant the destruction of the mother.

Case 3

I have known Carol for some years now. From the age of fourteen on I saw her irregularly, but several months ago she began to attend four times weekly. She is now eighteen years old. Carol is an identical twin.

From the time that she and her twin sister went to different schools, Carol felt miserable and empty, constantly wanting to do something to alleviate the tension she felt in her body. When she and her sister were together, she felt as if they made each other complete; by being together they could make each other happy and take care of each other. From early adolescence on, she consciously experienced her body and her feelings as not belonging to herself— it was as though these belonged partly to her sister, and she hoped that her sister felt the same way. When she began to masturbate in adolescence, she not only considered it horrible, but in the long run it made her feel worse and more tense. The conscious fantasy varied —her sister and she were near one another; she was being held by another girl; or she was being penetrated by a middle-aged man.

Later in adolescence, she became promiscuous. During intercourse she felt that it was not her body at all that was there with her —it was as if she had little to do with the feelings which she then had. For a time, she was convinced that she would become a lesbian, saying that she sometimes abhorred having to be penetrated and that she preferred the idea of being admired by another girl. Her promiscuity helped her temporarily to give up masturbation and to replace the masturbation fantasy with the fantasy of having intercourse with an older man while her mother and twin sister looked on and were furious.

In her treatment she recalled that when as a small child she had looked in the mirror, she had said to herself, "Who is that?" As young children she and her sister were, according to Carol, exactly alike, "and it was wonderful and horrible." She remembered how she would fix her eyes on her sister until she really knew what her sister was feeling, "and then I knew what to feel." She loved playing games with her father, but she often felt terrible while playing with him because she thought she could attract him sexually if she really tried. But when she had such thoughts, she also believed it was not really her body that might attract him—it was as if that body belonged to somebody else.

In her present relationship with a young man, she fears that to be successful sexually would bring an attack upon her by her mother and her twin sister. It is as if her mother and sister had to give her the permission to be sexually attractive and to be "female." But the conflict seems to have an additional meaning. Carol's genital sexual feelings interfere with her fantasy of oneness with the twin sister, a fantasy that also contains the wish for oneness with the mother. Breaking this tie would risk being left completely empty and vulnerable to an attack by her mother, a danger which is itself a projection of Carol's own feeling. Masturbation at this point in her life continues to confirm for her that she prefers herself, that is, her sister, to a man.

Case 4

Norman, aged eighteen, first sought help for migraine and depression as a result of which his school attendance was poor. Soon after his analytic treatment began (at the Hampstead Child-Therapy Clinic), he mentioned his compulsive masturbation and his weird behavior during masturbation as his most serious problems. He felt that his thoughts and actions during masturbation confirmed that there was something seriously wrong. Throughout his adolescence, there was a definite pattern to his actions and the fantasy which usually accompanied masturbation. Most often he masturbated in the nude. He liked to have his anus exposed and his buttocks very tensed. Sometimes he would hit himself on his back, but this was not very important for him to enjoy the masturbation. During masturbation he felt that "everything is perfect," but after ejaculation he felt that he was just sinking into nothingness, that he was weak, a girl. (He had the same feeling when he smoked marijuana or took methedrine.) It was as if some big person—he did not know who— had suddenly overpowered him and was either holding him or doing something to him.

Norman, who was talented at painting, conveyed his ambiguous male-female status by repeatedly painting a dark figure with undefined genitals. He said that this was almost like a self-portrait—he never was sure what his body was like, or what he wanted to be, that is, helpless and passive or in control and active. He grew up with a Christ fantasy, which in childhood and latency he enacted in various ways. He sometimes went to church after school, carried heavy books around the church until he was very tired, and then felt that this was how Christ must have felt. This fantasy, or its elaboration, dominated his sexual life, and more specifically his adolescent masturbation which always left him feeling helpless, a woman, and somebody who, like Christ, could reach the height of success and understanding through passivity and helplessness.

A short time ago Norman began to smoke marijuana, and more recently he began to take methedrine. During the time when he was "high," he felt that his body was not troubling him, that he did not have to do anything to his body to feel good, and that his penis was something separate from the rest of himself. It was as if the penis had a "mind of its own," i.e., that it could become erect or make him do things which had nothing to do with the rest of his life. The methedrine enabled him to feel "outside my body" and temporarily created the illusion that he was protected from the body's demands. The drug could also induce feelings that were similar to those he experienced during masturbation, but without his having to masturbate. When he put the drug into his body (whether by swallowing it or injecting himself), it was as though somebody else had taken over completely, and this "somebody" was producing a feeling that made everything perfect.

In the past, Norman had exposed himself, and he still feared that he might do it again. Comparing his penis with a vagina, he said: "The difference is that mine is outside and it's as if it doesn't belong to me, but a woman's vagina is all part of her. . . . My attitude to my penis is something like my attitude to my parents in the past [his father was dead], and to my mother now. Sometimes I hate her and feel like beating her, and sometimes I feel I like her and I want to protect her and make her feel good."

When he thought of suicide, he imagined killing a part of himself—sometimes he was not sure whether he would prefer to kill the man or the woman in himself—and then he would be left in peace.

Although some of his passive feminine thoughts were defensive and in part related to the fact that he was alone at home with his mother, as a child he had often felt that originally he had been a girl who, for some unknown reason, had been turned into a boy. His castration anxiety could be seen in his behavior and many of his activities, but at the same time there also was the very strong wish to be female—he would be helpless, taken care of, at peace. His mother had told him many years ago that if he had been a girl, he would have been called Helen, which was the name of his father's sister, a person whom his father loved very much. Norman had for many years suffered from "worms," and his mother had cleaned his anus with cotton wool: "I would just lie there and she would see to it."

In his masturbation fantasy, Norman was identified with the woman who was being penetrated by the big, powerful man. When Norman imagined this man entering his body, he seemed to be incorporating some of the power of this big man. This fantasy and the feeling of helplessness following masturbation temporarily offered him a great deal of satisfaction by enabling him to relive the feeling of being cared for by the mother who cleaned his anus. Although the regression was defensive in nature, it also afforded him the enormous gratification of feeling cared for and being at one with the mother.

DISCUSSION

Something went seriously wrong in the adolescent development of the patients whom I have reported. Each of them, no matter what he did, felt "stuck." Each described his entire adolescence as very painful. In each case, puberty seemed to set in motion a constant battle with something inside themselves over which they felt they had no control. These adolescents experienced their masturbation either as a confirmation of their abnormality or as a threat to their whole ego functioning, and specifically to their defensive organization (see especially the remarks by Lustman in Francis, 1968).

The treatment material of these adolescents contained two recurrent themes which were especially clear in the masturbation fantasies. First, they hated their bodies for forcing this activity upon them; and second, they felt helpless in the face of the abnormal fantasies, which inevitably would bring about a feeling of worthlessness and guilt. Moreover, the hatred of the body was equivalent to the hatred of the internalized parent. Norman talked of his penis having a life of its own—he could not control it; Susan hated her body for being what it was, and no matter what she did in masturbation, it always left her with the belief that she was damaged and horrible; Carol sought sexual experiences, but having sexual sensations simultaneously involved the risk of losing her mother or her twin sister and then being totally devoid of objects and empty.

Although the fantasies and the attitudes of these adolescents to their bodies could be viewed simply as representing defensive efforts against the positive oedipal wishes, something else occurred that produced this deadlock and strengthened this need to disown their bodies and body sensations: the onset of puberty apparently endangered the earlier defense against the aggression directed at the mother. When this aggression is reactivated in adolescence, it is experienced as something that could at any time take over and be put into action. Masturbation and the accompanying fantasies are further threats to these adolescents because the ensuing regression acts as a constant confirmation of their hatred and their abnormality. The mother, who originally was the stimulator and protector of the child's body (A. Freud, 1965; Hoffer, 1950; Winnicott, 1953), is now regarded as the persecutor. Susan believed that her mother would "die of shame" if she knew what her "special child" was doing or thinking; Alan was convinced that his mother was watching him when he had a nocturnal emission, and that he could never get away from her no matter how horrible he was to her.

Adolescents whose development has proceeded along more normal lines usually manage to keep their perverse fantasies under repression and, during masturbation, allow into consciousness only the more acceptable heterosexual fantasies that usually involve an appropriate love object. In treatment, it is often possible to undo some of the repression and to locate the perverse fantasies, which may be present. But the mere existence of these fantasies is not a sign of abnormality. While such fantasies may act as a threat, they are normally well defended against and therefore remain unconscious (Laufer, 1965). But the adolescents whom I have described react differently to their masturbation and the accompanying fantasies. The perverse fantasies do intrude into consciousness and, when they are experienced in relation to a physically mature body, the fantasy is nearly equivalent to an action. The fantasy feels real and dangerous.

This formulation—that the onset of puberty endangers the earlier defense against the aggression directed at the mother—seems to apply to both male and female patients. However, this implies that the resulting pathology will be different in boys and girls. The content of the masturbation fantasies enables us to reconstruct the child's conception of the primal scene and to determine which parent he or she is identified with. In the cases of Alan and Norman, their sense of helplessness in the face of their sexual sensations and the feeling of being completely overpowered following ejaculation served the function of denying their extreme castration anxiety. They lived out the fantasy of being like the mother with the phallus, a fantasy which also contained the notion that this made the mother more acceptable to the father. On a preoedipal level, there is the wish to be cared for, and this would perpetuate the relationship to the mother. But in order to understand the pathology in adolescence, it is necessary to view the conflict mainly in oedipal terms, which is that masturbation and the fantasy contain the identification with the mother who has a phallus. For some reason, this fantasy cannot be given up in adolescence but must be maintained. Greenacre's formulations about the development of the body image (1953, 1958, 1960), especially the faulty development in fetishism, are relevant in this context.

Susan and Carol regarded their mothers as the castrator as well as the protector. For both of them, the beginning of menstruation confirmed that their bodies were no good, and sexual feelings in adolescence simply reminded them of how horrible their bodies were. At the same time, they felt that their mothers knew everything about them, as if their mothers were with them all the time. To touch their genitals meant that they had to recognize that their mothers had given them bodies which were useless and abnormal. I believe that in the cases of both Susan and Carol, the onset of menstruation threatened the collapse of the identification with the mother with the phallus because it suddenly forced them to give up their belief that their bodies would change. Masturbation represented an additional danger because it confirmed the fact of their damaged bodies and thereby aroused the aggression against the mother. It is precisely this aggression which in turn tied these girls so completely to their mothers.

Another question must be raised. In the first place, what brings about such a solution, which then is disastrous for their adolescent development? My speculations, as well as some of the clinical data, point to the following possibilities: the actual observation of the primal scene during the oedipal phase; the parent's unconscious wish to have a child of the opposite sex; the mother handling the child's

body in such a way that the child felt overstimulated during the preoedipal period; the use of the child's body as a penis equivalent by
one of the parents; or the parents' rejection of their own bodies and
sex organs and their rejection of the child's sexuality. But further
clinical studies are required to help us understand which combination of factors is most important in determining the outcome.

BIBLIOGRAPHY

Arlow, J. A. (1953), Masturbation and Symptom Formation. *J. Amer. Psa. Assn.*, 1:45-58.

Bak, R. C. (1939), Regression of Ego-Orientation and Libido in Schizophrenia. *Int. J. Psa.*, 20:64-71.

Blos, P. (1967), The Second Individuation Process of Adolescence. *This Annual*, 22:162-186.

Bonnard, A. (1958), Pre-Body-Ego Types of (Pathological) Mental Functioning. *J. Amer. Psa. Assn.*, 6:581-611.

Bornstein, B. (1953), Masturbation in the Latency Period. *This Annual*, 8:65-78.

Brunswick, R. Mack (1940), The Pre-Oedipal Phase of the Libido Development. *Psa. Quart.*, 9:293-319.

Deutsch, H. (1944), *The Psychology of Women.* Vol. 1. New York: Grune & Stratton.

—— (1968), *Selected Problems of Adolescence.* New York: International Universities Press.

Eissler, K. R. (1958), Notes on Problems of Technique in the Psychoanalytic Treatment of Adolescents: With Special Remarks on Perversions. *This Annual*, 13:223-254.

Federn, P. (1952), *Ego Psychology and the Psychoses.* New York: Basic Books.

Francis, J. J. (1968), Panel Report: Masturbation. *J. Amer. Psa. Assn.*, 16:95-112.

Freud, A. (1949), Certain Types and Stages of Social Maladjustment. In: *Searchlights on Delinquency*, ed. K. R. Eissler. New York: International Universities Press, pp. 193-204.

—— (1952), The Role of Bodily Illness in the Mental Life of Children. *This Annual*, 7:69-81.

—— (1958), Adolescence. *This Annual*, 13:255-278.

—— (1965), *Normality and Pathology in Childhood.* New York: International Universities Press.

Freud, S. (1905), Three Essays on the Theory of Sexuality. *Standard Edition*, 7:125-243. London: Hogarth Press, 1953.

—— (1912), Contributions to a Discussion on Masturbation. *Standard Edition*, 12:239-254. London: Hogarth Press, 1958.

—— (1914), On Narcissism: An Introduction. *Standard Edition*, 14:67-102. London: Hogarth Press, 1957.

—— (1917), Mourning and Melancholia. *Standard Edition*, 14:237-260. London: Hogarth Press, 1957.

—— (1919), 'A Child Is Being Beaten.' *Standard Edition*, 17:175-204. London: Hogarth Press, 1955.

—— (1923), The Ego and the Id. *Standard Edition*, 19:3-66. London: Hogarth Press, 1961.

—— (1924), The Economic Problem of Masochism. *Standard Edition*, 19:157-170. London: Hogarth Press, 1961.

—— (1931), Female Sexuality. *Standard Edition*, 21:223-243. London: Hogarth Press, 1961.

Geleerd, E. R. (1956), Clinical Contribution to the Problem of the Early Mother-Child Relationship. *This Annual*, 11:336-351.
—— (1961), Some Aspects of Ego Vicissitudes in Adolescence. *J. Amer. Psa. Assn.*, 9:394-405.
Greenacre, P. (1953), Certain Relationships between Fetishism and the Faulty Development of the Body Image. *This Annual*, 8:79-98.
—— (1958), Early Physical Determinants in the Development of the Sense of Identity. *J. Amer. Psa. Assn.*, 6:612-627.
—— (1960), Further Notes on Fetishism. *This Annual*, 15:191-207.
Harley, M. (1961), Some Observations on the Relationship between Genitality and Structural Development at Adolescence. *J. Amer. Psa. Assn.*, 9:434-460.
Hartmann, H., Kris, E., & Loewenstein, R. M. (1946), Comments on the Formation of Psychic Structure. *This Annual*, 2:11-38.
Hoffer, W. (1950), Development of the Body Ego. *This Annual*, 5:18-24.
Jacobson, E. (1964), *The Self and the Object World*. New York: International Universities Press.
Jones, E. (1922), Some Problems of Adolescence. *Papers on Psycho-Analysis*. London: Ballière, Tindall & Cox, 5th ed., 1948, pp. 389-406.
Kramer, P. (1955), On Discovering One's Identity. *This Annual*, 10:47-74.
Kris, E. (1951), Some Comments and Observations on Early Autoerotic Activities. *This Annual*, 6:95-116.
Lampl-de Groot, J. (1950), On Masturbation and Its Influence on General Development. *This Annual*, 5:153-174.
—— (1960), On Adolescence. *This Annual*, 15:95-103.
Laufer, M. (1965), Assessment of Adolescent Disturbances: The Application of Anna Freud's Diagnostic Profile. *This Annual*, 20:99-123.
—— (1966), Object Loss and Mourning during Adolescence. *This Annual*, 21:269-293.
Levin, S. (1963), A Review of Freud's Contributions to the Topic of Masturbation. *Bull. Phila. Psa. Assn.*, 13:15-24.
Lichtenstein, H. (1961), Identity and Sexuality. *J. Amer. Psa. Assn.*, 9:179-260.
Lustman, S. L. (1956), Rudiments of the Ego. *This Annual*, 11:89-98.
Mahler, M. S. (1963), Thoughts about Development and Individuation. *This Annual*, 18:307-324.
Nagera, H. (1964), Autoerotism, Autoerotic Activities, and Ego Development. *This Annual*, 19:240-255.
Peto, A. (1959), Body Image and Archaic Thinking. *Int. J. Psa.*, 40:223-231.
Reich, A. (1960), Pathologic Forms of Self-esteem Regulation. *This Annual*, 15:215-232.
Ritvo, S. & Solnit, A. J. (1958), Influences of Early Mother-Child Interaction on Identification Processes. *This Annual*, 13:64-85.
Rubinfine, D. L. (1958), Panel Report: Problems of Identity. *J. Amer. Psa. Assn.*, 6:131-142.
Schilder, P. (1935), *The Image and Appearance of the Human Body*. New York: International Universities Press, 1950.
Schneer, H. I. & Kay, P. (1961), The Suicidal Adolescent. In: *Adolescents*, ed. S. Lorand & H. I. Schneer. New York: Hoeber, pp. 180-201.
Schur, M. (1955), Comments on the Metapsychology of Somatization. *This Annual*, 10:119-164.
Spiegel, L. A. (1959), The Self, the Sense of Self, and Perception. *This Annual*, 14:81-109.
Tausk, V. (1912), On Masturbation. *This Annual*, 6:61-79, 1951.
Winnicott, D. W. (1953), Transitional Objects and Transitional Phenomena. *Int. J. Psa.*, 34:89-97.
—— (1961), Adolescence. In: *The Family and Individual Development*. London: Tavistock Publications, 1965, pp. 79-87.

II

CONTRIBUTIONS TO PSYCHOANALYTIC THEORY

THE RELATION OF EXPLAINING
AND UNDERSTANDING IN
PSYCHOANALYSIS

Demonstrated by One Aspect of Freud's Approach
to Literature

K. R. EISSLER, M.D. (New York)

The question of whether psychoanalysis is a science or one of the humanities has been long debated and answered in various ways. The key to an answer seems to me to lie in the correct analysis of the place that is held in psychoanalysis by the functions of explaining and understanding. I would like to discuss this question in relation to the contribution that psychoanalysis can make to the study of works of literature. These works are outside the psychoanalytic situation, which excludes any third parties. All inferences can therefore be discussed with greater objectivity than is possible in clinical discussions, the subject of which is known only to the psychoanalyst who has treated the patient.

At the same time, I will seize the occasion to correct a widespread misconception that scholars seem to harbor with regard to Freud's approach to works of literature.

I

Psychoanalysis may make contributions to the explanation of works of literature in either of two ways, which are different in method, purpose, and result.

One I shall call exopoietic and the other endopoietic.[1]

This is an abbreviated section of a forthcoming book on *Hamlet,* to be published by International Universities Press, New York.

[1] I owe these terms to Mr. Harold Collins and wish to thank him for them.

In the former, all the explanatory factors are sought from outside the literary work itself. In exopoietic research, the literary work is taken as an embodiment of the creative mind. Exopoietic research in that sense aims at the reconstruction of the mental processes or other significant characteristics of the author.[2]

Endopoietic research does not go beyond the boundaries of the literary work; all explanatory factors remain within the givens of the literary work. The paradigm of psychoanalytic endopoietic research is to be found in Freud's explanation of an apraxia that the German playwright Friedrich von Schiller put on the stage (*Die Piccolomini*, Act I, scene 5) (Freud, 1916-1917, p. 37). This left no doubt that the slip of the tongue in question was caused by a disquieting idea on the part of the speaker, who tried to conceal it from the person with whom he was conversing. The slip was used deliberately by the playwright in order to let the audience know that the speaker had suddenly recognized a state of affairs previously unknown to him, but that circumstances forbade him to spell out his discovery in the situation in which he found himself at the moment. Curiously enough, Freud's endopoietic explanation did not contain anything that would not have been taken for granted by

[2] Is exopoietic research possible at all? I think Spurgeon's (1931, 1935) research proves that it is, although it also raises questions of the actual value of such research. Her discovery of the prototype of an unusual simile that Shakespeare used in *Lucrece* (1667-1673) in a still observable eddy under the eighteenth arch of the old Clopton Bridge (1935, pp. 97-99) is extraordinarily convincing and may be compared with an experimental validation. Her assumption is sound that "a dramatic poet . . . unconsciously 'gives himself away' in his images," and one cannot challenge her method "of collecting and classifying the images" on the grounds that "the poet unwittingly reveals his own innermost likes and dislikes, observations and interests, associations of thought, attitudes of mind and beliefs, in and through the images, the verbal pictures he draws to illuminate something quite different in the speech and thought of his characters" (1931, p. 173). She is also correct in her assertion that, by this method, we may learn "such as what in daily life thrilled him with pleasure, what offended and revolted him, what were his chief personal tastes" (1935, p. 201), and many other things that she enumerates.

It is true nevertheless that, in order to unearth data, we need a special method in Shakespeare's case, because his life is so poorly documented. These, after all, are data that we usually obtain from a poet's diaries and letters, and the accounts of his contemporaries. When Spurgeon proves that Shakespeare had an aversion against dogs (1935, pp. 195-199), this does not tell us anything about Shakespeare beyond the sentimental. Only data with regard to the structure of the personality are decisive and it is debatable whether or not such data can reliably be obtained by exopoietic research, unless there is unusually rich documentation. Some analysts doubt that it can be done even under such favorable conditions.

any reader, since Freud was explicating only what was clearly the playwright's purpose.[3] Yet this more or less trivial example can be taken as an "ideal-type" model of endopoietic explanation, along psychological lines, of one element of a literary work. The fact that this explanation coincides with commonsense thinking should not detract from its value as a model.

Exopoietic and endopoietic research are not always isolated from each other. By way of the latter, the unconscious meaning of a work can be established, and only after this has been done can the work be meaningfully connected with some particular element of the author's life. Hanns Sachs's (1919) endopoietic investigation of Shakespeare's *Tempest*, for example, brought to light the focal position that a daughter's marriage holds in the play, which discovery was then brought into meaningful connection with Shakespeare's relationship to his own daughter Judith.

The most frequent methodological mistake to be observed in exopoietic research is the assumption that genius follows in all essential respects the same psychological laws as those that are followed by the average person, whose mental apparatus is so familiar to the psychoanalyst. On the basis of this assumption, a large number of papers have been written, in which conclusions about the genius's personality have been drawn from an examination of his created works, without corresponding verifications of those conclusions from the biographical record. When such investigations are limited to the assertion that the artist had formed an oedipus complex or had disclosed aggression or such other universal emotions as envy or rivalry, little objection can be raised, since such formations are, after all, universal and they may be supposed to exist in one form or another in *every* human being. The question then can be whether or not the specific artistic element or structure can be connected genetically with the specific psychological element or structure to which it is supposedly related.

When Freud wrote the first extensive essay (1910a) in which he used the exopoietic method, he emphasized that his inquiry had to do only with that part of Leonardo's personality that he shared

---

3 It is remarkable that such a simple item as the slip which Schiller had one of his characters make, and which was easily understood for what it was by any schoolboy, contained *in nuce* the central ingredient out of which Freud built psychoanalysis.

with others, and excluded what we would call Leonardo's genius. From Freud's letters we know that he had had a patient in analysis who "seemed to have the same constitution as Leonardo without his genius" (Strachey, 1957, p. 60). This may sound strange today, since it is difficult to conceive of Leonardo without his genius; the interest has now shifted to what it is that makes Leonardo *different* from the rest of mankind. Whether or not Freud was right in his explanation of those elements that the genius shared with the rest of mankind, he demonstrated something that has since been confirmed—namely, that the flowering of genius depends on the early relationship to the mother. This was demonstrated by Freud negatively, perhaps, in that he showed how the growing child was hurt in that relationship and for that reason evolved inhibitions.

Since the problem was viewed in the light of observations made in the patient, the emphasis fell on those factors that stood in the artist's way and thus diminished the output of which he would otherwise have been innately capable. Such defects—if they were defects —were already well known from Leonardo's life. Yet one should not forget that there is a difference in principle between trying to explain why an artist completed relatively few paintings and concluding from the content of completed plays that the playwright must have gone through manic-depressive phases—especially when there is nothing known about him during the period in which he wrote these plays.

The tacit assumption is, first that there is a parallel between the prevailing mood in the playwright and the atmosphere conveyed in his plays.[4] Second, it is assumed that a genius's mind works, with regard to his extraordinary achievements, in the same way as the minds of subjects known to us from the intimacy of clinical observation. This may or may not be correct. For a conclusion to be made from an artist's achievement to the processes of his mental functioning, one would have to presuppose that we are as familiar with the psychic apparatus of the genius as we are with that of the average subject of psychoanalytic investigation.

Yet, since the psychic apparatus of the genius has been investi-

---

[4] Cf. Freud (1913, p. 187). Bühler (1927, p. 25) rightly warns against the assumption of a parallelism between a creative mind and its creations.

gated chiefly by way of an analysis of his achievements, it could be said that most of the psychoanalytic literature on genius is, methodologically speaking, circular. Since someone who is endowed with the capacities of genius does not generally come into psychoanalysis, it is necessary to use the few instances for which documentation is available in abundance and to reconstruct the genius's personality from his biographical record.

The situation is quite different in the field of endopoietic research. Here we have a fixed record, open to the inspection of anyone who is interested, and one does not have to go beyond what is given to establish links with an external frame of reference, such as the artist's personality or his society. Freud's first major contribution to the explanation of a literary work has to be assigned to endopoietic research, even though its original purpose was to inquire into the nature of the dreams that authors have their characters dream. The underlying idea was apparently to check whether the artist's conception of dreams showed any similarity with Freud's findings on that question. The novel *Gradiva* by Wilhelm Jensen (1837-1911), which had been published in 1903, seemed an appropriate choice, since it contained several dreams. In the hands of the master, however, the study went beyond this and became instead a comprehensive treatise (Freud, 1907). It can therefore be used instructively as a paradigm of endopoietic research.

The original purpose of the study led to a truly amazing result. The dreams that the novel's hero dreamed followed to an astonishing extent the theories that Freud had embodied in his *Interpretation* (1900). The interpretations of the hero's dreams that Freud presented were by no means strained; one does not discover a single trace of Freud's doing violence to the givens of the novel in order to establish some sort of agreement between it and his clinical findings. Even such an empirical detail as that the words spoken in a dream follow words that have been actually spoken or heard could be "confirmed" by the record investigated. Indeed, when one follows Freud as he takes apart the protagonist's two dreams, one can scarcely suppress the feeling that Jensen had studied Freud's book on dream interpretation and later applied his knowledge somewhat mechanically to a character that was allegedly born from his fantasy. Yet

the fact of the matter is that Jensen had no knowledge of psychoanalysis (see Freud, 1960, p. 252f.).[5]

Jensen (1907) wrote Freud about the way in which his story had
been born. It was written on a sudden impulse and within a short
time; he wrote it without reflection and in a somnambulistic way.
How then can one explain this strange coincidence: that the author
had his characters act and dream in complete accordance with the
scientist's detailed research into the vast orbit of the unconscious?
If Jensen had been applying knowledge, he would not have been
able to proceed with such speed and in such a somnambulant manner. Moreover, the parallel between an insight that was based on
science and the content of an artistic creation was not limited to
dreams; Freud had also discovered the same thing as Jensen presented, with regard to the appearance and disappearance of a delusion in the novel's chief character, as well as to the effect of erotic
experiences in early childhood on later psychopathology, and many
more such phenomena.

Yet what may be even more surprising is the fact that Freud
utilized, in his analysis of the novel, certain clinical findings that,
so far as I know, he had never referred to previously. He stated very
radically—if I may so describe it—in connection with the protagonist's vicissitudes that "when what has been repressed returns, it
emerges from the repressing force itself" or, in other words, that it is
easily possible "for the repressed to emerge behind the repressing
force and take effect by means of it" (1907, p. 35f.). Curiously
enough, Shakespeare had described this mechanism in detail some
300 years earlier, when he had Angelo say in *Measure for Measure*:

> O cunning enemy! that, to catch a saint,
> With saints dost bait thy hook. Most dangerous
> Is that temptation that doth goad us on
> To sin in loving virtue: never could the strumpet,
> With all her double vigour, art and nature,
> Once stir my temper, but this virtuous mind
> Subdues me quite.
>   [Act II, scene 2, lines 180-186]

[5] In order to explain the seeming coincidence, one could perhaps suggest a case
of cryptamnesia, but that can be ruled out here.

Later, Freud was to demonstrate something similar for certain diseases, but he would never again set up such a general rule. I feel uncertain as to whether Freud was right in his general statement, or was carried too far by the enthusiasm that the inquiry into the literary work apparently aroused in him. At any rate, it is a far-reaching and in fact splendid idea.

He also affirmed in this essay, for the first time, that "there is a grain of truth concealed in every delusion, there is something in it that really deserves belief" (p. 80).[6] He further demonstrated in his literary paper that the dream may contain a correct estimate and perception of reality, such as is denied in the delusion from which the dreamer suffers during his wakeful hours. Only many years later was Freud to make the observation that the dreams of a delusional patient are free of delusions—"that paranoia does not penetrate into dreams" (1922, p. 227)—an insight that he had apparently found one and a half decades earlier in the pursuit of dreams that the poet had assigned to an invented character.

I wish to make a categorical statement here. Freud has often been accused of "finding" in literary creations a confirmation of his theories, because he projected them into the subjects of his inquiry.[7] Freud was to anticipate this objection as early as in 1907 (p. 91): "It may be that we have produced a complete caricature of an interpretation by introducing into an innocent work of art purposes of which its creator had no notion, and by so doing have shown once more how easy it is to find what one is looking for and what is occupying one's own mind." If someone should raise this objection, nevertheless, one could point out that it is while he was analyzing the literary

6 Strachey (in a footnote to this passage) claims, however, that Freud had already expressed this view in his *Psychopathology of Everyday Life* (1901, p. 256), but in 1901 Freud, it seems to me, was referring to a formal quality, while in his *Gradiva* essay he was making a claim, with regard to content, that introduced a new aspect of the question.

7 Kenneth Muir (1952), in a thoughtful paper, the major part of which I agree with, warns against accepting "without reserve" any interpretation of Shakespeare's characters, whether it comes from Freud, Jung or Adler, since they differ completely but "conform . . . to the general theories of their authors" (p. 51). Reserve may be necessary in all scientific questions; Freud himself seems not to have been "without reserve" toward his own theories in view of his having changed them considerably and impressively. If I understand Muir's remark correctly as implying that literary works have been used by Freud merely as receptacles of cherished theories (which I would call an abuse), I would have to disagree, as the following aims to demonstrate.

work that Freud made discoveries for which he only later found clinical confirmation.[8]

For obvious reasons—as will be seen presently—I shall trace when and how Freud evolved his oedipal theory. His letter of October 15, 1897 to Wilhelm Fliess contains the theory for the first time as a universal proposition. In the same letter, he refers to the Greek tragedy *Oedipus Rex* and tries to explain why, among all tragedies of fate, this was the one that left such an indelible effect on the human mind. Then he continues: "Fleetingly it went through my head whether the same thing [the oedipal complex] might lie at the bottom of Hamlet" (Freud, 1950a; my translation). Some explanations then follow, in loose sequence, ending with a comparison between Hamlet's way of bringing about his self-destruction (to repeat his father's fate and to be poisoned by the same rival) and the behavior of hysterical patients.

The clinical theory and its application coincide literally, and thus an amazingly short time would have been left in order to evolve the sort of projections that some critics of Freud's Hamlet theory are wont to insist had occurred. I wish to stress here Freud's description of "fleetingly it went . . . ," which indicates that, at this stage, it was not yet a matter of a strictly discursive procedure, but rather of a groping for instances that may belong to the same type of problem.

Here it seems quite relevant to take note of a letter that Freud had written to Fliess twenty-four days earlier (September 21, 1897), in which he quoted within a significant context Hamlet's aphorism: "The readiness is all" (Act V, scene 2, line 224). He wrote: "I vary Hamlet's words 'to be in readiness' [the last four words written in English]—to be genial is all [*Heiter sein ist Alles*].[9] I could have every justification for feeling quite discontent" (Freud, 1887-1950a;

---

[8] So it seems to me, at least. It is very difficult—well-nigh impossible—to determine when a productive mind has taken in the seed of what will later become a cultural achievement, whether this be of a scientific or an artistic nature. I have the feeling that all consequential ideas are born "in their rough-hewn form" between adolescence and early manhood. While that may be an exaggeration, it is certain that the rudiments of great ideas move about more or less aimlessly in the unconscious for a long time before they are given definitive form.

[9] Unfortunately, this sentence was translated as: "I vary Hamlet's remark about ripeness—cheerfulness is all" (1950a, p. 217), which may sound as if Freud had confused King Lear with Hamlet.

my translation). Apparently, Freud felt at this juncture as Hamlet did when he was approaching the most fateful moment of his life —namely, killing Claudius—in a state of completed maturation.

Hamlet was thirty years old when he was "ready"; Freud was forty-one when he quoted the passage.[10] Hamlet's chances of accomplishing his life mission after weeks and months of groping, doubting, and searching had been at that moment reduced practically to nil. Yet he did not feel disheartened; instead he had a feeling of inner conviction that he was being carried along by a fate that was on his side. Freud felt himself to be, at that moment—after years of groping, doubting and searching—in an almost identical position, as he let Fliess know in the same letter. He had returned later than usual from an extensive vacation trip (Hamlet's journey to England?), and had come to recognize that the chief theory on which he had previously built his etiology of neurosis was wrong. The neurosis was *not* the consequence of the infantile trauma of seduction, as he had been certain only a short while before; with this seeming insight went the fruits of his long and laborious research.

From this new state of affairs he had also gained the conviction that hysteria cannot be cured by psychotherapy. He was on the verge of accepting hereditary disposition as the etiological determinant of hysteria, after thinking that he had successfully eliminated it as the preponderant etiological factor. All this meant that the fulfillment of his wishes, to which he had felt himself to be so very close, had instead vanished. Longingly, he meditated: "The expectation of eternal posthumous glory [Nachruhm] was so beautiful, as well as that of certain wealth, full independence, traveling, the children's rising above the grave worries that deprived me of my youth. This all depended on whether or not [the problem of] hysteria is resolved."

To his surprise, however, he did not feel ashamed, which might have been the most appropriate response to this recognition of failure. On the contrary, he felt "hearty and genial [frisch und heiter]," as he assured his friend in the first sentence, and this despite the fact that, in addition to his intellectual misfortune, he had no patients as something to worry about. Oddly enough—one might almost

10 From previous discussions of age in Shakespeare's time it will have become clear that the ages are really equivalent. Cf. Jones (1953, p. 267): "Eighteen ninety-seven was the acme of Freud's life."

say senselessly—he had "the feeling of victory rather than of defeat." Although psychoanalytic commonsense might explain this paradoxical feeling as the outcome of denial, I would still venture to explain it in the same way as I have interpreted Hamlet's equivalent reactions—namely, as the consequence of an unconscious anticipation or knowledge of the fact that he was standing at the threshold of momentous events.[11]

Thus, one seems entitled to postulate, on the basis of this letter, an almost exact replica of Hamlet's conversation with Horatio. And how *did* Freud fare? A little more than three weeks later, he held the theory in his grasp that, even though it did not bring him riches, did enable him to cure hysteria, as he had wished, and was to give him posthumous glory as well. What the theory said was that the male, as a boy, wishes to kill his father and to possess the mother. With this insight he not only dealt a blow to illusions that were held in high esteem by his culture, he also cut the rope that had kept his own neurosis attached to him. As I see it, he accomplished with this what Hamlet had accomplished, except that the scholar's work on his inner processes did not leave behind it the trail of blood that washes around Hamlet's corpse.

As the last point of similarity, which it seems unnecessary to characterize as perhaps the most important, Hamlet's father had died four or five months prior to his exchange of ideas with Horatio and Freud's father had died, to be exact, eleven months and two days before he felt "ready."[12] If we consider that *Hamlet* was written by Shakespeare either shortly before or shortly after his father's death, we may say that the circle is closed.

At this point one may ask whether Freud really applied his theory to *Hamlet*. Could it not have been the other way around— namely, that his identification with Hamlet[13] was one (and possibly not the least) among the many factors that made his great discovery

[11] As a matter of fact, Freud wrote in the same letter: "Can it be that this doubt merely represents an episode in advance towards further knowledge?" (1950b, p. 260).

[12] As a matter of fact, the oedipal theory was conveyed to Fliess one week before the first anniversary of the death of Jakob Freud.

[13] Identifications with characters from Shakespeare's plays should not be underestimated. In an unpublished manuscript, I tried to reconstruct the meaning of Freud's very puzzling identification with Macbeth, which I have found to be strongly suggested by two passages in Freud's correspondence (Freud, 1960, p. 6; Freud/Pfister, 1963, p. 35).

possible, or, at any rate, facilitated it? He wrote Fliess with regard to the oedipal involvement in *Hamlet* that he had not had it in mind to say that Shakespeare was following a conscious intention but rather that "the unconscious in him understood the unconscious in his hero" (1950b, p. 266). But did not the unconscious in Freud understand the unconscious in Hamlet, when he quoted, in a desperate situation, "the readiness is all"?

One may therefore go a step further and even speculate that Freud may have discovered the oedipus complex from his study of Shakespeare's tragic hero, as much as from his observation of clinical cases. In view of this possibility, it could very well be historically incorrect for Freud's interpretation of Hamlet's hesitancy to be called an "application of psychoanalysis." It may have been that Hamlet's oedipus complex, as it was brought to life in Shakespeare's tragedy, was *one of the sources from which Freud derived his insight*. That would be correct even if it were proved that Freud was not aware of this source.

In another instance, one is able almost to prove that literary figures were not used by Freud only to demonstrate his psychoanalytic theories and interpretations he had arrived at earlier, but instead that these figures became objects of clinical study, the results of which enforced profound changes in his theory. Indeed, the artist is always ahead of the psychologist,[14] and a genius who is a playwright may be able to perceive and to represent depths of the mind to which even sharpened clinical observation does not penetrate. That is to say, literary creations may bring to the surface phenomena of the human world that are so deeply submerged in actual life and therefore overlain by so many layers that they cannot be extrapolated from data actually observed. They make the arcane observable.

Thus Freud (1933, p. 105f.), in introducing the concept of a drive toward death in his *New Lectures*, exclaimed: "A queer instinct, in-

14 This can be demonstrated by way of some of Arthur Schnitzler's (1862-1931) writings. It is amazing to observe that at times Schnitzler described or presented psychic events that, only a few years later, would take a prominent place in Freud's theory formation. In the first play of the Anatol cycle: *The Question to Fate* [*Die Frage an das Schicksal*] (1889), Schnitzler takes as his theme the inhibition that a hypnotist suffers about asking the subject a question of whose answer he himself is afraid. This was written much earlier than Freud's research into countertransference and contains in a nutshell the problems of anxiety and resistance as an impediment to psychological research.

deed, directed to the destruction of its own organic home! Poets, it is true, talk of such things; *but poets are irresponsible people and enjoy the privilege of poetic licence"* (my italics). But what conclusion may be drawn from the fact that Freud refers immediately thereafter to the poets (it is only in the next sentence that there is a reference to pathophysiology), when he is searching for an ally in defense of his most improbable construct?[15]

When the history of Freud's theories about death is followed up (I will not do so here), one can observe that the first paper of Freud's in which death is assigned a central place is the one on the theme of the three caskets (1913), in which he presents his interpretation of Cordelia as a symbol of death.[16] I therefore believe that the poet "who talks of such things," and from whom Freud may have received the first impulse toward his theory of the drive toward death, might well have been Shakespeare.[17]

Enough has been said to demonstrate that, for Freud, literary works were by no means entities, to be used either for the purpose of proving the correctness of his views or as receptacles of projected theories. Many more instances could be enumerated of Freud's approaching literary works just as he did other objects he encountered —as stimulants toward inquiry. Just as an hour with a patient was an occasion to make a new observation, to find a new pattern of explanation, which did not fit in with the ones that were already part and parcel of psychoanalysis, so he was ever ready to learn from the creations of a literary mind, for he felt certain that in the writings of the great poets he would find more knowledge about man (although not in the form of explicit, scientific statements) than he himself would ever possess. He thus approached literary works as organic, live, real (the latter is here meant in a different sense from the one usually employed when one speaks of the "reality" of art). Shakespeare's creations may have been experienced by him, not as

15 Cf. Freud (1907, p. 8): "But creative writers are valuable allies and their evidence is to be prized highly, for they are apt to know a whole host of things between heaven and earth of which our philosophy has not yet let us dream. In their knowledge of the mind they are far in advance of us everyday people, for they draw upon sources which we have not yet opened for science."

16 For Lacan's conception of the development of Freud's thanatology—a conception that is quite different from mine—see Wilder (1966). See also Schur (1968).

17 It is noteworthy that, in his first division of drives into love and hunger, Freud followed, according to his own account of the matter, Friedrich Schiller.

figments of the mind, or as artistic illusions, but rather as sectors of a live world that has to be analyzed in the same way as one analyzes the minds of live and really existing people.

I shall now present another example of that sort, because it will bring us close to the question of the function of explaining in psychology.

Freud tried to make certain (and this is a question of principal importance) which elements of the literary works are due to so-called poetic license and which are actually representative of a human reality, a problem that can also be formulated as that of the limits of psychological interpretation. Freud found in Jensen's *Gradiva* two chief elements that, to his mind, fell outside the realm of interpretability: one was the identity of physical appearance between the woman who had been the protagonist's childhood sweetheart and the woman who was depicted in the ancient Gradiva bas-relief; the other was that the protagonist and the woman both take, at the same time and without knowing about each other, a trip to Naples. Consequently, they meet at the place where, in the hero's imagination, Gradiva had lived 2,000 years ago. Both elements, improbable as they are, of course, are necessary in order to be able to put together the framework of the story at all, and may therefore be dismissed as "nonmotivational" elements. Indeed, they do seem to be accidental, improbable events, enforced solely by artistic necessities.

Freud acknowledged this but added a remark that may incur the criticism of having overpsychologized. Since the protagonist takes flight to Pompeii from the woman who lived next door from him and of whose presence he had unconsciously been aware, and since Freud emphasized at that time the proximity of defense and the return of what had been warded off, he regarded with favor the author's use of a chance event, "for this chance reflects the fatal truth . . . that flight is precisely an instrument that delivers one over to what one is fleeing from" (1907, p. 42). Flight is *not* such an instrument, of course, although it cannot be denied that sometimes flight does lead to results of that sort. Freud was here applying a favorite theory, which, in this context, has scarcely any explanatory value.

In the other instance, the identity of physical appearance between a woman depicted on a bas-relief 2,000 years ago and a contemporary woman, Freud's ever-active ingenuity appears. He thought it would have been "a more sober choice" to limit that rather far-reaching resemblance to one single feature, such as the way both women put their foot on the ground when walking. Yet in following "the play of our own phantasy" (p. 42), he suggests "a link with reality." The girl's name *Bertgang*, which means "bright gait," describes someone "who steps along brilliantly"; the same thing also is signified in the name Gradiva. The name of the woman living in the present, Freud suggests, "might point to the fact that the women of that family had already been distinguished in ancient days by the peculiarity of their graceful gait" (p. 42). The girl's Germanic ancestors, one could suppose, were descended from a Roman family, one member of which was perpetuated on the ancient bas-relief. Since variations of form are interdependent and ancient types reappear, as can be observed, "it would not be totally impossible" for a contemporary person to reproduce not only the gait but all other bodily features as well of her Roman ancestors.

This train of thought may for many reasons be called typical of one aspect of Freud's thinking—namely, his ability to see through the coincidental and to reach that point of objective reality that is manifesting itself in what merely seems accidental. The "paradigm" (Kuhn, 1962) created in this instance then led to the awe-inspiring theory laid down in the *Moses* book (1939).[18]

The parallel between the Moses theory (a primordial trauma leaves a permanent trace in a people's history after a latency period) and the Gradiva situation (a woman's fate is decided by the fact that she has the same physical appearance as an ancestor had 2,000 years ago) may appear far-fetched, but the two have this one idea in common: that the past is ineluctable, even beyond the personal

---

[18] Stengel (1966) questions my assertion that this work of Freud's is the greatest achievement of psychoanalytic mentation. I do not know how Stengel would measure "mentation," but I had thought that the relation between the extent of one's premises and the extent of one's conclusions was a partially tolerable yardstick. The theory that Freud built upon one contradictory element in a legend was enormous. I think that there is no other work in which Freud built so much on so little, and with unsurpassable logic to boot; this is what permits one to accord a special place to the extraordinary mentation involved.

boundaries. The Gradiva theory brings forth—far more strongly than in Freud's previous writings—the idea of a repetition compulsion, which subsequently acquired a focal position in psychoanalytic theory and stood at the center of the Moses book. In *Gradiva* Freud seemed to have followed a sudden fancy, because he quietly dropped the thought as a mere speculation. The author, he felt, should be asked for the sources of this part of his creation; then, he suggested, we would be in a position to show that "what was ostensibly an arbitrary decision rested in fact upon law" (1907, p. 43). But Freud had done this independently of whatever the author's sources might have been, because "access to the sources in the author's mind is not open to us."

The explanation that he offered did precisely what he had suggested: it changed arbitrariness into lawfulness. It is not, of course, a question here of speculating whether or not Freud's explanation was correct but of emphasizing that, while a very good explanation may have been proffered, it does not contribute in any way to our better understanding either of the novel or of the personality of Gradiva. Thus in this instance explaining and understanding are disjoined. One could say that, in this instance, Freud's suggested explanation did not have anything to do with any psychic process, but referred instead to an improbable coincidence of two physical events.

This, of course, is quite true. But it has to do with a coincidence whose psychological meaning cannot be denied. Had the physical appearance of the woman and of Gradiva not been identical, she would never have regained the affection of her erstwhile childhood sweetheart and under particularly propitious circumstances, to boot, in that it facilitated displacement of her attachment to her own father. Be that as it may, the example demonstrates that explanation and understanding may not always coincide. With the raising of this distinction between explaining and understanding, we enter an area of decisive importance, which I shall now discuss as briefly as possible, because it cannot be discussed here in the depth and extension that it would deserve.

II

The one difficulty that haunts epistemological inquiry into the functions of explaining and understanding is linguistic. Both terms have a place in everyday language, and that place is filled by a variety of meanings that are sometimes contradictory and that may also deviate from the meaning assigned to them in the objective context of psychology and the theory of cognition. Contact between human beings, daily social life, is possible only because human beings understand each other. They have tools of communication, which consist of verbal language, gestures, facial expressions—that is, of signs expressed in a variety of media and possessing meanings that are shared by all group members and are therefore understood.

In most daily contacts, the function does not need to be explicitly activated; instead, it does its beneficial work silently. We say that we "understand" a man's rage and craving for revenge when we are informed that he was insulted in public, or that we "understand" a parent whose heart is filled with sadness and grief, when he hears of the loss of a child, even if it did occur a long time previously. There is thus a wide range of psychological connections that are "understood" by us without further inquiry or empirical study, when our understanding is explicitly activated. In other instances, however, understanding occurs only after a process of ratiocination of varying length. In order to "understand" Newtonian physics, one has to familiarize oneself with facts and go through a chain of explanations that are interconnected.

Finally, there are theorems, such as: When A equals B and B equals C, A equals C, which are understood with almost the same evidentiary certainty as the just cited emotional instances, even though the two contexts represent entirely different universes of discourse and therefore have nothing in common when they are investigated in epistemological terms. Explaining and understanding evidently constitute no problem at all in normal everyday life. When we feel puzzled, we make inquiries or ask others for explanations; as soon as we have obtained them, we respond with understanding. Nowhere are explaining and understanding experienced as constituting an antinomy or as being opposing functions.

This is different, however, when we are dealing with a scientific approach toward the world. The problem—or, as it may be called, the antinomy—of explaining and understanding is a crucial one in psychology. The basic work, "Verstehen und Erklären," the detailed study of which is indispensable for a grasp of the issues at stake, was written by H. Hartmann in 1927 and published in English as "Understanding and Explanation" (1964). It is a problem to which too little attention has been paid in this country, even though psychoanalysis as a science stands or falls with its outcome.

The problem started when Dilthey published his famous paper "Ideen über eine beschreibende und zergliedernde Psychologie" ("Ideas about a Describing and Analyzing Psychology") in 1894, and the antinomy between explaining and understanding was brought out precisely. I shall have to discuss the issue briefly. Dilthey distinguishes between explaining psychology and understanding psychology; for linguistic reasons, I shall call one *psychologia explanans* and the other *psychologia comprendens*.[19]

By *psychologia explanans* Dilthey meant all psychologies that work with the formation of hypotheses—that is to say, those that, being impressed by the rise of the natural sciences, use their methods. *Psychologia explanans* derives psychological phenomena from "a limited number of explicit explanatory elements of hypothetical character throughout" (p. 144). Yet aside from deriving psychological phenomena from a few hypothetical, well-defined elements, *psychologia explanans* may ignore the psyche altogether and derive psychic phenomena solely from physiological factors. Dilthey demonstrated the shortcomings of a *psychologia explanans* by discussing the psychological systems of the two Mills, Spencer, Herbart, Taine, and Wundt, all of whom had tried to explain psychological phenomena by the effect of factors or elements that were not directly observable or were not of a psychological nature at all. Thus, for example, they explained perception in terms of the stimulation of sense organs (or, in some instances, inner states) whose concatenations were interpreted as being parallel to processes in the nervous system.

Psychologia comprendens, by contrast, works without hypotheses. Its starting point is the totality of psychic life, as it reveals itself to

[19] This is necessary in order to avoid the monstrosities that may easily occur otherwise, such as "Understanding psychology understands mental life better than explaining psychology does."

consciousness. The first step is the exact description of the total live structural concatenation *(Strukturzusammenhang)*, which is not inferred from but represented directly in the ever-changing contents of consciousness. For the understanding of this structural concatenation no hypotheses are necessary, since the concatenation is given immediately and directly in the subjective experience. Once the structural concatenation is described in its totality, it can be analyzed *(zergliedert*—literally, dismembered), and thus its basic elements can be found without any need to introduce hypothetical or nonpsychological elements. Thus, Dilthey launched a vigorous attack against *psychologia explanans,* the fruitlessness of which he tried to demonstrate in all its forms, and he set forth the principles of *psychologia comprendens,* which he accepted as the only workable and scientifically justifiable psychology.

Psychologia comprendens, by starting out from the immediately given live structural concatenation, adjusted its method to the subject matter, an adjustment that is made in every science. Here then was the essential difference between psychology and natural science. External objects are not given to the direct subjective experience in the same way as the structural concatenation is. The psychic exterritoriality, so to speak, of all objects of science necessitates the formation of hypotheses; in matters of psychology, however, these are fruitless and even destroy a scientific psychology. Dilthey tried to show that a set of hypothetical elements that one school of *psychologia explanans* uses for the derivation of psychic phenomena is just as good as that of the other, and that the choice of hypotheses is only a matter of preference or bias, and without any consequence, since no one can explain psychic life, after all—at any rate, by means of such hypothetical elements.

When *psychologia comprendens* starts with a reliable and complete description of the live experienced total structural concatenation, and then works its way to the elements by taking apart the totality, it penetrates to the core of the personality. This Dilthey found to exist in the drives and feelings (p. 185), thereby establishing what was, at least in outward appearance, a surprising similarity with psychoanalysis.

I have simplified Dilthey's paper, which had such grave consequences for German psychiatry and psychopathology. No one can infer from my simple summary the subtlety and sophistication of his ratiocination and, of course, I do not refer here at all to his eminent position in the history of ideas. After all, he was the first, if I am not mistaken, to assert the indispensable and basic role of psychology in the humanities.

But, to return to Dilthey's principal differentiation between the basic mechanism in science and that in psychology (and therefore in the humanities in general), one has to regret his choice of terminology. When someone has explained the Pythagorean theorem to our satisfaction, or perhaps the laws of motion and gravitation, we not only feel but are entitled to say that we now *understand* that theorem or those laws. I assume that Dilthey would not have objected to this formulation, for if I understand him correctly what he wanted to do was to differentiate between two mechanisms that are both employed in order to arrive at knowledge.

> In the [subjective] experience, processes of the *entire psyche* act together. In it [the subjective experience] connection is a given, whereas the senses offer only a manifoldness of singlenesses. An individual process is carried experientially by the entire totality of psychic life and the connection in which it [the individual process] stands by itself, as well as with the totality of psychic life, belongs with the immediate experience. This is determined by the nature of the *understanding* of ourselves and of others. We explain by means of purely intellectual processes, but we understand by way of the acting together of all psychic forces in the act of apprehension. We proceed in understanding from the connection of the whole that is given to us as a living thing, in order to make out of it the single [element] comprehensible to us [My translation].

> [In dem Erlebnis wirken die Vorgänge des *ganzen Gemütes* zusammen. In ihm ist Zusammenhang gegeben, während die Sinne nur ein Mannigfaltiges von Einzelheiten darbieten. Der einzelne Vorgang ist von der ganzen Totalität des Seelenlebens im Erlebnis getragen, und der Zusammenhang, in welchem er in sich und mit dem Ganzen des Seelenlebens steht, gehört der unmittelbaren Erfahrung an. Dies bestimmt schon die Natur des *Verstehens* unserer selbst und anderer. Wir erklären durch rein intellektuelle Prozesse, aber wir verstehen durch des Zusammenwirken aller Gemütskräfte in der Auffassung. Und wir gehen im Verstehen vom Zusammenhang des Ganzen, der uns lebendig

gegeben ist, aus, um aus diesem das einzelne uns fassbar zu
machen] [p. 172].

Thus objects per se cannot be understood. By observation, experi-
mentation, induction, inference, and reasoning we may succeed in
explaining whatever there is to explain in the reality outside our
psyche. Yet it is the psyche that is given directly by way of inner
experience. All we have to do is to turn toward the totality of that
inner experience, describe it, and then take it apart; after that, we
will find the elements and their interplay, their effects and their
development. And anyone who follows Dilthey's reasoning closely
will agree with his momentous statement, which had such grave consequences for Central European psychiatry and psychopathology:
"Nature we explain; mental life we understand [Die Natur erklären
wir, das Seelenleben verstehen wir]" (p. 144).

The problem of *psychologia explanans* and *comprendens* has
found a revival in two recent papers by Kuiper (1964, 1965). By contrast with Heinz Hartmann—who has demonstrated that psychoanalysis is a *psychologia explanans*—Kuiper asserts that there is a
close affiliation between Dilthey's psychology and psychoanalysis.
Since psychoanalysis uncovers, according to Kuiper's reasoning, unconscious motives that make actions understandable, it is a *psychologia comprendens*. He therefore accepts as explanations only the
propositions of psychoanalytic metapsychology. In agreement with
Heinz Hartmann, I regard this conception of psychoanalysis as un-
tenable, in that it takes out of analysis its very gist and backbone.
Historically, it is certainly not correct. Dilthey did not take notice
of the beginnings of psychoanalysis, even though he died eleven
years after the publication of *The Interpretation of Dreams*. Perhaps
it never came to his attention; but even if it had, he would certainly have rejected it, as he did with every *psychologia explanans*.
And from his point of view he would have been correct in doing
so, for in epistemological terms, it is all the same whether conscious
psychic phenomena are derived from processes in the nervous system
or from the unconscious. This does not deny, of course, the well-
known and generally accepted fact that, in dropping his original
"Project for a Scientific Psychology," which Freud had written during
the fall of 1895, and which was essentially neurologically oriented,

and replacing it with an investigation into the broad area of unconscious repressed motives, Freud rendered an eminent service to
psychology.[20] Hartmann has very correctly pointed out that it is in
terms of a hypothesis that psychoanalysis finds the foundation of
mental processes to lie in instinctual ones (1927, p. 396), and I believe that one is entitled to say that any interpretation, in the
narrower sense, when it refers to the unconscious (whether this be
the repressed, the superego, or the unconscious parts of the ego),
is a construct and therefore hypothetical. To be sure, this construct
may sooner or later be confirmed to our satisfaction by the subject's
associations, actions or dreams. That satisfaction, however, is decep-
tive, as we shall later see.

First we have to take a closer look at the vexing problem of
explanation and understanding. In that regard, Dilthey seems to me
to have set forth a valid antinomy, even though the conclusions
that he drew, despite their correctness at the time he drew them,
were later proved to be wrong—at least so far as psychology is concerned, as the history of psychoanalysis demonstrates.

Historically it can be shown that explaining and understanding
have frequently been—and, as will be seen, from a certain point of
view always are—at loggerheads. The scholastic world view of the
Middle Ages provided a "full understanding" of the universe: there
were no gaps, no dark areas that might have puzzled man's mind.
Today we know that, despite its unrivaled source of "unlimited
understanding," that world view had no explanatory value at all.
Yet the degree of understanding that it did provide was greater
than that which the scientific approach will probably ever be capable

---

[20] In abandoning neurologizing psychology after having completed his "Project,"
Freud was not altogether original but followed the French example with which he was
familiar. Cf. Kris (1947, p. 336); cf. also Freud (1892-1894, p. 135): "The clinical observation of the French undoubtedly gains in self-sufficiency in that it relegates physiological considerations to a second place."

It has its own piquancy to consider the moves and countermoves in the history of
ideas during those last few years before the ending of the century: Dilthey read the
death sentence over *psychologia explanans* in 1894, while Freud, probably without
knowing of Dilthey's *psychologia comprendens*, plotted out, almost at the same time,
precisely a *psychologia explanans*, to its extremest consequences; by doing exactly what
Dilthey had warned most strongly against, Freud carried neurologizing psychology *ad
absurdum*, only to drop it and turn to creating a new *psychologia explanans*, which
was to fulfill Dilthey's specifications, through its extensive use of the function of understanding.

of producing—at least if current epistemological thinking is correct, with its alleged proof that a consistent system covering the universe as a whole is impossible, not only for practical but also for theoretical reasons. The consequence of this view is that science must be expected always to leave some areas unexplained. At this point one is forced to refer explanations to something objective, by contrast with understanding, which reflects solely a subjective state. The difficulty, of course, is that, in the common or literal sense, the understanding mind always has the feeling that it has been or is explaining.

The antinomy between understanding and explaining can be seen with particular sharpness if one considers Copernicus' heliocentric theory. It served one function brilliantly—namely, to explain the retrograde motions of the planets; but this advantage was almost trivial alongside the new unsolved problems that the theory created —for example, the state of rest of terrestrial objects (which was incompatible with a planet in motion), as well as the fact that an object that has been thrown vertically returns to exactly the point from which it has been thrown (which obviously could not happen if, in moving around the sun, the earth has changed its position). Thus a theory whose explanatory value was considerable—at least for a rather long period of time—initially left more phenomena unexplained than it explained, and certainly set new limits on the understanding of the universe, which seemed to have been understood quite well, before the advent of the new theory.

Here the antinomy of explanation and understanding becomes particularly clear: whether or not I *understand* something only I can decide, since understanding reflects a subjective state; whether or not an event is *explained,* however, cannot be decided in this subjective fashion but only objectively.

When Newton devised his theory of gravitational forces, he thereby made it possible to explain a wide area of observable data, and in due time these phenomena were "understood." It made sense to say that masses attracted each other and to speak of the gravitational force as drawing all things toward the center of the earth. It is questionable how many physicists would today suggest the existence of a gravitational force.

Scientific progress depends on two seemingly contradictory processes, as many have observed. These have to do with the ability to discover, almost to create disorder in states of seeming order and, by contrast, to discover—that is to say, to create—order out of states of seeming disorder. The scientist turns to areas of disorder within which no one has yet perceived order and in his research he is able to make new observations, or engage in speculations, which then will enable him to formulate new hypotheses and, ultimately, new theories. On the other hand, the scientist also discovers disorder in areas of seeming order: in what seems to others to be well explained, he discovers hitherto unnoted contradictory elements and, after he has proven the existence of such disorder, he aims at new explanations which will then re-establish a state of order at a higher level.

Freud proved his greatness in both directions: in discovering disorder in order and in establishing order in disorder. What is most remarkable is the fact that he did not allow himself to be seduced by the understanding he had obtained through his own research, but relatively quickly discovered and disclosed the disorder in the state of order that he had created not so long before. Sometimes a new theory was made necessary by a contradiction (state of disorder) that covered an area as amazingly small as that which led to his *Moses* book (1939); but when he had formulated that new theory, he then expanded its area of relevance as far as possible, pushing toward extremes of inference, only to admit later that he had learned once again how right Nestroy, the writer of comedies, who is beloved by the Viennese, was when he said: "Every step forward is only half as big as it looks at first."

The explanations set forth in the *Studies on Hysteria* (Breuer and Freud, 1893-1895), whatever their explanatory value may have been, did provide sufficient understanding of hysterical psychopathology to have served to satisfy one or two generations of psychiatrists. But only a few years later Freud produced, in *The Interpretation of Dreams* (1900), a far superior set of paradigms, which this time furnished understanding for two decades. *The Ego and the Id* (1923) might have provided understanding for longer than that, yet "Analysis Terminable and Interminable" (1937) definitely announced that Freud's unquiet mind was preparing for a new thrust. The direction in which it might have gone may be conjectured by an imaginative mind, yet it will remain forever no more than a hypothesis.

The sequence of phases in the evolvement of scientific insight seems to be: an extraordinary mind formulates explanations that offend common sense; if the formulator is lucky, he convinces a small group of similarly restless minds of the suitability of his formulations. The increase they make possible in predictive power; the increment in the ability to deal with processes that are taking place in the real world; and the inner state of harmony that is brought into being by the new formulations, as a consequence of their potential for temporarily eliminating contradictions within a limited area of the universe—all these gradually convince ever larger groups, until the new formulations, at one time rejected, are taught as absolute truths in the grade schools or high schools.

Thus the conversion of new explanations, earlier regarded as violating common sense, into commonsense understanding occurs at the very time when, at the top of the scientific hierarchy, these formulations are beginning to be recognized as internally contradictory and to be replaced by new ones, which will offend common sense as much as those that they will gradually replace did earlier.

What I have referred to, without any elaboration, as "explanations" and then again "formulations" have, of course, been made the subject of special inquiries by those who have a very serious concern about the theory of cognition. But whether one sees the progress of science as taking place through the creation of new paradigms (Kuhn, 1962), or defines the change from Newtonian to modern physics as the evolvement of a new system decoding the messages that Nature sends us—however different may be the theoretical outlook that underlies these approaches—it does not affect the line of thought pursued in this essay. For psychologically it is always the function of *explaining* that the subtleties and sophistications of modern theories of cognition revolve about.

One of the many remarkable features in Freud's scientific career is that in one lifetime his creative potential undertook and realized what is usually spread over several generations.

At this point it may be proper to refer briefly to a somewhat less important aspect of understanding. When a scientist discovers a new solution or a new explanation, and particularly when this has the dignity of a paradigm, in Kuhn's sense, he is often stirred to a temporary feeling of triumph. He has suddenly understood something that, only a short time before, had been an enigma. At that moment he is fully aware of the explanatory value of his finding. When paradigms become popular, however, and are absorbed by a whole generation; when they have become routinized—that is to say, made part and parcel of common sense—then these same paradigms become, at least psychologically, vehicles of understanding rather than of explaining. This is, indeed, one characteristic of the present phase of psychoanalysis. When Kuiper asserts that psychoanalysis is chiefly a *psychologia comprendens*—that in analyzing a patient we discover unconscious motives, which make it possible for both the analyst and the subject to understand better the latter's feelings, thoughts, and actions—most analysts, I assume, would agree. It may therefore sound paradoxical for me to say, in agreement with Hartmann, that psychoanalysis is nevertheless a *psychologia explanans*.

It would not be the first time that belief and reality have been in disagreement with each other. Psychoanalysis is now in a phase comparable to that in which physics was after Newton. Despite considerable differences of opinion and some rather large gaps in our knowledge, one has the impression that man's mind is now by and large understood. We do not have a well-defined yardstick, which would clearly demonstrate the lacunae of knowledge, as the physicist and the biologist have. Yet this is a reflection of the atmosphere during the heyday of Newtonian physics in the nineteenth century, when physicists did not "explain" but rather followed the common sense that had been created by Newton's "explanations." There is, by contrast, scarcely any analyst who, despite his basic agreement with Freud's work, does not disagree sharply with at least one of Freud's findings or theoretical positions.

If all these "proofs of error" were to be taken together, hardly any part of Freud's work would retain its validity. For this, it is not necessary to go so far as to include the critique of the neo-Freudian schools: I believe that an adding up of the varieties of criticism that Freud's work has found among those who would unhesitatingly regard themselves as closely following him would in itself produce that result. Curiously enough, no one critic would agree with the criticisms made by other critics. By and large he would say that to the best of his knowledge, only that part with which he himself disagrees is wrong; criticism of the other parts is unwarranted. No doubt, psychoanalysis finds itself, in this respect, in an odd position. Its disordered condition should not be equated with the divergence of opinions that is regularly to be found in all advancing fields of science. In my opinion, it is due rather to the decline that our science has suffered through having been perverted to a common-sense scheme and thereby losing its explanatory value.

From the psychological point of view, it seems to me that understanding in science almost always makes out of the content of explanations empathetic[21] processes. I am almost inclined to say that it is only when an explanation has been made empathetic that we evolve the feeling of understanding. Adler's psychological theories are much better suited for empathy than psychoanalytic theories are; this explains, on the one hand, their popularity and, on the other, the tendency of many psychoanalysts to simplify psychoanalytic theories in such a way as to make them hardly distinguishable from Adler's.

Some areas of psychoanalytic theory do not lend themselves well to empathy; these include the correlation that has been found between anality and avarice or pedantry (Hartmann, 1927, p. 394). The explanatory value of such constructs is enormous, even though they are scarcely to be described as empathetic.[22] On the other hand, constructs may be empathetic and yet wrong, because they do not *explain* anything.

Psychoanalysis is therefore a science only insofar as it *explains*, even though the temper of the times demands and expects from depth psychology empathetic statements. Kuiper (1964, p. 25) even goes so far as to defend psychoanalysis against the reproach of being a *psychologia explanans*—a reproach that has been raised in some quarters, in which Dilthey's axiomatic statement on the methodology and task of psychology has been accepted.

Kuiper ascribes only to psychoanalytic metapsychology the dignity of providing explanations; he criticizes psychoanalysts who put empathetic and metapsychological statements side by side.

It may appear as if he were right, when the structure of Freud's

21 By empathetic I mean what Hartmann's translator called "empathizable," when he was translating the German word *einfühlbar*.

22 It was precisely this construct that earned Freud the greatest amount of ridicule. It would be interesting to investigate whether or not the area covered by resistance is fairly identical with the unempathetic.

book on the *Interpretation of Dreams* is checked along these lines. Up to the seventh chapter, Freud presented all the observations he had made in his analyses of his patients' and his own dreams—such as the bearing of day residues, the differentiation of manifest and latent dream content, the variety of mechanisms involved in dream work and many more—only to declare suddenly, in the seventh chapter, that all that does not really explain the dream. He then proceeded to reconstruct the structure that a system must possess in order for it to be able to produce dreams.[23] The reader was able to follow Freud, in the first six chapters of his book, by way of "understanding." Just as in Newton's theories, forces (like animistic spirits) have effects on the movements of objects, the reader was able to visualize unpleasant memories as being cathected with energies that were then displaced upon other more neutral images, which fitted into other unpleasant contexts and thereby acquired at last sufficient energy to form a dream. In the seventh chapter, however, a different demand was put on the reader's "understanding." It was no longer a matter of understanding empathetic processes, but of grasping the structure of a system.

The break between the sixth and seventh chapters of *The Interpretation of Dreams* is thought-provoking and has particular bearing upon our subject matter. Freud (1900, p. 511) asserts: "To explain a thing means to trace it back to something already known." This strikes me as being particularly un-Freudian when I compare it with Nietzsche's (1869-1871, p. 253): "All enlargement of our knowledge originates from the making conscious of the unconscious [Alle Erweiterung unserer Erkenntnis entsteht aus dem Bewusstmachen des Unbewussten]." That was a most profound insight, which nevertheless did not prevent him from writing later (1884-1888, p. 127) —exactly as Freud was to do in 1900: *"Explanation:* The expression of a new thing by means of signs of something already known ['Erklärung': das ist der Ausdruck eines neuen Dinges vermittels der Zeichen von schon bekannten Dingen]." Yet Freud, as Hartmann (1927) has pointed out, did not always differentiate in his terminol-

---

23 This reconstruction was actually a mental *tour de force* of such proportions that since then analysts have sometimes tried to organize their own writing in such a way that their most pertinent conclusions were contained in the seventh section of these writings.

ogy between explaining and understanding; this can be observed
when he uses the term "meaningful" where "causally determined"
is what is actually meant (p. 400).[24]

I assume, in view of Freud's nomenclature, that what strikes the
reader as a break between the sixth and seventh chapters of *The
Interpretation of Dreams* was only apparent and not real, if it is
judged from Freud's vantage point. In his inquiry into or, better,
in his original attempt to cure neurotic patients, Freud found explanations for the patients' symptoms. Some or, probably, very many
of these explanations were of a kind that permitted empathy—that
is to say, they consisted of unconscious images, thoughts, wishes,
all of which are empathetic and can be re-experienced directly by
the observer as phenomena to which he could conceivably be subjected. That, in so doing, Freud did not proceed in the way that
Dilthey proposed, and that he probably did not even gain his insights primarily by empathy but rather by observation and the
search for causes—both these can be regarded as being almost
proven by the fact that he found "explanations" that are scarcely
empathetic and are therefore almost inaccessible to empathy. These
include the just mentioned transformation of the anal drive into a
well-delineated character picture. Since he was apparently guided
far less by understanding than by explaining, it is small wonder that,
despite all the insights that he had reported in the first six chapters,
he did not stop there, but acknowledged that the real work to be
done began now—exactly at the point at which "the merely understanding mind" would have stopped.

Metapsychology is not, as Kuiper asserts, an edifice built up of
explanatory statements, by contrast with the interpretations given
the patient, which, according to him, are part and parcel of a *psychologia comprendens*. In any interpretation that is given, a metapsychological statement is implicit. For obvious reasons, this built-in
metapsychology is only infrequently—if at all—verbalized to the
patient. But when a hostile intent, which is unconscious to the

24 It seems that Nietzsche, too, did not (at least at one point) differentiate between
explaining and understanding. Cf. the just quoted definition of explaining with the
following: " 'to understand' means naïvely only: to be able to express something new in
the language of something old and known" ["Verstehen" das heisst naiv bloss: etwas
Neues ausdrücken können in der Sprache von etwas Altem, Bekanntem]" (Nietzsche,
1884-1888, p. 11).

patient, is recognized by the analyst, and when the latter interprets it to the patient by way of a series of symptoms, dreams and let us assume also apraxias, in all of which psychic formations this hostility is shown to be the common element, then the patient may ask why he has not himself had any cognizance of that intent. If, at that point, we thought it technically advisable to answer the question, we would have to tell him that the intent has been repressed, that his conscience is opposed not only to these impulses but to many more. Some of these statements would be necessarily metapsychological by nature.[25]

Metapsychology should be no more than an abstract formulation of what the analyst's findings are.[26] Large portions of current metapsychology are the result of speculation and therefore open to question. It thus becomes questionable whether metapsychological statements are explanatory at all; if they are, however, it would be misleading to take this aspect as differentiating them from contents obtained by interpretations.[27] To be sure, the interpretation of sense perception that occurs when the bacteriologist observes a slide and the interpretation of free associations that is made by the analyst—similar or dissimilar as these two forms of interpretation may be, and a vast literature has accumulated around this question —what is essential is that both set out to explain objective data. If Freud had aimed at understanding, his mind would have come to rest much earlier; it was because he used the methods of natural science that he was propelled from one explanation to another. For one peculiarity of explaining is that there is no end to it, that no explanation is feasible that would be final. If science were approached from another vantage point, one would have to say that if one single phenomenon were *fully* explained, the whole universe would be.

The view that maintains that all parts of the universe, even the

25 Kuiper warns us against using technical language with the patient and I heartily agree; but the problem of what to tell a patient and what not to tell him is a technical one and has no place in an inquiry into the structure of psychoanalysis as a science.

26 I am aware that some problems of metapsychology may be purely speculative and that they cannot therefore be regarded as abstractions from observations (or from assumptions necessitated by observations). But the bulk of Freud's metapsychology was meant as an abstraction from the observable.

27 See Gedo et al. (1964) for a structuring of psychoanalytic psychology according to levels of abstraction.

smallest ones, are interconnected, that any change in any one part of the universe has effects upon the whole—that view is probably tenable and perhaps even a necessary assumption. If one takes into consideration, further, the fact that a full explanation of any element requires knowledge of its entire history, both past and future —that is to say, that the "complete" explanation of a simple apraxia would require knowledge not only of the subject's psychological history, but also that of his ancestors, as well as his ancestors' organic substructure (which would take us back not only to the origin of man but also to the beginnings of life and indeed of the planet)— then one will readily recognize that science has never succeeded in "truly" explaining anything.

What it has been able to do is to establish interconnections among some elements. Scientists are therefore forced to cut out of the universe a certain section of it, and to look at that section as if it were indeed self-contained. When psychoanalysis explains an apraxia, it follows it through only a short portion of its history and the explanation that it offers is of necessity only a partial one, since all scientific explanations are incomplete. In pointing out that a dream is overdetermined, Freud stated that one never knows whether or not a dream has been satisfactorily explained. Yet it is not only dreams, symptoms, and even apraxias that are overdetermined. If the method of psychoanalysis were that of understanding, as Dilthey recommended, we would indeed know when a phenomenon is "understood"; but there is no place in Dilthey's psychology for the concept of "overdetermination" that is basic and essential to psychoanalysis.

Kuiper sets forth a few clinical examples in order to demonstrate how the method of understanding works, and scarcely anyone who analyzes patients will differ with the examples he presents. Every analyst, of course, seeks to *understand* his patients' motives, and does so in a large number of instances, during almost every hour of his working day. If the term "to understand" is used in the vernacular of everyday life, Kuiper may be right. But his two papers, if I understand them correctly, are meant to solve problems of the theory of science.

Besides, one has to be aware that almost all psychoanalytic propositions are hypothetical—that is, except for an eventuality that I am not considering at this point. Freud was aware of such a possibility, as is known from his letters, in which he expressed doubt that very much of his work would prove to be lasting truths. Yet it is precisely in that, that the greatness of his work lies, even though it is overlooked by his critics and perhaps as well by many of his followers. Findings established by *psychologia comprendens* of the kind that Dilthey postulated will remain valid forever, because they do not *explain* anything but are merely descriptions. We know that accurate descriptions are not superseded; only explanations are. The fact that psychoanalysis is throughout a *psychologia explanans* makes it certain that it will be superseded by a new psychology. Understanding, however, finds an all too early satisfaction. When we experience understanding, we are admitting a limitation, a defect, because in so doing we are manifesting either indifference toward the contradictions in existing explanations or our belief that all the facts are now known.

If I knew for certain that the bulk of the psychoanalytic system, as we know it today, would still be valid in let us say one or two centuries, instead of being superseded by vastly improved explanations, I would be strongly inclined to agree with Kuiper that there is little explanatory value in psychoanalytic propositions. It may sound paradoxical to say that it is an unwarranted underestimation of psychoanalysis if one believes that its truth is permanent; up to now only descriptive statements have shown that quality. We may be certain that our textbooks of anatomy, as far as their description of structures and their topography are concerned, will not change greatly in the future; yet what a textbook of physiology will contain fifty years from now is anybody's guess. Understanding is *au fond* the enemy of explaining: it says that a satisfactory explanation has been found, even though we should know that there are no satisfactory explanations.[28]

One might therefore postulate that the truly scientific mind would discover new explanations and, at one and the same time, the defects necessarily contained in them. Ideal as this may appear to be,

---

[28] Nietzsche (1884-1888, p. 13) has put it in a nutshell: "Insofar as the word 'recognition' has any sense at all, the world is unrecognizable; but it is *interpretable;* it has no sense behind itself, but [it does have] innumerable senses [Soweit überhaupt das Wort 'Erkenntnisse' Sinn hat, ist die Welt unerkennbar; aber sie ist anders *deutbar,* sie hat keinen Sinn hinter sich, sondern unzählige Sinne]."

such a mind would live in chaos; it would never be capable of explaining anything. What seems like a defect of the human mind, as revealed in the experience of understanding, is actually an indispensable tool, for it enables us to make right choices. One needs a steering wheel of some sort, in order to be able to navigate among a huge number of explanatory possibilities. The history of science shows that correct explanations are often found at two or more places at approximately the same time; but it also shows that a great variety of different explanations for the same problem are often offered simultaneously, just as a variety of explanations all come at once to a man's mind, when he is in search of the right answer to a puzzling problem. If man's mind had at its disposal only the function of explaining, it would wander helplessly among a network of feasible explanations. Understanding makes it possible for him to steer through the bewildering variety of possible explanations, by pulling out of a large number of possible choices the one that best fits a particular situation, and thus setting the mind temporarily at rest. In the genius, that process does not take long and the arrest is therefore of short duration. Sometimes, however, it takes generations before the mind cannot any longer *understand* what had previously seemed to be so well explained.

In the long run, of course, understanding does not endanger scientific progress. The differences that separate generations stand in the way of any quiet settling down on found and fond solutions. Routinized explanations become boring, contradictions in the established theoretical edifice are discovered, and then new facts are found. A period of waiting sets in for the emergence of some richly endowed mind that will produce a new set of explanations or, better, paradigms.

It is well known that the atom still poses a number of unsolved problems; in all probability, science will never reach the point at which atomic physics can be said to have been completed. Is it likely that we have really made profound advances in the explanation of human behavior, if, after centuries of experimental research into physics, the atom still poses so many profound problems?

Common sense would therefore say that many a generation of research will have to pass before psychology will have created anything that can be even approximately compared to contemporary physics, in terms of exactness and profundity of understanding. Yet there is a faint possibility that we may be profoundly mistaken. Is a structure necessarily more complicated than its parts? Let's take a weathercock. It is easy to know everything there is to know about a weathercock; it is a simple instrument whose function and working can be understood by a child; it can be easily produced, even by an unskilled person. Yet if it is a weathercock—that is, one made out of metal—its parts are scarcely understood. One does not know for sure what a metal is, and once again we are face to face with the problem of the atom. *Mutatis mutandis,* one may conclude that it is an incredibly complicated substructure, the brain, that leads to a relatively simple organ, the mind.

It is needless to say that what I am about to suggest is highly improbable, except that improbability is not always the hallmark of error. There is a possibility, faint as it may be, that Freud cannot be spoken of as the Newton of psychology because he will not be followed by an Einstein or a Planck. Much will depend on what is found out about the infant. Is the infant's mind a more or less complicated structure than the adult's? Present-day common sense would say that, for many reasons, an infant is of course simpler than an adult. In general, I assume, the simple is better understood than the complex. Yet I think there is agreement that psychology knows more about the adult mind than about the infant's. That could perhaps be explained by the adult's rich ability to communicate, whereas the infant (like the animal) can be observed only from the outside and not from the inside. While that may be correct, one has to remember that the infant's mind is structured in such a way that it may develop into any of a number of different directions, whereas an aged mind can move in no more than a limited number of directions, and sometimes only one.

It is conceivable that a mind that possesses an unrealized potentiality for a huge variety of developments is more complicated than a mind that has already realized one of these and even exhausted its potential in one direction. It is also possible that the degree of complexity depends on the number of unrealized potentialities that a structure contains, rather than on its functional differentiation. If this were so, the historical comparison I made earlier between physics and psychology would have been wrong from the start. Be that as it may, the one conclusion that I would derive from all the foregoing reasoning seems valid: *one should describe as a true explanation only one that goes beyond the common sense of the historical period.* The scientist whose explanations move within the framework of contemporary understanding follows common sense; he is probably not activating the function of explanation, or only to a moderate degree. At this point, he should already have become puzzled by the loopholes that must gradually have become apparent to him in the set of explanations that have been degraded to commonsense thinking. Yet his "understanding" prevents him from becoming aware of precisely these areas of difficulty and the correct description would therefore be that he is applying his understanding but not explaining.[29]

III

This discussion of *psychologia explanans* and *psychologia comprendens* has not taken us as far from *Hamlet* as it may have seemed to, for there are critics who accept character analysis as a method of literary criticism only if it will lead to a better understanding. When Freud *explains* Hamlet's hesitation by reconstructing Hamlet's childhood oedipus complex, has he helped us to understand Hamlet any better? He has undoubtedly explained Hamlet's hesitation. If it were not known from innumerable other instances of people who have undergone psychoanalysis that children, during the process of growing up into psychological adulthood, regularly develop specific wishes and impulses of a sort that Claudius did carry out in reality, the analyst would never have arrived at the idea of finding in the defense against such impulses and wishes the key to Hamlet's hesitation.

---

29 In my opinion, this is one of the more characteristic features of present-day psychoanalytic research. The reproaches of rigidity, unoriginality, stagnation and the like, which have been raised against the school of analysis that follows Freud, are partly justified. A psychoanalytic common sense has evolved that now provides a sentiment of understanding, and, without intending to, impedes the search for new explanations. Yet this criticism should not induce anyone to accept the theories of those who want to break out of the stalemate, even at the price of false theories, only in order to evade the stigma of unoriginality. Nevertheless, it is to be expected that the mind that will provide a new push to psychology will probably be misunderstood initially, just as Freud was.

If we regard the tragedy as a self-contained system, one has to admit that one cannot find any direct clue to this solution of the problem. And therefore it becomes understandable if the reconstructed infantile oedipus complex sounds to many critics as alien to the development of the tragedy, as the assumption would be that an encephalitic inflammation must have taken place in Hamlet when he was a child. However, an astute scholar of comparative literature might well raise the question of whether the outspoken parent-child triangle that appears in *Oedipus Rex* and *The Brothers Karamazov* may not also lie at the basis of *Hamlet;* yet he, too, would face the charge of carrying into the tragedy an observation that he had derived from outside it. The only difference would be that, if one put Hamlet's oedipus complex in between two literary works and thus rested the proof of its existence on objects of the same class, the literary mind might have less trouble accepting an explanation that sounded annoying when it came from the medical profession, but would sound aesthetically acceptable when limited to three literary works of world renown.

The literary critics who rejected Freud's explanation were essentially correct in doing so, because it was an explanation that did not enlarge their understanding. For the analyst it is different: he has no doubt of the correctness of Freud's construct. Still, one facet of Freud's approach to literary works should be made clear. He did not—as he was accused of doing—abuse them by reducing them to agents through which to confirm pet theories of his. He approached them in the same spirit with which he approached everything else he encountered in life: as a possible source of new insights. The new insights that he derived from literary works fell, of course, into a broad network of assumptions—or better, interpretations—that he had formed gradually about life and man's mind. But even in this area he aimed at explanations, despite the fact that these may appear to the superficial eye in the guise of understanding. That he did not bend the literary work so as to make it fall into his already established explanatory schemata but responded readily to facets of the work that did not coincide with his accustomed explanations —this the reader may now be ready to accept with greater willingness than when he was reading the beginning of this essay, in which I presented the source material.

BIBLIOGRAPHY

Breuer, J. & Freud, S. (1893-1895), Studies on Hysteria. *Standard Edition*, 2. London: Hogarth Press, 1955.

Bühler, K. (1927), *Die Krise der Psychologie*. Jena: Fischer, 1929.

Dilthey, W. (1894), Ideen über eine beschreibende und zergliedernde Psychologie. In: *Wilhelm Diltheys Gesammelte Schriften*, 5:139-240. Leipzig-Berlin: Teubner, 1921-1934.

Freud, S. (1892-1894), Preface and Footnotes to the Translation of Charcot's *Tuesday Lectures*. *Standard Edition*, 1:129-143. London: Hogarth Press, 1966.

—— (1900), The Interpretation of Dreams. *Standard Edition*, 4 & 5. London: Hogarth Press, 1953.

—— (1901), The Psychopathology of Everyday Life. *Standard Edition*, 6. London: Hogarth Press, 1960.

—— (1907), Delusions and Dreams in Jensen's *Gradiva*. *Standard Edition*, 9:3-95. London: Hogarth Press, 1959.

—— (1910a), Leonardo da Vinci and a Memory of His Childhood. *Standard Edition*, 11:59-137. London: Hogarth Press, 1957.

—— (1910b), A Special Type of Choice of Object Made by Men. *Standard Edition*, 11:163-175. London: Hogarth Press, 1957.

—— (1913), The Theme of the Three Caskets. *Standard Edition*, 12:289-301. London: Hogarth Press, 1958.

—— (1916-1917), Introductory Lectures on Psycho-Analysis. *Standard Edition*, 15 & 16. London: Hogarth Press, 1963.

—— (1922), Some Neurotic Mechanisms in Jealousy, Paranoia, and Homosexuality. *Standard Edition*, 18:221-232. London: Hogarth Press, 1955.

—— (1923), The Ego and the Id. Standard Edition, 19:3-66. London: Hogarth Press, 1961.

—— (1933), New Introductory Lectures on Psycho-Analysis. *Standard Edition*, 22:3-182. London: Hogarth Press, 1964.

—— (1937), Analysis Terminable and Interminable. *Standard Edition*, 23:209-253. London: Hogarth Press, 1964.

—— (1939), Moses and Monotheism. *Standard Edition*, 23:3-137. London: Hogarth Press, 1964.

—— (1950a), *The Origins of Psycho-Analysis: Letters to Wilhelm Fliess, Drafts and Notes, 1888-1902*, ed. M. Bonaparte, A. Freud, & E. Kris. New York: Basic Books, 1954.

—— (1950b), Extracts from the Fliess Papers. *Standard Edition*, 1:175-280. London: Hogarth Press, 1966.

—— (1960), *Letters of Sigmund Freud* [1873-1939], ed. E. Freud. New York: Basic Books.

—— /Pfister, O. (1963), *Psychoanalysis and Faith* [1909-1939], ed. H. Meng & E. Freud. New York: Basic Books.

Gedo, J. E., Sabshin, M., Sadow, L., & Schlessinger, N. (1964), "Studies on Hysteria": A Methodological Evaluation. *J. Amer. Psa. Assn.*, 12:734-751.

Hartmann, H. (1927), Understanding and Explanation. *Essays on Ego Psychology*. New York: International Universities Press, 1964, pp. 369-403.

Jensen, W. (1907), Drei unveröffentlichte Briefe. *Psa. Beweg.*, 1:207-211, 1929.

Jones, E. (1953), *The Life and Work of Sigmund Freud*, Vol. 1. New York: Basic Books.

Kris, E. (1947), The Nature of Psychoanalytic Propositions and Their Validation. In: *Psychological Theory*, ed. M. H. Marx. New York: Macmillan, 1951, pp. 332-351.

Kuhn, T. S. (1962), The Structure of Scientific Revolutions. *International Encyclopedia of Unified Science*, Vol. 2, No. 2. Chicago: University of Chicago Press.

Kuiper, P. C. (1964), Verstehende Psychologie und Psychoanalyse. *Psyche*, 18:15-32.

—— (1965), Diltheys Psychologie und ihre Beziehung zur Psychoanalyse. *Psyche*, 19:242-249.

Muir, K. (1952), Some Freudian Interpretations of Shakespeare. *Proc. Leeds Philosophical Soc.*, 7:44-52.

Nietzsche, F. (1869-1871), Gedanken zu "Die Tragödie und die Freigeister." *Gesammelte Werke*, 3:232-259. Munich: Musarion Verlag, 1920-1929.

—— (1882-1886), Erkenntnistheorie. *Gesammelte Werke*, 16:87-133. Munich: Musarion Verlag, 1920-1929.

—— (1884-1888), Der Wille zur Macht. *Gesammelte Werke*, 19. Munich: Musarion Verlag, 1920-1929.

Sachs, H. (1919), The Unconscious in Shakespeare's *Tempest*. *The Creative Unconscious*. Cambridge, Mass.: Sci-Art Publishers, 1951, pp. 243-323.

Schnitzler, A. (1889), Die Frage an das Schicksal. *Die dramatischen Werke*, 1:30-41. Frankfurt: Fischer Verlag, 1962.

Schur, M. (1968), *The Problem of Death in Freud's Writings and Life*. New York: International Universities Press (in press).

Spurgeon, C. F. E. (1931), Shakespeare's Iterative Imagery. In: *Studies in Shakespeare*, sel. & intr. by P. Alexander. London, New York, Toronto: Oxford University Press, 1964, pp. 171-260.

—— (1935), *Shakespeare's Imagery and What It Tells Us*. Cambridge: Atheneum University Press, 1966.

Stengel, E. (1966), Review: *Medical Orthodoxy and the Future of Psychoanalysis*. *Brit. J. Med. Psychol.*, 39:264-265.

Strachey, J. (1957), Editor's Note [to Freud, 1910a]. *Standard Edition*, 11:59-62. London: Hogarth Press, 1957.

Wilder, A. G. (1966), Freud, Signorelli, and Lacan: The Repression of the Signifier. *Amer. Imago*, 23:332-366.

NOTES ON THE THEORY OF DEFENSE

WILLIE HOFFER, M.D.†

Freud's conception of defense is one of the cornerstones of psychoanalytic theory. In the hierarchy of psychoanalytic concepts, it is at the apex, together with those of the unconscious, the instinctual drives, and the development and structuralization of personality. In the area of therapy, since 1926 it has superseded the theory of repression. The theory of defense had a revolutionizing impact on psychoanalytic technique due to Anna Freud and her book, *The Ego and the Mechanisms of Defense* (1936); familiarity with this work is a prerequisite for the understanding and clinical application of the theory of defense.[1]

THE CONCEPT OF DEFENSE

In 1896, Freud described *defense* as "an attempt to repress an incompatible idea which had come into distressing opposition to the patient's ego" (p. 162). Yet, in 1926, Freud wrote:

> In the course of discussing the problem of anxiety I have revived a concept or, to put it more modestly, a term, of which I made exclusive use thirty years ago when I first began to study the subject but which I later abandoned. I refer to the term 'defensive process'. I afterwards replaced it by the word 'repression', but the relation between the two remained uncertain. It

This paper was first published under the title "Bemerkungen zur Abwehrlehre." In: *Hoofdstukken uit de hedendaagse psychoanalyse,* edited by P. J. van der Leeuw, E. C. M. Frijling-Schreuder, and P. C. Kuiper. Arnhem: van Loghum Slaterus, 1967, pp. 20-30. We wish to thank the editors and publishers of this book for permission to translate this paper. The translation was prepared by Ruth S. Eissler, M.D.

[1] The Bibliography appended to this paper contains a selection from among the many additional publications dealing with the theory of defense.

will be an undoubted advantage, I think, to revert to the old concept of 'defence', provided we employ it explicitly as a general designation for all the techniques which the ego makes use of in conflicts which may lead to a neurosis, while we retain the word 'repression' for the special method of defence which the line of approach taken by our investigations made us better acquainted with in the first instance [p. 163].

Thus, in 1896 (and already in 1894), defense was a term that designated the psychological process (the defense process [*Abwehrvorgang*]) of repression; in 1926, however, defense became a concept comprising a variety of analytically observable defense mechanisms (repression, isolation, undoing, etc.); furthermore, the defensive process was viewed as originating in the human's anxiety and in the mastery of anxiety arising from internal dangers; this process was localized in the ego. So much for the concept of defense.

THE DEFENSE PROCESSES

The processes of defense are not accessible to direct observation, not even to self-observation; they take place in the unconscious. Yet the postulation of defense mechanisms becomes convincing if one observes the derivatives of the defensive process—the defense mechanisms—in psychoanalytic therapy, traces their effect on mental life, and is confronted by the fact that changes in the defense mechanisms coincide with changes in behavior.

The distinction between defense processes and defense mechanisms seems justified especially if one follows Freud's thoughts concerning the origin and the vitally important functions of defense. In *Inhibitions, Symptoms and Anxiety* Freud attempted to demonstrate that the defense processes have a primal and causal relation to the preparedness for anxiety (traumatic or danger situation) and the mastery of anxiety; that the defense processes protect the ego functions from traumatically being put out of action—that is, from being overwhelmed, especially by internal "overstimulation"; and that the defense processes thus serve adaptation, the regulation and satisfaction of instinctual drives ("inner adaptation").

In present-day psychoanalysis, however, particularly in clinical reports, the concept of anxiety is still frequently used as if it derived from the observations described by Freud in 1894. At that time Freud spoke of "incompatible ideas" and thoughts, and saw the goal of psychoanalytic therapy in the overcoming of this defense so that these ideas could be recognized and integrated. In other words, recognition of the inner conflict was to replace the defense (the resistance) and thus to institute the solution of the conflict. Thus, defense was *defense against thoughts* and its direct relation to anxiety was not formulated.

Something similar took place when, starting in 1905, the instinctual drives and their development became the center of interest and when the idea of *defense against instincts* [*Triebabwehr*] (one spoke of drive repression) became prevalent. In particular, the newly discovered vicissitudes of instincts, the fixations and regression of instincts, and their importance for therapy, confirmed and illustrated the defense against instincts. In therapy, the defense against instincts could now achieve for the understanding of obsessional neurosis what the idea of defense against thoughts had accomplished for the understanding of the hysterias. Yet Freud's model of defense thereby became more complicated: defense against thoughts could still be viewed as defense against whatever was felt to be embarrassing, shameful, and forbidden; but defense against instincts is a biopsychological concept; defense now became a life-preserving process of self-preservation; and repression was necessary no longer for social reasons or object-related motives, but because it preserved life; Alfred Adler foundered on this enlargement and complication of the theory of defense.

The idea of defense against instincts remained prevalent for at least ten years: until Freud's paper "On Narcissism" (1914) and beyond that. In looking back one can say: until the time when ego psychology gradually made its appearance. One may regard Freud's *Inhibitions, Symptoms and Anxiety* (1926) as a report giving an account of this development; the experiences with perversions and psychoses (Schreber [1911], the Wolf Man [1918], "A Child Is Being Beaten" [1919]) represented its clinical basis. The ideas of defense against thoughts and defense against instincts were thereby in no way discarded but only further specified.

What constituted the progress that was expressed in this development? First, one no longer needed to conceive of defense as primarily directed against an idea (or thought), or, for that matter, against instinctual impulses, but saw it as a psychic process of protection (according to J. Sandler [1960], a process in the service of "safety") which, linked with an unobservable "anxiety signal," was to counteract the development of anxiety and ultimately to prevent the ego functions from being paralyzed by traumata. Secondly, from this point forward one considered not only that which was defended against, but also that which did the defending, and localized the latter in the ego. This development had incisive consequences for psychoanalytic technique and in particular for the method of interpretation. One could now ask under what conditions, during treatment, the defending ego could be induced to tolerate that which it had warded off—primarily anxiety; the therapeutic alliance (R. Sterba, 1934) and the transference appeared in a new light. This did not simplify psychoanalytic technique, but interpretation was made more effective. Symptom analysis was definitely replaced by "analysis of the total personality," and new dimensions were opened up for the indications for psychoanalytic treatment (child analysis, psychoses, dissociality).

Thus, if we speak of defense processes, we are not referring to observable psychic processes; rather, we place them as neutralized instinctual processes in the ego organization. They serve the integrity of the ego, regulate (in terms of safety) the mental drive representations, and give them direction. They represent a function of the ego organization in the service of instinct regulation. They are not really "inimical to instincts," but because of their connection with the affect of anxiety they are "sensitive to instincts." They are the manifestation of a general responsiveness or sensitivity or anxiousness toward disturbances within the ego's organization. Like the organs of perception, the defense processes are in the service of the protective shield against stimuli; however, being directed inward, they recognize instinctual stimuli, give signals, and selectively participate in their management and satisfaction. Freud (1905) expressed this very impressively and much more simply in the following words: "Defensive processes are the psychical correlative of the

flight reflex and perform the task of preventing the generation of
unpleasure from internal sources. In fulfilling this task they serve
mental events as an automatic regulation, which in the end, incidentally, turns out to be detrimental and has to be subjected to conscious thinking (p. 233).

When, in a presentation such as that attempted here, one strives
for an integration of the theses on defense, he has to accept a complication which the theory of defense has in common with the theory of
the ego: we have to resort to assumptions, "probabilities" and "possibilities" and a moderate degree of speculation, to fill the gaps of our
knowledge.

The prehistory of the ego is shrouded in darkness. In order to
understand the defense processes and to do justice to clinical impressions, we have to bear in mind two such assumptions: (1) that the
infantile ego, sensitive to instinctual drives, close to helplessness,
growing toward control and regulation, is exposed to nonobservable,
silent traumata; and (2) that the developing ego is capable of counteracting the danger of trauma and the internal conflicts derived
from it by ego splitting.

In connection with superego development, ego splitting is generally accepted. One can then imagine the ego as if it simultaneously
strove—like a Janus face—for instinct discharge (modification of
instinct) and instinct defense. The objection that repression is capable of actually suppressing the instinctual discharge is not valid;
the intention of the process of repression—avoidance of anxiety engendered by the danger of trauma—must not be confused with the
result of repression. This distinction is important for psychoanalytic
technique and for the therapeutic alliance; "the return of the repressed in the symptoms" is after all an obvious indication of ego
splitting and the unreliability of repression. Do we not speak of
"afterrepression, countercathexis, and reaction formation"? Thus,
if we speak of the "localization of defense in the ego," we do not
mean "the entire ego" but only one aspect of the ego activities, and
for this reason we can speak of a defense organization in the ego.
Hartmann (1950) incisively drew attention to these conditions in the
ego. The early traumata and ego splittings are very important for
the understanding of ego pathology and thus for therapy.

The Mechanisms of Defense

We cannot answer the questions: "Whence came the mechanisms of defense? What is inborn, what developmental, what acquired?" Edward Glover (1947) and Heinz Hartmann (1950) say that—strictly speaking—a "mechanism" cannot be reduced to more primitive simpler elements. The defense mechanisms are merely organized defense processes, and an "organization" ceases to function when it is dissolved into its parts. Whatever we know from clinical observations, in particular from observation of children (Anna Freud, 1965), demonstrates that there is a *chronology* of defense mechanisms; that, for instance, identification with the aggressor develops much later than identification per se, and that repression precedes denial and even more so negation.

If we adhere to the observable and wish to avoid speculations, we are inclined to speak of "precursors" of defense mechanisms. Heinz Hartmann (1950) describes as precursors of repression the neonate's closing of the eyelids whenever too intense a light stimulus reaches his eyes. René Spitz (1965) also refers to such precursors. Accordingly, one should distinguish between precursors, physiological models of defense, and defense mechanisms that appear early in life. Introjection, projection, displacement, and condensation were described as the earliest defense mechanisms (e.g., by Nunberg, 1932). Could we say that defense processes are related to the strengths of affects (unpleasure, pain), while defense mechanisms are also related to ideational or thought content? It is difficult to assume the existence of defense processes and defense mechanisms in the neonate and the infant; I believe Freud did so.

At this point I would like to mention a personal experience: in the 1930s the Vienna Academic Society for Medical Psychology founded a reading seminar which was chaired by Hartmann and myself. We had worked through to the last pages of Freud's *Inhibitions, Symptoms and Anxiety* when we encountered the following mysterious sentence: "It may well be that before its sharp cleavage into an ego and id, and before the formation of a super-ego, the mental apparatus makes use of different methods of defence from those which it employs after it has reached these stages of organization" (1926, p. 164). When we were asked what Freud meant by this, I had no answer available. Heinz Hartmann, though, did: introjection and projection! The role of these early defense mechanisms is now generally recognized in the psychology of infants.

The distinction between precursors of defense (physiological models) and early defense processes seems to be influenced by the extent of the significance that is attributed to the phase of ego-id differentiation; it would appear that this phase is regarded as not really belonging to ego psychology and that it holds a special position—somewhat like Wales to England. Similar problems are presented by the concepts of signal anxiety (Schur, 1958) and trauma (Spitz, 1965). Whatever the result of such considerations, the idea remains that defense processes are protective processes and exert a controlling function on the mutual interaction between the internal world and the external world. This mutual interaction is particularly important with respect to an adequate assessment of the role which the mother plays in the development of the child's defense mechanisms. It cannot be seriously maintained that the mother takes over the first protection against dangers. Would this not be an exaggeration? After all, she cannot "digest" for the infant, she only can support or disturb this process. Moreover, the mother is herself a "danger situation"; she can increase or decrease the stimuli, particularly the object stimuli, and induce both anxiety of object loss and, by overstimulation, anxiety of loss of self. With regard to the asocial or dissocial child Freud, as early as 1911, pointed to overstimulation, spoiling, and thus indirectly to the defect in the infantile defense organization. It thus seems permissible to speak of the relative autonomy of defense.

The observations of the chronology of defense mechanisms lead to the vicissitudes of the defense mechanisms, namely, to the fact that defense mechanisms may become inactive and—as Hartmann (1947, 1950) demonstrated—undergo a change of function. However, our knowledge ends at this point.

The precocious and premature defense mechanisms must be distinguished from the precursors and the early mechanisms of defense. Anna Freud pointed to their importance in the psychopathology of childhood. The chronology of defense mechanisms has its clinical importance, but the number of variables makes it very difficult for the observer to trace the conditions for the preparedness for anxiety and the development of defense.

A special case of precocious, premature defense is the combination of defense mechanisms which is characteristic of an unusually early appearance of genuine superego formations. One gains the impression that all the defense mechanisms participating in the formation of the superego are forged into one single mechanism: introjection and turning against self (aggression, self-criticism), plus identification, plus intensive repression, plus turning of self-love (narcissism) into masochism (Jacobson, 1964). A combination of anxieties, the reaction to a multitude of inner dangers (loss of self, loss of object, loss of the object's love, loss of the genital, the latter also including female genitality)—all of these mobilize, comparable to a chain reaction, defenses which in normal superego development take place only step by step. The precocious development of the superego bears out Kurt Eissler's (1953) conclusions, namely: that the defense mechanisms may protect but also destroy the ego.

A hierarchy or the development of a rank order of defense mechanisms was already considered by Edward Glover (1937); a kind of "sense of order" in the use of the different defense mechanisms can be observed, as was indicated in the development and unfolding of the superego. The assumption of a rank order of defense mechanisms, however, claims no more than that some defense mechanisms are particularly important—hold, so to speak, "cabinet rank" in government—whereas others—like "ambassadors"—can be activated according to need or play a less central role. In the assessment of pathology, according to Anna Freud (1965), one must distinguish between defense against specific anxiety situations and defense against all anxiety-provoking instinctual impulses; in this way the idea of a hierarchy of defenses gains clinical interest and significance. The gradual formation of a hierarchical order of the defense mechanisms can obscure and blur the chronology in a confusing manner, a result leading back to the inadequacy of our means of observation. The more we know about the defense activity, the more we will be able to sharpen and to make use of our observational apparatus. Only in this way can one protect oneself from becoming dulled in clinical work.

The Defense Organization

The clinical-therapeutic importance of defense mechanisms cannot be rated highly enough; yet one should not identify the defense function of the ego with the ego functions and the ego organization as a whole; even less should one identify the defense mechanisms with ego pathology and place them in opposition to a healthy ego. P. J. van der Leeuw (1965) rightly said that "the defense is not the illness itself." Ego pathology is rooted in unsuccessful as well as in successful defense; we know that in the obsessional neurosis and in the perversions the defense is exceedingly successful, whereas it is the contribution of unsuccessful defense that makes the pathology of the ego so incisive. There is an advantage to having recourse to a construct, i.e., to assume a "defense organization" which comprises all aspects of defense. Accordingly, the defense organization is one facet of the ego organization, its origin and prehistory are obscure, but its function can be formulated precisely, namely, regulation of anxiety, not total avoidance of anxiety. It has a developmental history which, on the basis of observations, we are able to reconstruct from the earliest age on, provided we assume traumata in infancy. The developmental vicissitudes of the defense organization are co-determined by modifications of the internal world and by the mutual interaction between inner and outer world. We must not be seduced into attributing too much significance to the changes occurring in the external world simply because they are accessible to observation and depend neither on the possibilities for communication nor on introspection. We also have to conceive of the defense organization (as part of the ego organization) in terms of a mutual interaction between id and superego (the intersystemic relations, according to Hartmann, 1951), and even more important: in mutual interaction with the other facets of the ego organization as, for instance, ego autonomy (Hartmann, 1950), with the instinct-integrating activity of the ego (gratification and transformation of instincts), and, furthermore, as important special cases, with socialization and sublimation (neutralization), including the newly created structures (Hartmann, 1955). Here the conscious and unconscious fantasies certainly find their place.

A less general and more specific justification for the assumption of a defense organization may be found in observations made by Anna Freud (as far as I know, she has reported them only in her lectures to the students of the London Institute of Psycho-Analysis). I have previously (1954) referred to this point, which P. J. van der Leeuw (1965) subsequently took up and enlarged upon. I point to the fact that the defense mechanisms not only regulate the instinct-ego relationships but simultaneously enrich, enlarge, and strengthen in a positive and constructive sense the ego organization as well. The implications for our therapeutic technique are enormous, though we are usually not sufficiently aware of their impact when we give an account of our therapeutic work.

BIBLIOGRAPHY

Eissler, K. R. (1953), The Effect of Structure of the Ego on Psychoanalytic Technique. *J. Amer. Psa. Assn.*, 1:104-143.
Freud, A. (1936), *The Ego and the Mechanisms of Defense.* New York: International Universities Press, rev. ed., 1966.
—— (1965), *Normality and Pathology in Childhood: Assessments of Development.* New York: International Universities Press.
Freud, S. (1894), The Neuro-Psychoses of Defence. *Standard Edition,* 3:43-68. London: Hogarth Press, 1962.
—— (1896), Further Remarks on the Neuro-Psychoses of Defence. *Standard Edition,* 3:159-185. London: Hogarth Press, 1962.
—— (1905), Jokes and Their Relation to the Unconscious. *Standard Edition,* 8. London: Hogarth Press, 1960.
—— (1911), Psycho-Analytic Notes on an Autobiographical Account of a Case of Paranoia (Dementia Paranoides). *Standard Edition,* 12:3-82. London: Hogarth Press, 1958.
—— (1914), On Narcissism. *Standard Edition,* 14:67-102. London: Hogarth Press, 1957.
—— (1918), From the History of an Infantile Neurosis. *Standard Edition,* 17:3-123. London: Hogarth Press, 1955.
—— (1919), 'A Child Is Being Beaten.' *Standard Edition,* 17:175-204. London: Hogarth Press, 1955.
—— (1926), Inhibitions, Symptoms and Anxiety. *Standard Edition,* 20:77-175. London: Hogarth Press, 1959.
Gero, G. (1951), The Concept of Defense. *Psa. Quart.,* 20:565-578.
Glover, E. (1937), In: Symposium on the Theory of the Therapeutic Results of Psycho-Analysis. *Int. J. Psa.,* 18:125-189.
—— (1947), Basic Mental Concepts. *Psa. Quart.,* 16:482-506.
Greenson, R. R. (1958), Variations in Classical Psycho-Analytic Technique. *Int. J. Psa.,* 39:200-201.
—— (1960), Problems of Dosage, Timing and Tact in Interpretation. Abstract in: *Bull. Phila. Assn. Psa.,* 10:23-24.
Hartmann, H. (1947), On Rational and Irrational Action. *Essays on Ego Psychology.* New York: International Universities Press, 1964, pp. 37-68.
—— (1950), Comments on the Psychoanalytic Theory of the Ego. *Essays on Ego Psychology.* New York: International Universities Press, 1964, pp. 113-141.

—— (1951), Technical Implications of Ego Psychology. *Essays on Ego Psychology.* New York: International Universities Press, 1964, pp. 142-154.

—— (1955), Notes on the Theory of Sublimation. *Essays on Ego Psychology.* New York: International Universities Press, 1964, pp. 215-240.

Hoffer, W. (1954), Defensive Process and Defensive Organization. *Int. J. Psa.,* 35:194-198.

Jacobson, E. (1964), *The Self and the Object World.* New York: International Universities Press.

Kris, E. (1951), Ego Psychology and Interpretation in Psychoanalytic Therapy. *Psa. Quart.,* 20:15-30.

—— (1956), The Recovery of Childhood Memories in Psychoanalysis. *This Annual,* 11:54-88.

Lampl-de Groot, J. (1965), *The Development of the Mind.* New York: International Universities Pres.

Loewenstein, R. M. (1951), The Problem of Interpretation. *Psa. Quart.,* 20:1-14.

—— (1954), On Defences, Autonomous Ego and Psycho-Analytic Technique. *Int. J. Psa.,* 35:188-193.

—— (1966), Defensive Organization and Autonomous Ego Functions. In Panel: Defense Organization of the Ego and Psychoanalytic Technique, rep. E. Pumpian-Mindlin. *J. Amer. Psa. Assn.,* 15:150-165, 1967.

Nunberg, H. (1932), *The Principles of Psychoanalysis.* New York: International Universities Press, 1955.

Sandler, J. (1960), The Background of Safety. *Int. J. Psa.,* 41:352-356.

Schur, M. (1958), The Ego and the Id in Anxiety. *This Annual,* 13:190-220.

Spitz, R. A. (1965), *The First Year of Life.* New York: International Universities Press.

Sterba, R. F. (1934), The Fate of the Ego in Analytic Therapy. *Int. J. Psa.,* 15:117-126.

Van der Leeuw, P. J. (1965), Zur Entwicklung des Begriffs der Abwehr. *Psyche,* 19:161-171.

Zetzel, E. R. (1954), Report of Panel: Defense Mechanisms and Psychoanalytic Technique. *J. Amer. Psa. Assn.,* 2:318-326.

THE ECONOMIC POINT OF VIEW
AND DEFENSE

SEYMOUR L. LUSTMAN, Ph.D., M.D. (New Haven)

The energic propositions of psychoanalytic theory are perhaps among the most problematic of Freudian conceptualizations. In view of the nature of recent attention given the topic, it might be more appropriate to start with a "defense of economy" rather than the "economy of defense."

Perhaps the most pervasive problem of the economic point of view stems from a failure to accept that the division of psychoanalytic theory into five metapsychological points of view is an artifact. It was most recently stressed by Rapaport and Gill (1959) for essentially two purposes. The first was the hope of making discussion easier, and the second was to stress that no psychoanalytic discourse was complete—no description or explanation complete—that did not use *all*. Each of the "points of view" is permeated with the others. For example, the dynamic point of view has within it some of Freud's richest genetic (libidinal development), adaptive (object relations), structural, and economic propositions. Such divisions as are necessary for discussion are *our* divisions—not an inherent divisibility of psychic phenomena. When we single out one point of view, we must remain aware of the distortions we thus introduce. However, even taking these considerations into account, the economic point of view has certainly been the single most attacked formulation in the literature.

The exclusive use of economic concepts is justifiably criticized as a misuse of metapsychology. There can be no doubt that the economic view lends itself to glib and excessively simplistic explanation —if used alone. It has also been the set of concepts most frequently

Professor of Psychiatry, Yale University Child Study Center and Department of Psychiatry.

used alone. Schur (1966) also urged that we "discourage the assumption that an economic formulation can be sufficiently meaningful per se without a consideration of the other metapsychological points of view" (p. 201). I shall return to this issue since I feel that it is only in the neonatal period that economic propositions may predominate.

For the purposes of this essay, I would like to address myself to only three areas of discontent. The first I will label as quantitative; the second, the relationship to science; and the third, the relationship of theory to phenomena.

A major and valid critique has been Kubie's (1947), to the point that the concept of psychic energy places us in a quantitative idiom at a time when we have no measurement of such quantities. This is true. The economic view carries the quantitative burden within psychoanalytic theory, and is a source of great embarrassment for many. Yet, this is a quandary that psychoanalysis shares with every clinical science which rests on clinical judgment. Given any human trait, characteristic, affect, illness, or what have you, people rarely have it or don't have it—they have it in varying degrees. In spite of the availability of reasonably exact blood-glucose measurements, clinical diabetes is still *judged* to be mild, moderate, or severe. One can superimpose a quasi-quantification through the use of expert judges and scalar techniques for those more comfortable four places to the right of the decimal point—but this is a technique for assuming validity from established reliability. It is not the kind of quantification that concerns and eludes us. Nevertheless, in spite of the embarrassment, quantified judgments will remain in clinical work because they are useful in dealing with the reality of observable phenomenology. The clinician has to assess the degree of anxiety, depression, defense, etc., because those quantitative estimates, however crude, have great predictive and prognostic value.

Some analysts are also embarrassed by what they refer to as psychoanalysis not changing its concepts to fit the "newer" concepts of the rest of science. This ignores the fact that the phenomenological fields are very different and gives the impression of some monolithic, "Big Science," unified and cohesive, and which, for some perverse reason, analysis refuses to accept. While most scientists accept a unified concept of science as a philosophical position, this is not true of their work. For example, if we turn from the obvious interdisciplinary differences to the small, well-circumscribed area of particle physics, the diversity of interest and conception as related to empiricism is well described by Greene (1968): "Aside from the common difficulty in treating a system of many interacting particles, the form and even the statement of the problem are different in different areas. Nuclear physicists are usually interested in the energy of a particular state, and their problems have to do with the complicated forces and large degeneracies. Atomic physicists know the forces, but have to deal with degeneracies and a relatively small system. Solid-state physicists, on the other hand, are frequently less interested in ground-state energies than in the spectrum of the elementary excitations and in the temperature-dependent response of a large system to external stimuli" (p. 153). One need not bemoan this characteristic of science since the debate always has heuristic value. But one can wonder what global energy concept we are to conform to that all the rest of science conforms to.

I remain impressed with the defensiveness of many psychoanalysts in the face of such criticisms as "this is unlike any other form of energy." In a discussion such as this, it always seems necessary to restate somehow the fact that pychoanalytic energic concepts refer *exclusively* to that scientific, mythical construct—the psychic apparatus. They are not equated with biological or physical concepts of energy, nor do they have to be congruent with the new energy concepts of other disciplines since they are not addressed to the same phenomena. While such a unity of science may one day come about, until that more propitious moment we are left with the perplexing semantic problem of using the same words for very different purposes. In this sense, energy may be a contaminated word—but I know of no better one for psychoanalytic theory.

Accordingly, one may expect to continue to hear the criticism that psychoanalytic energy obeys no known laws of (physical or biological) energy concepts. One can only say that at this stage of scientific development, the phenomenological domain of psychoanalysis has not extended to enzyme systems, electric light bulbs, or nuclear physics—any more than the phenomenological domains of those disciplines have extended to the quantitatively intense alterations of the function of psychic defense in adolescence. As a psychoanalyst, one can only be productively concerned with the utility of concepts to the uniquely human phenomena with which the field deals. By this I do not for one moment mean to imply that more useful concepts will not emerge when more is known—or that these future concepts will not demonstrate a cross-disciplinary convergence. I simply think a cross-disciplinary sterilization—as would occur with premature borrowing or discarding—is to be avoided until that moment of more advantageous cross-disciplinary fertilization.

I think this longing for acceptance by psychoanalysts is related to what Allport (1947) noted about psychology when he stated, "The machine model in psychology had its origin not in clinical or social experience, but rather in adulation of the technological success of the physical sciences" (p. 259f.).

The body of concepts we call the economic point of view was developed because of certain phenomenological characteristics noted by Freud in clinical psychoanalytic treatment, symptoms, dreams, slips, humor, the perversions, and literature. They did not develop, as is implied and stated, because of cross-disciplinary influences on Freud. Freud was not misled by the philosophical, neurological, and physical theoreticians of his day. I do not believe that the evolution of the economic point of view was primarily dictated by the state of scientific and philosophical theory of the era in which Freud worked. Nor do I think he was preoccupied with trying either to cast his observations into, or reconcile them with, the predominant theories of his era (Lustman, 1967).[1]

Freud's theory building arose from an empirical base, and the vicissitudes of that lifelong effort were always intimately related to this empirical base. In the main, the theoretical development always reflected his increasing awareness of newer or more clearly defined *clinical* phenomena, and the development of more sophisticated and abstract conceptualizations which were broad enough to permit fitting clinical data into the context of everyday life.

By now, they include aspects of the pleasure-pain principle, the reality principle, primary and secondary process, cathexis, hyper-

[1] It should be noted that the only time Freud made the attempt, early in his career, to cast psychological formulations in the predominant neurophysiological theories of his era, he discarded the "Project" (1895).

cathexis, anticathexis, libidinal and aggressive sources of energy, the "reservoir" and the "flux," degrees of neutralization and deneutralization, fusion, transformation, and crucial aspects of ego autonomy and conflict-free or conflict-ridden functioning. Such concepts are not in themselves phenomena—they are simplifying, organizing guidelines which exist only in the minds of investigators. However, it is true that as used, they are in part descriptive, in part explanatory. Nevertheless, if properly used, they are capable of predictive use related to *specific phenomena*.

In this sense, Freud developed the economic concepts in order to work theoretically with phenomena which were characterized by increase, diminution, discharge, and displacement. When one looks at the clinical data of psychoanalysis—which I consider its basic phenomenological field (I shall speak more of this later)—I wonder if the situation is very different than it was in 1894 when Freud noted, "I refer to the concept that in mental functions something is to be distinguished—a quota of affect or sum of excitation—which possesses all the characteristics of a quantity (though we have no means of measuring it), which is capable of increase, diminution, displacement and discharge, and which is spread over the memory-traces of ideas somewhat as an electric charge is spread over the surface of a body" (p. 60). The crucial aspect of this basic statement is its phenomenological referent, not its electrical analogy; and as theory, it must be judged by its utility and relevance.

I quite agree that we must not hold to concepts for sentimental or authoritarian reasons; and I agree that some of our concepts are weaker (in a scientific sense) than others; and further, that they do not all have the same probability of survival. However, I continue to feel that we should base our modifications or elimination of concepts on the criteria suggested by Hartmann, Kris, and Loewenstein (1953): that the existing concept contradicts established empirical knowledge; that it is no longer useful in the scientific sense; that new, modified, and more useful concepts have been proposed—concepts which in the same area of inquiry suggest better and more useful hypotheses.

Given this, it seems to me that the major difficulties are related to the hope of rewriting psychoanalytic theory as a general theory of man. While this was clearly a goal of Freud's, it was one he did not achieve. Perhaps it would be more appropriate to say that the degree to which he succeeded depends on one's definition of a general theory of man.

My personal view is that although psychoanalysis is the most comprehensive theory available to date, it is not a general theory. Nor do I see the possibility of such a theory in the foreseeable future from any source. The so-called "information explosion" pierces some disciplinary barriers but makes massive correlations, integration, and synthesis a larger problem. The idea of a "general psychological theory" of man has become a limiting rather than a broadening concept. It is a contradiction in terms since for "general theoretical" considerations, man can no longer be considered primarily a psychological animal—although he can for specific theoretical purposes. Even within psychology itself, appropriately or inappropriately—for better or for worse—there have been massive shifts toward biology (neurophysiology and pharmacology) and sociology.

All of the branches of science that look at man look at a *part* of him, and say something valid about this incredibly complex, intricate animal. All of the separate divisions of such disciplines as biology, psychiatry, psychoanalysis, psychology, sociology, anthropology, history, political science, economics, have "one leg of the elephant." Psychoanalysis can be proud of its impact on the world of theories about man, but it does not have the method or the theoretical power to replace them. Each has its own view of man, and each has theories that are useful and relevant to that segmental view because man is all of these things, and more.

The most reasoned, even if excessively ambitious, effort at a general theory is implied in the "systems theory" approach. However, the status of this effort as well as the relationship of psychoanalysis to it are not within the scope of this paper.

Of greater import is the question currently being posed by theoreticians: How much of man, as a phenomenological field, can psychoanalysis encompass and remain psychoanalysis?

As an example, one can contrast the Piaget and the Freudian concepts of moral development. Since Piaget is concerned with thought, he arrives at a beautiful developmental progression of what children consciously *think about* moral values and judgments. Since he is a marvelous epistemologist, his theoretical constructs are models of theory construction. His phenomenological field is clear, circumscribed, and legitimate. However, it is only tangentially related to the empirical base of psychoanalytic superego theory. Piaget is not concerned with how people behave, or where they get their values or controls from within; nor is he concerned with guilt and shame. Psychoanalysis *is* concerned with these things. The analyst knows that our jails are filled with people who know and can abstract all the rules. As a matter of fact, to be a certain type of confidence man, one must know these.

The correlation of abstract thought to inner control and behavior is not easily established. One can only say that the two systems, each a legitimate area of inquiry, are addressed to different areas of phenomenology. The analyst must be interested in thought, but that is not enough for him. His theory has to deal with the source of cognitive content, identification and internalization processes, unconscious as well as conscious thought, impulse, and the progression from shame to guilt (Piers and Singer, 1953). Since his empirical base is more complicated, his theories are more complex.

The utility and relevance of psychoanalytic theory varies with the distance any incorporated phenomenon is from the conceptual intrapsychic structure of man as analysis sees it. At its base, psychoanalysis is an internal or intrapsychic conflict theory of man. As such, it is an eminently useful theory. As it is extended from this base, the conceptual problems become those of redefining the phenomenological field. Accordingly, psychoanalytic propositions are most congruent with intrapsychic processes; their applicability becomes less specific and less useful as the field is shifted. For example, as one shifts from the individual to small group phenomena (except for the family), to large group phenomena, to nations, etc., the congruence between empiricism and theory deteriorates. Scientists who deal with large group phenomena, such as societies and nations, have less use for a concept like psychic energy precisely *because* it is an intrapsychic concept.

The same shift in utility and relevance is possible within ego psychology. Although ego psychology is a crucial part of psychoanalysis, it is quite possible, by placing an exclusive or primary focus on cognition, to be an ego psychologist without being a psychoanalyst. For example, an ego psychologist can construct a developmental dimension along the lines of ego interests to skills. In contrast, consider an analyst faced with a Shakespearean scholar who has moved from a productive career, through an "interest" in pornography, which then became his "hobby," and ultimately brought him to psychoanalytic treatment because of an inability to work due to a driven obsession with pornography. The analyst will find such concepts as sublimation, deneutralization, cathexis, hypercathexis, sexualized, driven thought useful. Psychic energy and concepts of economy are relevant and useful to the one phenomenon, and apparently less so to the other.

In reading the literature of that part of ego psychology which attempts to avoid using economic propositions,[2] I am less impressed with the relative absence of energic concepts than I am with the more striking absence of sex, psychosexual or libidinal development, the genetic history of object relationships, problems of identification, character, the neuroses, etc. This does not mean that the theories proposed are wrong or not useful for the specific area; it suggests rather that the phenomenological area has been changed, and classical theory has been found wanting for the newer area by these workers. Whether this demands a change in classical theory involves the question which is the tail and which is the dog. Perhaps we are obliged to construct a hierarchy of psychoanalytic phenomena ranging from basic to extended.

As one way of looking at this problem, I would propose that the major explanatory and predictive value of economic propositions lies in that dimension of Freudian conceptualization which ranges from *displacement* phenomena to the *transference neurosis* phenomena, with its shifts in intensity, aggression, love, and degrees of discharge in varying forms of expression. Since this is one of the most basic data of psychoanalysis, there may be some value to using it as a target phenomenon. If in all of our attempted expansions of psychoanalytic theory, we would agree on retaining the nuclear posi-

---

2 See especially the contributions to *Motives and Thought*, edited by R. R. Holt (1967). In this same volume there is a touching memoir of David Rapaport in which the essence of the humanness of the man is described in terms of his "passion, intensity, enthusiasm"—all terms related to what psychoanalysis considers the economic point of view.

tion of this phenomenon, then one would say that any attempt to completely replace energic concepts (or any other) should be better able to explain and to predict the transference neuroses phenomena than do the current economic propositions.

As it has broadened its concept of man, psychoanalysis has had to formulate a conflict-free sphere (Hartmann, 1939) of ego activity. However, conflict is so ubiquitous in human development that analysts have tended to view all ego activities from that perspective. But if we grant that there are areas of conflict-free ego functioning (that have not so developed through change of function or secondary autonomy), then we have a major theoretical problem of fitting special theories into the major, larger theory. This is no easy task and introduces the need to evaluate alternative theories as well.

For example, does a psychoanalytic theory of cognitive development cover the same ground as Piaget? If so, which does what better? If we develop a limited psychoanalytic learning theory, or a theory of cognitive development, can we use some concepts for one area and not another and retain the sense of a cohesive theory?

It is in this area of selected phenomena that the conceptual problems arise. Ego psychology includes cognition—it also includes defense. Although both are ego functions, and must have conflict involved in their development, it is possible (at least it appears so from the literature) to conceptualize the theoretical needs differently. It is even possible, by defining the type of intellectual development one is concerned with, to be eclectic enough to use Piaget for one thing and Freud for another.

However, if we try to fit this into a theory which also deals with transference, I remain unpersuaded that Piaget, cybernetics, existing learning theories, cognitive styles, or ethology will help us any more than solid-state physics. They simply do not deal with identical aspects of man. As indicated above, the study of man, as the most complex area of scientific endeavor, has fruitfully developed more separate scientific disciplines than all of the rest of science.

Ego psychology as it relates to defense is different from ego psychology as it has been extended to cognition and other circumscribed developmental areas. It should be possible to develop and incorporate a limited learning theory and a relevant theory of cognitive development within psychoanalysis. However, one cannot redevelop a psychoanalytic theory out of a cognitive learning theory. The base is too narrow. It would result in the same type of inverted pyramid personality theory that has characterized all learning theories in the past.

I have selected defense as an aspect of ego psychology precisely because of its relationship to conflict theory. To continue to use the model of internal conflict (as well as aspects of external conflict) required certain theoretical assumptions. Loewenstein (1965) recently formulated this as follows: "In order to account for the direct and indirect manifestations of psychic conflict, it had to be assumed that the ego, like the drives, possesses forces capable of dynamic effects, . . . such as inhibiting and even arresting the development and the discharge of instinctual drives. Hence, it was necessary to hypothesize the existence of a special form of energy proper to the ego" (p. 40f.).

The more general necessities imposed by this have been succinctly stated by Rapaport and Gill (1959): since (dynamic) "forces have a direction, cannot account for displacements and transformations, and energies which (by definition) are directionless quantities cannot account for directional phenomena, we need . . . both energy and force concepts" (p. 156).

It is from these considerations that the economic propositions emerge. I would like to make my approach to the economy of defense through the perceptual processes of man which, by definition, we attribute to an ego apparatus of primary autonomy—but which developmentally will involve conflict and eventually achieve a status of secondary autonomy. In Freudian theory, perception—inner-directed and outer-directed—has never been a passive phenomenon, but an active process which depends on the availability and function of what we define as attention. This is a quantitative concept, and Freud quite early and consistently called this active process *hypercathexis*. To recover a memory requires a hypercathexis —or increase in attention cathexis. The withdrawal of attention cathexis brings about a decrease in the potential for awareness.

In relation to defensive functioning, the ego must perceive the primary stimuli as well as the affect signal developed by the ego. Then the automatic, unconscious mobilization of defensive mechanisms prevents further perception of, or modifications of, what is perceived. But defense is not accounted for by vicissitudes of attention cathexis alone. In economic terms, a defense such as repression is an interaction of withdrawal of hypercathexis with, more importantly, the establishment of a countercathexis—the relative permanence of which we conceptualize as structuralization. Thus a defense would be considered a substructure of the structure ego.

In psychoanalytic terms attention cathexis fulfills the criteria for a nonvectored, roughly quantitative energy concept. The quantitative aspects can be demonstrated in multiple task situations. It can better be demonstrated in the learning of any complicated, multiple task skill. For example, when one learns to drive an auto, one's interest is "invested" in steering, shifting gears, braking, etc. It is only after this has achieved the state of a stable autonomous function that attention can become available to permit concentration on where one wants to drive or the sights one encounters on the trip.

It was with this quantitative concept in mind—of the unavailability and deployment of attention cathexis at the extremes of the pleasure-pain continuum—that I previously (1957) called "imperceptivity" in the neonate a precursor of defense. The implication is a quantitative one, i.e., that more attention cathexis becomes available with increased *autonomy* of ego functions and is inversely related to the intensity of pleasure-pain experienced (although demonstrable most clearly at the ends of the continuum). Much of the concept of ego autonomy rests on such concepts of attention cathexis.

A further difference between attention in the service of relatively conflict-free ego function (such as some forms of problem solving) as contrasted with the pre-emption of attention in conflict (as in an obsessional preoccupation) demonstrates precisely the utility of such economic propositions as degrees of neutralization or instinctualization of energy. In other words, psychoanalysis also remains interested in the fact that skill with wheels can be more than transportation, i.e., the Hell's Angels.

Developmentally, defenses are not the only, but are a distinct class of controlling, delaying substructures of the ego. The idea of control comes from Freud's statement that the ego *"can only cathect an idea if it is in a position to inhibit any development of unpleasure that may proceed from it"* (1900, p. 601). Here, too, pain is purely an economic proposition referable to unbearable, overwhelming increase in tension. The richness of this vein of thought is apparent in the psychoanalytic research around the fundamental issue of trauma (see Furst, 1967).

The basic *economic* definition of a defense would have to do with the ability to control and maintain increases in tension in a *conflict situation*. Certainly all ego structures to some degree control and maintain tension, i.e., thought. However, as a substructure of the ego, defense is the most readily available for study and remains central for psychoanalytic theory because it is central to conflict. It includes a threshold concept, and states that those peremptory, cyclical, consummatory activities (which we attribute to drive) demonstrate quantitatively increasing characteristics which become noticeable when the threshold is reached (Rapaport, 1960b). Theoretically, a defense operates as a substructure or function—as a countercathexis which raises the threshold.

Again, I do not wish to imply that the economic propositions are not problematic, or that they can be applied to defense to the exclusion of other points of view. They remain useful for a theory of defense—but defense is much more and has many other research implications. For example, they are rich sources for developmental research.

However, since my arbitrary purpose is to speak of economy rather than the relationship to the other points of view, I would like to refer in passing to the possibility of an economic developmental sequence. Ignoring for the moment the question of whether they lead to variations of normality or pathology—developmentally, defensive function appears to parallel the development of the secondary process which leads to delay, binding, and subsequent detour. I refer to the developmentally determined series or continuum of defenses based on economic modes of functioning as conceptualized in the primary and secondary process. As Anna Freud (1936) points out, some defenses, such as displacement, operate by primary process mechanisms and are very close to instinctual forms of functioning. As defenses, they have in addition discharge characteristics. Others, such as rationalization or intellectualization, are closer to secondary process manifestations in economic mode of functioning.

Another major research and clinical advantage is the value of quantity or intensity, as a concept, as one of the four criteria Anna Freud (1965) suggested as a way of determining the pathogenicity or normalcy of a defense mechanism: "*Intensity.* Whether defense leads to symptom formation rather than to healthy social adaptation depends on quantitative factors even more than on qualitative ones. Any overdoing of drive restraint, regardless of the mechanism used, inevitably leads to neurotic results" (p. 177f.).

At the same time, one of the major undefined problems of the economic view is the problem of man as a tension-seeking animal. The economic point of view is most explicitly predicated on the issue of keeping the organism *relatively* free of tension. In terms of regulatory principles, defenses are among the ego mechanisms which relate to tension maintenance—but not explicitly to tension seeking. As indicated above, this proposition has great relevance to the psychoanalytic concept of trauma. To approach this issue, one must readdress oneself to the problems of the regulatory principles (Schur, 1966). One may question whether the two principles are adequate to explain these relationships, or whether we must follow Jacobson (1964) and speak of equilibrium as a principle of psychoeconomics.

In summary, for lack of a better word, I will continue to talk of energy, and I hope that in the future we can address ourselves to the complex and thorny problems of the source of what we define as bound energy in defense; the transformation of such energies as implied in sublimations, neutralization, and deneutralization (as when a working sublimation breaks up into its component raw drives); the structuralization, stability, or autonomy of defensive structures; discharge phenomena within defense, or as they bypass defense (as in jokes or Greenson's description of enthusiasm [1962]); the epistemological need for nonvectored concepts as concomitant concepts to the vectored concepts of drive; the economic impact on the ego of defense, as in impoverishment or deformation of other structures such as memory, judgment, attention (i.e., attention span or quantity of attention); and the impact of freed energy when a defense is analyzed and altered. For example, some feel that this energy then becomes available to the ego as neutralized energy and can be assumed from increased recall of memory, greater and more focused attention, etc. Others, principally Hartmann (1950), have suggested that analysis of a defense may lead to a release of aggressive energy previously bound in countercathexis, which may be first indicated in the analytic situation by a negative transference reaction.

In closing, I would like to repeat that the discussion above has a forced emphasis. The economic point of view was never put forth to explain all of human behavior; it is one of five points of view, which, with the others, is brought to bear on the problems. I repeat, such divisions as are necessary for discussion are *our* divisions—not an inherent divisibility of psychic phenomena. It is imperative that we remain aware of the distortions we introduce when we do this.

BIBLIOGRAPHY

Allport, G. W. (1947), The Emphasis on Molar Problems. In: *Theories in Contemporary Psychology*, ed. W. H. Marx. New York: Macmillan, 1963.
Freud, A. (1936), *The Ego and the Mechanisms of Defense*. New York: International Universities Press, rev. ed., 1966.
—— (1965), *Normality and Pathology in Childhood*. New York: International Universities Press.
Freud, S. (1894), The Neuro-psychoses of Defence. *Standard Edition*, 3:43-68. London: Hogarth Press, 1962.
—— (1895), Project for a Scientific Psychology. In: *The Origins of Psychoanalysis*. New York: Basic Books, 1954.
—— (1900), The Interpretation of Dreams. *Standard Edition*, 4 & 5. London: Hogarth Press, 1953.
Furst, S. S., ed. (1967), *Psychic Trauma*. New York: Basic Books.
Greene, M. P. (1968), A Problem in Theoretical Physics. *Science,* 161:153 (July 12).
Greenson, R. R. (1962), On Enthusiasm. *J. Amer. Psa. Assn.,* 10:3-21.
Hartmann, H. (1933), An Experimental Contribution to the Psychology of Obsessive-Compulsive Neurosis. *Essays on Ego Psychology*. New York: International Universities Press, 1964, pp. 404-418.
—— (1939), *Ego Psychology and the Problem of Adaptation*. New York: International Universities Press, 1958.
—— (1950), Comments on the Psychoanalytic Theory of the Ego. *This Annual*, 5:74-96.
—— (1964), *Essays on Ego Psychology*. New York: International Universities Press.
—— Kris, E., & Loewenstein, R. M. (1953), The Function of Theory in Psychoanalysis. In: *Drives, Affects, Behavior*, Vol. 1, ed. R. M. Loewenstein. New York: International Universities Press, pp. 13-37.
Holt, R. R., ed. (1967), *Motives and Thought: Psychoanalytic Essays in Honor of David Rapaport* [*Psychological Issues*, Monogr. 18/19]. New York: International Universities Press.
Jacobson, E. (1964), *The Self and the Object World*. New York: International Universities Press.
Kris, E. (1955), Neutralization and Sublimation: Observations on Young Children. *This Annual*, 10:30-46.
Kubie, L. S. (1947), The Fallacious Use of Quantitative Concepts in Dynamic Psychology. *Psa. Quart.,* 16:507-518.

Loewenstein, R. M. (1965), Observational Data and Theory in Psychoanalysis. In: *Drives, Affects, Behavior,* Vol. 2, ed. M. Schur. New York: International Universities Press, pp. 38-59.
Lustman, S. L. (1957), Psychic Energy and Mechanisms of Defense. *This Annual,* 12:151-165.
—— (1967), The Scientific Leadership of Anna Freud. *J. Amer. Psa. Assn.,* 15:810-827.
Piaget, J. (1932), *The Moral Judgment of the Child.* Glencoe: Free Press, 1948.
Piers, G. & Singer, M. (1953), *Shame and Guilt.* Springfield: Thomas.
Rapaport, D. (1960a), *The Structure of Psychoanalytic Theory* [*Psychological Issues,* Monogr. 6]. New York: International Universities Press.
—— (1960b), On the Psychoanalytic Theory of Motivation. In: *Nebraska Symposium on Motivation,* ed. M. R. Jones. Lincoln: University of Nebraska Press, pp. 173-247.
—— (1966), *The Collected Papers of David Rapaport,* ed. M. M. Gill. New York: Basic Books.
—— & Gill, M. M. (1959), The Points of View and Assumptions of Metapsychology. *Int. J. Psa.,* 40:153-162.
Sandler, J. & Joffe, W. G. (1966), On Skill and Sublimation. *J. Amer. Psa. Assn.,* 14:335-355.
Schur, M. (1966), *The Id and the Regulatory Principles of Mental Functioning.* New York: International Universities Press.
Wolff, P. H. (1960), *The Developmental Psychologies of Jean Piaget and Psychoanalysis* [*Psychological Issues,* Monogr. 5]. New York: International Universities Press.

FORM AND CONTENT

An Ego-Psychological View

RAFAEL MOSES, M.D. (Jerusalem)

In 1923 Groddeck wrote: "There you have the essential quality of the doctor, a propensity to cruelty which has been just so far repressed as to be useful, and which has for its warder the dread of causing pain" (p. 8). This astute formulation illustrates the problem of form and content in psychoanalytic perspective. The content of unconscious drives is the all-important determinant of behavior, but its specific functional influence is determined by the form it takes; by its quality, its quantity, its juxtaposition with other drives or other forces; as Groddeck puts it, by "this delicate interplay"—in his example, the interplay of cruelty and dread. It is the multiplication of such delicate interplays that determines personality and character as well as the specific forms of psychopathology. These interplays are mediated by what Rapaport (1960) calls ego structures and by the processes and energies which become available through these structures.

It is my thesis that it is useful to distinguish between form and content, even though they may at times come to stand for each other. The tendency to cruelty, in Groddeck's illustration, represents at the same time the content of the drive and its motivating energy. The fear of hurting another person and the repression of cruelty result from ego and superego intervention. The drive content has been given specific form as a result of processes emanating from ego structures, so that it now exerts its function on behavior: *repressed* cruelty, *dread* of causing pain. These structures also determine the "delicate interplay of forces," i.e., the quantitative relationships

Hadassah Hebrew University Medical School and Rothschild Hadassah University Hospital.

Lecture delivered to the Israel Psychoanalytic Society, Haifa, February 11, 1967.

which largely determine the recurring forms or styles of behavior patterns characteristic of the individual, in our example, physician. I believe that form or style, as an aspect of ego psychology, should become an important object of our study.

In the early years of psychoanalysis, the emphasis was mainly on the discovery of new meanings of content; and for many years thereafter, the interest shown in form rather than content reflected the wish to know what form revealed about content. The beginning of a change in this respect can be dated to 1939, when Hartmann's *Ego Psychology and the Problem of Adaptation* was published. This change continued with the further development of ego psychology. I hope to show that the formal aspect of behavior and its phenomena are in meaningful ways (though not exclusively) related to the functioning of the ego; that specific advantages are to be gained if these formal aspects are approached separately from content; and that such an endeavor properly belongs within the framework of ego psychology.

I have looked up the subject of "form and content" in a variety of reference works, both encyclopedic and specialized, with very few tangible results. Clearly, the dichotomy of form and content originates in philosophy. Aristotle is quoted widely as having distinguished between matter and form (*hypokeimenon* and *eidos* or *morphe*). To Aristotle, form was the arrangement or organization of the elements of the thing. Form was also the end or aim; it had a teleological aspect, which today we would attribute to function. In this sense, according to Aristotelian psychology, the soul was a form of the body: that which exists in the body as a mere potentiality appears in the soul in full activity and reality; it has become manifest, or its potential has been realized, we would say today. This viewpoint leads Aristotle to the odd-sounding statement that God is pure form.

We can follow the views on matter and form through the philosophers of all ages (Hoffding, 1894). What strikes the reader is that, as an eminent representative of aesthetics (Croce, 1922) has put it, content and form seem to reverse their meanings at times. Aesthetics is indeed that branch of philosophy which has assumed the concern with the dichotomy of matter and content. In Germany, there was talk of a "war" between the aesthetics of content (*Gehaltsaesthetik*)

and that of form *(Formaesthetik)* (Hoffding, 1894). The proponents
of the first view considered content to be paramount, and saw content
threatened or even demolished by form; whereas the aesthetes of
form, the realists, emphasized the importance of form as outshining
content.

Clearly, we can use our psychoanalytic interpretative tools to
detect personal meanings of content (i.e., unconscious meanings) in
each of these opposing stances. I mean that for those who see form
as destroying content, content often symbolizes unblemished beauty,
omniscience, and goodness, whereas form symbolizes the bad drives,
destructive and castrating, which mar the wholeness of content. Anthropomorphically, this group sees a beautiful soul (the content)—
the beauty being displaced upward from below—in danger of being
destroyed by the ugly, imperfect, castrated body (the form).

In the second group, the reverse often seems true. It is form
which represents goodness, wholeness, and perfection; whereas content represents the bad, ugly, and forbidden inner drives which mar
the beautiful external appearance, just as, anthropomorphically, outer
bodily perfection seems marred by inner dirt and destructiveness.[1]

This "content interpretation" of the two opposing attitudes of
the parties to the dichotomy of form and content hints at the probable reasons for the intensity of the "wars" waged as well as the confusion which reigns at times. As Croce (1922) put it: "The relation
of content and form is most disputed in aesthetics."

In logic, a differently based philosophy, however, form is the
central notion of the subject. This is so because logic is the study
of the rules of argument, of its form independent of the subject
matter involved. The validity of the argument thus depends on
formal properties and relations. It is also for this reason that symbolic notations (leading to mathematics) are used to show independence from subject matter. In other words, mathematics and the
use of symbols in general are the most formal ways of looking at
relations (Rothschild, 1950, 1958). (In contrast to my understanding,
Noy [1966] views mathematical thinking, because of its formal
aspects, as akin to primary process thinking.)

---

[1] See, for example, Deri (1931), Ehrenzweig (1948-1949), Fairbairn (1938a, 1938b),
Lesser (1957), Read (1951), Rickman (1940), Sachs (1942), Stokes (1955), Tarachow
(1949), Thorburn (1925).

In literature, form is defined as the schema or structure chosen for the presentation of content—a definition which seems much simpler; it also holds true for the graphic and plastic arts and, I believe, for psychoanalysis as well.

After reference books on philosophy and aesthetics, I turned for references relating to form and content to the *Index of Psycho-analytic Writings* (Grinstein, 1960). I was surprised and pleased to find a paper entitled "Form and Content in Psychoanalysis," read by Margarete Stegmann at the 6th International Psycho-Analytical Congress, held in The Hague in 1920. Though the paper does not seem to be available, I did find the author's summary in the *Internationale Zeitschrift für Psychoanalyse* (1920). Stegmann defined *content* as the complexes, the material aspect of experience, the What of neurosis. She defined *form* as "the structure which expresses itself in the experience." She pointed out that the content is the same in neurotic and in healthy people. It is form which is characteristically different. She quoted Freud as saying that an increased concern for the individual rules of form would be very fruitful for therapeutic practice, and cited as an example Ferenczi's active analysis. According to Stegmann, "the recognition and the making conscious of the rules of form elevate the drives to a higher level of conscious formation." Does she mean that the recognition and the interpretation of symptomatic and patterned behavior result in the neutralization of drive energy and therefore in "more healthy defense mechanisms"? Or am I superimposing ego-psychological terminology on id-psychological formulations?

In a general way, Stegmann's formulations seem to tie in with a view of the complexes, the drives, the basic unconscious conflicts as content. However, the summary is too short to allow us to understand what importance Stegmann attaches to form and whether she attributes relevance to form beyond a deepening understanding of content.

Next I shall turn to Freud. In the context of discussing the dream work, he said: "Even if it [the manifest dream] has an apparently sensible exterior, we know that this . . . can have as little organic relation to the internal content of the dream as the façade of an Italian church has to its structure and plan. There are other occasions when this façade of the dream *has* its meaning, and reproduces

an important component of the latent dream-thoughts with little or
no distortion" (1916-1917, p. 181).

In the same lecture on dream work, Freud also used the term
"form" for the dream as a whole when he said: "One cannot give
the name of 'dream' to anything other than the product of the
dream-work—that is to say, the *form* into which the latent thoughts
have been transmuted by the dream-work" (p. 183).

When Freud compared creative writers and daydreaming (1908a),
he added an emphasis on a function of form that subsequently became the basis for the analyses of the function and role of form in
art and in literature. He said: "the essential *ars poetica* lies in the
technique of overcoming the feeling of repulsion in us. . . . The
writer softens the character of his egoistic day-dreams by altering
and disguising it, and he bribes us by the purely formal—that is,
aesthetic—yield of pleasure which he offers us in the presentation
of his phantasies" (p. 153). In *Jokes and Their Relation to the Unconscious* (1905) Freud used the same phrase, i.e., that the form or
technique of the joke bribes our critical faculties, so that we can
overcome our inhibition and thus release the psychic energy saved
through laughter. Weiss (1947) and Noy (1966) see the same phenomena of a saving of energy in aesthetic pleasure as in the joke.

Freud began his essay on "The Moses of Michelangelo" (1914)
by saying: "I have often observed that the subject-matter of works
of art has a stronger attraction for me than their formal and technical qualities, though to the artist their value lies first and foremost in these latter." Freud wanted to discover and to interpret the
meaning and the content of that which is repressed.

Thus, in his dream book (1900), Freud asked "what certain
formal characteristics of the method of representation in dreams
signify in relation to the thoughts underlying them" (p. 329). In
other words, Freud raised the question of the symbolic meaning of
form, and this constituted a considerable part of his contribution
to the understanding of dreams. In this category Freud also placed,
e.g., the perceptual intensity of the dream picture and the clarity
of its parts. Freud cited the dream of a female patient who, in an
unclear, confused dream, did not know whether a man was her
father or her husband. The lack of clarity was part of the dream
thought—the lack of clarity as to who was her father. Freud con-

cluded that the form of the dream is used with surprising frequency for the representation of the hidden content (p. 332). Or: "it [the dream work] is giving a manifest form to a portion of the latent content" (p. 436).

Similarly, form is seen as representing content in the dream within the dream, in which "the dream-work makes use of dreaming as a form of repudiation" (p. 338). And form, of course, represents content and symbolizes content. The best known examples are the various sexual symbols, but there are innumerable others.

It is in relation to the façade of the dream that Freud mentioned secondary elaboration, which he compared to a connective material that joins different unconnected parts into a whole (pp. 488-508). This function, clearly related to form, reminds us of what Nunberg (1930) described as the "synthetic function of the ego" which gives (good) form to unorganized, chaotic content, and of what Hartmann (1947) has called the "organizing function."

Glover (1950, p. 111) mentioned secondary elaboration as occurring so near the point of waking that it has "practically the whole range of intellectual operations at [its] disposal." In other words, Glover viewed secondary elaboration as an ego function, and elsewhere (p. 21) he contrasted this structure of mind with unconscious content.

Freud also compared secondary elaboration to the work of thinking in waking life. Just as we correctly and rationally fill in gaps in material presented to us in our waking life, secondary elaboration fills in the gaps of dream material to make a whole, to provide unity of form for the dream. Secondary elaboration thus is responsible for the formal unity of the dream; it is related to the functioning of thought processes in waking life, to consciousness, and to the ego.

Freud also described the formal aspect of dream work in general: "it [the dream work] restricts itself to giving things a new form"; in summary he stated: "Little attention is paid to the logical relations between the thoughts; those relations are ultimately given a disguised representation in certain *formal* characteristics of dreams" (p. 507). Even in this early work Freud compared the dream with the plastic arts. It is of course in the area of the arts that form has been studied most intensively by psychoanalysts as well as others.

I now turn to another basic work of Freud in which form plays an important part, namely, *Jokes and Their Relation to the Unconscious* (1905). In jokes, as in dreams, Freud paid much attention to form or technique. However, here too he used the different forms mainly to discover their hidden meanings and the unconscious functions of the different kinds of jokes. At least part of what Freud termed the technique seems to be what we would call the form of wit and jokes. The form here relates to the various categories of jokes which Freud listed (aggressive jokes, masochistic jokes), i.e., to the function of jokes. Form also relates to the number of persons and actors involved (e.g., the person who tells the joke, the listener, and the person about whom the joke is told); i.e., form relates to the structure of the joke situation and the different functions which the joke serves for each participant.

At this point, however, we are faced with the question whether the id is indeed only content, whether the id is chaotic and formless. As one examines the mechanisms of dreams, of jokes, of art, of children's play or of symptoms—in short, of all those phenomena which derive from the id, the unconscious, it is evident that they are by no means formless content. True, it can be argued that the drives are modified by the ego as they become accessible to our conscious exploration. Yet we are all familiar with the mechanisms of unconscious functioning—condensation, displacement, symbolization—described by Freud many years ago (1900). These mechanisms, to my mind, shape the content and give it form. They represent formal rules relating to unconscious content. Although clearly different from, they are as clearly analogous to, those rules of form which govern conscious activity or thought.

Let me summarize my main points so far:

1. Form and content are often confused and even reversible in their meaning, especially in philosophy.

2. In literature and art, as in psychoanalysis, we can define form as the schema or structure chosen for the presentation of content. Or, we can say with the painter Ben Shahn (1957), redundantly yet appropriately, "Form is the shape of content."

3. Psychoanalysis made one of its most important early contributions by interpreting form with reference to content. Content was shown to be universal. It could be rediscovered in form—in dreams,

jokes, symptoms. In addition, in art as well as in jokes, it was seen that form was bribing us with aesthetic pleasure so that we could enjoy that content which, without having been bribed, our censor would prohibit us from enjoying.

4. In dreams, jokes, and symptoms, the formal aspects referred to as secondary elaboration or revision are related to the ego, whereas content, the universally recurring conflicts, is related to the id.

This relationship—of content to id, of form to ego—is valid, but only partially. This brings us to the center of another innovation of ego psychology. In the early formulations, the id was seen as chaotic, as lacking organization and differentiation. The newborn infant was seen psychologically as all id, as dominated completely by uncontrolled and unorganized drives. The ego was seen as developing out of the id under the influence of contact with reality. This would fit in with a concept of the id as wholly content, as being without form. Ego psychology, on the other hand, saw both ego and id as developing out of an undifferentiated matrix (Hartmann, 1939). In this view, we could expect form, or structure, or organization to evolve in both id and ego as they develop and differentiate; that is to say, we would expect early primitive forms of both id and ego.[2] We would then assume and look for formal rules governing unconscious id material as well as formal ego patterns. Indeed, we can find such rules in the modes imposed by the mechanisms of displacement, condensation, substitution, symbolization, and overdetermination— in brief, the modes of primary process functioning. Magical thinking is based on the principles of similarity and contiguity. These are organizational forms that differ from those of secondary process functioning, but they are organizational forms nonetheless.

The comparison of the two processes can be followed in another area. In attempts to understand some of the differences between ego and id in energic terms, Freud (1895, 1900, 1911, 1915a, 1915b) introduced the concepts of free and bound cathexis, which he ascribed to Breuer. Kris (1952) took up this question and reiterated that "unconscious processes use mobile psychic energy; preconscious processes bound energy. The two degrees of mobility correspond to two types of discharge characterized as the primary and secondary

---

[2] See, for example, Rapaport (1960), Jacobson (1964), Schur (1966), Klein (1967), Holt (1967).

processes. We are thus faced with the delimitation between the id
and the ego" (p. 305). Kris added that, to Hartmann, Rapaport, and
himself, "Hypotheses of transitions between extremes seem . . . pre-
ferable" to extreme (process) formulations (p. 305f.). In other words,
Kris postulated a continuum rather than mutually exclusive extremes.

Holt (1962, 1967) elaborated in considerable detail on the problem of bound versus mobile cathexis. However, in line with Kris's
reservation, I propose analogous formulations for id and ego in
this respect. Just as I regard id material as being subject to some
orderly principles of organization and form, though these differ from
the modes operating in the ego, I believe that the id of the adult,
the drive cathexes at his disposal, cannot be viewed as fully mobile.
They are mobile only relative to the more bound cathexes of the
ego. I believe that this is so because in none of those areas in which
id derivatives are discernible—dreams, symptoms, art, jokes, the
play of children—are drive energies freely transferable from one
element to another, nor do they move freely to discharge. True,
there is more freedom in the drive organization, e.g., of memories,
than in the more constricted, conceptual organization of memories;
the latter is limited in displaceability and in not striving toward
direct and complete discharge (Rapaport, 1951a, p. 697). Holt (1962)
reached the same conclusion after a lengthy and detailed discussion
of Freud's different and varied uses of the terms "free," "mobile,"
and "bound" cathexes in the "Project for a Scientific Psychology"
(1895) and the *Outline* (1940).

Allow me to break off here and tackle the problem from yet another angle. Among the many writers both within and outside psychoanalysis, Kris was one of the few who questioned the widely accepted dichotomy of form and content. He suggested that instead
of accepting the division of form and content, we should establish
their interrelation (p. 22). In Kris's view, psychoanalysts have tended
to minimize the contrast of form and content; "even the formal
characteristics tend to lead the psychoanalyst into content" (p. 105),
e.g., the translation of the formal characteristics of the dream into
latent dream thoughts. Kris also referred to the views of others;
Karl Bühler (1927) considered psychoanalysis to be content-bound,
as did Herbert Read (1951). Discussing the preconscious mental

processes, Kris spoke of the "period in psychoanalysis when interest was centered on the id, when only the repressed was considered as 'real' psychic material, when defense was seen as a screen, resistances was considered a force of evil, and when what was a phase in the development of psychoanalysis was declared to be the only legitimate and relevant field of investigation" (p. 303f.).

It was Kris's view that "Whereas the common elements relate to the id, we might say that the differences are determined by the ego" (p. 105f.). It is this view which leads ego psychology into the area of character, i.e., to structural problems (in Rapaport's sense of structures) and to style—both personal, idiosyncratic style and collective style, e.g., that of a given period in history, or of a given culture or subculture. Kris dealt with the aspect of style when he discussed the personal and historical determinants of the formal characteristics of Messerschmidt's series of busts (1952, Chapter 4), and thus approached the relation of content to form.

There are phenomena, perhaps more easily discernible in art, where the interrelation of content and form can be examined more closely. Form and content may be related in different ways. (1) In most works of art form reiterates the message of the content. Obvious examples are those paintings of the Middle Ages in which the Trinity of Father, Son, and Holy Ghost is the content, and in which triangular or tripolar formal characteristics recur in the painting. Here, content and form share a communicative aim, a harmony which is distinctive for most literary and musical works as well as in the plastic arts. However, the communicative aims of form and content need not always converge and enhance each other. (2) Each may convey messages that conflict, the degree of conflictedness depending on their qualities and admixtures. For example, when the form of a joke "bribes our critical faculties," the conflicting messages ally themselves to bring about the effect of laughter. Similar conflicting messages bring about the effects of parody and satire. (3) When the messages of form and content are divorced from each other, we seem to find ourselves within the field of psychopathology. Whereas a person telling a funny story with a serious mien will often enhance the comical effect (and thus be categorized in our second group), when a sad story is told smilingly or with laughter, we have no difficulty in discerning psychopathology. The same effect is obtained in many of the drawings or paintings of psychotic persons (see, e.g., figures 52 to 61 in Kris, 1952).

In the past, however, definite formal aspects were often dealt with only, or mainly, in terms of their content. Freud (1908b) stated that "the permanent character-traits are either unchanged prolongations of the original instincts, or sublimations of those instincts, or reaction-formations against them" (p. 175). Abraham (1921), following Freud, considered character in terms of its drive origin, i.e., its content, acknowledging its formal characteristics only indirectly. Reich (1933) "makes use of the form of expression exclusively, but uses this form in order to penetrate to the decisively important infantile experiences." To Reich, the *how* of saying things is as important "material" for interpretation as *what* the patient says. However, form serves as an avenue of approach to the unconscious content which is at the root of character.

The same approach has been used in psychological testing (see, e.g., Rorschach, 1923; Zulliger, 1950). Those who worked with the Rorschach test clearly pioneered in the evaluation of form, as distinct from and in addition to content (Rapaport et al., 1945-1946). It was in this area that the ego qualities of good form were emphasized and systematically utilized both for diagnostic and prognostic purposes, an approach that is strikingly absent in descriptions of our clinical work (though rarely in actual practice). Yet, even in Rorschach's and Zulliger's psychoanalytically oriented papers, the symbolic content of the response is evaluated in terms of its meaning, whereas the formal aspects fall by the wayside.

The same is true of the studies of Schilder and Bender (1936), Stokes (1955), Rosenthal (1951), Paneth (1929), and others. Rapaport (1951b) was one of the few who told us that the "lack of interest in theoretical foundations [in psychoanalysis] is early expressed by the disregard of thought-processes in favour of thought-content" (p. 292). Is Rapaport telling us that it is our interest in therapeutic work rather than in theoretical underpinnings which leads us to focus on content? Is it our medical and therapeutic motivation which leads us away from an interest in form—to which at least some nonmedical psychoanalysts try to bring us back? Perhaps some of the latter are better equipped to look at and deal with theory by virtue of their training in academic psychology, or by virtue of the motivation which made them choose a theoretical rather than a pragmatic approach. I became aware in myself of how difficult it was to counterbalance my attraction to therapy and pragmatism and to rediscover an interest in theoretical formulations.

But let us turn from this digression to the problem of style. Style, as character, is clearly an aspect of form. We are most directly confronted with style in art—literary styles, musical styles, painting styles.

The earliest paper dealing with the psychoanalysis of style which I found is by Josef Körner from Prague, who wrote on this subject in *Das Literarische Echo* in 1919. Clearly no Freudian analyst, Körner recommended the use of psychoanalytic investigations of literary style at a time when expressionism was becoming fashionable. But the purpose of such investigation was "to discover the underlying personal psychological motivation of the author or poet." In other words, form (here style) was to lead to an understanding of unconscious content, i.e., motivation.

Federn, in 1931, lectured on "the neurotic style" at a conference on applied psychopathology. In his view, "the direct investigation of normal style presupposes the creation of a psychoanalytic theory of character and of expression." Federn, therefore, confined himself to a discussion of neurotic—and not of normal—style. He quoted Schopenhauer, Nietzsche, and others who examined the style of authors in order to accuse them of such vices as immaturity, cowardice, meanness, and falsehood. Federn referred to a book entitled *The History of a Style,* in which Woodrow Wilson's secretary, Hales, took revenge on his one-time employer. Interestingly enough, from our present point of view, this author used counting methods; he counted the number of "needless repetitions and meaningless abstractions." Federn, too, used some counting methods to demonstrate quantitatively how neurotic trends made written style needlessly cumbersome, vague, and difficult to understand. Federn emphasized the importance of recognizing such disturbances of style since, owing to psychoanalysis, they could now be corrected. The author's hesitant compromise finds expression only in the style, Federn commented, and not in the content of the communication, "because the facts undoubtedly needed to be said"; perhaps it would be better to say, "because consciously the author was convinced that the facts needed to be said; while his unconscious doubts about these facts expressed themselves in cumbersome style."

Federn, too, dealt with style in its implications for content and saw drives as determinants of style. However, if we wish to heed his postulation of the need for a psychoanalytic theory of character and of expression, we must return once more to Kris, this time to his paper on "Laughter as an Expressive Process," read in 1936 (see 1952, Chapter 9). Kris cited the shaping which the physiological act of laughter undergoes through the agency of the human ego as a clear and impressive example of the fact that everything we recognize as a process giving form and shape to psychic material is to be regarded as an ego function. Developmentally, too, the language of the body is replaced by the language of words. Expression which is more under control of the drives, of the unconscious, of primary processes, is replaced by expression under the dominant control of the ego, of consciousness, of secondary processes. Here, then, is a beginning of a psychoanalytic theory of expression.

Lesser (1957) has given us an excellent study of form in fiction. In line with Federn and Kris, Lesser defined form as the "devices used to structure and communicate expressive content." He also pointed out that in its formal aspects, narrative art approaches the nonverbal character of other arts and he documented his point very convincingly (Chapter 5). Lesser also re-emphasized and detailed that psychodynamic function of form which Freud was the first to point out: the bribing of our critical faculties. Lesser postulated three functions of literary form: (1) to give pleasure; (2) to avoid or relieve guilt or anxiety; (3) to facilitate perception. These functions are implicitly related to the conflictful content which narrative art necessarily portrays. Such functions of form relate to the influence which form or style has on the audience: on the reader of fiction, on the listener to a joke, on the viewer of a painting.

I wish now to return to the expressive aspects of style, i.e., to what it is that style demonstrates or tells us with regard to its subject —the person who uses style to express himself and to communicate. Clearly, we can discern style in a variety of areas: motor styles of speaking and writing, artistic styles in the media of art such as painting, sculpture, music, and again writing. Moreover, all of us recognize both individual and collective patterns of style—mostly without being aware of the cues to such recognition. We recognize by its sound the step of a familiar person without seeing him, we recognize his patterns of motility by sight, his patterns of speech, of coughing, or of clearing his throat.

The same is true for works of art. We recognize a work of music as being, say, by Bach—before we know which particular piece it is. We recognize that it is classical before we can decide whether it is by Vivaldi or Bach. We recognize a painting as impressionistic or expressionistic; and recognize a Modigliani or a Cezanne painting because of its specific style (see Noy, 1966). Similarly, we can recognize characteristic styles of dreaming in our patients (Gumbel, 1967). Yet most of us cannot spell out what constitutes the basis for our sure judgments. We can distinguish between a variety of styles, but would find it difficult to categorize them in a systematic way.

If form, and therefore style, is related to ego; if it is a relatively enduring quality of a person, and one that can be reliably recognized —then surely it must be related to what Rapaport called structures. Rapaport and Gill (1959) spoke of structures as configurations of a slow rate of change, such as character traits and defenses. A faster rate of change is characteristic of free drive cathexes, of primary process. The stability, the enduring quality, the cohesiveness and predictability which we associate with style and character are typical of the ego, of secondary process, and therefore of energy processes which are far removed from free drive cathexes. I have previously indicated my belief that we should not equate the free drive cathexes and the primary process as they occur in infancy with those that occur in adulthood, just as regressive phenomena in an adult cannot be equated with the corresponding developmental phase in his childhood.

The distance of secondary processes, of bound cathexes, of style, from the drive cathexes of the id can be seen as bridged by structures. Rapaport (1960) stated that organisms "postpone and obstruct the operation of the entropic tendency [the pleasure principle] . . . by being structured and by building further structures" (p. 93). He viewed bound energy cathexes as being tied up in structures which "produce" more neutralized energy cathexes as the structures become more differentiated. Developmentally, we would expect increasing differentiation and organization (Hartmann, 1947), increasing structure building (Rapaport, 1960), which can then be seen in stable and enduring forms and styles of expression.

Thus, ego structures can be seen to function and to mediate on different axes. The complexity of this conception must be further increased in order to account for one more axis, namely, for the variations in the degrees of pathology we encounter. In other words, we must envisage at least three axes along which differentiation of structure can be followed: (1) developmentally: i.e., (a) phylogenetically as well as (b) ontogenetically, from infant to child to adult; (2) the different degrees of differentiation which can be observed from primary process to secondary process in the adult; and (3) degrees of pathology, ranging from the psychoses on the less differentiated side, to the neuroses and personality disorders, to the more healthy persons on the side of increased differentiation. This last axis is perhaps least clear. Clinical experience teaches us that psychoses as well as severe character disorders tend to show extremely stable and even rigid structures which are very resistant to change; in this sense, they contrast with what we term the flexibility of the more healthy personality. At the same time it is logical to assume that such rigid structures possess a lesser degree of differentiation (i.e., of specialization of function) than do similar structures which serve as the basis for the more flexible behavior of persons with less pathology. While, therefore, stability is associated with increased differentiation, this is true only up to a point, to a certain degree. At the same time, we need only remind ourselves of the labilities of behavior and affect which we see in some very disturbed persons to realize that along the third axis, that of differentiation of structure from pathology to health, we can also find lability, as we would expect, associated with dedifferentiation.

As clinicians, we tend to focus more on drives and on unconscious content than on formal aspects. This focus may be responsible for our neglecting another dimension of form—the transcultural one. I have been impressed by the fact that we focus on the same universal contents and conflicts in patients in many different cultural settings, at the expense, so it seems to me, of the specific cultural forms (again mediated by ego structures) which the attempts to deal with such conflicts take.

The relative neglect of the formal aspects of clinical phenomena, especially in transcultural work, allows me to return at this point to a special facet of clinical study and clinical findings. Wynne and Singer (1963; see also Singer and Wynne, 1960, 1963, 1964, 1965, 1966) have over a number of years staked out, defined, and applied a methodological approach to the understanding of the thought disorders of schizophrenics, particularly in their genetic, familial, and communicative aspects. By assuming that "shared focal attention" provides the conditions for "learning to learn," and by addressing themselves to stable, enduring patterns of verbal expressive behavior, these workers have been able to specify important aspects of communication defects that presumably are related to the genesis of thought disorders in schizophrenics. What seems to me of particular importance in their work—and relevant to my topic—is the fact that they have consistently addressed themselves to the formal characteristics of their subjects. They have reasoned that these formal aspects are related to stable, enduring aspects of personality. They have pointed out that content has a tendency to draw our attention away from form. Formal aspects can, with some discipline and methodological technique, be sorted and rated reliably. In this way, Singer and Wynne (1963, 1966) succeeded in "blindly" selecting the parents of childhood schizophrenics, adult schizophrenics, neurotic and aggressive children.[3]

Style and form can thus be examined in verbatim, standardized interviews, as in the verbatim protocols of psychological tests. Similarly, stylistic aspects of therapeutic interviews (Singer and Wynne, 1960), of children's stories, of children's dreams, or of passages from literature can be studied. The analysis of verbatim transcripts of psychoanalytic hours can, I believe, yield data on the relationship between the appearance and the differential handling of affects within the hour and variations in expressive form or style.

Such analyses, intended to clarify and map the different axes

[3] I have had the pleasure and the privilege of working with Wynne and Singer and their co-workers. This paper is evidence of some of the stimulating influences to which I have been exposed, and of some of the opportunities of which I could avail myself in this period of collaboration.

along which structure formation and differentiation seem to take place, require both categorization and quantification. Categorizations in this area should help in our understanding of how expressive, formal characteristics vary both in the course of development and in different pathological states. They should also bring the theoretical framework from which they are applied into closer proximity with the empirical categories which they label. Quantification has been shown by Rapaport (1960, pp. 90-100) to be related to the need for clarification of the process of structure formation; its problems are numerous and its ramifications complex.

In summary, psychoanalytic ego psychology as it stands today provides us with the theoretical framework for an exploration of the formal aspects of behavior as distinct from its motivational content. These formal aspects can be linked to ego functioning and ego structures. What I wish to stress is not that we ignore content, but instead that we bear in mind how content and form are interrelated. The formal aspects of expressive behavior seem to lend themselves more easily to systematization and perhaps even to quantification than do the content and the motivations of behavior. Such investigations can be expected to deepen our understanding of the practical implications of ego psychology and to expand its theoretical basis.

BIBLIOGRAPHY

Abraham, K. (1921), Contributions to the Theory of the Anal Character. *Selected Papers on Psycho-Analysis.* London: Hogarth Press, 1927, pp. 370-392.
Baudouin, C. (1924), *Psychoanalysis and Aesthetics.* New York: Dodd, Mead.
Bühler, K. (1927), *Die Krise der Psychologie.* Jena: Fischer.
Croce, B. (1922), *Aesthetics as Science of Expression and General Linguistics.* London: Macmillan.
Deri, M. (1931), Naturobjekt und Menschenwerk. *Imago,* 17:5-40.
Ehrenzweig, A. (1948-1949), Unconscious Form-Creation in Art. *Brit. J. Med. Psychol.,* 21:88-109, 1948; 22:185-214, 1949.
Fairbairn, W. R. D. (1938a), Prolegomena to a Psychology of Art. *Brit. J. Psychol.,* 28:288-303.
—— (1938b), The Ultimate Bases of Aesthetic Experience. *Brit. J. Psychol.,* 29:167-181.
Federn, P. (1931), Der neurotische Stil. *Abhandlungen aus der Neurologie, Psychiatrie und ihren Grenzgebieten.* Berlin: Karger, pp. 194-201.
Freud, S. (1895), Project for a Scientific Psychology. *The Origins of Psychoanalysis.* New York: Basic Books, 1954, pp. 347-445.
—— (1900), The Interpretation of Dreams. *Standard Edition,* 4 & 5. London: Hogarth Press, 1953.
—— (1905), Jokes and Their Relation to the Unconscious. *Standard Edition,* 8. London: Hogarth Press, 1960.

—— (1908a), Creative Writers and Day-Dreaming. *Standard Edition*, 9:141-154. London: Hogarth Press, 1959.

—— (1908b), Character and Anal Erotism. *Standard Edition*, 9:167-175. London: Hogarth Press, 1959.

—— (1911), Formulations on the Two Principles of Mental Functioning. *Standard Edition*, 12:213-226. London: Hogarth Press, 1958.

—— (1914), The Moses of Michelangelo. Postscript (1927). *Standard Edition*, 13:211-238. London: Hogarth Press, 1955.

—— (1915a), Repression. *Standard Edition*, 14:141-158. London: Hogarth Press, 1957.

—— (1915b), The Unconscious. *Standard Edition*, 14:159-215. London: Hogarth Press, 1957.

—— (1916), Some Character-Types Met with in Psycho-Analytic Work. *Standard Edition*, 14:309-333. London: Hogarth Press, 1957.

—— (1916-1917), Introductory Lectures on Psycho-Analysis. *Standard Edition*, 15 & 16. London: Hogarth Press, 1963.

—— (1917 [1915]), A Metapsychological Supplement to the Theory of Dreams. *Standard Edition*, 14:217-235. London: Hogarth Press, 1957.

—— (1925), A Note upon the 'Mystic Writing-Pad.' *Standard Edition*, 19:227-232. London: Hogarth Press, 1961.

—— (1926), Inhibitions, Symptoms and Anxiety. *Standard Edition*, 20:77-175. London: Hogarth Press, 1959.

—— (1940 [1938]), An Outline of Psycho-Analysis. *Standard Edition*, 23:141-207. London: Hogarth Press, 1964.

Gill, M. M. (1963), *Topography and Systems in Psychoanalytic Theory* [*Psychological Issues*, Monogr. 10]. New York: International Universities Press.

Glover, E. (1950), *Freud or Jung*. New York: Norton.

Grinstein, A. (1960), *Index of Psychoanalytic Writings*, Vol 5. New York: International Universities Press.

Groddeck, G. (1923), *The Book of the It*. New York: Funk & Wagnalls, 1950.

Gumbel, E. (1967), Personal communication.

Hartmann, H. (1939), *Ego Psychology and the Problem of Adaptation*. New York: International Universities Press, 1958.

—— (1947), On Rational and Irrational Action. *Essays on Ego Psychology*. New York: International Universities Press, 1964, pp. 37-68.

Hermann, I. (1922), Ordnungssinn und Gestaltungswert im Zusammenhang mit der Sittlichkeit. *Z. angew. Psychol.*, 20:391-400.

Hoffding, H. (1894), *History of Modern Philosophy*. New York: Dover, 1955.

Holt, R. R. (1962), A Critical Examination of Freud's Concept of Bound vs. Free Cathexis. *J. Amer. Psa. Assn.*, 10:475-525.

—— (1967), The Development of the Primary Process. In: *Motives and Thought* [*Psychological Issues*, 18/19:344-384]. New York: International Universities Press.

Jacobson, E. (1964), *The Self and the Object World*. New York: International Universities Press.

Klein, G. S. (1967), Peremptory Ideation. In: *Motives and Thought* [*Psychological Issues*, 18/19:78-128]. New York: International Universities Press.

Körner, J. (1919), Die Psychoanalyse des Stils. *Literarisches Echo*, 21.

Kris, E. (1952), *Psychoanalytic Explorations in Art*. New York: International Universities Press.

Langer, S. (1953), *Feeling and Form*. London: Routledge & Kegan Paul.

Lesser, S. O. (1957), *Fiction and the Unconscious*. Boston: Beacon Press.

Mayer, F. (1930), Das Formale in der Psychoanalyse. *Zbl. Psychother.*, 3:132-147.

Noy, P. (1966), A Theory about Art and Aesthetic Experience (mimeographed).

—— (1968), The Development of Musical Ability. *This Annual*, 23:332-347.

Nunberg, H. (1930), The Synthetic Function of the Ego. *Int. J. Psa.*, 12:123-140, 1931.

Paneth, L. (1929), Form und Farbe in der Psychoanalyse. *Nervenarzt*, 2:326-337.
Plokker, J. H. (1965), *Art from the Mentally Disturbed*. Boston: Little, Brown.
Rapaport, D., ed. & tr. (1951a), *Organization and Pathology of Thought*. New York: Columbia University Press.
—— (1951b), Paul Schilder's Contribution to the Theory of Thought-Processes. *Int. J. Psa.*, 32:291-301.
—— (1960), *The Structure of Psychoanalytic Theory* [*Psychological Issues*, Monogr. 6]. New York: International Universities Press.
—— & Gill, M. M. (1959), The Points of View and Assumptions of Metapsychology. *Int. J. Psa.*, 40:153-162.
—— —— & Schafer, R. (1945-1946), *Diagnostic Psychological Testing*, rev. ed. by R. R. Holt. New York: International Universities Press, 1968.
Read, H. (1951), Psycho-Analysis and the Problem of Aesthetic Value. *Int. J. Psa.*, 32:73-82.
Reich, W. (1933), *Character Analysis*. New York: Noonday Press, 1949.
Rickman, J. (1940), On the Nature of Ugliness and the Creative Impulse. *Int. J. Psa.*, 21:294-313.
Rorschach, H. (1923), Zur Auswertung des Formdeutversuchs für die Psychoanalyse. *Z. Neurol. & Psychiat.*, 82:240-274.
Rosenthal, M. (1951), Relationships between Form and Feeling in the Art of Picasso. *Amer. Imago*, 8:371-391.
Rothschild, F. S. (1950), *Das Ich und die Regulationen des Erlebnisvorgangs*. Basel: Karger.
—— (1958), *Das Zentralnervensystem als Symbol des Erlebens*. Basel: Karger.
Sachs, H. (1942), *The Creative Unconscious*. Cambridge: Sci-Art.
Schilder, P. F. & Bender, L. (1936), Form as a Principle in the Play of Children. *J. Genet. Psychol.*, 49:254-261.
Schur, M. (1966), *The Id and the Regulatory Principles of Mental Functioning*. New York: International Universities Press.
Shahn, B. (1957), *The Shape of Content*. Cambridge: Harvard University Press.
Shapiro, M. (1952), Style. In: *A Modern Book of Esthetics*, ed. M. M. Rader. New York: Holt, pp. 336-346.
Singer, M. T. & Wynne, L. C. (1960), Principles for Scoring Communication Defects and Deviances in Parents of Schizophrenics: Rorschach and TAT Scoring Manuals. *Psychiatry*, 29:260-288.
—— —— (1963), Differentiating Characteristics of the Parents of Childhood Schizophrenics, Childhood Neurotics and Young Adult Schizophrenics. *Amer. J. Psychiat.*, 120:234-243.
—— —— (1964), Stylistic Variables in Family Research. Presented at a Symposium at Marquette University, Milwaukee Psychiatric Hospital.
—— —— (1965), Thought Disorder and Family Relations of Schizophrenics: III. Methodology Using Projective Techniques. IV. Results and Implications. *Arch. Gen. Psychiat.*, 12:187-212.
—— —— (1966), Communication Styles in Parents of Normals, Neurotics and Schizophrenics: Some Findings Using a New Rorschach Scoring Manual. In: *Family Structure, Dynamics and Therapy*, ed. I. Cohen. Psychiatric Research Reports, No. 20, pp. 25-38.
Stegmann, M. (1920), Form und Inhalt in der Psychoanalyse. Read at 6th International Psycho-Analytical Congress, The Hague, 1920. Author's abstract in: *Int. Z. Psa.*, 6:401.
Stokes, A. (1955), Form in Art. In: *New Directions in Psycho-Analysis*, ed. M. Klein, P. Heimann, & R. M. Money-Kyrle. New York: Basic Books, pp. 406-420.
Tarachow, S. (1949), Remarks on the Comic Process and Beauty. *Psa. Quart.*, 18:215-226.
Thorburn, J. M. (1925), *Art and the Unconscious*. London: Kegan Paul.

Weiss, J. (1947), A Psychological Theory of Formal Beauty. *Psa. Quart.*, 16:391-400.

Wynne, L. C. & Singer, M. T. (1963), Thought Disorder and Family Relations of Schizophrenics: I. A Research Strategy. II. A Classification of Forms of Thinking. *Arch. Gen. Psychiat.*, 9:191-206.

Zulliger, H. (1950), Psycho-Analysis and the Form-Interpretation Test. *Int. J. Psa.*, 31:152-155.

THE CONCEPT OF EGO APPARATUS
IN PSYCHOANALYSIS

Including Considerations Concerning the
Somatic Roots of the Ego

HUMBERTO NAGERA, M.D. (Ann Arbor, Mich.)

DIFFERENT USES OF THE TERMS APPARATUS
AND EGO APPARATUS

The term *apparatus* is frequently encountered in psychoanalytic literature. It is used in a variety of ways, usually forming compounds such as the mental apparatus, apparatuses of the mind, ego apparatuses, etc. As I pointed out in another publication (1967), it was Hartmann who, in 1939, introduced the term "ego apparatus," though Hartmann as well as others, especially Rapaport, have used "apparatus" interchangeably with "structure." In the same publication, Hartmann stated that the further development of "inborn ego apparatuses" takes place, to some extent, in what he called the "conflict-free sphere of the ego." He said:

The newborn infant is not wholly a creature of drives; he has inborn apparatuses (perceptual and protective mechanisms) which appropriately perform a part of those functions which, after the differentiation of ego and id, we attribute to the ego [p. 49]. The human individual, at his birth, also has apparatuses, which serve to master the external world. These mature in the course of development [p. 50]. We know that maturation processes are not

The present paper is part of a larger series entitled "The Structural Theory: Some Clarifications and Reformulations." It forms part of the ongoing research on "Assessment of Pathology in Childhood" conducted at the Hampstead Child-Therapy Clinic in London. The investigation is supported in part by Public Health Service Research Grant, M-5683-06 from the National Institute of Mental Health, Washington. An earlier paper of this series entitled "The Concepts of Structure and Structuralization: Psychoanalytic Usage and Implications for a Theory of Learning and Creativity" appeared in *This Annual*, Vol. 22, 1967.

entirely impervious to environmental influences. Yet they are independent factors which, both before and after birth, bring the inborn apparatuses successively into play, and determine at least grossly the rhythm of developmental processes [p. 104].

[Later, in 1952, he stated:] Generally speaking, the apparatus serving perception, motility, and others that underlie ego functions, seem, in the infant, to be activated by instinctual needs. . . . But they are not created by the needs. These apparatus, as well as those that account for the phenomena of memory, are partly inborn; they cannot be traced, in the individual, to the influence of the instincts and of reality, and their maturation follows certain laws which are also part of our inheritance. They will gradually come under the control of the ego; on the other hand, they act on the ego and its subsequent phases of development [p. 167].

According to Hartmann, the inborn ego apparatuses include perception, laying down of memory traces, motility, thinking, and consciousness.[1]

Hartmann (1939) clarified the relationship between ego apparatuses and adaptation when he stated that "adaptation (speaking now mainly about man) is guaranteed, in both its grosser and finer aspects, on the one hand by man's primary equipment and the maturation of his apparatuses, and on the other hand by those ego-regulated actions which (using this equipment) counteract the disturbances in, and actively improve the person's relationship to, the environment" (p. 25), adding that the "psychoanalytic study of those primary disorders of ego apparatuses which result in failures of adaptation has barely begun" (p. 39f.).

Hartmann further maintained that ego development and drive development are partly based on somatic maturational processes.

Let us consider first the somatic processes of maturation: just as the phases of libido development depend upon somatic maturation processes (for instance, the anal-sadistic phase develops "ob-

[1] With regard to the system of consciousness Gill (1963) stated: "In present-day terminology, *Cs.* would be described as a primarily autonomous ego apparatus, as are the apparatuses of perception and motility" (p. 66). On the basis of the observation that *Cs.* can be stimulated in abnormal conditions and during sleep, for example, by contents invested with drive energy and organized according to primary process, Gill adds the interesting comment that "In a sense, then, we may say that these apparatuses belong not to the ego but to the entire psychic apparatus, even though they are usually under the control of the ego" (p. 66).

viously in connection with the cutting of the teeth, the strengthening of the musculature, and the control of the sphincters"
[Freud, 1932, p. 135]), so ego development too is connected with
the somatic maturation of certain apparatuses [p. 46 f.]. [He
wondered] whether or not the defense processes are influenced
by the maturation and exercise of the apparatuses of the conflict-
free ego sphere. . . . It is possible that the developmental rhythm
of these apparatuses is one of the determinants of the sequence in
which defense methods arise [p. 106].

Furthermore, he saw ego development as a complicated process
of differentiation in which primitive regulating factors are increasingly replaced by more effective ego regulations: "Differentiation
progresses not only *by the creation of new apparatuses to master new
demands and new tasks, but also and mainly by new apparatuses
taking over,* on a higher level, functions which were originally performed by more primitive means (p. 50; my italics). He also thought
that the study of the disorders of automatized actions due to organic
brain disease would, for example, "give us important information
about the function of the somatic apparatuses involved in action,
while we learn about the function of the mental apparatuses involved from developmental psychology and from psychoanalysis
(particularly of psychotics)" (p. 88).

The closest Hartmann came to defining his concept of mental
apparatus is in the following statement (1939): " 'Mental apparatus'
is a particularly fitting description of the preconscious automatisms
(and not only of those which pertain to action); however, since it
implies structure and formedness, as all concepts of apparatuses do,
it is hardly applicable to what is occasionally termed the automatic
character of the id" (p. 100). He remarked that little attention had
been devoted to the study of somatic and mental apparatuses, stating
that:

. . . if we take the conflict-free ego sphere into consideration and
if we want to develop a general psychology of action, the study of
these apparatuses becomes imperative, because otherwise all our
statements about action include an unknown.
   [He made it quite clear] that the apparatuses, both congenital
and acquired, need a driving force in order to function; and that
the psychology of action is inconceivable without the psychology
of instinctual drives [pp. 100 f.]. [The] psychology of the ego

apparatuses seems to me a good example of the interlocking of conflict and adaptation (and achievement) . . . [p. 107].

He insisted (1939), following Freud (1937), on the crucial role that hereditary factors play in the ego's constitution and apparatuses. Thus he says: "Let us now return to the inherited ego characteristics in general" (p. 105). Similarly, in "Psychoanalysis as a Scientific Theory" (1959), he points out that "It is likely that in man not only instinctual factors are in part determined by heredity, but also the apparatus of the ego underlying the functions just mentioned" (p. 329).

At times it is not clear whether Hartmann means to include "physical apparatuses" as an integral part of the ego organization. Some of the statements to be found in his monograph (1939) seem to point in that direction, for example: "The functions of all the *mental and physical ego apparatuses* mentioned can become secondarily sources of pleasure" (p. 46; my italics). A similarly ambiguous statement is the following: "The use of a term is after all a matter of definition; the term 'automatism' here is applied only to *the somatic and preconscious ego apparatuses . . .*" (p. 90; my italics). At other times he clearly specifies that the somatic apparatuses are used by the ego, thus implying that they are outside the ego organization. He says, for example: "The ego uses somatic apparatuses to execute actions. I will discuss first the motor apparatuses . . ." (p. 87), and on p. 100: "In action the ego uses both somatic and mental apparatuses." Or: "The individual does not acquire all the apparatuses which are put in *the service of the ego* in the course of development: perception, motility, intelligence, etc., rest on constitutional givens" (p. 101; my italics). But the question remains: are these somatic and mental apparatuses an integral part of the ego organization or are they outside of it and only used by the ego organization when appropriate?

Further, Hartmann (1939) has used the term apparatus in referring not only to ego apparatuses in general or to the inborn ego apparatuses in particular (p. 49f.) but also to physical (p. 100) or somatic ego apparatuses (pp. 87 and 90), mental ego apparatuses (p. 100f.), congenital ego apparatuses, acquired ego apparatuses (p. 101), and inherited ego apparatuses (p. 105), etc. Further, he quotes (p. 100) Bleuler who coined the term "occasional apparatus" to explain the process of abreaction.

Although questions such as those raised above are occasionally a source of contention and argument in analytic discussions, they seem to me to be more of a rhetoric nature than of fundamental significance. There are advantages in considering the ego in purely psychological terms and in viewing it as being in charge of the control and organization of the multiplicity of functions of which humans are capable; nor is there any reason not to consider all the somatic apparatuses whose functions finally come under the ego's control and are placed at its service as outside the ego organization properly speaking. The ego remains a psychological agency that uses, organizes, and controls all the functions that these apparatuses can perform according to specific sets of rules and regulations that take into account the demands of the other agencies (id and super-ego) as well as those of external reality. But the decision to define the ego in these terms must not obscure the fact that the qualities, abilities, and functional capabilities of any particular ego are never-theless determined to a large extent by the basic nature, quality, and intrinsic characteristics of all those physical organs that lie at its root. Obviously, no ego organization could exist were it not for the functions that can be performed by these underlying somatic organs or structures. It is equally obvious that because of this dependent relationship the damage to any of these somatic apparatuses (i.e., the organs of vision or of other brain structures, etc.) leads to atypical and deviant ego organizations. Hartmann (1952) stated that: "In the ego's relationship with the body, we can now describe three aspects: the postulated physiological processes underlying activities of the ego; those somatic apparatus that gradually come under the control of the ego and which in turn influence the timing, intensity, and direction of ego development; and, third, but not necessarily inde-pendent of the two others, those special structures that underlie what we call the body ego" (p. 169).

Although I have previously singled out a few ambiguous quota-tions from Hartmann's *Ego Psychology and the Problem of Adapta-tion,* it is clear to me that the study of Hartmann's work shows be-yond doubt that his conception of the ego is in line with Freud's formulations and that the ambiguity referred to results only from

the difficulties inherent in the attempt to show the dependent relations between the ego agencies (as a psychological construct) and the
somatic structures that underlie them.

Brenner and Arlow in their monograph *Psychoanalytic Concepts
and the Structural Theory* (1964) showed a marked predilection for
conceptualizations in terms of functions. Thus, they rarely use the
term ego apparatus and instead usually refer to ego functions. These
authors use apparatus primarily in expressions such as psychic apparatus, mental apparatus, or apparatuses of the mind, etc. Thus,
for example, they say: "According to the structural theory, those
mental functions which are called the ego, which normally form a
coherent and integrated whole, . . . develop from the apparatuses
of the mind which have to do with an individual's response to the
world about him. Thus the ego may be characterized in either of
two ways. (1) It may be defined as a group of functions of the mind
which are usually associated with one another in situations of mental
conflict; or (2) it may be defined as the group of mental functions
which in one way or another have to do with mediating between
the demands of the id and those of the outer world" (p. 41).[2]

The terms apparatus or ego apparatus also do not appear in the
index of Fenichel's *The Psychoanalytic Theory of Neurosis* (1945).
An examination of the actual text shows a similar absence of the
concept of ego apparatus in Hartmann's sense, though occasionally
Fenichel employed the term apparatus in expressions such as "It
[the ego] operates as an inhibiting apparatus" (p. 16), or "The mental functions represent a progressively more complicated apparatus
for the mastery of stimuli" (p. 34).

A similar situation exists in Nunberg's *Principles of Psychoanalysis* (1932). Apparatus or ego apparatuses are not listed in the index
of the book, though the bibliography includes references to Hartmann's work, including Hartmann's *Ego Psychology and the Problem of Adaptation* in its German edition.[3] In the actual text very

---

2 Their arguments here seem to me to be obscured by the fact that they fail to
specify what they mean by apparatuses of the mind and that they do not define their
use of "mind" as a concept and its relation to the concept of ego.

3 Fenichel, too, lists in the bibliography of his book the German edition of Hartmann's monograph (the English translation appeared in 1958). In Nunberg's case, the
English version of his book (1955), though not representing a word-for-word translation,
is based on his German text published in 1932, that is to say, before Hartmann's
monograph appeared in German.

few references to ego apparatuses are to be found such as the ego
"possesses a receptive, defensive, and inhibitory apparatus for mastering . . ." (p. 118). Occasionally instead of referring to the ego
apparatus concerned with thought processes, he will refer to a "thinking organ" or instead of the *perceptive apparatus* he refers to "the
system of perception" (p. 128).

Even in Waelder's more recent and very fine textbook, *Basic
Theory of Psychoanalysis* (1960), the concept of ego apparatus is not
discussed.

THE BIOLOGICAL MODEL OF AN APPARATUS: ITS INFLUENCE ON THE PSYCHOLOGICAL MODEL AND OTHER CONSIDERATIONS

As we see, apparatus is a term that has a variety of connotations.
These are derived from the fact that it is used in different sciences,
such as physics, biology, and especially medicine. The Gould's Medical Dictionary (fifth edition) defines apparatus as "1. A collection of
instruments or devices used for a special purpose. 2. Anatomically
the word is used to designate collectively the organs performing a
certain function. . . ."

Generally speaking, expressions such as the organ of vision or
the apparatus of vision usually mean for the lay man the eyes, while
for the biologist or neurophysiologist a great deal more is included,
that is, the optic nerve, the specific occipital brain areas to which
the stimuli received in the eye are transmitted, the links with other
areas of the brain, etc.

In medicine, an apparatus, such as the apparatus of vision or
the respiratory apparatus, includes several anatomical entities, organs
that combine in coordinated ways the functions they are capable of
performing individually to accomplish some other, more elaborate,
and specific set of functions. In other words, different organs perform
a number of functions specifically assigned to them and simultaneously work as part of a more complex apparatus. Although these
different apparatuses are complex anatomophysiological units in
themselves with a number of specific functions, they keep at the
same time the closest relationships with other somatic apparatuses,
some of whose services and functions are essential for the performance of their own specific tasks. Thus, for example, the physiological

processes carried out by the respiratory apparatus (i.e., the exchange of gases) are dependent on the normal activity of the circulatory apparatus which pumps the blood at different rates through the lungs, etc.

What I wish to highlight here is the interdependence between the different apparatuses and their functions because this type of model is implicit in our concept of ego apparatus. What we call an ego apparatus is an extremely complex organization, to which several physical organs or apparatuses may contribute their functional capabilities in different degrees and combinations. But we should note that in the case of the circulatory apparatus, for example, these functional capabilities are described as the physiological processes of which the corresponding anatomical structures are capable, while in the case of many of the somatic organs subserving the mind more directly, for example, the brain, some of the physiological processes have a concomitant psychological equivalent—a fact that is of the greatest significance.

We assume that to start with the "inborn apparatuses" (Hartmann, 1939) which later form part of the ego organization are rather primitive in their functional possibilities. These are in any case essentially determined and closely linked to the physical organ or organs on which they are dependent. This rather obvious statement is made only to emphasize the very close connection that exists at the very beginning between function and specific organs. As ego development progresses, many other apparatuses and functions become integrated in the performance of the perfected form of the function. That is to say, the contribution of the somatic apparatus, say of visual perception, essential as it remains in terms of the reception of visual sensations, is nevertheless relative when contrasted with the contributions that are made to actual visual perception by other ego apparatuses and functions. In Hartmann's (1939) words: "Ego development is a differentiation, in which these primitive regulating factors are increasingly replaced or supplemented by more effective ego regulations. . . . Differentiation progresses not only by the creation of new apparatuses to master new demands and new tasks, but also and mainly by new apparatuses taking over, on a higher level, functions which were originally performed by more primitive means" (p. 49f.).

As mentioned above, our conception of the ego apparatuses has
striking similarities with the explanatory construct of the somatic
apparatuses, but there are also striking differences that deserve some
further consideration.

We have no conscious awareness of the many physiological
processes that take place in the different apparatuses of our organism,
for example, while we breathe or digest. Mostly silent and automatically regulated, these processes find no conscious expression in
our minds unless something is at fault, in which case we perceive
feelings along the unpleasure-pain series. In other words, the possibility of translating these physiological processes into psychological
terms, into terms that the mind can manipulate, is extremely restricted.

A completely different situation exists with regard to the mental
apparatus, as I have already suggested. We are of course not aware
of the innumerable physiological processes in the brain that underlie
our mental activities per se. Yet, many of these underlying physiological processes are retranslated—by means that escape us so far—
into what I can describe only (lacking a better and more accurate
expression) as the psychological language of the mind, the language
of the ego organization. These are phenomena of which we frequently can become conscious, which have acquired a certain independence, which can be manipulated in different ways, which form
part of our psychical processes. In other words, when certain physiological processes are retranslated, transformed, or raised to the level
of the psychological, they are perceived in the mind, the mental
apparatus (or rather that part of it which we call the ego), as ideas,
thoughts, visual or auditory images, memories, feelings, etc.

SOMATIC APPARATUSES AND PSYCHOLOGICAL EGO APPARATUSES

Although we all have some notion of what is meant by ego apparatus, there remains a great deal of obscurity and ambiguity with
respect to this concept. I shall use *visual perception* as a concrete
example to illustrate the difference between somatic and psychic
apparatus and to consider the distinct roles played by these ego
apparatuses in the performance of this ego function. We agree, first
of all, that the physical apparatuses, the somatic organs involved in

the perception of visual stimuli, must reach an appropriate degree of maturation before they can appropriately perform the basic functions involved in visual perception. We agree, furthermore, that the mere fact of the physical apparatus having reached maturity and therefore being potentially ready to perform its function does not imply that this function will immediately be performed in all its complexity. Visual perception is an extremely complicated process that needs exercise and learning for its perfection. Such learning takes time and requires a coordinated interaction with several other apparatuses and mental processes that must themselves reach a certain maturational level and organization before they can contribute to the performance of visual perception as a perfected function.

At the beginning of life, the somatic organs[4] concerned are capable of receiving and carrying different types of visual stimuli (light, dark, color, shapes, etc.), but the sensory impressions that these stimuli produce in the organism are devoid of specific meaning. Whatever sensation they create, it is not understood without an appropriate relation to a given context, in short, unless it is organized and integrated with other mental phenomena. As other apparatuses develop, as increased discrimination is possible, as memories are laid down, perceptions become integrated and processed in interaction with other mental processes that take into account previous experiences and knowledge. This is naturally a gradual process of development becoming more and more complex and refined.

In this way we learn to perceive not just primitive and simple sensory impressions, but impressions that can now be discriminated in terms of form, shapes, color, depth, spatial relations, causal connections, meanings, and the like. This not only allows for the identification of objects according to their different qualities, in the abstract so to say; but more important, by means of complicated processes of association with other memories of other objects, experiences, and things, all these impressions have for each person a special individual meaning that belongs in the life context of his own experiences and knowledge.

---

[4] The somatic organs of vision naturally include not only the eye but the nervous pathways carrying the sensory impression to the appropriate areas in the occipital cortex and the multiple links between these areas and other centers in the brain.

We have seen the role played by the somatic ego apparatus of vision in terms of receiving the stimuli and producing specific sensory impressions, but we could not have failed to notice that without the contribution of other physical apparatuses, of other mental functions and processes, without the organization of the stimuli perceived visually according to certain laws, without the necessary coordination and integration with the content of innumerable other experiences, past, present, and even future (through the function of imagination), perceptive processes would have remained at the level of *primitive sensory impressions* registered by the *somatic apparatus* concerned with vision. What raises visual perception from the level of primitive sensory impressions conveyed by the somatic organ to the sophisticated, invaluable process that we know as vision is the existence of the *psychological ego apparatus* of perception. By this I mean an intangible, nonmaterial organization, with a *functional structure* of its own, which regulates its own activities and those of the multiple somatic structures or organs it utilizes according to a well-established (though largely unknown) hierarchy of regulating principles and laws; a preordained set of processes that has structured itself slowly and gradually through development; a functional structuralization that has been earned, partly perhaps through trial and error (though not exclusively) and whose basic regulating principle during its organization (and perhaps afterward as well) was its adaptive value, even its survival value. Much of the development of the psychological ego apparatus of visual perception can be assumed to follow, at least in part, a preordained course determined by the genetically controlled maturational unfolding of the physical structures that will allow for a gradual and increasing complexity and integration of those mental processes that such maturational unfolding makes possible.

The quality of the psychological ego apparatus concerned with the function of perception will vary enormously from one individual to another. These variations are dependent, on the one hand, on the "quality" of the somatic ego apparatuses underlying some of these processes (the quality being itself determined by constitutional and hereditary factors in interaction with environmental influences insofar as their physical maturation is influenced by it) and, on the other hand, on all those factors that generally influence development and more specifically the development of the ego apparatuses concerned with the function of visual perception. Among these are suitable stimulation, accumulation of all sorts of experiences, opportunities to practice the skills involved in order to perfect them further—in short, factors that influence learning, in this particular case, learning to perceive and to organize percepts in a meaningful way.

What I have described for perception applies, I believe, to all other ego functions. Although at present we do not have as much knowledge about the physical structures underlying such mental activities as ideation, thinking, etc., as we have about visual perception and the physical structures and physiological processes underlying it, I have little doubt that the day will come when these relationships will be understood. Such an understanding will enrich psychoanalytic and psychological propositions dealing with these aspects of mental functioning. Nevertheless, in the absence of such knowledge, we are still forced to operate at a level of abstraction that occasionally seems to carry with it the danger that some of our working hypotheses might acquire metaphysical or mystical connotations, as it were, and these could hinder our scientific development.

I would like to end this section by applying to my discussion what Hartmann (1939) said: that many of these "lengthy—but still incomplete—considerations are not psychoanalytic in the narrow sense, and some of them seem to have taken us quite far from the core of psychoanalysis" (p. 108). Following him, I would add that psychoanalysis as a general psychology and as a developmental theory can no longer avoid branching out into different directions and borrowing from biology, neurophysiology, and other sciences whatever is necessary for its further development on its own independent lines.

THE DEVELOPMENTAL APPROACH TO THE EGO AND ITS SOMATIC ROOTS

Many analysts have attempted to describe and understand the developmental steps leading from the rudimentary ego at birth to the final ego organization. While a full description of these attempts is beyond the scope of this paper, these studies have made it quite clear that ego development is predicated on a number of factors interacting with one another. I single out the physical maturational processes taking place in the somatic structures whose functional capacities will at the appropriate time become integrated into the ego organization. I have mentioned earlier that physical maturation itself is not enough, that the performance of the function must be learned and perfected, and that experiencing and different forms of stimulation play essential contributory roles.

It is in relation to the *physical* maturation occurring simultaneously in various organs and in interaction with each other that we observe the beginning of certain psychological activities that I refer to as primitive or elementary ego functions. Further maturation, stimulation, learning, experiencing, and practice in the use of these physical apparatuses lead to greater efficiency of their functioning and to the slow and gradual development of the ego structure. This naturally includes an increasing and more efficient interaction and integration of the various functions and apparatuses which contribute to the building of the ego structure until we reach, at the appropriate time, the "final" ego organization. At this point the ego has acquired the capacity to use, control, and command all the resources available and functions with an amazing degree of complexity. Even then we have to qualify the statement, "the ego in its final form," because we know that the capacity of the mature ego structure in terms of learning, imagining, and functioning in ever more complex ways continues to increase for many years and in some fortunate individuals throughout their lives.

Among biologists, neurologists, and neurophysiologists there seems to be a measure of agreement that actual physical maturation of the brain structures and other elements of the central nervous system is more or less completed during the first year and a half of life.[5] Since the level of ego development reached at this stage is very limited, we appreciate the degree to which development in the human depends upon learning, on constant stimulation, on a great variety of experiences, and on the constant exercise of the ego

---

[5] It is hardly necessary to remind the reader that the young of the human species is born with a degree of immaturity that has no equivalent in any other mammal species. To reach a degree of physical maturation equivalent to that of other species at birth, he takes a good year and a half of extrauterine life, a factor of the greatest psychological significance.

organization dealing with new situations in more complex ways. These experiences are recorded and laid down, so that this storehouse of memories and knowledge can be used to deal with further new experiences in more purposeful and adaptive ways. In this manner, the ego widens its ability to understand and master the complexity of new situations and stimuli that reach it.

Two aspects deserve further discussion. The first one concerns the fact, referred to earlier, that in the physical maturation of somatic structures appropriate stimulation by the mother or mother substitute seems to play an essential role. Many studies and observations have shown that, in the absence of such stimulation, the development of several somatic apparatuses, initially having a normal potential, is delayed to a point where they are quite incapable of performing certain functions (Provence and Lipton, 1962). Since it is these functional capabilities that constitute the very essence of the ego structure (when a certain level of functioning and organization has been reached), we can see the close association between external stimulation, the development and maturation of the somatic apparatuses, and their final functional expression, that is, their ego dimension.

These functional capacities are qualitatively very different in different individuals because the constitutional givens as well as the quantity and type of stimulation received vary. The developmental continuum I have tried to describe highlights the dangers and oversimplification implicit in a conception in which the psychological ego organization is totally divorced from the somatic apparatuses on which it depends not only for its inception but also for its more mature functioning. In this respect, Hartmann (1939) stated: "It is obvious that these apparatuses, *somatic and mental,* influence the development and the functions of the ego which uses them; we maintain that these apparatuses constitute one of the roots of the ego" (p. 101; my italics). In 1950, he added:

The problem of maturation has a physiological aspect. Speaking of this aspect we may refer to the growth of whatever we assume to be the physiological basis of those functions which, looked at from the angle of psychology, we call the ego; or we may refer to the growth of such apparatus which sooner or later come to be specifically used by the ego (e.g., the motor apparatus used in action). However, the role of these apparatus for the ego is not limited to their function as tools which the ego at a given time finds at its disposal. We have to assume that differences in the timing or intensity of their growth enter into the picture of ego development as a partly independent variable; e.g., the timing of the appearance of grasping, of walking, of the motor aspect of speech (see also Hendrick, 1943). Neither does it seem unlikely that the congenital motor equipment is among the factors which right from birth on tend to modify certain attitudes of the developing ego (Fries and Lewis, 1938). The presence of such factors in all aspects of the child's behavior makes them also an essential element in the development of his self-experience. We can assume that from the earliest stages on the corresponding experiences are preserved in his system of memory traces. We have also reasons to think that the reproduction of environmental data is very generally fused with and formed by elements of that kind, e.g., the reproduction of motor experiences [p. 121].

By obscuring these links we deny ourselves a better understanding of what we call the ego organization, of how it is established, how it acquires the special qualities that characterize it as a finished product and distinguish it from all other ego organizations. Further, by depriving ourselves of understanding these processes of interaction throughout development, we place out of our reach the possibility of learning how we can favorably influence the processes or at least prevent detrimental influences.

As long as psychoanalysis was primarily concerned with the neurotic conflicts of the adult personality (the finished product)—as was certainly the case in 1923, when Freud introduced the structural model of the mind—it could afford to conceive of the ego structure without expanding on the relationship between the ego's functions and the apparatuses.[6] At that point in the development of psychoanalysis it was sufficient to say that such apparatuses were at the service of the ego organization and under its control. But with the move of psychoanalysis in the direction of a *psychoanalytic psychology* and more especially of a *developmental psychoanalytic psychology,* the situation changed and what had been a most useful set of formulations pertinent to the problems dealt with was no longer sufficient. Further study and elaboration of our propositions con-

6 Hartmann also refers to this problem in 1939.

cerning the ego are necessary if we are to meet in a more systematic way the requirements of child development, normal as well as psychopathological.

We have only to think of some children with minimal brain damage whose egos are atypical because of the primary defects in the somatic apparatuses on which the ego structure is based. These ego deviations cannot possibly be understood without reference to the organic structures that support it. Further, the indiscriminate extension of the formulations concerning the ego structure of normal or neurotic adults to this type of case may lead—and, I believe, has in fact occasionally led—to serious misconceptions about the true nature of these children's basic disturbances. They consist, in these brain-damaged children, of primary defects and abnormalities of the somatic apparatuses, which naturally enough produce atypical ego organizations lacking in certain functions and having defects in the integrative capacities. The same arguments apply to *some* of the so-called "borderline," "autistic" children or children with "atypical" personalities. These terms are purely descriptive classifications based on behavioral manifestations; they are meaningless with regard to etiology because each such group can contain children whose disturbances were caused by very different factors. With such cases, too, no headway can be made without a better understanding of the close relationship between the final ego organization and the different somatic apparatuses that sustain it and make it possible. The symptomatology of some of these cases may in fact also be due to primary deficiencies in the apparatuses.[7]

Another example may further clarify the issues involved. At the Hampstead Clinic we have had the opportunity to observe and study a number of children who were blind, some of them from birth. The lack of the organ of vision, one of the somatic apparatuses at the disposal of the ego at later stages, tends to distort the development of these children in practically every area of their functioning at least for some time. Most of these blind children lag behind sighted children in all their achievements. Their drive development

---

[7] These primary deficiencies need not always be due to organic disturbances. They may be due to insufficient or excessive stimulation at the inappropriate stage, to overwhelming traumatic experiences which, if they occur at certain periods, may completely disrupt development.

deviates from the norm, and so does their ego and superego development.[8] It is particularly interesting to note, by means of the contrast with the sighted, the essential contribution that sight makes to the development of a multitude of other ego apparatuses and functions. Without this fundamental contribution from the organ of sight many of these functions do not develop or are faulty and incomplete. Sometimes the ego handicap remains for life. In these cases we cannot fail to appreciate the intimate dependence between apparatus and function and, even more important, the essential contribution that the organ of vision makes to the development of other apparatuses and functions.

As I have tried to demonstrate with these examples, it will prove profitable for the further development of psychoanalysis as a developmental psychology to focus some of our interest on the close correlation between the physical and the psychological. Moreover, in this way we might succeed in further closing the artificial gap that still exists between the concepts of body and mind, of physical and psychological, and thus re-establish the natural continuum between them.

Obviously, there were many reasons why the formulations in *The Ego and the Id* were not aimed at closing this gap. I have already referred to the fact that they adequately dealt with the type of problem they were meant to deal with (neurotic conflicts, especially in the adult). They did not involve the type of problems and interactions that could not be escaped when analysis branched out in several new directions. Insufficient knowledge in other disciplines also did not favor attempts at integration.

Hartmann, Kris, and Loewenstein (1946) have pointed out that Freud was by no means unaware of these problems, quite the contrary. They stated: "In adopting the *functions* exercised in mental processes as the decisive criterion for defining the psychic systems Freud used physiology as his model in concept formation. However, this does not imply any correlation of any one of the systems to any specific physiological organization or group of organs, though Freud considered such a correlation as the ultimate goal of psychological research. Psychological terminology, he assumed, has to be main-

<hr/>

[8] For more detailed account of these deviations in the blind, see Nagera and Colonna (1965).

tained as long as it cannot be adequately substituted by physiological terminology" (p. 15). Yet, in my opinion, attempts to correlate *psychological structures (id, ego, superego) and specific areas of the brain, anatomical structures, or physiological processes* are ill-advised and bound to fail. They do not seem, at least to my mind, to take full account of the functional-psychological nature of our conceptualizations of these agencies or, for that matter, of the true significance of recent neurophysiological advances.

To equate or correlate, for example, the brain cortex with our ego agency may occasionally be quite tempting because many of the functions of the cortex and the physiological processes taking place there are usually accompanied by psychological experiences and functions that we attribute to the ego. However, these striking similarities are due only to the fact that all psychological phenomena have a physiological substratum, which in some cases can be located in one or another area of the brain. But our ego concept cannot be tied down to any area or areas of the central nervous system, nor can it be restricted to or identified with the functions performed by them. As a functional construct, the ego cannot be localized anywhere or made identical with any area (or groups of them) since what it utilizes for its performance is the *psychological translation* of a physiological process or groups of physiological processes located in the central nervous system. What is important is not the location of the physiological processes underlying the psychological retranslation (which the ego uses for its operation), but the psychological laws that regulate the organization of these psychological processes, giving them distinct qualities[9] that characterize a given mental process as the product of the ego organization. As a psychological construct it deals only with psychological phenomena and not with the neurophysiological processes underlying it. As such and without in any way wanting to deny the close links with such processes, we can say that it has simultaneously acquired in *conceptual terms*, and otherwise, a marked independence from them.

I emphasize once more, to avoid misunderstanding, that the developmental approach to the ego and its somatic roots that I am suggesting here does not have as its aim a correlation between the

[9] These were well defined by Freud (i.e., secondary processes, delay, binding of mental energy, etc.).

ego or any other psychic agency (id and superego) with specific anatomical or anatomophysiological localities of the central nervous system. But it does try to correlate (not equate), relatively and within
limits, the interrelations between what psychoanalysis conceptualizes
as "ego functions" and the underlying physical structures and physiological processes on which the former are dependent.

BIBLIOGRAPHY

Brenner, C. & Arlow, J. A. (1964), *Psychoanalytic Concepts and the Structural Theory*.
New York: International Universities Press.
Fenichel, O. (1945), *The Psychoanalytic Theory of Neurosis*. New York: Norton.
Freud, S. (1923), The Ego and the Id. *Standard Edition*, 19:3-66. London: Hogarth
Press, 1961.
—— (1937), Analysis Terminable and Interminable. *Standard Edition*, 23:209-253.
London: Hogarth Press, 1964.
Gill, M. M. (1963), *Topography and Systems in Psychoanalytic Theory* [*Psychological
Issues*, Monogr. 10]. New York: International Universities Press.
Hartmann, H. (1939), *Ego Psychology and the Problem of Adaptation*. New York:
International Universities Press, 1958.
—— (1950), Comments on the Psychoanalytic Theory of the Ego. *Essays on Ego
Psychology*. New York: International Universities Press, 1964, pp. 113-141.
—— (1952), The Mutual Influences in the Development of Ego and Id. *Essays on Ego
Psychology*. New York: International Universities Press, 1964, pp. 155-181.
—— (1959), Psychoanalysis as a Scientific Theory. *Essays on Ego Psychology*. New York:
International Universities Press, 1964, pp. 318-350.
—— (1964), *Essays on Ego Psychology*. New York: International Universities Press.
—— Kris, E., & Loewenstein, R. M. (1946), Comments on the Formation of Psychic
Structure. *This Annual*, 2:11-38.
Nagera, H. (1967), The Concepts of Structure and Structuralization: Psychoanalytic
Usage and Implications for a Theory of Learning and Creativity. *This Annual*,
22:77-102.
—— & Colonna, A. (1965), Aspects of the Contribution of Sight to Ego and Drive
Development. *This Annual*, 20:267-287.
Nunberg, H. (1932), *Principles of Psychoanalysis*. New York: International Universities
Press, 1955.
Provence, S. & Lipton, R. C. (1962), *Infants in Institutions*. New York: International
Universities Press.
Waelder, R. (1960), *Basic Theory of Psychoanalysis*. New York: International Universi-
ties Press.

III

ASPECTS OF NORMAL
AND PATHOLOGICAL DEVELOPMENT

CHARACTER FORMATION IN ADOLESCENCE

PETER BLOS, Ph.D. (New York)

The problem of character formation is of such a vast scope that almost any aspect of psychoanalytic theory is related to it. This fact tells us at the outset that we deal with a concept of enormous complexity or with integrative processes of the highest order. It is a sobering and welcome limitation to concentrate on the adolescent period and investigate, in this circumscribed domain, whether this particular stage of development affords us insight into the formative process of character, and consequently throws light on the concept of character in general. It would not be the first time in the history of psychoanalysis that the nature of a psychic phenomenon becomes illuminated by the study of its formation.

Whoever has studied adolescence, regardless of theoretical background, has been aware of changes in the maturing personality that are generally identified with character formation. Even the untutored observer of youth, or the adult who retrospectively contemplates his own adolescence, cannot fail to notice that, with the termination of adolescence, a new mode of dealing with the exigencies of life is in evidence. Behavior, attitudes, interests, and relationships appear more predictable, show a relatively greater stability, and tend to become irreversible, even under stress.

The psychoanalytic observer of adolescence can attest to these findings. However, he asks himself which psychic mechanisms or which maturational processes are at work in character formation. The process of formation, indeed, raises the question of "what takes form" and "what gives form"; furthermore, what are the preconditions for the formation of character, and why and to what extent does it occur at the stage of adolescence? Precursors of character can be

Presented at the Fall Meeting of the American Psychoanalytic Association, New York, December 16, 1967.

discerned abundantly in childhood. However, we would not attribute to these rather habitual ways in which the ego deals with id, superego and reality the designation of character, because the integrated, rather fixed pattern of its disparate components is still lacking. Due to the adolescent forward step in the organization of character traits, Gitelson (1948) referred to "character synthesis" as the essential therapeutic task during the adolescent period. Empirically, we all have come to similar conclusions. However, I believe that the formation of character in adolescence is the outcome of psychic restructuring or, in other words, it is the manifest sign of a completed, not necessarily complete, passage through adolescence. We all had occasion to observe how the analysis of an adolescent, especially of the older adolescent, moves toward its termination by the silent emergence of character. What do we mean by this obvious something that emerges? This question forces us to consider some pertinent aspects of psychoanalytic characterology.

CHARACTER TRAITS AND CHARACTER

The etymological root of the word "character" in the Greek verb of "to furrow and to engrave" has always remained part of the concept of character in regard to the permanency and fixity of pattern or design. These permanencies are represented, in terms of personality, by distinctive traits or qualities and by typical or idiosyncratic ways of conducting oneself. Even the style of life and temperamental attitudes were here and there brought into the broad scope of character.

In the psychoanalytic literature on character we encounter an imprecise and inconsistent use of terms. The interchangeable use of "character," "character type," and "character trait" has been particularly confusing. We can, roughly, distinguish four approaches to classical psychoanalytic characterology. In one approach (Freud, 1908; Abraham, 1921, 1924, 1925; Jones, 1918; Glover, 1924), the character trait is traced to a specific level of drive development or drive fixation (e.g., oral character traits); in another (W. Reich, 1928, 1930), the defensive aspect of the ego represents the decisive factor (e.g., the reactive character); in the third (Freud, 1939), it is the fate of object libido that determines the character (e.g., the narcissistic or anaclitic character); and in the fourth (Erikson, 1946), it is the influence of environment, culture, and history that engraves a patterned and preferential style of life on people (the psychosocial definition of character). Of course, these four determinants of character traits and of character are not mutually exclusive; on the contrary, they appear in various admixtures and combinations. The salient feature of each characterological formation is the implicit ego syntonicity and absence of conflict, as distinct from neurotic symptom formation, and the patterned fixity of the characterological organization.

Two widely accepted definitions of character read as follows:

". . . typical mode of reaction of the ego towards the id and the outer world" (W. Reich, 1929, p. 149).

". . . the habitual mode of bringing into harmony the tasks presented by internal demands and by the external world, is necessarily a function of . . . the ego" (Fenichel, 1945, p. 467).

Character originates in conflict, but, by its very nature, it prevents the arousal of signal anxiety through the codification of conflict solutions. The automatization of dealing with idiosyncratic danger situations represents a considerable forward step in personality integration and functioning. Indeed, character formation can be conceptualized from an adaptive point of view, and clinical evidence in support of such a thesis is easily obtainable. The economic gain inherent in character formation frees psychic energy for the expansion of adaptive inventiveness and the actualization of human potentialities. The economic gain involved in character formation was stated clearly by Freud (1913): "repression either does not come into action [in character formation] or smoothly achieves its aim of replacing the repressed by reaction-formations and sublimations" (p. 323). Having observed these substitutions in the analysis of adolescents, I wonder whether the countercathexis of the reactive (defensive) character does not restrict rather than expand the adaptive scope of self-realization. I shall return to this question.

The transformation of drive fixations into character traits is so universal and so well documented that it requires little comment. It might, however, not be superfluous to mention that instinctual predilections in combination with special sensitivities constitute inherent aspects of human development. When drive fixations are transformed into character traits, the qualitative and quantitative factors due to endowment bestow on each character a highly individualistic countenance.

We are familar with the host of character traits that take their origin, separately or mixed, in the various levels of psychosexual development. Secondarily, the ego makes use of such proclivities by drawing them into its own realm and employing them for its own purposes. We then speak of the sublimation type of character. If the instinctual predilection gives rise to conflict, then the automatization of defenses marks the character in some decisive fashion, as is exemplified in the reactive character. We can see that the fixed ego attitude of dealing with danger (e.g., "avoidances") has a broader, more inclusive scope than a character trait derived from drive transformations (e.g., "obstinacy"). Yet, we cannot discern such circumscribed, enduring, and fixed ego reactions in children because the child's ego remains partly and significantly interlocked with parental and environmental object dependencies up to the age of puberty. We certainly can discern distinct character traits in the child. However, what appears as character in childhood is mainly a pattern of ego attitudes, stabilized by identifications, which, as we know, can undergo a most radical revision during adolescence. Here lies one further reason for the fact that character formation and adolescence are synonymous. Precocious character consolidation occurring before puberty should be looked at as an abnormal development, because it precludes that essential elasticity and flexibility of psychic structure without which the adolescent process cannot take its normal course.

The distinction between character traits and character corresponds with the developmental line of demarcation drawn by adolescence. Character traits, then, are not identical with character per se, nor is character simply the sum total of character traits. Of course, we can trace in each individual oral, anal, urethral, and phallic-genital characteristics or character traits, but neither one of these characteristics suffices, nor can it do justice to a person's character as a monolithic structure. If we recognize in a person a degree of orderliness, stubbornness, and frugality, we no doubt are confronted with anal character traits. However, we hesitate to call that person an anal character unless we know more about the economic, structural, and dynamic factors, indeed, the degree to which these traits are still cathected with anal erotism and the extent to which these traits became emancipated from infantile bondage and in time acquired functions far removed from their genetic source.

We are reminded here of Hartmann's (1952) statement that defensive ego functions can lose their defensive nature in time and become valuable and integral ego assets serving a far wider function than the original defensive one. Similarly, it can be said that "reactive character formation, originating in defense against the drives, may gradually take over a host of other functions in the framework of the ego" (Hartmann, 1952, p. 25), namely, remain a part of the personality despite the fact that its original *raison d'être* has vanished. Hartmann's point of view opens up two avenues of thought: either the defensive nature of the character trait is altered because it is emptied of its countercathexis; or, on the other hand, the id component is afforded a nonconflictual gratification in the exercise and maintenance of character. Could it be that the attainment of the genital level of drive maturation during adolescence facilitates either one of these outcomes? Furthermore, could it be assumed that these transitions or modifications of character traits into character formation are the cardinal achievement of adolescence? We certainly ascertain in character formation integrative processes, structurings and patternings that belong to a different order than a mere bundling together of traits, attitudes, habits and idiosyncrasies. Lampl-de Groot (1963), following a similar line of thought, modified the earlier definitions of character (W. Reich, 1929; Fenichel, 1945) by saying that character is the habitual way in which integration is achieved.

The Function of Character

My remarks, up to this point, about character formation have carried an implicit assumption that should now be stated directly and affirmatively. It should, however, be borne in mind that these propositions are laid down here only in order to pave the road to the central theme of this investigation, namely, the relationship between the adolescent process and character formation.

It is assumed that character, as a definitive component of adult psychic structure, performs an essential function in the mature psychic organism. This function is manifested in the maintenance of psychosomatic homeostasis, in patterned self-esteem regulation (A.

Reich, 1958), in the stabilization of ego identity (Erikson, 1956), and in the automatization of threshold and barrier levels, both shifting in accordance with the intensity of internal or external stimuli. This regulatory function includes the containment of affective fluctuations within a tolerable range, including depression, as a major determinant in character formation (Zetzel, 1964).

The more complex a psychic formation, the more elusive to the observer becomes the total configuration or organization. The concept of character is a case in point. We have to content ourselves with the study of components or, more precisely, with a description of the whole in terms of the function of its constituent parts. The whole can be assembled as a psychic entity from such fractional comprehensions (Lichtenstein, 1965). Two investigative approaches are now open to us; one, to study observable functions in order to impute structure (dynamic, economic principle); and, two, to trace the growth of a psychic formation and see how it comes into its own (genetic principle). These approaches are not the result of an arbitrary choice, but they are forced upon us by the nature of our subject. Character formation is, generally speaking, an integrative process and as such aims at the elimination of conflict and anxiety arousal. We are reminded of Anna Freud's (1936) statement that the ego cannot be studied when it is in harmony with id, superego, and the outer world; it reveals its nature only when disharmony between the psychic institutions prevails. We are faced with a similar dilemma in studying character. Here, too, we can clearly describe pathological character formation, while the typical process of character formation remains elusive. In the analysis of adolescents we cannot fail to notice how character takes shape silently, how it consolidates proportionate to the severance from and dissolution of infantile ties: like Phoenix rising from its ashes.

Let us return now to the question why the formation of character occurs at the stage of adolescence or, rather, at the termination of adolescence. Generally, we recognize developmental progression by the appearance of new psychic formations as the consequence of differentiating processes. Drive and ego maturation always leads to a new and more complex personality organization. Adolescent drive progression to the adult genital level presupposes a hierarchical arrangement of the drives, as is reflected in the formation of forepleasure. Ego maturation, distinctly influenced but not wholly determined by drive progression, is reflected in qualitative cognitive advances as described by Inhelder and Piaget (1958). Looking at development and maturation in terms of differentiating and integrative processes, we can now ask the question which of these processes in adolescence are preconditional for character formation.

I shall approach this problem by investigating some aspects of typical adolescent drive and ego progression that make character formation not only possible but mandatory for the stabilization of the newly attained personality organization of adulthood. If it is possible to describe character in terms of observable functions, and character formation in terms of preconditions or of epigenetic sequences or abandoned developmental stages, then the aim of this exploration would be closer within our reach. Zetzel (1964) has emphasized the developmental aspect of character formation and speaks of a developmental task which, I think, belongs to the phase of late adolescence. Zetzel's expansion of the definition of character formation is noteworthy; she stated: "Character formation . . . includes the whole range of solutions, adaptive or maladaptive, to recognized developmental challenges" (p. 153).

The Adolescent Process and Character Formation

I have chosen four adolescent developmental challenges which I have found to be closely related to character formation. In fact, character formation remains stunted or takes on some abnormal slant if these challenges are not met with reasonable competence. It should be evident that I look at character formation from a developmental point of view and see in it a normative formation that reflects the result of progressive ego and drive development at adolescence. One might compare it to the emergence of the latency period as a result of the oedipal resolution. Whenever the oedipal stage is prolonged beyond its proper timing, latency development remains incomplete or defective. We are accustomed to consider the decline of the oedipus complex as a precondition for latency to come into its own. In a comparable and similar perspective I introduce here four developmental preconditions without which adolescent character formation cannot take its course.

The Second Individuation

The first precondition which I shall discuss encompasses what has been called the loosening of the infantile object ties (A. Freud, 1958), a process which, in its wider scope, I have conceptualized as the second individuation process of adolescence (Blos, 1967). The developmental task of this process lies in the disengagement of libidinal and aggressive cathexes from the internalized infantile love and hate objects. We know how closely infantile object relations are interwoven with psychic structure formation as demonstrated, for example, by the transformation of object love into identification. I do not have to remind you that object relations activate and form ego nuclei around which subsequent experiences coalesce, and that they induce and sharpen idiosyncratic sensitizations, inclusive of preferences and avoidances. The most dramatic and fateful formation derived from object relations is, of course, the superego. Conflicts of the infantile period and of childhood give rise to the many character traits and attitudes which can, at those times, be easily observed *in statu nascendi*.

We recognize in the disengagement from infantile object ties the psychological counterpart to the attainment of somatic maturity, brought about by the biological process of puberty. The psychic formations that not only were derived from object relations, but, more or less, still maintain close instinctual ties to infantile object representations are affected, often catastrophically, by the second individuation of adolescence. Again, the superego demonstrates, by the degree of its disorganization or disintegration at adolescence, the affective affinity of this structure to infantile object ties. I can only hint here at the fact that many controls and adaptational functions pass over from the superego to the ego ideal, namely, to a narcissistic formation. The love of the infant's parent is, partially at least, replaced by the love of the self or its potential perfection.

The psychic restructuring, implicit in what I have described above, cannot be accomplished without regression. The relentless striving toward increasing autonomy through regression forces us to view this kind of regression in adolescence as regression in the service of development, rather than in the service of defense. In fact, adolescent analysis demonstrates convincingly not only the adolescent's defense against phase-specific regression, but also the task of the analysis to facilitate regression.

Adolescent regression not only is unavoidable, it is obligatory, namely, phase specific. Adolescent regression in the service of development brings the more advanced ego of adolescence into contact with infantile drive positions, with old conflictual constellations and their solutions, with early object relations and narcissistic formations. We might say that the personality functioning which was adequate for the child undergoes a selective overhaul. The ego's advanced resourcefulness is brought to bear on this task.

In the course of adolescent psychic restructuring the ego draws drive propensities and superego influences into its own realm, integrating these disparate elements into an adaptive pattern. The process of the second individuation proceeds via regressive recathexis of pregenital and preoedipal positions. They are, so to say, revisited, lived through again, but with the difference that the adolescent ego, being in a vastly more mature state vis-à-vis infantile drives and conflicts, is able to bring about shifts in the balance between ego and id. New identifications ("the friend," "the group," etc.) take over superego functions, episodically or lastingly. The adolescent's emotional and physical withdrawal from, or opposition to, his world of childhood dependencies and security measures makes him, for some time, seek a protective cover in passionate, but usually transient, peer associations. We then observe shifting identifications with imitative and restitutive connotations as expressed in posture, gait, gesture, attire, speech, opinion, value system, etc. Their shifting and experimental nature is a sign that character has not yet been formed, but it also indicates that social adaptation has transcended the confines of the family, its milieu and tradition. These social way stations, significant as they are, have outlasted their usefulness with the unfolding and implementation of a life plan, with the capacity for adult object relations, and with a realistic projection of the self into the future. Then we know that a consolidation of the personality has come about, that a new forward step in internalization has been taken, that inner consistencies and uniformities have become stabilized, that behavior and attitudes have acquired an almost predictable countenance, reliance, and harmony.

Residual Trauma

I shall now turn to the second precondition for adolescent character formation which will throw light on the function of character.
I hope to show that the character takes over homeostatic functions
from other regulatory agencies of childhood.[1] In this connection we
have to consider the effect of trauma on adolescent character formation. The usage of the term "trauma" in this paper corresponds with
Greenacre's (1967) definition. She writes: "In my own work I have
not limited my conception of trauma to sexual (genital) traumatic
events, or circumscribed episodes, but have included *traumatic conditions, i.e., any conditions which seem definitely unfavorable, noxious, or drastically injurious to the development of the young individual"* (p. 128).

Clinical observation gave rise to the theoretical formulations that
follow. The analysis of older adolescents has demonstrated to me that
the resolution of the neurotic conflict, the weaning from infantile
fantasies, will bring the analytic work to a good end, without, however, having eliminated all residues of the pathogenetic foundation
on which the illness rested. These residues remain recognizable in special sensitivities to certain stimuli, external or internal, as well as in
affinities to, or avoidances of, experiences and fantasies, or in somatic
proclivities, despite the fact that all these aspects were dealt with
exhaustively in the analysis. By the end of the analysis, these residues
have lost their noxious valence due to ego and drive maturation. In
spite of this, they do require constant containment, which is to say,
they still are factors to be reckoned with in the maintenance of
psychic homeostasis. It is my contention that the automatization of
this containment process is identical with the function or, more precisely, with a part function of character. Such sensitizations to special
danger situations of a permanent traumatic valence are to be found,
for example, in object loss, passive dependency, loss of control, decline of self-esteem, and other structurally and affectively injurious
conditions.

It is assumed here that trauma is a universal human condition
during infancy and early childhood, leaving, under the most favor-

---

[1] Again, I have to condense here what I have developed at greater length elsewhere
(1962, pp. 132-140).

able circumstances, a permanent residue. The adolescent process, unable to overcome the disequilibrizing effect of this residue, assimilates it through characterological stabilization, namely, by rendering it ego syntonic. I draw here on Freud's distinction between a positive and a negative effect of trauma. The negative reaction aims at the removal of any memory or repetition of the trauma, a reaction that leads to the reactive character formation via avoidances, phobias, compulsions, and inhibitions. The positive effects "are attempts to bring the trauma into operation once again—that is, to remember the forgotten experience, . . . to make it real, to experience a repetition of it. . . . [The effects] may be taken up into what passes as a normal ego and, as permanent trends in it, may lend it unalterable character traits" (Freud, 1939, p. 75).

The high noon of this integrative achievement lies in the terminal period of adolescence when the enormous instability of psychic and somatic functions gradually gives way to an organized and integrated mode of operation. The residual trauma ceases to alert the ego repetitiously via signal anxiety once it has become an integral part of the ego. The residual trauma has become an organizer in the process of character formation. A state of helplessness and vigilance has been counteracted by character formation. Character, then, is identical with patterned responses to signal anxiety or, generally, with the conquest of residual trauma: not with its disappearance, nor its avoidance, but with its continuance within an adaptive formation.

Residual trauma lends its persistent and relentless push toward actualization to that formation within the personality which we designate as character. Due to its origin character always contains a compulsive quality; it lies beyond choice and contemplation, is self-evident and compelling: "Here I stand, I cannot do otherwise" (Luther). The psychic energy required for character to take form is derived in part, from the cathexis which the residual trauma contains. Those adolescents who sidestep the transformation of residual trauma into character formation project the danger situation into the outside world and thus avoid the internal confrontation with it. By failing to internalize the danger situation, the chance for coming to terms with it is forfeited. This impasse results in what Erikson (1956)

has described as the adolescent moratorium, which either leads to belated character formation or to a pathological outcome. We gain the
impression that the formation of character encompasses more than
superego influences, identifications or defenses. We are now ready to
state that in character formation there is an integrative principle at
work which bends the various contributing and confluent components to a broadening of the ego's secondary autonomy. Erikson's
concept of ego identity (1956) belongs in this realm of clinical impressions.

In the analysis of older adolescents we can observe the luxuri-
ant fantasy life of adolescence shriveling up with the consolidation
of character. Greenacre (1967) comments on the fact that whenever a traumatic experience was associated with an underlying
fantasy, the fixation on the trauma is more persistent than in cases
where the trauma was bland and incidental. Is it possible that in
adolescent character formation not only the experiential side of the
residual trauma, but also the fantasy associated with it, are absorbed
in the ego organization? The thought has often been expressed that
instinctual drives find expression in the exercise of a so-called healthy
character. At any rate, we are now willing to say that the characterological stabilization of residual trauma advances the independence of
man from his environment, from which the traumatic injury originally emanated at a time when pain was identical with the outside
of the self or with the nonself.

Ego Continuity

I now come to the third precondition for adolescent character
formation. Again, clinical observation has shown the direction and
cleared the path to a conceptual formulation. I have described certain cases of adolescent acting out in which the maladaptive behavior
represents an effort via action language to contradict a distortion of
the family history that was coercively forced upon the child's mind.
I have designated such conditions as "family myth" (1963). It differs
from the classical family romance in that the distortion is forced on
the child from the outside, calling in question the validity of the
child's own perception. The study of a considerable number of such
cases has convinced me that adolescent development can be carried

forward only if the adolescent ego succeeds in establishing a historical continuity within its realm. If this is prevented, a partial foreclosure of adolescent development follows, namely, the psychic restructuring of adolescence remains incomplete. Besides delinquency, much of the quandary and adventurousness of youth as well as its creative, especially literary, productions can be studied from this point of view.

The establishment of historical ego continuity appears, of course, in every analysis, but in adolescent analysis it has an integrative and growth-stimulating effect that lies beyond conflict resolution. One adolescent spoke for many in saying that one cannot have a future without having a past. Again, we observe a tendency toward internalization or, conversely, toward a disengagement (on the ego level) from the adult caretaking environment (usually the family) which has acted as the trustee and guardian of the immature ego of the child. It seems that ego maturation, along the lines I have just described, gives rise to the subjective sense of wholeness and inviolability during the adolescent years, when the envelope of the family has outlived its usefulness. Of course, the sense of wholeness and inviolability has much in common with the psychological qualities that we ascribe to the reflection of character on subjective feeling states.

Sexual Identity

In order to complete the set of preconditions that promote adolescent character formation, a fourth one has to be mentioned, namely, the emergence of sexual identity. While gender identity is established at an early age, it has been my contention that sexual identity with definitive, i.e., irreversible, boundaries appears only belatedly as the collateral of sexual maturation at puberty. Before physical sexual maturity is attained, the boundaries of sexual identity remain fluid. Indeed, a shifting or ambiguous sexual identity, within limits, is the rule rather than the exception. This is more apparent in the girl than in the boy. I have only to remind you of the acceptability, socially and personally, of the tomboy stage in the girl and of the deep repression of breast envy in the preadolescent boy. At any rate, puberty represents the demarcation line beyond which bisexual admixtures to gender identity become incompatible

with progressive development. Clinically, this can easily be observed
in the adolescent's growing capacity for heterosexual object finding
and in the decline of masturbation, both of which advance parallel
with the formation of sexual identity.

It is not the purpose of this paper to trace the origin or the
resolution of bisexuality. But it needs to be said that, as long as the
ambiguity or, indeed, the ambivalence of sexual identification lasts,
the ego cannot escape being affected by the ambiguity of the drives.
The maturational exigencies of puberty which normally lead to
integrative processes of increasing complexity are not able to perform their function as long as sexual ambiguity prevails; that is to
say, maturational processes will be defeated all along the line. Sub-
jectively, this is experienced by the adolescent as identity crisis or
identity diffusion, using Erikson's (1956) terms. In the pursuit of
our subject we would conclude that the formation of character presupposes that sexual identity formation has advanced along a narrow-
ing path, leading to masculinity or femininity.

At this juncture, in late adolescence and postadolescence, we can
observe how persistently remnants of the bisexual orientation have
been debarred from genital expression and been absorbed in character formation. The role of the ego ideal, the heir of the negative
oedipus complex (Blos, 1963), so important and decisive at this
turning point of late adolescence, can only be hinted at because the
pursuit of it, relevant as it might be, exceeds the limits of this
exposition.

The Genealogy of Character

The four preconditions which I have outlined rest on antecedents that reach back into the earliest history of individual life.
We have good reason to assume that, beyond these experiential
aspects, there are also embedded in the character structure components that hark back to biological givens. It follows from this
view that adolescent character formation is affected, adversely or
beneficially, by constitutional conditions as well as by infantile
antecedents and their lifelong effect on psychic structure and conflict. The characterological stabilization of drive and ego vicissitudes
is not, however, identical with character. The four, by no means

definitive, preconditions must be transcended in some fashion before the homeostatic function of this new formation that we then call character is regulated. The credentials of character are to be found in the postadolescent developmental level which, if attained, renders character formation possible; in other words, character formation reflects the structural accommodations which have brought the adolescent process to a close. The extent to which the four preconditions have been fulfilled, or the extent to which the four developmental challenges have been met, will determine the autonomous or defensive nature of the character that ensues. With the termination of childhood during the pubertal period, adult somatic structure and functioning are reached; this attainment has its psychological counterpart in the consolidation of the personality or in the formation of character.

It must have become clear during this presentation that in talking about character, one is constantly tempted to speak of healthy or pathological character formation. I have not offered in my schema any explicit accommodation of the so-called character disturbances, character disorders, or the vast spectrum of the pathological character. Proceeding from clinical observation of adolescents and on the basis of analytic data, I have arrived at conclusions and formulations which I have submitted. These have to be brought into harmony with observations of similar substance but derived from other characterological phenomena and from other periods of life. This lies beyond the scope of my present investigation.

The Evolutionary Aspect of Character

I realize with apprehension that I have not heeded my initial admonition too well and have burdened this presentation with a vast array of theoretical concerns. This is the risk one runs in discussing character formation. There remains, however, still one further comment on this subject to which I shall now turn.

I have approached character formation as a corollary to drive and ego maturation at the stage of puberty. In doing so I have lifted it out of its ontogenetic matrix and assigned to it a function that is commensurate with the concurrent biological, namely, sexual, ma-

turation and the morphological attainment of adult status. Each
stage of maturation increases the complexity of the psychic organization. Character reflects on the level of personality development the
attainment of the highest form of physical structure formation and
functioning. References, explicit or implicit, to the complex structure and function of character can be found in the analytic literature
that attributes to character a holistic, integrative principle of various
designations: the synthesizing function of the ego, fitting together
(Hartmann), identity formation, organizing principle, consolidation
process, the self, the whole person, etc. All these connotations have
in common the subjective experience that one's character is identical
with one's self. Psychic life cannot be conceived without it, just
as physical life is inconceivable without one's body. One feels at
home in one's character, or *mutatis mutandis* one's character is one's
home and is, indeed, a dependable and reliable protector of the self.
One accepts a shortcoming of one's character the way one accepts a
physical imperfection. One does not like it, but there it is. When
Lawrence Durrell was asked whether he is aware of any specific weakness as a writer, he gave the following answer: "My great weaknesses
come from my character, not from lack of talent; I am hasty, rash,
impulsive at moments when I should be timid, reserved and objective, and vice versa. My prose and poetry clearly show this weakness" (*Réalités*, April, 1961). We cannot fail to detect in this statement a note of pride for possessing the courage to accept one's
weakness. A comment by Lichtenstein (1965) is pertinent to this
observation: "Insofar as we are perceiving such an invariant as a
characteristic of our own inner world (Hartmann), we tend to refer
to it as the *experience* (Erlebnis) of our Self" (p. 119). Character
formation establishes new invariants in the psychic life, and thus
heightens and stabilizes the experience of the self. This, essentially
identical, experience was derived in childhood from the invariants
—reliability and sameness—of the environment.

Character structure renders the psychic organism less vulnerable
than it had ever been before, and the maintenance of this structure
is secured against any interference from any quarter, internal or
external. If must be, one dies for it before letting it die. The over-
valuation of one's own character makes it apparent that character

formation is cathected with narcissistic libido and that narcissistic gratification is a legitimate gain derived from the exercise of character.

I am aware that I have spoken above in anthropomorphic metaphor instead of psychological concepts. This I shall correct by pointing out that the four preconditions are essentially a forward step in internalization and consequently in a furtherance of independence from the environment. A higher level of integration is thereby reached which contains new homeostatic possibilities. In this sense we can say, applying the genetic point of view, that the utter dependence of the human infant on environmental, protective stability has achieved in character formation its contraposition, namely, the internalization of a stable, protective environment. While content and pattern of character are socially determined, it is only internalization that renders the psychic organism greatly independent from those forces that brought it into existence. While character structure is of a most durable and irreversible kind, only a degree of openness and flexibility assures its enrichment and modulation during adult life.

The evolutionary aspect of character formation lies in the internalization of dependencies and the formation of a progressively complex psychic structure. The function of character lies in the maintenance of this psychic structure that is self-regulatory, namely, automatized, and thus reduces the infliction of psychic injury to a minimum. It goes without saying that the level of psychic organization thus achieved facilitates the unfolding of man's boundless potentialities.

In character formation we observe, on the ontogenetic level of personality development, an evolutionary principle that has its parallel, on the phylogenetic level, in advancing independence of the organism from the conditions of its environment. This evolution has reached its apex in man. Claude Bernard (1859) has expressed this principle by saying that "The constancy of the internal environment is the condition of the free life." In this sense, we can view character formation in an evolutionary perspective and contemplate it as a closed system that, through its operation, maintains its adaptive function, which is to facilitate the creative use of the human potentiality. The processes of internalization and automatization in character formation establish and stabilize the psychic internal milieu, thus enabling man to shape his environment, singly and collectively, by impressing on it those conditions that correspond most favorably with the inviolability and integrity of his personality.

BIBLIOGRAPHY

Abraham, K. (1921), Contributions to the Theory of the Anal Character. In: *Selected Papers on Psycho-Analysis.* London: Hogarth Press, 1927, pp. 370-392.
—— (1924), The Influence of Oral Erotism on Character-Formation. In: *Selected Papers on Psycho-Analysis.* London: Hogarth Press, 1927, pp. 393-406.
—— (1925), Character-Formation on the Genital Level of Libido. In: *Selected Papers on Psycho-Analysis.* London: Hogarth Press, 1927, pp. 407-417.
Blos, P. (1962), *On Adolescence: A Psychoanalytic Interpretation.* New York: Free Press of Glencoe.
—— (1963), The Concept of Acting Out in Relation to the Adolescent Process. *J. Amer. Acad. Child Psychiat.,* 2:118-136.
—— (1967), The Second Individuation Process of Adolescence. *This Annual,* 22:162-186.
Erikson, E. H. (1946), Ego Development and Historical Change. *This Annual,* 2:359-396.
—— (1956), The Problem of Ego Identity. *J. Amer. Psa. Assn.,* 4:56-121.
Fenichel, O. (1945), *The Psychoanalytic Theory of Neurosis.* New York: Norton.
Freud, A. (1936), *The Ego and the Mechanisms of Defense.* New York: International Universities Press, rev. ed., 1966.
—— (1958), Adolescence. *This Annual,* 13:255-278.
Freud, S. (1908), Character and Anal Erotism. *Standard Edition,* 9:167-175. London: Hogarth Press, 1959.
—— (1913), The Disposition to Obsessional Neurosis. *Standard Edition,* 12:311-326. London: Hogarth Press, 1958.
—— (1931), Libidinal Types. *Standard Edition,* 21:215-220. London: Hogarth Press, 1961.
—— (1939), Moses and Monotheism. *Standard Edition,* 23:3-137. London: Hogarth Press, 1964.
Gitelson, M. (1948), Character Synthesis: The Psychotherapeutic Problem of Adolescence. *Amer. J. Orthopsychiat.,* 18:422-431.
Glover, E. (1924), Notes on Oral Character Formation. In: *On the Early Development of Mind.* New York: International Universities Press, 1956, pp. 25-46.
Greenacre, P. (1967), The Influence of Infantile Trauma on Genetic Patterns. In: *Psychic Trauma,* ed. S. S. Furst. New York: Basic Books, pp. 108-153.
Hartmann, H. (1952), The Mutual Influences in the Development of Ego and Id. *This Annual,* 7:9-30.
Inhelder, B. & Piaget, J. (1958), *The Growth of Logical Thinking.* New York: Basic Books.
Jones, E. (1918), Anal-Erotic Character Traits. In: *Papers on Psycho-Analysis.* Baltimore: Williams & Wilkins, 5th ed., 1948, pp. 413-437.
Lampl-de Groot, J. (1963), Symptom Formation and Character Formation. *Int. J. Psa.,* 44:1-11.
Lichtenstein, H. (1965), Towards a Metapsychological Definition of the Concept of Self. *Int. J. Psa.,* 46:117-128.
Reich, A. (1958), A Character Formation Representing the Integration of Unusual Conflict Solutions into the Ego Structure. *This Annual,* 13:309-323.

Reich, W. (1928), On Character Analysis. In: *The Psychoanalytic Reader,* ed. R. Fliess. New York: International Universities Press, 1948, pp. 129-147.

—— (1929), The Genital Character and the Neurotic Character. In: *The Psychoanalytic Reader,* ed. R. Fliess. New York: International Universities Press, 1948, pp. 148-169.

—— (1930), Character Formation and the Phobias of Childhood. In: *The Psychoanalytic Reader,* ed. R. Fliess. New York: International Universities Press, 1948, pp. 170-182.

Zetzel, E. R. (1964), Symptom Formation and Character Formation. *Int. J. Psa.,* 45:151-154.

PARALLEL AND DIVERGENT PATTERNS
IN BLIND AND SIGHTED INFANTS

SELMA FRAIBERG (Ann Arbor, Mich.)

I

Through studies of infants blind from birth we are attempting to explore certain psychoanalytic problems in early ego development which can be isolated through the study of a visual deficit.

In any consideration of the ego's adaptive functions we assume intactness of the biological equipment and a human environment that provides at least minimal conditions for adaptive functioning in the human infant. The apparatuses that serve perception, motility, and vocalization play a primary role in the earliest adaptive behavior of the infant (Hartmann, 1939). Long before we can speak of an ego in the sense of personality organization we can speak of adaptation on a sensorimotor level. As an ego, properly speaking, emerges from an undifferentiated state, these apparatuses remain central in the organization "ego" and, in a certain sense, as Hartmann points out, they constitute the rudiments of the ego at birth. The biological equipment, then, constitutes the infant's state of adaptive readiness.

On the environmental side we have compelling evidence that certain minimal conditions in nurture must be provided during the early formative period of ego development in order to insure adaptive capacity in the infant and to bring about ego organization. From the studies of infants reared in institutions and pathological homes

Supported by the National Institutes of Child Development and Health, Grant # HD01-444-02, by the Earhardt Foundation, and by the General Research Fund of the Department of Psychiatry, University of Michigan Medical School.

I am deeply indebted to colleagues in the Child Development Project who have participated in the primary research and the evaluation of data: Dr. Marguerite Smith, Dr. Ralph Gibson, Mrs. Edna Adelson, Mr. Morton Chethik, Dr. Barry Siegel, Dr. Eric Lenneberg, and Mrs. Barbara Wasylenki.

Professor of Child Psychoanalysis, Department of Psychiatry, University of Michigan Medical School, Ann Arbor, Michigan.

we have learned that the deprivation of human partners and human love will result in marked impairment of adaptive capacity and the self-regulatory functions of the ego. In cases of the most extreme deprivation there will be developmental arrest and deterioration of functioning regardless of the constitutional adequacy of these children at birth. The findings among a large group of studies tell us that intactness of the biological equipment affords minimal guarantees for adaptive functioning when the environment can provide only the minimal guarantees for attachment to human partners.

The study of infants with sensory or motor deficits can tell us another part of the story. In the case of the blind babies on whom I shall report here, we can study the process of early ego development when one of the systems that serve the organization of experience is absent. The study of the deficit will also tell us, of course, about the role of vision in the development of intact infants.

II

The Sample

The data which are summarized in this report are derived from a study of eight babies (five boys and three girls), the youngest of whom is now eighteen months and the oldest six years. (This group includes one child who was studied in New Orleans [see Fraiberg and Freedman, 1964].) So far as possible, we have brought babies into the study as soon after birth as possible, but the actual age at the point of referral has ranged from three days to six months. Within the range of medical certainty we do not accept babies for the longitudinal study who have any other deficits in the sensory or motor spheres or in whom any suspicion of neurological damage exists. Again, within the range of medical certainty, we have selected *babies who are totally blind from birth or who have light perception only.*

Our sample, then, is highly selective and our findings cannot be generalized for a blind infant population. (In a typical blind child population we will have children with a range of useful vision who are still legally classified as "blind," and we will have a high incidence of multiple handicaps and neurological damage.) Our babies, then, are advantaged in a blind child population by the intactness of other systems and are disadvantaged as a group by having no pattern vision. These restrictive criteria have given us a small population even under the circumstances in which we worked within a major medical center. With the cooperation of the Department of Ophthalmology and the Department of Pediatrics of the University of Michigan Medical School our screening and referral processes were highly efficient. Between March, 1964 and January, 1968 we had available to us all blind babies admitted for outpatient or inpatient service at our hospital who satisfied these restrictive criteria. A total of ten babies have been followed to date. Since two of the babies are under six months of age at the time of this writing, I have selected for this report data on the eight babies who have passed the eighteen-month mark.

It is important to note that we have provided a concurrent educational and guidance service for all babies in the research program. We know that the early development of blind babies is perilous. In a blind child population we see a very high incidence of deviant and nondifferentiated personalities and arrested ego development, even when we exclude cases of brain damage and multiple handicaps which are also common in this population. As our own research progressed, we were able to link certain developmental roadblocks with a clinical picture seen in the older blind child (Fraiberg and Freedman, 1964). Very briefly, we now know that not blindness alone but tactile-auditory insufficiency in the early months will prevent the blind baby from making the vital attachments to his mother and to the human world. We must insure adequacy in this area through our work with the parents. We now know that adaptive hand behavior follows a very different pattern in the blind infant and the hands must be educated in special ways. We know that certain gross motor achievements are impeded by the absence of vision and we know how to facilitate these achievements. We know that the blind baby remains helpless and defenseless before the most ordinary dangers of early childhood and we can introduce prophylactic and remedial measures which build adaptive capacity. In short, we have studied the unique adaptive problems of the blind infant in our research and translated these findings into educational measures for the blind baby.

In doing this we have certainly altered our field in this investigation. But no benefits to the research could have justified withholding this knowledge. We have reason to believe that our counseling and educational work have been highly effective in promoting the development of our blind babies. We can, for example, compare our babies with a group of blind babies who have not had special measures introduced into their rearing. These are the babies who are brought to us for consultation or psychological evaluation and who, for geographic reasons or age at the time of referral are not suitable for the longitudinal study. These children, too, have informed us very largely about the developmental hazards for a blind infant.

What we can say, then, is that the observations in this report are derived from a group of healthy, otherwise intact blind infants; their families represent a good range of socioeconomic conditions; their mothers are at least adequate and in three cases would be rated as superior; and the development of these babies has probably been favored by our intervention.

Areas of Study

Our longitudinal study covers these areas of development: human object relations; behavior toward inanimate objects, toys; feeding; sleep; affectivity; language; gross motor development; prehension; self-stimulating behaviors; object permanence.

Observational Procedures

Observers: Each baby is assigned to a team of two observers. The primary responsibility for observation is placed in a senior professional staff member who is present at each visit. Of the six staff members who have participated in this phase of the investigation, three are psychoanalysts (including the project director) and three are clinical psychologists. (Graduate or undergraduate students in psychology are sometimes employed as assistant observers as part of our training program for students. In other cases a second senior staff member sits in as "assistant observer.")

By placing the primary responsibility for observation in our senior professional staff we have insured as far as possible a high degree of sensitivity and clinical judgment in the work of data collection.

Methods: The baby is visited in his home at twice monthly intervals. (We travel within a radius of 100 miles to cover our home visits.) We try to time our visits to coincide with a morning or afternoon waking period and to fit our observations into the normal routine of that period. Nearly all of the data required for our study can be obtained through observing a feeding, a bath, a playtime with mother, a diapering or clothes changing, and a period of self-occupation with or without toys. A small amount of time in each session may be employed for testing procedures by the examiner in the areas of prehension and object concept.

The observation period begins with an informal session with the mother in which we obtain her picture of the baby's development in the two-week interval and communications regarding her concerns for the baby, her pleasure in a new achievement. Her selection of material to report to us as well as qualitative aspects of her mothering enter into the recording. The mother's report is recorded in a detailed narrative. During this period the second observer is recording the baby's activity in his crib or play table at a time when his mother is not interacting with him; often he may be in another room.

We then begin to follow the baby in certain typical routines of this waking period as described above. The observers record a continuous narrative with descriptive detail. To insure coverage of all items which must be gathered for comparative developmental study, the observers have memorized our coding schedule with particular reference to the developmental period under study in this observational session. We do not use a "checklist" as such. This would defeat our objectives in observation. We do not follow any specific order or sequence in data collection except for formal testing procedures.

This method allows us to cover the qualitative aspects of the baby's behavior and the mother-child interaction through a descriptive narrative, and to obtain statistical data for comparison within the group and for comparison with sighted developmental norms. I have found that the method allows me maximum freedom to observe without constriction, to be open to novelty and surprise, yet assures uniform data collection where this serves the purposes of the investigation. With experience, I found that I could cover nearly all the items needed for statistical coverage without disturbing the baby's routines and without imposing a formal pattern on the observational session.

At monthly or twice monthly intervals (depending upon age of the child) we record film samples of behavior in the areas of mother-child interaction in feeding or play, prehension, gross motor achievements, self-occupation. The photographing *does* impose a degree of artificiality on the observational session and we try to keep this within the minimum required for useful documentation and study (approximately 450 feet of film per month or a total of 15 minutes of film recording per month).

The film record is reviewed on a variable speed projector at the scheduled case review of each baby with all staff members present. The film record has proved indispensable for certain areas of our study. In the study of prehension, for example, the patterns of adaptive hand behavior in the blind infant were entirely new to the professional student of child development who had been trained in observation of sighted infants. We needed to draw inferences from subtle, fleeting hand and finger movements which could be obtained only through slow-motion study.

The cinema record serves data collection in two other ways: (1) the film itself is available for repeated study and comparison; (2) a recorded narrative of each film is transcribed and the protocol that results is entered into the baby's record as a separate document. The transcript is obtained as follows: As the film is reviewed at one-third normal speed, with all staff members present, the senior investigator of the baby's research team records on a dictaphone a complete narrative of the film sequence in fine detail. Where there is any disagreement among the viewers regarding a specific detail, the disputed film sequence is run over again until there is agreement. The transcribed narrative of the film becomes a flexible document which serves the retrieval of any items of information recorded on film and as source material for coding and evaluation.

Our guidance program becomes a third source of information in following the baby's development. In principle, we try to separate the research visits and personnel from the guidance visits. Since all the senior investigators in the research are also trained clinicians we try to assign staff ourselves so that X, who is senior researcher on teams (a), (b), and (c), serves as guidance worker for a family covered by team (d). However, in two instances it has been necessary for the educational work to be carried on by one of the team members (usually in separate visits to the home).

The number of guidance visits per month to each family varies with the needs of the baby and his family. Typically, there may be one to four regularly scheduled visits per month. We do not provide psychotherapy for our families. We consider ourselves consultants to the families on problems of rearing a blind infant and young child and our work can be described as "education."

The observations of the guidance worker augment the data of the observational sessions in vital areas. In the relative privacy of the home interview, the mother is free to talk about her relationship to the baby, her own reactions, her own concerns. If the baby is present for part of the time, there are additional observations of mother-baby interaction to augment our baby records. Sometimes the father joins these sessions. On other occasions we may schedule a private session for the father alone. The effects of a blind baby on his parents and his siblings can be read through the guidance record. The subtleties in parent-child interaction appear in the clinical records of these visits.

Testing Procedures

Developmental tests: Since there are no developmental tests standardized for our population (infants totally blind from birth, infants with light perception only) and no reliable instruments for the general blind infant population, our use of developmental tests is qualified and conservative. We use modified items from the Cattell, the Griffiths, the Vineland Social Maturity Scale, and the Maxfield-Buckholz Scale of Social Maturity for use with Preschool Blind Children for obtaining a profile of development. In general, we can have more confidence in the assessment when the child shows a consistent performance in the average to superior range and when there is harmony in the developmental test profile in all sectors of development. With all these qualifications the developmental tests have usefulness as a structured observational setup, for comparing babies within our sample in each sector of development, and for comparison of our babies with sighted babies in certain sectors of development with particular reference to nonvisual experience.

Out of our own experience at the Child Development Project we find that our testing procedures for the study of adaptive hand behavior in the blind infant are yielding criteria which permit us to compare babies within our sample in this crucial area during the sensorimotor period. A full description of these procedures will be reported in future publications.

Evaluation of Data (Coding Procedures)

The indexing and tabulation of data are performed by student assistants under the supervision of a senior staff member. A rigorous training in the use of our code schedule is a prerequisite for this work. Frequent cross-checks are made to insure agreement and the use of standard criteria among the coders. Questions of judgment in coding are referred to senior staff members.

The organization of data begins with the detailed descriptive records. Assistants read the protocol and classify the data into the major categories of our study by means of marginal symbols. In the tabulation of data the categories are further broken down into subdivisions following the code schedule. This, of course, enables us to make comparisons within age periods of each of our babies in each sector of development.

The statistical data give us a short-hand summary which serves certain purposes of the investigation. At the same time each item tabulated in code must have a cross-reference by page and line to the original protocol so that the descriptive and qualitative aspects of the behavior studied can be given separate treatment.

In many areas of the study the detailed analysis of the descriptive material has greater significance than a statistical summary. For example, while it is useful to know that x number of cases showed clear discrimination of mother and stranger between the ages of six and eight months, it is more important for the purposes of our study to know *how* the blind baby made these distinctions, what information he employed in discrimination, what specific affective expression was manifest. For this information we need to consult the detailed protocol.

III

Development of Object Relations

We have strong evidence in the study of human infancy that the healthy, sighted baby establishes his capacity for libidinal object ties during the first eighteen months of life. From the maternal deprivation studies we know that the absence of human partners or a rupture in the early love ties will produce permanent effects in the capacity to form enduring bonds in later life.

To a very large extent, the establishment of libidinal object relations in infancy utilizes visual experience. From the third month on, the baby responds to the visual configuration of the human face through smiling. The smile undergoes a progressive course of differentiation during the first year and becomes, increasingly, a selective smile for the mother and other significant figures in the child's environment, which means, of course, that the unique characteristics of this face or that face are gradually selected from the sea of human faces and recognition memory is established. We know from the maternal deprivation studies that if a child does not have human partners who give emotional import to this visual experience, there will be a marked delay in the visual discrimination of faces (Provence and Lipton, 1962). By the time a sighted baby has reached the middle of the first year, he will demonstrate his attachment to his mother, his father, and other special persons. At the sight of their faces he becomes joyful and excited, he makes greeting noises, and he shows special gestures of affection. When these faces disappear from his field of vision, he is equally noisy in his complaints and his grief. When confronted with strange faces he will no longer produce his indiscriminate smile. He will look solemn or quizzical or may even set up a howl. Somewhere in the second year, possibly earlier, the indelible tracing of these faces can be evoked by memory itself, independent of the visual presentation and perception of these pictures. The storage and evocation of these picture memories are the final achievements of this period of sensorimotor intelligence.

When I now summarize our findings on the human object relations of eight blind babies, I should stress again that we have provided educational guidance for the parents of our babies and that for this reason the findings should not be regarded as characteristic of all blind infants. Because our guidance has probably influenced the generally favorable picture in human object relations at the end of the first year, our intervention should be described as a component of the picture.

Typically the blind baby is "a very quiet baby" during the early weeks of life, as our mothers reported to us and we ourselves could verify. The danger for the blind child is that he can live for a perilously long time in something like a void. We helped the mother to see that the baby needed physical closeness through holding, that he needed to be talked to, played with, placed in the center of family activity during his waking hours. He needed more stimulation from his environment than a sighted child normally does. This does not mean, of course, "overstimulation" but a qualitatively rich and varied experience with his human partners to give pleasure and meaning to his waking hours. As the baby began to respond to his human partners, we saw, in each case, how response began to elicit a "dialogue" (in Spitz's terms [1963]) between the baby and his partners.

We had a wide range of adequacy in mothering within our group of blind babies. At one end of the scale were two depressed mothers; at the other end of the scale three experienced and highly intuitive mothers. We have reason to believe that even in the case of two depressed mothers we were able to insure a kind of "minimum adequacy" in nurture and stimulation as demonstrated by the good performance of these two babies on objective tests.

When we speak of "adequacy" in the human environments of our eight babies, we mean simply that the experience provided these babies in a wide range of homes afforded at least the essential nutriments for development during the sensorimotor period as demonstrated by the baby's performance at the end of the first year. In addition to criteria employed in assessing human object relations (described later), seven of the eight babies were within the average to superior range for blind children, and our confidence in the assessment is supported by the general picture of harmony in the developmental test profile and consistent gains. As still another criterion of "adequacy" in environmental stimulation we offer our observations on the sleep-waking patterns of these children. In any given quarter of the first year of life the distribution of sleeping and waking hours during the twenty-four-hour day approximated that for sighted children. At the end of the first year nearly all of our mothers brought in complaints that the baby disliked his naps and stalled in getting to sleep at night. When we congratulated our mothers, they were surprised.

Each of the blind babies in our longitudinal study has shown a phase-by-phase human attachment during the first year, paralleling in significant ways that of sighted babies. There are qualitative differences which I shall describe later, and these are of great interest to us, but we are impressed to see how, given adequacy in nurture, the first milestones in human attachment are negotiated by each of these babies.

In evaluating the responses of our blind babies to human objects we employed criteria developed for the sighted child by psychoanalytic investigators (Anna Freud, René Spitz, Sally Provence, and others) and adapted the Objectal Scale of Thérèse Gouin Décarie (1965) and items selected by Mary Ainsworth (1963), both of whom employ psychoanalytic criteria for a sequence of differential responses of infants to their human environment. The criteria drawn from these sources were generally in agreement regarding the significant signs of human attachment during the first year of life. When the criteria employed visual stimuli and visual discriminations, we allowed the blind baby to teach us what kinds of sense information he used when he made selective responses to his mother, his father, and other significant persons in his environment, how he differentiated mother and stranger, how he reacted to separation from his mother, how he demonstrated affection, joy, need, grief, anger, and the range of human emotion that will normally tell us about the quality of human bonds during the first year of life.

The blind baby can demonstrate a clear response smile to the sound of his mother's voice in the early weeks of life. Our findings show close correspondence with those of Peter Wolff (1963) who has reported that at four weeks of age the sighted baby shows a selective smile to the sound of his mother's voice. This response smile to voice precedes the response smile of the sighted infant to the visual presentation of the human face at six weeks. As early as four weeks our blind Richard demonstrated a response smile to his mother's and father's voices, as we saw clearly in a cinema record of this observation. When I, a stranger, tried repeatedly to elicit a smile through my own voice, there was no smile. When we repeated the experiment several times with the mother's or father's voice, the smile appeared.

In the early months of life, the blind baby shows discomfort in the arms of a stranger. Here, we think, he is using postural cues; even when the investigator tries to employ the same postures in holding that the mother uses, there appear to be subtle differences which register and cause the baby to squirm or to cry. Sighted babies will also react to these postural differences at the same age.

During the first year of life the blind baby shows increasingly selective and well-differentiated responses to his mother, his father, intimate persons, and strangers. In addition to voice cues, the blind baby begins to inform himself through his fingers around five months of age and explores the faces of intimate persons with his hands. Between six and eight months he shows clear preference for his mother when confronted with mother and stranger. In the arms of a stranger he will squirm, stiffen, or protest. Three of our babies (Toni, Kathy, and Richard) reacted with manifest anxiety to the stranger. The smile itself becomes more and more selective in the second half of the first year. Yet, among all of our babies we have few observations of spontaneous smiles in response to the investigators. The smile in greeting, the smile in response to voice or a game appears in relation to the mother, the father, or siblings and clearly connotes selectivity and value—an exclusive sign of affection.

All this, too, compares favorably with the differential responses of sighted babies of the same age, but there are essential differences. Our babies, we know, do not smile as frequently as sighted babies do, and even when we have all the criteria for a mutually satisfying mother-child relationship, the smile strikes us as a muted smile. The joyful, even ecstatic smile that we see in a healthy sighted baby is a comparatively rare occurrence among blind babies. We know that the sighted infant in the early months of life responds to the smiling face with a smile of his own; the smile as visual stimulus evokes a response smile. The contagion of smiling is clearly dependent upon visual experience. But beyond this, we see in our blind infants that smiling is something that must be elicited, induced through interaction with another person, and it is not easily generalized to inanimate objects such as toys. A nine-month-old blind baby, playing on the floor with his assembled toys, may present a picture of absorption, interest, even inquiry, but rarely will the toy or his activity with the toy produce a spontaneous smile. In a fifteen-minute interval we may see nothing more than an impassive face and busy hands.

In the second half of the first year the blind baby can make overt demonstrations of affection. Among sighted babies we consider the child's ability to make affectionate gestures a favorable sign of his taking an active partnership in love. When Richard's mother says, "Give mommy a kiss," our blind Richard opens his mouth and reaches with his mouth to his mother's face. Again this closely parallels the behavior of the sighted child. But there is this difference: at a slightly later age (eight to twelve months) where the sighted baby will initiate affectionate games or hold up his arms in the universal gesture to be picked up or embraced, our blind babies do not. In this respect and in all similar tests of initiative the blind baby does not yet perform. From other evidence in our study we believe that the slowness in initiative is the result of not being able to see the consequences of one's actions, to feel that one is an effector, that one can cause events.

The vocalizing of our blind babies follows in all essential respects that of the sighted child. Since the language sector of development provides sensitive criteria for the evaluation of the baby's interaction with his human environment, it is significant that seven of our eight children followed language norms for sighted children throughout the first year of life. Among our blind babies we have excellent examples of "dialogues" with the mother around the middle of the first year, or "questions and answers" between mother and baby following speech cadences, in a parody of English. Naming of objects falls within the range for sighted children, with this difference: in the second year when we expect to see a rapid acquisition of new words in the child's vocabulary, the blind child lags behind for a period. When he becomes mobile and the range of his explorations brings him in contact with more and more objects, his vocabulary expands and it is our impression and that of Eric Lenneberg who has studied the language achievements of preschool blind children that at the age of three the blind child's vocabulary is within the range for sighted children.

From these descriptions, it is clear that blindness need not be an impediment to the development of libidinal ties. Yet there is one area of human object relations in which the parallels between the blind and sighted children break down. In the second year of life we expect to see in the sighted child some evidence of growing independence from his mother. The sighted child who has strong ties to his mother can also tolerate brief separations from her such as ordinarily occur in the course of a day. A sighted child who clings to his mother and must have proof of her whereabouts for most of his waking hours is a child who is showing more than typical separation anxiety for his age. Yet, as each of our blind children moved into the second year, we saw periods or episodes of desperate clinging to the mother and a panic during actual or anticipated separation for which we could find no true equivalence in a healthy sighted child. Later, I will cite clinical examples of this behavior. This acute separation anxiety appears in children who have shown good overall development and is relatively independent of the quality of the mothering, which in three of our cases would be rated as very superior.

We believe that the severe and sometimes protracted separation anxiety of our blind young children can inform us considerably about the role of vision in forming stable mental representatives.[1] For the blind child in the second year will also tell us through objective tests that he lags behind the sighted child in the construction of an object concept (Piaget, 1937). The blind baby who is reduced to helplessness and panic when he loses his mother will also demonstrate a revealing behavior toward the inanimate object. For most of the second year our blind young children demonstrate that they cannot yet believe in the existence of an object when it leaves their perceptual field. Between sixteen and eighteen months, the sighted child conducts a kind of search for lost objects that tells us that he can believe in the existence of the object when it no longer manifests itself to him, and his ability to carry out a search for the vanished

[1] Here, our data appear to provide confirmation of a hypothesis introduced by Omwake and Solnit (1961) that a mental representation based upon nonvisual experience has less stability than one that is organized through visual experience.

object tells us that he has a mental representation of the object, that he can evoke the memory of the thing lost independent of the visual presentation. This stage in the development of the object concept is called "permanence" by Piaget. In the case of human object relations psychoanalysis employs the term "object constancy" to embrace both the libidinal investment of the mother and a mental representation of the mother. The sighted child in the second year has a mental representation of the mother which aids him in adapting to the brief separations of a normal day. The blind child, who is delayed at least a year in developing a concept of permanence, is reduced to helplessness and panic when he cannot verify the existence of his mother.

We see, then, that under the most favorable circumstances and adequacy in mothering, blindness need not be an impediment to the establishment of libidinal object ties in the first year of life. But the stability of these ties, and hence the stability of the early ego organization, can be imperiled through the prolongation of infantile dependency and helplessness and the limited adaptive solutions open to a blind child.

Yet, if we have demonstrated that the blind baby in the first year makes the vital human connections in ways that parallel those of the sighted child, we are confronted with the implications of such an achievement. For while it is true that everything that goes into human attachment in sighted infants is predicated upon the role of vision, the blind child informs us of the degree to which *nonvisual* experience can enter into the attachment. It is very likely, it seems to us, that what we see as a sequence of visual recognitory experiences which establish the identity of "mother," for example, is a progressive synthesis of visual-auditory-tactile experience in which the picture unites all sensory data. The term "synesthesia" is exact here, and should be rescued from usage as exotic sense experience and brought back within the framework of developmental psychology, as Heinz Werner (1948) attempted to do some years ago.

Motor Development

The study of gross and fine motor development in the blind infant has provided valuable insights into the role of vision in facilitating maturational patterns. During the first eight or nine months of life, the gross motor achievements of our blind babies follow a maturational pattern and timetable that closely parallel those of the sighted child. The elevation of the head in prone position, rolling over, sitting independently, appear without significant delay. This tells us, of course, that these motor achievements are relatively independent of vision.

Then, in the last quarter of the first year, each of our babies reached a developmental impasse. In spite of demonstrated postural readiness for creeping, at a point where the baby can support himself well on hands and knees, the blind baby is unable to creep. Thus, in one of our film documentaries, we saw Robbie, the acrobat of our group, balancing himself on hands and knees, then poised beautifully with one leg extended in mid-air—yet unable to move forward. The examiner placed a favorite sound-making toy within easy reach. Robbie was attentive to its sound, but made no gesture of reach. Between nine and eleven months Robbie maintained an easy posture on hands and knees, rocking himself back and forth, the apparatus energized but unable to perform. No incentive provided by the environment or through experimental testing could yet bring this intelligent and healthy blind baby to creep. At eleven months of age Robbie demonstrated for the first time his ability to locate, reach for, and attain a bell on sound cue. Three days later he began to creep. In the next observational session we recorded a sequence on film in which a bell was rung a few feet away from Robbie who was sitting on the floor. Robbie immediately got into creeping position and took a direct, linear route to the bell. He retrieved it expertly, turned over on his back with a huge smile on his face, and kicked his feet with joy.

The developmental impasse which I described in Robbie appeared in each of our blind babies. In general the retrospective histories of blind children support our findings that there is a marked lag in the achievement of creeping, and that, in fact, many blind babies do not creep at all. For all blind children the achievement of independent walking is markedly delayed.

Why shouldn't the blind baby propel himself forward? For a while we could only come up with half the answer. If we reconstruct the beginning of creeping in the sighted child, we obtain this picture: at the time the sighted baby has learned to support himself on hands and knees he is also expert in reaching and attaining an object on sight. That reaching for the out-of-range object propels him forward and the early creeping pattern looks something like this: a reach and a collapse, a reach and a collapse, a pattern which gradually smooths out and becomes the motor pattern for creeping.

Clearly for the blind baby with motor maturational readiness for creeping, there was no stimulus for reaching. But why should not an attractive sound-making object substitute for the visual stimulus of reaching?

While we were puzzling out this problem, another part of the story was emerging from our study of prehension in the blind baby and our study of the adaptive substitution of sound for vision.

At approximately five months of age the sighted infant can reach for and attain an object "on sight." Everything that we know about this achievement is predicated upon the role of vision. Our study of prehension in the totally blind infant has given us important information regarding maturational patterns and the role of vision in facilitating adaptive hand behavior.

We are impressed to see with each of our blind babies that the grasping *mode*, for example, follows the maturational timetable for sighted children. If we use two ten-month criteria to summarize, we can demonstrate that a full-term blind baby employs pincer grasping when he makes contact with a test cube and that he uses his index finger to explore the hole of a pegboard. By contrast with a sighted baby, the grasp is awkward and uncertain in the blind baby, but the pattern has emerged.

We were puzzled, however, to see in the early stages of our work that our totally blind babies did not spontaneously bring the hands together at midline. Typically, the blind infant maintains his hands at rest at shoulder height in a neonatal posture. Many blind children retain this posture at later stages of childhood. Sustained mutual fingering at midline, which is seen in the sighted child at sixteen weeks, was not observed in our totally blind babies. If the blind baby's hands made a *chance* encounter with each other, there might be fingering, but there appeared to be no pleasure bonus for the blind infant, and the chance encounter of the two hands did not lead to voluntary repetition of the act, which is essential for the finger game. Yet one of our babies who had light perception in one eye played the finger game by bringing his hands very close to that eye, producing for himself a kind of shadow game.[2] There is good reason to believe, then, that the mutual fingering game and the organization of the hands at midline are largely facilitated by vision, and that the tactile encounter and engagement of the fingers requires the simultaneous visual experience to insure its pleasurable repetition.

For the sighted child, the finger game at midline is one of a number of activities in which the hands are brought into the visual field. Sustained hand regard and an alternation of hand regard and visual fixation of an object facilitate the coordination of vision and prehension and prepare for intentional reaching in the subsequent stage.

If we compare our blind babies and sighted babies at five months of age, we find that there is no behavior in the blind infant that is equivalent to "reaching and attaining an object on sight." *There is no adaptive substitution of sound for vision at this age.*

At five months if we experimentally introduce a sound object within easy reach of the blind baby's hand, the characteristic behavior is alertness and attention; but there is no gesture of reaching and no swiping in the direction of the sound. The hands remain motionless. In film study, when we slow down the projector to about one-third normal speed, we can see that, typically, there is not even a fleeting activation of the fingers in response to the sound. If we introduce a favorite rattle or a cherished musical toy, or if we jingle the bell on his cradle gym a few seconds after the baby himself has set the trapeze in motion and heard the bell, we will not elicit any behavior that tells us that the sound connotes a thing that can be grasped!

During the same period, however, there occurs another behavior which is promising. If a toy, a sound-making toy or a soundless toy, is removed experimentally from the baby's hands, he will sometimes make a fleeting gesture of pursuit. This is not an intentional reach; he has no directional cues for recovery of the object; he is actually producing the motor pattern which is induced as an object is pulled away from his grasp and the resistant arm is extended forward. But

2 Described also by D. G. Freedman (1964) in an infant with congenital cataracts.

even this involuntary behavior will assist the baby in the next stage of his development because if he acquires the motor pattern for reaching, he will begin to make accidental contact with objects and will even begin a kind of random search for objects in the six-to-eight-month period.

The beginnings of search in the six-to-eight-month period are dictated by certain requirements. If a toy has been removed from the baby's grasp and placed on the playtable, the baby will now explore the table surface. It does not yet matter whether the toy is a sound object or a soundless object. The only requirement is immediately *prior manual tactile experience of the object.* This behavior tells us that the baby has begun to attribute some kind of substantiality to classes of objects which have been previously grasped, "tactile objects," so to speak, and that he has learned that the surface of his playtable is "a place" where things can be found and re-experienced through grasping. But again, if we squeak his favorite bed toy, and place it on his tray, and if he has *not* had an immediately antecedent tactile experience with that toy, he will make no search. Typically, there is no gesture of reaching, and the hands are not activated in any way by the sound of the toy.

We begin to see the adaptive problem for the blind baby. First of all, the absence of vision becomes a major impediment to localizing sound and obtaining directional cues for the source of sound. As early as the second month of life, the sighted child turns toward the source of sound with the "expectation" that the sound will produce a visual experience. The blind baby in the early months of life has no information that can help him place sound or organize sounds into a meaningful experience. Second, we see that sound alone does not confer substantiality to an object at this phase of development. Before the blind baby is able to achieve a direct reach on sound cue alone he must solve a conceptual problem. When he hears the sound of his favorite musical toy "out there," the sound must connote a thing which has certain tactile and acoustical properties which constitute its identity and its wholeness. It cannot be one thing when he is grasping it, and another thing when it only manifests a familiar sound. And as we watch the blind baby during the period approximately eight to ten months we begin to see the idea emerge.

We are now able to predict when a baby is getting ready to reach on sound cue alone. At the sound of a bell, or rattle, or favorite sound toy, the baby's fingers begin to move. Sometimes there is only a fluttering of the fingers, sometimes a grasping, ungrasping motion of the hands, which tells us that the "graspability" of the object is beginning to register when the sound is heard. The baby does not yet reach toward the source of sound; he may not even make a swiping motion toward it. But we can predict that within a few weeks he will coordinate reaching, grasping, and directional cues on sound which will lead him to his first success in attaining an object on sound cue.

When does the blind baby give his first demonstration of reaching on sound cue alone? The range for eight babies is 6 months, 21 days to 11 months, 20 days, with six of the babies in the range of 9 months, 18 days to 11 months, 27 days (see Table I).

TABLE I

Age of Attaining an Object on Sound Cue Alone

Lawrence	6 months 21 days
Richard	7 months 0 days
Cathy	9 months 18 days
Toni	10 months 3 days
Keith	10 months 26 days
Robby	11 months 7 days
Sally	11 months 20 days
Jack	11 months 27 days

It should be mentioned that we credited the baby with a success if he gave only *one* demonstration of successful attainment on sound cue alone during a one-and-a-half-hour observational session. The number of trials afforded in the test situation alone might run as high as twenty to thirty using a variety of toys and objects. The only limitation in number of trials was the baby's tolerance. Here, of course, we were not following standard testing procedure in scoring since our investigation is concerned only with the problem "How does the blind baby solve the problem for the first time?" But if we wish to compare these findings in "acoustically directed prehension in the blind child" with "visually directed prehension in the sighted child," it should be noted that these first achievements in reaching on sound cue alone are by no means equivalent to the demonstrations required in standard testing procedure for the sighted child. The number of trials and the single demonstration in the case of our blind babies would actually correspond to the very early stages of visually directed prehension, *under* five months, when a sighted baby swiping at an object within range makes a first lucky contact with the object, grasps it, and brings it to his mouth. Between five and six months the sighted baby can "reach on sight" with a high degree of success on every trial.

We can see then that a blind baby traverses a long and difficult route to get to a point where the hand can locate and attain objects and serve as the vital bridge between the self and outer world. Where vision guarantees adaptive hand behavior, the visual deficit requires a complex adaptive solution. From the clinical evidence, this is a perilous route. Some blind babies never find the adaptive solution and these children will be found in every population of blind children. These are the blind children who have "blind hands," hands that do not explore objects, hands that serve primarily to bring objects to the mouth for sucking, hands that are maintained in infantile postures, with inutile, bizarre fingering, all of which testifies to the failure of the hands to attain and to find meaning in experience.

For a dangerously long period in the first eight months of life, the blind baby's hands can give him only a small part of the information he needs for learning about his world, and his hands during this period do not serve intentionality or as executive organs of the personality. Compared to the sighted child, the blind baby lives in a sensory void in which things happen to him, sounds occur around him, objects emerge from the void and make accidental contact with his hands, or the hands in random movements make accidental contact with objects. Because these hands give him impoverished information about a world beyond his own body, there is the danger that in this early period of ego formation the personality may remain centered in body sensations and appetites, and that the bridge between the body and an external world may be unstable or may not be found at all.

If we now return to the problem raised at the beginning of this section, it becomes clear that *the blind baby's delay in locomotion which raised such important questions is actually linked to a problem in prehension and to the circuitous route that leads a blind baby to locate an object on sound cue alone and to reach for and attain an object.*

We can test this further through one of our educational interventions. If we have a blind baby who has attained the posture for creeping (i.e., supporting himself ably on hands and knees) and if that baby has begun to demonstrate his ability to reach for and attain an object on sound cue alone, we can initiate the creeping pattern by placing a desirable sound object just beyond his reach on the floor. At this point the sound stimulus will substitute for a visual stimulus as an incentive to direct linear creeping. Conversely, if we have a baby who can demonstrate the posture for creeping without a demonstration of reaching on sound cue alone, no external stimulus will propel that baby forward. *We have no baby in our series who learned to creep before he gave us a demonstration of reaching on sound cue alone.*

We should emphasize that these findings are valid only for our group of totally blind babies or babies with light perception only. Our observations of babies with only a small amount of useful vision tell us the degree to which vision can be utilized by a baby. These children, still legally blind, tend to follow the developmental patterns for sighted children with some lag in following developmental norms. One case from our own series is instructive. Susan, who was excluded from this report, began to show signs of some useful vision around eight months of age. We were able to follow Susan through the first year. Her visual range at nine months did not exceed her arm's reach and, from our observations, an object visualized at that range was probably not much more than a blurred figure. (When she wanted to examine an object she would bring it close to her eyes.) At just under nine months Susan demonstrated postural readiness for creeping. Without any significant delay, active creeping was recorded by us at nine months and three days.

In our educational work with the mothers of our babies we translated our clinical observations into an education of the blind baby's hands. To encourage midline organization of the hands we employed a number of strategies which would facilitate mutuality, reciprocity, and coordinate use of the hands. We encouraged patty-cake games and other games that insured pleasurable contact of the hands at midline. We encouraged the presentation of toys and interesting objects at midline. Through the device of a playtable with a broad surface and a rail around the edge we created for the blind baby "an interesting space"—for want of a better term. On the table surface we placed attractive toys and objects. The baby's reach at midline or a search of the tray practically guaranteed an encounter with a toy and the grasping of that toy. We have reason to believe that our education of the baby's hands has had a significant effect in facilitating adaptive hand behavior. A comparison between the adaptive hand behavior of the babies in our longitudinal study with that of babies in our "consultation" group in which no special educational measures have been employed shows that our babies are consistently advanced in attaining objects at the end of the first year and in getting information through the fingers.

Adaptation and Defense

By the time a sighted baby enters the second year of life he has moved a long way from the condition of helplessness and total dependence that characterizes the early months of life. From the point of view of simple mechanical mastery of his body and his environment the sighted baby is mobile on all fours and is beginning to take independent steps; he can pursue objects that interest him and attain them within a certain range. He has begun to feed himself. He has a small and useful vocabulary to designate people and things that are desirable to him. If he is frustrated, he can already fight back. (He can, for example, deliver a well-aimed smack to a sneaky sibling who swipes a toy from him.) He knows anger; he knows self-assertiveness. And while it is entirely correct to say that he is dependent upon his mother and dependent upon her love, he is not reduced to total helplessness if his mother should leave the room for a while or go out for the afternoon or evening. The small degree of autonomy which he possesses in the second year gives him a measure of independence. And the ability to act upon his environment provides a kind of defense against danger.

If we turn our attention to the blind child in the second year, we see some parallels and some striking differences. If we make some allowance in the maturational timetable for the handicap of blindness in achieving independent locomotion, we note these parallels: the majority of our blind babies are mobile on all fours or walking with some form of support before the age of fifteen months, with independent walking achieved between seventeen months and two years. Mobility gives the blind baby a great push toward discovery of things and the organization of space. A healthy blind child in the second year will be "into everything," our mothers report with some exasperation. He will track objects through sound and pursue his mother through the house using sound cues. He has begun to feed himself. His vocabulary is within the normal range for sighted children.

Here the parallels between the blind child's achievements and those of the sighted child are impressive. If we describe points of divergence, even in these patterns, we begin to see some of the unique adaptive problems of the blind baby in the second year and the areas of vulnerability in early ego development.

The healthy blind baby can track objects on sound in the second year, but there is a type of pursuit which he cannot demonstrate. He will track an object only to the place where he last heard it. If a toy that he values is soundlessly moved, he will scream with frustration, or flip over in a tantrum on the floor, or switch his attention to something else—but he will not search. The sighted child, from sixteen months on, will conduct a search for the lost object, which means that he can believe that the object must exist someplace, even when he cannot perceive it (Piaget's Stage VI). But we have seen only one blind child between the ages of sixteen months and three years of age who will conduct such a search.[3] Search is futile, for the child of this age, because he cannot deduce the displacements of an object in space. The failure of search leaves the blind child with a temporary handicap in cognitive development; he cannot believe that an object exists when it does not manifest itself to him, and this conceptual problem becomes a temporary barrier to the development of spatial concepts and notions of causality. We have reason to believe that the blind child evolves some kind of stable

3 Not in our series. Reported by David A. Freedman with film documentation.

object concept between the ages of three and five, but we do not yet know how he does it; our children are not yet old enough to teach us.

Apart from the problems in cognitive development which are presented here, we have a correlate in ego development that has important implications. This means, of course, that a blind child lives for a very long time in a world of magic, where people and things manifest themselves by emerging from a void and returning to a void. It means, above all, that the human figures in his environment are also subject to this capricious causality, and that the protectors against danger evaporate in some mysterious way when they do not manifest themselves to the child and reconstitute themselves in some mysterious way when they return. When we consider that even the sighted child reacts with anxiety to prolonged separation from his mother, we are impressed by the vulnerability and helplessness of a blind child whose protectors behave like spirits in a ghost world.

How does the blind young child defend himself against danger? Under any circumstances in which the human protectors are absent in the moment in which he experiences anxiety, or cannot for other reasons defend him, what means does he possess to protect himself or act upon his environment? We have collected a number of clinical examples from our work with blind children in the second year. From these I select a few examples which tell a sobering story of the perils of blindness in childhood and which, in themselves, illuminate some aspects of ego defensive measures in normal development of young children.

In each of the clinical illustrations which I shall present we can see how the condition of helplessness produces transient pathological states in the young blind child. When we now describe the forms of pathology encountered among these children, it is important to stress again that these are children who have been reared under the most favorable circumstances we could provide; they are neurologically intact, the overall development of these children falls within the average to superior range for blind children, and the pathological states that occurred were relatively independent of the quality of mothering. Three of the mothers would be rated by us as superior or very superior in their demonstrated capacity to meet the blind child's needs.

Jack: Diagnosis—retrolental fibroplasia.

At seventeen months Jack, who had been making good strides in development, had a severe setback. Jack's mother was called away suddenly when her father died and she was gone for three days. During that time Jack was in the care of various friends and relatives who helped out in the emergency. Soon after the mother returned Jack showed alarming symptoms and began to regress in nearly all areas of development. He had screaming fits which lasted for hours. Our own observers found them nearly indescribable. These were screams or shouts of a repetitive, chanting character, and were practically unceasing for most of his waking hours. During these attacks the child's face was curiously immobile and expressionless. The repetitive rhythmic pattern in the shouting and the immobile face gave the clinical impression of a tic. When the mother held Jack, there was a brief respite, but at these times he would crawl desperately all over her body as if trying to get as much as possible of his own body surface in touch with his mother's body. This frenzied crawling was as nerve wracking to the mother as the shouting. Meantime, Jack abandoned his toys and showed no interest in games or any of his former activities. He was wakeful for long periods at night. He lost interest in food and after a few mouthfuls would vomit. In short, there was a pathological regression in nearly every sector of development and the ticlike shouts were themselves of a highly pathological type.

This morbid picture persisted for days until the mother sought our help. From our clinical observations we had one clue which we thought we could utilize in helping the baby over this crisis. The ticlike shouting, our observers felt, had a quality of helpless rage. If the observers were right, why was rage discharged through shouting? A sighted child, of this age, even in a tantrum will not only yell but kick the floor or bang with his hands, in which case we could see rage discharged through the skeletal muscles. But with Jack, as with our other babies in the second year, we rarely saw a blind baby who employed the motor patterns of fighting.

We gave the mother a suggestion which was based on our clinical hunch. When Jack begins his shouting, she should provide him with pots and pants or banging toys and encourage him to

pound and bang with his hands and his fists. We asked the mother
to report back to us as soon as possible. Within a few days the mother
called us. The banging games, she said, "worked like magic." The
shouting had stopped and Jack had taken to pounding and banging
with an enthusiasm that surprised her. And while the pot banging
created its own noise, this was the kind of noise that a mother could
tolerate. But more than this, banging provided adequate discharge
of tension; it was not necessary, for example, for Jack to bang pots
all day in the same way that he had shouted all day. He used his
pot banging when he needed it. And within a few days, Jack began
to show signs of improvement in all areas. The shouting was now
rare, the desperate clinging to the mother had disappeared, he was
playing actively again and seemed to be his old self, according to
the mother and our observers. It is interesting to note that Jack
remains one of our rare babies in the second year who has the motor
patterns of aggression and who can fight back if necessary.

A clinical picture of the kind I have described in Jack would
rarely be found in a healthy, sighted baby. The sighted baby of this
age would also react to temporary loss of his mother, but only in the
most extraordinary cases would we find the kind of total regression
I have described in Jack.

Yet, we have a number of other examples of transient regressive
states among our blind young children. I shall briefly describe the
clinical picture in some of these cases because it leads us into very important considerations of defense and adaptive functions of the ego.

Robbie: Diagnosis—bilateral agenesis of the optic nerves

When Robbie was thirteen months old our observers became
alarmed by an abrupt change in his personality and regression in
nearly all sectors of development. For most of his first thirteen
months Robbie had been an alert, responsive baby and his general
performance would put him in the high-average range for blind
children. This good developmental picture was all the more remarkable when we consider that his mother had depressive features in her
personality which she warded off through eating and a kind of forced
cheerfulness and hilarity. Until thirteen months we can say that
whatever conflicts the mother may have had, she functioned adequately as a mother for Robbie, and his development was not im-

peded. At thirteen months Robbie became apathetic and virtually mute. The few words he possessed dropped out. He was solemn, unsmiling, unresponsive. In testing situations he was unable to solve problems involving memory which he had successfully passed on the eleven- and twelve-month level. A type of rocking appeared which had distinctly pathological features.

Our observers saw that the mother withdrew from Robbie for large periods of the day and cared for his needs in a forced and mechanical way. There were clinical signs of a depression in the mother. Our staff caseworker worked closely with the mother on a supportive basis to help her move out of her depression and come into contact with her baby once again. As the mother improved and restored her earlier relationship with Robbie, the morbid symptoms, including the rocking, dropped out and Robbie began to move apace with his development. Within a two-month period his overall development placed him again in the high-average range for blind children.

In Robbie's case, we see how the mother's depression had the effect of making her an absent mother or a lost mother for the blind baby. When she lost touch with him through holding and talking to him, she was virtually an absent mother. It is true that a sighted baby, too, will show reactions to a mother's depression through withdrawal and anxiety, but very rarely will we see a sighted baby with a history of a very favorable development, as in Robbie's case, who will present a picture of sudden morbid decline and pathological regression in all areas.

At this point certain clinical questions can be fairly raised. How much of this clinical picture belongs to blindness and helplessness before danger, and how much may be attributed to environmental factors? How do we know, for example, that we have made the correct assessment of the mother's contributions to the child's pathology? We could not know, of course, unless we had a range of environments in which we could assess the environmental contribution and the qualities of mothering.

At this point I propose to describe three other cases of transient regressive states which appeared in children whose mothers are rated by us as "superior." The judgment is based not only upon demonstrated capacity to meet the blind baby's special needs but upon our assessment of the mother's capacity in rearing older children.

Toni: Diagnosis—ophthalmia neonatorum

Toni, in the New Orleans study (Fraiberg and Freedman, 1964), was a healthy, bright, and active child who acquired a pathological symptom in the second year. Again, as far as we can judge, the symptom appeared in connection with a brief absence of the mother and always reappeared in association with absence of the mother. Later it became generalized to other situations of danger. The symptom was a type of pathological sleep. We saw it as observers. Soon after we would enter the room as strangers, Toni would creep into her mother's arms and instantly, as if a light were switched off, she would go into a stuporous sleep. At night, when the mother would go out and leave her with the older children or a sitter, Toni would cry briefly, then fall into a stuporous sleep. This pathological sleep could be induced in the middle of active play if Toni felt overwhelming anxiety for one reason or another. In all other respects, Toni's development was excellent. Toni's mother was a warm and sensitive woman who had reared five healthy older children. She had shown extraordinary intuition in her rearing of her blind baby and as Toni reached the second year the mother flexibly encouraged independence and learning in Toni at the same time that she provided necessary support and protection. But danger for Toni immediately signaled the onset of pathological sleep.

Kathy: Diagnosis—retrolental fibroplasia

Kathy can be rated as one of the most superior of our blind babies. In the second year of life her language and social skills would easily put her in the superior range for sighted children. Her adaptive hand behavior was very superior for blind children. Her mother would also be rated as the most intuitive and expert of our mothers, and her experience in rearing four other children had given her a sense of competence and poise in any emergency, and a perspective for observing her blind baby's development.

When Kathy was twenty months old, she was walking only with

support and her parents showed patience and a very good under-standing of the problem posed for a blind child in establishing independent walking. In all respects she was a joy to her parents. They were quite unprepared, and so were we, for a crisis which appeared around twenty months. Kathy had begun a kind of desperate clinging to her mother, following her mother's every move, clutching a skirt, a leg, any part of her mother's body that would bring her in direct physical contact. Through every waking hour she demanded to be held, or to be in touch with her mother's body or her voice. She wanted only her mother. She refused to have anything to do with her father in spite of the fact that she had always had a strong attachment to him. It was an exclusive, desperate holding on to the mother. When her mother held her, Kathy would crawl frantically over her mother's body, in a way reminiscent of Jack's behavior, trying in every way to get as much of her own body sur-face in touch with her mother's. The anxiety was so intense that Kathy begged to go to sleep at all odd hours of the day and the mother, a very wise mother, felt that this retreat to sleep was not healthy. The mother discouraged the excessive sleeping and did everything possible to keep Kathy awake and interested and close to her since it brought her comfort. The mother, a very good observer, told us that she had a strong feeling that this anxiety was connected with walking. The mother had picked up a number of clues that told her that Kathy had a terror of taking her first independent steps, of moving out into space.

And the mother was right. Soon after Kathy took her first inde-pendent steps, the anxiety dissolved, the desperate following and clutching of mother ceased, and the longing to crawl into her own bed disappeared.

It would be hard to find a parallel among sighted children for this kind of anxiety in connection with independent walking, or to find such severe symptoms in an otherwise healthy child confronted with a problem. In a sighted child, at the most we might see some anxiety in connection with his new-found independence and the cutting of his moorings to his mother, but I can think of no exam-ples of a healthy sighted child who resorted to desperate clinging and crawling over his mother's body, or retreat into sleep.

Patty: Diagnosis—retinoblastoma

Patty is not one of the children in our longitudinal series. She became blind at eight months of age when both eyes were enucleated. We have followed her since the onset of blindness because of our interest in her and because of her mother's wish to consult us.

At fifteen months, Patty was a vivacious little girl, beginning to walk independently and already speaking in good simple sentences. The advantages of at least six months of vision were seen in a mobile, expressive face and a skill in adaptive hand behavior of a kind we never encounter in a child blind from birth. The mother was tender, very sensitive to her blind baby's signals and needs, and had already demonstrated her competence as a mother with two older children.

When Patty was eighteen months old, her mother called our social worker in great alarm. For over a week Patty had manifested a strange symptom. The symptom as the mother described it, and later as we saw it, was a ticlike lateral rotation of the head and trunk which persisted in an automatic, agitated fashion throughout her waking hours.

Patty was seen at our hospital promptly. Pediatric and neurological findings were negative. A psychiatric review of the recent developmental pictures provided some important clues. The mother had been conducting an energetic campaign in toilet training Patty. Later we learned that Patty had been spanked for soiling herself. Then, "almost overnight," as the mother reported it, Patty became toilet trained. Almost simultaneously with this achievement the tic appeared. And while we were trying to understand this complex development, the whole situation reversed in a dramatic fashion. Patty began to resist going to the toilet. And when she soiled her pants, she spanked herself and said "bad girl" very severely. As the toilet training broke down, the tic disappeared completely!

In putting together the several pieces of this puzzle we were sure that the tic was closely connected with anxiety over the toilet training. Yet, in our clinical experience, we would rarely encounter an otherwise healthy child who developed such a severe symptom as the result of a conflict over toilet training. In a typical population of sighted children there must be a large number of instances in which punitive measures have been used, sometimes by otherwise understanding and stable mothers like Patty's mother. Yet, in our clinical experience with sighted children, we would rarely encounter a pathological regression and a symptom of such severity as we saw in Patty. Typically, when a mother has been punitive in toilet training, there will be a contest between the sighted baby and his mother. The baby may become very aggressive and fight the mother. He may develop temper tantrums. He may fight back through retention of his stool. He may develop an eating disturbance. In each of these typical reactions or symptoms there is the factor of rebellion, refusal, fighting back.

But Patty did not fight back at first. Patty's anxiety, we think would have been considerably greater than that of a sighted child. Typically, a blind child at eighteen months cannot understand the use of the toilet. Even a sighted child may consider the whole business a piece of nonsense, but how can a blind child make sense out of this procedure? The blind child has never seen his stool. It is the rare mother of a blind child who will permit the child to touch his stool. Usually, the mother needs to wait until the blind child is two and a half to three and a half with enough language facility so that patient explanations can be given. Patty, at eighteen months, only knew that she was being led to a roaring monster, that she was supposed to make some obligatory sacrifice to the monster, and that, if she did not, she would be spanked for being a bad girl. Her anxiety and confusion must have been very great. In the face of this terror we cannot imagine how she was able to learn what was expected of her, but this obedience under pressure of anxiety produced a pathological regression; anxiety was discharged through a primitive motor act.

Why didn't Patty rebel or "fight back" as other two-year-olds might do? Typically, our blind young children do not "fight back." The absence of aggression in blind children has been remarked upon by Dorothy Burlingham (1965). The fate of aggression in the blind young child should open up important avenues to the study of the role of aggression in adaptation and defense (Hartmann, Kris, Loewenstein, 1949).

At this early stage of our study of defense in the blind young child we begin to discern the outlines of the adaptive problem for

the blind child. Blindness maintains the child in the condition of
infantile helplessness for a perilously long period in the second and
third years of life. The blind child must use his human protectors
against danger at an age where the sighted child already has ego
defensive measures and defense mechanisms. In our clinical examples, covering a wide range of environments and a range of blind
babies with good to superior overall development, we have an
extraordinary picture of helplessness and defenselessness. In the
absence of other defenses, the blind young child is most frequently
reduced to primitive forms of regression as a defense against danger.

From the clinical evidence at this point in our study, blindness
robs the child of two primary modes of defense in the second year.
First, we have clinical evidence and empirical data from testing that
the blind child is slow in achieving a stable mental representation
of the mother and a belief in objective permanence. In the simplest
terms, this means, of course, that when mother is absent she ceases
to "exist." The sighted child in the second year has already moved
far beyond such elementary notions of space. He can sustain brief
absences from his mother with minimal anxiety because he can
evoke the picture of his mother when his mother is not physically
present. Somewhere between two years and four years a healthy
blind child will achieve notions of "permanence" with regard to
human and inanimate objects, but the construction of the concept
of permanence must be a long and protracted experiment for a
child without vision. Vision practically insures the construction of
spatial concepts and belief in permanence. Beyond this, we can see
that a sighted child who has achieved a mental representation of
mother has the possibility of acquiring defense mechanisms in which
identification plays a role. To possess the stable picture of the mother
and human protectors is equivalent in psychic terms to having the
loved person within the ego and, by identification, to experience
"protection" as the magical consequence of possessing and evoking
the picture of the protector. The variety of imitative and imaginative games which a sighted child in the second year demonstrates
tells us how he incorporates the qualities and characteristics of his
human protectors and makes them his own. We have no parallels
for the blind child in the second year and we begin to see fragmen-

tary forms of such identifications only in the third and fourth years.

The second aspect of defenselessness in the blind child of the second year emerges from our clinical observations on aggression and the defensive aspects of aggression. In the remarks that follow I cannot do more than sketch the problem for the blind child and touch on some promising leads for study which our children have given us. We are all aware that there are many gaps in our understanding of the role of aggression in the early development of sighted and intact infants.

We might begin with an illustration of the characteristic behavior of a sighted child confronted with an ordinary type of objective danger. If a sighted child in the second year is confronted with a bullying older brother, he has some means for defensive action. If his older brother grabs a toy from him, he can try to grab the toy back. He can smack the older brother. He may still not get the toy back, but aggression is mobilized in this situation of danger and is discharged toward the older brother who is clearly identified as the source of trouble. Within a few months—and with the rich opportunities for practice afforded by an older brother—that baby can often put up a respectable fight for his property and his rights. It is not even unheard of that an older brother will take flight before the fury of this lilliputian attack.

A blind baby may be well endowed with aggression, but in the second or the third year and even later, we will see a very different pattern of discharge from that of the sighted child. We have almost no examples from our blind young children of "fighting back." In the most typical situation in which a valued toy is taken out of his hands, or a pleasurable activity interrupted, there will be certain typical reactions. The blind child in the second or third year will have a tantrum in which he stiffens, arches his back, flails his arms and legs, and screams. The pattern is one of gross discharge of rage, without aim or object. In a ghostly world of presences there are rare chances to "fight back," and these depend upon close physical proximity at the point of conflict. And how, in fact, does the child without vision construct a causal sequence in which he can attribute to someone outside of himself an action or a sequence of actions that have affected him and frustrated his own wishes? What we see in the blind child's characteristic tantrum is something very close to that which we see in the sighted child during the first six to eight months of life, before drives are directed toward objects and before the infant intelligence has constructed notions of causality.

In short, the blind child in the second year who experiences danger in a moment at which his human protectors are not present cannot defend himself through "fighting back," and what we see in some of the clinical observations I have reported is a motor discharge of aggression without the motor patterns for aggression. In the defense model "fight" or "flight," we see that *regression remains the chief defense of the blind young child* in our clinical examples of the second year. Aggression is discharged along primitive motor pathways, as we see in the tantrums or the ticlike symptoms produced by two of our children.

We know that this condition of helplessness before danger in the second and third years of life need not be the fate of the blind child. From the evidence of a number of healthy blind children at school age, we know that an ego organization emerges and the child is not reduced to helplessness and pathological regressions when confronted with ordinary dangers. This means that the ego acquires some measures of defense and defense mechanisms. How does the blind child achieve this? How does he acquire a stable mental representation on the basis of nonvisual experience? How does he find the motor patterns of aggression for defensive action? How does aggression become neutralized in the service of defense and sublimation? These are the problems that lie before us as we follow the development of our blind infants in the preschool years. We are hopeful that longitudinal studies of blind children will illuminate a number of problems in early ego organization and the evolution of defense mechanisms.

Summary

The study of the ego as the agency of adaptation is approached in this investigation from the side of the biological equipment that serves the later ego organization and from the side of the human environment that must provide conditions for development and organization of personality. The visual deficit in each of the children studied has created extraordinary adaptive problems in the areas of human relations, gross motor achievements, adaptive hand behavior, the construction of an object world, and the development of defensive action and defense mechanisms by the end of the second year of life. The adaptive problems appeared in each of the children studied, in a range of human environments that permitted some assessment of qualitative factors in mothering. It is not blindness alone that imperils the child's development, but the absence of vision as an organizer of experience, the absence of vision as the facilitator of gross motor achievements and prehension, the absence of vision in constructing a stable mental representation, and the obstacle to finding motor pathways for aggression that can lead to defense and neutralization of aggression in the service of the ego. The clinical examples of severe pathological regressions in five children show the helplessness of the blind child in the face of objective danger and the vulnerability of the blind child's ego for an extended period in early childhood.

BIBLIOGRAPHY

Ainsworth, M. (1963), The Development of Infant-Mother Interaction. In: *Determinants of Infant Behavior*, ed. B. M. Foss. New York: Wiley, 2:67-104.
Burlingham, D. T. (1965), Some Problems of Ego Development in Blind Children. *This Annual*, 20:194-208.
Fraiberg, S. & Freedman, D. A. (1964), Studies in the Ego Development of the Congenitally Blind Child. *This Annual*, 19:113-169.
—— Siegel, B. L., & Gibson, R. (1966), The Role of Sound in the Search Behavior of a Blind Infant. *This Annual*, 21:327-357.
Freedman, D. G. (1964), Smiling in Blind Infants and the Issue of Innate vs. Acquired. *J. Child Psychol. & Psychiat.*, 5:171-184.
Gouin Décarie, T. (1965), *Intelligence and Affectivity in Early Childhood*. New York: International Universities Press.
Hartmann, H. (1939), *Ego Psychology and the Problem of Adaptation*. New York: International Universities Press, 1958.
—— (1952), The Mutual Influences in the Development of Ego and Id. *This Annual*, 7:9-30.
—— Kris, E., & Loewenstein, R. M. (1949), Notes on the Theory of Aggression. *This Annual*, 3/4:9-36.
Omwake, E. B. & Solnit, A. J. (1961), "It Isn't Fair." *This Annual*, 16:352-404.
Piaget, J. (1937), *The Construction of Reality in the Child*. New York: Basic Books, 1954.
Provence, S. & Lipton, R. C. (1962), *Infants in Institutions*. New York: International Universities Press.

Spitz, R. A. (1963), Life and the Dialogue. In: *Counterpoint*, ed. H. S. Gaskill. New York: International Universities Press, pp. 154-176.
—— & Wolf, K. M. (1946), The Smiling Response. *Genet. Psychol. Monogr.*, 34:57-125.
Werner, H. (1948), *Comparative Psychology of Mental Development*. New York: International Universities Press, 1957.
Wolff, P. H. (1963), Observations on the Early Development of Smiling. In: *Determinants of Infant Behavior*, ed. B. M. Foss. New York: Wiley, 2:113-134.

CONSCIENCE DEVELOPMENT

CARL P. MALMQUIST, M.D. (Minneapolis)

Where the theoretical problems of the past several decades have involved an expansion and clarification of the concepts and applications of ego psychology, the present situation seems to be shifting toward a "superego psychology." This will not be quite as dramatic a shift in emphasis, but will probably lead to attempts at clarification of the interactions between these agencies and a general re-evaluation of theory. The genesis and functions ascribed to the construct superego will be examined, and clinical experience will aid in explanations of why certain pathological deviations occur as well as how. This implies a coalescence of developmental data and developmental psychology. This paper will elaborate upon the clinical and developmental manifestations of "conscience" in the child until approximately six years of age. The focus will figuratively be on the developmental anatomy and physiology of conscience in the young child. Emphasis is upon the susceptibility to experiential influences which affect the manner in which the human biological organism achieves discharge, mastery, and control over its impulses. A process of perfection of such a mental structure occurs with respect to prohibitions but also for ideals and positive strivings.

Early "moral activities" of the child are viewed as amoral. Behavior is initially believed to be governed by such fundamental biological strivings as pleasure seeking or its converse of pain avoidance. Tendencies to relive and cope with experiences by their repetition also appear to operate and these may not be congruent with the avoidance of pain. Fundamental questions thus arise: How is it that feeling states of guilt and a subsequent need for penance arise, and what are the psychological processes which propel this development?

From the Institute of Child Development and Department of Psychology, University of Minnesota, Minneapolis, Minnesota.

In a broader sense, the question is asked how a child becomes socialized and acquires a control system? The explanatory model is taken from clinical and developmental data.

THEORETICAL ISSUES

During the oral phase of development, a groundwork is laid for the formation of inner controls. The first humans with whom an infant becomes intimate inculcate in him feelings of trust and confidence, basic feeling states responsible for how the world comes to be viewed. From work done in the areas of maternal deprivation, it is apparent that the infant can sustain multiple and critical injuries which will predispose him to emotional disturbances. The debatable issue at present is whether we can find techniques to predict which type of psychopathology will develop from specific unfortunate experiences occurring at vulnerable stages of development. What disturbances of later conscience functioning result from certain influences operating at particular ages or what were once thought to be "critical periods" of development?

The concept of infantile narcissism has relevance to conscience formation because it is believed that "narcissistic disturbances" originate from conflicts in this early phase. For developing a control system and later difficulties with controls, struggles with narcissism appear to be of great significance for the template of a conscience. Primary narcissism may be viewed as a hypothetical state of psychological equilibrium in the organism analogous to that of an ideal intrauterine existence. Since in the postnatal state conditions of relative bliss are unattainable, "objects" are used for gratification so that a narcissistic balance can be maintained. Empirically, the earliest interactions with objects for receiving and taking, as well as loving and being loved, are put into operation. Infantile omnipotence is compromised repeatedly by the gradual realization of dependency on others for satisfaction. The antithesis of narcissism is not an object existing but rather a quality of object love. Such qualitative relationships with objects are what allows an infant to experience a narcissistic equilibrium rather than merely to seek a profusion of object contacts (Kohut, 1966). Early narcissistic injuries are believed to contribute toward many later clinical phenomena, such as proneness to depression, acting out, and schizoid withdrawal. Each of these is also accompanied by anomalies of conscience functioning.

How external objects and their multiple representations and associated feelings are transmitted and absorbed into the mental life of a child is still an unsolved psychological problem. Its answer is relevant to the entire topic of how we socialize and interpersonally affect each other. Clinical discussions of the development of progressive controls over feelings and impulses presuppose that some type of differentiation process occurs within a mental structure. Ego psychology assumes that the infant possesses inhibiting apparatuses even before an ego has emerged from an "undifferentiated matrix" (Hartmann, 1939). This type of theorizing receives its greatest criticism from behavioristically oriented psychologists for whom the very term "conscience" is unacceptable because of its surplus meaning and implications of a unitary structure controlling behavior. References to "inner controls" are viewed as reifications; only descriptions of "self-control" defined in terms of self-generated stimuli which observably control certain responses are permitted. "If any of the critical responses or response-produced stimuli are not observable, then no application of the concept of self-control can justifiably be made" (Bijou and Baer, 1961, p. 80). Inhibition of certain acts without an accompanying verbal indicator of the response-produced stimulation would be considered an unwarranted inference. This parsimonious type of theorizing cannot be quarreled with if the limits to which it is applicable are clear. It would hold for very discrete situations in which a child is willing to oblige with various observable stimulus and response patterns which the experimenter considers necessary for a description of functional relationships. There is some acknowledgment of difficulties with physiological processes in this regard, but the behaviorists apparently hope that more of such processes will become observable in time, even though they are intraorganismic.

A clinician would feel greatly restricted in attempting to confine his data to "nothing but" observables as defined above, even though the rigorously empiricist part of him may resonate to the neatness of this approach. However, clinical data are not neat, nor are they often directly observable; they usually are quite complex and multiply determined. This is particularly so when efforts are made not merely to describe such phenomena as why a child chooses various alternatives, but to account for and make predictions as to why he has developed or might develop certain types of controls or their deviations. At present there does not appear to be a valid philosophical criticism to utilizing concepts with surplus meanings which many other scientific theories also employ. If critics object to them, it becomes a matter of empirically demonstrating the usefulness, or lack of usefulness, of employing specific hypothetical constructs which allow for cognitive referents beyond observable data.

"Internalization" is a concept derived from empirical data such as the overtures of children who begin to imitate parental behavior verbally and nonverbally; they also directly observe incorporative acts when objects are literally ingested, such as in eating. Internalization also encompasses the psychological processes referred to as "introjection" whereby mental representations occur apart from external and observable data. This permits data such as fantasies to be treated as significant and usable. Thus, if theorist X was to hold that such data are not observable and therefore not scientific, theorist Y can only reply that he finds the construct useful since it allows him to derive further empirical propositions which are connectable to observables and which, moreover, are subject to such scientific criteria as testability, preciseness, predictability, generality, coherence, and consistency. Internalization is a principle operating with imitation, introjection, and identification in a defensive as well as developmental manner. It is related to the development of a control system by virtue of these processes which allow for the gradual replacement of control based solely on the presence of external supports (Hartmann and Loewenstein, 1962). In place of, or in preference to, a dependency on the outside world or stimuli for regulation by societal threats or coercion, an autonomy or gradual independence of control is gained as a progressive developmental landmark. Whether this is an ideal that can entirely be attained is another debatable issue.

OBSERVATIONAL DATA

Empirical evidence indicates that in infancy a primitive struggle for impulse control sets in. This may occur in the context of frustration and lead to initial attempts at "taking it out on oneself." A common example is the physiological need to bite which appears at approximately six months and which is not only pain-relieving to tender gums but pleasurable in its own right. Yet the response of the mother sets sharp limits to this activity which is "punished." Erikson (1950a) feels that "this point in the individual's early history can be the origin of an evil dividedness, where anger against gnawing teeth, and anger against the withdrawing mother, and anger with one's impotent anger all lead to a forceful experience of sadistic and masochistic confusion leaving the general impression that once upon a time one destroyed one's unity with a maternal matrix. This earliest catastrophe in the individual's relation to himself and to the world is probably the ontogenetic contribution to the biblical saga of paradise, where the first people on earth forfeited forever the right to pluck without effort what had been put at their disposal; they bit into the forbidden apple, and made God angry. . . . A drastic loss of accustomed mother love without proper substitution at this time can lead (under otherwise aggravating conditions) to acute infantile depression or to a mild but chronic state of mourning which may give a depressive undertone to the whole remainder of life" (p. 79 f.). This would seem fatalistically to predispose each individual to a potential feeling of badness and depression based on his infantile impulses to bite. The nurturer must be viewed as a source of both gratification and deprivation depending on whether the situation is one of pleasure or of inflicting pain in some manner as an "enemy" might. Such potentials might be actualized in varying degrees depending upon the intensity of the infantile losses, but they would also seem to be contingent upon subsequent experiential components.

At some time between nine and twelve months infants begin to shake their heads from side to side as though communicating "no" by gesture. This is then associated with behavior which the parents condemn in the form of a verbal "no-no." The head shaking is based on a biological pattern which earlier led the infant to rotate his head sideways toward the nipple and by six months to rotate his head away from the breast when satiated as an expression of withdrawal. Spitz (1957) viewed the "no-no" as the first semantic symbol that functions on an abstract level in contrast to such global expressions as "ma-ma" which have innumerable meanings. That a process of internalization that goes beyond the initial imitative efforts has begun as well is evident when the child is subsequently observed to shake his head as he approaches a forbidden object. Thus, a ten-month-old child who has knocked over a lamp and been punished by getting a slap may subsequently be observed standing near the tempting object shaking his head, or a fourteen-month-old who has turned on the burner of a stove and been similarly reprimanded may be seen standing in front of the stove saying "no-no" verbally and physically. Efforts to conceptualize this behavior purely as a change from a social positive reinforcement of receiving parental attention to a social negative reinforcement based on discriminating punishment do not seem adequate even at this early age, nor do they serve as a sufficient explanatory premise for the meaning of the "no-no." Rather, they appear to be descriptions of what is immediately observable. Even with this type of theorizing, the situation is more comparable to a conflict situation where the infant must choose between alternatives such as to touch or not to touch, but parental attention is also sustained along with a negative reinforcement so that the child is not confronted merely with a mutually exclusive choice. Such maintenance of parental attention is believed conducive to internalization.

Subtle attempts to conceal or escape may also emerge in infancy. Thus, a child of one year who has been caught doing something that has been prohibited may seek to run away from the parent, or he may hide his hand behind him when he has touched a forbidden object. Struggles to control impulses and to evade external control begin to appear. Thus, a twelve-month-old girl was forbidden to touch a light socket. The child was then observed repeatedly pushing a toy closer and closer to the socket and gingerly reaching out toward it. When the parent was not watching, the girl was observed to smile and touch the switch.

Another facet of the early phase of such a struggle for internalization can be seen in self-punitive behavior. During the first year, disturbances in the motor sphere in the form of head banging, head rolling, and self-hitting are rather frequent occurrences. These may progress to bruises and other injuries which may be viewed as a maladaptive pattern in handling aggression. Cases in which such a pattern is due to organic factors such as headaches or otitis media are not being considered here. Originally, such behavior was believed to be a response to frustrating conditions or stimuli when the child miscarries his attempt to express hostility toward those around him or against external objects; it was hypothesized that the hostility was retroflexed against the initiator himself. This mechanism of coping with anger would appear to be an early prototype for one type of depression associated with defective internal regulation of affect. However, the concept of retroflexed aggression when external expression is blocked may be a gross oversimplification (Cain, 1961). Such behavior may be viewed as simply discharge-oriented irrespective of the recipient, or it may be viewed as a response to the need for stimulation as a counterirritant to offset some other psychological or physiological state. As an external object becomes incorporated or introjected, retroflection of an impulse may refer to directing aggression against this internalized psychic representation, or to defensive identification with an external object. In some cases, autoaggression may also function as an aid to delineate body boundaries, or to "project" blame from one part of the body to another. Thus, an eighteen-month-old child who has touched a forbidden object may be observed hiding his hand as though he were saying, "My hand [not I] did it." When caught for such a misdeed, some children will slap the "guilty" hand with the "innocent" one.

Theorists differ as to whether such turning inward of aggression can occur before or only after the existence of a functioning superego. The above observational and developmental evidence indicates that it occurs much before that time. Psychophysiological skin disorders can be used to illustrate a similar mechanism. Such an infant compulsively scratches himself when he is angry or pushes his fists into his eyes. Undoubtedly, equipmental sensitivities and situational factors subtly combine in the individual infant to focus on the skin as a place to express feelings. More dramatic are instances of self-biting which often result in bleeding. Such phenomena have too frequently been passed off as extreme degrees of pathology confined to retarded, brain-damaged or psychotic children and adults. However, many sporadic instances of similar behavior can be observed among infants and children without such malignant diagnoses and taken from normative investigations. Whatever varied and individually determined motivation such autoaggressive activity may have, the self-aggressive element is overtly evident. Although it may be theoretically impossible to direct aggression against the *self* (ego) before a distinct concept of the self and its boundaries exists, aggression may be directed against the *body* from the earliest period of life. Attacks upon the psychological structure of the ego necessitate a higher degree of psychological structuralization and some understanding of masochism as a mental process.

THE STRUGGLE FOR CONTROL

The entire period from the second to the fourth year is crucial for molding a conscience template. I shall not discuss all the ramifications of this period, but focus only on selected aspects pertaining to conscience formation. This period is associated not only with the "battle of the pot," but also with the more general increase in motor, language, and perceptual activities. The very act of walking allows for a broader field in which conflict or forbidden behavior can be expressed. Similarly, the emergence of communicative language allows for verbal opposition, or the capacity to comply verbally but not in deed. Language development also permits the utilization of another mode than motor discharge for handling feelings; it may allow for an acceptance and confirmation of such feelings by those with whom the child is most intimate and in this respect makes a contribution to the child's ability to accept such feelings as part of his own inner reality. In contrast to primitive societies where older children lead the young ones into the bushes without the complicated paraphernalia of modern bathrooms, the setting for toilet training is further complicated by the cultural impact of the need for cleanliness. The child can now use sphincter control as a potent weapon in coercive, defiant, or manipulative attempts. Control over feeding is a relatively mutual process between mother and infant, but with sphincter control the balance is tipped in favor of the child. Anxieties related to lack or loss of body control become equated with lack of sphincter control and a concern that things might always remain this way. This may be reinforced by parental behavior which conveys shame and disgust, and by their use of such techniques as cajolery, bribery, and begging as models for exercising control over others and for dealing with oneself.

Quite literal sensations of having an uncontrollable monster within may be related to fantasies that develop at this age. Feelings of alienation may be present in attempts to isolate oneself from this "foreign body." Struggles over impulse mastery may persist into latency and adolescence with secret fantasies that when one is threatened by the possibility of impulse expression, an animal takes over. In some severely conflicted adolescents this fantasy may be experienced very concretely and be associated with a pictorial image of a specific animal or a specific name. An overtly obsessional boy revealed a secret fear from early latency in which he suspected that a dead animal, probably a rat, had remained in his bowel for years. He believed that when he was about three years old this animal had crawled into his anus from the toilet bowl and this accounted for the smell associated with bowel movements. Intellectually he realized this was not so, but the feeling state persisted in isolation and undiminished in intensity for years. (Abstract world systems and various communal practices of purifying a contaminated body before acceptance or redemption may have some genetic psychological connection with these efforts to "get rid of the enemy within.") Such children develop a distorted body image and may feel compelled to wage a constant war against an evil inside of them which is yet part of them. The self-hatred thus generated may induce the child to seek punishment or to project hate onto others so that he feels external objects hate him—the origin of the persecutor. Nor can the transactional element be ignored with respect to the feeling that one is hated. The hate is generated not only in attempts to control forbidden instinctual strivings, but it is also sensed in the feelings of those on whom one is dependent. A chronically hostile, conflicted parent may induce self-hate in a child. By four years of age, a child may thus candidly tell a parent, "Daddy, you don't like me and then I don't like myself." Such reciprocal exchanges of affect between parent and child appear to begin in the earliest imitations, and to continue in multiple ways throughout a person's emotional development. In most cases they are not so explicitly put in words.

During this period, a rudimentary system of self-regulation arises which Ferenczi (1925) designated "sphincter morality." This refers to the child's self-esteem being contingent upon complying with the toilet-training requests of the parent. "I am good only if I have a bowel movement in such and such a place, and bad if I do it in my pants." In a context of mutual trust and respect, rather than hatred and rage, the child's control over his body functions progresses with only vestigal remnants of oppositional behavior. Preponderantly "negative emotions" such as hate, rage, or jealousy are later perpetuated via overt defiance and "sneaky behavior." The association of such characterological traits with resistance to socialization and later antisocial behavior is apparent. The stage is set for acting out the feelings of rage linked to conflicts of whether to "give in or not." Such emotional paralysis connected with helplessness promotes behavior leading to its alleviation. A feeling of gross injustice or the need to "get even" for past attacks may be derivatives of such struggles. Anal components breaking through a deficient control may contribute to the acting out of both children and adolescents.

Encopresis may be viewed as a symptomatic expression involving many of the conflicts of this stage which have not been resolved. In such cases the parents and child may play morality games by hiding soiled underwear or throwing it away. Usually there are sadistic elements, e.g., the parent may force the child to wash the soiled underclothing with his bare hands, or demand that he show such clothing to neighbors or visitors. One eleven-year-old encopretic girl, without signs of organic or mental deficiency, would crawl under her porch steps and defecate crouching and barking like a dog; at the same time she also accumulated a large collection of soiled underclothing in her "hideaway." An adolescent boy when angered at his teachers would leave a stool lying on the washroom floor thus conveying his hate and contempt. Fecal "calling cards" may be left at the scene of a robbery conveying similar feelings. Soldiers abandoning an area to "the enemy" may leave feces scattered about as an expression of their feelings; or, as in the Viet Nam conflict, primitive traps with wooden spikes smeared with feces may convey such impulses along with the attempt to poison. The discomfort and humiliation attendant upon such conflicts about obedience and authority are one source of lasting resentment and a persisting desire for vengeance.

Strivings for autonomy may be discerned in the changed manner in which the two- or three-year-old begins to use the word "no." Coping attempts to master the impulse to negate appear in the form of "games" which the child plays. At three years of age children about to go to bed may be heard to state repetitiously, "No, no, no, no"; or they may indulge in games of reversal, such as looking in a mirror and calling the image a copycat or a "not me" as part of the struggle to differentiate themselves by separation. These are childhood attempts to observe himself as part of reality testing. Cognitive and affective splits occur in the ego preparatory to observing and evaluating oneself. When developed, these processes may be viewed as superego functions. Depersonalization is developmentally connected with these experiences.

About fifty percent of American children apparently learn "no" as their first word, which is an interesting cultural observation in its own right. However, for the individual child, this may initially not be negativistic but rather illustrate strivings for autonomy. He may be "flexing his controls" in an effort to test whether he can make a decision. For example, a child refuses to accept something which we are quite sure he really desires. This may indicate a struggle to master his own impulses in a learning situation with other people. It is the beginning of his ability to say "no" to his impulses. A similar principle may be operating in a three-year-old who constantly "changes his mind." Behavior which an adult interprets as antagonistic may in reality be functioning as a self-testing device for the child at this age. Thus, after repeatedly asking for permission to go outside, an adult may agree, but then find the child responding with a "no" after he has received the desired permission. However, if the adult then accepts this at face value, he may be chagrined to find the child protesting and reiterating, "I want to." The child creates innumerable such situations which can be handled in different ways by the adult. One alternative is angrily to quash and ridicule such strivings for autonomy. From the standpoint of conscience development, the use of *shame* as an educational technique seems to result in an affective state of nakedness and humiliation with respect to one's impulses and the self from which they originate. This leads to feelings of worthlessness and hatefulness toward oneself rather than to condemning certain acts. Such a device for controlling behavior says, "You as a person are worthless and shameful." Feelings of social ostracism and alienation become the norm. Another result may be the repetitious seeking for ways to get away with things since detection brings such painful humiliation; or the child may brood about getting even when the supposed infallible authorities are gone.

A more specific danger for conscience structure is that of the precocious or overmanipulative conscience. "Denied the gradual and well-guided experience of the autonomy of free choice, or weakened by an initial loss of trust, the sensitive child may turn against himself all his urge to discriminate and to manipulate" (Erikson, 1950b, p. 70). Repetitiveness becomes an end for its own defensive sake rather than serving any productive purpose, and perfectionistic trends emerge. These qualities may also be used in attempts to manipulate authorities when they are viewed as arbitrary and unjust. When he wishes to deceive others, even the wish may lead to attempts at negation in his search for inner controls. The child then alternates between pseudohumility and feelings of shame, and his apologetic manner is coupled with fears of exposure; this may be punctuated by precipitous attempts to achieve a defiant autonomy.

Obsessional devices are also used developmentally as part of the control mechanisms at the disposal of the child. Magic words and rituals are used to counter talion fear. The element of caricature is also present to taper as well as ridicule the external authority's demand for conformity and cleanliness. Early obsessional behavior may thus also be a mimicry to taper the standards being placed upon the child prior to their defensive use. "I will not only clean my hands but wash them five times before every meal." This parody of a moral system led Freud (1907) to describe the obsessional neuroses as a private religion. Such behavior is also related to the function of observing oneself in action as well as on reflection. Multiple levels of discharge and control then operate such as the aggressive discharge when the five-year-old demands her mother participate in her handwashing rituals as well as angry outbursts if the mother does not so comply; the raw, red hands of the child also effect a self-punitive regulatory mechanism for transgression.

It is apparent that a good deal of "civilized behavior" is based on the fear and avoidance of being caught. Since an external agency is still the prime regulator of behavior, one cannot yet speak of a functioning superego, which is conceived to be an internal agency. Moreover, for the preoedipal child, his feelings and impulses have often greater reality than external objective criteria. Not until the fourth year is the child cognitively aware of what truth is in the sense of differentiating external reality from his own inner experiences, desires, fancies, and aspirations (Woolf, 1949). This may be seen in straightforward factual contradictions which the child denies. At times, drive strength coupled with a weak ego determines deviations even when an externalized control is present; hence the phrase that the pleasure was "worth the price." Behavioral regulation based primarily on "not getting caught" suffers from several unfortunate consequences from the standpoint of the individual child who does not progress beyond it, and also from that of the society in which he lives. Parental prohibitions are often greatly exaggerated so that the child fears horrible punishment for transgressions which have overtones of oral or anal destruction, such as being eaten or blown apart, etc. A six-year-old psychotic boy whose behavior fluctuated between autistic withdrawal and devious ward behavior repetitively expressed his fears verbally and in play therapy of being "bombed by shit"; he had panic episodes in which he lay crouching in a corner or under a table. Minor reprimands led to his smearing feces on himself.

External authority may be evaded, however—a fact which reveals the weakness of this device as a regulator of social behavior—while the danger of detection by some type of magnified and distorted inner authority is an ever-present reality. The child may develop various guises to appease authority which further contribute to "sneaky qualities." He may put the emphasis on externals and become a "stickler," or pretend to feel sorry while he actually experiences no such feelings. Ferenczi once stated, "And out of this lie morality came into existence" (see Fenichel, 1945, p. 102). Such feigning of regrets must be distinguished from the emerging capacity for genuine *empathy,* another forerunner of superego development. The child becomes capable of partially identifying with another person and of sensing that person's painful feelings; he then indicates that he is "sorry." Such concern is viewed as a step leading to an ability to console oneself when needed (the loving aspects of the superego) by "identification with the comforter" (Furer, 1967). To insure the continuance of gratifications from pleasure-giving objects in the environment, there is a continuous introjection in fantasy. The threat of separation from these objects engenders anxiety which may be one factor contributing to the nucleus for later propensities to act out. The presence of conscious fantasies of merging with love objects is part of normal development up to three years of age. Beyond that age level, transitory fusions between the self and external objects occur and these contribute to an individual's empathic capacity to relate to others. The tendency toward fusion always remains and under stressful conditions (catastrophies, authoritarian regimes) may be seen in efforts of individuals to merge with each other or with their persecutors. This may explain some cases of false confession as well as group regressions in moral standards (Jacobson, 1964).

At this developmental level of conscience categorical judgments begin. People and objects are either "good" or "bad" and compromises are not tolerated. A child feels he is a "bad boy," regardless of whether his behavior was motivated by an attempt to control "bad" impulses or was actually a forbidden "bad" activity. Unsophisticated and blatant attempts to manipulate adults in the environment make their appearance. A four-year-old may overtly and unabashedly tell an adult how much he loves him shortly after having performed a prohibited act, or prior to carrying out forbidden behavior. Such behavior is the beginning of bribery, which is first directed toward external objects and later toward the agency of the superego. The goal is to obtain permission from a poorly integrated authority, external or internal, to perform or think prohibited acts or thoughts. A similar defect is seen in the "corruptibility of the superego" in which the discharge of an impulse necessitates an act of atonement which is then used as permission for further transgressions in a vicious cycle. This may also have components of bribing the superego: the child performs a meritorious act, but punishes himself to "purchase" the pleasure he is seeking. A comparable attitude is seen in children who begin to "store up" little acts of denial as the price for future indulgences.

As the defensive capacity of the ego develops, certain defenses may be used in the service of the consolidating superego to alleviate the discomfort attendant upon wishes or acts which have been prohibited. These are defenses directed against guilt feelings which are the *sina qua non* of a developing conscience. These defenses make their appearance at about three years of age, when, e.g., projection of blame is quite common. "You shouldn't have left the cookie jar out for me to take one," implying that the mother herself is thus responsible for the child eating the cookie. The same mechanism can be seen in adult patients who are struggling to control their behavior, e.g., the woman who carries on an affair when her husband is out

of town and blames him for putting her in this situation of temptation. Displacement and externalization are seen in the child's efforts
to hypostasize an external control system which will "catch" him or
pursue him if he misbehaves—hence, the games and associated fears
of being detected by bogeymen or policemen. Externalization is employed to portray the conflict emerging between certain impulses and
their prohibition. Theories of the "good guys" versus the "bad guys"
are repetitively re-enacted, with the forces of evil often being represented by some type of thief, monster, or beast over which smaller,
but more virtuous individuals (perhaps toy soldiers or cowboys) triumph in the end. As soon as we realize that in the psychic life of the
child, actually committed acts, wishes, fantasies, and words are
equated, and have the same economic-dynamic function, the universality of such mechanisms in children becomes clearer. Themes of
guilt and atonement attain prominence and are seen in dreams and
play activities of children at this transitional stage of conscience development, and in play therapy if the child is in treatment. Such devices as Pinocchio's Jiminy Cricket may be invented to help an immature conscience decide what to do and admonish it when the
control system falters. Questions pertaining to power and submission
become frequent when the child's psychological structure is solidify-
ing, a process that is reinforced by religio-cultural norms. A five-year-
old may ask such questions as, "Who is more powerful than God?"
Or he will come up with such unanswerable philosophical questions
as, "Who punishes God when He is naughty?" or, "Why is swearing
bad to do?"

Another phenomenon seen in an immature conscience, as well as
in those with defects, is superego isolation. This allows prohibitions
to be experienced at one time but not at another. By temporarily
vacating controls, the child is allowed to discharge impulses he would
not otherwise be capable of acting upon. In some children such
periods of temporary license remain as a consolidated structure
within the personality. This is similar to the behavior of "suffering
first" as permission for later indulgence, or the need to expiate after
having experienced pleasure. Such patterns also appear in the course
of therapy with patients of all age groups who use the suffering engendered by therapy as a justification for indulgence. Another ex-

ample of such a maladaptive pattern is compulsive hard work which either precedes or follows indulgence in pleasure. These measures are reinforced by cultural practices such as holidays of indulgence, or by such cultural myths as that hard work is always rewarded or that success cannot be achieved by any other means.

The behavior of carrying out condemned acts with equanimity under certain conditions is similarly based on dissociation of certain superego functions. In such cases we usually find the child's identification figures are unsatisfactory or defective, so that a license to carry out behavior varies with the situation the child is in. For this reason the child does not progress to a consistent internalization of controls. Instead he develops a hybrid of standards which lend his character unpredictability. Laymen and teachers are perpetually amazed when a nine-year-old boy who is in every respect a model and an outstanding student is caught hanging cats, or when a girl who is known only for her assiduous hard work and shyness is found to enjoy "experiments" of burning live animals. Many of these behaviors reveal reaction formations against and breakthroughs of impulses that were not renounced and toward which adequate defenses and adaptations were never accomplished. This is especially true with respect to the handling of aggression. Thus, a sixteen-year-old honor student with a lifetime of laudatory reports suddenly takes a rifle, hides on a hill, and kills several pedestrians before committing suicide. These are extreme examples of the struggle that to some degree occurs in all children, though most of them achieve greater synthesis. Such dissociation of conscience has been portrayed effectively by Richard Hughes in *A High Wind in Jamaica*. In this book, Emily, a quite proper, moral little girl, who is shocked by unconventionality and terrified of her conscience, is nevertheless capable of homicide and allowing innocent men to be hanged for her misdeed. In a similar fashion, it can be said the most civilized nations reward their citizens for carrying out antisocial acts for their country. The ease of vacating the internalized standards vary widely among different men; at one end of the scale are those who reveal they were never able to pull a trigger or that they shot over the enemy's head; at the other end we find men who idealize such expressions of their aggression by referring to them as noble causes or serving a higher purpose.

CULTURAL ASPECTS

A culmination of such precursors of conscience activity occurs during the oedipal period. The attempt of Freud in *Totem and Taboo* (1913) to establish an ultimate phylogenetic basis of all guilt is today rarely accepted without much qualification. He originally speculated that the claims for religious and moral codes which gave them cogency were based on a primeval act of parricide and the appropriation of the women who belonged to the father; this would then establish guilt and an everlasting need for repentance in mankind. One obvious point of difficulty in this explanation lies in its failure to account for the basis of guilt in women since Freud did not hypothesize that the females of the tribe practiced matricide. In variation of this theme, Margaret Mead (1963) hypothesizes, on the basis of recent paleological and ethological work, that an actual deed of parricide may have occurred, although not in the time perspective of our species, but possibly at an earlier time when no physiological latency occurred; during this period the young prehuman may have repeated "the act" for hundreds of thousands of years. The orthodox viewpoint holds that the establishment of a moral system within the individual is related to his attempts to resolve the oedipal struggle, so that at the beginning of the oedipus situation one cannot yet speak of a superego. Conscience development is contingent upon the subsequent utilization of the hatred felt at that time for rivals within the family setting. The two specific components of the oedipal conflict—incestuous wishes toward the parent of the opposite sex, and death wishes toward the parent of the same sex—are believed to be crucial for conscience structuralization. There are then fears of retaliatory punishment as well as fears of losing parental love and support. The resultant ambivalence is believed to be the driving force that impels the child toward the finalization of an internal mental structure which is a conglomerate of functions in the service of self-control and self-esteem. Psychoanalytic theory assumes that the process of introjection of parental standards is continuous and progressively solidified by an identification with the oedipal introject. Castration anxiety in the boy, and its analogue in the girl, is posited to the phase-specific fear that provides the motivational impetus to renounce oedipal strivings. In theoretical terms, this is stated as a

318   CARL P. MALMQUIST

shift of instinctual cathexes from the original objects to their identification models within the ego; these later become part of the superego, a structure which is thus the heir of and substitute for oedipal
relationships. Further ongoing identifications crystallize the superego
and lend it strength for control of behavior. Drive neutralization and
the enlargement of conflict-free ego functions are also promoted. The
ego comes to behave toward the superego as an internal and irre-
vocable, although not unmodifiable, educator. Maturation in such
ego functions as reality testing, synthesis, memory, conceptual capacity, and the experiencing of affect also contribute to a stabilized
conscience, so that superego development cannot actually be discussed apart from ego development.

What is introjected at this stage is largely the values, conflicts, and
conscience defects of the parental figures. This process thus contributes a stabilizing, conservative element in the sense that similar
values are perpetuated and preserved. However, there is also the
potential of a disorganizing effect if the adult educators transmit
their conflicts to the child. Moreover, there is an element of inevitability: if the parents express some tenderness and affection to a
child, he apparently cannot escape some degree of socialization and at
least a rudimentary conscience. Closely related is the question of the
universality of the oedipal situation. The wide ramifications of this
issue will only briefly be noted by reference to problems of conscience development in different cultures.

If conflict about oedipal objects plays a crucial role in the solidification of conscience, then the different types of conflicts in various
cultures will determine which processes pertain to conscience formation. Phrasing the question in the expectation of either a positive
or a negative answer about universality may in itself be fallacious.
Several of these issues were debated in the 1920s between Ernest
Jones (1924) and the anthropologist, Bronislaw Malinowski, but they
have remained confused. The issue is not solely a matter of semantics
but is partially a matter of how data should be interpreted as well as
a controversy about the nature of oedipal objects. One of the issues
pertains to the question whether the oedipal struggle takes place
only with biological parents and whether it is necessary to explain
all variations as denials or displacements from this one relationship.
With the increasing work on the relationship between personality

and culture and the expansion of ego psychology, a wider framework has evolved, but even with the primarily instinctual approach of early psychoanalytic theory a greater latitude was possible. Instincts were always viewed in terms of having a source, aim, or object (external or internal representation), all of which could be displaced. And this factor allowed for a great number of variations in different societies with different family and social patterns (Parsons, 1964). Clinical observations as well as social studies show that a number of objects—not only the biological parents—can be the focus of oedipal strivings. Thus, the developing personality is based on multiple identifications with different aspects of different persons. Such an approach does not sacrifice instinctual strivings and infantile sexuality for a purely "culturalist" position. Cultural absolutism appears to oversimplify the situation by viewing personality as strictly determined by social situations. On the other hand, the concept of a mental apparatus which is constructed to control drives and operates within a social framework does justice to the drive vicissitudes as well as to the multiple objects that significantly influence the child's development.

DEVELOPMENTAL PSYCHOLOGY

Theorists in the fields of learning and developmental psychology have presented various ideas about the development of "moral standards." Most typically, controls are viewed as a form of learned social behavior which emerges as a result of reward and punishment as well as of secondary and vicarious reinforcement. Conscience development is ascribed to such factors as the desire for parental approval and praise, and, conversely, anxiety in response to parental rejection and criticism. Elaborate empirical and laboratory data have been amassed by utilizing social learning theory in an effort to describe the acquisition and maintenance of self-control as well as transgressions (Bandura and Walters, 1963). A thorough discussion would require another paper since this is a separate but tangential approach to the problem of the development of controls. Various measures are used in attempts to delineate conscience growth, such as resistance to temptation, guilt, sex-typing, adult role formation, and prosocial aggression, which are believed to be reflections of identification processes.

One of the difficulties in using the concept of identification is inherent in the different referents to which it is applied. In the above discussion of the development of an internalized control system, identification has been used as a process by which external models in their great complexity become part of the psychological structure of the child. This is an anaclitic type of identification which serves a developmental function: the child thinks, feels, and behaves as though the characteristics of another person or group of people belong to him; he patterns his behavior, consciously and unconsciously, after such a model (Bronfenbrenner, 1960). Many other usages have become rampant since Freud's delineation of the defensive process as he observed it in depressions. These other usages have mainly been in nonclinical areas. Thus, some think of identification as merely behaving like another person, while others have extended the concept to have motivational implications such as the need to be like another person; the concept has also been confined to the belief of a child that the attributes of a model belong to the child himself (Kagan, 1958).

Social learning theorists posit similar motives and correlations with regard to such behaviors as seeking praise and acceptance, fear of rejection, sex-typing, and the learning of moral standards. It is assumed that identification proceeds from a desire to emulate actions and behaviors that have acquired a positive reward value for the child, such as power to control others, environmental mastery, and obtaining love. These formulations contribute some knowledge of the way children become like their parents. They lack the cogency of psychodynamic explanations which are rooted in conflict situations. There does not appear to be a satisfactory theory to account for why such processes as imitation of a model commence in which the explanation is not circular. It may be that resort to a biological theory such as imprinting and its derivatives is needed. An element of circularity is inherent in much of the theory of anaclitic identification. Thus, it states, "I want to be like my parents and therefore I identify, and I identify because I want to be like them." It is not much of an improvement to say that the child behaves in the way parents do because that gets their approval and avoids their disapproval. Apart from overt situations such as those obtaining in classical conditioning or instrumental learning, the *how* and *why* of the manifold variations seen in the development of control systems do not seem accounted for. Explanations to account for pathological phenomena which are believed to be related to identification problems also seem insufficient if the explanation restricts itself to acquiring the attributes of another. This is not to deny that adaptive and defensive identifications occur in learning situations; however, I believe that a theory with additional explanatory power is necessary.

Identification with the aggressor as a defensive maneuver usually begins during the second year and is believed to be of great significance for crystallization of a superego. It builds on the attachment the child has earlier made to a parent, and is almost always described in the oedipal context of the boy fearing castration from his father as a retaliation for his sensual wishes toward his mother. The wish to eliminate the rival is repressed and gives rise to guilt. The coexisting affectionate tie permits the child to identify with the threatening parent as well as with the mother who is loved by both child and father. The establishment of this defense within the ego is viewed as necessary but not sufficient for the actual development of internalized controls (Spitz, 1958). This method of handling anxiety by adopting behavior of the person who is feared offers an explanation of how a child can identify with an adult with whom he has had unpleasant experiences. One of the most common examples is the child playing doctor, which allows him to change from a helpless, passive state to one of active mastery. He can then repetitively re-enact on his playmates the unpleasure and anxiety which he has experienced. The child puts himself in the role of an aggressor and does to others what the adults have done to him. Similar behavior is repeated in many spheres as the child matures. It may later play a role in the identity crises of adolescents who begin to act like athletes, heroes or movie stars. Such processes originate in the infant's helplessness and are primitive attempts to master a situation by becoming the protective or frustrating adult. Such a change from passivity to activity allows aggression to be discharged against external objects, but also against the self. The defense which initially was directed against a feared object is now available to the child's own psychological self as a restrictive mechanism. In economic terms, energy is withdrawn (decathected) from the external objects by a process of desexualization and deaggressivization. This energy then becomes available to the superego for its own internalized primitive aggressive and loving activities (Hammerman, 1965). Guilt is not experienced until this level of development is reached when the ego can direct against itself some of its functions. A separate group of functions are then developed under the control of the superego, such as self-observation, self-evaluation, self-punishment, a need to expiate for transgression of standards, the bestowing of self-esteem for virtuous thoughts, acts, and wishes, and withholding it for their contraries. Intersystemic conflicts now supersede intrasystemic ones (Beres, 1966).

The loss of the object sustained during the oedipal period has elements in common with the mourning process that accompanies the actual loss of object. The renunciation of a loved object is facilitated by becoming like that object. This is seen quite commonly in persons who take on qualities or symptoms, of those they mourn. Put in more theoretical terms, the loss of the oedipal objects entails an instinctual defusion which liberates the child from the aggressive attachment to parental figures. The fate of the liberated aggression and the precise mechanism utilized by the individual child in his attempts to neutralize it are of great significance. One result may be an intrapunitive superego which wars against its introjects. A control structure which does not allow sufficient discharge of aggression will permit this aggression to be used against part of itself. The harshness of the educators, premature attempts to develop inner controls, anger generated by repeatedly inconsistent or disappointing parents, use of shaming techniques, masochistic adaptations to authorities, and parental conflicts with respect to handling their own impulses—these are some of the factors that contribute to the quality of conscience established in the child.

The attempts to look at conscience formations from the external aspects of socialization and conformity may have delayed a conjoint consideration of the complex psychological processes that are involved in the emergence of controls—the aspect with which the clinician is more familiar. The investigators who followed the classic study of Hartshorne and May (1928) viewed "moral character" in terms of overt conformity, such as adherence to rules and not cheating on school tests, i.e., in terms of resistance to temptation. Clinicians working with children during the period when conscience is developing are interested in such behavior, but are more curious to understand the meaning of such outward conformity. They would be aware of the fact that such external rule-following can be present in children, as well as adults, yet be accompanied by severe conscience deficits, as witnessed repeatedly in therapeutic work with children and families. In fact, conformity to moral rules seem to have little correlation with the strength of verbalized beliefs in rules or the intensity of guilt feelings following transgressions. Judgments and verbalizations about what a moral act is are of little value in predicting whether the individual child or adult will actually act in such a manner. Rather, knowledge of morality is indicative of the child's cognitive and cultural background and of his desire to make a good impression (Kohlberg, 1964).

Another issue is the extent to which cognition and intellect are involved in the development and function of conscience. Theorists who believe in the primacy of cognitive functions over affective factors, such as anxiety and guilt, stress the sequence of stages in the genesis of conscience formation. These, they believe, are patterned according to the child's social experiences. Such theories emphasize intelligence, social class, and peer relationships as preconditions of "moral development," but the child's level of moral judgment is distinguishable from these factors. The term "moral character" may not be equivalent to what clinicians call superego, which implies an internalized, psychological apparatus that can moderate impulse expression and deal with affects, such as anxiety, guilt, and shame. If moral character actually refers to a *knowledge* of moral acts, clinicians would be interested in knowing the age norms when children can at least verbalize certain standards; if moral character refers to *performance* of acts that are judged virtuous (moral conduct), the clinician would be interested in which acts a given culture considers so, and in sociological data about which classes of children behave in such ways. Yet, he would still be left with the feeling that the problem of conscience has merely been skimmed and that only tangential material has been dealt with.

Some have attempted a synthesis by viewing "moral character" as part of the developing ego strength of the child. This would then actually place moral behavior, or the effectiveness of a control system, within the ego rather than the superego. This is consistent with a theory that emphasizes a cognitive rather than an affect-motivated system of controls. The primary basis of behavior of all types is then seen in the decision-making processes of the ego; hence, the stronger one's ego, the more moral will be the child's behavior insofar as that behavior is subject to the controls and the sanctions of society. A mature superego is then contingent upon the organization of the ego which has achieved a level of development that corresponds to the psychosexual stage of development and is adequate to the task of handling impulses and external pressures.

A degree of conceptual capacity is undoubtedly needed before an operational conscience can be present. However, many of the functions indicating some type of control system are precursors of the actual conscience. The viewpoint of developmental stages is still crucial, since the superego is a structural part of mental functioning which evolves in the early years of life. Certain ego functions, such as reality testing, memory, and judgment, are necessary for the elaboration of conscience, but to say that these are equivalent to conscience gives a totally different perspective on a mental agency that functions in the realm of personal values, ideals, and social controls. Furthermore, it is not an agency merely concerned with conformity as judged by externals, such as cheating on school tests, but refers specifically to part of an intrapsychic system that develops in contact with the social environment and the inner world of wishes and strivings. Moreover, at a certain point in a person's development, this structure survives in its own right independent of the specific social and environmental pressures.

THE ROLE OF AFFECTS

In the young child diverse manifestations of controls exist prior to a functioning superego. As noted, some inhibition of direct impulse expression can be observed in children during the infantile period. This is originally based on imitation and fear and later expands to the stage of an inner danger. Since warning functions are attributable to the ego, impulse-controlled behavior or conformity does not by itself signify superego activity or anticipation of superego restriction. It is rather that ego development is a precursor of superego development. Outward social conformity may thus be a protective device of the ego and not be influenced by the

superego. Similarly, the existence of defenses does not imply a superego since these too are ego functions. What does seem to occur in
the course of development is that the superego lends a more skilled
and specific direction to these ego activities. The presence of a
superego can be detected by a different kind of warning signal
experienced by the ego—the affect of guilt—in contrast to many
other affects which are experienced by the ego. Defenses, moreover,
are not always initiated by or in the service of the superego; they can
be employed by the ego when the latter is in conflict with the environment. Thus, reaction formation may result in strict cleanliness
to counter the expression of anal impulses when these are prohibited by a strict environment and need not be the response of a
harsh superego. It may thus be very difficult to distinguish whether
a certain observed behavior is due to the influence of the superego
or that of a defensive ego function. To make this evaluation we need
to know whether other superego functions pertaining to ideals or
controls, such as self-evaluation, prohibitions and injunctions, social
feelings, and the necessary sense of guilt are present. Only these will
give us a clue to the developmental level that has been attained.

The morality of the preoedipal child, or of those who remain
on this level of moral functioning, implies an absolutism that not
only can be uncomfortable but actually portrays a lack of personal
controls and values. This is in part due to a disturbance or lack of
stabilized identification processes. These disturbances become manifest when a separate identity fails to develop. This statement does not
imply that the entire process must be completed by six years of age;
we all know that subsequent periods, particularly adolescence, are
of great importance. What it does imply is that unless the child can
progress beyond the level of object relationships based solely on
identification, he will be incapable of autonomous moral functioning
and be continuously subject to the environmental models that significantly influence him at a given time, or that are retained in
fantasy as objects to mimic. Such children may be considered to
have "preceptual superegos" which constantly plead for external
percepts to guide their behavior (Beres, 1966). A most striking feature of such immature morality is not only the harshness, as noted
in many studies of obsessionals, but the essential indecisiveness inherent in such a conscience. There is a perplexity as to how one

should behave and an inability to decide, which by no means are merely cognitive defects. Such children vacillate between groping for and rejecting the opinions of others and never really achieve any consistent synthesis. Their relationships to others involve not only ambivalent submission, but also envy of those who have greater freedom to choose.

If a sense of guilt is the hallmark of an internalized conscience and value system, as well as one of the most important problems in civilized societies, its development and function in a child may be one of the most important problems of child development. Guilt has been viewed in an ultimate sense as serving the biological survival of men who must live together with restrictions on their behavior. Some have gone beyond this by holding that the price of civilization is a heightening of the sense of guilt (Freud, 1930). Such broad questions are beyond the scope of this paper, which is focused on the development of guilt as part of the regulating mechanisms in the mental physiology of the child. Psychologically, guilt is an affective state which is believed to denote equilibrium between ego and super-ego, or a feeling of anxiety in the ego with respect to the superego. There may be a conscious awareness of guilt, or derivatives of unconscious guilt may manifest themselves in inferiority feelings, self-depreciation, self-punishment, or depressive states. Guilt as an affective state is also related to the ego ideal. This has been viewed as a substitute for the lost narcissism of childhood in which the child took himself as his own ideal. Guilt may then also express tension between ego and ego ideal.

Evidence of conscience development, which proceeds simultaneously with other developmental processes, can be observed in the three- to six-year-old child. A child who has transgressed may look "guilty," or he may be led to communicate his deed in a manner that contains the seed for future subtle deceptions about his behavior. For example, when a child of four who has taken an object that does not belong to him comes to his mother hiding it behind his back and asks, "What will happen to so-and-so [a friend] if he takes my gun?" the child seems to be groping for some help and direction with respect to control of his impulses. A child may transgress and then verbalize in a choked voice, and a tear or two, how he feels "bad." If one asks him what this is like, he may answer, "It's like I feel lonesome when mommy is gone," illustrating his fears of abandonment because of a misdeed.

If the child in this age group is punished, he may express hostile feelings and say something like, "I don't like you," with an angry look. Such anger appears to serve as a defense against a fear of losing the loved object and express the child's hope that the parent will seek reconciliation. It is as though his anger initially denied the possibility of such a loss. When the child has not been accepted back into a close relationship for some time, he may be unable to separate, e.g., resistance to falling asleep. Unresolved sleep disturbances may be associated with parents who utilize such situations to prolong the discomfort of the child and do not allow him to get closure in some manner. Such parents are often identified with this "bad" part in the child and punish themselves for their own unresolved infantile conflicts and transgressions. When sleep will not come, the child may in time "swallow his anger" and repeatedly come out of his bedroom until "things are good again," or he may provoke punishment which "soothes his conscience." The child uses all of these devices to restore himself to the good graces of the people who nurture him, and to his own internalized need for such reconciliation.

What is it that makes the need for restoring a good relationship with dependency objects occupy so prominent a place in the motivational structure of the child? If such behavior is conceptualized as due to fear of losing love, are we helped at all in understanding it? It could be argued that since survival is ultimately the key to all behavior, maintenance of a dependency relationship is necessary for existence. This would be a variation of the earlier ego-instincts approach. However, such an abstraction seems to lack the vitality of the actual feeling states which accompany observed behavior. This has led to a concept of guilt as a feeling state so painful and threatening to the ego that failure to resolve it produces feelings of annihilation and emptiness which are akin to death. The association of guilt feelings with gastrointestinal complaints was noted by some clinicians early in their work with depressed patients. It was also found in the "masked depressions" of children who typically present recurrent abdominal pains for which organic pathology is not demonstrable; such children have been labeled "little bellyachers" by some clin-

icians. Guilt feelings over a transgression are initially related to a
state of starvation on an emotional level. It is as though the child
were saying, "Unless you are restored to your parents' good graces,
you will starve. You will be empty and isolated." The concept frequently used to explain this is loss of self-esteem which regulates
the intrapsychic hunger for or feeling of well-being. Guilt or lack of
self-esteem come to be anticipated by signal affects which may also
lead to an elaboration of defenses against affect. A "bad conscience"
is then equivalent to a feeling of emotional hunger; to relieve it,
the child seeks to be restored to a loving relationship in which he
will be fed, physically and emotionally, so that he can again think
and feel well about himself.

With the appearance (at four to six years) of superego anxiety
(guilt), in contrast to the fear of an external authority, a major
landmark has been achieved in the anatomy of a conscience. The
brief period in the life of the child before an internalized, automatized conscience is present, is analogous to the problem that existed
with prehistoric man. Breasted (1933) noted that as the first social
codes to guide behavior evolved in the fourth millennium B.C.,
there were no such words as "right" and "wrong." Rather, such
phrases as, "He who does that is *loved*," and "He who does that is
hated," were used to approve or disapprove of behavior. These were
transitional periods on the way toward an internalization of individual standards. It would appear that the group conscience and
the standards of society since then can be as inconsistent and riddled
with conflicts as the conscience of the individual, but this question
would lead far afield from the problems of conscience development
in the individual child. The events and feelings that each child
experiences in the course of his development are reflected and
result in some type of internalized mechanism for guiding behavior
in both a prohibitory and a striving manner. That there are defects
and deformities does not seem as surprising as the fact that such
a process and structure can result.

A by-product of successful internalization is that the child is now
allowed to sin in "thought, word, and deed" as institutionalized religions emphasize in their prayers. Not only actual transgressions but
also fantasied ones are now followed by feelings of discomfort which
serve multiple functions; they may serve as a warning against the

deed and thought; or they may represent a concomitant punishment via the displeasure for even having the thought. In those developmental anomalies which result in an overdeveloped conscience, we can see that such persons are in a state of dysphoria, always lack satisfaction, and feel a chronic need to do something like fulfilling an obligation. "It also expresses itself in an exaggerated helpfulness and an exaggerated generosity, and in spending money. Some patients have the feeling that they must give their innermost souls to free themselves from the unbearable tension. The aim of all these strivings and actions is reconciliation. The feeling of guilt may appear in a variety of other forms, in forebodings of disaster, humility, suffering, striving for punishment, repentance, self-sacrifice, compulsion for purification, etc." (Nunberg, 1934, p. 137). At the point of time when such guilty feelings are manifested, a discordance between the ego and superego can be discerned. The mechanisms to achieve reconciliation often betray the urgency to accomplish this. Moreover, by five to six years, the ways in which the child handles conscious and unconscious misdeeds also give us a clue to how he will consolidate his character traits. Regressive phenomena such as merging with protective authorities, delusional systems with magical overtones, the beginning use of formalized religious devices, and sublimatory activity now achieve prominence, as do the acute awareness of loneliness and fear of social ostracism. The need of the child to belong and to be accepted in a group thus acquires deeper significance; at the same time it brings with it the propensity for many pathological neurotic disturbances.

Not only a hated authority, but also a loved one has been internalized. Schafer (1960) states that in the young child the *ego* is loved by the id as one has earlier loved external parents, and by the superego as one has wished to be loved by parents. "In the hostile aspect of the superego, object hate is turned around and transformed into self-hate; in the benign aspects of the superego it is object love which is turned around and transformed into that aspect of self-love or narcissism felt as pride and security in relation to society and destiny as well as one's own conscience and ideas. The superego builds and upholds as well as splits and tears down, just as the ego does" (p. 187f). A great many psychopathological and clinical conditions result if the hating aspects of the superego are predominant. In

330   CARL P. MALMQUIST

young children the need to suffer takes the form of psychophysiological and neurotic illnesses, as manifested in such behavior as the
constant courting of punishment or humiliation, or "accident proneness." Future "delinquent" behavior may be foreshadowed by defects
in the emerging superego, such as those related to faulty object
relations which hamper the development of a structurally intact
superego, internalization of defective parental models, an overriding
sense of guilt which leads to compulsive criminality, as well as acting
out in connection with disillusionment of ideals.

SUMMARY

In this paper the process of acquiring a conscience has been explored as a developmental phenomenon. The emphasis has been on
developmental observations and clinical material of children until
the age of six, although I have also pointed to the implications for
later normal and pathological functioning. The wealth and diversity
of data from this age period have led to the development of different
theories in different branches of psychology. The approach utilized
most frequently in this paper emphasizes the emergence of structuralized mental agencies, but it also takes into account the contributions made by learning theory and experimental investigations of
moral development. Current theoretical issues such as the cognitive
or affect-based theory of controls have been elaborated. I have emphasized the need for understanding the vicissitudes of normal conscience development from infancy onward in order to comprehend
the diverse clinical syndromes with conscience defects. The broader
cultural and anthropological questions about the origins of conscience were discussed in relation to the oedipal period. The emergence of guilt as a phenomenon of conscience has been viewed as
indicating the establishment of a delineated and functioning superego in its idealized and prohibitory aspects.

BIBLIOGRAPHY

Bandura, A. & Walters, R. H. (1963), *Social Learning and Personality Development.*
    New York: Holt, Rinehart & Winston.
Beres, D. (1958), Vicissitudes of Superego Functions and Superego Precursors in Child-
    hood. *This Annual*, 13:324-351.

—— (1966), The Functions of the Superego. In: *Psychoanalysis in the Americas,* ed. R. E. Litman. New York: International Universities Press, pp. 275-288.
Bijou, S. W. & Baer, D. M. (1961), *Child Development: A Systematic and Empirical Theory.* New York: Appleton-Century-Crofts.
Breasted, J. H. (1933), *The Dawn of Conscience.* New York: Scribner's, 1947.
Bronfenbrenner, U. (1960), Freudian Theories of Identification and Their Derivatives. *Child Develpm.,* 31:15-40.
Cain, A. C. (1961), The Presuperego 'Turning-Inward' of Aggression. *Psa. Quart.,* 30:171-208.
Erikson, E. H. (1950a), *Childhood and Society.* New York: Norton, 2nd ed., 1963.
—— (1950b), Growth and Crises of the Healthy Personality. In: *Identity and the Life Cycle* [*Psychological Issues,* Monogr. 1]. New York: International Universities Press, 1959, pp. 50-100.
Fenichel, O. (1945), *The Psychoanalytic Theory of Neurosis.* New York: Norton.
Ferenczi, S. (1925), Psycho-Analysis of Sexual Habits. *Further Contributions to the Therapy and Technique of Psycho-Analysis.* London: Hogarth Press, 1926, pp. 259-296.
Freud, S. (1907), Obsessive Actions and Religious Practices. *Standard Edition,* 9:115-127. London: Hogarth Press, 1959.
—— (1913), Totem and Taboo. *Standard Edition,* 13:1-161. London: Hogarth Press, 1955.
—— (1930), Civilization and Its Discontents. *Standard Edition,* 21:59-145. London: Hogarth Press, 1961.
Furer, M. (1967), Some Developmental Aspects of the Superego. *Int. J. Psa.,* 48:277-280.
Hammerman, S. (1965), Conceptions of Superego Development. *J. Amer. Psa. Assn.,* 13:320-355.
Hartmann, H. (1939), *Ego Psychology and the Problem of Adaptation.* New York: International Universities Press, 1958.
—— & Loewenstein, R. M. (1962), Notes on the Superego. *This Annual,* 17:42-81.
Hartshorne, J. & May, M. A. (1928-1930), *Studies in the Nature of Character,* 3 Vols. New York: Macmillan.
Jacobson, E. (1964), *The Self and the Object World.* New York: International Universities Press.
Jones, E. (1924), Mother-Right and the Sexual Ignorance of Savages. *Essays in Applied Psycho-Analysis,* 2:145-173. New York: International Universities Press, 1964.
Kagan, J. (1958), The Conception of Identification. *Psychol. Rev.,* 15:296-305.
Kohlberg, L. (1964), Development of Moral Character and Moral Ideology. In: *Review of Child Development,* 1:383-432. New York: Russell Sage Foundation.
Kohut, H. (1966), Forms and Transformations of Narcissism. *J. Amer. Psa. Assn.,* 14:243-272.
Mead, M. (1963), *Totem and Taboo* Reconsidered with Respect. *Bull. Menninger Clin.,* 27:185-199.
Nunberg, H. (1934), The Feeling of Guilt. *Practice and Theory of Psychoanalysis.* New York: International Universities Press, 1948, pp. 137-149.
Parsons, A. (1964), Is the Oedipus Complex Universal? In: *The Psychoanalytic Study of Society,* 3:278-328. New York: International Universities Press.
Schafer, R. (1960), The Loving and Beloved Superego in Freud's Structural Theory. *This Annual,* 15:163-188.
Spitz, R. A. (1957), *No and Yes: On the Genesis of Human Communication.* New York: International Universities Press.
—— (1958), On the Genesis of Superego Components. *This Annual,* 13:375-406.
Woolf, M. (1949), The Child's Moral Development. In: *Searchlights on Delinquency,* ed. K. R. Eissler. New York: International Universities Press, pp. 263-272.

THE DEVELOPMENT OF MUSICAL ABILITY

PINCHAS NOY, M.D. (Jerusalem)

Ernst Kris (1925) wrote: "the study of art is part of the study of communication. There is a sender, there are receivers, and there is a message" (p. 16). As a medium of communication, music, like any language, is spoken and listened to. He who is capable of creating structures, of finding original forms of expression in this language, is a creative artist; he who knows how to speak it, through making its signs audible and intelligible, is a performing artist; while the perceiver, who is sensitive enough to hear and understand it, is the "listener." Yet, all three, the creator, the performer, and the listener, although having command of this language and mastering its secrets, do so without awareness of what this language is, what it is saying, how it is saying what it says, and how the listener comprehends that of which he does not know what it is. And all three are incapable of translating the language of music into any other intelligible language.

To provide answers to these questions, to disclose the intrinsic essence of this language, requires investigations penetrating the secret of the artist's peculiar ability to create and perform, and of the listener's ability to comprehend, enjoy, and respond emotionally. Evidently, such problems cannot be resolved without thorough study of the multiple issues involved. No one branch of science can provide an all-embracing resolution; only a multidisciplinary approach devolving on musicology, psychology, sociology, anthropology, and other sciences has a chance of attaining conclusive information.

Lecturer in Psychiatry, Department of Psychiatry, Hebrew University and Hadassah Medical School and Hospital, Jerusalem.

Thanks are due to Mrs. M. Frisch and Dr. M. Kaufman for their help in completing this paper.

Read before the fall conference of the New England Music Therapy Association, Medfield, Mass., September, 1967.

The purpose of this paper is to examine one aspect out of the multiple facets, in an attempt to find an answer to part of the problems, through utilizing the theoretical, clinical, and experimental knowledge that has been accumulated in psychoanalysis. The paper will deal only with the origin of musical language and the developmental roots of musical ability and talent.

THE MUSICAL LANGUAGE

Most authors who concerned themselves with the origin of musical language traced it to preverbal communication. Racker (1951) writes: "We may also assume that music uses means prior to the spoken word and to object representation" (p. 150). Gutheil (1954) designates music "a communication of which we know that it is non-verbal, or perhaps pre-verbal" (p. 98). In accord with this opinion, Masserman (1955) refers to music as "this nonverbal, non-analogic form of communication" (p. 616). Margolis (1954), in an attempt to summarize the pertinent psychoanalytic ideas, states, "Most authors feel that music is related to the very earliest periods of psychological organization when the ego cannot as yet distinctly delineate the boundaries between self and reality" (p. 286).

This early source of musicality requires a discussion of what is known about the infantile ways of communication. Various authors have dealt with the specific modes of the central perceptual and organizational processes in infancy. In spite of differences in terminology to explain the peculiarities of the processes, the affinity of ideas is evident. Schachtel (1959) terms the primary mode of perception "autocentric perception," and describes it as follows: "In the autocentric mode there is little or no objectification; the emphasis is on how and what the person feels; there is a close relation, amounting to a fusion, between sensory quality and pleasure or unpleasure feelings, and the perceiver reacts primarily to something impinging on him" (p. 83).

René Spitz (1965) refers to this primary organization as the "coenesthetic organization," of which he writes: "Here, sensing is extensive, primarily visceral, centered in the autonomic nervous system, and manifests itself in the form of emotions" (p. 44).

The reader can easily accede to the fact that these statements also contain a true description of the experience of music, although this was not intended by the authors. That such an association is possible may have to do with the probable origin of musical perception in those primary modes of perception.

Observation of a six-month-old shows that the infant apprehends and "understands" his mother and other members of the family. The infant "understands" and distinguishes whether the mother approaching him is happy and merry or tense, angry, and impatient, and he responds to her love with a smile and to her tension with crying. Every mother feels that her baby "understands" her talk and distinguishes between words of love and manifestation of anger. But the infant not only is sensitive to extreme variations, he is already aware of slight changes in mood as these are expressed in the mother's voice. Since the infant still lacks the capacity of relating to language as a semantic system, to its symbols and concepts, he is indeed responding merely to the various sound components—intensity, pitch, rhythm, and timbre. Hence the remark of Spitz (1965): "Signs and signals that reach and are received by the infant in the first months of life belong to the following categories: equilibrium, tension (muscular or otherwise), posture, temperature, vibration, skin and body contact, *rhythm, tempo, duration, pitch, tone, resonance, clang,* and probably a number of others of which the adult is hardly aware and which he certainly cannot verbalize" (p. 135; my italics).

But these coincide with what musicologists refer to as the elements of the musical language—tone, pitch, intensity, timbre, rhythm, and duration. All these are part components of the preverbal, auditory, communicative medium of the infant, gathered by Spitz under the umbrella term of "coenesthetic communication." Dealing with these components of primary communication, Spitz states: "Adults, who have retained the capacity to make use of one or several of these usually atrophied categories of perception and communication, belong to the specially gifted. They are composers, musicians, dancers, acrobats, fliers, painters and poets" (p. 136).

It thus may be concluded that music is a language whose origin goes back to the auditory channel of communication at the preverbal infantile stage, i.e., at the oral and beginning anal phases. This early origin in a period preceding logical thinking may explain why it is so difficult to grasp this language by means of logical thinking and to translate its signs into the secondary terms of speech. It is highly improbable, in fact, that any language preceding the period governed by logic can be comprehended logically. Yet if we could turn back and identify with the infant, hearing the world around us through infantile ears, might not the secrets of music unveil themselves before us, enabling us to understand its paths of expression? Let us try and follow this fancy in an attempt at understanding the meaning of musical structures in analogy to infantile modes of perception.

Three examples will suffice to demonstrate briefly a new principle —to draw conclusions pertinent to the meaning of musical structures from the auditory experience of the infant. For if music as a language has its roots in the "language" of the infant, it seems right to assume that it may arouse and revive experiences originating in those early periods.

1. A frequently heard musical rhythm—the same tone repeated in short, evenly spaced beats followed by a longer accentuated tone— is regarded as portending "fate," as the opening of Beethoven's *Fifth Symphony,* for instance, or of Mahler's *Fifth Symphony,* or of the *Appassionata,* and of many others. Such structures bestow on the listener a dim feeling of anxiety, of apprehension, a sense of "fatefulness" and impending tragedy. If, ignoring the verbal content, we now try to imagine ourselves listening to a mother chiding her baby, we will hear the rhythmical repetition of the same, mostly high tone, followed by a long, intensive, and usually lower one. Does this analogy not suggest that our reaction to music of this kind with a dim feeling of anxiety may be due to a re-enactment of the apprehension with which we responded as infants to mother's rebukes?

2. In many scores, particularly in those for cembalo and piano, we find movements of fast, bouncing configurations, accentuated by a fast, steadily repetitive rhythm, played by the right hand within the span of soprano. The accompanying left hand, in sonorous and slow basses, proceeds in large, confident, and rhythmical movements (e.g., Couperin's *Les Barricades Mystérieuses),* which bestow upon us an experience of calmness and repose. Returning once again to infancy, we can imagine the concord of voices—the baby's high, shrill, emotion-ridden shrieks and the mother's comforting, reassuring, and restraining cooing in low, quiet, and slow tones. May we

not assume that it is the echo of an emotional experience of this kind that reverberates in the sounds of such music?

3. For centuries the fugue has been a favorite of musicians, transmitted from one period to the next, surviving and adapted to all styles and fashions. A form so attractive to composers and listeners alike over hundreds of years should express a deep psychological truth and gratify some basic need. Like the canon, the fugue, as its offspring, is founded on a single theme, carried by each voice and each instrument, yet taken up by each one after the other at evenly spaced intervals, so that at one and the same time it accompanies itself and is always behind itself at the same unchanging step. Turning once more to the infant and his development, we now recall the stage of first free mobility, crawling and toddling the first steps. As soon as the toddler achieves some mastery over his movements, he insists on being left on his own; he rejects support and the helping hand and is upset by any attempt to guide him. At the same time, however, he still wants his mother to stand by, ready to protect and pick him up the moment he stumbles. He wants to walk on his own, but be assured that the "big one" follows his steps at an equal and safe distance, lending him the feeling of security that makes him continue to walk "alone." Returning to the fugue, may we not assume that its specific structure of accompanying itself at a constant distance is reminiscent of some of this early experience of security, the re-assurance that there is someone to follow, to look after and protect us?

A similar, not far-off experience lies in the religious belief in the Divine Providence, in the guardian who watches man's steps (which is identical with the Ur-defense suggested by Masserman [1955], "the delusion of the omnipotent servant"). This experience, basic to all religions, may explain the fact that it was especially in the service of the church that the fugue developed and reached its height and prime.

That music is apt to induce regression to experiences dating back to earliest infancy has often been put forth in the psychoanalytic literature. Pfeifer (1923) believes that music achieves its specific effect by inducing regression to narcissistic-erotic pleasure. In his opinion, music can do this by virtue of its property to symbolize the libido of the pregenital phases preceding the stage of object relation. Germain (1928) maintains that music inspires regression to the weaning period, while Sterba (1939) suggests that music is conducive to regression reaching back to the stage when the ego was not yet differentiated from the outside world. It is due to this particular regression that music bestows on the listener a deep experience of becoming united with the outside world, of being at one with the universe.

Kohut (1955) writes: "Music, however, as an extraverbal mode of mental functioning, permits a specific, subtle regression to preverbal, i.e., to truly primitive forms of mental experience while at the same time remaining socially and aesthetically acceptable" (p. 20).

The preverbal origin of the musical language explains its universality, its ability to cross frontiers, cultures, epochs, and language barriers, its being a language intelligible to everyone. Yet although it originates in a "language spoken" by every human being at one time, there are enormous individual differences in the specific capability to use it. Not everybody hearing it is sensitive enough to enjoy listening to it, to understand it, and to respond to it. Only a few people can reproduce musical sounds, and even fewer are gifted enough to be creative in it. The ability to use this language, be it as the creator, the performer, or the discriminating listener, is by no means a property common to all mankind. Rather, it requires a special talent, of which those endowed with it have each their own measured share. And those gifted with musical talent are not a priori aware of possessing an ability that not everyone has. Discriminative hearing, the capacity to distinguish sounds, to listen to numerous sounds at one and the same time, and to store and reconstruct them in the mind—these are for the gifted natural activities, as hearing and seeing are for ordinary people. But the person who lacks these faculties regards the gifted as exceptional, blessed, and favored with a "gift from the Gods."

The question about the source of such special artistic endowment was rather neglected in classical psychology. It was generally accepted that man was born with such properties, that he had inherited them. This was the belief of psychologists like Seashore (1938) and Schoen (1940), who both devoted their works to the study of music. In fact, this opinion was shared by a number of psychoanalysts, who regarded specific artistic talent as due to constitutional factors. Other authors, however, denied any constitutional basis and maintained that musical ability, like others, is acquired in the course of the learning process. Lundin (1953) collected a considerable amount of literature to prove this point.

From more recent psychoanalytic studies it appears that there is more to the problem and that matters are not so one-sidedly clearcut. Artistic endowment is viewed as an end product that is determined by various factors, some constitutional, some environmental. These two factors, i.e., the constitutional background and the environmental influence, will here be presented separately in order to facilitate the discussion, yet they are always interrelated.

THE CONSTITUTIONAL BACKGROUND

Psychoanalytic research has endeavored to investigate those constitutional factors that are later affected by various environmental influences into promoting artistic talent. At present there is rather general agreement that the most important coefficient, probably the only one, is the presence of "a special sensory endowment which determines the perceptual organization of the individual" (Rosen, 1964, p. 4). This endowment grants the artist "greater sensitivity to sensory stimulation . . . [and] unusual capacity for awareness of relations between various stimuli" (Greenacre, 1957, p. 53).

Bergman and Escalona (1949) pointed out that children showed individual constitutional variations in their sensitivities in different sensory modalities. These variations in sensitivity may concern several senses or merely one specific sense, while the individual exaggeration of response is specific for the quantity of a given stimulus, its quality, or for both together. The oversensitivity is independent of a particular acuteness of the sensory perception (as differences in acuteness of vision, for instance); it depends, rather, on a specific reaction to stimuli and the ability to assimilate and withstand stimuli of a particular quality. The authors assume that the variations in response stem from a difference in the thickness of the "protective barrier against stimuli," or, in other words, they assume a barrier that checks the penetration of stimuli and permits no more to penetrate than can be best assimilated and integrated. A person having a lower than normal threshold will be overrun by stimuli that do not threaten to overtax another individual's toler-ance. Such a sensitive person is liable to be hurt by an impact of stimuli that for a less sensitive person may still be within the normal range. The authors present a number of cases to demonstrate that extreme oversensitivity in various modalities is apt to impede the normal development of the ego and may result in psychotic develop-ment even in childhood. Yet when the deviation is less extreme, the ego succeeds in achieving normal development, although it will have to build up specific defenses to protect itself against its unusual sensitivity in order to reject, neutralize, or master the redundant stimuli.

In a mere footnote the authors put forth a tentative suggestion: "It is attractive to follow the idea of a 'thin' protective barrier against stimuli as a possible constitutional fundament of special gifts. To do so would lead to an assumption of this sort: Only the individual liable to suffer from 'bad' stimuli in a certain modality would be likely to be able to develop sufficient interest in procuring or pro-ducing 'good' stimuli. For example, only he who suffers from noise would be likely to become a good musician" (p. 348).

It seems to me, however, that this hypothesis deserves further attention, since it can provide the basis for a theory of the constitu-tional background of artistic endowment; in my opinion, this as-sumption fits in with all we know about the development of percep-tual modalities, with the observations gathered in other realms of psychology, particularly with those of Gestalt psychology.

Perception is an active process requiring internal regulatory mechanisms to absorb and screen percepts, rejecting them in part and, with the remainder, establishing the Gestalts that enter con-sciousness. Much effort has been invested in Gestalt psychological investigation of this process. Hartmann (1939), linking such con-ceptions with psychoanalysis, described perception as an active regu-latory function on the part of the ego (p. 58).

The newborn is exposed to a multitude of stimuli, all working on his sense organs. In the developmental process the perceptual field becomes more and more recognizable and intelligible. This compre-hension requires, in turn, much activity to organize the perceptual field. The infant must develop the capability for focusing his atten-tion on numerous percepts, preventing the redundant ones from being absorbed and organizing those assimilated into simple Gestalts that he can recognize, remember, and compare.

In the auditory field, in which we are interested here, the infant absorbs tens or perhaps hundreds of stimuli at any given time. His capability for listening to certain stimuli depends, first of all, on the development of the ability *not* to hear, to shut out, all other stimuli. This is a natural faculty for every adult who, attending a lecture, for instance, listens to its presentation while being deaf to outside noises like the rattling of cars in the street, banging of doors, his neighbor's creaking chair, etc. To put it schematically, one might suppose that a person who, at a given time, is simultaneously exposed to let us say fifty auditory stimuli will succeed in shutting out forty-eight or forty-nine, while his attention is absorbed by only one or two.

To the extent that the protective barrier against stimuli differs from one individual to another, it may be assumed that children differ in the ability *not* to hear the redundant stimuli. There are, thus, variations in the degree to which the child is capable of ignoring the surfeit stimuli; or such a selection, while easily carried out by one child, may prove to be too much of an effort for another. It may just as well be imagined that a child is simply incapable of shutting out the forty-eight or forty-nine stimuli, that he can do so with no more than thirty at a time. The child thus remains exposed to about twenty simultaneous stimuli. In that case he has only two alternatives —either to submit to "break down" or to develop specific abilities in the ego to overcome and master the threatening results of a constitutional deficiency. The only way out of this dilemma is an effort toward orientation in and mastery of the auditory perceptual field. The infant will have to develop an ability to concentrate his attention to directing and mastering twenty different, simultaneously occurring sound stimuli.

An extreme example of such an accomplishment is presented in the person of the prominent conductor of an orchestra, who has the extraordinary gift of simultaneously listening to the orchestra as one body and to each of the instruments separately, distinguishing each by its playing as if he concentrated on it alone—an achievement that the ordinary person can neither imagine nor grasp how it is being brought off.

The ego, exposed to the impact of auditory stimuli, is compelled to attain considerable abilities in order to protect itself and to build up a second line of defense to replace the primary, the deficient barrier against stimuli. In that case the ego develops a superior capability to organize auditory stimuli, to discern among their various shades, and, in particular, to transform "painful" stimuli so that he can derive gratification and pleasure from them. It may be assumed, therefore, that specific musical abilities are part of coping mechanisms which the ego is forced to develop as a defense for mastering oversensitivity.

This theory is borne out by the common observation that people with a flair for music are, in general, sensitive to sound stimuli and easily "irritated" by exceptional noise. Biographies of musicians brim with anecdotes about such oversensitivity. Macalpine and Hunter (1952) described one example of the composer Rossini, who suffered from phobic fear of the noise of trains, and a severe compulsion expressed in the auditory sphere.[1]

Some similarity may be found between the theory suggested here and the formulations put forth by Kohut and Levarie (1950), Kohut (1957), Niederland (1958), and Berezin (1958) with regard to enjoyment. These authors regard listening to music as an activity of the ego in the service of mastering auditory stimuli that, in their deeper meaning, are threatening and frightening. These writers, too, are convinced that, owing to constitutional and environmental factors alike, this threatening implication is attributed to various noise stimuli. Still there is an essential difference between their theories and the present one. Whereas they maintain that listening to music is an activity which, like playing, serves the ego's needs for mastery, it is here contended that the musical talent itself stems from the essential need of the ego to achieve mastery. Unlike playing, mastery of this sort is not primarily intended to attain pleasure; it is definitely enacted out of the defensive need, to help the ego cope with the onslaught of a surfeit of auditory stimuli.

---

[1] It is dangerous to depend on biographies, which are frequently retrograde glorifications of childhood genius, as a scientific source for conveying facts about the predecessors of artistic achievement. But it would be possible and worthwhile to plan an anterograde research in which predictions could be made based on young children's specific sensitivities. These predictions would be related some years later to the possible emergence of musical abilities.

THE ENVIRONMENTAL BACKGROUND

The environmental factors influencing the development of musical ability have been rather neglected in the psychoanalytic literature. The few authors who have dealt with the subject stressed the influence of the primary mother-child relationship.

Racker (1951) discusses music as a communicative medium antedating the spoken word and object representation. He concludes that "the sharpening, or more exactly, the erotization of hearing may possibly have one of its roots in the attention a small child pays to the arrival of his mother" (p. 150).

Anna Freud (1965), dealing with the lines of development in children, states that such lines of development "are included in their constitution as inherent possibilities" (p. 86). The proportionate strength, however, of the one or the other developmental line depends on environmental factors, most important among which is the mother and her primary relation to her baby: "In the beginning of life, at least, the infant seems to concentrate on the development along those lines which call forth most ostensibly the mother's love and approval. . . . This implies that activities which are acclaimed by the mother are repeated more frequently, become libidinized, and thereby stimulated into further growth" (p. 86).

Among the examples used by Anna Freud to demonstrate these influences, we find the following: "It is not unknown that early contact with the mother through her singing has consequences for the later attitudes to music and may promote special musical aptitudes" (p. 87).

In the light of the opinions quoted above it seems safe to assume that among the environmental factors it is the primary preverbal mode of communication between the infant and his mother that initiates the development of musical talent. Rather little was done in psychoanalysis to investigate these modes of communication until René Spitz (1965) observed that they differ essentially from later ones. The primary modes communicate no more than affects, expressed in patterns of coenesthetic organization through the various sensory channels—hearing, seeing, touching, etc.

From observations of mother-child dyads it appears that there are individual differences in the modes of communication. Each dyad shows a preference for one particular channel of communication, which then becomes dominant in this specific relationship while others are used considerably less. Such individual differences are due to specific factors which vary from mother to mother and from infant to infant. Some mothers like to talk to their babies, to whisper and sing to them, whereas others do not open their lips while handling their babies. Often we hear a mother reply to our question about her contact with her child: "Naturally, I won't talk to him, he doesn't understand anything yet." Similar differences are found with regard to tactile contact. Some mothers enjoy keeping the baby in their arms, cuddling, and fondling him, whereas others handle the baby as little as possible and only when it is really asked for. (Such mothers will not hesitate to find a rational excuse like the danger of infection, etc.) Because of the individual differences in the mother's contact with her baby, every infant "receives" the mother differently. As stated above, there usually is one dominant channel of communication through which the infant affectively "receives" the mother and, through her, the outside world; yet that channel is different for every baby.

Primary communication is mutual, as is communication in general, since the baby expresses his needs through the same channels— sounds, movements, contacts, etc. Even such a primary ability as that of expression is subject to individual variations; Korner (1964), e.g., observed that infants vary in their abilities to demonstrate their inner states, some conveying "their needs more readily to their caretakers" than others (p. 65). It may be assumed, furthermore, that children differ in their capacities for utilizing the various modes of communication, yet every baby eventually succeeds in making himself understood through signs of one or the other sort. Some children convey their needs mainly by vocal means, while others resort more frequently to movement. These variations seem to stem from constitutional factors, on the one hand, and from the experiences the infant has had with regard to the mother's readiness to respond to his various "messages," on the other hand. Hence the specific pattern of communication characteristic of each mother-child dyad is modeled on a combination of two factors, those contributed by the mother and those inherent in the infant.

When the auditory channel is the supreme mode of primary com-

munication, it may be assumed that the child is predisposed to building musical ability. In an infant who related affectively to his surroundings through the auditory channel of communication and who
"received" the mother mainly through auditory stimuli, this channel
may continue to play a prominent role in his emotional exchange
with the outside world. And later, when the adult is stirred up by
longings for the lost paradise of oral infancy, for that symbiotic
mother love, such longings may take on the shape of craving for those
"fondling tones." Music, with its sound patterns set according to primary design, can thus bring him back to that primary period when
through the sensory modality of hearing he had felt reassured by his
mother's love.

Psychoanalysts who have musical patients in treatment certainly
observe a periodical increase in the pressing need of their patients to
hear and enjoy music. With several patients I have had the experience that such periods were marked by concurrent diffuse and indis-
tinct longings, such as "I feel like yearning for I don't know what;
nothing can please me but music." Some time later all these patients
vividly recalled early memories of their long-dead mothers.

Interestingly, it is not through musical ability alone that the
preservation of infantile auditory modes of communication is manifested by those persons. They have other characteristics that retain
traces of auditory coenesthetic perception. While talking with others,
they are unusually sensitive to the various components of speech,
such as sound, timbre, intensity, and rhythm. This perception, without necessarily being conscious, is actively engaged in, though it
serves a communicative function. Whenever I am told by a patient
about impressions such as "I can't complain, he is kind with me, but
I feel that he is really mad at me; something in his voice tells me
so . . . ," I usually ask the patient whether he is fond of music. And
it has always proved to be true that those who are more sensitive and
responsive to the sounds of speech rather than to its content have
some affinity to music.

INTEGRATION OF THE FACTORS

The constitutional and environmental factors do not exist independently of each other, and it is obvious that they mutually influ-

ence each other. A specific sensory sensitivity that is considered to be determined by a constitutional factor is permanently subjected to environmental influences. Spitz (1965) maintains that the primary barrier against stimuli forms an integral part of the structure of the sensorium. Within a very brief span of time, though, the protective task is taken over by the "ego nuclei," so that the protective barrier is turned into a function of the ego. Since in the course of development the ego is exposed to numerous environmental factors, these will certainly exert an influence on the specific ability of the protective barrier to screen stimuli, to reject or to assimilate them. It may therefore be concluded that the unusual sensory sensitivity that is assumed to be at the root of musical ability is given at birth as an Anlage and is molded into its final shape through the mutual influences of a variety of environmental factors.

On the other hand, it is rather improbable that the specific mode of communication of the mother-child dyad can be singled out as a mere environmental factor. This specific mode is not established solely by the mother's habitual approach to her child; it is no less determined by the infant's modes of expression, and these depend to a considerable degree on constitutional factors. In reality, however, as was indicated briefly, it is impossible to distinguish between constitutional and environmental factors because every single etiological factor bears distinct evidence of the mutual and interwoven influences of constitution and environment.

In spite of this mutuality of influences it seems worthwhile to distinguish between the primary sensory sensitivity and the mother-infant mode of communication, and to view them as two separate factors, each being instrumental in the development of musical ability. The proportionate degree to which each of them exercises its influence varies from one individual to another; accordingly, countless variations of individual patterns of musical ability are observed.

In some people musicality is many-sided; they have a "natural" capacity for absolute pitch, for pitch discrimination, etc., yet they show little interest in music and are not particularly keen on it, whereas others enjoy nothing better than music and even become "addicted" to it. Some persons get tense and irritable if for some reason they are prevented from listening to music for some time, but in musical aptitude tests they show no particular musicality, a factor that may be responsible for their falling short of performing or composing music, although they eagerly endeavor to do so.

Between these extremes multi-shaded variations are observed in the combination of primary ability and the need for attaining gratification through listening to music. Those combinations presumably mirror the varieties of integration of the two factors that determine the development of musical ability. Apparently, the specific musical capability owes its development to the unusual sensory sensitivity, whereas the specific interest in music and the ability to attain gratification from listening to it are based in the primary modes of communication. In reality we scarcely ever see a case in which one of the two factors can be isolated as the single determinant of development. It is not surprising, then, that a person will rarely display considerable musical talent while denying all interest in music, just as it is highly improbable that a person greatly interested in music will be denied all musical talent.

The opinions presented here are merely hypothetical, though they are rooted in the clinical and theoretical knowledge gathered in the field of psychoanalysis; yet they lack experimental confirmation. Certainly, every assumption will be scientifically better founded when it has withstood the test of controlled experiment. In fact, such an experimental investigation of the psychoanalytic conceptions about art and artists has not been undertaken. It seems, however, that the assumptions presented here might serve as the basis for designing a research project to examine and prove the constitutional roots of musical talent and to demonstrate the effects of primary modes of communication on the development of musical ability. I realize that considerable effort would need to be invested in an experimental study of this kind. Yet I think it worthwhile because the results, beyond yielding additional information about music and musical ability, may shed light on the problems of the developmental background of artistic talent per se and of gratification through art in all its forms.

BIBLIOGRAPHY

Berezin, M. A. (1958), Some Observations on Art (Music) and Its Relationship to Ego Mastery. *Bull. Phila. Assn. Psa.*, 8:49-65.
Bergman, P. & Escalona, S. K. (1949), Unusual Sensitivities in Very Young Children. *This Annual*, 3/4:333-352.
Freud, A. (1965), *Normality and Pathology in Childhood: Assessments of Development.* New York: International Universities Press.
Germain, P. (1928), La musique et la psychanalyse. *Rev. Franç.*, 2:751-792.
Greenacre, P. (1957), The Childhood of the Artist. *This Annual*, 12:47-72.
Gutheil, E. A. (1954), Music as Adjoint to Psychotherapy. *Amer. J. Psychother.*, 8:94-109.
Hartmann, H. (1939), *Ego Psychology and the Problem of Adaptation.* New York: International Universities Press.
Kohut, H. (1955), Some Psychological Effects of Music and Their Relation to Music Therapy. *Music Ther.*, 5:17-20.
—— (1957), Observations on the Psychological Function of Music. *J. Amer. Psa. Assn.*, 5:389-407.
—— & Levarie, S. (1950), On the Enjoyment of Listening to Music. *Psa. Quart.*, 19:64-87.
Korner, A. F. (1964), Some Hypotheses regarding the Significance of Individual Differences at Birth for Later Development. *This Annual*, 19:58-72.
Kris, E. (1952), *Psychoanalytic Explorations in Art.* New York: International Universities Press.
Lundin, R. W. (1953), *An Objective Psychology of Music.* New York: Ronald Press.
Macalpine, I. & Hunter, R. A. (1952), Rossini: Piano Pieces for the Primal Scene. *Amer. Imago*, 9:213-219.
Margolis, N. M. (1954), A Theory on the Psychology of Jazz. *Amer. Imago*, 11:263-291.
Masserman, J. H. (1955), *The Practice of Dynamic Psychiatry.* Philadelphia: Saunders.
Niederland, W. G. (1958), Early Auditory Experiences, Beating Fantasies, and Primal Scene. *This Annual*, 13:471-504.
Pfeifer, S. (1923), Musikpsychologische Probleme. *Imago*, 9:453-462.
Racker, H. (1951), Contribution to Psychoanalysis of Music. *Amer. Imago*, 8:129-163.
Rosen, V. H. (1964), Some Effects of Artistic Talent on Character Style. *Psa. Quart.*, 33:1-24.
Schachtel, E. G. (1959), *Metamorphosis.* New York: Basic Books.
Schoen, M. (1940), *The Psychology of Music.* New York: Ronald Press.
Seashore, C. E. (1938), *Psychology of Music.* New York: McGraw-Hill.
Sterba, R. (1939), Toward the Problem of the Musical Process. *Psa. Rev.*, 33:37-43, 1946.
Spitz, R. A. (1965), *The First Year of Life.* New York: International Universities Press.

ON AN EARLY GENITAL PHASE
With an Addendum on Genesis

HERMAN ROIPHE, M.D. (New York)

One of the best established sets of constructs in psychoanalysis is that large body of work in which the genital phase, along with its appropriate dynamic content, is delineated. It is my purpose in this paper to reconsider some aspects of these constructs against the background of a body of clinical experience, with the aim of suggesting some extensions of our understanding of genital development.

The most generally accepted theory of the development of sexuality is that the two sexes develop in much the same way until the onset of the phallic phase at about three years of age. At this time children of both sexes would seem to be little boys (Freud, 1933). The child's observation of the anatomical differences between the sexes (Freud, 1925) and the consequent castration complex have a fateful impact on the by now divergent lines of male and female sexual development (Abraham, 1920; Freud, 1931, 1933; Lampl-de Groot, 1927). This genital sexual current is from the beginning crucially involved with the familiar oedipal triangle.

Thus far the conceptual lines are direct and clear and have served to organize and elucidate a bewildering array of phenomena of normal and pathological development. Freud himself began to disturb this conceptual clarity when, in 1931 and 1933, he concerned himself with the preoedipal development of the girl, emphasizing that the early attachment to the mother did not terminate as early or as decisively as had been thought, but rather continued on into

This paper was presented before The New York Psychoanalytic Society, October, 1967. The data on which this paper is based were collected at The Masters Children's Center. The interpretation of these data is entirely my own and in no way reflects the views of Margaret S. Mahler, M.D., Director of Research of The Masters Children's Center.

Assistant Clinical Professor of Psychiatry, Albert Einstein College of Medicine.

the phallic phase and in some cases was never relinquished. In addition, he referred to reports of other investigators about early vaginal sensations in little girls. Both Jones (1927) and Melanie Klein (1928) cited evidence of genital sensations in little girls in the second year of life which are associated with oral and anal phase developments. Their view is, however, complicated by their invocation of an oedipal constellation in the second year of life which is concomitant with this genital arousal. While their conceptual framework is open to serious question, it is not so easy to dismiss the observational underpinnings of a genitality that manifests itself earlier than has generally been supposed and that is involved with preoedipal developmental currents.

Discussing observations at variance with established analytic findings concerning chronology, Anna Freud (1951) reports, "Penis envy, which we expected to see in girls in the phallic phase, appeared with extreme violence according to some of our recordings in girls between eighteen and twenty-four months. In these cases, the responsible factor may have been the bodily intimacy between boys and girls as it exists in a residential nursery where the opportunities for watching other children being bathed, dressed, potted, etc., are countless" (p. 27f.). Anna Freud has tentatively suggested that the provocative force of the observation of the anatomical difference between the sexes produced the extremely violent reactions of penis envy in these children. Such a thesis does not, however, explain the curious age clustering, nor, for that matter, does it establish the conditions for the high narcissistic cathexis of the genitals which is implied in such a reaction.

Lisbeth Sachs (1962) has reported in considerable detail a case of severe castration anxiety in an eighteen-month-old boy. This youngster had achieved rather solid bowel and bladder control by eighteen months. He suddenly refused to use the toilet, and would not even enter the bathroom. He became generally tense and panic-stricken and repeatedly expressed the fear that he would lose his penis, that he would be flushed down the toilet, or that he would lose an arm, fingers or nose. He resisted his mother's efforts to remove his soiled diaper with the expressed fear that his penis would fall off. He also worried that his penis would fall off in the bath and go down the drain. He soon developed a severe sleep disturbance. He would awake from sleep screaming for his mother, although her approach frequently provoked a more intense panic. Apparently he awoke from nightmares of noisily barking dogs, bells, and shooting guns and was frightened by dreams of butterflies touching his body. His fear of noises soon spread to the daytime sounds of screeching brakes, airplanes, the vacuum cleaner, and the washing machine.

This is a classical description of profound castration anxiety in a young boy and would be unremarkable were it not for the unusually early age of its onset. Unfortunately, there is a hiatus in this otherwise rich and detailed clinical study. There is no delineation of what factors served to provoke this catastrophic castration reaction. There is, however, some indirect evidence that the little boy had seen his mother exposed. Once when his mother had scolded him a great deal, he cried, "I don't want my penis. I want to wee-wee from my toushy like mommies do." Sachs would seem to explain the castration anxiety in this youngster as arising out of an oedipal conflict, a far-reaching assertion for which the protocol does not offer sufficient clinical evidence. In any case, the fact that this eighteen-month-old boy suffered a severe castration reaction is established beyond any reasonable doubt. It should be noted that the time of onset falls within the age cluster of the cases reported earlier by Anna Freud.

In another paper (1968) I reported a case of a moderately severe castration reaction in a nineteen-month-old. The reaction in this little girl is in most details similar to the case reported by Sachs. Kate had by nineteen months achieved fairly solid bowel and bladder control. One day she spent the afternoon at the house of a little boy, a familiar playmate of her own age, who on that occasion walked around without any clothes, and later in the afternoon both children were bathed together by the little boy's mother. When Kate returned home, she made repeated direct references to the little boy's penis. However, within a short while this direct, undistorted acknowledgment of the genital difference was replaced by a defensive denial and displacement of profound force. She now referred to his penis as his "three belly buttons" and his birthmark; it should be noted that she had a somewhat protuberant umbilicus and a birthmark on her hip, neither of which the little boy had. The formal structure of this denial and displacement, that she had something just like the little boy had, became remarkably pervasive and tended to organize the child's perceptions, thoughts, and relationships.

The denial was incapable of containing the disruptive force of the child's observation of the genital difference, and within a brief period she became incontinent. Concomitant with the incontinence was an intense and intractable negativism, which made even the most rudimentary operations such as dressing and bathing major daily crises. A sleep disturbance of moderate severity also developed.

After several months, active reparative fantasies and behavior became much more evident. Along these lines there were indications of her belief that her mother and other grown women had a hidden penis with the suggestion that she might still grow one. There were hints of a stool-phallus equation, with the underlying assertion that she had one. Kate demonstrated behavior suggestive of an incipient syndrome of penis envy, with the aggressive impulse to seize the penis for herself.

In my discussion of the case I attempted to demonstrate that the underlying disruptive, dynamic force of Kate's observation of genital difference stemmed from the threat of object loss with which she was confronted. At the same time, the utter collapse of the child reflected the severe narcissistic injury and the undermining of the self representation, particularly the body self, which followed the traumatic experience.

The castration reaction in this child falls within the same age cluster as the other cases discussed above. Any explanatory thesis not only will have to account for the age specificity, but must also establish the conditions for the high narcissistic cathexis of the genitals which is implied in such pronounced castration reactions.

In a paper on early female sexual development, Greenacre (1950) raised a number of points relevant to the whole question of a genital arousal earlier than our usual genital phase constructs would lead us to expect. In a summary statement, she wrote of:

> (a) the possible early vague awareness of the vagina, which however is not subjectively adequately differentiated from the rectum; (b) the influence on vaginal awareness and reactivity by states of oral stimulation or frustration . . . by direct stimulation of the rectum and anus, and by a surcharging of the organism by massive stimulations greater than can be cared for through ap-

propriate [i.e., mature] channels of discharge, so that immature discharge mechanisms [i.e., genital] may be prematurely stimulated. As a corollary to this, there is the implication that there may be distortions of the regular sequence of preoedipal development, or in the extreme, different types of preoedipal organization. This leads to (c), the consideration that clitoris and vagina may have varying relationships to each other, with a patterning which has a far-reaching influence on the sexual response of the woman and a deep, sometimes decisive effect on her character [p. 134 f.].

We have reached a point where we must begin to find a place in our genetic constructions for these many observations which run contrary to our present developmental concepts. It is my purpose to propose a regularly occurring, normal genital phase appearing some time between eighteen and twenty-four months of age. The specific dynamic content of this phase concerns itself with questions of self and object representation and is, as far as I have been able to determine, free of any oedipal resonance, although I do believe that the developmental precipitates specific to this phase may have fateful implications for the later genital-oedipal phase.

Clinical data from the treatment of a three-and-a-half year-old pseudoautistic psychotic girl, Alice, highlighted a number of developmental features which ultimately suggested to me both the necessity and the usefulness of the proposed early genital phase, not only in understanding aberrant patterns of development but also in elucidating important aspects of normal development.

Alice was a firstborn child, whose development, in retrospect, was already aberrant in the second half of the first year. Although her physical growth was entirely normal, her social responses were atypical. She was from very early a sober-faced child, who very rarely smiled. When she woke, either in the middle of the night or in the early morning, she never cried or called to her mother, but would sit quietly in her crib until someone came to her. Even when she had an ear infection, which on physical examination revealed an angry red bulging eardrum, the child did not cry. By the end of the first year the pediatrician who had seen Alice since birth made the diagnosis of childhood autism. She did develop speech in the beginning of the second year, but did not appear to use it in a communicative fashion. Her parents separated when she was two years old. Thereupon her use of speech, such as it was, quickly diminished, so that when she appeared for treatment a year and a half later, she was mute except for unintelligible vocalizations and shrieks. She was at three and a half incontinent and wore diapers both during the day and night. She never appeared to manifest any awareness of bowel and bladder functions, even when her mother made an effort to train her.

Alice was three and a half years of age when she was started in an intensive treatment program, as part of a research investigation of the separation-individuation phase in normal and psychotic children (see Mahler and Gosliner, 1955; Mahler and Furer, 1960; Pine and Furer, 1963). She was a well-developed child and physically attractive, except for the vacant, unfocused gaze and immobile features which gave her appearance a curiously unappealing quality. While she was largely oblivious to her human environment unless it impinged too closely or vigorously upon her, she carried with her everywhere a burdensome collection of plastic baby bottles, a shredded blanket and toy duck, objects from which she could not bear to be parted. Her activity alternated between an aimless wandering and a concentrated and almost endlessly repetitive filling and emptying of her baby bottles with dried peas or dirt, painstakingly collected from crevices in the concrete-floored playground.

After several months of extremely patient work with her warm, sensitive, and devoted therapist, the child began to show some cracks in her autistic shell. Alice began to use the therapist to fetch objects which were out of reach, to join in mutual rhythmic play; and occasionally she would burrow in her therapist's embrace in a relaxed, dreamy, infantile attitude.

In this general climate, Alice was one day observed frantically running about the playroom with a searching, darting gaze, as if she were looking for something. She suddenly stopped, her gaze focused, she momentarily strained at a bowel movement, and then resumed running about as before. Previously Alice had not manifested even the slightest awareness of bowel or bladder functions, nor had she shown any observable behavioral reflections of these functions. When it was pointed out to her that she was looking for something outside herself, when, in fact, what she was responding to was the inner stimulus of bowel urgency, Alice flew into a panic tantrum of awesome dimension. From that time on it was possible, in an emotionally meaningful climate, to delineate interpretively for Alice such primal ego discriminations as inside-outside, self-nonself, animate-inanimate. In the process, the behavioral concomitants of and her attitudes toward the bowel urgency became sharply focused in a well-defined sequence of cause and effect such as had never before been observed in her autistically organized state. For a time the sequence, bowel urgency-interpretation-panic tantrum, became much more frequent, so that the several hours which Alice spent daily at the treatment Center were entirely consumed in the most intense conflict over holding on and letting go. Gradually she seemed to resolve the conflict by withholding her bowel movement until nighttime, when she was asleep in her bed, wearing diapers.

As the conflict over bowel urgency receded, behavior and conflict very similar in many details, at least at the outset, were manifested around urinary urgency. Much the same interpretative ground was covered as was the case with the bowel conflict. Naturally, the primal polarities of self-nonself, inside-outside, were traversed in a much more telescoped fashion, but the problems of the threat of object loss and of the disintegration of the sense of self, particularly the body self, were only painfully slowly and partially worked through.

In this general setting, with the gradual withholding and control of the urinary function, a new developmental feature, central to my formulation of an early genital phase, arose. As Alice became increasingly able to withhold the immediate discharge of bladder urgency, she began for the first time to manifest unmistakable and unambiguous indications of genital arousal. For the first time she was observed to masturbate openly and she began to examine with extraordinary curiosity and concentration the genital area of the playroom dolls. There were also signs of a developing penis-envy syndrome. She could be seen to interrupt her masturbation and dart into the adjoining playroom of a young boy, where she would steal a model airplane, a car or toy soldiers of his, and return to her room in an excited and euphoric mood.

In view of the foregoing, I would draw the general inference that with the delay in the immediate discharge of bowel and bladder

tension in the early phase of toilet control, there regularly and normally occurs a spread in excitation to and arousal of the genital
organs. I tend to believe that this is a neurophysiological developmental given. I am also inclined to believe that after several months
of more firmly established mastery of sphincter control, there follows
a loosening in the association of sphincter, rectal, and bladder tension, on the one hand, and genital arousal, on the other. Furthermore, I have the impression that this loosening association of the
two leads, in varying degrees, to a brief period of latency as far as
genital arousal is concerned, which then erupts again in the familiar
phallic-oedipal phase.

It may be criticized that such a relationship, which I have inferred from the highly chaotic and atypical development of a psychotic child, cannot have relevance for normal development. I would
maintain that the study of the severe neuroses and the psychoses may
serve to focus for us many features of very early development, just as
the study of the transference neurosis served to clarify the importance of the later oedipal constellation in normal development.

The association of anal sensations with genital sensations is by
no means a novel observation. Freud (1933) wrote, "there are a few
isolated reports of early vaginal sensations as well, but it could not
be easy to distinguish these from sensations in the anus or vestibu-
lum" (p. 118). And Jones (1927) stated, "The anus is evidently identified with the vagina to begin with, and the differentiation of the
two is an extremely obscure process, more so perhaps than any other
in female development; I surmise, however, that it takes place in
part at an earlier age than is generally supposed" (p. 443). Brunswick
(1940) also called attention to vaginal sensitivity arising early, associated with anal stimulation. Greenacre (1950) anticipated many of
my own findings, without quite making the association of a regularly
occurring early genital phase. She found evidence of very early
vaginal awareness, hazy and unverified though it is. She noted that
vaginal awareness was increased in those patients who in infancy
had been subjected to repeated stimulation of the rectum and anus;
when this had occurred before the phallic phase, a strong oral-vaginal
response developed in reaction to primal scene observations.

A major developmental precipitate of the early genital phase is
the integration of the genital representation into the body schema.

Loewenstein (1950), in a charming observational vignette, which I have in several instances been able to confirm, described a ten-month-old boy's discovery of his penis and the whole process of his experimental confirmation that the penis belongs to his body. This level of integration of the genital into the body self, as he described it, is mediated through tactile, kinesthetic, and, most importantly, visual incorporation. The importance of the visual mode for this level of genital integration into the body image must incidentally play a small role, if any at all, for the little girl, since she cannot readily see her own genitals. In any case, I believe that the contribution of this level of experience to the ultimate genital schematization must be weak indeed. It is for this reason that I take exception to Loewenstein's assertion that the boy's castration anxiety in the phallic phase takes as its model the infantile uncertainty that the penis is an indissoluble part of his own body: i.e., if Loewenstein means by this that there is a dynamic relationship between the two, as he seems to suggest, rather than a merely formalistic and analogic relationship. On the other hand, the centrality of the early genital phase for the genital schematization rests on the fact that during this phase there is, I believe, a normal and regularly occurring genital arousal, with the implied maturation of the genitals as a channel for tension discharge and pleasure possibility. From this point onward, all major experiences of the child will have a genital reflection.

I have already indicated that the genital arousal central to this phase is a developmental precipitate, so to speak, of the whole process of sphincter control. In the clinical sketch of Alice's developmental progress in her therapy, her relationship to her own stool paralleled and was directly bound up with the level of her object relations. The first behavioral reflection of a bowel movement was manifested only after months of therapeutic work, which resulted in a relatively solidly established need-satisfying relationship with her therapist. While Alice could periodically retreat into her autistic shell, she was just as often driven outward again by her object hunger. From this time onward, the stool, the concretization of the oral attachment to the nourishing object, could no longer pass through the body without psychic registration, since the primal attachment to the object results in a structuralization within the ego.

For many months thereafter, the conflict around the stool-object

raged; Alice could not ignore it, and she could not resolve it. Painstaking interpretative work dealt with a variety of reincorporative
and destructive fantasies. The panic centered essentially around the
threat of object loss and the related threat to the integrity of the self.
With the partial working through of these conflics, the ego's margin
of control, as manifested in the gradually improving sphincter control, was enhanced. Much of this was touchingly confirmed when
Alice had her first bowel movement in the toilet. With this loss she
developed for the first time a profound sadness, which could be
empathically recognized as such, and which lasted for several days.

The major thrust of development up to this point has been the
differentiation of the self from the object and the internalization and
solidification of the object representation as signaled in the achievement of sphincter control. With the latter, there is the developmental
precipitate of the early genital phase, which opens the channel of
genital arousal. At this juncture, the specific anxieties of the two
contiguous phases, object loss and castration, are indissoluble. The
later castration anxiety of the phallic phase is genetically linked to
that of the early genital phase, and, by virtue of this, has a direct
developmental connection to the anxiety of object loss. In *Inhibitions, Symptoms and Anxiety* (1926), Freud discussed the analogic
relation between the anxieties of object loss and castration. I have
here attempted to demonstrate that this relationship is more than a
formal one, that it is an actual and developmentally a prototypic one.
Nevertheless, the castration anxiety in the phallic phase no longer
has the direct and immediate resonance of object loss as it did in
the earlier genital phase, since in the intervening period the object
representation has become further solidified so that the constancy
of the representation is to a large extent insured.

At this point it may be useful to reconsider the observations of
early and violent castration reactions reported by Anna Freud,
Lisbeth Sachs, and myself in the light of the early genital phase
which I have proposed. Ordinarily a child will pass through the
early genital phase with very little observable behavioral reflection
of the important dynamic currents of this phase. However, symptomatic castration reactions, at times of extreme violence, will develop
when the following three conditions, to be discussed in more detail

below, exist: (1) There is a genital arousal which is universal and characteristic of this early phase. (2) The child, at this point in development, observes the anatomical difference between the sexes. (3) At an earlier phase in his life the child was subjected to experiences which served to produce an instability in the self and object representations.

The first requirement of any explanatory thesis must be that it establish the conditions for the high narcissistic cathexis of the genitals which is implied in such reactions. This condition has been adequately satisfied, I believe, by my assertion of a normal and regularly occurring genital arousal at this early age, with the implied maturation of the genitals as a channel for tension discharge and pleasure possibility. Another feature that was noted in these cases was the clustering of the reported castration reactions between the ages of eighteen and twenty-four months. This is, of course, the age range in which at least preliminary sphincter control is ordinarily established, and with it the consequent genital arousal. There are those special situations in which sphincter control is enforced much earlier or delayed until well after this age range. It would be of particular interest to determine the implications of these special situations for the early genital phase development, but this must be left for future investigation.

I have previously described a severe castration reaction in nineteen-month-old Kate, a reaction which was undeniably triggered by the disruptive traumatic observation of a little boy's penis. With the proposal of the early genital phase, with its high narcissistic cathexis of the genitals, the narcissistic injury and the undermining of the self representation which resulted from the observation of the anatomical difference between the sexes are readily understandable. In this sense, the situation is hardly different from that of the phallic-phase child, who is traumatized by his observation of the sexual difference precisely because there is such a high narcissistic evaluation of the genitals. In the cases from the Hampstead Nursery in which violent penis-envy reactions in little girls were observed in the second half of the second year, Anna Freud similarly felt that the responsible factor may have been the observation of the genitals of children of the opposite sex. In Sachs's case of severe castration anxiety in an eighteen-month-old boy, the provocative experience was not delineated, but there was indirect evidence that he had observed his mother urinating and clearly saw that she did not possess a penis.

In addition to these two preconditions necessary for the symptomatic outbreak of a castration reaction during this early genital phase, there must have been in the child's prehistory some conditions or experiences which distorted or interfered with the self and object representations. The nineteen-month-old girl, Kate, who developed a severe castration reaction, had some four months earlier shown a marked separation reaction when her father left for the Army. The little girl undeniably reacted to the loss of her father, but the major impact of the experience stemmed from the implied threat of losing the more highly invested maternal object. A major developmental thrust at this period in the child's life is the separation from and the casting off of the infantile symbiotic relationship to the mother (Mahler and Gosliner, 1955), in the process of which the child leans increasingly heavily on the father. With the loss of her father, Kate was thrown back to her mother and was as a consequence much more threatened by her maturing independent strivings. When this child reached the early genital phase, her reaction to her observation of the anatomical difference, with its implied threat to her sense of body integrity, was markedly intensified by the earlier threat of object loss. At this juncture in development, castration and object loss have the same resonance as a Gestalt figure-ground pattern.

Similarly, the reactions of a child in the early genital phase to the observation of anatomical distinctions will be immediately intensified if in his prehistory there were experiences or conditions such as pain, convulsions, fevers, etc., which create severe disturbances in the sense of the body self, with feelings of imminent dissolution. At this point in development, castration and annihilation fears converge and are indissoluble. In the phallic phase, with the further solidification and constancy of the self and object representations, the castration fear, powerful and organizing as it may be, no longer carries the immediate, more global meaning of threatened object loss and self-annihilation, as is the case in the early genital phase. It is one of the most striking phase-specific characteristics of the early genital development that the genital schematization and the sense of self are largely coextensive. This characteristic is very reminiscent of the state of affairs in male perversions, particularly in the fetishist, and in certain severe neuroses in women. For this reason, I believe that the concept of an early genital phase will prove crucial in the further elucidation of these psychopathological conditions.

In a definitive series of papers on fetishism Greenacre (1953, 1955, 1960) emphasized a specific combination of genetic influences. She pointed to disturbances in the first eighteen months of life which produce instability in the formation of the body image, lead to uncertainty of outline and fluctuations in the subjective sense of size, and which by bringing about complementary disturbances in the phallic phase result in an exaggeration of the castration complex. The genital area of the body image is less certain in the early months of life than most other parts of the body. Under normal conditions the genital schematization becomes consolidated during the phallic phase, due to an increase in the spontaneous endogenous sensations arising at that time.

Under the conditions of disturbed pregenitality which she described in some detail, the overly strong castration anxiety of the phallic phase is combined with the body-disintegration anxiety from the earlier phases and depletes rather than reinforces the genital schematization. This felicitous reconstruction of the prehistory of the fetishist would serve to explicate, as I understand it, the major crises in his pathological development. I would like to suggest that the disturbances which in the first eighteen months of life resulted in an instability in the formation of the body image must, with the onset of the early genital phase in the second half of the second year, already result in a faulty genital outline of the body at a time in life when normally the genital schematization undergoes a primary consolidation due to the normal increase in the endogenous sensations. I believe that at this juncture in development there would already be manifest that combination of castration anxiety and body-disintegration anxiety which is characteristic of the early genital phase anxiety.

This link can also be observed in certain neurotic women who early in analysis manifest a massive and virtually all-encompassing castration complex. In such patients there is a rapid and often chaotic shifting between castration reactions and separation reactions, with the threat of object loss. I have noted over and over again that even brief interruptions of the treatment, such as a short holiday, or at times even the weekend break, provoke major storms. The underlying fantasy frequently proved to be either a fellatio fantasy or one of biting the penis, which during the course of the hour or even within minutes shifted to a fantasy of sucking at or biting the breast. The history of these patients revealed major disturbances in the early mother-child relationship in the first year and a half, such as the emotional unavailability of the mother or illness of the child, with hospitalization and surgical intervention—factors which resulted in an instability in body outline. These women had an early, intense, although ambivalent attachment to their mothers, which was followed by a similarly strong and tenacious oedipal attachment to the father, which generally was only partially and poorly resolved. In these women the experiences of the first eighteen months of life resulted in an unstable body image and strong dissolution fears. With the onset of the early genital phase, there is, I believe, a complementary instability in the initial genital schematization. The traumata which these women experience in the phallic phase result in overly strong castration reactions, since there is an underlying resonance of the earlier dissolution fears and the earlier instability in the genital outline of the body.

I have, with the construct of an early genital phase, attempted to organize the numerous observations of my own and other workers that could not be readily understood in terms of existent genetic constructs. I am aware of the fact that at certain points this has involved an imaginative leap and also that there are many gaps in my understanding of this developmental passage. I trust that further work, by means of both direct observation and analytic reconstruction, may serve to confirm and fill in the outlines which I have here sketched.

An unexpected dividend of my work on the early genital phase was the elucidation of several paradoxical features of the creation myth in Genesis, which had long puzzled me. I shall quote below the relevant passages from the First Book of Moses (Authorized King James Version):

> . . . And God said, let us make man in our image, after our likeness; and let them have dominion over the fish of the sea, and

over the fowl of the air, and over the cattle, and over all the earth, and over every creeping thing that creepeth upon the earth. So God created man in his own image, in the image of God created he him; male and female created he them [1:26].

And the Lord God formed man of the dust of the ground and breathed into his nostrils the breath of life; and man became a living soul. And the Lord God planted a garden eastward in Eden; and there he put the man whom he had formed. And out of the ground made the Lord God to grow every tree that is pleasant to the sight and good for food; the tree of life also in the midst of the garden and the tree of knowledge of good and evil. And the Lord God commanded the man, saying, of every tree of the garden thou mayest freely eat; but of the tree of the knowledge of good and evil, thou shalt not eat of it; for in the day that thou eatest thereof thou shalt surely die. And the Lord God said, It is not good that the man should be alone; I will make him an help meet for him. And out of the ground the Lord God formed every beast of the field, and every fowl of the air; and brought them unto Adam to see what he would call them: and whatsoever Adam called every living creature, that was the name thereof. And Adam gave names to all the cattle, and to the fowl of the air, and to every beast of the field; but for Adam there was not found an help meet for him. And the Lord God caused a deep sleep to fall upon Adam and he slept; and he took one of his ribs, and closed up the flesh instead thereof; and the rib which the Lord God had taken from man, made he a woman, and brought her unto the man. And Adam said, This is now bone of my bones, and flesh of my flesh; she shall be called woman because she was taken out of man . . . And they were both naked, the man and his wife, and were not ashamed [2:7-25].

Since I was a little boy I had been troubled by the perplexing juxtaposition of the two paradoxically different creation stories. There they stood, side by side, apparently contradictory, without any acknowledgment of the disparity. The first creation myth, "male and female created he them," is curiously matter-of-fact, reflecting the way in which little children learn to accept that this is how things are. It contains, in addition, that hard-won reality assertion that little boys and girls are born that way. The second myth, which ends with Eve's creation out of Adam's rib, is wildly fantastic, irrational; the phantasmagoric stuff that dreams are made of.

The first myth is, I believe, a reference to the physical birth of man. Man's birth is here but a step in the orderly process of creation and evolution, although great promise is held out to man in that he is to have dominion over the world. This first myth is devoid of rich fantasy, an elegant literary device, which suggests that with physical birth man has not yet attained those attributes of self-awareness, consciousness, and separateness—in short, a psychic life —which are so uniquely human. This, then, is a Biblical reference to the undifferentiated phase. The second creation myth is a highly condensed, startlingly economical allegory of the personal birth of man.

Let us consider the second creation myth in detail. In this version God created Adam alone, out of dust, and breathed into his nostrils the breath of life, and man became a living soul. This assertion contains the brilliant reference to that one factor in the fateful passage from prenatal to postnatal life that determines viability and in fact defines the physical birth, and that is the establishment of respiration. With the premature baby in the incubator we can to a remarkable degree approximate the conditions of fetal life, such as temperature regulation, feeding, and insulation from undue stimulation, but the one function we are helpless to facilitate is the establishment of respiration, and that is the miracle of the physical birth. The fact that Adam is the only man, and male at that, recognizes that the newborn continues for a time in a state approximating the completeness and wholeness of fetal narcissism; there is no self-awareness, no separateness.

Adam is placed in the Garden of Eden, the symbol of oral plenty. Curiously, in this garden there is the tree of knowledge, from which he must not eat under the penalty of death. In the first months of life there is the repetitive, rhythmic pattern of need arousal and satiation, out of which there grows the dawning awareness of the other, the nonself, the outside, and this is the beginning of that second passage, the personal birth. This Old Testament God is starkly unsentimental; in placing the tree in the garden, he only acknowledges that out of the repetitive pattern of need arousal and satiation must come the ultimate knowledge of one's separateness. The penalty of death that comes with knowledge is not a moral issue; rather, it states the bald truth that the awareness of self contains the threat of self-annihilation. This general interpretation is confirmed by the very next verse, in which God says it is not good that man should be alone, i.e., with the knowledge of our separateness begins our loneliness. After this major breach in the primary narcissism of the infant, there is a touching reference to the brief respite which is afforded by a fleeting phase of infantile omnipotence, in which the infant staves off his loneliness and helplessness through his omnipotent control of the object. God brought every living creature to see what Adam would call them, and that was to be their name.

But still Adam was lonely, and God created out of Adam's own body a woman, Eve. The whole process of personal birth, which results in our sense of separateness, in our awareness of self and object, is allegorically signaled by the birth of the second person, Eve, out of Adam's own body. This mythic conjunction of the two currents, the creation of the other person and the awareness of the sexual difference, can be understood in terms of the construct of the early genital phase, which I have suggested. The whole process of self and object awareness results in the internalized mental precipitate of a self and an object representation which is concretized in the functional control of bowel and bladder. Out of this control, as I have indicated above, is set in motion the whole process of genital arousal and the recognition, at least potentially, of the sexual difference. In chapter 3, with a tragic inevitability, Adam and Eve eat the apple from the tree of knowledge, which was, after all, planted from the beginning. When they eat the apple, they know not only their own separateness, but also the sexual difference, and they sew, in shame, an apron of fig leaves.

BIBLIOGRAPHY

Abraham, K. (1920), Manifestations of the Female Castration Complex. *Selected Papers on Psycho-Analysis*, London: Hogarth Press, 1927, pp. 338-369.

Brunswick, R. M. (1940), The Preoedipal Phase of Libido Development. *Psa. Quart.*, 9:293-319.

Freud, A. (1951), Observations on Child Development. *This Annual*, 6:18-30.

Freud, S. (1917), Mourning and Melancholia. *Standard Edition*, 14:239-258. London: Hogarth Press, 1957.

—— (1923), The Ego and the Id. *Standard Edition*, 19:3-66. London: Hogarth Press, 1961.

—— (1925), Some Psychical Consequences of the Anatomical Distinction between the Sexes. *Standard Edition*, 19:243-258.

—— (1926), Inhibitions, Symptoms and Anxiety. *Standard Edition*, 20:77-175. London: Hogarth Press, 1959.

—— (1931), Female Sexuality. *Standard Edition*, 21:223-243. London: Hogarth Press, 1961.

—— (1933), New Introductory Lectures on Psycho-Analysis. Femininity [Lecture 33]. *Standard Edition*, 22:112-135. London: Hogarth Press, 1964.

Greenacre, P. (1950), Special Problems of Early Female Sexual Development. *This Annual*, 5:122-138.

—— (1953), Certain Relationships between Fetishism and the Faulty Development of the Body Image. *This Annual*, 8:79-98.

—— (1955), Further Considerations Regarding Fetishism. *This Annual*, 10:187-194.

—— (1960), Further Notes on Fetishism. *This Annual*, 15:191-207.

Jones, E. (1927), The Early Development of Female Sexuality. *Papers on Psycho-Analysis*. London: Ballière, Tindall & Cox, 5th ed., 1948, pp. 438-451.

Klein, M. (1928), Early Stages of the Oedipus Conflict. *Contributions to Psycho-Analysis*. London: Hogarth Press, 1948, pp. 202-214.

Lampl-de Groot, J. (1927), The Evolution of the Oedipus Complex in Women. *The Development of the Mind*. New York: International Universities Press, 1965, pp. 3-18.

Loewenstein, R. M. (1950), Conflict and Autonomous Ego Development during the Phallic Phase. *This Annual*, 5:47-52.

Mahler, M. S. & Furer, M. (1960), Observations on Research Regarding the 'Symbiotic Syndrome' of Infantile Psychosis. *Psa. Quart.*, 29:317-327.

—— & Gosliner, B. J. (1955), On Symbiotic Child Psychosis: Genetic, Dynamic and Restitutive Aspects. *This Annual*, 10:195-212.

Pine, F. & Furer, M. (1963), Studies of the Separation-Individuation Phase. *This Annual*, 18:325-342.

Roiphe, H. (1968), Castration Complex and Object Loss (in press).

Sachs, L. J. (1962), A Case of Castration Anxiety Beginning at Eighteen Months. *J. Amer. Psychoanal. Assn.*, 10:329-337, 1962.

IV
CLINICAL CONTRIBUTIONS

THE RE-EDUCATION
OF A RETARDED BLIND CHILD

DOROTHY BURLINGHAM (London)

In Collaboration with ALICE GOLDBERGER

This paper describes in detail a backward and withdrawn child, born with multiple handicaps and subjected to pain, frustration, and lack of stimulation in her early childhood. Her therapy, carried out by Alice Goldberger within the Hampstead Child-Therapy Clinic, aimed at counteracting past damage and promoting any urge toward normal development which lay dormant in her.

PARENTS' REPORT ON PERSONAL HISTORY

The first report which the parents gave to us on Judy's history was rather scanty.

At the time of the child's birth, they were already in their middle forties, with two teenage daughters, seventeen and eleven years old. They lived as a close-knit family in a modest house of their own, together with the maternal grandmother.

Due to the mother's high blood pressure, Judy was born in the hospital by Caesarian operation. She was "blue" at birth (not due to strangulation). Her feet were deformed, one toe folded under each foot. There was some (undefined) malformation of her mouth. At age six weeks she was found to be suffering from *congenital cataract* with her sight reduced to some light perception.

The work with the blind children is part of the Educational Unit of the Hampstead Child-Therapy Clinic and as such is maintained by the Grant Foundation, Inc., N.Y. The research work with the blind is assisted by the National Institute of Mental Health, Bethesda, Md. An additional grant for the musical and further education of Judy was received from Mr. and Mrs. Norman Clement Stone, Atherton, California.

Presented at the third annual scientific meeting of The American Association for Child Psychoanalysis, Inc., New Haven, Conn., on April 20, 1968.

According to the parents, Judy was extremely difficult to rear
from the beginning. Soon after birth, she developed a raw and blis-
tered skin, which made her shrink from any touch, scream when
handled, and dread contact with the bath water. (In later life she
could not bear a clip put in her hair or a cap placed on her head.)

It puzzled the parents that her development did not resemble
that of their older children. She never explored her surroundings
by either smelling, licking, or touching anything. She never raised
her arms to be lifted, carried, or cuddled. When she had learned
to stand, her hands hung limply at her sides. She by-passed the crawling stage, but walked at age two and a half. She was at all times
oversensitive to sound and terrified of any noise to which she was not
accustomed. So far as feeding was concerned, the deformity of her
mouth, and later of her teeth, prevented any enjoyment of the
process. The mother fed her passively until a late age and urged the
intake of food to "prevent her from starving."

Toilet training was persistent, but led to no result.

When speech began, Judy acquired a fairly large vocabulary
fairly quickly, but it did not serve communication. Words were
strung together without meaning in what the parents called her
"gabble talk."

With all that, the parents stressed that the child was neither
aggressive nor destructive, nor had outbursts of temper. When
thwarted, she reacted with hurt withdrawal.

First Visit to the Clinic

Judy was four and a half years old when she was accepted by
the Clinic for observation. She was at the time a nice-looking, well-
built, sturdy little girl, with large blue wide-open eyes (unseeing),
appropriately and attractively dressed.

She came to the Clinic in an odd way, walking stiffly and awk-
wardly beside her mother, who did not hold her hand, but instead
guided her by holding on to a tassel on top of her pixie cap.

When, during the interview, Judy sat on her mother's lap, she
did so impersonally, treating the mother's body as if it were a piece
of furniture. Her face remained expressionless while she chattered

incessantly in a high-pitched voice; occasionally an isolated, un-connected word could be singled out from her gabble talk.

Each of her hands held an object which she did not discard dur-ing the visit: one the plastic body of a headless and limbless doll, the other a cup. She showed no interest in any toy offered to her. Only when a tambourine was softly drummed near her to gain her attention did she react—by lifting an arm in front of her face as if warding off a blow.

A Period of Observation
(approximately one year)

In spite of the many oddities in Judy's appearance and behavior, it was the therapist's impression that she was neither a mentally de-fective nor an autistic child, and that contact could be made with her. Since touch was obviously unwelcome and words were tol-erated, the latter means was chosen as appropriate for an approach.

The therapist, in a simple way, commiserated with Judy for hav-ing to meet a stranger. When the child "gabbled" in answer and the father admonished her to "talk sensibly," the therapist, again very simply and directly, explained that there was no need for this intervention, that Judy played with words as other children play with toys, and that this was her pleasure. The therapist was gratified when there appeared an answering flicker of expression in the child's face.

Her next move was to pick out random words from the child's talk and turn them into nursery rhymes. At this Judy smiled and even attempted to construct such a rhyme herself. Contact seemed established, and further words could be used to attract her atten-tion and amuse her. Since in her gabbling Judy gave obvious signs of copying conversations, even the intonations of TV announcers, the therapist used the device of assuming their role, thereby insinu-ating herself into the child's imaginary world.

On following visits, stories were made up concerning everyday events: how Judy got dressed, came to the Clinic, made her thera-pist wait, was welcomed by her, etc. Judy obviously began to enjoy this entertainment, looked forward to it, and even tried to join in. The therapist realized that she had gained a first point when Judy exclaimed at the end of a session: "Next week I see you again."

It was much more difficult to elicit positive responses to touch. When a ball was rolled toward Judy, she would lift her arms in a rejecting gesture and shout: "No, no, next week!"

Picking up fallen objects presented another difficult task. When the therapist prevented the mother from picking up what had dropped from the child's hand, Judy most reluctantly followed the directions given her for searching ("One step toward Mummy," etc.). Gradually she accepted the therapist's interest in her clothing and began, together with her, to touch her "soft and cuddly sweater" without shrinking from the contact.

It took time until Judy cooperated in even the simplest games of the toddler stage, and there were many setbacks to be encountered on the way, Judy expressing displeasure in the place of enjoyment.

Since chocolate seemed the only sweet she liked, a piece of it was dropped into the cup she held in her hand to encourage her to take it out. Unfortunately, the chocolate rattled in the cup and the noise caused her to drop both in fright. Another time, a piece of chocolate, willingly accepted and placed in her mouth, was simply let fall out.

When a toy lorry was loaded with the chocolate and wheeled toward her to be invited to "come in," she was cunning enough to defend herself by saying that she was "out, not at home." It took some time until she complied to the extent of saying: "Come in, lorry," and touched the chocolate gingerly.

Although Judy had a firm grasp on the two toys which always accompanied her, her fingers remained lifeless in contact with other objects.

Some use could be made of her perception of light. When the therapist noted some reaction on Judy's part to the turning on of lights, she tried to engage her interest in the action of the light switch and to guide her toward manipulating it herself. The father's delighted surprise about this led him to construct a special light switch for her at home, which she proceeded to turn on and off endlessly.

In any exploration of her surroundings, Judy was much hindered by her fear of sound. Any strange voice, any unexpected noise, even the wind rustling in the trees, caused a state of panic, in which she covered her ears, crouched down and begged: "Turn it off, off!"

It seemed possible to the therapist that Judy's frequent immobility marked a state of intense listening, i.e., an attempt to identify noises, thereby reducing their frightening character. With this idea in mind, she embarked on the verbalization and explanation of sounds as they presented themselves. When Judy tapped with her foot, she remarked on it and then did the same, entering into an exchange of tapping sounds. When Judy entered the room and set the chimes in motion, their soft tinkle was explained, explored, and turned into something expectable, etc. Even though these attempts were often greeted with the usual "No, no, off, off," a growing fascination with rhythmical sounds and music gradually became apparent.

On the whole, during this observation period it was possible to collect a large amount of data concerning the functioning of Judy's ego apparatus, her anxieties, and her avoidance measures.

Another gain of these first weeks was a clearer picture of the parental handling of the child and of the parents' own personalities. On the one hand, there was no doubt that Judy was given conscientious and loving care, and that the parents spared no efforts in dealing with her handicap. On the other hand, the mother emerged as a depressed and rigid person, unable to show physical affection or to respond sensitively to the child's real needs. It was easy to picture her initial shock and revulsion when she discovered that she had given birth to an abnormal child and when she found herself unable to comfort the distressed and screaming infant. Her concern that the child would starve to death, and her success in keeping her alive by feeding can be taken as active reactions against her guilt feelings and hostile wishes.

The father, in contrast, was affectionate and warmhearted. He tried to play with Judy, to amuse her, even to make her behave normally. But he too was handicapped in his attention to the child. Faced with his wife's severe illness at the time of her confinement with Judy, he was above all concerned with the danger to her life. Faced with her depressive reaction afterward, he attempted above all to cheer her up. This made him assume a more or less forced gaiety as a reaction to strain and worry. He approached the child on this basis, and tried to elicit the same response from her. But

Judy, according to her own nature, was generally unable to respond to his efforts.

A Period of Re-education

Judy's re-education was built on the assumption that in her early infancy she had missed out on those pleasurable experiences around which the nuclei of a normal personality are formed. There was little pleasure to be gained from a mother who was herself despairing, guilty, and withdrawn. Judy's skin condition precluded any positive sensations connected with cuddling, being handled, bathed, etc. Sucking was interfered with by her mouth condition. With vision absent, all that was left to link her with the environment was sound, but in the absence of security and comfort, sounds were as frightening as they were stimulating. Under these conditions, her own body as well as the figures of the external world remained uncathected with positive libido.

The therapist accordingly set out on a program of introducing Judy to pleasurable experiences. She kept the relationship to herself playful, joyful, and companionable. She introduced sounds soft enough to be nonfrightening and pleasurable (playing a mouth organ for her, an autoharp, etc.), and toys which were pleasant to the touch. Chocolate, as described before, was used to stimulate her functioning. Contact with other adults or children in the Clinic was avoided to exclude upsets and disturbances.

Judy reacted to these arrangements with an affectionate attachment to the therapist, which took the parents completely by surprise. Their hopes were awakened and they were eager (though not always able) to follow any suggestions for different home management which were made to them. Nevertheless, it was necessary at this time to warn them that even under the most favorable circumstances a readjustment such as that necessary in Judy would take years, and that even then the outcome remained unpredictable. Ego functions would have to be coaxed into action and learning processes initiated long past the time appropriate for their emergence. Libidinal ties would have to be strengthened and widened to draw the child out of her isolation. Control of her body functions had to be established and, above all, her hands and fingers stimulated to assume their proper role.

In fact, some of these advances were made spontaneously by Judy as a by-product of her relationship to the therapist. As this developed and stabilized itself, the soiling ceased (almost immediately after attendance at the Clinic began), the wetting became intermittent, and her (archaic) fears decreased perceptibly.

What follows are illustrations extracted from Judy's attendance at the Clinic during the next two years. They are selected to highlight advances made but also to show the inevitable difficulty and slowness of the task.

Fear of the Unknown

It was never possible for Judy to touch anything that she encountered for the first time. Her answer to such a request was invariably: "No, no, thank you." Nevertheless, if the same thing was presented to her repeatedly, on different occasions, in the form of a game, etc., she could accept it finally and make use of it from then onward. The discouraging point was that this learning process did not extend from one object to the next. Whatever was new had to be introduced to her in the same laborious way.

It is known, in fact, that all blind children show a certain hesitation in handling new objects, probably because the reassurance provided by sight is missing. In the majority of cases this is overcome quickly. It was the therapist's surmise that in this respect Judy was handicapped more than others owing to her painful experiences with all skin contact in early infancy.

Advances in Speech

Judy's advances in verbal communication were slow but steady. Where before she had expressed her wishes with the use of one sharp word, such as "box," "door," she would now say: "Give me the box." Where before she had panicked at the sound of an aeroplane, she would now say: "The aeroplane is very noisy." Her gabble talk continued, but became less frequent, resorted to only when she was confused or frightened, or when too much was demanded of her. Although she still copied what she heard in conversation, on the wireless or on TV, she was gradually able to use these snatches, not out of context, but with understanding.

Advances in Self-Awareness

Even at the age of four and a half, Judy had seemed not to possess an inner image of her own body. When playing body games with the therapist, she was unable to differentiate her own fingers, legs, etc., from the latter's. She behaved at times as if her clothes were part of her body. In this period she was oblivious of physical pain (in contrast to her infancy) and therefore also lacked this powerful guide to self-awareness. It was therefore a great advance when she ceased to speak of herself in the third person and used the first person instead. When she was heard to say to her therapist: "I love you and I love myself," it was felt that she had made the forward move of differentiating herself for the first time from another person.

Denial of Emotion

In the course of Judy's attendance at the Clinic she was observed to be capable of occasionally producing a complete denial of reality. For example, when she was told that the gramophone was broken and that she would be unable to dance to her favorite tunes, she nevertheless moved the furniture around to begin dancing. When told that the therapist was going on a holiday and could not see her for a while, she reacted by saying: "See you tomorrow." When told that the therapist had been taken ill and that she would have to return home, she refused to budge, appeared stunned and speechless, and insisted on waiting until the therapist "would come."

Advances in Self-Assertion

In contrast to her former reactions of hurt withdrawal in the face of frustration, Judy gradually became able to assert herself more vigorously. When told by her father to stop twiddling with the wireless, she answered: "I did not twiddle, I put it louder so you could hear the news better." When urged to eat an apple, she said: "She does not want the apple, take it away." When offered a doll, she screamed: "I don't want the doll, I don't like dolls, and I don't want to be talked into it."

Relations with the Mother

Under the influence of the therapist, the mother began to make demands on her daughter which were long overdue, such as fetching things, washing her hands, helping to dress herself, etc. Judy was able to comply, but apart from this there was still little warmth in their relationship.

Oedipal Attitudes toward the Father

In contrast, Judy's relationship to her father made a forward move and took on all the aspects of an oedipal attachment. When he approached, her face lit up with pleasure. She cuddled in his arms, kissed him, and called him sweetheart. She sang and danced with him. On one occasion, when told that he had to leave, she burst into tears, sobbed bitterly, and begged him not to go. On another occasion, when her mother had just got her fully dressed and she heard his voice, she proceeded in a flash to take off every single piece of clothing which her mother had laboriously put on her. She insisted: "Daddy must dress me."

It is interesting to note that this was done by the same child who, under less cathected circumstances, showed herself quite unable to undo a button or manipulate her underwear.

Wetting

For a considerable period Judy's "intermittent" wetting defied explanation. Finally, it became possible to link the occurrence of loss of bladder control with stress and confusion in her life. So long as she had no other free outlet for her feelings, notably while she was unable to weep (as she was initially), wetting served this purpose.

Early in Judy's treatment, the maternal grandmother who had shared the family's life died. There was the usual commotion in the house, excitement, crying, the coming and going of neighbors. Nothing of this was explained to Judy, who was thought to be unaware of the event. Here the wetting recurred, after having stopped a while ago. It persisted until the therapist took over the task of explaining and verbalizing for Judy the emotions which she felt around her and to which she responded on a body level.

She also wet before a visit to the dentist, which brought back a former occasion when she had been held down forcibly.

She wet during the long summer vacation when separated from her therapist and stopped wetting when she returned to her.

Again, she wet when a paternal uncle was found asphyxiated in the garage.

Altogether, her dry periods coincided with the times when she felt comparatively untroubled, happier, and relaxed; her wetting was associated with states of tenseness, disorientation, fear, and loneliness.

Nursery School

At the age of five years and ten months, after more than one and a half years of individual work, it was decided to let Judy enter our Nursery Group for Blind Children under the direction of Annemarie Curson. Although Judy was chronologically of school age, her performance was considered to be nearer to nursery school level or, if anything, below it.

For a considerable period, her attendance there was anything but a success. Although introduced to the new life gradually, by means of first once weekly, then twice weekly visits accompanied by her therapist, she was unable to show or to maintain her gains in the new surroundings, or to make use of the often undivided attention given to her by the nursery school teacher. The noise made by the other children, their talk, etc., confused her, and she shrank from contact with them. She could often be found standing around, withdrawn and expressionless. She again resorted to gabble talk. When induced to work with Montessori insets or to sort out beads (using her color perception), she did so, listlessly, her fingers stiff, awkward, and seemingly unable to manipulate material.

It was puzzling that, in spite of this apparent rejection of her surroundings, Judy always wanted to come to the nursery school, insisted on being taken there even when she was ill, and that she was fond of her teacher. It led us to believe that what appeared as inactivity and indifference was, in essence, an active form of listening, and that this attempt to grasp what was going on was Judy's only way of participation.

There was only one game, on the toddler level, which Judy was ready to play with the teacher, and to repeat unendingly. It was called by her "Hello, good-bye." She would pretend to leave, saying good-bye. The teacher had to remark how sorry she was to have her go, whereupon Judy would rush back with a happy "hello" and had to be greeted lovingly. What she played out in this way was probably a fantasy of the gay, happy, affectionate reciprocal mother-infant relationship which she had never had occasion to experience.

With tremendous effort, patience, and encouragement on the part of the teacher, Judy finally succeeded in joining in some of the nursery school activities, such as climbing, jumping, counting, taking turns, etc. Although little pleasure was involved in this, she could feel pleased when praised. Spontaneous enjoyment appeared only when musical activities, dancing to music, etc., were introduced.

MUSIC

As mentioned before, music played a part in Judy's re-education from the outset when her therapist played softly for her on the mouth organ to help Judy overcome her fear of noises. Gradually, passive listening was changed to the active production of sounds by means of a musical box, a tambourine, a drum, and a xylophone. Primarily these served enjoyment, secondarily they also promoted the use of her fingers for handling the musical box, manipulating the drumsticks, and pressing down the keys on the keyboard of the xylophone. Music was also used to introduce simple tasks of orientation, such as tracing the location of instruments played in different parts of the room.

When introduced to a piano, Judy refused at first to touch the keys. But she soon learned to pick out tunes wtih one finger, and her parents were so surprised and delighted with this that they bought a piano for the home.

Her love for music took a big step forward when one of the psychiatrists of the Clinic, an active musician himself, joined forces with her therapist and came at regular intervals to play the piano for her. Judy was eager to dance to his playing. When doing this, she held herself rigid and moved her arms and legs stiffly, as if she were a puppet. Nevertheless, she kept perfect time, tapped with her feet, as in tap-dancing, and responded to every change in the rhythm with abandon.

She also sang, accompanied by the piano, learned the text of a number of songs quickly and easily, and had no difficulty in beating time to the music. According to her mood of the day, she would ask with discrimination for her favorites, such as "church music" (meaning Bach), Mozart's country dances, etc. After a holiday (age five years and ten months), she entered the room singing most appropriately "Glory, glory, hallelujah."

At the age of six years and eleven months, Judy was started on formal piano lessons with Professor F. Rauter, a well-known piano teacher with experience in teaching backward children. His report on her activities with him runs as follows:

The way I approached Judy was through asking her questions in the form of a played short melody, which could be understood as such a question. Unfailingly her answer was given in the same way. The conversation could take the form of a little opera and it gives joy to both sides. Judy seemed to know the essentials of music without ever having been instructed.

Out of the "talking" to her through improvised melodies little special compositions arose which I put down on paper and which I numbered. Although we have recently started to learn a "real" minuet by Bach, these little pieces which I wrote for her still remain her favorites.

Judy can name and recognize each note on the piano, that is, she has perfect pitch. She is also able to find the right notes of any scale without being told, as well as to give the notes played in a chord. She plays with both hands, that is, her hands work independently in playing easy pieces. She is able to transpose single melodies into any other key. She has an excellent memory, she recognizes many symphonies and other classical music from listening to the wireless, can name them, and knows the composers. She is also aware of the various instruments which are played in an orchestra and can tell you which they are.

The inner experience of music has formed Judy's hands. It is an aesthetic pleasure to watch them when she plays as she does naturally, what sometimes needs weeks or months of teaching. Her hands are firm and when she has learned a new piece, her confidence increases and seems to spread from her fingers over her whole body and her mind. It is quite amazing how little Judy is spoilt by the music which blares from the radios and TV sets in her surrounding. She develops more and more a good taste for good things and the time has come where I have to introduce her into a world of other composers which may be beneficial for a further development of her inner life.

What was striking to us in the Clinic was Judy's enthusiastic attitude toward her lessons and her marked expressions of enjoyment. Although, like most children, she preferred at times to play what was easy, she also tried seriously to comply with the teacher's wishes, to please him and to learn. She apologized for her mistakes and offered to "do it again." She smiled when praised, and listened entranced when a piece appealed to her. She said once: "I love Dr. Rauter and I love myself," using the same words as she had used initially to express her feelings toward her therapist.

We were left, then, with a double impression. On the one hand, there was this nursery school child, now seven years and eleven months, withdrawn, backward, unable to manipulate buttons or toys, or to mount the climbing frame without active help, scoring a mental age of three years ten months on the Williams intelligence scale for children with defective vision. On the other hand, the same little girl was also alert, interested, her body flexible, her hands graceful, her fingers strong and purposeful, the whole personality animated by what her teacher called "high musical intelligence."

While one part of her life seemed singularly devoid of libidinal cathexis and lay barren, the cathected part flowered and developed. The question was left open whether some of the impetus could, in the long run, be extended from there to cover other areas of her ego development.

FATEFUL EXTERNAL EVENTS

In the year that followed (age eight years), Judy's life was shaken by three profoundly disturbing events: the death of her father; an operation of her own; and her mother's severe illness and hospitalization.

Father's Death

The father's death occurred suddenly and without preparation. One day, when Judy and her mother returned from the Clinic as usual, he lay dead following a heart attack. In the ensuing confusion, Judy was sent to the neighbors where, on entering, she burst into tears and cried bitterly.

After this first outburst, Judy was found by the mother to lack mourning responses. The mother complained that the child was sitting in the living room listening to the transistor radio instead of sharing in the family's grief. On the day of the funeral she returned to her denial reaction by insisting that her Daddy should "take her to the seashore." When her therapist verbalized the happenings for her, she reacted with an obviously learned response that "my Daddy was here last year, now he is dead, he is with the angels." It was more spontaneous when she reported to her therapist two months later that "my Daddy has been with me the day before," and again at another time that "he was singing" with her. Both reports presumably referred to dreams.

Apart from this, the shock showed in regressed behavior, such as clinging to the mother, wetting, return of the gabble talk, etc. It did not affect her musical ability. After a while she was able to declare sensibly: "I miss my Dad and my Mummy misses him too."

Operation

Judy had always been under medical care for her eye condition, her irregular teeth, and her foot deformities. At age eight and a half she was now faced with a corrective operation on her feet, and this aroused concern in us that the hospitalization, coupled with the many investigations and interferences, might lose her the gains which she had achieved.

Surprisingly enough, she enjoyed the first hospital visits, including physiotherapy. She allowed herself to be handled by the medical staff and obeyed their instructions to walk, tiptoe, skip, etc. Leaving after one of her visits, she said: "Good-bye, doctors. I am coming to see you again."

Since the operation was delayed for many months, owing to the father's death, Judy's own intermittent illnesses, and other events, there was ample time for the therapist to prepare her for the event. Fear was denied by Judy. On the contrary, she looked forward to being visited in the hospital by her therapist, to being brought her musical box, and on the very day of entering the hospital, she persisted in her denial by calling it "going on holiday."

She remained seemingly unconcerned after the operation as well, even though wires were sticking out of her toes. When the therapist accompanied by Judy's mother visited Judy, she inquired only whether the therapist had really brought the musical box, as promised. She did not mind the commotion of the busy ward, nurses pursuing their activities, children running around, etc. But she was badly put out finally by a small defective boy who declared that she was blind. She reacted to this with indignation: "He says I am blind. I am not blind."

The subject of her blindness, which had been raised unsuccessfully with her many times before, suddenly, due to the operation, seemed to have acquired significance. Possibly, also, the direct attack of the little boy had pierced her denial and laid bare a fantasy that the visit to the hospital would help her to gain sight. (This would explain much of the pleasurable anticipation.) When Judy was told by the staff that nothing could be done for her eyes, she pleaded whether instead her teeth could not be made better.

There was no doubt that Judy was aware of her defects and wanted to be improved.

Mother's Illness and Hospitalization

During the following holiday, soon after Judy's own operation, Judy's mother fell severely ill with high blood pressure and had to be hospitalized. Since the therapist, absent from London, could not be reached, Judy was left without support in this first separation from her mother.

Her eldest sister, by now married and with two young infants of her own, took Judy in, but she did so most unwillingly. Her home was crowded as it was, the children upset by Judy's arrival and reacting badly to their mother's preoccupation. Moreover, Judy wet, was uncooperative, regressed, and frozen; she showed no concern for her mother and refused to visit her in the hospital. In her terror that the mother might die and Judy be left on her hands, the sister talked incessantly in the child's hearing of sending her to an institution.

Altogether, this was a devastating experience for Judy.

When she could return to her own home, with the mother discharged from hospital, Judy was unable to mention any of it and referred to her own recent hospitalization instead. "People turned lights on all the time and they gave me pricks." "Some wind was blowing and I went to sleep," etc. Moreover, Judy's sister continued with her entreaties that the only sensible course of action was to send Judy to a residential home for retarded blind children. The child was well aware of this, and displayed her suspicions of her sister by shrinking from her, refusing to board a bus with her, etc.

It needed the therapist's return from holiday to put an end to this planning. She succeeded in convincing the family that even normal children find themselves unable to cope with an accumulation of events such as separation, loss of a parent, change of routine, entry into a strange household, etc.; that in Judy's situation nothing could be expected under the circumstances short of massive regression.

While the household gradually settled back into its normal routine, the therapist began to examine ways and means of safeguarding Judy's continued stay at home, her music lessons, and her therapy. Since Judy had outgrown the nursery school, nothing except a suitable day school promised to answer the need.

Entry into School

After much searching, the Gatehouse School, Dallington Street, London, E.C.1. was willing to accept Judy. It is a private Montessori school which makes a practice of including one handicapped child in every class of normal pupils. Judy entered on trial, at age nine years, looking forward to the event with mixed feelings of fear, excitement, pride; leaning heavily on the support of her therapist, who accompanied her.

To our surprise she adapted to the school more easily than she had to our nursery school. According to the school report, she progressed well using the Montessori sensorial material and her sense of touch in particular is much stronger and more accurate. Instead of listening passively she seems to enjoy doing things. She wants to talk to the teacher and is keen to listen to what she is told. She likes being asked what she thinks, or does, and answers in a reasonable manner.

Above all, she makes progress in learning braille, uses the braille machine quite confidently and has learned many letters. Reading back her braille still presents difficulties, but her tactile sense is improving. She has also advanced in her understanding of numbers.

She relates easily and in a friendly manner to the other children who respond well to her. She is always ready to play on the piano any song the children ask for and she even played for the parents in the school concert.

Discussion

ALICE B. COLONNA (London)

Dorothy Burlingham's interesting and detailed account of Alice Goldberger's painstaking work and success in awakening this difficult and sad little girl bring up many questions.

One is struck and surprised by the way in which Judy was able to respond when she was offered a musical outlet, training, and an instrument. Of course, many months of preparation preceded this. Nevertheless, it was as though the capacity for and understanding of this medium of expression had always been there in Judy, but had not been utilized. It makes one wonder how many other potentials exist in these early years, unknown and untapped, waiting to be made use of.

Various methods help us ascertain what is missing in early ego development because of the lack of visual stimulation and give many hints how some of these missing ingredients can be supplied in the place of what develops automatically with sight from the start of life. Does the work with Judy and her reaction mean that through the means of music she might actually relive and relearn some of those feelings and experiences that she missed at the appropriate time in her development? Can some of these be provided now? Or is it an ingredient that, unless it is supplied at a particular moment, leaves a permanent defect and deficiency? Should one be satisfied that Judy has found one enjoyable activity that will make her life more interesting and much richer within the framework of a retarded and somewhat abnormal personality structure? Or ought one to assume that she will be able to respond to further interpretation and clarification of inner and outer reality in such a way as to make the aims of work with her the same as those with other normal or neurotic blind or sighted children—that is, to present her with the prospect of looking forward to a relatively independent future in which satisfying work and relationships can be expected? Judy's needs seem very special; and work with the mother has enabled the latter to provide a more protected environment in which some of these needs can be satisfied.

One of the problems is whether one can and should try to provide Judy with some sort of sheltered future. The mother, on whom so much depends now that she is the only person to look after Judy since the father's death (the sister obviously does not want her and cannot cope with her), seems to be a very ill woman whose blood pressure may at any moment render her quite incapable of caring for Judy. Ought one and could one prepare Judy for such a likelihood? Does she now fear that her mother might die? How could one prepare a child for this?

A blind toddler who is withdrawn and who does not use touch to explore and learn, cuts herself off from the world much more effectively than does a neurotic child. Verbalization does not develop normally and her thought processes remain primitive. She stops effective learning and imitation. The facial expression remains vacant and she becomes unable, literally, to grasp at and master the situations confronting her. In what way is the ego thereby permanently shaped? Judy's passivity seemed so marked that the therapist constantly had to stimulate her over a period of years of work. Will Judy be able to take over this function for herself?

Time does not permit a Profile of Judy, but a brief discussion organized in terms of some of the main Profile headings may indicate certain salient points.

Leaving aside the history, the description, etc., which have been discussed, I shall first take up the possible significant *environmental circumstances*. As Dorothy Burlingham said, the ordinary requirements of mothering are not sufficient for a blind child born with multiple handicaps, and being a parent of a blind child of this type calls for skills and a personality that not all normal mothers can be expected to have. Judy was born to an elderly mother who had grown daughters. Despite this woman's devotion, care, concern, etc., she herself was, it seems, subjected to many additional problems that made her unable to understand her handicapped child's special needs. Her ill health is an additional environmental factor. The father's ill health and sudden death not only affected the mother in her attitude to the child but also represented a tremendous loss for Judy. There is the death of the grandmother and that of the paternal uncle. The sister's role and the attitude of her children were further environmental factors. The separations, hospitalizations, and medications were all of obvious significance in these unfortunate early years.

We have come to expect that the *level of libidinal development* will look rather different for the bind child who retains gratifications from earlier levels while moving much of the libido forward. Judy is no exception to this, though it will be recalled that she was able to give up the soiling and wetting while she was in treatment. She needed encouragement before she could enjoy satisfaction of her oral needs. There appear to be instances which point to her having made some moves from the mother as the oedipal object toward the father. Treatment evidently helped her loosen the close tie to the mother and made this move possible. It is difficult to assess how far her personality as a whole has been shaped by the way she experienced this oedipal phase. However, in some respects she shows certain features of latency in the sublimatory interest in music, even though she could not be called a latency child if one compared her to a normal child of her own age.

Cathexis of self has certainly been grossly disturbed. She was an ailing and miserable infant who rarely, if ever, experienced a sense of well-being. The mother, despite her good intentions, was not able to serve as protector against painful stimuli or as stimulator toward positive development. Judy's whole body appears to allow for little pleasure and, except for the musical instruments which she touches with so much care and interest, there has been a massive withdrawal, reluctance, and refusal to use her body, and especially her fingers, either to explore her own or the object's body or to learn about the wider world.

Cathexis of objects. Judy has responded very positively to Alice Goldberger's overtures and apparently she had a warm relationship with her father. Although contact seems to be initiated by the other person more than by Judy, it is a positive sign that, after therapy, she shows the wish to be with other children and adults.

Aggression. It would appear that there is a good deal of aggression against the mother which finds partial expression in Judy's stubbornness and obstinacy. It may be a feature of the touching inhibition and of the clinging and fear of separation. Qualitatively, her aggression seems to contain elements from all phases. Her fear of mother having an accident may stem in part from the oedipal death wishes, though it contains elements from the anal and oral phases as well. Aggression does not seem to be obviously directed against the self in that Judy is not a child who gets hurt frequently and she is not accident prone. However, the inhibitions and restrictions in her personality may contain an element of this. Aggression is not directed toward the object world either.

Aggressive expressions are, of course, always particularly conflictful for the blind child because of his great dependence on the sighted world. Some blind children are helped in this conflict when they are able to look forward to a time when they will be more independent and will not experience so much need of the sighted adult world.

Ego. The ego apparatus is defective due to the blindness, but no other known defect exists. The ego functions are impaired not only by the blindness but by the withdrawal and the touching inhibition. Her IQ is not known. The function of memory is good,[1] as is the case with many blind children. There is a discrepancy between the type of auditory synthesis shown in her musical capacity (i.e., finding chords from the start, etc.) and the lack of such integrative attempts in all other areas. The fact that learning did not extend from one object or situation to another is characteristic of the concrete thinking which in most blind children persists longer than in the sighted.

Emergent defensive mechanisms are evident in the denial, projection, withdrawal, displacement (wetting, not crying) reaction formation, regression, repression, and sublimation in the musical ability.

If one tries to assess the nature of Judy's *conflicts,* one finds it difficult to know how much the retardation and abnormality are the result of inner psychic conflict and how much they are due to an arrest in development resulting from the unsatisfactory early infancy and restricted first years of life when the normal child would be making independent moves in reaching out, moving, etc. There is obviously conflict over her aggressive feelings and a fear of annihilation, not uncommon in small blind children who have limited means

[1] Good in the sense that isolated pieces of information are retained rigidly intact over a period of years, but not good in the sense of helping the ego retain useful information in a flexible, adaptive, and meaningful way. The two are often confused.

of knowing what to expect. It may be that Judy experienced any moves to independence as aggressive, but one cannot be sure about it.

The *general characteristics* are also difficult to assess. Judy's positive response to treatment and to the frustration involved indicates that she has a capacity for frustration tolerance. Treatment also shows how much frustration and anxiety Judy has been subjected to and how few of her needs have ever been recognized and satisfied. As to the progressive versus regressive forces, there are certainly progressive forces in her case.

In conclusion, to return to the remarkable response to music, it has been pointed out by Warren Brodey[2] and others that there are two ways of approaching cognition and learning: the visual and the auditory.[3] Ours is a visual cultural approach, Nagera points out, but in many social systems and for many people the auditory process of thinking and integrating, understanding of time, distance, space, etc., is more valid. Brodey feels that many of the difficulties that appear in the development of blind children of this type stem from the total lack of communication between the family and the child from the very start. Certain forms of behavior which may be valid ways of learning are discouraged, and the blind child is made to conform, to take on a kind of stereotype façade in the hope that his handicap will not be noticed or commented upon, thereby buttressing the denial of the defect altogether. Many of the blind children use this as a means of expressing aggression, sensing how much it means to their parents that they cease to behave in odd, abnormal, and self-conscious ways. Accordingly, those who help this type of child need to overcome much resistance in order to convince the child of the wish to understand and help, as Alice Goldberger has succeeded in doing.

2 In a personal communication.
3 H. Nagera has discussed this frequently in our work on ego functions in the Clinical Concept Research Group at the Hampstead Child-Therapy Clinic.

A BLIND CHILD GOES TO THE HOSPITAL

ALICE B. COLONNA, M.A. (London)

Much has been written in recent years to demonstrate conclusively the traumatic effects of hospitalization, even for relatively brief periods, on the development of the very young child. It has become clear that one of the major factors in this is the separation the small child has to suffer from his objects, mainly from his mother. When mother and child can be together in the hospital, the experience has a completely different effect on the psychic development of the child. Surgical interventions and treatment, even when prolonged and painful, do not always in themselves produce traumatic and permanently damaging effects, provided that certain necessary arrangements are made.

If the importance of the presence of the mother has been so clearly demonstrated in the case of the young sighted child, how will it be in the case of a blind child? One would expect that without the aid of vision to help the child master the new unfamiliar hospital surroundings, with its unfamiliar noises, etc., the anxieties, loneliness, and loss would be much greater and the aftereffects more profound and lasting. Sighted children often find comfort at night

The work with blind children is part of the Educational Unit of the Hampstead Child-Therapy Clinic and as such is maintained by the Grant Foundation, Inc., New York. The research work with the blind is assisted further by the National Institute of Mental Health, Bethesda, Md. (Grant # M-5683-06). I am most grateful to Mrs. Dorothy Burlingham for regular help during the period of work with Richard and to Miss Anna Freud for suggestions concerning this paper. Special thanks are due to Dr. H. Nagera for his assistance in some of the theoretical formulations concerning aspects of this child's ego functions and capacities, and for his aid with the organization of this paper. Mrs. Anne Marie Curson and Mrs. Mary Fyvel, Richard's nursery school teachers, worked closely with the author in visits to Richard during his stay in the hospital. I am grateful for their permission to quote from their reports. Discussions with members of the Research Group on the Study of Blind Children have provided many valuable suggestions and ideas.

when there is a light in the room, for example, but all such props are denied to the blind.[1]

The different effect that such an experience has on a blind child would need to be assessed in terms of the child's drive and ego development and the level of his object relationships.

The blind child who will be described was subjected to many hospitalizations in early life. At such times his parents, because of their own anxieties, were not even able to visit him regularly, much less to stay with him. He was in the hospital at regular intervals for most of the time between the age of fourteen months and two and a half years, but this study centers around the hospital experiences that took place when the child was four years eleven months old.

According to our observations, this child did suffer profound unhappiness during the three separations from home that occurred at this point in his life. There was, to start with, the fear that he was being sent to the hospital as a punishment and would never be allowed to return home—a fear that was intensely real for him. In his fantasy life this rejection and punishment were associated with his blindness and his family's feelings toward him because of this handicap. Moreover, there was, of course, the fact that his blindness had made him different, had distorted his development, and had introduced a handicap in his capacity to understand and assess his and other people's feelings as well as the world of reality outside of himself.

What impressed us most—indeed, seemed remarkable to us— was that Richard ultimately has emerged from these negative experiences with a positive balance. With some help we provided, he appears to have been able to turn what might have been a damaging life experience into one which has increased his insight and made him more capable of dealing with the problems of being handicapped.

---

[1] Freud remarked on the connection between loneliness and darkness. In the context of elucidating his early theory of anxiety, he stated: "In children the first phobias relating to situations are those of darkness and solitude. The former . . . often persists throughout life; both are involved when a child feels the absence of some loved person who looks after it—its mother, that is to say. While I was in the next room, I heard a child who was afraid of the dark call out: 'Do speak to me, Auntie! I'm frightened!' 'Why, what good would that do? You can't see me.' To this the child replied: 'If someone speaks, it gets lighter'" (1916-1917, p. 407).

Before proceeding further a few general remarks are necessary. Richard was a member of our nursery school for blind children. In addition to the regular educational and group activities provided within the school, each child is given individual "special help" by a child therapist who sees the child four times a week. This work does not follow the usually accepted technique of child analysis for the neurotic child, but is modified to fit the special requirements of the blind. The special help given often includes support, reassurance, and many measures of a purely educational character. The latter in particular are designed to improve the blind child's ego development, which is usually distorted and in many ways retarded. In the specific case of Richard, the sessions were not confined to the treatment room but included walks in the street and parks, drives in the therapist's car, and visits to her home.

Similarly, when the hospitalizations to be described were about to take place, the decision was taken to give full support to Richard by visiting him for long periods of time and continuing the special help right at the hospital. A number of reasons made this advisable. We knew of the family's inability to prepare him appropriately for these experiences because they tended to deny their frightening character. While Richard's father and mother were in many respects excellent parents, they were not able to tolerate the expression of any distress, fear, or anxiety in the child. As a consequence Richard did not dare to verbalize his feelings to them, even though he suffered from severe distress, as could be seen in the sessions preceding the hospitalizations. Finally, and more important, we knew of the mother's previous inability to visit the child in the hospital and feared that this would be the case again. As will be seen, during the first hospitalization, the parents did not visit Richard until six days after the operation. In these circumstances and in the hope of avoiding as much as possible the potential traumatic effects of such a situation, the therapist felt it important to perform tasks and accept roles that are not part of the normal therapist-patient relationship in child analysis.

THE HISTORY OF THE BLINDNESS AND ITS EFFECTS
ON THE MOTHER-CHILD RELATIONSHIP
THE MOTHER'S WITHDRAWAL AND MOURNING

We learned from later material that the onset of Richard's blindness when he was fourteen months old led to an immense alteration
in the parents', particularly his mother's, relationship to him. The
blindness was the result of a retinoblastoma, an extremely malignant
growth arising from the posterior part of the retina. The tumor cells,
generally found only in very young children under the age of five,
may grow backward along the optic nerve and invade the brain and
rapidly cause death unless there is surgical intervention. As soon
as Richard's condition was diagnosed (when he was fourteen months
of age), one eye was removed immediately. The other eye was treated
regularly with cobalt ray in the hospital. This proved unsuccessful
and when Richard was two and a half years old, the second eye was
removed.

We have by now come to expect that the mothers of blind children experience profound and often prolonged periods of depression.[2] During this abnormal state the capacity to perceive and respond to the child's needs may be markedly impaired. Unless the
mother is given help at the right time, the small child who, like
Richard, loses his sight some time after birth suffers not only from
this loss: while he finds himself in a bewildering new world of
darkness, he simultaneously suffers the loss of the mother and her
help just when he needs it the most. This applies to the child's
need for an auxiliary ego to orient himself in the new world of
blindness and to his need to learn about and identify his own and
other people's affective responses. We know that much of this
process takes place automatically in the rich visual and auditory
interaction between the normal mother and her child. An immense
range of shadings and variations of affect are expressed through various sounds and colors and subtle distinctions between them. The
tone and sound of the mother's voice convey important messages to
the child.

Unfortunately, in some of the blind children we observed, the

2 Solnit and Stark (1961) have discussed this type of problem.

mother's withdrawal meant that the verbal communication decreased markedly and the child also suffers from lack of auditory contact. When the mother is depressed, as Richard's mother was, her voice can become flat and affectless.[3] Or she can be silent altogether for long periods of time, which deprives the child of communication on any perceptual level. From the study of Richard we can learn that it is possible for another person to "teach" the blind child much about his affects and inner world and that careful verbalization can open up areas of contact which seemed to be drastically limited. This was evident in Richard's case; but it should also be noted that he had the advantage of a good mother-child relationship during the first fourteen months of life and perhaps the benefit of some sight during this period. Further, Richard himself, possibly for the above reasons, never withdrew markedly from contact with the object world as some other blind children do. The situation may be different in the sense of having more permanent damaging effects when the child is blind from birth and certainly when the mother-child relationship is damaged from the beginning.

As we had not known Richard's mother before his blindness, we formed a picture of her as a rather withdrawn, depressed, colorless, and disturbed personality. It was only some years later, when the depression had passed, that we saw another woman. At present she looks quite different, with color in her face and variety and interest in the tone of her voice. The interaction with her children is lively and animated. We observed her very slow recovery, and the change in her personality is startling and dramatic. Richard evidently lost a cheerful and contented mother and after a satisfactory fourteen months of infancy, he suddenly had a different mother.

For the mother, on the other hand, this blind child was not the same infant she had so delighted in. Thus the mother had a different child and the child a different mother. Although he could not at such an early age give verbal expression to his feelings, he perceived correctly that he was no longer loved in the way he knew and that this was related to a change in himself and to his handicap. He had

[3] A similar situation was observed in the case of Winnie, a blind child treated at the Clinic by Cecily Legg. The mother, who was deaf, was eventually persuaded to get a hearing aid, but she continued to turn it off for long periods of time in order to remove herself from the situation.

an overwhelming fear of being discarded by his parents, and he experienced the hospitalization as such a real danger. This perception of himself as a broken object to be finally discarded was partly related to the fact that he was in the anal-sadistic phase of development when his eyes were found to be malignant and were removed (and discarded). It was appropriate to the level of ego development that he formed his concepts of events in anal terms. As a blind child, moreover, his thinking remained much more concrete than that of the sighted child (see Nagera and Colonna, 1965).

Thus, in his further development, he not only had to struggle with the normal problems inherent in the move to the phallic-oedipal phase; in addition, he had to cope with the problems of understanding his own handicap and its meaning in terms of his future as a damaged male. Having lost his mother because of his handicap, the blindness further affected his capacity to identify with a sighted father and brother.

Much of what will be described can be seen as Richard's longing to find again and reunite with the lost mother. This inevitably contained elements from the early need-satisfying phase of object relationship as well as the emergent phallic-oedipal factors appropriate to his stage of development.[4]

In any case, Richard's developmental progression took place largely through a series of difficult identifications which ultimately led him to a masculine position. At present he seems to have found his way back to his mother on the age-adequate level of latency. Through verbalization, clarification, and interpretation of inner and outer reality, many missing links of his psychic life were gradually re-established. It is of interest to note that the working through of much of this was done by the child himself after he left our unit at the Hampstead Clinic and went to a boarding school at the age of five years.

---

[4] Freud described how different levels of object relationships and the concomitant anxiety and fear of separation and loss of love are intertwined with each other. He said: "If a mother is absent or has withdrawn her love from her child, it is no longer sure of the satisfaction of its needs and is perhaps exposed to the most distressing feelings of tension. Do not reject the idea that these determinants of anxiety may at bottom repeat the situation of the original anxiety at birth, which . . . also represented a separation from the mother. Indeed, . . . you may add the fear of castration . . . , for a loss of the male organ results in an inability to unite once more with the mother (or a substitute for her) in the sexual act" (1933, p. 87).

History

As already stated, the first fourteen months of Richard's life were satisfactory. He was the second son of middle-class parents living in a London suburb. His paternal grandparents lived nearby and were very much attached to Richard. When Richard went to the hospital at the age of fourteen months, he stayed for two weeks, his recovery being complicated by his contracting measles on the ward. Subsequent to this, he went in for a period of three or four nights every fortnight for cobalt-ray treatment for over a year. During this period his parents retained every hope that one eye could be saved. They were able to provide him at home with many opportunities for exploration, free movement, and play with his elder brother, Jack, age eight.

However, when Richard ran straight into a chair for the first time, his parents noted the change in his orientation and took him to the hospital. The examination disclosed that the cobalt-ray treatment had caused a hemorrhage, and the second eye had to be removed. Richard was then two and a half years old. According to the parents, there was no sign of regression during this period, although they felt that his walking was delayed by the loss of vision.

Entrance to Nursery School

Richard began daily attendance at our nursery school when he was three years old, about six months after the removal of his second eye. He seemed particularly ready for school and appeared to adapt to it easily and confidently.

Four months after he entered nursery school, his younger sister Louise was born. At that time his grandmother stayed at their home and was able to give him the attention which in infancy he had received from his mother. Some months later, when Louise became mobile and active, Richard began to show signs of distress. He developed a speech difficulty, described as a stammer when he tried to talk very rapidly. Some observers felt that his behavior was excessively manic, while at the same time there were increasingly frequent periods of withdrawal, when his expression seemed very

sad. I began to see Richard in individual treatment on a daily basis
when he was four years old.

Introductory Period of Individual Treatment

The first weeks of work provided the opportunity to see how an
intelligent blind child can adapt to an entirely new experience, that
is, an unfamiliar person, different surroundings and activities, a wide
range of freedom in his play, and encouragement to verbalize his
ideas, fears, and feelings. He came to the sessions quite easily and I
learned only much later that he had feared being left with me permanently. Despite this, he was eager for the contact.

His mode of exploration and orientation seemed very adequate.
He was cautious in feeling his way in the unfamiliar building, and
in his treatment room he explored the area with much care, touching all the objects on the level of his arms. To the observer this behavior resembled the sweeping glance of the sighted person in a new
room, though the information gained was of course limited by the
possible range accessible to touch. The laborious tactile exploration
replaces the visual impressions which convey at once an immense
amount of information, enabling the sighted child to proceed directly. There was a striking difference in Richard's behavior in the
first and second sessions. In place of his initial cautiousness, he
showed confidence and pleasure. The child must obviously first feel
safe before he can further explore a new situation or materials and
find new ways to use them.

We noted rapidly that the treatment room suited to the sighted
neurotic patient was not inviting enough to the blind child. Richard
was soon restless and impatient to leave, wanted to visit my home,
drive in the car or take a walk. It was necessary to modify the treatment technique, adapting it to provide the educational help which
seemed to be required. We felt that in Richard's case, outer reality
needed a great deal of clarification before the inner problems could
be seen more clearly and taken up in treatment. For example, together Richard and I found ways of gaining information about the
room as an enclosed space with windows and doors. We used ladders,
bounced balls against different walls and against the ceiling. We
attached objects to a string and threw these out of the window. In
this way he acquired a better concept not only of the dimensions of

the room but also of the relation between ceiling, floor, and walls, etc. Similarly, we searched for more ways by which Richard could gain a better knowledge of the space in the room, its construction, its relationship to the house, that is to say, a concept of distances.[5] During this period of work Richard seemed impatient with toys and he never entered into any form of play.

Reactions to the Younger Sister

Gradually, through activity which seemed at first incomprehensible, Richard showed that he was trying to cope with what was for him a painful and confusing situation—having a sighted sibling who was rapidly becoming mobile and was able to move more quickly and efficiently than he. Interestingly enough, he showed this by very noisy behavior in which he was re-enacting the changed situation as he perceived it. At home there was now an active infant capable of producing many new confusing and disturbing sounds. He began to shout, to slam doors, to kick, throw objects, and break toys. Simultaneously, he made great efforts to contain and control his behavior, feelings, and thoughts. His noisy behavior was a complex, highly overdetermined expression of his inner life. It conveyed not only his auditory perception of the different environment but also the inner tensions this created. While this behavior appeared to be aggressive, it was more an expression of his fear and anxiety of disintegration and of his perplexity than a real outburst of aggression. Some of his noisiness also was a way of conveying the concern he felt when his little sister cried and screamed at night or when he was confronted with her reaction to his inadvertently

[5] The conceptual confusion of the blind child is frequently underestimated. The blind child acquires words and language with apparent ease, but it is not always realized that the small blind child learns and parrots words and sentences without having sufficient knowledge to understand their meaning. As was described in a previous publication (1965), sight plays an essential part in the acquisition of the meaning of words. While the blind child may acquire words denoting colors, shades of light and darkness, etc., it is extremely difficult—if not impossible—for him to acquire the corresponding concepts. Hence, we find conceptual confusion and impairment of other complex ego functions.

Development, especially ego development, is a gradual building up and expansion of the previous achievements. In the blind, the foundations are faulty, and as a consequence later ego development is poor, retarded, distorted or impaired in various ways (Burlingham, 1961, 1965). In view of these factors, the therapeutic work with the blind must of necessity include much clarification of external and internal reality as well as other educational measures.

falling over her while she crawled silently about the home. This resulted in some restriction of the freedom he had previously had in his home.

In his libidinal development Richard had never fully given up the satisfaction and concerns of earlier phases as he progressed in some measure to the next one, a factor characteristic of the young blind child. For this reason, Louise's toilet-training problems became a source of great concern to him. He made many references to the noises and smells and to the continual question of whether Louise had been "good" or "naughty." He shouted anal words and jokes. He enacted in the treatment the way in which he would ascertain whether or not Louise had performed when she sat on the pot and he showed that he touched her body and helped her, then reported his findings to his mother.

His confusion about her "good" eyes and his "bad" ones that had had to be removed now appeared in the sessions and was taken up in this context. "Good and bad eyes" included elements and fantasies pertaining to the anal and the phallic-oedipal phases of development. By such means he introduced another question of great concern to him, namely, that of the imminence of another hospitalization with its resultant anxiety and fantasies concerning the reasons for it. So far the family had not informed me about this pending hospitalization.

The Threat of Hospitalization

I learned then that he would have to go to the hospital for a skin-grafting operation. Its purpose was to build up in his eyesocket the tissue which had been burned during the earlier radium treatment. The only purpose of the operation was to improve the appearance of the eye.

It was typical of this family that they had not appropriately discussed this with Richard. The parents denied that he would in any way feel anxiety or unhappiness about the hospitalization and operation, claiming that he would accept it as an inevitable necessity, just as they themselves did. Naturally, his anxiety was increasingly evident in the sessions, where it appeared in concrete terms relating to castration anxiety on the libidinal side and to its various symbolizations and manifestations on the ego side. Richard seemed to personify and see himself in every damaged object or toy. He was petrified when I happened to mention that my car had a dent in a fender and would have to be repaired at the garage. He was quite unable to touch the dent, shrinking back in terror. He used his little engine to show me how, when it was removed from the rails, it also banged into objects the way he did. Whenever Richard ran into anything, he always blamed himself for being careless. He feared his engine was so damaged that it would have to be relegated to the dustbin. In this way he indicated his fantasies that he too would be discarded by the family because of his damage, and at the same time revealed his fear that he would be abandoned in the hospital.

His difficulties in verbalizing affect were constantly in evidence, partly because of the concretization of thought generally found in blind children of this age.[6] When I verbalized his anger during the time of some very rough play with his engine, Richard refused to play with it again. We learned that he had had a playmate whom his mother forbade to enter the house because he had used bad language. When Richard's grandmother initiated a game in which she called Richard by this child's name, Richard became very anxious and asked his grandmother to stop calling him by that name because he feared that he too would be banned from the home by his mother. This type of reaction, common enough in all children, is particularly frequent and marked in the blind child because of the usual concretization of his thought processes. For this reason such fears are not based merely on an unconscious association but are often "real" conscious fears.

Richard's fear of being found out, punished, and discarded increased. He expressed the fear that the receptionist would come and take him away when he was noisy and naughty during the sessions. Sometimes he listened attentively for her steps on the stairs.

Once he heard a child cry in the Baby Clinic and said: "What is somebody doing to that little boy?" On another occasion, but in

[6] For this reason we have earlier emphasized the need for conceptual clarification of what is going on in the external as well as in the internal world. One must help the blind child (as one does with much younger children) to understand, conceptualize, and verbalize his inner overwhelming experiences and affects so that he can acquire the appropriate means of expressing such feelings. The therapeutic value of such measures is well known and is particularly important in the case of the blind child.

the same general context, he also referred to his "Daddy" and to the "ragman."

The fear of what the angry father might do to the naughty little boy showed the intensified castration anxiety that the blind boy experiences in the phallic-oedipal phase. On the one hand, Richard conveyed that he had already experienced the damage and suffered the castration and the punishment. On the other hand, the blindness made him much more apprehensive and fearful of external dangers since he felt continually unable to anticipate external attack. Furthermore, he was convinced that his wrongdoing could be observed by others without his having knowledge of it. While the sighted child also has such beliefs, the blind child has in actuality many experiences that convey to him that others know what he is doing without any understanding on his part how they do. In the blind child, therefore, the superego as an external agency persists much longer than it does in sighted children. In Richard's case, these notions were linked to his fear of the punishing doctor who would perform the castration, as he had removed the "bad" eyes.

I saw evidence of the punishing, condemning, external all-seeing nature of his superego in the therapy sessions: Richard was terrified, and he barricaded the door of our room with tables and chairs. He also became increasingly unable to control his outbursts of anxiety, which made his functioning in nursery school very difficult.

The Fear of Being Discarded

This fear, it emerged, was personified in the figure of the rag and bone man who Richard feared would come and take him because of his bad, aggressive behavior. He became quite terrified whenever he heard the ragman call out. His grandmother and others tried to help him overcome this educationally, encouraging him to feel the horse and cart, but this usually active and outgoing child would stiffen and pull away in fear. Interpretation of the fear of being taken away as punishment for angry and naughty feelings helped relieve his anxiety. Another form of verbalization that provided some relief was the clarification and discussion of his blindness and of his feeling that he was a broken toy and therefore only good for the dustbin. Together we named in concrete terms the "good" parts of himself, his ears, nose, hands, feet, in contrast to the "bad" eyes, and commented on the unlikeliness of anyone with so many good functions being discarded.

However, the fear of being discarded remained to some extent, and on later occasions when Richard's anxiety was at a peak, he became altogether panicked again on hearing the rag and bone man's cry. On one such occasion he began to sob convulsively and could be calmed down only by being picked up by the therapist. When I attempted to talk to him about this, he said, "Let's talk about my nice daddy," and further avoided the subject by wanting to know where all the members of his family were.

It was as though all his love objects at home and at the Clinic were experienced as one. He wanted to keep them all together and with him, to feel reassured. He calmed down only after barricading doors and windows. It was at this point that for the first time he was able to verbalize his feelings that it was "silly" to go to the hospital. He longed to have his mother stand by him and insist that she would not let him leave all the persons he loved in order to go to the hospital. He also wanted to know whether I would take this stand if I were his mother. Furthermore, he verbalized many worries about his naughty behavior, such as slamming doors, which his parents had specifically forbidden. Yet, he had a constant desire to throw things and to slam doors.

A few sessions later, just before the summer holidays, he said at the end of one session, "I'm a little bit afraid of going home" because he feared that the post would have brought a letter requesting him to come to the hospital.

In the car when he tooted the horn, he became fearful that a policeman would come and take him to prison. The ragman, the doctor, and the policeman were all frightening external figures who had the power to punish and banish him. In Richard's fantasies, neither the mother nor, in a sense, I would save him from dangers, particularly the oncoming hospitalization, but both of us would give way. The reality facts for a blind child, who is so extremely dependent and therefore so defenseless, seemed particularly cruel to Richard at this point.

When his sessions were interrupted for the summer holidays, no one knew whether or when the hospitalization would take place.

Difficulties over Aggression

Immediately after the summer holiday Richard told me, while playing with the toy train, that he had gone by two trains and one bus to visit the hospital. When I inquired whether he had slept there, he said he had not done so but would have to next time. He said this with little show of affect, requesting that I come to visit him and bring a gift to him in the hospital. He expressed worry about the Clinic doctor, became anxious, and wanted to leave the Clinic building altogether. In these sessions one saw his conflict over aggression. His anger, sense of frustration, and fear made him long to get away and yet at the same time because of his blindness he felt completely dependent upon the adult world.

This is naturally an acute problem for the young blind child. All young children, including the sighted, are to some degree dependent upon the adult world, but they can look forward to the time when they will be independent. The blind child, because of his handicap, feels particularly tied to and dependent upon the sighted object world and cannot see his way out of this situation. Much time was therefore devoted to reassure Richard and to explain that in spite of his handicap there were ways and means by which he could become more independent and eventually almost self-sufficient. For example, in due time he would learn Braille and become able to read his own books. All this was welcome to Richard, who had such a strong wish for independence.

The dependence of the blind child on his sighted objects makes it particularly difficult to express aggressive wishes, fantasies, and feelings. This dependence usually transforms itself into the fear of being abandoned by those whose ill-will has been provoked by aggression. Richard was, of course, no exception to this.

A new type of play began to emerge in the treatment hours. Richard would sit in the driver's seat in the therapist's car and drive to "Cantontown" (a name similar to Richard's family name). From time to time he wanted to get out of the car, to feel the pavement underneath and explore it; but the fear that I might drive off and leave him behind was constantly evident.

During these weeks he persisted in frequently throwing objects on the floor or out of the window. I discussed this with him in terms of his feelings about the hospitalizations and his fear that it was he who was being thrown away and discarded. His anxiety that the home would change and that he would be replaced during his absence was verbalized. He listened intently. When I talked in reality terms about the fact that it feels horrible to have to sleep in the hospital for two to three weeks, as he well knew from past experiences, he also recalled reassuringly that he went back home each time and had never been replaced in his absence. We spoke repeatedly and in detail about the fact that his bed, his room, place at meals, etc., were all kept for his return. He seemed to need the very concrete details in order to conceptualize this possibility in his own terms.

He asked many appropriate questions and was more able to verbalize his feelings. For instance, he said, "Mr. S. [the surgeon] is away on holiday. Isn't that a shame?" When I asked what he thought was a shame, he said, "Isn't it a shame I have to go to hospital. Mr. S. and hospitals are horrible." We agreed to keep these thoughts and feelings about the hospitalization to ourselves since his family found it so painful to hear how horrible it would be.

It was interesting that this "secret" talk led the next day to his wish to turn the lights on in the car "to see a little." I commented that he must wish that the doctor could help him see. He asked, "Do you wish I could see?" to which I replied that I did indeed wish this for him and so did other people. He said his mother wished it, and we spoke of all the family and friends and doctors who wished it, and how unfortunate it was that the time in the hospital would not make it possible.

Affect of Sadness

A day or so later he bumped his chin, crying pitifully and wishing to sit on my lap and be comforted. Since his reaction was excessive, I discussed it with him in terms of his sadness and wish for protection from the pain of separation from home as well as of his fear of the physical pain he would suffer in the hospital. Thus, I tried to prepare him for the discomfort awaiting him in the hospital, where the skin grafting would be performed. Throughout this time he was increasingly able to talk about his blindness and to mourn for his lost sight.

The pain involved in separations could often be verbalized when he left his sessions to go home. His behavior at this time was particularly difficult. Asked why he thought it was so hard, he relaxed and once said, "Miss C., it *is* difficult leaving."

Richard's destructive and restless behavior at home and in school became more evident after I had had an interview with his father. Richard questioned me whether we had talked of how he "worries" his mother and "gets under her feet." In this period he told me that he disliked Saturday and Sunday because we did not meet on those days. Some of the destructive behavior, i.e., breaking plates, knocking over chairs and tables, was also understood as his attempt to anticipate the coming events, an indication of the feeling he would be broken up further in the hospital as a punishment. Similarly, in this context, he played shopping, buying, and selling, which also appeared to indicate his feeling of being sold or given away to the rag and bone man.

Richard talked more and more about the operation and demonstrated that he had recently learned to distinguish between the right and the left eye. He explained that the operation was necessary because his right eye "is growing" and the left one, called the "little eye," would be made the same as the other. Other concerns and interest about big and little objects of all sorts were expressed, with special reference to my car and his father's larger car. He revealed his concern about being seen and watched by adults and his wish to get away from them. Moreover, he gave clear indications of his feeling that sighted adults are omnipotent and magical since they can so easily perform so many tasks that the blind child can do only with great difficulty. After throwing furniture and toys around Richard described once how he "helps" his mother in vacuuming and then replacing furniture which she has had to move for the cleaning. The implicit wish was to make up for his anger and bad wishes. Repeatedly during this time he attempted to make his teachers in school and myself angry in order to test if we would "throw" him away because of it.

One day Richard spoke in great detail about his new shoes, new socks, new trousers, new coat, and he said he had a new tummy. In this way he indicated his concern about the change in his eye socket and the "new eye" that would be fitted in the hospital.

(Previously there had been regular fittings for new eyes as the sockets grew.) At the same time he talked to his playing with his brother and friends at home, showing his sadness about his blindness and the degree to which it handicapped him in playing. The wish for a new eye could be discerned and was now taken up in treatment.

Blindness and Castration Fear

The link between his blindness, his masturbation guilt, and his fear of castration was apparent when Richard compared his own body with that of his sister Louise. It came up in the context of forbidden behavior in the car (such as pulling knobs, etc.). He said, "the wiggley gone . . . eyes gone." He also said he knew he had lost the "little thing behind his eyes."

During the next weeks the castration theme was accompanied by more numerous phallic-oedipal manifestations in his relationship to the therapist. He began to play a game in which he was taking me on holidays in the car, he being the driver, the daddy, etc. He became very polite and solicitous, as phallic-oedipal children often are, but then shifted to wildly anal behavior such as screaming, giggling, laughing, etc. The shift seemed related to his anger about being blind and unable fully to identify with the father role.

Mixed with the fear of the imminent hospitalization was the threat of being sent to a boarding school which loomed as an equally frightening reality. His brother told him stories of headmasters who beat and punish naughty boys. Both the hospital and the elementary school authorities had told the parents that they would be informed the moment a vacancy appeared. In Richard's feeling, this meant that life was somehow suspended indefinitely, that a fearful unknown future threatened.

The throwing and kicking behavior now emerged as his rage reaction to the frustrated wish to do what his big brother did; i.e., to engage in masculine activities that are dangerous and nearly impossible for a blind child, such as football. It included Richard's fury and sense of impotence engendered by his inability to use his body in the age-adequate aggressive outlets permitted the sighted in sports, etc. In play with me he was the chauffeuring father, picking up sons and their friends. A great wish to be a normal ordinary boy was shown in play, and verbalized as "I'll be the boy and you be the mommy," riding a bicycle, etc. In addition, he frequently enacted being the man around the house who performs such heavy tasks as filling the coal bin, etc.

HOSPITALIZATION

When the letter from the hospital finally arrived informing Richard's parents that he would be expected in the hospital in two or three days, his initial reaction was one of denial. He said it was going to be "lovely," a statement that was quickly followed by an outburst of uncontrolled behavior. In the last days before his departure what seemed to help him most was a concrete discussion of hospital routines and ward arrangements. We embarked on a project that consisted in making a book about hospital life. This book contained actual objects which Richard could feel, such as his washcloth, toothbrush, medical implements from a toy doctor kit, etc. He took this with him when he reported to the hospital. The intention here was to give him some intellectual knowledge of hospital routines, medical instruments, etc., which might help him control the natural anxiety provoked by the new environment. It is particularly difficult for the blind child to orient himself in and familiarize himself with a new environment—a difficulty which is further intensified by fear or anxiety.

First Hospitalization

What follows are excerpts from the observations I made during the period of his hospitalization.

When I went in on Monday afternoon at four, expecting to stay only a few minutes, I saw Richard being taken by the hand by a man (I later learned, the father of another patient) to the lavatory. He was very pleased at my arrival.

It was clear that he was completely confused by the situation. He did not know the time of day (proved by his asking me to come later and his hope that the parents would return later, though it was nearly his bedtime). He had had no help in orientation to the new place and no idea of where his bed was, where he could find the lavatory, or where the toys were kept. He played with some of the large toys which were lined up in the middle of the ward. The other children, who could see, did not find this arrangement confusing or difficult, but Richard kept bumping into things, being run into, and obviously stayed in his crib when I was not there. He had lost his own teddy bear. Briefly, he appeared completely bewildered.

The next day when I arrived he was asleep, recovering from the anesthetic. When I returned the following day, he was lying quietly in his bed, but was eager to talk to me and still very confused. He looked very pale and pathetic. I gave him the toy he had asked me to bring and told him that I had come the day before and had seen him sleeping. He seemed impressed and pleased about this and repeated it several times. He had to stay in bed. Whenever he needed to defecate or urinate (he seemed to have a slight diarrhea), he wanted me to get the pot for him, not welcoming bodily handling from strangers. Similarly, he wanted me to get him his milk or juice and resented anyone else offering it to him. He asked for whatever he wanted very quietly and it was my impression that had I not been there, he would never have asked. His mouth seemed sore and the drinks seemed to soothe it.[7] He did not have with him a single one of his belongings[8] from home despite all our talk and preparations of what he would take with him. His coat and clothing had been taken home by the parents, and he was dressed in very large pyjamas which required being tied. He longed for his own possessions, particularly for his own biscuits, which had been taken away by the nurse. Before I left he cried a little for his mother and begged me to stay with him, offering me a place in his bed. Bedtime was the most difficult for everyone and the ward was a chaos of sobbing children.

By Thursday he was up and could go to the lavatory. We encountered a little girl in the bathroom who was dressing to go home. When I told Richard that she was going home, he said crossly, "No, I shall not go home." By this time he was able to count the number of beds he had to pass before reaching his own bed. He appeared to know the names of some of the other children and he told me that he sat at the table with them at lunch. (It was of interest to me that all the children were quite different in the presence or absence of

7 Skin was taken from inside the mouth for grafting.
8 Except his book.

their parents. When they were alone, they were friendly and open to adults. When their parents were present, the children were unfriendly to adults and children alike.)

Richard and I frequently spoke about his parents and how much his family missed him and how happy they would be to have him at home again. The question of why his mother had not come to visit him came up. I said that it was a pity, but that it made her so sad to see him unhappy. During these days we spoke at length about the routines of the home and about the roads and the buses and trains between home and hospital. It seemed necessary to make the family and the home alive for him, for they seemed so remote from his life in the hospital. Similarly, I talked to him at length about my home and my own activities, and the journey from my home to the Clinic.

Richard insisted that on Saturday I come at two o'clock sharp, when visiting hours start, although his parents were coming that day. In fact, I spoke to them briefly on this occasion. The father obviously was glad that I had been able to visit and seemed to appreciate the importance of this for Richard. His mother still said that the time of his stay in the hospital was short and that he needed the rest. When I returned at bedtime, after the parents had left, Richard was sobbing.

Early in the second week of the hospitalization Richard was again examined under anesthetic, and it was found that the skin grafting was unsuccessful. The procedure would have to be repeated in a few weeks' time.

Reaction to First Hospitalization

Richard's first reaction to being home in time for Christmas was pleasure and delight at the reunion with his family, and his voice when he telephoned me on Christmas morning was happy and relieved. It was always a strange paradox that this family was so capable of providing him with affection and care at home and so incapable of supporting him during the times away from home in the hospital. Because I was away for a few days at the beginning of the following term, Richard returned to nursery school before he resumed the treatment sessions. The following observations were made and reported by one of his teachers, Mrs. Fyvel.

On the first day back Richard arrived with a bandage over his eye. Soon after he arrived he told her: "In hospital I had a big bandage on my eye, but now I have a small one." I asked him if he would like to play hospital with me and he accepted this suggestion with alacrity and as soon as it was possible—after snacks—he said, "Come on, I want to be the doctor and you can be Richard." We went into the other room and he asked me to find a large bandage and pad. He accepted as suitable a folded handkerchief and my long scarf, which he proceeded (with my help) to put over one of my eyes. When he found that the bandage was covering my mouth, he said, "I only want it as far as the bridge of your nose" and proceeded very gently to move the bandage to the correct place. He arranged a bell on the door by threading through the handle the two small cymbals on a string, and each time he opened the door he took great care to make the bell ring. He told me that the other room was his "office" and he frequently went to fetch things from it.

He explained that he was going to do an operation on me and went to fetch his "tools," which turned out to be the box of counting sticks; he used them as thermometer, stethoscope, instrument for examining my ear, and a syringe for injections. He only named the "injections," but his actions made quite clear what he was doing. I was struck by the gentle, tender way in which he treated me. He would lean over me, gently pushing the hair from my face and acting as though he were peering at me. He did occasionally give me a fierce jab when he was giving me an "injection," but he always explained first, "It may be a bit hard this time." When I responded by saying that I couldn't help crying a bit, he told me, "Never mind, when I am finished I will bring you something to make you happy again." And each time he would go off and fetch me something. He brought a good many of the jigsaw puzzles and he sat beside me "showing" me how to do them (which he did most competently, including one or two new ones which I had not seen before). When he was trying to fit a piece, I said, without thinking, that he should *feel* where to put it, whereupon he answered: "I don't have to feel, I am the doctor, I can see."

I asked when I could go home. He told me that he must go into his "office" and "look at his notes." When he came back, he went over the days of the week correctly and showed me that I would have to be in the hospital for ten days.

In the midst of this game Richard mentioned that he knew the others were having music time, but he did not want to join them; he added, "I want to go on playing this game until it is time to go home, I am enjoying it so much," and we went on playing for nearly an hour and a half.

On the following two mornings, Richard again asked to play
"doctors" and much the same actions were repeated with certain
additions. On one occasion he suddenly said to me, "Did you get a
smack in hospital?" I expressed surprise, and asked whether he had
been smacked. He told me, "No, but Lisa was." He then explained
that Lisa was a little girl of two who had been in the bed on one
side of him, and Robert, aged five, was on the other side. Apparently
Lisa had cried a lot "for her mummy, of course," but as he was
"four and three quarters, and Robert five, we did not cry."

He mentioned the name of the nurse who had been mainly responsible for his care and also "sister" whom he knew from previous
hospitalizations, but it was clearly the "doctor" who had made the
deepest impression on him and whose role he now played with such
intensity. I asked his grandmother whether there had been a house
doctor who had had a lot to do with Richard and she replied most
emphatically that there had been one whom she had seen when she
visited Richard and who told her about Richard: "That child is a
smasher."

Another observation of Richard in the nursery school was supplied by Mrs. Curson, who reported:

One morning Richard and I were alone, the other children having gone to the hospital for the day. Richard said, "Aren't you lucky
I didn't have to go to hospital?" When I agreed it was nice for me
to have at least one little boy with me, he added that he would have
to go back to the hospital some time; he said to me, "You have a
Stephen who is going to be a doctor, haven't you? Well, I want to be
a doctor like your Stephen."

This type of play made it clear to us that Richard was now
capable of understanding the doctor's role not only in terms of pain
and fear: the positive aspects in terms of healing, making things
better, were now included. As we have seen, he identified himself
with the good, gentle doctor and showed this not only in his play but
also in his relation to a younger girl on his ward. I believe that this
step significantly helped him in coping with this hospital experience.

As is to be expected, it took some time in his treatment sessions
before Richard was able to discuss with me some of the anxieties and
his distress about the experience, but his reaction could be seen in

the great concern he showed toward the end of his sessions. He attempted to prevent the separation from the therapist by taking my keys and hiding them. When I verbalized his feelings for him, he was able to separate the anxiety linked with the past hospital experience from his reaction to separation from me after the sessions. I showed him that at present he was not really being left alone and desolate, as he had felt in the hospital, but he was reliving again the feelings of helplessness and despair which he had experienced then. He was heard to repeat this to himself later.

I felt that I had to take into account that this blind child had far fewer cues in reality to separate past from present. Moreover, he and I were together for some time each day in the treatment sessions, as we had been in the hospital. For this reason, the current situation felt to him just as the hospital setting had. Referring to his wish for me to sleep in his cot in the hospital, he now stated that I should stay beside his bed in a chair while his parents should come into his bed. (When I visited him in the hospital, he had invited me to share his bed.)

A few days after his return to the Clinic, Richard had to go into the hospital again for a day for further examination. The surgeon told the mother that he thought that at least for the time being it would not be necessary to operate again. He hoped that through the fitting of a larger artificial eye, the socket might stretch sufficiently without surgery. Both mother and child were confused and anxious about precisely what this might involve and whether or not this would be a painful procedure. Richard then began to talk again about the period he had spent in the hospital and showed that for him there had been at least one positive aspect to the experience. This was his memory of some of the other children he had met in the hospital. This pleasant impression seemed to help him in understanding and anticipating what the boarding school would be like, a concern always in evidence. The general impression that he conveyed was that he had taken some inner step which now made him look forward with more confidence to school and to growing up.

In the context of this last one-day hospital visit we did some more work exploring his concern about size, big and little, etc., and relating it to his confusion about the two eyes (a little one and a big one) and the series of operations and treatments undertaken for the purpose of making them the same.

A few days after he had visited the eye technician who was to fit him with an artificial eye, there was another change in the hospital arrangements.

It transpired that the eye technician had considered it an impossibility to fit a larger size eye to the socket in its present condition. He insisted that further surgery was needed before he would be able to do so. When I spoke to Richard about this in the following session, he at first expressed surprise, adding, "You mean I do have to go to hospital to *sleep there?*" He was then reluctant to speak about it and began to play a game in which he piled toys onto a lorry and brought them to my "house." This game went on for a short while until, in an attempt to bring back the subject, I said it was nice of him to deliver things to me to cheer me up because I was feeling sad.[9] He asked why, and I replied, "Because you will have to go to hospital again to sleep." He said, "Last week they said I wouldn't have to and now they say I do have to." I sympathized with his disappointment and emphasized how difficult it was to have hopes raised and dropped. I said that I believed the surgeon must have felt so bad about Richard having had to go through so much again that he hoped he would be able to avoid another operation. He meant well, but the results were terribly disappointing for Richard. At this point his play changed and he had to go to hospital on account of an earache. I used this opportunity to verbalize Richard's own situation, i.e., he goes to the hospital not because of any aches or pains, but to make his eye look better, which must be confusing for him since he cannot see how his eye looks.

In his play he came upon some plasticine and wanted to cut it with his folding knife. In attempting this he cut his thumb slightly, and this brought on a strong reaction of tears and sobbing. (I was reminded of how he had felt in the hospital when he so longed for his mother to be with him. He was then in some pain and kept saying, "I want my mummy.") He proceeded to push me away, saying he

9 As is well known, children who would not tolerate a discussion of their feelings are frequently able to do so if their feelings are externalized and attributed to somebody else to start with.

would never come to me again; that I should not let him play with a knife; and that he wanted to go to Mrs. Curson. We could see his anger with his mother, who exposed him to the medical manipulations and hospital experiences, leaving him there alone.

The next day he arrived with a suitcase, "not" for the hospital, he said, matter-of-factly, because there they provided him with pyjamas. We could now talk again about the next hospitalization. I said I felt that now he could also talk to his mother about his feeling of longing for her to visit him. We would try to make a "schedule" so that he could know the exact days when she would come and see him; in addition, his grandmother would come, and his teachers and I would come since it seemed to help him cope with the time better. I also indicated again how sorry I was that he had cut his thumb. Yet, his tears had shown not only his feelings about the hospital and the fear of damaging himself but how hard it was for him to learn to do things for himself without getting cuts, bumps, etc. I praised him highly, saying that I thought he was brave and how good it was that he continued to try in spite of the many difficulties he encountered. Gradually, through repetition of this type of interpretation and variations of it in play, some of the dread of the hospital seemed to diminish.

A few days later Richard telephoned me and said, "I've something sad to tell you about. I'm going into hospital tomorrow. The letter just came today. If it had come earlier, I could have told you about it." I talked to his mother, who explained that they would take him in at 10:30 in the morning and it was all rather a rush. She thought it would be difficult to find somebody to stay with his younger sister Louise, etc. It seemed clear that she might again avoid going to see him in the hospital. I then suggested that I would visit him in the afternoon. She was very relieved and said they would go to see Richard on the weekend (the operation was to be on Saturday).

When Richard heard that I would come to see him, he said he would show me all around because there was a great deal I had not seen before and did not yet know about the hospital. He asked me to bring his cat, Muffins. He then wanted to know exactly where I was when I heard he was on the telephone and where I was now and he wished to speak to the Clinic receptionist. He told her about the hospital and said he was very sorry that he had not seen her that morning. On this occasion, his effort to master his anxiety and his acceptance of his feelings of sadness were striking.

The Second Hospitalization

This period in the hospital was characterized by a much more positive approach on Richard's part.[10] Not only had he been able to ask his mother to come and visit him, but together we all made up with Richard a kind of schedule in which he could tell, by the feel, who would visit him and on which day. The fact that during the periods when he was alone he was able to go over this, to anticipate who would be coming, seemed to be of great help to him. All of us who participated in this were symbolized in the book by a little figure or other object which he was familiar with and associated with a particular person. He seemed much more active in his overtures to the other children on the ward and in our visits we tried to encourage this. In fact, Richard succeeded in really helping one little girl who was particularly lost and unhappy. When he heard this child cry and cling to any adult, including those who came to visit him, Richard had at first pushed her away. Gradually, however, he began to accept her, perhaps by taking over our attitude. For instance, when little Frances asked for biscuits, we gave them to her, then encouraged her to ask Richard, hoping that this would carry over to the times he was alone, as indeed it did. It was also obvious that Richard now found it somewhat comforting that all the other children on the ward were sobbing for their mothers. Perhaps this made him feel not only less alone, but also less guilty about his own lack of control.

During my visits we did a great deal of walking around so that he could become better oriented. He knew the hall, where the baby ward and big children's ward were, the lavatory, bathroom, kitchen, doctor's room, etc. This was reassuring to him. He was interested in the door to the lift and the stairs which were barricaded. He showed a different type of behavior toward me in that he seemed to want physical contact with me. We sat for a very long time on a long wooden bench in the hall and he put his head on my lap and

---

10 He was able to do this even though we had not known about the fact that this time skin would be grafted from his leg and therefore had been unable to prepare him for this.

talked.[11] He said he would go down the stairs and take a bus and go home; then he talked of throwing his music box down and how it would all break. This showed his anger as well as his fear of what would happen to him if he tried to go. We talked about the other children and their fears and he helpfully pushed one tiny girl about in a cart.

During this period Richard seemed much closer to tears than he had been during his first hospitalization. He expressed greater distress whenever a person left him. He was no longer so frightened of being discarded if he made demands or expressed his fears and feelings. He clearly had more access to his own affects, and this in turn brought him closer to the other children in the hospital. Repeatedly he played a game which he called "prison," in which he expressed his own feelings about being in the hospital. We also talked frequently about his fantasy and evident fear that this experience was a punishment for his angry thoughts. I reassured him that this was not so and that in fact everyone admired and liked him for his bravery. His aggression found outlets in a game where he was a driver (on his tricycle) who runs into and hurts a pedestrian who then has to go to the hospital for treatment. In this same game he was sometimes a man on the men's ward and sometimes a little boy who wanted to be cared for and sheltered.

When Richard's mother finally came to visit him, it was clear how very difficult it was for her to bear not only his sadness, but all the unhappiness of the other children on the ward. When Richard showed signs of a trembling lip, his mother admonished him rather tensely not to cry and to "be a good boy." She said she had not heard another child crying when his parents left, and she wanted to tell Richard's father that he had not cried either. Richard was able to go to the door with her and maintain his control.

After she left, he did cry and even expressed anger, though not against his mother. He wanted to hit the door and to run desperately out to call her to come back. This was not enough outlet for his anger, and for the next hour we had to walk about the hospital wing, exploring all the lavatories and other rooms available.

---

11 Quite apart from the obvious phallic-oedipal implications, it must be taken into account that this small child was in great need of comfort from the mother. In her absence he attempted to give me her role.

Through motility he found some release for his aggressive affect. But he still showed much concern about his aggression and when he asked for a story, he worried what would happen to a beetle if he were to smack it and what a little boy's mommy would say if he came in and said that the beetle was dead. On this occasion he was very concerned about when I would leave him, asking me many times beforehand and sobbing when I left.

Throughout this second hospitalization Richard was more outgoing than he had previously been, and for this reason the sisters and nurses on the ward generally seemed more sympathetic and aware of him and of his plight. However, they were unable really to reach out and make appropriate contact with him. I should note the extreme variability of his mood at this time and how quickly he moved from sadness to anger, to interest, to tears, to smiling, etc. He now seemed to experience affects profoundly and showed little of the desperate and desolate control that had been manifest during the first hospitalization.

There was another change in Richard. With my help he succeeded in making overtures to the nursing staff when he wanted something. He learned that there were some sisters who would help him and others who seemed too busy, and this clearly made the experience more manageable for him.

During this second hospitalization there were many occasions when Richard could enter into a sort of conspiracy with me over some hospital routine; together we agreed that it was "silly," but that it would be better to adapt to it in order to avoid difficulties. Gradually we drew his mother and grandmother into this conspiracy, and this also helped him to cope with the overwhelming feeling that he was alone against the world. He told me that sometimes he wanted to shout on the ward and that he would loudly refuse sandwiches at mealtimes.

Reaction to the Second Hospitalization

The second period in the hospital conveyed more about Richard's thoughts, anxieties, and feelings than the first one. His reaction this time was both more profound and more moving. On Sunday he telephoned me from home to say that he was no longer in the hospital. His tone of voice conveyed a sense of gratitude for being permitted to be home again and to experience the relief of the absence of so much psychic pain and tension. This time his tension and anxiety were rather more in evidence, shown in some play of "naughty" animals, in his wish to use more infantile toys and equipment, and in an increased fear of trying new things. However, there was an overall sense of relief and pleasure in being out with people and away from the monotony and sheer misery and sense of deprivation he felt in the hospital. There was much talk about prison, and he conveyed a kind of resignation about it.

On returning to his sessions Richard heard the rag and bone man again. To my surprise he said that he would like to be the rag and bone man when he grew up. This seemed to be related to his wish to be the doctor; in both roles he desired to be the person who wants to have the damaged and broken in order to mend them. At this time he was wearing an eye shade and the skin around it was red and looked very raw and painful. He absolutely refused to talk about the eye or how he felt. The condition of the skin became worse and on the last day of the week I heard that the eye socket had become swollen. The sister in the hospital was contacted and she suggested that he be brought in immediately for an examination.

Third Period in the Hospital

Shortly afterward the eye socket became infected and Richard was hurried back to the hospital, where he was given regular treatment. When I visited him he said that this time he had been given quite "a shock," which meant that the surgeon had been horrified to note the condition of the eye socket. He was admitted to the hospital without delay. He said that the hospital could care for his eye "better than mommy," and this time there was the suggestion of relief at being back in the hospital where he was confident of being given treatment. He conveyed his notion that the doctor cared when he dropped his eye shade and then quickly picked it up, wiped some tea from it, and said: "Dr. ——— will go mad if he knows my eye shade got tea on it." In the days just before the parents took him back for examination of the infected eye socket he had shown very clearly in his sessions that he did not wish to call attention to his eye condition, his discomfort, and pain. He was indeed very worried and anxious about doing so and about the parents' possible reaction.

At the hospital he played his "punishment game" repeatedly, judging and then jailing us for "a million trillion years" for motoring offenses such as running into people, a crime he enacted by riding on his own tricycle in the hospital hallway.

At bedtime he was usually extremely sad, whimpering for his mother and repeating "mommy, mommy" sadly but without affect. At times he appeared to pretend that I was his mother for the moment.

POSTHOSPITALIZATION PERIOD

In the initial period after these hospitalizations Richard enjoyed the relief of having this experience over. Now his primary interest and concern related to his oncoming move to primary school. Although it was not certain when this would take place, it was possible for us to arrange some visits to the school together and this was a comfort to Richard who then knew that some of his former friends were there and that the teachers were initially impressed and pleased with him.

Follow-up Contact and Current Picture

When quite suddenly he did start school as a five-day boarder, we agreed to a period when there would be little contact other than telephone calls initiated by Richard when he was home over the weekend. The parents felt that this was important for him during the period of adjustment to the school. We were given reports that the teachers were delighted with Richard. This in itself made an immense difference to both parents who felt great concern about his future. After a few months occasional visiting was arranged, and this has continued at varying intervals. Richard is now eight years old. He went through a difficult period in school, but his recent development has been extremely positive and hopeful.

The mother reports that Richard concentrates better than his elder brother did at his age. His Braille reading is excellent. (To some extent this may be related to the restricted and limited activity that blindness imposes on him. Sighted children of this age may find concentration for long periods difficult because of the vast range of inner and outer stimuli to which their attention is directed and among which they have to choose.)

From the point of view of Richard's own inner development, his achievements are very considerable. He now has a much higher degree of self-esteem and there seems to be a sense of having mastered and achieved many difficult tasks, of being a valuable and worthwhile person with something to offer and to contribute. He does not appear to feel that he is in danger of being discarded or thrown aside, as he felt as a small child. Neither does he now need to assert himself as superior to other children. This had been characteristic during some of his stay at the nursery school. For a time he needed to insist upon being better or more clever than his older brother, Jack, and in school he was known to be rather aggressive toward other children, sometimes even tearing up their work, etc. Apparently this had a defensive quality and at present it is not a feature of his personality.

Richard has achieved a surprising familiarity with and knowledge about football. This is the favorite sport of his father and his brother and is an activity that is highly cathected by the entire family. Richard knows a great deal about the game and can converse about it very knowledgeably indeed. The father has been remarkably imaginative, patient, and helpful in teaching Richard about the plays, scoring, etc. Richard practices kicking the ball for long periods of time. He listens while the family watch TV matches. He has a little game, designed by his father, with the players, goal posts, net, etc., and he has learned all about it in this way. He is taken with his brother to all the matches and he even met the members of one of the teams and felt the ball. He knows the names of all the players on various of the famous teams.

It seems that this gives him the real entry into the world of men and makes him an integral part of the family. Visiting the family now, one has a totally different feeling about them. This is reflected in the way they talk and relate to the child, their pride in him, and the enjoyment of this activity. The mother indeed looks like a different person. The home itself also looks quite different now that she is able to take interest in it; with the father's help, the house was altered structurally, giving an impression of space, light, and air, where previously the feeling of gloom and depression had been predominant. The family was making plans to go abroad on the next holiday in a totally different spirit; earlier such occasions were approached as a great chore and effort, something that had to be done but in a pleasureless way.

Conclusion

It has been remarked that living and working with a blind child requires an effort very different from that with a sighted child of the same age, and this certainly continues to be evident. It is clear that without a very great active effort on the part of the environment, Richard would probably still tend to lapse into inactivity even though he has more resources at his disposal.

BIBLIOGRAPHY

Burlingham, D. (1961), Some Notes on the Development of the Blind. *This Annual*, 16:121-145.
—— (1965), Some Problems of Ego Development in Blind Children. *This Annual*, 20:194-208.
Freud, S. (1916-1917), Introductory Lectures on Psycho-Analysis. *Standard Edition*, 15 & 16. London: Hogarth Press, 1963.
—— (1933), New Introductory Lectures on Psycho-Analysis. *Standard Edition*, 22:3-182. London: Hogarth Press, 1964.
Nagera, H. & Colonna, A. (1965), Aspects of the Contribution of Sight to Ego and Drive Development. *This Annual*, 20:267-287.
Solnit, A. J. & Stark, M. H. (1961), Mourning and the Birth of a Defective Child. *This Annual*, 16:523-537.

NONVERBAL, EXTRAVERBAL, AND AUTISTIC VERBAL COMMUNICATION IN THE TREATMENT OF A CHILD TIQUEUR

PAULA ELKISCH, Ph.D. (New York)

This paper draws on data gathered during the course of a project in psychological research and psychotherapy which I conducted from 1940 to 1943 with thirty-two schoolchildren between seven and twelve years of age. I studied these children in individual sessions. Their undirected free expressions were assessed in terms of projections—in the sense in which this term is used in the concept of "projective techniques" (Elkisch, 1943). Within that framework, I focused specifically on the significance of certain form elements, as they became discernible in the children's drawings and paintings (Elkisch, 1945, 1947, 1948, 1952, 1960). In addition, my study threw some light on other questions, such as those of verbal communication, or its absence or its distortion, and on the way in which the children's verbal communications were accompanied, supplemented, or replaced by other media.

The case of Kenneth demonstrates how communication may be established when the faculty of intelligible speech is impaired or absent in a child, or when he uses language in an autistic noncommunicative way.[1]

I treated Kenneth while he and I were at a boarding school. At the beginning of treatment he was seven and a half years old. Kenneth's parents were divorced. His mother, who had been diagnosed as schizophrenic, had been hospitalized several times. After Kenneth's birth, she had her first breakdown, a postpartum psychosis. The

---

This paper was read at the Meeting of the American Association for Child Psychoanalysis, Aurora, Ohio, June 4, 1967.

[1] I have previously (1947) discussed the case of Kenneth, although in a different frame of reference.

father, a professional man, had been taking care of the child and continued to assume responsibility for him while he was at the boarding school. He wished to keep in contact with me; the mother, however, refused to meet me.

Kenneth had attended five different schools before he came to the boarding school. He was introduced to me as a schizophrenic boy suffering from a severe tic syndrome. In general, he was extremely fidgety; at times, the tics gripped the entire upper part of his body and threw him into something that bordered on convulsions. He also made strange noises with his tongue and throat, mixing these noises with nonsense and obscene words. At other times, eruptively and without any apparent reason, he would burst into paroxysmal laughter, laughing and giggling to himself. Occasionally, he withdrew completely and hid under chairs and tables, where he remained in a catatoniclike state of motionlessness and muteness.

Despite these disturbances, Kenneth succeeded, at times, in his attempts to relate to his teachers and schoolmates; he even pleased them. Of superior intelligence, he was interested in his schoolwork and was regarded as a good student. But his object relations were often, and always suddenly, disrupted. People became alienated by him. Subject matters in which he had previously shown an interest were at those times handled by him in an autistic manner. The same was true in regard to his verbal communication; periods of muteness seemed to alternate with periods of autistic verbosity. He displayed a peculiarly sensitive relationship to language—so peculiar, in fact, that language itself became a specific medium of his expressions and productions and was only rarely a means of direct verbal communication.

It seemed that since speech, in this tiqueur child, was unintelligible most of the time, his urge to express himself, if not verbally, then at least vocally, had found an outlet in his vocal tic.

Through claywork and drawing, however, Kenneth became able to communicate intelligibly and with great eagerness and directness. In his drawings, he presents us with some autobiographical picture stories, as it were, and with illustrations of his tic syndrome. In her comprehensive studies on tiqueur children, as well as in conversations with me, Mahler, in collaboration with other authors, has described certain features as characteristic of the tiqueur's behavior and attitudes,[2] features which are dramatically expressed in Kenneth's art work:

increased motor urgency;

indications of latent mental coprolalia (that is, the involuntary repetition of obscene utterances, a mechanism that Charcot called a "tic of ideas");

the specific role that the relationship of mother and child plays in the formation of the tic syndrome.

With regard to the topic of motor urgency, the motor, the machine, was by far the most prominent object represented in Kenneth's drawings. But it was not just the motor itself, it was the dynamic language of the motor, obviously reflecting the boy's uncontrollable, involuntary motor impulse, of which he felt himself to be a victim. For example, he made a drawing of a car, and he recalled the horrible day when the car stalled and he was blamed for the stalling and spanked severely by his father.

DRAWING A

While he was drawing, the twitching, shaking, and grimacing, in fact, his entire gestural tic, usually diminished considerably; his vocal tic, however, his noisy phonation and coprolalia, and also his

[2] See Mahler (1944, 1949), Mahler and Rangell (1943), Mahler and Gross (1945), Mahler, Luke, and Daltroff (1945), Mahler and Luke (1946).

neologistic treatment of language stayed with him and accompanied his drawing activity. Yet, by strange contrast with these most unintelligible communications, quite often, while he was drawing, his speech became increasingly coherent and intelligible. For example, referring to Drawing A, he explained: "This is a goofy car. You have never seen such a thing, it is between a house and a car. It has chimneys for gas, water, and steam. There is always explosion. These many fasteners—they should stop it. It is a car with seventeen motors —seventeen motors! Think of that! Next time I'll draw you a car with eighty motors."

The next time we met he announced: "I'll draw you a car with a hundred motors." Kenneth drew this car without any further comment. But he did express noisily his excitement and delight about so many motors (Drawing B).

DRAWING B

On another occasion he depicted his catatonic state in the image of a car (Drawing C). "I make a scary car, so scary that nobody would dare to come near—look—these tires—flat—flat." In fact, the flat tires are reminiscent of his hiding positions, in which he used to remain almost motionless.

DRAWING C

Likewise, Kenneth's dreams were pervaded with electricity, explosive speed, blockade, death. In one of his dreams he was to be electrocuted by a "man in the machine." While he was making Drawing D, he commented, "The man electrocuted my leg, but I could get out and rushed away. . . . I'm shrinking—you see—running—shrinking. He'll eat my leg."

DRAWING D

Immediately, he proceeded to make Drawing E. "This was the man. Fat—I make him fat, extremely fat. He's a piggy.. He wants to eat everything. He wants to eat me up."

DRAWING E

The experience of being overwhelmed by his motor impulses, which are personified by "the man in the machine," is identical for Kenneth with the experience of being castrated. Both "Eat Nothing" and "Piggy Stuffit" are images of orality, at opposite poles. Intricately and nonverbally, Kenneth communicates here the meaning, or rather meanings, of his oral tic, which was most likely related to early deprivations. Some time later, Kenneth illustrated this by remembering that when he was very little, his mother had told him that she "could not have him any longer" because she was mentally sick. Running, shrinking, being castrated, "Eat Nothing"—these seem to refer to experiences of annihilation. And through the name "Piggy" Kenneth communicates not only the all-devouring machine in himself, but also his own oral cravings, mixed with sadistic fantasies (both oral and anal), which express themselves in the symptom of mental coprolalia.

In tune with the model of free association, although on the nonverbal level, I once suggested to Kenneth that he put one hand over his closed eyes and wait a little while, until he saw something that perhaps he could draw. While he was holding his pencil over the drawing paper, with his eyes closed, he said, "You mean I should draw my mind?" I said, "Draw whatever you think or what you see now." After a while he opened his eyes and drew an animal defecating through various openings of its body (Drawing F).

DRAWING F

Kenneth commented, "I can't draw my mind, but this was on my mind. This is a horse, maybe—I don't know—it's you and me—it's dirt—plork—this horse has many holes, you see." In this drawing, Kenneth was exploiting—or so it seemed to me—his noisy vocal tic in order to imitate the horse's defecation. The two Y signs in the upper right corner meant something "very bad and dirty." The animal's "many holes" refer not only to elimination but also to a sex play between him and other boys to which he had given the name "holekin."

Obviously stimulated by this product, Kenneth suggested one day that he would like to draw "his mind." While he was making Drawing G, he explained: "There is a door—and then all my thoughts. . . . They are all sizes according to their going out of my mind." When he made the black spot in the center, he said, "This is bad, this is devilish, this is all black. I cannot get rid of it. Mock. I am very, very sure of. Whack. But there are others which I am unsure of; they may become devilish." It was for these uncertain thoughts that he made the odd signs, the Y's and the swastikalike forms. He said: "When I am talking, my thoughts shrink—they go out the door. Only the black one doesn't. It cannot get rid of itself. It wants to get rid of itself. It is impossible."

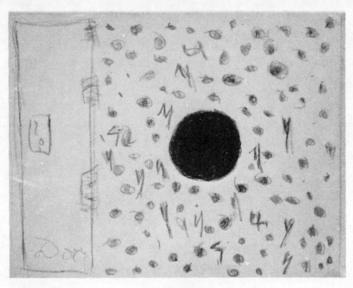

DRAWING G

This drawing conveys certain essential messages. If we hear the child's comments on it and remember the blackness of the car (Drawing C), which represents standstill, death, then Drawing G communicates Kenneth's ambivalence and conflict about verbalizing his thoughts, his being possessed by coprolalia and the concreteness of his thinking. "When I am talking my thoughts shrink—they go out the door," he said. This conveys that talking, even though it may unburden him, also impoverishes him, leaves him empty. This statement makes us think of the painfulness of his failure to communicate through intelligible speech; it might be related to his autistic language distortions; for, if he distorts and thus does not communicate, perhaps he may be able to keep his thoughts from fading away and leaving him empty. Still, there is one thought that ought to fade away, yet will not: the black evil thought. If only he could talk about it! But that he finds impossible. Instead, the thought has taken possession of him: it is in the center of his mind, and apparently presents the ideational content of his coprolalic tic.

At this point in the treatment I suggested that we talk about the black thought. While drawing the spot in the center and making explosive noises, Kenneth had thrown in two words, "Mock" and "Whack." Being now confronted with his black thought, he uttered, with a most furious expression, "When I am mocked"—and he performed the outrage he used to feel when the boys teased him, while he had to refrain from the urge to "whack" them, because "If I ever did, I'd become too bad." But instead of talking further about it, Kenneth wanted to draw another picture.

In this next drawing (H), he localized the black spot. "I'll draw you a picture when I was three," he said. "Mom and Pop are com-

DRAWING H

ing from the other room." The parents are obviously frightening the child, who feels guilty, because he has been masturbating. Allegedly, they are concerned about a "black spot" on the wall where noises come from—"szzz" noises from "unseen people in the dark." Kenneth here reversed his primal scene fantasies, confounding them with the noises he himself might have produced when he was masturbating. Just as he externalized or projected his motor tics onto his drawings of the car, so in this picture (Drawing H) he projected his own noisemaking onto the wall.

He then asked me, "How do you like my belly button? It's bigger than my head—no, it's bigger than me. Goofy, isn't it? I'll show you how big." Then he drew another picture, Drawing I, roaring with laughter mixed with indescribable noises.

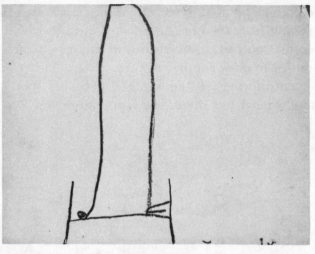

DRAWING I

If we try to visualize the last four pictures, synoptically, as it were, we may be able to perceive this child's representation of what he calls "his mind," through understanding, by inference, the meaning of the black spot. By starting with the "horse" that was "on his mind" (Drawing F) and following through the primal scene picture (Drawing H), and that of the overgrown penis (Drawing I), we have a graphic representation of the boy's sadomasochism, his castration fear (being "mocked"), and his phallic wishes ("whacking" the boys) —wishes that he had to suppress because of his anal-sadistic impulses. Thus the black spot constitutes a symbolic pictorial condensation, analogous to Kenneth's neologistic word condensations.

Fear of the dark, of being abandoned by the mother, is common in tiqueurs. When Kenneth mentioned to me that his mother had told him that she could not stay with him any longer, he recalled how he had been waiting for her to come. (Note the reappearance of the black car in Drawing J.) While he was still waiting, he had been taken back to the house by Ella, their maid.

DRAWING J

While working on Drawing J, he said: "This is Ella, our maid. She was old and I didn't like her. I was three then. She shook me. She always shook me when she punished me. I went out to look for my mother. But she didn't come. Then Ella got me and shook me awfully. I make her hair stand up. She was furious." One of the most prominent features of Kenneth's tic impulsions was the shaking of his head and of his entire body. This particular motor impulse most likely goes back to the shaking experience of waiting in vain for his mother—a waiting that had coincided with his being exposed to the fury of an angry maid. It cannot be by accident that, in this drawing, the child depicted himself in the womb. It is the womb of the "bad" mother.

Years later, when Kenneth stayed at the boarding school, and was in treatment with me, his mother came to visit him. Since she had refused to see me, I took the opportunity to observe from a distance the meeting of mother and son. They had not seen each other for more than two months, a comparatively long time. Kenneth's tics had left him for fifteen days. Their meeting took place on a hot summer day. The mother, dressed all in white, was standing in the shade of a fir tree waiting for Kenneth to come. Now he came running toward

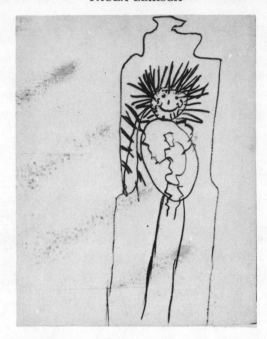

DRAWING K

his mother and jumped into her arms. While she hugged him, his body started to twitch violently and uncontrollably. His tics had taken hold of him again.

When Kenneth came to his session the following day, he drew a picture which he named "A Ghost in the Dark." Drawing L strongly evokes the meaning of the figure-ground reversal, as it is known in Rorschach responses.[3] Furthermore, displacement may be noted. The black center spot of Kenneth's drawing "My Mind" (Drawing G) has been displaced here and "turned white," as it were; the center of Drawing L is occupied by the white mother-ghost. One may speculate about the significance which is thus added to our understanding of the drawing "My Mind" through this dark-light reversal, as well as through the displacements. It seems as if Kenneth is implicitly ex-

---

[3] Schafer (1954) observed the expression of "denial . . . accomplished through a figure-ground reversal. The dark (unpleasant, anxiety-arousing area) is related to the background, the space (bright, light, decorative . . .) is called into the foreground. . . . The perceptual figure-ground reversal would seem to correspond in part to the mood reversal—good spirits covering depression—which is common in settings where denial is heavily emphasized" (p. 243).

pressing here the relation of his "mind" (or his representation of it) to his experience with his mother and his intense conflict in this (ghostly) experience.

DRAWING L

SOME THOUGHTS CONCERNING THE THERAPEUTIC INTERVENTION

In the treatment of Kenneth, the various forms of unconventional, "private" communication that he exhibited—nonverbal, extraverbal, and autistic verbal—proved to be therapeutic tools.

Most of the time, Kenneth felt tortured by his tics and he was often teased and humiliated for them by others. In his drawings, however, he had found an ego-syntonic way of expressing his otherwise alien, painful motor impulses. It seemed as though his gestural tic, which became so noticeably reduced while he was drawing, was neutralized, transformed into, or merged with his drawing activity; one might even say that it was sublimated into this activity. Thus, the boy had found an adequate medium of self-expression, which was actually an expression and illustration of his sensory and affectomotor disorder—a disorder that he tried to reconstruct, as it were, historically and etiologically.

Likewise, Kenneth's private, autistic, and noncommunicative vocal inventions were as meaningful as were his drawings. Through my subsequent study of Kenneth's cryptic linguistics, it became clear in retrospect what he had communicated to me in his sessions, by way of his, at times, primary process form of talking: it was his own diagnosis.

It was precisely the content of this diagnosis, his tic neurosis, that he had revealed by means of his private unintelligible idiom; and it was precisely the content of his diagnosis that he did not want to, and indeed was not able to talk about, just as he could not talk about the black spot in the center of his "mind." At the same time, however, he was forced to do so, mercilessly, by the impulsions of his vocal tic.

Thus, paradoxically and inadvertently, the very same means that were designed to defend him against the onslaught of his urge to talk gave him away, so that he would burst helplessly into vocalizations that were themselves symptomatic. He used the entire gamut of audible, imitable, and imitative noises, or sounds or words—or rather, he seemed to be used by them in his echolalic compulsions. These ranged from primitive preverbal sounds, animal sounds, and even inanimate noises, to multi-meaningful word condensations— namely, his sophisticated neologisms which, after they had been deciphered, proved to be a highly symbolic language (Elkisch, 1947).

We rarely have the opportunity to see a conflict at work as clearly as we can see it here: the conflict of communication versus noncommunication, of verbalizing thoughts versus not verbalizing them. I had the impression that Kenneth did find, at least for some moments, a kind of solution to his conflict—though it was a pseudo-solution—when in his private, autistic idiom he voiced words that betrayed elements of his diagnosis. At these moments he must have felt that he could talk about the black spot, and what it stood for, without really talking about it.

Such a compromise seemed to give him instantaneous satisfaction. At the same time, however, this hypersensitive, highly intelligent boy must also have felt deeply ashamed of his own nonsense talk. He must somehow have known what it communicated—namely, his inability to defend himself against his own urges, so that once more he had to succumb and again to be the passive victim of these paroxysms of ambivalence.

One may raise the question of the extent to which Kenneth might have been mimicking his mother's illness, since he did exhibit an extraordinary number of mimicry reactions—for instance, in his direct motor imitations and through his onomatopoeic phonation. I raise this question in view of his sudden relapse into his tics while his mother was hugging him. Mimicry, I surmise, is rooted in the symbiotic phase, which in Kenneth's case was pathologically prolonged. It was this prolongation that was preventing the separation-individuation process from taking its normal course.

BIBLIOGRAPHY

Elkisch, P. (1943), Certain Projective Techniques as a Means of Investigating the Psychodynamic Status of Children. Unpublished doctoral dissertation, University of Michigan.
—— (1945), Children's Drawings in a Projective Technique. *Psychol. Monogr.*, Vol. 58, No. 1, Whole No. 266.
—— (1947), Diagnostic and Therapeutic Values of Projective Techniques: A Case of a Child Tiqueur. *Amer. J. Psychother.*, 1:279-312.
—— (1948), The "Scribbling Game": A Projective Method. *Nerv. Child*, 7:247-256.
—— (1952), Significant Relationship between the Human Figure and the Machine in the Drawings of Boys. *Amer. J. Orthopsychiat.*, 22:379-385.
—— (1960), Free Art Expression. In: *Projective Techniques with Children*, ed. A. I. Rabin & M. R. Haworth. New York-London: Grune & Stratton, pp. 273-288.
Mahler, M. S. (1944), Tics and Impulsions in Children: A Study of Motility. *Psa. Quart.*, 13:430-444.
—— (1949), A Psychoanalytic Evaluation of Tic in Psychopathology of Children: Symptomatic and Tic Syndrome. *This Annual*, 3/4:279-310.
—— & Gross, I. H. (1945), Psychotherapeutic Study of a Typical Case with a Tic Syndrome. *Nerv. Child*, 4:359-373.
—— & Luke, J. A. (1946), Outcome of the Tic Syndrome. *J. Nerv. Ment. Dis.*, 103:433-445.
—— —— & Daltroff, W. (1945), Clinical and Follow-up Study of the Tic Syndrome in Children. *Amer. J. Orthopsychiat.*, 15:631-647.
—— & Rangell, L. (1943), A Somatic Study of Maladie des Tics (Gilles de la Tourette's Disease). *Psychiat. Quart.*, 17:579-603.
Schafer, R. (1954), *Psychoanalytic Interpretation in Rorschach Testing*. New York: Grune & Stratton.

OBJECT CATHEXIS IN A BORDERLINE TWIN

ANNA MAENCHEN, Ph.D. (Berkeley, California)

Object cathexis in borderline children was found to be inadequate, weak, or arrested in its development. Therapeutic work with borderline children is fascinating but not rewarding because these children improve only to a limited extent, and even if the level of their functioning is successfully raised, they remain odd people. The therapist's fascination lies in theoretical issues. A picture of the borderline child as a special entity seems to be emerging from a series of converging observations. Our diagnostic tools are being sharpened and a special technique is gradually developing. Many questions will be answered by more research, and probably not only by psychoanalytic research. Still, the problem of the origin of the disorder can now at least be approached in the area of the "experiential": environment and fate.

Early development is best studied by combining the method of reconstruction of the past in the analysis of children and adults with that of direct observation. My case can offer neither: the long therapy was not analysis proper, not much reconstruction was accomplished, and the observational material is scanty. I saw the patient once or twice a week for over five years of therapy.

The term "borderline" is used rather loosely. Where does the border run and what does it divide? Obsessional symptoms observed in borderline cases are also found in neurotic and schizophrenic children (Sandler and Joffe, 1965). The common denominator in the borderline cases seems to be a severe disturbance in ego de-

A version of this paper was presented at the meetings of the West Coast Psychoanalytic Societies in San Francisco, October, 1966. I am very grateful to my colleagues Jose Barchilon, Bryce L. Boyer, Dorothy Burlingham, Victor Calef, Rudolf Ekstein, Merton Gill, and Margaret S. Mahler for their valuable suggestions and criticisms. I specially want to acknowledge many stimulating discussions with Lillian Weitzner on her profile of the case; they were fruitful for the interpretation of the data.

velopment, but a definition on this basis is too general to be meaningful. We must attempt to specify the defects. (We seem to be dealing with a qualitative difference and possibly with a quantitative one that is so extensive as to change the quality.) Borderline children suffer from a specific defect in the ego function, different from the impairment of ego function that results from childhood neurosis. It is useless to compare the borderline and neurotic children as to the degree of their illness. The borderline children are ill in a different way: for instance, something is wrong with their stimulus barrier (Bergman and Escalona, 1949); they are more sensitive to light, noise, and smell; some experiences are more traumatic to them than to other children; they seem to be affected not by a single trauma but by many traumata or simply by ordinary events that are experienced as traumatic (Kut Rosenfeld and Sprince, 1963) because of their inadequate defenses very early in life. In normal development the mother serves as a protective stimulus barrier. Here we are faced with the recurrent problem of the interplay between constitution and environment.

The symptoms of borderline children are varied: overwhelming primitive anxiety comparable to that of neonates (Spitz, 1945, 1946; Winnicott, 1953, 1965), states of panic, bizarre behavior, distortions in the body ego and in the sense of self, language difficulties, and inadequate defenses against impulses. The question concerning delusions is still open. Some investigators described hidden delusions.[1]

CASE PRESENTATION

A twelve-year-old boy is sitting on the couch in my study, talking rapidly and incessantly. His tongue is out, he drools, picks his nose, and eats the mucus, unraveling a thread of his sweater or socks. He does not play. At times he slides to the floor, gets on all fours, and shows me his behind, making anal noises to accentuate his flatus. He fingers and smells everything and at times he mouths objects.

[1] From the extensive literature I refer here only to the work done by the researchers at the Hampstead Clinic (Singer, 1960; Kut Rosenfeld and Sprince, 1963, 1965; Thomas et al., 1966), Geleerd (1946, 1958), Ekstein and Wallerstein (1954, 1956), Boyer (1956), Searles (1963), A. Freud (1965), Boyer and Giovacchini (1967), Bonnard (1967), Kernberg (1967).

The same boy is a very gifted musician; he has perfect pitch and an understanding of classical music rarely found in children. He fails in school. This is Pat as I met him seven years ago.

Pat Y. was one of male twins born six weeks prematurely to a couple expecting their first child, one child. The father was a brilliant scientist, the mother an accomplished musician who subordinated her career to the rearing of her children, the twins and their younger siblings. Since adolescence, she had suffered from a severe inhibition in performing music. The parents were told to expect twins only one week before delivery; they had no time to prepare themselves emotionally. Mrs. Y. could not accept the fact at all and developed the theory that the boys were conceived at different times, even a year apart, as she revealed in a slip of the tongue. Faced with unwanted multiple births, the parents conscientiously did the best they could. What could not have been prevented was the depression of the mother after delivery.[2] The first year in the life of the twins has remained a nightmare in her memory. Everybody denied that they were identical twins. But when the analyst treating the other twin and I found much psychological identity between the two boys, we checked the hospital records and found that they were indeed monozygotic.

The boys were named Chris and Pat; the parents tried not to treat them as one, even though they had difficulty in telling them apart. Chris was born first, Pat followed eight minutes later and remained "the younger brother," an extra child, a bargain, and a surplus.

The two boys were in psychotherapy with a male colleague and myself for four to five years. The material I collected grew, and my courage to deal with the voluminous folders declined steadily.

The similarity between the twins was striking: they looked very much alike, wore the same glasses, behaved in a very similar way, and had the same symptoms and confusion in reality testing. Their first psychological tests were also similar. Their reactions to their therapists were the same, although one therapist was a young man and the

[2] At the time of the writing of this paper, Mrs. Y. is recovering from a severe depression which required prolonged hospitalization. So far, it has not been possible to gain insight into her depression during the first year of the twins' life, except her recollection that this early depression was connected with her inability to nurse them.

other an older woman. They used each other in the same way, their mutual attachment being both narcissistic and genuinely affectionate, but they did not quite complement each other—they were two halves which did not make a whole. The differences between them were only a matter of degrees, but the difference in age (the precious eight minutes!) played an important part, as it always does in twins, and constituted a decisive environmental influence. It was, after all, the appearance of Pat that resulted in a multiple birth. Pat's singsong at the beginning of therapy, "I am Pat, and I live in a garbage can," expressed his feelings.

At birth Pat was the heavier of the two and looked more developed. According to a note in the medical records, however, he suffered anoxia. Certainly, the birth experiences were different. Chris was overactive, Pat underactive, from the start. Both were extremely sensitive to stimuli. They were bottle-fed; contact with their mother's body was limited. There was no extra help in caring for them, and they had to be left alone, but together, much of the time. The mother recalled that from the beginning Chris could not be satisfied; he cried a lot in great distress. Pat as a baby and a small child "just sat," as she put it.

I was intrigued by the fact that during the first four years of life these twins had an exclusive language of their own that was not intelligible to anyone else. They started to speak when they entered nursery school (age four). This childhood language of the twins has persisted as an exciting verbal game until the present. It consists of guttural and nasal sounds and gestures accompanied by great glee and excitement. The twins can seduce each other into this game by making these sounds, and then they are off, lost to the world around them. It is significant that in this verbal game they offer each other strange-sounding foods.

Pat's symptomatology was dominated by overwhelming anxiety, at times by panic, resulting in complete disorganization, which Pat called "falling apart." At the height of his anxiety and at the low point of his functioning he expressed the wish to give up the struggle and to be cared for in an institution.

Pat attached himself to the therapist as he had to his twin. Any similarity in experience or possessions could reduce his anxiety; he was not alone, he was merging with me. He had to lean against somebody or something for support. He had to be close to me bodily, and this produced a somewhat comical picture: since he soon became taller than I, he practically surrounded me. He was handsome but overweight, physically awkward, poorly coordinated, and had a bad posture. In addition, he gestured, grimaced, snatched food from the family table, and was in general sloppy.

Pat feared body injury, illness, his own aggression, and insanity. Early in therapy an intense fear of death emerged, but the signal anxiety was lacking. He was also afraid of poisoning himself or being poisoned by others. This was not only a reaction formation (to oral sadism), but was also influenced by infantile sexual theories (he walked into my study stomach first, like a pregnant woman). The infantile sexual theories were still attached to the mother. Pat was afraid of being chased by big boys or a big dog, but there was no paranoid system. He suffered most from his severe obsessions—a musical instrument had to be secured to the wall, the car radio checked, etc. Most of his obsessions were connected with bedtime rituals requiring the constant help of his parents. He was compulsive about his therapy sessions, possessive of every second of his time with me. (The hour with me seemed short to him, waiting for it endless.)

Pat's speech was rapid, monotonous, at times garbled, and accompanied by motor activity. Only after two years of our work could he describe something without gesturing. He managed to be overactive even without moving from his favorite spot on the couch.

The problem of communication with Pat was considerable. When he was excited he did not hear me; and when he did, he often took the words literally, mechanically repeating what I had said as if by mimicry. Firmness in my voice could quiet him down more than the meaning of my words. I wondered about the significance of sounds in his early life: the mother's voice or the sounds of her music, and most importantly, the sounds of the twin and the language they had in common. Since he wanted me to be powerful and to "fix things" in his life, he also looked for magic in my words. It was difficult for him to think abstractly. In a magazine in my waiting room he saw an advertisement of a bathroom, and he smelled the picture of the toilet. The thought became an act. He obviously had a disturbance in thought processes and perception.

The sleep pattern in infancy was erratic in both babies. They disturbed each other—Chris, the restless baby, usually awakening Pat, the placid one. During latency, Pat had an episode of sleeping for several days (after measles at the age of eight). The possibility of encephalitis was considered at that time. Later he suffered from sleepiness during the daytime and was given medication; this was diagnosed as an allergy, and wool articles and pets were removed from the home. Drowsy and apathetic as he was during the day, he would come to life at bedtime, full of fears, going through his rituals, and complaining endlessly to his parents, who complied with his wishes to reduce his distress. I took Pat's reluctance to fall asleep as a positive sign (an autistic child will often sleep in a strange place). His sleep disturbance had oedipal features and contained reactions to what must have been particularly traumatic experiences for him— tonsillectomy (age six), birth of siblings (ages six and nine), medical examination for the possible need of repair on his penis because the circumcision in infancy was not successful (his penis looked different from that of his twin), "fall from a mountain" at the age of seven, small injuries. The sleep problem disappeared during therapy; some of the rituals reappeared at times of stress.

Intolerant of any delays, Pat was impatient, and his needs were urgent. The ego was incapable of postponing action by thought processes. Neither was gratification in fantasy possible. The waiting was made bearable only by compulsive talk. In the "primary- to secondary-process continuum" (Gill, 1967) he easily reverted to the primary process.

Pat felt poor and wanted many things of high quality, but they had to be purchased at a bargain price. The electronic kits he ordered always proved useless to him and were a "letdown," although he waited for them with impatience bordering on frenzy. He thought of himself as inadequate ("I am only a half") and felt hopeless. His self-esteem was extremely low. The fantasy of greatness seemed a solution, and he clung to it. He saw himself as a great musician. This interfered with reality testing, and in turn exaggerated his fears. He wanted to be the greatest without working for it, work being degrading to him. His wish was to be born great. He had talent, but could not work. He lacked the ability to predict, could not see cause and effect, and in general was incapable of mastery.

First I thought that the boy's fantasy of greatness was a defense against a castration anxiety. Later I found it to be a more primitive fear of body disintegration. Pat translated everything into defectiveness of body and mind (brain equals electronics). The things had to fill and improve the body like food. Any body waste was threatening (he ate his mucus). He felt empty. There was a severe disturbance in his sense of self. He had no pleasure in himself, and no continued sense of pleasure in anything. He anticipated pleasure, but did not achieve it—a fact that might explain the affect of sadness uncovered in therapy.

Pat regarded his father as a genius, felt hopeless about ever measuring up to him, and resorted to boasting and to fantasy, "I am a genius musician." He exaggerated his craziness to complement his notion of a genius, and in his boasting he rammed Bach and Vivaldi down people's throats and taunted and belittled everybody. He denied his helplessness in everyday existence and expressed his aggression; he identified himself with powerful functions of people and of inanimate objects. His hi-fi had to have a perfect tone, possess a powerful amplifier, and be heard all over town. At the same time he was physically timid, easily tired, afraid to use his muscles, and at war with physical education teachers.

Pat taunted his father incessantly with his own inadequacies and pseudoidiocy. His attempts to identify with his father were apparent in his wish to walk next to him in an academic procession, as if seeing himself in his father. His genius fantasy was also an expression of his identification with his father. In the transference he made fun of my husband, taunted him in absentia, called him sarcastically "the Professor," and at the same time expressed the wish to be "recognized" by him.[3] He showed identification with his mother in his serious interest in music, in shopping for food, and in cooking (mother's function as provider of food). At times he could be kind and motherly to his younger siblings.[4] His real identification (and empathy), however, was with his twin.

[3] Here transference is used as a general term. It would be more correct to speak of externalization as a "subspecies of transference" (A. Freud, 1965).

[4] It seems to be characteristic of borderline children to identify not with persons but with functions and moods (compare Mahler and Elkisch, 1953; Elkisch and Mahler, 1959).

Pat's relationship to parents, teachers, and later foster parents, was sadomasochistic. He played dumb and wore a sadistic grin on his face whenever he was wrong. At the same time he could show knowledge and concern about social issues, especially civil rights. He feared loss of his parents' love, but he was powerless to comply with their wishes. He feared abandonment—an archaic fear of a person not equipped to take care of himself. He trusted only one person—his twin. The family was divided into two groups; parents and younger siblings on one side and the twins on the other. The twins looked after each other, and it was Chris who at the family's outing would shout, "Wait for Pat." Pat hoped never to be separated from Chris.

Except for some underhanded aggression against the younger brothers, Pat's aggression was mostly of the tormenting type. He simply drove people crazy, and tried his best to do the same with his therapist. His means were mocking, ridiculing, and pounding a subject (my house was cheap, poorly built, and ugly; everything in my office was of poor quality; my car was old and foreign). All of these expressed aggression, low self-esteem, an effort at merging with me, demandingness, and, later in therapy, also rivalry with his twin ("Who has a better and more powerful therapist?"). He wanted to take my desk to his room, to have all my possessions, and later he expressed a strong wish to move into my house. Actually, he was underaggressive in action (he broke only my old wire recorder, which was nothing compared to the number of his own things he broke "by accident" at home). He was overaggressive in tormenting, underaggressive in actually destroying things belonging to others or in hurting somebody physically. His aggressive weapon was his speech.[5]

I wondered why he never could conceive of a relationship without aggression. I first thought only of projected rage in infancy, but now I believe that the answer lies in the twin relationship. The two infants were constantly together, playing with each other, intertwined,[6] and hurting each other. At times their mother had to separate them for their safety.

My impression is that in infancy and early childhood these twins

[5] Concerning the power of speech in the service of aggression, see Loewenstein (1956).
[6] "Intertwinned," as Ekstein suggested in a personal communication.

showed less than normal autoerotic activity, such as thumb sucking, that their playing with each other was more prominent than any autoerotic activity, which possibly added to the early difficulty in the development of the body ego (Hoffer, 1950).

During the years of therapy with Pat, the themes shifted slightly from oral to anal to genital, not the other way around. The oral demandingness did not appear as a regression during therapy, it was always present.

During the years I treated Pat I felt that no drastic environmental changes should be made, and I attempted merely to help Pat separate himself from his twin psychologically before he was separated from him physically. In this I failed. The parents reached the point where they had to protect the integrity of the family and the welfare of the younger children from the chaos the twins created and therefore had to separate them. Chris was sent to an out-of-town special boarding school. Pat stayed at home, and later was placed in a foster home where he could continue his therapy with me. He repeated the previously described pattern of behavior with his foster parents, and hardly changed his relationship to me, although he reproached me for not preventing his eviction from his family. During therapy, the oral demand first changed from water and cookies to paper and a few rides in my car, then diminished. He no longer had to fill himself, he was able to stick to a diet, and he lost 30 pounds. During the period of dieting, he looked sadly at his diminishing middle, expressed sorrow about the lost pounds, and comforted himself by "replacing" them with the special electronic equipment promised him as a reward. In the main Pat used me as a source of ego supplies and for reality testing, especially for testing other people and their reactions. He also used me to prevent dangers in his life and to influence his parents; and he would have liked to have me as a protector in school to achieve good grades. Even today, at the age of nineteen, when he comes for a session once in a great while, he still, in spite of some improvement and maturation, wants to use my "power" to protect him and to arrange things in his favor.

I have already referred to the fact that Pat accepted interpretations easily and repeated them *ad nauseam*. I had to be careful with interpretations of contents because of his insufficient defensive structure.

I have also mentioned previously that some affects of sadness and longing were uncovered during therapy. The thought of being separated from Chris could evoke these feelings and so could listening to records, which he could not stop playing for hours (compare Mahler, 1961). He defended himself against sadness by clowning, which was easy for him. Dreams and fantasies were not distinguished clearly from reality and therefore were considered dangerous. His obsessions stemmed from anal-sadistic impulses; some internalization had taken place at that stage. The ambivalence was striking and unadorned; he could make yes-no responses in one sentence. His defenses against anal wishes were weak (flatus, shame about elimination, and sexual curiosity restricted to the wish to see girls on the toilet).

Only analysis could have answered the question whether his hi-fi represented the twin or whether the music represented the mother. All I could see was that Pat used the hi-fi in a magical way. That use was not based on the fantasy of a neurotic child; as mentioned before, in Pat's case the hi-fi had to fill his body and replace its bad parts. Pat's talking was libidinized and could be regarded as action, while the usual play and acting out in child therapy were absent. The talking was Pat's doing (and his undoing).

Pat developed some competitiveness toward Chris when the psychological separation from the twin began, although it was not completed. The rivalry between the twins resulted in a cold war, not in open hostility. Pat was afraid to lose the interdependence with Chris.

Some degree of a belated internalization was achieved in therapy and with it a measure of autonomy of behavior, but Pat's superego (even now at the age of nineteen) is still dependent on authority figures around him. At the end of therapy he was able to check his responses to his environment and to adjust to it to a moderate degree.

In trying to bring order into a case which seemed almost chaotic and to introduce an observer and evaluator of the material collected I asked Lillian Weitzner to do a profile. I greatly profited by the Profile and the stimulating discussions resulting from it. The clinical notes of the third year of therapy were chosen by Mrs. Weitzner for a detailed study. She felt that "previously, the quality and quantity of anxiety were so pervasive and perceived as so destructive, that it colored and interfered with the observation of the ego function.

Treatment reduced the extent of anxiety to a sufficient degree so that Pat's disturbed body ego and thought processes were now more observable for study."

The Profile on Pat at the age of fourteen speaks for the value of Anna Freud's Developmental Profile as a delicate diagnostic tool. It helped me in structuring my thinking on the case and drew my attention to some features I would not have seen as clearly without it.

The Profile showed that:

1. Pat's annihilating anxiety was linked with the glaring insufficiency in self-regard (insufficiency of primary and secondary narcissism) with unsuccessful attempts at self-esteem regulation.

2. Self-awareness was experienced as body sensations and contained elements of visual perception.

3. Motility (especially self-touching) gave him assurance that he existed (apart from the twin).

4. The core tie was to his twin, and the representation of other objects contained that of the twin. All later ties were pseudo ties.

5. The Profile suggested that the verbal game was used as a defense against feeling abandoned or depressed, the highly libidinized sounds filling the gap of the lost object. Moreover, poor internalization of the parents might be responsible for this attempt to use the remnant of a highly cathected symbol (the common language being the mutual product of the twins in the past).

In general, the Profile showed that varying levels of maturity coexisted in Pat's libidinal structure and his ego functions. Especially prominent were the restriction and instability of the defenses and disordered ego boundaries.

DISCUSSION

What was the effect of twinning on object cathexis?[7] As early as 1933, Hartmann wrote of the striking similarities in the mental illnesses of twin pairs, the frequency of *folie à deux,* and the problem of interidentification. Dorothy Burlingham showed that twins, while

---

[7] The literature on twins is enormous. I will call attention here only to the work of Hartmann (1934-1935), Burlingham (1946, 1949, 1952), Burlingham and Barron (1963), Arlow (1960), Benjamin (1961), Leonard (1961), Joseph and Tabor (1961). Much of what I observed in Pat's case has been described by these authors as well as by others.

"working as a team," are not amenable to outside influence and that the twin relationship usually delays or holds up the personality development of twins. The continued copying is based on dependence. She also stressed the contagion of feelings. Leonard (1961) described the environmental influence on twinship: the cultural attitude, the parental attitude, the physical sameness, and the socioeconomic situation. In Pat's case, all these factors were unfavorable for normal development: in his cultural milieu twins were not regarded as a blessing; the parents denied the identicity; the physical sameness made it difficult to tell them apart; and the socioeconomic situation prevented alleviation of the burden of caring for two infants at one time.

Much material is available on the difficulties of identical twins in perceiving the twin as another child. According to Leonard, "Continued visual incorporation with the mirror image leads to identification through visual incorporation. . . . This [primary] identification with the twin often retards the maturation of individuals, causing language difficulties and interfering with the formation of other object relationships" (p. 308 f.). Pat said to me: "If I die, I won't see myself."

It has been shown that a special kind of mothering is needed in bringing up twins: it consists in keeping the twins separate and developing an intimate relationship with each infant separately, that is, establishing two mother-infant couples.

As we have learned from Mahler (1952, 1967) and Mahler and Gosliner (1955), a child fixated in the primary identification with the mother develops a psychosis of a symbiotic type. Applied to twins, fixation on the intertwin identification would probably have made them autistic. The object relationship to the mother had to break through this strong intertwin identification. The twins under discussion were not autistic, which proves that they were relating to their mother in some degree. An important environmental aspect may account for the fact that Pat's disturbance was more severe than that of Chris. It was easier for the mother to identify with Chris because of the acute distress he suffered as an infant. It was Pat's fate that he had even less of his mother than Chris. Neither twin had enough to provide for the imitation (and mutuality in imitation) between child and mother, so important for the development of the child (Spitz, 1945, 1946, 1962, 1965; Spitz and Wolf, 1949; Jacobson, 1954, 1964). There was too much imitation in gesture and sound with the twin, and not enough with the mother. The verbal game also developed into grimacing and clowning as a way of relating to other people. It probably started as lallation, continued as echolalia, and became a "preverbal language."[8]

Like other twin pairs, Chris and Pat at times represented two parts of one person: active-passive, masculine-feminine, right- and left-handed. When one was acutely upset the other was relatively calm, like a seesaw. It was during adolescence, after both had had years of therapy and after their forced separation, that Pat finally wanted to be Pat, separate but equal. He then made use of his talent for music. But any meeting with Chris brought about some regression, including the verbal game. The difference between the twins in the general activity-passivity pattern remained. Chris learned to use tools, to drive a truck, and to defend himself by fighting; he is altogether more independent. Pat cannot do any of these things. He is consumed by passive fantasies and is in general less capable.

As we know, the infant's awareness of his body is a step in differentiation from the mother. The symbiotic child is psychologically not differentiated from her. The mental representation of the mother is not separated from the self, and therefore no external objects exist to be cathected.

Pat's case came close to twin symbiosis. The twin relationship provided gratifications of a kind that led to a symbiosis—with the subsequent difficulties in separation—and therefore obstructed normal development. Instead of identification with a competent adult, instead of mutuality of imitation between mother and child, we see here identification with an equally helpless twin.[9]

Pat was unable to maintain an object in its absence. Each time I was leaving for a vacation he wanted to write to me; he would proudly carry off an airletter with my address on it, but he never wrote. The airletter meant at the moment either my money or myself rather than a means of communication. As a twin, Pat inevitably had to share his mother: his passivity in early life removed him even

---

8 The discussion of the secret language of the twins and Pat's use of language in general and in therapy would require another paper.

9 As Merton Gill suggested in a personal communication.

further from her. Here we see the two possible sources of the faulty object cathexis: the twinship and the passivity. We cannot say that his passivity alone pushed him to the border, because the other, active twin was also there. Passivity was Pat's first handicap in the development of object relations.[10] I am referring to the imbalance in the first contact with objects, but I do not wish to exaggerate: there was contact. Because of the extra sensitivity, the twinship, and the mother's depression, Pat as an infant must have experienced distress and expressed it in a way different from that of his noisy twin. We cannot measure the normal amount of stimulation needed, but we can say that Pat got too little from his mother and too much from his "mirror image."

In the narcissistic unity between child and mother, the child does not distinguish between himself and the environment. In twins, the unity with the twin can occur at the expense of the unity with the mother, as it did in Pat's case. In this account we must of course also consider the effect of the child's psychopathology on the mother. To be sure, the way the mother saw the child interfered with her empathic relationship. But the *folie à deux* was not between mother and child—it involved the twins. In his relationship to me Pat tried very hard to make me his twin.[11]

The twins' prolonged inability to talk to their parents increased the disturbance of thought processes, limited their hold on reality, and interfered with binding of anxiety. The early verbalization is important for the contact between mother and infant and facilitates the speech development of the child (Katan, 1961). Pat lacked this stimulus. Instead, for four years he "talked" with his twin. It is intriguing that for a long time he circumvented speech only to become a compulsive talker and a musician. It was as if he sought contact with mother through music, and possibly through his hi-fi.[12] As mentioned above, for Pat, objects remained associated with functions, attributes, or possessions. Before separations from the family

10 I think Nagera's (1963) expression "the chain effect" could be applied here.

11 A. Freud (1965) described how borderline patients use the therapist for a *folie à deux* relationship.

12 Mahler (in a personal communication) suggested that for Pat the hi-fi might literally have been the "mechanized" mother making music for him at his will and with which he could do as he pleased, even ruin it and replace it. In her experience, this is typical for the borderline "psychotic kind of fetish." Compare also Elkisch and Mahler (1959).

and the therapist (in camps and placements), he was afraid that his needs would not be fulfilled, instead of experiencing object loss with an appropriate affect. He went through libidinal stages of development, but there was never a phase specificity. Tied to his twin more than to his mother early in life, he never developed strong friendships. A late adolescent at present, he is as egocentric and eccentric as a child. The absence of the common separation anxiety in his childhood is understandable because until adolescence the twin was always there. People were interchangeable when they satisfied his urgent needs. The tormenting possessiveness which during the anal stage can be observed in every child's relationship to his mother remained in Pat's case affixed to all relationships, men as well as women. It seems that the fusion of libido and aggression was not accomplished: object constancy was not achieved.

In evaluating the case of Pat I found the observations made by Kut Rosenfeld and Sprince (1963, 1965) helpful. The phallic material in their borderline children has an "as if" quality; the "unstable primacy of phallic development . . . gives way to either anal or oral features"; the "oedipal manifestations remain within the realm of fantasy" (1963, p. 616f.). My case does not quite fit these findings. It is, I think, the bisexual conflict in Pat which makes him somewhat different from the borderline children studied at Hampstead, and this difference is probably due to twinning. In Pat, the oedipal involvement was contaminated by the twin, who was the most highly cathected object.

Anna Freud (1963, 1965) showed that the difficulty in maintaining object cathexis interferes with the development of object relationship. The borderline children, she suggests, are on the border between object cathexis and primary identification. When they revert to identification with the object, the merging sets up a panic. I believe that the ego development is even more obstructed in identical twins because of the continued presence of the living mirror image. Pat's case brings together the problem of object cathexis both in borderline cases and in twinning.

When Pat told me that the wires in his brain were crossed, that he could not pick and choose what he thought, he obviously spoke of his difficulty in screening stimuli. It produced confusion which was frightening to him. The confusion between the inside and the outside stimuli was, of course, increased in Pat by his always having the mirror image of himself outside. (I had to learn that what looked like an ordinary and clear projection was complicated, in Pat's case, by the other twin outside.) Here, again, we have to return to the twinning which confuses the distinction between self and object.

During therapy, Pat acquired some degree of self-observation: he learned to distinguish between internal and external reality, between how he felt and what he did, and how he was seen by others. He became aware of his own hostility and more capable in general; and I felt that I became more of a real person to him. (He finished high school and is now in a junior college where he enjoys a course in cooking; he lives in a cooperative boarding house.) But even these modest achievements are not quite on solid ground. We have to consider the biological foundation of the potential for ego development and, more specifically, an additional organic source of the disturbance: anoxia after birth. Although repeated neurological and psychological studies were negative, the last psychological test showed similarities with tests of brain-damaged children; a recent seizure warrants this consideration.

SUMMARY

Analysts have for a long time been interested in identical twins as representing an "experiment in nature." Benjamin (1961), among others, was fascinated by the possibility of studying the interaction between the innate and the experiential. Twins also present material for studying the problems of differentiation, interidentification, and interdependence. But important as twinship is for personality development, we should not be carried away. Hartmann warned against attributing too much to it. Psychological twinning, after all, occurs even outside of twinship, as, for instance, in siblings close in age, or even in some old married couples.

One could, I think, compare the role of twinning in Pat's case with the disturbances shown by the six concentration camp victims described by Anna Freud and S. Dann (1951). These six children grew up in a group (like sextuplets, one could say), were interdependent and interidentified, mothered each other, and related to adults only on the most primitive need-satisfying level. One could even say that they had a "group body ego."

We are usually skeptical when human babies are compared to monkeys. But René Spitz's (1962) use of Harlow's experiment is of special significance. When two rhesus monkeys of the same age were raised by a surrogate mother, they clung to each other, were unable to form any other relationships, and did not engage in play, sexual or other, with monkeys of their own age or older. Spitz asks: "What is missing here? Surely not reciprocity—if anything, there is too much of it" (p. 292). He found that the monkeys were arrested at what in man would be called the primary narcissistic level. Each of these monkeys became an obstacle to the object relation of the other as a result of what Spitz calls "the anaclitic gratification" offered in the together-together relationship. "If object relations proper are to become effective, anaclitic gratifications of a narcissistic nature must be abandoned. . . . There is no frustration [in this relationship] and therefore neither incentive nor push to form different relations" (p. 295). Spitz applies to human babies that the interaction between the Rhesus mother and her baby "opens the road to individuation, to social, and sexual relations."

I think Spitz would agree with my application of his findings to twinship in a specific environment. The mutual overstimulation of the twins did not "open the road to individuation"; it did not produce a social response; rather, it obstructed the process of socialization of the child.

The lack of gratification, the failure to anticipate gratification, and the lack of frustration interfere with the development of object relations and with the evolution of normal personality. The result is archaic anxiety. Furthermore, the first recognition of the mother is more difficult for twins, and so is the "recognition" of the individual child for the mother of twins. Each individual twin has a different environment, of course, even *in utero*. If a twin symbiosis occurs, however, it plays a decisive role in the origin of a defect in object cathexis. The twin symbiosis drains or replaces entirely the mother-child symbiosis.

Our case was aggravated by one more adverse condition. The boys were premature twins. Whatever the constitutional determinants of maturation may be—for instance, for the perceptual apparatus—the need for a more protective environment is greater in premature children. And much more of the exceptional empathic ability is needed to provide two mother-child couples at one time for prematures.

The borderline features in the case presented have psychological as well as organic roots. Twinning played an additional specific and decisive role in the genesis of the disorder: defect in object cathexis.

BIBLIOGRAPHY

Arlow, J. A. (1960), Fantasy Systems in Twins. *Psa. Quart.*, 29:175-199.
Benjamin, J. D. (1961), The Innate and the Experiential in Development. In: *Lectures on Experimental Psychiatry*, ed. H. W. Brosin. Pittsburgh: University of Pittsburgh Press, pp. 19-42.
Bergman, P. & Escalona, S. K. (1949), Unusual Sensitivities in Very Young Children. *This Annual*, 3/4:333-352.
Bonnard, A. (1967), Primary Process Phenomena in the Case of a Borderline Psychotic Child. *Int. J. Psa.*, 48:221-236.
Boyer, L. B. (1956), On Maternal Overstimulation and Ego Defects. *This Annual*, 11:236-256.
—— & Giovacchini, P. L. (1967), *Psychoanalytic Treatment of Schizophrenic and Characterological Disorders*. New York: Science House.
Burlingham, D. (1946), Twins. *This Annual*, 2:61-73.
—— (1949), The Relationship of Twins to Each Other. *This Annual*, 3/4:57-72.
—— (1952), *Twins: A Study of Three Pairs of Identical Twins*. New York: International Universities Press.
—— & Barron, A. T. (1963), A Study of Identical Twins. *This Annual*, 18:367-423.
Ekstein, R. & Wallerstein, J. (1954), Observations on the Psychology of Borderline and Psychotic Children. *This Annual*, 9:344-369.
—— —— (1956), Observations on the Psychotherapy of Borderline and Psychotic Children. *This Annual*, 11:303-311.
Elkisch, P. & Mahler, M. S. (1959), On Infantile Precursors of the "Influencing Machine" (Tausk). *This Annual*, 14:219-235.
Freud, A. (1952), The Mutual Influences in the Development of Ego and Id: Introduction to the Discussion. *This Annual*, 7:42-50.
—— (1963), The Concept of Developmental Lines. *This Annual*, 18:245-265.
—— (1965), *Normality and Pathology in Childhood*. New York: International Universities Press.
—— & Dann, S. (1951), An Experiment in Group Upbringing. *This Annual*, 6:127-169.
Geleerd, E. R. (1946), A Contribution to the Problem of Psychoses in Childhood. *This Annual*, 2:271-291.
—— (1958), Borderline States in Childhood and Adolescence. *This Annual*, 13:279-295.
Gill, M. M. (1967), The Primary Process. In: *Motives and Thought*, ed. R. H. Holt [*Psychological Issues*, Monogr. 18/19]. New York: International Universities Press, pp. 259-298.
Hartmann, H. (1934-1935), Psychiatrische Zwillingsstudien. *Jb. Psychiat. & Neurol.*, Vols. 50 & 51. Translated in part as: Psychiatric Studies of Twins. In: *Essays on Ego Psychology*. New York: International Universities Press, 1964, pp. 419-445.
—— Kris, E., & Loewenstein, R. M. (1946), Comments on the Formation of Psychic Structure. *This Annual*, 2:11-38.

Hoffer, W. (1950), Development of the Body Ego. *This Annual,* 5:18-24.
Jacobson, E. (1954), The Self and the Object World. *This Annual,* 9:75-127.
—— (1964), *The Self and the Object World.* New York: International Universities Press.
Joseph, E. D. & Tabor, J. H. (1961), The Simultaneous Analysis of a Pair of Identical Twins and the Twinning Reaction. *This Annual,* 16:275-299.
Katan, A. (1961), Some Thoughts about the Role of Verbalization in Early Childhood. *This Annual,* 16:184-188.
Kernberg, O. (1967), Borderline Personality Organization. *J. Amer. Psa. Assn.,* 15:641-685.
Kut Rosenfeld, S. & Sprince, M. P. (1963), An Attempt to Formulate the Meaning of the Concept "Borderline." *This Annual,* 18:603-635.
—— —— (1965), Some Thoughts on the Technical Handling of Borderline Children. *This Annual,* 20:495-517.
Leonard, M. R. (1961), Problems in Identification and Ego Development in Twins. *This Annual,* 16:300-320.
Loewenstein, R. M. (1956), Some Remarks on the Rôle of Speech in Psycho-Analytic Technique. *Int. J. Psa.,* 37:462-468.
Mahler, M. S. (1952), On Child Psychosis and Schizophrenia. *This Annual,* 7:286-305.
—— (1961), On Sadness and Grief in Infancy and Childhood. *This Annual,* 16:332-351.
—— (1967), On Human Symbiosis and the Vicissitudes of Individuation. *J. Amer. Psa. Assn.,* 15:740-763.
—— & Elkisch, P. (1953), Some Observations on Disturbances of the Ego in a Case of Infantile Psychosis. *This Annual,* 8:252-261.
—— & Gosliner, B. J. (1955), On Symbiotic Child Psychosis. *This Annual,* 10:195-212.
Nagera, H. (1963), The Developmental Profile: Notes on Some Practical Considerations Regarding Its Use. *This Annual,* 18:511-540.
Sandler, J. & Joffe, W. G. (1965), Notes on Obsessional Manifestations in Children. *This Annual,* 20:425-438.
Searles, H. F. (1963), The Place of Neutral Therapist-Responses in Psychotherapy with a Schizophrenic Patient. *Int. J. Psa.,* 44:42-56.
Singer, M. B. (1960), Fantasies of a Borderline Patient. *This Annual,* 15:310-356.
Spitz, R. A. (1945), Hospitalism. *This Annual,* 1:53-74.
—— (1946), Hospitalism: A Follow-up Report. *This Annual,* 2:113-117.
—— (1962), Autoerotism Re-examined. *This Annual,* 17:283-315.
—— (1965), *The First Year of Life.* New York: International Universities Press.
—— & Wolf, K. M. (1949), Autoerotism. *This Annual,* 3/4:85-120.
Thomas, R. et al. (1966), Comments on Some Aspects of Self and Object Representation in a Group of Psychotic Children. *This Annual,* 21:527-580.
Winnicott, D. W. (1953), Transitional Objects and Transitional Phenomena. *Int. J. Psa.,* 34:89-97.
—— (1965), *Maturational Processes and the Facilitating Environment.* New York: International Universities Press.

V

PSYCHOANALYSIS AND JURISPRUDENCE

PSYCHOANALYSIS AND JURISPRUDENCE
On the Relevance of Psychoanalytic Theory to Law

JOSEPH GOLDSTEIN, Ph.D., LL.B. (New Haven)

Psychoanalysis endeavors to provide a systematic theory of human behavior. Law, both as a body of substantive decisions and as a process for decision making, has been created by man to regulate the behavior of man. Psychoanalysis seeks to understand the workings of the mind. Law is mind-of-man-made. There is in law, as psychoanalysis teaches that there is in individual man, a rich residue which each generation preserves from the past, modifies for the present, and leaves for the future. An initial, though tentative assumption that one discipline is relevant to the other seems therefore warranted. The congruence of their concern for man, his mind, his behavior, and his environment may justify this assertion of mutual relevance. But it does nothing to demarcate the potential limits of psychoanalysis as an aid to understanding the meaning and function of law. This essay explores some of the contributions psychoanalytic theory may make to jurisprudence and, perhaps more significantly, seeks to locate and examine the boundaries which mark the potential area of any such contribution.

Although law is stereotypically perceived as being concerned with an *external* and psychoanalysis with an *internal* image of man, each

Justus S. Hotchkiss Professor of Law, Yale University.

This essay is an elaboration of my paper entitled "Psychoanalysis and Law—A Subject For Study?" read at the Hampstead Child-Therapy Clinic, London, 1965, and of a paper entitled "On the Relevance of Psychoanalytic Theory to Law," presented at the Annual Meeting of the American Psychoanalytic Association in Detroit, May, 1967, and at the joint meeting of the Boston and Western New England Societies of Psychoanalysis in Stockbridge, Mass., October, 1967. It is an outgrowth of my work with Jay Katz and Alan Dershowitz and with my students over the years in a seminar entitled: Psychoanalysis and Law. An essay on the same subject matter but with a substantially different emphasis is simultaneously being published in the *Yale Law Journal*, Vol. 77, 1968, pp. 1053-1077.

discipline is in fact concerned with both faces of man. While law training, practice, and research concentrate primarily on man's external world, the substance and process of law rest heavily on assumptions about man's internal world. While psychoanalytic training, practice, and research focus primarily on an internal view of man, the theory and therapy of psychoanalysis have always had an ear and an eye to outer reality—and increasingly so with the development of genetic and adaptive vantage points in metapsychology. Both disciplines then must cross common intellectual territory. Thus *lawyers* enter the field, for example, when they ask of *law* in terms of its so-social control function what *psychoanalysts* might ask of *man* in terms of his adaptive capacities: "To what extent are internal mechanisms of control reflected in and affected by the development and efficacy of external controls?"

Yet the integration of psychoanalysis and jurisprudence is not close at hand. It has hardly begun and only at a relatively superficial descriptive level. It may be that psychoanalysis as theory is too young and incomplete. It may be that problems in jurisprudence are not sufficiently defined or too bound by linguistic analysis and functionless questions. It may be that psychoanalysis as a data-gathering technique is inadequate to provide a general psychology of man. It may be that psychoanalytic theory of man as an individual is too complex to permit productive explorations of what may be even more complex—groups of human beings interacting in the legal process. Or it may be that well-charted terrain for each discipline becomes no-man's land upon a mere mutual exchange of maps—a no-man's land in both of its usual meanings, an area separating hostile and opposing forces and an area of ambiguous and indefinite character for which frequently no one claims responsibility.[1] Thus, in searching for a common ground between psychoanalysis and jurisprudence the assumption of mutual relevance must be constantly challenged. The no-man's land may be mined with frustration or even raked by cross fire. But hopefully the possible ambit of, as well as the limits to, the contribution psychoanalysis may make to law will begin to emerge.

I turn first to jurisprudence, to the task of defining law, then to

---

[1] The reference to no-man's land was suggested by Hartmann's observation (1939) about psychoanalysis in relation to sociology.

some questions about law in the light of psychoanalytic theory, and finally to the major purpose of this essay, which is to locate and to draw the boundaries marking the potential area of the psychoanalytic contribution to jurisprudence.

I

Before exploring the ways psychoanalysis may enrich the law, the variegated nature of each must be heeded. Neither the concept of psychoanalysis nor the concept of law is unitary. In theory, in practice, and in research, psychoanalysis, like law, is both a set of concepts and a process of interaction. Psychoanalysis is a theory of man as an individual, how he may have become what he is, and how he may change or be changed. Psychoanalysis is also a mode of therapy, a means pre-eminently of helping an individual understand what he is and why, and thereby liberating him to accept the strengths and limits of his potential and perhaps to change himself. Finally, psychoanalysis is a method of investigation, a research tool to further theory and to improve therapy (see Freud, 1923).

Law too appears in many garbs. It is part of man's reality, a mechanism for molding and reinforcing controls over himself in relation to others, a process of assigning to man-made authority, the state, the power to decide why, under what circumstances, to what extent, and by what means man, as a private person, is to be restrained or encouraged in the making and implementing of his decisions as an individual. Law is, in turn, a device for controlling the state, or, strictly speaking, the individuals who act as decision makers for the state, in the exercise of its power over man. The underlying question always confronting these decision makers and those concerned with the study of law is whether, how, and to what extent the state should not or should be authorized to intervene in what would otherwise be the private ordering of a man's life—i.e., to regulate the relations of man.

The study of law focuses on these decision makers, the problems they seek to resolve, their guides for decision, and their decisions. These law subjects are not as traditionally perceived only the work of judges, primarily the appellate judge and his opinions. Rather they are in criminal law, for example, (1) the work and procedures of the *legislators* who decide what conduct under what circumstances is to constitute an offence, what official conduct may be authorized to determine whether such an offence has occurred, and what official responses by way of sanctions, i.e., deprivations of liberty of varying degrees and purposes may be imposed and by whom; they are (2) the work and procedures of the *police and the prosecutor* who, with varying degrees of discretion, may invoke the process and in effect seek review by *court, judge,* and a *jury* of their decisions both substantive and procedural; they are (3) the work and procedures of the *appellate courts* who review the decisions of all those who have participated in the process to this point, including the legislature; they are (4) the work and procedures of the *administrators,* e.g., the warden, probation officer, prison official, executioner, parole or pardoning agencies who, following an affirmance of conviction, have to decide how to implement it in accord with its purposes. Finally, these decisions—and there are analogous points and agents of decision in all fields of law—are subject to review by students of law and ultimately by the legislature which ought to be continually appraising the consequences of its decisions (Goldstein, 1960). Thus the process of decision in law moves along a human continuum which schematically is circular and thus has no beginning or end. Law then is an official process for determining to what persons or agencies should be assigned the role of promulgating, invoking, implementing, and appraising decisions to grant or restrict the power of man over man (Lasswell, 1956). "Indeed," as Katz and I (1965), have noted, "law may be perceived as a response to 'the family's' success or failure in providing each *child* with internal mechanisms of control sufficient for each *adult* to be a law unto himself" (p. 1).

Law is at the same time the guardian of a powerful substantive heritage as well as a generator and regenerator of fundamental societal values. It is a continuous and continuing process both for meeting man's need for stability in the external world through the creation and application of *rule* and *precedent* and, at the same time, for meeting man's need for flexibility, growth, and development by creating for each *precedent* a *counterprecedent,* for each *rule* a *counterrule* (Kessler, 1944), and for each *agency of decision* an *agency of review.* Of course, the degree of flexibility and continuity in law varies over time as to the subject matter and as to the points in the process of decision. Thus, from the community's point of vantage, the decision maker at every level from the most general to the most specific has and is compelled to a greater or lesser extent to make a choice between available alternatives and often among conflicting goals—a discretion which hopefully he can exercise with some awareness of the values in issue and of the external and internal pressures at work. For to the extent that law provides a proper mix of continuity and flexibility, it provides a process for a stable, vital, and viable society capable of keeping its revolutions peaceful. The study of law focuses, or should focus, upon the ways in which the process meets or fails to meet these needs.

In 1881, when a young medical student, Sigmund Freud, was conducting research on the nerve cells of crayfish, Oliver Wendell Holmes, Jr., who was later to become a Justice of the United States Supreme Court, spoke of the law as psychoanalysis has come to speak of man. He observed:

> The life of the law has not been logic: it has been experience. The felt necessities of the time, the prevalent moral and political theories, intuitions of public policy, avowed or unconscious, even the prejudices which judges share with their fellow-men, have had a good deal more to do than the syllogism in determining the rules by which men should be governed. The law embodies the story of a nation's development through many centuries, and it cannot be dealt with as if it contained only the axioms and corollaries of a book of mathematics. In order to know what it is, we must know what it has been, and what it tends to become. [T]he most difficult labor will be to understand the combination of the two into new products at every stage. [T]he degree to which it is able to work out desired results depend[s] very much upon its past.
>
> The rational study of law is still to a large extent the study of history. [I]t is a part of the rational study, because it is the first step toward an enlightened skepticism. [W]hen you get the dragon out of his cave on to the plain and in the daylight, you can count his teeth and claws, and see just what is his strength.[2]

[2] Interestingly, in "Analysis Terminable and Interminable" (1937a), Freud writes: "What has once come to life clings tenaciously to its existence. One feels inclined to doubt sometimes whether the dragons of primeval days are really extinct" (p. 229).

Since the law, including decisions that the state has no role to play, is concerned with *every* aspect of human activity,[3] since its decisions are not rigidly bound by sterile logic, and since the decision maker, or, in any event, the student of law, must always ask: "What is the purpose of the decision?" and "What must I learn to make a decision compatible with that purpose?" the work and the findings of many disciplines are not only appropriate but essential sources of data. This is meant to imply not that a lawyer ought indiscriminately to collect data, but rather that he first determine what he seeks to do and then pose for himself a series of questions which should be tested by the underlying question: "In what way would any answer to the question posed be relevant to that which the lawyer (on behalf of society, the state, an individual client, himself or any combination of these) seeks to accomplish?"

Law, in the idiom of psychoanalysis, might be discussed as a secondary process phenomenon, as a function and product of the *ego* enhancing its control over *id* impulses. It could be perceived as a generally nonviolent external means for regulating the discharge of aggression by mouth as well as by hand and arm. These organs, as Hartmann, Kris, and Loewenstein (1949) have noted, may function as instruments for the discharge of aggressive energy. But while psychoanalysis supplies in this fashion new words to describe the loud voice, the heavy hand, and the long arm of the law, it does not necessarily furnish new insights about law. Long before the law had a psychoanalytic window, it was viewed as an adversary process, as a substitute of trial by words for trial by combat. Indeed, Freud (1893), in an early writing attributes to an unnamed Englishman the observation that "the man who first flung a word of abuse at his enemy instead of a spear was the founder of civilization" (p. 36). The vividness and the richness of this prepsychoanalytic remark should, however, not obscure the need for a systematic theory which provides an opportunity for gaining a greater and detailed understanding of what is thus implied about the dynamics of law as a human product, and about the meaning of justice for man who is, at one and the same

[3] The law, as a subject for study, includes any problem for decision which may confront any agency of the state, as well as any decision which explicitly, implicitly or by default places certain areas of human activity outside the ambit of official concern or regulation.

time "law making," "law abiding," and "law breaking." For this purpose and with cautious expectations I have, with my colleagues Katz and Dershowitz (1967), framed the following questions about law in the light of psychoanalytic theory:

Are there forces in man interacting within him and among men which require the creation of some external authority to administer man in his day-to-day relations with himself and others? [p. 5].

To what extent does, can, or should the State take into account the unconscious in the promulgation, invocation and administration of its law?

Should the unconscious be taken as a characteristic common to all human activity, and thus deemed of no special significance to decisions in law?

Should the law seek to authorize different responses for the variety of unconscious manifestations in individual human behavior?

Under what, if any, circumstances, should the legal process seek to probe the unconscious of any of its participants? [p. 51].

Does law develop out of a recognition, express or implied, that id out of control would destroy us as individuals and as a society?

Does law rest on the assumption that man has both an ego and a superego which require nutriment for the control of id?

Does law, though a part of reality, develop as do ego and superego, out of a continuous interaction with id and reality? [p. 87].

And I would add: "Do exceptions to legal proscriptions in such forms as defenses, excuses, and justifications serve to preserve the autonomy of the ego from environmental pressures which ultimately might reduce the autonomy of the ego from the id?"

In pursuing the answers to these and many subquestions, it is important to locate the limits of psychoanalytic theory in understanding the dynamics of law as a product of, stimulator of, and regulator for human behavior. Marking the limits will at the same time delineate the area of potential contribution.

II

Law cannot find in psychoanalysis, or for that matter in any science, the moral, political or social values upon which to base or evaluate its decisions. Psychoanalytic theory cannot provide guides to "good" or "bad." Yet in appraising decisions designed to serve the "good" and undermine the "bad," psychoanalysis may provide insights to prompt a modification of the ways and means by which society, through law, seeks to fulfill its goals.

Nothing in psychoanalytic theory, for example, can provide the law with underlying moral values for guiding its decision in the debate about whether and why abortion should or should not be singled out, from among other surgical procedures, for special social controls. Nor can it provide the ethical or moral standards for conducting experiments on human beings or animals.

And the psychoanalyst, as scientist, cannot say what conduct, if any, should be considered a ground for divorce, a crime, an excuse for a crime, or who should be held or relieved of responsibility, or what consequences for what purposes should attend a finding of responsibility. He cannot, to take a specific example, provide the law with guides for deciding whether homosexual acts between consenting adults should be subject to criminal sanction. Yet some might erroneously declare Freud's *Three Essays on Sexuality* (1905) as an affirmative vote for genitality and thus as a justification for official social condemnation of what he neutrally labels "a perversion—a pathological disorder." As Szasz (1961) so dramatically argues,[4] the failure of the decision maker in the legal process to recognize that psychoanalysis is not a source of moral values and of the psychoanalyst to make clear to himself and others when he speaks as scientist and when he speaks as citizen, who happens to be a psychoanalyst or a psychiatrist, has contributed to much of the confusion, chaos, and injustice which surrounds the administration of our mental health laws. Less prominently, though not necessarily less significantly, these blurred identities have cast doubt on the work of some psychoanalysts and psychiatrists writing about problems in law. They abandon their scientific point of vantage and, without so advising their readers and possibly themselves, they present their personal value preferences camouflaged in the language of psychoanalysis. Freud, the scientist, makes this point and thus marks one of the important though oft-forgotten limits to the use of psychoanalysis in

4 See also Waelder (1952).

law in his essay on "Moral Responsibility for the Content of Dreams" (1925). He writes, albeit somewhat sarcastically, "The physician will leave it to the jurist to construct for social purposes a responsibility that is artificially limited to the metapsychological ego" (p. 134).

Psychoanalysis, however, may help the decision maker in law by forcing into view conflicts between existing rules and preferred values which he may not see or may not wish to acknowledge. Thus while a judge will not turn to psychoanalysis to determine whether it is desirable to design a trial process which makes "belief beyond a reasonable doubt" a requisite of finding a person guilty of a criminal offense, he may, given this value preference for minimizing the chance of error in ascertaining guilt, draw on insights from psychoanalysis. A judge has, for example, refused to convict a father for sexual violation of his daughter solely on her uncorroborated accusation. He relied primarily on clinical findings, without requiring a theoretical explanation for the gap between an individual's psychic and external reality, that some women tend to translate fantasy of sexual assault or seduction into belief and report it as a reality.[5]

Similarly, a judge has re-examined the evidentiary rule which imputes guilt to flight. Judges and legal commentators have assumed, on the basis of what they call "common" experience: (1) that a person who flees shortly after a criminal act is committed or after being accused of a crime does so because he feels some guilt about that act and (2) that one who feels some guilt concerning an act is guilty of committing that act.[6] In 1963 the Court of Appeals for the District of Columbia re-examined this doctrine and decided to modify the rule in accord with its underlying purpose. The Court recited and responded to Freud's warning to lawyers in 1906 that:

> You may be led astray by a neurotic who, although he is innocent, reacts as if he were guilty, because a lurking sense of

[5] State v. Anderson 137 N.W. 2d 781 (Minn. 1965).

[6] Wigmore, a leading authority on evidence in law, summarized the traditional judicial view thus: "The commission of a crime leaves usually upon the consciousness a moral impression which is characteristic. The innocent man is without it; the guilty man usually has it. Its evidential value has never been doubted. The inference from consciousness of guilt to 'guilty' is always available in evidence. It is a most powerful one, because the only other hypothesis conceivable is the rare one that the person's consciousness is caused by a delusion, and not by the actual doing of the act" (see Wigmore, *On Evidence*, § 173 [1940]).

guilt that already exists in him seizes upon the accusation made
in the particular instance. . . . It can be that he has in fact not
committed the particular crime with which you have charged him
but that he has committed one of which you know nothing and
of which you are not accusing him. He therefore quite truthfully
denies being guilty of the one misdeed, while at the same time
betraying his sense of guilt on account of the other [p. 113].

Accordingly, without altering the function or purpose of the
rule, the appellate court changed its content to recognize a more
complex image of man as a guilt-feeling animal:

> When evidence of flight has been introduced into a case, . . .
> the trial court should . . . explain to the jury . . . that flight does
> not necessarily reflect feelings of guilt, and that feelings of guilt,
> which are present in many innocent people, do not necessarily
> reflect actual guilt.[7]

The implications of psychoanalytic insights about the relationship between feeling guilty (or, for that matter, not feeling guilty)
and actually in a legal sense being guilty are still to be explored in
important areas of the law—confessions, pleas of guilty, and particularly admissions of guilt by juveniles in delinquency proceedings.

What Hartmann (1960) said of psychoanalysis as therapy in relation to an individual patient's moral code may be said of the relationship of psychoanalysis, as theory, to the state's legal process. Psychoanalysis cannot provide "the ultimate ends for the moral aspects
of personal, social, or political behavior. But . . . contributions toward clarification and organization, in the framework of a given
system of valuations, or, more specifically in the framework of given
moral codes, . . . can be gained simply and directly from psychoanalytic knowledge" (p. 100 f.). Thus despite the limitation which psychoanalysis shares with all science, a very significant sector of potential
and actual application to law emerges.

Quite another but related limitation which also defines a potentially significant contribution can be discerned in the manner in
which the court applied psychoanalytic knowledge about feelings of
guilt to the evidentiary rule on flight. The appellate court limited its

---

7 Miller v. United States, 320 F. 2d 767, 773 (D.C. Cir. 1963).

use of such knowledge to revise a generally held legal assumption about the nature of man. It did not concern itself with the meaning of flight as a psychic act for the particular defendant in the particular case. Nor did it advise the trial judge or jury to engage or invite experts to engage in such curbstone psychoanalysis—i.e., the interpretation of an individual's conduct or feelings without access to the one source of evidence which distinguishes psychoanalysis from all other disciplines: the individual's associations obtained and observed over a very substantial period of time in a very special setting.[8]

It is, for example, a tempting and potentially destructive abuse of psychoanalysis, for a teacher examining the decision in a famous attempted murder case to suggest that when the defendant, the estranged husband of the victim, shouted, "It won't fire. It won't fire," as he held an *unloaded* pistol at his wife's head and pulled the trigger, he was revealing his sexual impotence.[9] Such remarks are of no potential value in examining the function and purpose of the criminal law of attempts, and are of no relevance or reliability so far as the criminal responsibility of the particular defendant is concerned. The pseudo interpretation may be salvaged by using it to illustrate a major contribution of psychoanalysis, which is that man is complex and that the conduct of an individual person is multifunctioned and cannot be understood at least in terms of the dynamic play of intrapsychic forces on the basis of a chance remark or of superficially gathered data.

That Freud was aware of the danger of such misuse of psychoanalytic insights is made explicit in his observations concerning a homicide case in which expert testimony on the universality of the oedipus complex and of death wishes of sons toward fathers was used to indict and convict Philip Halsmann of murdering his father despite the absence of objective proof that he had in fact killed his father. Freud (1931) warned:

> Precisely because it is always present, the Oedipus complex is not suited to provide a decision on the question of guilt. The situation envisaged in a well-known anecdote might easily be

[8] Cf. Anna Freud (1965a): "The analyst is tied to his own laborious and slow method of observation and sees no more without it than the bacteriologist, deprived of his microscope, sees of bacilli with his naked eye" (p. 12).

[9] See State v. Damms 100 N.W. 2d 592 (Wisc. 1960).

brought about. There was a burglary. A man who had a jemmy
in his possession was found guilty of the crime. After the verdict
had been given and he had been asked if he had anything to say,
he begged to be sentenced for adultery at the same time—since he
was carrying the tool for that on him as well [p. 252].

It may seem paradoxical that, while psychoanalysis is a theory
based on individual personal introspective data, an important limit
on the contribution of psychoanalysis to law is the general inapplica-
bility of its concepts to specific participants without infinitely more
information (internal data) about them than is generally available.
Yet, since law is primarily concerned with men in groups and the
resolution of group problems or the group resolution of external
conflicts, the contribution of psychoanalysis as a general theory of
human behavior can be assured only if this very significant limitation
is acknowledged. This position implicitly includes and is reinforced
by two important general findings of psychoanalysis which must be
made explicit.

1. The first is that similarly described behavior (whether perceived as a symptom or a sign of health) may for different people be
a reflection of and response to a wide range of different, even opposite unconscious forces. Likewise, different conduct on the part of
different individuals may be a consequence of similar underlying
psychic factors (Hartmann and Kris, 1945). The law, depending on
its purposes, may appropriately take this into account.

For example, the Supreme Court of the United States,[10] in con-
struing the Congressional exemption for conscientious objectors
from combatant service, does not try to distinguish or require draft
boards to distinguish between those whose pacifism, for example,
might be a "reaction formation against impulses of the anal-sadistic
phase," or "to the wish to attack or to the fear of being attacked," or
those for whom pacifism might have become a relatively independent
structure through what Hartmann (1939) calls "the phenomenon of
change of function." Although such information may be of use for
diagnostic and therapeutic purposes, it cannot assist Congress, the
courts, or draft boards in finding a meaningful compromise between

10 United States v. Seeger, 380 U.S. 163 (1965).

two basic values they seek to safeguard: the conscience of the individual and the security of the state. By failing to consider the unconscious origins of each individual applicant's pacifism, the law does not deny the existence of unconscious forces; rather, it recognizes that the universality of such internal forces makes them (not unlike the adulterer's tool) irrelevant to the problem for decision, which is a claim, not to therapy, but for exemption. Unconscious forces are taken as a given, a common denominator of all human conduct, and prime focus is placed, without greater specificity, for purposes of the legislative and judicial design, on conscious reflections of the conscience. Thus Hartmann (1939), in observing that defenses may be converted from means to goals, re-emphasizes the insight from psychoanalysis for law that similar conduct not only may have multiple functions but also that conduct cannot be relied on as the basis for making generalizations about the unconscious motivations of any specific individual.

Further, in accord with the general finding that like manifest conduct does not necessarily reveal a like interplay of psychic forces in different individuals, Anna Freud, in warning psychoanalysts, alerts students of law, particularly those concerned with statutory design and research in criminal law, the law of juvenile delinquency and the administration of mental health laws, to the limitations of categorizing individuals in terms of overt behavior. She writes (1965a):

> . . . the descriptive nature of many current diagnostic categories runs counter to the essence of psychoanalytic thinking, since it emphasizes the identity of or difference between manifest symptomatology while neglecting those of the underlying . . . factors. It is true that in this manner a classification . . . seems orderly and comprehensive to the superficial glance . . . . whenever the analyst accepts diagnostic thinking at this level, he is inevitably led into confusion in assessment and subsequently to erroneous therapeutic inferences [p. 110 f].[11]

11 However, see W. L. Pious, M.D., who states in a letter (dated March 13, 1968) to the author: "While I generally agree with your and Anna Freud's position with regard to the problems inherent in diagnostic classifications and other attempts at descriptive categorization, I would also suggest that these categorizations have value which should not be ignored. It is a fact that human behavior does lend itself to classification and that the basis for this relative uniformity of behavior patterns, arising from multiple and often unrelated motivations, remains a riddle."

Of course, this warning does not lead to the conclusion that all legislatively defined categories—such as thief, murderer, rapist, conspirator, juvenile delinquent, or committable mentally ill person—are inappropriate for all purposes. But it does highlight an often overlooked limitation of such legal classification. It may be a useful and workable legislative strategy to create such categories as a basis for sorting out those who are entitled to one legal process or another; or who may or may not be considered appropriate objects of community anger for differing lengths of time (as in let the punishment fit the crime, not necessarily the specific individual criminal). Yet it is a limitation of the strategy that such categories cannot (as they often seem to do) serve as a basis for determining, for example, who should be provided with what therapeutic regime or assigned what institutional setting for rehabilitative purposes.

The laws governing sex offenders and juvenile delinquents illustrate well the frequent failure to recognize this limitation. It is confusing then to turn to psychoanalysis and to find studies and research programs which rest on the assumption that "juvenile delinquent" is a viable diagnostic category. On the other hand, it is encouraging, for example, to find emphasized in the "Report on the President's Commission on Law Enforcement" (1967) a position consistent with the essence of psychoanalytic thinking, which is: "No single formula, no single theory, no single generalization can explain the vast range of behavior called crime." To the extent that the law is concerned with therapeutic goals as a function of its response to the "criminal" or the "juvenile delinquent" or to the "mentally ill" it becomes of enormous value to heed Anna Freud's warning not only in directing research but in framing procedures and institutional responses. Thus the psychoanalytic generalization that one cannot generalize about the nature of an individual or the causes of his conduct on the basis of his overt conduct makes a significant contribution to law by forcing into view the limitations of conduct-based categories. Here the psychoanalytic contribution can press the law in theory and in practice to focus more sharply on those decisions and points of decision in which the individual must be decategorized and perceived as the highly complex human being that he is if the function and purpose of the law is to be fulfilled.

2. The second general finding is but another face of the first. It is that the meaning of an actual experience in giving direction to a person's life rests, as seems obvious once said, on countless internal and external variables. Not only may what appears to be a similar event have different significance for the same person depending upon his stage of development at the time of its occurrence, but it may also have different implications for different people at similar stages of development.[12] Implicit in this observation is an insight of substantial significance to anyone seeking to evaluate the consequences of decisions in law. It points to a limitation frequently obscured in assumptions in empirical studies about the impact or likely impact of a statute, judgment, or administrative ruling. Unless such decisions are perceived as external events in the lives of many people—events which have different meanings for different people—statistical evidence of success may include, without recognizing a distinction, a number of people upon whom the decision had no impact; and, even more significant, it may include in the failure column a number upon whom the decision had a direct impact contrary to that sought —not just no impact.

For example, in evaluating a decision to impose a criminal sanction against a specific offender for purposes both of satisfying the punitive demands of the community and of deterring others from engaging in the offensive conduct, the student of law can or ought to assume that the decision may for some satisfy, for some exacerbate, and for some have nothing to do with punitive wishes, and may for some restrain, for some provoke, and for some have no impact on the urge to engage in the prohibited conduct. Recognition of the multiple consequences of every law-created event makes comprehensible both the never-ending search for multiple resolutions of what is perceived to be a single problem in law and the resultant need to

12 Cf. Freud (1920): "So long as we trace the development from its final outcome backwards, the chain of events appears continuous, and we feel we have gained an insight which is completely satisfactory or even exhaustive. But if we proceed the reverse way, if we start from the premises inferred from the analysis and try to follow these up to the final result, then we no longer get the impression of an inevitable sequence of events which could not have been otherwise determined. We notice at once that there might have been another result, and that we might have been just as well able to understand and explain the latter. The synthesis is thus not so satisfactory as the analysis; in other words, from a knowledge of the premises we could not have foretold the nature of the result" (p. 167). See also Hartmann and Kris (1945) and Anna Freud (1958, 1965a).

find an ensemble of official and unofficial responses which on balance come closest to achieving the social control sought.

It would seem that the value of the psychoanalytic insight has often been lost in the stock criticism of psychoanalysis that psychoanalysts whatever the facts can always use or fashion them to fit the theory (see Freud, 1937b; Waelder, 1962). What is lost to the critic engaged in the fruitless exercise of establishing that psychoanalysis is not a science and what is ofttimes lost to the unwary psychoanalyst is the finding that a symptom common to different people may reflect a variety of different dynamic explanations or causes and that a single "traumatic" event may reverberate in different ways in different people. The need for re-emphasizing this finding is pointedly illustrated by the Bullit-Freud book on Wilson (1967)[13] and the Zeligs volume misleadingly entitled *An Analysis of Whittaker Chambers and Alger Hiss* (1967). This is not to say that a highly skilled and artistic psychoanalytic observer with access to reliable manifest and secondary data about a particular individual cannot make perceptive and probably valid guesses about unconscious content (see Anna Freud, 1965a). But it seems clear that in both of these books, one of which is based on a major legal confrontation, the data were neither sufficient nor of sufficient reliability to justify the specific assertions made about specific individuals concerning specific events. As Hartmann and Kris (1945) have warned: "This is the reason why a superficial collection of anamnestic data concerning an individual's childhood is frequently misleading" (p. 25).

Psychoanalytic theory makes manifest the complexity of man and the unreliability of conduct-based or event-based categorizations as sources for predicting conduct and for understanding the intrapsychic meaning of the conduct or event for any specific individual. That generalization rests upon generalizations about the intrapsychic processes at work in all individuals—about the dynamic interaction of id, ego, and superego, about the functions of the ego and mechanisms of defense, about the pleasure principle and the reality principle, etc. These generalizations, particularly those drawn from the genetic points of vantage in metapsychology concerning the process of growth and development from birthhood to adulthood, hold the

13 For fascinating and conflicting views of Freud's contribution to this book see Erikson (1967) and Roazen (1968).

most immediate promise of applicability to problems for decision in law. Those problems are concerned with the process and substance of the disposition of children in a variety of legal settings, from the initial legal assignment of each child to his natural parents to child custody decisions ordered or acquiesced in by the state in proceedings labeled, for example, neglecting parent, juvenile delinquency, adoption, foster care, separation, and divorce.

To the extent that legal decisions regarding child custody are to comply with an official policy preference for the *child's best interest*, psychoanalytic theory and research findings have a contribution to make to both substantive guides and procedures for decision. Anna Freud's work (1965b) on growth and development, for example, demonstrates the need of every child for unbroken continuity of affectionate and stimulating relationships. Her formulation pours content into that aspect of the law's standard which is concerned with psychological well-being. It calls into question decisions which split the custody of a child between two parents or which provide a noncustodial parent with the right to visit or to force the child to visit. It casts doubt upon traditional procedures which never finalize a custody decision in divorce but instead allow the court to retain jurisdiction to modify and remodify custody. Such official invitations to discontinuity in the life of a child are but illustrative of many decisions in law which persistently run contrary to the professed purpose of these decisions, to serve the child's best interest (see Goldstein and Katz, 1965).

Since dispositions are frequently rendered in divorce proceedings without presenting the decision makers with adequate data about both the child and the available alternative custodians, a presumption should be established to favor relatively long-standing and continuing ongoing relationships. *Painter v. Bannister* is an interesting and celebrated case in point.[14] There a father sought to regain the custody of his seven-year-old son who, at the time of court decision, had been living with his grandparents for two and one half years following the death of his mother. The court was confronted with a request to interrupt a satisfactory ongoing "parent-figure"-child relationship and to make an abrupt change without any plan for transi-

[14] 140 N.W. 2d (Iowa 1966).

tion to allow for the gradual re-establishment of a relationship between natural father and son. At the outset the appellate court made clear that its guiding principle would be the child's best interest. The household of the grandparents was described as "stable, dependable, conventional, middle-class, midwest" and that of the father as "unstable, unconventional, arty Bohemian, and probably intellectually stimulating." The court correctly asserted: "It is not our prerogative to determine custody upon our choice of one of two ways of life within normal and proper limits and we will not do so." It concurred with the trial judges finding that both parties were proper and fit. While acknowledging a preference in law for the natural parent, the court weighed more heavily the child's best interest and concluded that the existing relationship should not be disturbed. The court declared:

> Mark has established a father-son relationship with [the grandfather] which he apparently had never had with his natural father. He is happy, well-adjusted and progressing nicely in his development. We do not believe it is for Mark's best interest to take him out of this stable atmosphere in the face of warnings of dire consequences from an eminent child psychologist and send him to an uncertain future in his father's home. Regardless of our appreciation of the father's love for his child and his desire to have him with him, we do not believe we have the moral right to gamble with this child's future . . . [at 158].

Despite provocative newspaper headlines charging the court with depriving a Bohemian parent and member of the American Civil Liberties Union of his child because of his style of life, it follows from the opinion that the court's decision would have been the same even if the characterization of the competing parties had been reversed. Evaluated in the light of Anna Freud's need-for-continuity formulation, the decision can be understood as a determination made in accord with the overall mandate of the state—the child's best interests.

In noting that the problems concerned with the legal disposition of children offer a major opportunity for the application of psychoanalytic knowledge to law, the word "opportunity" is used advisedly, for there is in this area a great amount of judicial and student resistance. Judicial decisions abound in which the judge, unhampered by any procedural barriers to the introduction of psychoanalytic evidence of a general or specific character, will patiently hear all the evidence and then render a decision as if the record were free of such guides as those provided by Anna Freud. There intrudes, and perhaps correctly so in areas of compulsory state action, the judge's express concern for parental rights or for the policy of a foster care agency seeking to preserve the natural parent's right to the ultimate return of her child, however remote the possibility.[15] Such disregard of the evidence may, in some instances, reflect a fear that approving the widespread use of psychoanalytic guides will somehow in other contexts empower the state to mold whatever kind of adult the state may want at any given time.

Yet it is precisely in this area that effective communication between law and psychoanalysis can begin to remove such misunderstandings, to the extent that they are real. If the law student (who is also hopefully the future judge) were to study the primary sources of psychoanalysis, he would see that at most and at best a psychoanalytically informed definition of the child's best interest would assist a court or adoption agency in deciding which disposition among available alternatives is likely to provide the child, whatever his endowments, with the best available opportunity to fulfill his potential in society as a civilized human being.[16] The diverse conglomeration of procedures for handling children which have haphazardly entered the statute books require examination in the light of this knowledge.

III

Briefly then, I have tried to define law, to pose some questions about law in the light of psychoanalytic theory, and to identify the area of—as well as to locate some limits to—the potential contribution of psychoanalysis to jurisprudence. While the boundaries and the size of the area remain unclear, it becomes clear that he, in law, who turns to psychoanalysis for a completed theory offering a com-

[15] See, e.g., In re Jewish Child Care Association, 5 N.Y. 2d 222, 156 N.E. 2d 700 (1959) and the discussion by Ritvo (1965).

[16] See Goldstein and Katz (1965): It may prove less awesome, more realistic and thus more amenable to relevant data gathering were the guide to decision in the child's best interest cast in terms of "that which is the least detrimental alternative for the child" (p. 4). See also Erikson (1950).

478 JOSEPH GOLDSTEIN

plete explanation of any and all human activity will either be duped or disappointed. But the legal scholar and practitioner who, with his traditionally critical but open eye, sees psychoanalysis as a rich body of knowledge and hypotheses about man will have found another analytic tool to enrich his never-ending work to better understand and to better the law.

BIBLIOGRAPHY

Erikson, E. H. (1950), Growth and Crises of the Healthy Personality. In: *Identity and the Life Cycle* [*Psychological Issues*, Monogr. 1]. New York: International Universities Press, 1959, pp. 50-100.
—— (1967), The Strange Case of Freud, Bullitt, and Woodrow Wilson. *N.Y. Rev. Books*, 8:3-5.
Freud, A. (1958), Child Observation and Prediction of Development. *This Annual*, 13:92-124.
—— (1965a), *Normality and Pathology in Childhood: Assessments of Development*. New York: International Universities Press.
—— (1965b), Cindy. In: *The Family and the Law*, by J. Goldstein & J. Katz. New York: Free Press, pp. 1051-1053.
Freud, S. (1893), On the Psychical Mechanism of Hysterical Phenomena. *Standard Edition*, 3:25-39. London: Hogarth Press, 1962.
—— (1905), Three Essays on the Theory of Sexuality. *Standard Edition*, 7:125-243. London: Hogarth Press, 1953.
—— (1906), Psycho-Analysis and the Establishment of the Facts in Legal Proceedings. *Standard Edition*, 9:97-114. London: Hogarth Press, 1959.
—— (1920), The Psychogenesis of a Case of Homosexuality in a Woman. *Standard Edition*, 18:145-172. London: Hogarth Press, 1955.
—— (1923), Two Encyclopaedia Articles. *Standard Edition*, 18:235-259. London: Hogarth Press, 1955.
—— (1925), Some Additional Notes on Dream-Interpretation as a Whole. *Standard Edition*, 19:125-138. London: Hogarth Press, 1961.
—— (1931), The Expert Opinion in the Halsmann Case. *Standard Edition*, 21:251-253. London: Hogarth Press, 1961.
—— (1937a), Analysis Terminable and Interminable. *Standard Edition*, 23:211-253. London: Hogarth Press, 1964.
—— (1937b), Constructions in Analysis. *Standard Edition*, 23:255-269. London: Hogarth Press, 1964.
—— & Bullitt, W. C. (1967), *Thomas Woodrow Wilson, Twenty-eighth President of the United States: A Psychological Study*. Boston: Houghton Mifflin.
Goldstein, J. (1960), Police Discretion Not to Invoke the Criminal Process: Low Visibility Decisions in the Administration of Justice. *Yale Law J.*, 69:543-594.
—— & Katz, J. (1965), *The Family and the Law*. New York: Free Press.
Hartmann, H. (1939), *Ego Psychology and the Problem of Adaptation*. New York: International Universities Press, 1958.
—— (1960), *Psychoanalysis and Moral Values*. New York: International Universities Press.
—— & Kris, E. (1945), The Genetic Approach in Psychoanalysis. *This Annual*, 1:11-30.
—— —— & Loewenstein, R. M. (1949), Notes on the Theory of Aggression. *This Annual*, 3/4:9-36.

Holmes, O. W. (1881), The Common Law and Collected Speeches. In: *The Life of the Law*, ed. J. Honnold. New York: Free Press, 1963, p. 3.

Katz, J., Goldstein, J., & Dershowitz, A. M. (1967), *Psychoanalysis, Psychiatry, and Law*. New York: Free Press.

Kessler, F. (1944), Natural Law, Justice and Democracy—Some Reflections on Three Types of Thinking about Law and Justice. *Tulane Law Rev.*, 19:32-61.

Lasswell, H. (1956), *The Decision Process: Seven Categories of Functional Analysis*. College Park, Maryland: Bureau of Government Research, University of Maryland.

Ritvo, S. (1965), Discussion. In: *The Family and the Law*, by J. Goldstein & J. Katz. New York: Free Press, p. 1032.

Roazen, P. (1968), *Freud: Political and Social Thought*. New York: Knopf.

Szasz, T. S. (1961), Statement at Hearings before the Subcommittee on Constitutional Rights of the Mentally Ill of the Senate Committee on the Judiciary, 87th Cong., 1st Sess., pt. 1, pp. 251-272.

Waelder, R. (1952), Psychiatry and the Problem of Criminal Responsibility. *Univ. Pa. Law Rev.*, 101:378-390.

—— (1962), Psychoanalysis, Scientific Method, and Philosophy. *J. Amer. Psa. Assn.*, 10:617-637.

Zeligs, M. A. (1967), *Friendship and Fratricide: An Analysis of Whittaker Chambers and Alger Hiss*. New York: Viking Press.

CONTENTS OF VOLUMES I–XXII

PINE, F. & FURER, M.
 Studies of the Separation–Individuation Phase: A Method-
 ological Overview (1963)   18:325–342
PLANK, E. N.
 Memories of Early Childhood in Autobiographies (1953)   8:381–393
—— & HORWOOD, C.
 Leg Amputation in a Four-year-old: Reactions of the Child,
 Her Family, and the Staff (1961)   16:405–422
—— & PLANK, R.
 Emotional Components in Arithmetical Learning as Seen
 Through Autobiographies (1954)   9:274–293
PLANK, R.
 On "Seeing the Salamander" (1957)   12:379–398
 See also PLANK & PLANK (1954)
PRENTICE, N., see JESSNER, LAMONT, LONG, ROLLINS,
 WHIPPLE, & PRENTICE (1955)
PROVENCE, S. & RITVO, S.
 Effects of Deprivation on Institutionalized Infants: Disturb-
 ances in Development of Relationship to Inanimate Objects
 (1961)   16:189–205
 See also COLEMAN, KRIS, & PROVENCE (1953), RITVO &
 PROVENCE (1953)
PUTNAM, M. C., RANK, B., & KAPLAN, S.
 Notes on John I.: A Case of Primal Depression in an Infant
 (1951)   6:38–58

RAMZY, I. & WALLERSTEIN, R. S.
 Pain, Fear, and Anxiety: A Study in Their Interrelationships
 (1958)   13:147–189
RANGELL, L.
 A Treatment of Nightmare in a Seven-year-old Boy (1950)   5:358–390
 The Scope of Intrapsychic Conflict: Microscopic and Macro-
 scopic Considerations (1963)   18:75–102
 Structural Problems in Intrapsychic Conflict (1963)   18:103–138
RANK, B.
 Aggression (1949)   3/4:43–48
—— & MACNAUGHTON, D.
 A Clinical Contribution to Early Ego Development (1950)   5:53–65
 See also PUTNAM, RANK, & KAPLAN (1951)
RAPPAPORT, S. R.
 Behavior Disorder and Ego Development in a Brain-injured
 Child (1961)   16:423–450
REDL, F.
 The Psychology of Gang Formation and the Treatment of
 Juvenile Delinquents (1945)   1:367–377
REICH, A.
 The Discussion of 1912 on Masturbation and Our Present-day
 Views (1951)   6:80–94
 A Character Formation Representing the Integration of Un-
 usual Conflict Solutions into the Ego Structure (1958)   13:309–323

P9-DOF-572

What Is Structural Exegesis?

by
Daniel Patte

Fortress Press
Philadelphia

Contents

95197   5408B76   Printed in U.S.A.   1-462

Editor's Foreword

The first three volumes in this series dealt respectively with form criticism, redaction criticism, and literary criticism. And now we come to structural exegesis (or interpretation or criticism), which has been intensively used in France for some years and is being employed increasingly in other countries, including the United States. It might be helpful at the outset to relate structural exegesis to the other three disciplines in a very sketchy way.

Form criticism has been to some extent a literary discipline because it has concerned itself with the formal patterns in the pericopes of the Gospels (or other New Testament literature). But I would judge that it has been more strongly historical than literary because of its interest in the *development* of a given unit or form, and in the influence of the setting in life on both the origin and the development of both the form and content of the units of the Gospel tradition. Redaction criticism has likewise been both literary and historical, but again I would deem the historical concern to be the dominant one, although some recent redaction-critical studies have manifested a more genuinely literary-critical approach. Redaction criticism is literary in its intention to observe and analyze how the final author of a Gospel (or other document) shaped and modified his source materials (tradition) and put them together. How does the author give expression to his theological interpretation of Jesus through his stylistic and compositional techniques? But redaction criticism is also fundamentally historical in nature because it wants to separate tradition from redaction (the author's contribution)—rather than looking at the text as a unified whole—and to assess the connections and tensions between the two as well as to investigate the historical relationship between the author and his community and the history-of-thought relationships among the Gospels. I believe that most form and redaction critics have operated, implicitly or explicitly, with the assumption that the language of their texts was exercising primarily the referential function. The texts refer beyond themselves to events, situations, conflicts, ideas—and meaning is not really available apart from this reference.

The volume on literary criticism gave some attention to the kind of inquiry that biblical scholars have traditionally called literary criticism—such as the search for sources behind the Gospels. This is, however, really a kind of historical criticism because it is concerned with the temporal process through which the Gospels came into existence. Nevertheless, this volume was devoted principally to what we might call aesthetic literary criticism (although I do not want to impose that term or exactly this understanding of literary criticism on Professor Beardslee).

Aesthetic literary criticism sees its texts as exercising primarily the poetic linguistic function, or at least it is able to throw this function into relief. Language exercising the poetic function attracts attention intransitively to itself and does not refer it to some object beyond the text. Poetic language (using the term *poetic* broadly to include narrative and various kinds of imagistic language) is able to grasp the attention in this way because the various linguistic elements are locked into each other centripetally so that attention does not escape easily to the outside. This internal organization makes the text an organic unity and gives it a semi-autonomy. The text is grasped as a whole or totality, as people read it, rather than as something to be analyzed (into tradition and redaction), and meaning is seen to be a function not of the relationship between text and historical setting, but primarily of the union of form and content in the text itself. Form is not a separable container for the content but is itself the shaping or patterning of the content. All of this is to say that aesthetic literary criticism is concerned with the surface structure of the text, the manifest union of form and content.

Structural criticism I take to be a mode of literary criticism, but its object is not primarily the surface structure of the text. It focuses rather on the relationship between the surface structure and the "deep" structures which lie implicitly or unconsciously beneath, around, or alongside of the text. Structural criticism wants to articulate the larger implicit structure which in some way generates the text under consideration. How and to what extent does the given text manifest the reservoir of formal possibilities that belong to literature as such? There is a sense in which structural criticism is referential, but it does not derive the meaning of a text from its reference to something nonliterary, that is, something historical, sociological, or ideational. It discloses rather how the text "refers" to the reservoir of formal literary possibilities. I should like to add that all "structuralists" cannot be pressed into the same mold, and surely not all of them would agree with my brief formulation here.

It should not be thought, in my judgment, that historical and literary disciplines mutually exclude each other. But one thing that structuralism has taught us is that the two must be kept distinct, separate, and unconfounded. This is because the meaning which an item has in its own meaning system (its synchronic connections) is not the same as the meaning which it has as part of a historical process (its diachronic connections). For example, the prologue of the Gospel of John, which foregrounds the divine pre-existence of Jesus, receives a part of its meaning from its *relationship* to the story of the foot washing which belongs to the same larger narrative. But in the history of christological thought, which we may see developing from one Gospel to another, the pre-existence of Jesus is a *substitute* for the virgin birth and/or baptism of Jesus. The picture is further complicated by the fact that items which do or might belong to the same diachronic process may be *treated* synchronically, as related to each other in the same meaning system. But that carries us beyond the purposes of this brief foreword.

iv

DAN O. VIA, JR.

Preface

Structuralism is necessarily an interdisciplinary endeavor. Structural methods can only be developed by a team of specialists in several fields. The interdisciplinary project "Semiology and Exegesis" at Vanderbilt University, a project supported by a grant from the National Endowment for the Humanities, provided this necessary interdisciplinary context. The preparation of this book has benefited from the collective methodological research of two interdisciplinary seminars and a colloquium, at Vanderbilt University, and of a three week international colloquium on Biblical Semiotics (Annecy, France, July 1974).

The following colleagues at Vanderbilt University have participated in the seminars: W. von Raffler Engel (professor of Linguistics), J. Kaplan and D. Thomas (both professors of Anthropology), L. Crist and R. Poggenburg (both professors of French Literature), J. Engel (professor of German Literature), J. Post (professor of Philosophy), P. Krolack (professor of Systems and Information Sciences), C. McCorkel (professor of Fine Arts), J. Crenshaw (professor of Old Testament), C. Hambrick (professor of Religious Studies), and L. H. Silberman (Hillel professor of Jewish Studies). The colloquium at Vanderbilt University featured two speakers: S. Wittig (professor of English Literature, University of Texas at Austin), and D. Via, Jr. (professor of Religious Studies, University of Virginia). The international colloquium on Biblical Semiotics included twenty-eight scholars, the majority of whom belonged to the Association for the Structural Study of the Bible (a group of French scholars also known as ASTRUC), a group from Vanderbilt University, and scholars from various European Universities. J. Delorme and J. Calloud (both professors of Biblical Exegesis, Catholic University, Lyon, France) were the conveners; J. Geninasca (professor of French Literature, University of Zurich, Switzerland) was a guest speaker; and M. Rengstorf (assistant of Professor A. J. Greimas, University of Paris) was a consultant.

Each page of this work reflects this collective research. It is with gratitude that I acknowledge that this book owes much to the insights of each of them. Special thanks are due to Dan Via who offered a detailed criticism of a first draft of this book which led to many improvements, and to J. Delorme, J. Calloud, and M. Rengstorf who taught me so much. I have nevertheless to assume the responsibility for the content of this book.

Last, but not least, five persons who collaborated closely with me in my research: my wife Aline, and four Ph.D. candidates, John Jones, Ed McMahon, Judd Parker, and Gary Phillips. The "form of the expression" of this book owes much to them: my wife typed it and re-typed it; the others helped me with the English style and language. The "form of its content" also owes much to the constant encouragement and critical insights that each of the five gave me.

I

The Place of Structural Methods in the Exegetical Task

We designate as "structural exegesis" that which employs those exegetical methods which are deliberately derived from the methodologies of the linguist Ferdinand de Saussure, and of the anthropologist Claude Lévi-Strauss.

In biblical exegesis we are accustomed to making use of a series of methods: for instance, text criticism, literary criticism, form criticism, and redaction criticism. When confronted with various types of structural analysis our spontaneous tendency is to classify these new methods alongside the others. Thus we are attempting to evaluate the validity and usefulness of structural methods in terms of their ability to answer questions raised by the traditional methods—and we become perplexed. At the outcome of a very involved structural analysis we find that very few (if any!) such questions have been answered. Consequently we are tempted to dismiss structural methods as useless. Yet, if we resist this temptation and examine more closely the structuralist methods we discover that our initial assumption was misguided. Structural methods do not fit into the series of traditional exegetical methods. Text criticism, literary criticism, form criticism, and redaction criticism belong together because they all assume a historical paradigm with a specific pre-understanding of the biblical text. That is, they presuppose that biblical texts are to be seen primarily as sources for reconstructing some kind of historical process. By contrast the structural methods assume a linguistic paradigm, that is, that expression in language is to be taken as a fundamental category and not as an access to something else, e.g., history. Thus the very introduction of structural methods in exegesis implies a shift in the exegete's preunderstanding of the biblical text. This shift needs to be elucidated and evaluated in order to determine if it is legitimate and potentially fruitful for the exegete to involve himself in these methods which are still in process of formulation. Such an evaluation will entail defining the nature of the exegetical task and setting forth some criteria for evaluating the methods. On this ground we intend to show that in the present cultural situation neither traditional nor structural exegesis alone can successfully carry out the exegetical task to its end. By contrast it will appear that the combination of traditional and structural methods is neither a luxury nor a fad but a "must" if one wants to carry out the exegetical task in the contemporary culture. We shall also suggest that the exegetical methods (primarily reformulations of traditional methods) which resulted from the research of the New Hermeneutic themselves witness to this methodological shift.

IN A NEW CULTURE, A NEW EXEGESIS

Contemporary Culture

The goal of the present chapter is to *interpret* the significance of the present diversification in exegetical methods. As in any interpretation, the present one will be involved in a hermeneutical circle; my evaluation is necessarily based upon preunderstandings which I need to elucidate at the outset by stating them briefly.

Our culture is man-centered rather than cosmos-centered. Our preunderstandings are therefore man-centered: they depend upon our "view of man" (rather than upon our "world view").[1] Modern convictions about man can be characterized as dialectical. Man is perceived at once as a creator of "significations" (that is, of meaningful entities, cultural values, symbols, etc.) and as a conditioned being upon which significations are imposed.[2] We are not concerned here to justify philosophically such a dialectical view of man. We simply suggest that it is prevalent in our culture. The recent debate over the work of B. F. Skinner can serve as an illustration. Many of Skinner's behaviorist theories are used for educational and advertising purposes. We assume with Skinner that man is conditioned; however, this assumption is taken seriously only insofar as it does not threaten to destroy our dialectical view of man. There is no objection to saying "significations are imposed upon man" as long as one can also imply "and man is a creator of significations." But as

---

1. Our view of man (as a whole or in one of its specific aspects) is a conviction: although it can be conscious—it can be an understanding or a philosophy—most of the time it is simply self-evident.

2. Although one cannot date cultural changes precisely, it is significant to note that this view of man imposed itself relatively recently upon our society. In this paragraph we use the term "signification" without its technical connotation discussed in Chapter II.

soon as Skinner argues (as in *Beyond Freedom and Dignity*)[3] that man is totally conditioned, objections are raised from all sides.

Our other presuppositions are simply corollaries of this dialectical view of man. For instance, let us consider the nature of language. Without denying that man is an author (he uses language to express what he means), we need also to affirm with Heidegger and his disciples the ontological nature of language (meaning is not poured into language by the author but belongs intrinsically to it).

When applied more directly to the object of our investigation, the dialectical view of man demands that we consider exegetical methods as a specific type of language. The exegete (as subject) chooses and creates his methods, although concurrently these methods impose themselves on the exegete: each specific set of methods symbolizes a specific preunderstanding of the text. Changes in methods entail changes in preunderstanding (or, at least, changes in that part of the preunderstanding which is involved in exegetical methods). This is why we stated above that introducing new exegetical methods implies a shift in preunderstanding of the biblical text, and that it is illegitimate to test the validity and usefulness of a specific exegesis in terms of its ability to answer the questions raised by another exegetical method. What is still needed are criteria which will allow us to evaluate the legitimacy of various exegeses. In order to establish them we shall discuss first the nature of the exegetical task (and specifically its relationship to the hermeneutical task), and second, the relationship between exegetical methods and the exegete's culture.

Exegesis and Hermeneutic

The process of interpreting a text—a single phenomenon—can be viewed as including two approaches: exegesis and hermeneutic. Exegesis aims at understanding the text in itself, while hermeneutic attempts to elucidate what the text means for the modern interpreter and the people of his culture. Exegesis and hermeneutic must be distinguished from each other despite the fact that the very function of exegesis is to lead to hermeneutic. This is not to say that our distinction between two modes of interpretation should be identified with that proposed by nineteenth-century scholarship. The difference lies in the presuppositions which lead to such a distinction.

A characteristic formulation of nineteenth–century position can be found in W. Dilthey's work.[4] Hermeneutic and exegesis were seen

3. B. F. Skinner, *Beyond Freedom and Dignity* (New York: Alfred A. Knopf, 1971).

4. Cf. Wilhelm Dilthey's 1900 essay entitled "Origin and Development of Hermeneutics," German original in *Gesammelte Schriften*, vol. V.

in a subject-object schema. Dilthey proposed to distinguish between a) an interpretation as *explanation* of the text; and b) an interpretation as *appropriation* of the text. His concern was to distinguish as clearly as possible the former (which he associated with the scientific explanation of natural phenomena) from the latter (which he called a "science of the mind": *Geisteswissenschaft*), in order to establish the scientific character of the appropriation of the text despite the fact that it is not readily comparable to the natural sciences. Consequently these two types of interpretation were primarily seen in contrast and opposition to each other.

The sharpness of Dilthey's distinction was rapidly eroded when the discussion focused on the problem of the hermeneutical circle. Thus for Bultmann exegesis and hermeneutic are closely related, although the distinction between them is still necessary. As the New Hermeneutic has shown, Bultmann was ultimately able to maintain such a distinction because of his understanding of language as an objectification of the existential self-understanding; language conceals the latter. The obstacle posed by this objectification has to be overcome by exegesis in order to uncover the existential self-understanding hidden in the text. In such a case, exegesis (which is no longer understood in terms of the subject-object schema) leads directly to hermeneutic. As a result of exegesis the existential self-understanding of the text confronts the interpreter's existential self-understanding.

With the New Hermeneutic one needs to challenge Bultmann's understanding of language and consequently his understanding of the relationship of exegesis to hermeneutic. Following Heidegger and Gadamer the New Hermeneutic acknowledged the *ontological nature* of language. In theological terms one can then speak of the incarnation of the Word of God in language. The Word is not to be found beyond the human language but in it—in the "language event" as Fuchs puts it. In other words, the meaning of the language that the hermeneut wants to appropriate belongs to the language itself and not to a pristine realm beyond language. In such a perspective, exegesis—understood as explanation and clarification which allow the overcoming of the objectification of language—is not the necessary prelude to hermeneutic. The transmission of the meaning of the text (hermeneutic) does not depend upon its objective analysis (traditional understanding of exegesis). On this we agree with the New Hermeneutic school. Nevertheless the hermeneutic of a text is not directly possible: it needs to be preceded by an exegesis, although the exegetical task is no longer that envisioned by Dilthey and Bultmann.

As long as the language under consideration is a "living language" (a speech), hermeneutic is directly possible. I, as listener, enter into a speech's dimension of meaning and attempt to take it upon myself. As Gadamer wrote, "Understanding means primarily to understand each other on the subject matter [hermeneutic] and only secondarily to clarify and understand the view of the other person as such" [traditional exegesis].[5] In this case there is no doubt that the speech is addressed to me; exegesis is secondary. It is not a necessary prelude to hermeneutic.

When one considers the hermeneutic of a text, however, Gadamer's analysis can no longer be directly applied. A text is *not* living language: it is *"dead language."* It is no longer a speech. I, as reader, cannot enter directly into the text's dimension of meaning. It is self-evident that a speech is addressed to me. Not so, in the case of a text. The distance which separates the text from the reader should not be overlooked. In order for a hermeneutic of a text to take place it is first necessary that its dead language be brought back to life. Such is the task of exegesis.

This understanding of exegesis is clearly different from Dilthey's and Bultmann's in that it assumes the ontological nature of language. The discourse of the text is not to be *overcome* by exegesis but to be *revitalized* by it. With Ricoeur we can indeed define hermeneutic as the prolongation of the discourse of the text into a new discourse.[6]

In a dialogue, I prolong the discourse of my interlocutor into my own discourse; we understand each other on the subject-matter. Ultimately in a dialogue I apprehend myself in a new way. This is hermeneutic. To use a metaphor, the other party in the dialogue becomes a mirror in which I can see myself. Reading is similar to dialogue: the text likewise becomes a mirror in which I can see myself, a discourse that I can prolong into my own discourse. Yet it is different in the sense that this mirror is not the "fugitive other" who in his freedom confronts me on his own. The text is fixed and therefore I have to approach it. In dialogue the hermeneutic is instantaneous but quite superficial: such a "fugitive" mirror does not

5. H. G. Gadamer, *Wahrheit und Methode*, pp. 277 f., quoted by J. M. Robinson, "Hermeneutic since Barth," in *New Frontiers of Theology*, vol. II, *The New Hermeneutic*, ed. by J. M. Robinson and J. B. Cobb, (New York: Harper and Row, 1964), p. 75.
6. Paul Ricoeur, "Problèmes actuels de l'interprétation," *CPED* 148 (1970), pp. 163–82: "Lire c'est en tout hypothèse enchaîner un discours nouveau au discours du texte," p. 176. Cf. also his collection of essays, *Le conflit des Interprétations. Essais d'Herméneutique* (Paris: Seuil, 1969); "Du conflit à la convergence des méthodes en exégèse biblique," and "Contribution d'une réflexion sur le langage à une théologie de la parole," *Exégèse et Herméneutique* (Paris: Seuil, 1971), pp. 35–53 and pp. 301–19.

allow more than a glance at myself. In reading, by contrast, the hermeneutic demands an effort on my part. I need to approach the text. Yet because it is a fixed mirror I, as reader, have the possibility of apprehending the size, the shape, and the form of the mirror in which I discover myself. I have the time to place myself within the perspective of the text, to evaluate what part of myself will be revealed by the mirror and with what kind of "distortions." All this is exegesis. To put it another way, we could say that by exegesis I have time to apprehend the vectors of the discourse of the text. By hermeneutic I will later extend these vectors up to myself. This will be done in a legitimate way if I respect the original direction of these vectors as defined by exegesis.

In short, exegesis determines the discourse of the text, its nature, its semantic potentialities. As such, exegesis considers the text as a "closed system" of signs. Then, in a second step, the hermeneutic prolongs the discourse of the text into a new discourse. The fact that the results of exegesis determine what the hermeneutic will be does not authorize us to assimilate these two types of interpretations. On the other hand, exegesis is not an end in itself even though it is a scientific investigation of the "it" of the text. When exegesis does not lead to hermeneutic—that is, when exegesis does not bring back to life the dead language of the text—it has failed. It is not a legitimate exegesis in that it does not carry out the exegetical task to its end, that is, lead to hermeneutic.[7] We have here a first criterion which will help us to determine the legitimacy of an exegesis.

Exegesis and the Exegete's Culture

This first criterion for the legitimacy of exegesis is not sufficient by itself: there are illegitimate exegeses which lead to hermeneutic. A second and complementary criterion can be defined by examining the relationship between exegesis and the exegete's culture.

As noted above, the exegete can choose or create methods of interpretation. In so doing he assumes a specific attitude toward the text, a specific preunderstanding. Yet, concurrently, a preunderstanding of the text is imposed upon the exegete by his culture.[8] As creator of significations, the exegete can adopt a specific set of methods and therefore a specific preunderstanding which is different from the preunderstanding demanded by his culture. Yet as a man

---

7. On other grounds it can be a legitimate study of the text, yet it is not an exegesis. The dynamic connotation of *exēgeisthai* (lit. to lead out; to guide) needs to be preserved.
8. We use the term "culture" in the broad sense of the set of convictions (and their symbolizations) which characterizes a given society.

6

upon whom significations are imposed, the exegete cannot help but assume this latter preunderstanding. We would like to propose that an exegesis is legitimate only when the preunderstanding implied in the methods is identical with (or at least closely related to) the preunderstanding demanded by the interpreter's culture. When the methodological and the cultural preunderstandings are at odds with each other—that is, when the exegesis is obscurantist in that its methods ignore the demands of the exegete's culture—either the exegesis of the text is based upon a faulty way of thinking or it fails to lead to hermeneutic. This criterion of legitimacy can be verified by briefly applying it to a clearly illegitimate type of exegesis: the fundamentalist exegesis of the Bible (which is often integrated with an implicit hermeneutic).

One aspect of our culture and of what Van Harvey termed its "new morality of knowledge"[9] demands that the past be evaluated in terms of its historicity. The fundamentalist interpreter, unlike the biblical scholar, refuses to comply with the demands of historiography. He affirms that a religious reading of the Bible is the only valid one. Yet, paradoxically, such an attitude is intended to protect the "historicity" of the Bible. For instance, the fundamentalist interpreter as exegete affirms, against the historian, the historicity of the virgin birth and of the empty tomb. Why? Because he abides by the modern historical conviction which can be summarized in the phrase: *if it is historical it is true,* even more than does the historian! For this fundamentalist exegete, truth and historicity are so much identified with each other that he is led to conclude: *if it is true* (according to my faith), *it is historical.* Jesus' resurrection is a cornerstone of his faith. Consequently the empty tomb must be a historical fact. This obscurantist attitude which intended to provide a biblical interpretation free from the modern culture ends by being bound to that culture. It is now assumed that the modern historical conviction belonged intrinsically to the biblical faith! This obscurantist attitude can be termed "historicism" since it absolutizes the modern historical conviction in its very attempt to dismiss it.

When combined with a conviction about the literal inspiration of the Bible, such historicism leads, nevertheless, to a hermeneutic which is accepted as meaningful by a sizable section of our society. This puzzling phenomenon can be understood if one notices that it integrates both poles of the dialectical view of man, however ille-

9. Van A. Harvey, *The Historian and the Believer: The Morality of Historical Knowledge and Christian Belief* (New York: Macmillan Co., 1969), Chaps. II and III.

gitimately. The doctrine of literal inspiration assumes that significations are imposed upon man, while historicism manages to project an appearance of historical perspective which, as we shall see, assumes that man is creator of significations. As long as such a fundamentalist believer can remain in his religious world structured by his interpretation of the Bible, the weakness of this interpretation remains concealed.

Another sizable section of our society, while refusing to withdraw from modern culture, adopts the historicist interpretations of the Bible (often simply because of a reluctance to be involved in the complexity of a critical study) but as a consequence dismisses the Bible (or most of it) as meaningless because it is not historically true. Except for a number of moral teachings, the biblical text does not make sense to them. Let us emphasize it: no hermeneutic takes place. It is not that a given meaning of the Bible has been found to be unacceptable because it is incompatible with modern culture. Instead, by using an obscurantist interpretation (identifying true with *historically* true) it is not possible to tell whether the text is incompatible with modern culture or not.

It appears therefore that an obscurantist exegesis is illegitimate either because it involves a faulty way of thinking or because it prevents the exegesis from leading to a hermeneutic. By contrast, an exegesis is legitimate when methodological and cultural preunderstandings are attuned to each other. In such a case the exegete indeed depends upon his culture (significations are imposed upon him), but he is not bound to it (he is a creator of significations). To continue the preceding example, let us note that scholarly historical exegesis dispels the specific obscurantism which hinders the fundamentalist interpreter. By assuming historical methods, the exegete avoids absolutizing the modern historical conviction. Not only does he become aware of this specific preunderstanding, but also, like any historian, he recognizes that such research does not yield any absolute result but only probabilities. In this way he overcomes historicism and its absolute equation of "historical" and "true."

This second criterion—the criterion of obscurantism—is decisive. In some instances it can be applied directly, specifically when the faulty reasoning is obvious. In other instances, obscurantism assumes very subtle disguises. While struggling to avoid any incorrect reasoning by carefully scrutinizing our methodological preunderstanding, we, as exegetes, may fail to notice the cultural changes around us. If our methodological and cultural preunderstandings have come to be at odds with each other, we may, despite our efforts, become trapped in obscurantism (as defined above). Thus when no faulty reasoning is apparent we will need to use our first criterion for a preliminary diagnostic: if a given exegesis does not lead to hermeneutic, it is suspect of obscurantism.

These two criteria, together with our observations about the nature of the exegetical task and about the contemporary culture, will allow us to evaluate the shift in preunderstanding which is implied in the present process of diversification in exegetical methods.

AN EVALUATION OF THE DIVERSIFICATION IN EXEGETICAL METHODS

In the narrow limits of this chapter we cannot indulge in a discussion of the specific preunderstanding of the biblical text implied in each of the specific exegetical methods. This would require us to take carefully into account the nuances given to each method by the various exegetes. The object of our investigation is rather to identify the broader preunderstandings which characterize the two main sets of exegetical methods: the traditional historical methods (in which we include redaction criticism), and the new exegetical methods (in which we include reformulations of the traditional methods, as well as various structuralist methods).

Traditional Historical Exegesis:
Diachronic Exegesis

By the term "traditional historical exegesis" (or in short "historical exegesis") we designate the exegesis which is characterized by the following methods: text criticism, philological study, literary criticism, history of traditions, form criticism, and redaction criticism. These methods (as originally understood by their creators and not as recently reformulated)[10] are still used by a majority of exegetes. We qualify this exegesis as "historical" in the specific sense that it is a study of the biblical text according to the demands of the now traditional historiography as formulated by Ernst Troeltsch (among others). Van Harvey's[11] analysis of the various attempts of the exegete to conform to such a historiography illustrates the characteristics of historical exegesis.

Historical exegesis is a deliberate attempt to interpret the Bible in terms of the morality of knowledge demanded by modern culture and understood as "the morality of historical knowledge." The legitimacy of historical exegesis is to be tested by the norms and warrants which pertain to historiography. Such an exegesis should

10. Cf., for instance, the revised formulation of literary criticism by W. A. Beardslee, *Literary Criticism of the New Testament* (Philadelphia: Fortress Press, 1970).
11. Van A. Harvey, *The Historian and the Believer.*

unfold itself naturally into a modern hermeneutic which would reveal the meaning of the biblical text for modern man (irrespective of its adoption or rejection). But such is not in fact the case: the believer (layman, minister, or theologian) seems paralysed, unable to cross the threshold which separates historical exegesis from hermeneutic. The cause of this failure cannot be the incompatibility of the Bible with modern culture; such a verdict would presuppose that a given meaning of the Bible has been found to be unacceptable, i.e., that a hermeneutic has taken place. Instead, the nature of this text as defined by historical exegesis appears to be *meaningless*: no hermeneutic takes place. Applying our first criterion, we have to conclude that historical exegesis is suspect of obscurantism. Could it be that its methodological preunderstanding is at odds with the contemporary cultural preunderstanding? To answer this question we need to elucidate the methodological preunderstanding implied in historical exegesis.

At the outset we need to note that historical exegesis as historiography is a "field-encompassing field."[12] Eventually, directly or indirectly, the historian makes use of methods borrowed from each of the human sciences. Consequently the historian is often satisfied that historiography reflects the *whole* modern view of man which is symbolized in these various methodologies. Thus, at first it seems impossible to suggest that the historian may have neglected in his methodology some essential aspects of the modern view of man. This is an illusion that we have to dispel. For if historiography (and historical exegesis) is indeed "field-encompassing," it is nevertheless a field. In borrowing from each human science the historian is selective. All the methods that he uses have to fit and be cast into the specific structure which governs and motivates his historical research. It is at the level of this structure that the methodological preunderstanding implied in historical exegesis lies.

A first characteristic that the various historical exegetical methods have in common is that each can be qualified as descriptive. Each is an attempt to determine as objectively as possible the "what" of the text.[13] Despite the fact that the contemporary historian never claims absolute objectivity but only different degrees of probability,

---

12. Ibid., pp. 54–59.
13. 1) What is the authentic text, or better, what is the original text?—*text criticism*. 2) What is the "language" of the text? Here, the historical evolution of the meaning of the terminology: *philological study*. 3) What is the literary genre of the text? At this level the style and literary structure as well as the grammatical aspects of the text are studied: *literary criticism*. 4) What are the origin and history of the traditions used in the text? This permits an understanding of the evolution of the signification of these traditions from their origins up to the text: *form criticism* and *history of traditions*. It is to

he remains convinced that "truth" is defined in terms of objectivity. This he implies further when he acknowledges that no absolute "historical truth" can be reached; "historical" is always understood in terms of objectivity, i.e., in positivistic terms. This limits considerably the historian's field of investigation: it necessarily includes only the data which are susceptible to being apprehended objectively, i.e., only those which allow for objective verification. Such is indeed the case with the data that the above methods propose to examine. For instance, it is legitimate to investigate the "personality" of a man of the past: this can be established by taking into consideration what he did and said in specific circumstances. One can even discern the "psychological motives" of this man: they can be deduced from the data. Yet, when in the name of an existentialist historiography someone claims that "the self underlying the personality" should be taken into consideration, the historian's reply is quite sarcastic. James Robinson made such a claim. Van Harvey, in the name of the historian, responds:

> The personality, he [Robinson] writes, is merely one's "empirical habitus," the "inescapable medium through which the self expresses itself but is not identical with the self" (Robinson, *New Quest*, 68). But how does one get at this self underlying the personality except by some kind of reflection on the conscious beliefs, intentions, and motives of the "personality"? Surely it would be meaningless to talk about a decision in complete abstraction from motives.[14]

In other words, Robinson, according to Harvey, unduly exceeded the limitations of historiography. We agree that these limitations do have some validity for biblical exegesis; yet, in order to avoid any confusion, one should acknowledge that there are additional legitimate approaches which are not "historical." Van Harvey's criticism is quite valuable here in that it brings into sharp focus the limitations of the historian's field of investigation to "the *conscious* beliefs, the (*conscious*) intentions, and the (*conscious*) motives of the 'personality'." For the historian it is "*meaningless* to talk about a decision in complete abstraction from (*conscious*) motives." To put it negatively, the historian refuses to take into consideration what we could call the unconscious. (We shall be more specific below.) This

be noted that such a method owes much to the insights borrowed from the research conducted in anthropology, sociology, and history of religion. 5) What did the author want to say? At this level it is essential to understand who the author was, what his theology was, what the circumstances were which presided over the elaboration of this text, and who the addressees were: *redaction criticism*.

14. Van A. Harvey, *op. cit.*, p. 191. See also the whole of Ch. VI, "The Morality of Historical Knowledge and the New Quest of the Historical Jesus," pp. 164–203.

focus of historical research on the conscious level[15] is not accidental. It is demanded not only by the positivistic character of historiography, but also by the view of man on which it is based.

The specific view of man which is implied in the historical exegetical methods can be summed up in the phrase: *man is a creator of significations*. The author wants to say something: what he expresses is his own *creative* and *free* response to a specific situation. He is free to come to a decision and to act accordingly. The author creates new symbols. He also *uses* in his own way the symbols which are available to him, ascribing to them specific meanings which suit *his* argument. We could say that it is assumed that for him the symbols (and the larger symbolic units which are the traditions) are like construction blocks. Earlier they were arranged by others to form the edifices which they chose to build. Now the author, discarding the old edifices, reuses these blocks for another purpose, giving them new places, new functions, new meanings. In the same way he *uses* the language as a whole as well as literary techniques. In short, he is "making a coherent deformation of the language"[16] in order to express a new thought or idea. In order to be able to grasp what is specifically the author's, one therefore has to evaluate on the one hand the extent of this deformation of the language by comparing the author's uses of terminology, literary genres, traditions, and symbols with those of previous authors (or groups), and on the other hand the historical circumstances to which he responds. In brief, traditional historical exegesis assumes that man, either as an individual or as a group (in the case of a tradition), is primarily an *author*, i.e., the "originator" or "creator" of significations. He is a semantic agent.

The focusing of historical inquiries on the conscious level is coherent with this view of man as *author*. Furthermore, it is not surprising that the historian's major concern should be to determine the *origin and evolution* of an institution, of a tradition, of a symbol, or of an idea. Describing the origin, he reaches the "author" (as an individual or a group): there is no need to go further. Describing the evolution, he evaluates the impacts of subsequent "authors." History is made up of a succession of "authors": to reach them is to reach the very fabric of history.

15. Here we follow Claude Lévi-Strauss. In his essay "History and Anthropology" (in *Structural Anthropology* [New York: Basic Books, 1963], pp. 1–27), Lévi-Strauss distinguishes historical from anthropological research on the ground that the first deals primarily with the "conscious" level while the second is focused primarily on the "unconscious" level.
16. This phrase is attributed to André Malraux by Merleau-Ponty in *Signs* (Evanston: Northwestern University Press, 1964), p. 91.

In order to emphasize the preunderstanding implied in traditional historical methods we can qualify these methods as diachronic.[17] The genetic concern of such an exegesis (its constant concern with origins—the original text, the origin of a tradition, etc.) is one aspect of this diachronic attitude toward the text. Further, even though the historical exegete may often be involved in studies which are not focused on a succession of times, his attitude toward the text is diachronic. The text is studied in the context of the dynamic history made up of a succession of authors. Any aspect of the text, as well as any historical phenomenon, can be understood only in terms of what precedes and what succeeds it.[18] It is in the dynamism of diachrony that the historical exegete expects to reach the very nature of the text, i.e., what, for modern man, is potentially significant in this text: man as the author of significations.

One could object that the historian acknowledges that "significations are imposed upon man": he points out what and who influenced the author. Yet this is done in order to determine better the specificity of the author's creation. For the historian man is so predominantly the semantic agent that the semantic potentiality of the text is strictly limited to what the author (as an individual or as a group) *meant*.

Historical exegesis is confident that an exposition of this semantic dimension of the text (what the author meant) will lead to hermeneutic (what the text means). Yet it does not. Keeping in mind our observations about the contemporary view of man, we can suggest that this failure to carry out the exegetical task to its end (the hermeneutic) finds its roots in the fact that the methodological preunderstanding is only partly attuned to the cultural preunderstand-

17. Ferdinand de Saussure made a distinction between diachronic and synchronic *linguistic* studies. Yet the very fact that we shall use this terminology to designate various approaches to the study of a text (as speech)—rather than to the study of language—demands an adaptation of these concepts. Thus the evolution of language is not the fact of the direct intervention of the speakers: "linguistic changes are wholly unintentional" (F. de Saussure, *Course in General Linguistics* [New York: McGraw-Hill, 1959], p. 85); a linguistic diachronic study examines an impersonal dynamic force which imposes a language with new features on the speakers. By contrast the historical exegete—by the very fact that he studies a text and no longer a language—is concerned with the evolution of the text, of the symbols, of the traditions, as media of signification: these changes are conceived by the historical exegete as the manifestation of the semantic creativity of the authors. A diachronic exegetical study has as ultimate object to point out what the author *meant*, and therefore the *intentional* changes in symbols, traditions, and ideas. Again, for the traditional historical exegete, man is primarily a creator of significations and consequently his exegesis, as attempt to capture this creativity, is characteristically diachronic.
18. This is the "principle of correlation," one of the three principles that Ernst Troeltsch saw as the basis of any historical investigation. Cf. E. Troeltsch, "Historiography," *Encyclopedia of Religion and Ethics*, ed. James Hastings, (New York: Charles Scribner's Sons, 1914), Ch. VI, pp. 716–23.

ing. To be sure, the historical exegete in his diachronic approach acknowledges with our culture that man is a creator of significations, but he fails to affirm concurrently (through other exegetical methods) that significations are also imposed upon man.

The structural methods are in sharp contrast to the traditional historical methods. We shall see that rather than being diachronic they are synchronic: their methodological preunderstanding of the text assumes that significations are imposed upon man. We shall also suggest that the reformulations of traditional historical methods (results of the research of the New Hermeneutic) are themselves synchronic. Thus the structural methods belong together with these reformulations. One of our conclusions will be that the structural methodological preunderstanding demands a plurality of exegetical methods. Accordingly, a complete exegesis is perceived as involving a plurality of synchronic approaches as well as the plurality of diachronic approaches discussed above; synchronic exegesis does not intend to supplant the traditional historical exegesis.

Structural Exegesis:
Synchronic Exegesis

As before, we are not concerned in this chapter with the methods themselves (how a structural exegesis is performed) but with the methodology (structuralism). We shall therefore limit ourselves to a number of observations about the preunderstanding of the text implied in the various structural exegeses.

A first striking characteristic of a structural exegesis is the absence of the traditional semantic concern: the exegesis no longer aims at what the author meant. Herein lies the radical difference from traditional exegesis which is always, at least indirectly, aimed at uncovering what the author (as an individual or as a group) wanted to say. Nevertheless this does not mean that there is no semantic dimension to structural studies.

The structural exegete attempts to uncover, for instance, the linguistic, narrative, or mythical structures of the text under consideration. Whether or not these structures were intended by the author is not a relevant question. In fact, in most instances it appears quite likely that the author was not aware of using such complex structures. Indeed he was preoccupied with conveying a meaning. Yet his "speech" (*parole*, in de Saussure's terminology) could not but use the "language" available to him which "gives unity to speech."[19]

---

19. de Saussure, *op. cit.*, p. 11.

This language imposes itself upon him.

> Language is not a function of the speaker; it is a product that is passively assimilated by the individual. It never requires premeditation, and reflection enters in only for the purpose of classification. . .[20]

The structural analyst studies this language without concern for what the author meant (the traditionally understood semantic dimension of the text). Yet language itself has a semantic dimension. When language imposes itself upon man, significations are also imposed upon man. Studying language as a system of signs, the structuralist brackets out the question of the significations of the "speech" and thus the traditional semantic question. In the process of pointing out the structure of the language he exposes the semantic dimension of the language. In fact the "meaning" of a language (its "value" in de Saussure's terminology) is nothing else than its structure (which is one of contrasts, distinctions, and oppositions) because the elements of language always exist in relation to one another.

Similarly, when structural analysis is applied beyond a sentence to a discourse, its "structural meaning" is nothing else than the various intra-textual and extra-textual correlations.[21] Likewise in the analysis of a text as a system of mythical representations, the mythical structure is a "meaning" of the text.[22]

A last characteristic of "meaning" as viewed by the structuralists must be noted: as opposed to the unicity of the historical meaning (the author meant one thing), the structuralists acknowledge the plurality of "structural meanings."[23] The different levels of structural studies point out different structural meanings. Furthermore, each structural study aims at exposing a plurality of "meanings." The structures of a text are the semantic potentialities of this text. All these structural meanings were passively assimilated by the author. He assumed them while he, as a creator of significations, was concerned to communicate a specific meaning. Although this meaning is not the object of his study, the structural analyst would nevertheless not deny its existence.

---

20. Ibid., p. 14.
21. Roland Barthes, "L'analyse structurale," *Exégèse et Herméneutique*, (Paris: Seuil, 1971), p. 185.
22 Cf. Lévi-Strauss, "The Structural Study of a Myth," *Structural Anthropology*, pp. 206–31.
23. Barthes, "L'analyse structurale," *Exégèse et Herméneutique*, p. 188, and François Wahl, "La philosophie entre l'avant et l'après du structuralisme," in *Qu'est-ce que le structuralisme?* (Paris: Seuil, 1968), p. 316.

These brief observations should suffice to suggest that the basic preunderstanding implied in structural exegesis is that "significations are imposed upon man." Methodologically, the antithesis "man is a creator of significations" is bracketed out. As Lévi-Strauss emphasized—when adapting the Saussurian methodology for anthropological studies[24]—the historical and the structural approaches need to be clearly distinguished. Confusing them leads to the exclusion of one of the two approaches.[25] They should be kept in a dialectical tension: the tension between a diachronic and a synchronic approach.

The synchronic approach can be briefly characterized in contrast to the diachronic approach. Instead of understanding a phenomenon in terms of a succession of times, a synchronic study considers it in terms of the various elements with which it is related in a mutual and simultaneous interdependence. Instead of a linear horizontal historical study, a synchronic study is in-depth, vertical. This does not mean that a synchronic study is necessarily limited to a specific time span (for this reason some authors substitute "achronic" for "synchronic"). The structural exegete often enriches his study of a specific structure by comparing or contrasting it with other similar structures even though they do not necessarily belong to the same time span. In so doing he has no genetic concern; indeed the time sequence has absolutely no relevance. At the structural level, time can be viewed as reversible.[26] Thus in a structural study of a discourse, the inter-textual correlations with any texts present similar structures. Whether they were written before or after the text under consideration is of no importance. This is in sharp contrast to the historian's genetic concern, which is based on a non-reversible time, viewing history as a succession of authors. Consequently a synchronic study is also characterized by the fact that it aims not at what arises from the author's creativity, but at what imposes itself upon him.

24. Lévi-Strauss, "History and Anthropology," *Structural Anthropology*, pp. 1–27.
25. Cf. de Saussure's warnings: *Course in General Linguistics,* pp. 96 ff.
26. Lévi-Strauss, "The Structural Study of a Myth," pp. 211 ff. This implies that there is a dynamic aspect to the structure which does not negate the wholeness of the structure. Piaget expresses it as follows: "As a first approximation, we may say that a structure is a system of transformations. Inasmuch as it is a system and not a mere collection of elements and their properties, these transformations involve laws: the structure is preserved or enriched by the interplay of its transformation laws, which never yield results external to the system nor employ elements that are external to it. In short the notion of structure is comprised of three key ideas: the idea of wholeness, the idea of transformation, and the idea of self-regulation." Jean Piaget, *Structuralism* (New York: Basic Books, 1970), p. 5.

The preceding observations lead us to another characteristic of the preunderstanding implied in structural methods. In order to account fully for the significations, the ideas, the decisions, the acts, the discourses, the personality of a man one needs to reach beyond the conscious belief, beyond the conscious intentions, beyond the conscious motives. In brief, one needs to apprehend the unconscious elements which impose significations upon man. We shall be more specific below on this point.

We termed the traditional historical exegesis diachronic because diachrony appeared as the central characteristic of its preunderstanding of the text. In the same way we term the structural exegesis as synchronic. This qualification sums up its specific preunderstanding of an approach to the text. A synchronic exegesis is thus characterized by a specific notion of time, as well as by a specific concept of the semantics of a text which demand that we take into consideration unconscious elements.

A Plurality of Synchronic Methods
among the Exegetical Methods

It remains for us to evaluate the general orientation of the process of diversification in exegetical methods. The preceding discussion of the preunderstanding implied in structural methods suggests that this diversification might be the result of the correlation or juxtaposition of a synchronic preunderstanding with a diachronic preunderstanding of the text. To clarify that this is indeed the case we need to emphasize the plurality of synchronic approaches.

As noted above, structural analysis implies a plurality of meanings, therefore a plurality of semantic potentialities. Each structural study aims at exposing a plurality of meanings at a specific structural level: again, a given structure is a set of semantic potentialities. Yet an analyst studying a specific structure does not pretend that his study exhausts the semantic potentialities of the text. He is aware of the diachronic semantic dimension of the text (what the author *meant*). Furthermore, he acknowledges other synchronic semantic dimensions. If he is a linguist, the structuralist is aware that there are literary structures (studied by Roland Barthes), narrative structures (studied by A. J. Greimas), psychological structures (studied by Jacques Lacan), sociological structures (studied by Lucien Goldmann), mythical structures, and anthropological structures (studied by Lévi-Strauss). Beyond the structuralist approaches it appears that other methods of the social sciences are also concerned to elucidate the role of various "unconscious elements which impose significations upon man."

There is no need to demonstrate that the various disciplines present different preunderstandings of this unconscious element. Further, in a given social science the various schools often have fundamentally divergent opinions on this question. Thus this unconscious element may be innate, it may belong to man *qua* man (for instance, it may be a deep anthropological structure aimed at by Lévi-Strauss), or rather, it may characterize man in a specific religion, or even characterize man as an individual. This unconscious element may be buried in the depth of the unconscious; it may belong to the twilight zone between conscious and unconscious. The fact that these various methodological preunderstandings are assumed and implicitly accepted as valid in our culture (as long as the scholars who use them do not deny that man is also the creator of significations) suggests that the modern convictional view of man lacks any specificity regarding what imposes significations upon man. Better, it appears that this convictional view of man implies a plurality of unconscious elements which impose significations upon man. These various methods of the social sciences can be seen as incorporating—in various ways (dialectical or not) and at various levels—synchronic approaches (synchronic being understood as discussed above and not in the specific Saussurian sense).

In this light, the diversification of exegetical methods appears to be provoked by the emergence of a plurality of synchronic exegetical methods, either used in correlation with or juxtaposed to the traditional diachronic methods.

The reformulations of the traditional exegetical methods under the impact of the research of the New Hermeneutic appear to be an attempt to complement the traditional historical methods with synchronic methods in such a way that the exegetical methods might be coherent with an Heideggerian ontological understanding of language. Because they were aware that language includes an essential semantic dimension the new hermeneuts formulated exegetical methods which integrate diachronic and synchronic approaches. For instance, literary criticism can no longer be content to consider literary genres as tools used by the authors: literary genres are also viewed as having a semantic power in themselves.[27] Thus, as Beardslee has shown, an important part of the meaning of the "beatitudes" is provided by their literary genre. They are words of authority which establish the reality "blessedness" for those to whom they are addressed.

27. Cf., for instance, Beardslee, *Literary Criticism*, and Dan O. Via, *The Parables: Their Literary and Existential Dimension* (Philadelphia: Fortress Press, 1967).

The preceding remarks should suffice to suggest that the diversification in exegetical methods results from the introduction of various synchronic methods. That such a process of diversification is a must has been shown. In order to be attuned to the cultural preunderstanding the methodological preunderstanding must be dialectical: man is viewed as a semantic agent upon whom significations are also imposed. To be legitimate an exegesis must be at once diachronic and synchronic. Further, since our cultural preunderstanding implies a plurality of synchronic semantic dimensions, an exegesis should include several synchronic approaches.

Finally, the exegesis must be free from any faulty reasoning. The legitimacy of historical exegesis is to be tested by the norms and warrants which pertain to historiography. Similarly the legitimacy of synchronic exegesis is to be tested by norms and warrants, in most instances, those developed by the various synchronic social sciences. Among the synchronic methods, the structural methods are the more rigorous: because they are directly based upon linguistic models they can be tested by the norms and warrants which pertain to linguistics. Furthermore the exegete needs to acknowledge scrupulously the limitations of each method. For instance, "psychologism" (i.e., the absolutizing of a model for the unconscious) must be as carefully avoided as "historicism." Historicism results from dogmatizing the historical conviction. The historical exegete properly relativizes such a conviction. He clearly distinguishes the historical methods from the philosophies of history. Similarly, in order to avoid faulty ways of thinking in a synchronic approach, the exegete must clearly distinguish the synchronic methods from the various philosophies which are extrapolated from the results of these methods, or which gave rise to them. Thus in structural exegesis the exegete needs to respect the norms and warrants which pertain to the sciences of language. In this way the exegete may hope to dispel the power of the convictions which gave rise to such methods and which are part of our culture. The exegete should also heed the warning of the structuralists. Diachronic and synchronic approaches should be clearly distinguished in order to avoid the dismissal of one or the other. During the exegesis, diachronic and synchronic approaches should be kept in a dialectical tension reflecting our dialectical view of man. The synthesis emerges in the hermeneutic. For indeed we can hope that such a dialectical exegesis will open toward a hermeneutic.

Through the broad evaluation of the present diversification in exegetical methods we have suggested why, in our view, it is imperative to develop synchronic exegetical methods and more specifically structural methods. Without such methods, the exegete cannot hope to carry out his task to its end: the leading to a hermeneutic of the Bible in the present cultural situation. Beyond this theoretical discussion there are (as we shall see below) indications that the results of structural exegesis when combined with the results of diachronic exegesis do indeed open important hermeneutical possibilities. Yet in most instances we cannot expect these results immediately. They will appear clearly only after extensive use of structural methods. Prior to this, the structural methods need to be further developed and the criteria for their use more sharply formulated. The recently published exegetical structural studies are to be viewed as various quests for and attempts at formulating these new methods.

Our second chapter will present a broad outline of the structural methodology in which we shall introduce the main methodological concepts. Following this theoretical chapter we shall present two specific structural methods and show how they can be used for the exegesis of New Testament texts.

II

From Structuralism to
Structural Exegesis

Meaning Effect
and Structures

A rough distinction between diachronic and synchronic exegeses has been proposed above in an attempt to show how they are complementary. We have seen further that this distinction revolves around the concept of *meaning* understood either as what is consciously meant by the author or as what imposes itself upon him. It should be clear by now that, when considering a text (although the following remarks apply to any cultural phenomenon), what we call the "meaning of a text" includes both the author's intentionality as well as various unconscious constraints upon him. By contrast, the common reader apprehends the meaning of a text as an indivisible whole. A text usually appears to have a single meaning which is spontaneously perceived as an entity. The preceding chapter should suffice to suggest that the "meaning of a text" is not an entity poured into the form "text" or hidden behind the text, but rather, in Greimas' terms, that it is a "meaning effect" ("*effet de sens*," that is, an "effect" offered to our perception, e.g., comparable to a "sound effect"). An analogy, despite its limitations, might help us to grasp the concept of meaning effect, which is closely related to the concept of structure.

A text may be compared to a hand-woven blanket. Its colorful design that we apprehend as a whole would be its "meaning." The "design effect" is the result of the intentional combination of colored threads. Yet the "design effect" is also determined by the limited possibilities offered by the loom and the set of colored threads available to the artisan. In such a case we could say as a first approximation that the "meaning effect" results from the interaction of the weaver's (author's) intentionality and of two structures (loom and set of colored threads). The two structures are constraints upon the weaver. His creativity is limited by these structures and simultaneously is realized within these structures. The weaver's art is the creative use of these two structures. For instance, within the limits of the possibilities of the loom, he can choose to build a warp with a specific number of threads. Similarly he can choose specific colored threads from the set available to him, and so on. In other words, the creation of a specific blanket is the actualization of some of the potentialities of the two structures. The design effect indeed reflects the weaver's creativity, but this creativity can take place only as a *manifestation* of some of the potentialities of the structures. Consequently, following Greimas, we shall use the term "manifestation" as a technical term to designate the finished product as the actualization of some of the potentialities of the structures.

Before going further let us emphasize that the "structures" we are speaking about (loom and set of colored threads) are something quite different from the "stylistic structure" of the design. Stylistic structures are structures of the "manifestation" (that is, of the finished product). *The structures studied by the structuralists are those structures which offer their potentialities in quest of actualization to the author's* (the weaver's) *creativity and which are also constraints limiting the author's creativity.* We shall use the term "structure" in this second sense exclusively.

It should be also noted that a given manifestation never exhausts the potentialities of the structures (e.g., a given blanket does not exhaust the potentialities of the loom).

Let us carry our analogy a step further. We have pointed out two structures: the loom and the set of colored threads. In fact there are other structures which preside over the weaving of the blanket. For example, we can readily distinguish between Indian blankets and Persian blankets because their designs present specific characteristics. Some of these differences might be explained by variations in the two structures discussed above: the Indian weavers might have a set of colored threads slightly different from that of the Persian weavers. Yet we have to acknowledge the role of two different "cultural structures" which offer their potentialities to and limit the weaver's creativity. These "cultural structures," even though they are much more subtle, are also manifested in the designs of the blankets.

The design "effect" of a blanket—and the meaning effect of a text—can therefore be viewed as resulting from the interaction of three types of constraints:

1) The constraints of the weaver's creativity which also includes the concrete situation in which he is (*Sitz im Leben*). In the case of a text or discourse, these constraints can be termed *structures of the enunciation* (that is, the constraints imposed upon the discourse by the author and the situation that he wishes to address).

2) The constraints of *cultural structures* also termed *cultural codes*.
3) The constraints of other structures which impose themselves on any blanket weaver: in our *analogy* we assume that the loom and the set of colored threads are such structures (even though it may not in fact be the case). In the case of a text or discourse, these are the *deep structures*, i.e., the constraints which impose themselves on any author or speaker.

Despite all its shortcomings, this analogy can suggest some of the characteristics of the structures that the analysts propose to study. A text is the *manifestation* which results from the interaction of various structures as some of their potentialities are actualized in the text. This analogy should also suggest how the structures interact. As a constraint each structure excludes a number of possibilities. The loom excludes all other weaving techniques. The set of colored threads excludes the colors which it does not contain. The cultural structure excludes foreign designs, etc. When combined, these structures exclude a part of each other's potentialities. For instance, the cultural structure might exclude specific combinations of colors even though they are possibilities offered by the set of colored threads. Similarly in a text, the various structural levels which superimpose themselves upon each other progressively reduce the number of possibilities offered to the author's creativity. This limitation of the author's freedom is compensated by the added potentialities offered by each additional structure. The structures might be compared to the lenses of a microscope. As one adds lenses the field of vision is progressively reduced, but magnification is increased and one can discern smaller details, the image is sharper. Similarly the meaning effect of a text becomes sharper and sharper as more and more structures are at work in it. The interaction of the structures can also be compared to a filtering process. For indeed the vocabulary of a natural language is very ambiguous. Without the limitations imposed by various structures, each word has a quasi infinite number of potential semantic connotations (also termed *semantic features*) since it can theoretically be defined in terms of all the entries in the dictionary. The structures function as a filtering process which drastically limits the number of semantic features for each word. We could say that the structures *select the pertinent semantic features*, i.e., the semantic features which will participate in the meaning effect. Thus the "meaning effect" of a text can be apprehended by the readers insofar as when reading the text, they are using the very structures which the author used.

The preceding remark suggests that the concept of "meaning effect" must be understood as a term of communication. The author intends his text to be a meaningful text that he proposes to others in order to communicate with them. Already at that level an important selection of elements of the meaning effect is performed by constraints such as the author's intention and his situation in life. These constraints, which we term *"structures of the enunciation,"* are studied by means of traditional methods. In order to apprehend the meaning effect intended by the author the reader must, as far as possible, be aware of these constraints.

The meaning effect of the text also results from the interaction of other structures, i.e., the text presupposes these additional structures even though they might be manifested only indirectly or partially. Yet the text as manifestation suggests these other structures in a way that is sufficient to evoke them for the readers who can then apprehend those dimensions of the meaning effect to whose production these structures contributed. For instance, a text might manifest only a few elements of the narrative structure: this is enough for the reader to identify it as a narrative. In terms of our previous analogy when the weaver gives the product of his work to another person, this person can identify it as a blanket and eventually decide to buy it because its design is pleasing to him (i.e., its design is "meaningful"). These woven threads suggested or evoked structures which allowed the buyer to acknowledge the *value* of this thing. (We use value as a technical term: the value of something is its place in a structure.)

Thus, a text is meaningful only insofar as it evokes for the readers not only *the structures of the enunciation,* but also other structures which presided over its creation. In most instances this process is not conscious: one simply acknowledges a text as being meaningful. This implies that both the author and the reader could refer to these structures. Some of these structures are common only to a group of people. These are the *"cultural codes"* or *"cultural structures"* which are generally conscious structures and are also studied by means of traditional methods.

There are still other structures which every man seems to presuppose and which appear to be buried in the unconscious of man *qua* man. For this reason they have been compared with the Jungian archetypes (despite important differences between the Jungian and structuralist theories).[1] Since these structures belong to man *qua* man they have the property (among others) of being *achronic* (transhistorical) and their specific actualizations can be apprehended as a whole in the *synchrony* of any specific point of history. Since these structures are buried in the unconscious they

1. Cf., for instance, R. J. Z. Werblowsky, "Structure and Archetype" in *The Gaster Festschrift (The Journal of the Ancient Near Eastern Society of Columbia University,* vol. 5, 1973): 435–42.

are usually termed *deep structures*. These structures are the primary object of structural studies.

The fundamental theoretical tenets on which the structural analysis of text is based can now be summarized as follows. A meaningful text is a text which has a meaning effect. The meaning effect is produced by the complex interaction of a series of structures. These structures as constraints select from the potential semantic features of each word the features which will participate in the meaning effect. There are *three types of structures* (we could also say "three structural levels"): the *structures of the enunciation* (the constraints brought about by the author as an individual or as a group, and his situation in life); the *cultural structures* (the constraints which characterize a specific culture); the *deep structures* (which characterize man *qua* man). The structures of the enunciation and the cultural structures are most commonly studied by means of the traditional methods. Consequently, in this short book, we shall not discuss them. Yet it should be emphasized that structural analysis at these two levels (and especially at the level of cultural structures) is quite useful because it allows for a more systematic study. The deep structures are the primary objects of structural studies. We shall focus our presentation upon them so as to show how a knowledge of these structures can be used in biblical exegesis. The structural methods are thus to be seen as analytical tools analogous to—but operating on a level different from—the methods of form criticism, tradition criticism, text criticism, etc.

Syntagm and Paradigm

A structural analysis of a text is thus the study of the structures which presided over its creation. It can be viewed as the deconstruction of the meaning effect of a text. The text is decomposed into its basic elements which are then identified as belonging to various structures. The reader first apprehends the basic elements of the text as organized according to an order which manifests primarily the author's intentionality (e.g., the logical order of an argument). This order is produced by the structures of the enunciation. Each element of the text is associated with the elements which precede and follow it in the text. This is what the structuralists often call the *syntagmatic* order: the linear, chain-like order of the manifestation. The text as a whole is viewed as a *syntagm* in which each element receives its *value* through its relationship with what precedes and what follows.

The elements of the text can also be viewed as being associated with each other by various cultural structures and deep structures. In such a case these elements are not simply viewed as being associated with what precedes and follows them in the syntagmatic order of the text, but also with the other elements scattered throughout the text which belong to the same *system* characterized by a specific structure. Gathering the elements which belong together in a given system is performed through a *paradigmatic* reading of the text, i.e., a "vertical" reading which does not follow any longer the linear, horizontal syntagmatic order of the text.

A paradigmatic reading gathers together the elements which manifest in the text a given structure. Yet it should be kept in mind that *these elements manifest only a part of this structure*: they evoke, suggest, and presuppose the structure. Thus in the paradigmatic reading of any text one cannot expect to find the whole structure. The structure has to be reconstructed from the few of its elements which are manifested. Let us take an example by analyzing an aspect of the following text.

> The tourist after much hesitation chose a blanket. Its price, five dollars, seemed quite reasonable. Pulling a five dollar bill from his wallet he gave it to the artisan, took the blanket and drove away.

In the syntagmatic reading the five dollar bill is associated with the blanket and is an element of the transaction. But it is also assumed throughout this brief text that the five dollar bill has a *value* because it belongs to the monetary system. The value of the bill is determined in opposition to the respective values of other bills and coins. This monetary system is manifested by only one of its elements (the five dollar bill) although it is presupposed in its entirety. Without such a presupposition the text would lose an essential part of its meaning.

The preceding example presents in the simplest terms a very rough approximation of structural analysis (a monetary structure is part of a cultural structure). Nevertheless it should suffice to illustrate that a cultural or deep structure needs to be *reconstructed*. And indeed the models that the analyst proposes for such structures are *constructs* that he is always ready to modify in view of new evidence (discovered, e.g., through the analysis of other texts). For example, we shall propose below models of two deep structures: the narrative structure and the mythical structure. Each model will have to be considered as the theory which, at the present stage of research, best represents in our view the corresponding structure. They account for what is manifested in the narrative and mythological texts studied so far. Yet they should not be construed as absolute laws. When used for the analysis of texts they have proved to be adequate, although we may discover that these models need to be revised. In this approach our procedure is similar to that of scientists in other fields. For instance, there are several theories about the phenomenon of electricity. These theories remain theories even though their approximate descriptions of the phenomenon present the possibility of using electricity in various ways. Similarly the paradigmatic structures, even though they are constructs, enable the analyst to apprehend more precisely the meaning effect of a text.

It is in linguistics (the study of language at the level of the sentence and of smaller linguistic units) that paradigmatic structures were first identified and that the very concept of paradigmatic structure has been established. The linguistic model is the basis of any structural analysis and needs therefore to be briefly discussed.

Linguistic Model

The present section does not intend to describe the series of linguistic theories (of F. de Saussure, L. Hjelmslev, R. Jakobson, A. Martinet, E. Benveniste, and other linguists) which are the basis upon which structuralist research is being developed. Our sole intention is to present the broad linguistic model which is assumed by the structuralists in fields other than linguistics and increasingly in biblical research. For this purpose we need to venture briefly into a domain foreign to many biblical scholars, that of linguistic theories. We shall limit our presentation to the concepts and the terminology absolutely necessary for the understanding of this fundamental model. Several of the following statements result from opting for certain linguistic theories as opposed to others, from deciding to emphasize certain aspects of the linguistic theories rather than others. We cannot discuss here these options and decisions. Suffice it to say that the model presented here does not pretend to be more than a theory, a construct, which in the view of a significant group of scholars adequately accounts for a part of the linguistic phenomenon.

The basis for this theory was laid by Ferdinand de Saussure in his *Course in General Linguistics*. He proposed the distinction between *speech* (*parole*), i.e., the language as used by an individual speaker in order to convey a specific message, and *language* (*langue*), i.e., "the sum of word-images stored in the minds of all individuals." Thus language is social. "Language is not a function of the speaker; it is a product that is passively assimilated by the individual."[2] Focusing his research at the level of "language," de Saussure pointed out that it is not merely a *list* of words, but an organized whole, a *system* of words which are related to each other in specific ways. The relational network which organizes the words into a system is

2. Ferdinand de Saussure, *Course in General Linguistics* (New York: McGraw-Hill, 1966), pp. 13–14.

what we call a structure of the language (a paradigmatic structure). Yet the situation is more complex because words are not the basic units of language. By progressively deconstructing language into its basic units we shall present the relational network which is the linguistic structure.

The words of a language are signs. They have two related components: a sound-image (a sound when it is articulated, a graphic image when written), and a concept. De Saussure termed the sound-image *signifiant* (commonly translated as *"signifier"*), the concept *signifié* (translated as *"signified"*), and their relation *signification*. A sign is commonly represented as follows:

$$\frac{\text{signifier}}{\text{signified}}$$

Thus the sign "tree" has for signifier the sound-image "tree" and for signified the concept "tree."

Other scholars (following Hjelmslev) represent the sign as a *relation* (de Saussure's signification) between the *expression* (de Saussure's signifier) and the *content* (de Saussure's signified).

$$\frac{\text{signifier}}{\text{signified}} \quad \begin{array}{l}\text{Expression} \\ \text{Relation} \\ \text{Content.}\end{array}$$

The signification can be viewed as a process which unites signifier and signified into a sign. The relation between signifier and signified is part of the linguistic structural network because it is *arbitrary* (not motivated), since the two components have different "natures," that is, there is no inherent relation between the sound or expression "tree" and the concept or content "tree." Hence in different languages various successions of phonetic (or graphic) elements are related to similar concepts. Furthermore this relation is *necessary*. A signifier cannot exist without a signified (it would not be a signifier but a sound without signification). Similarly a signified cannot exist without signifier (i.e., without some kind of expression). This relation is a part of the linguistic structural network.

The meaning of a sign includes not only its signification (as defined above) but also its *value* which is determined by the correlation (or opposition) of this sign with other signs into a system characterized by a structure.[3] This distinction between signification

3. Obviously "signification" and "value" are closely interrelated since both belong to the sign. We introduce the term "meaning" to express this combination of signification and value. At first F. de Saussure did not emphasize the concept of value, but progressively he pointed it out as the very characteristic of the sign to the point that it included the signification. Without denying this view, we believe it to be necessary in the process of deconstructing the linguistic phenomenon to mark clearly the distinction between signification and value.

and value is the most important of de Saussure's contributions. We are spontaneously aware that words have significations but we have the tendency to neglect the fact that they also have values. At the level of the signifieds, for instance, the fact that in English the word "education" is first of all associated with "school," "teacher," "books," determines the value of the word "education" in a way quite different from the value it has in another language in which "education" is first of all associated with "good manners." Similarly, at the level of the signifier, in a specific language, certain sounds are spontaneously associated with other sounds and certain combinations of sounds are possible while others are not. The structure of a system of signs is purely *formal*: it is made up of correlations and oppositions. Or in de Saussure's words:

> The conceptual [signified] side of value is made up solely of relations and differences with respect to the other terms of language, and the same can be said of its material [signifier] side.[4]

The preceding quotation suggests that in a system of signs the value of a sign is determined at its two levels, that is, in terms of the correlations of its signifier with the other signifiers and of its signified with the other signifieds.

Thus in order to carry de Saussure's theory to its logical end we have to go beyond it with another linguist, L. Hjelmslev.[5] His theory about the sign can be schematized as follows:

$$\text{Expression (or signifier)} \begin{cases} \text{form} \\ \\ \text{substance} \end{cases}$$

$$\text{Content (or signified)} \begin{cases} \text{form} \\ \\ \text{substance} \end{cases}$$

This schema implies that the sign is a complex linguistic entity. Both signifier ("expression" in Hjelmslev's terminology) and signified ("content" in Hjelmslev's terminology) are defined by their position in their own systems. The *form* of a signifier (or formal internal organization of the signifier) is determined by its position in a *system of signifiers*. Thus the *form* of a given signifier is *a specific manifestation of the structure of a system of signifiers*. The form of the signifier organizes a "substance" (for instance, one or

4. de Saussure, *Course*, pp. 117–18.
5. Louis Hjelmslev, *Prolegomena to a Theory of Language* (Madison: University of Wisconsin, 1961); also, L. Hjelmslev and H. J. Uldall, *Outline of Glossematics* (Copenhagen, 1957).

several *phonemes*, i.e., one or several phonetic units) which can be apprehended independently of its form. The same is true of the signified: it has a form (a specific manifestation of the structure of a system of signifieds) and a substance (one or several *semes*, that is, one or several semantic units). Before giving an example, let us emphasize that the value of a sign is twofold: it is the combination of the form of its signifier (its "value" in a system of signifiers) with the form of its signified (its "value" in a system of signifieds). In other words, in order to determine the value of a sign one needs to study two structures: the structure of the system of signifiers and the structure of the system of signifieds.[6]

Hjelmslev's theory was partly in response to the research in phonology (especially by N. S. Trubetzkoy, A. Martinet, and R. Jakobson)[7] which had demonstrated that the sign was not the basic linguistic unit. For instance, the sign "veau" (French for "calf") has as its signifier two phonemes (/v/ and /o/). These two phonemes are the substance of the signifier. The form of the signifier is determined by the French phonetic system and its structure which opposes this specific combination of phonemes to other phonetic units. Hjelmslev (and following him Greimas) emphasized that the same is true of the signified. The signified of the French word "veau" is made out of three semantic units usually called *semes*: /male/young/cattle. These three semes are the substance of the signifier. The form of the signified is determined by a semantic system and its structure which opposes this combination of semes to other semantic units.

These structures of the systems of signifiers and signified perform a partial selection of the linguistic features which participate in the meaning effect of a discourse expressed in a specific language. As the five dollar bill is defined by its position in the monetary system, so is each word (or sign) defined by its position in *two* systems: a system of signifiers and a system of signifieds. The structures of these systems—respectively the phonetic structure (a structure of the expression) and the semantic structure (a structure of the content)—relate one word with other words in specific ways.[8]

6. In this perspective one understands why the signification and the value of a sign cannot be strictly separated from each other (cf. Note 3 above).

7. N. S. Trubetzkoy, *Principles of Phonology* (Berkeley: University of California, 1969); A. Martinet, *Eléments de linguistique générale* (Paris, 1961); M. Halle and R. Jakobson, *Fundamentals of Language* (The Hague: Mouton, 1956). Cf. also O. Ducrot and T. Todorov, *Dictionnaire encyclopédique des sciences du langage* (Paris: Seuil, 1972), pp. 219–27, from which the following example is borrowed.

8. For the various theories about linguistic structures, see O. Ducrot and T. Todorov, *Dictionnaire encyclopédique*, pp. 115–70, 219–27.

From the Linguistic Model to Semiology

The science of signs, semiology (also called semiotics), is not limited to the study of natural languages (linguistics). In other words, the linguistic model briefly described above can be applied to other levels of the phenomenon of culture which can be viewed as a phenomenon of communication. Such was in substance the assertion of Claude Lévi-Strauss who introduced structural methods in anthropology and in so doing paved the way for structural research in still other fields. He took this decisive step forward in the study of kinship in his massive book, *The Elementary Structures of Kinship*.[9] The following remarks on this work are intended to suggest how and why Lévi-Strauss introduced a broad linguistic model in his anthropological study.

The prohibition of incest is at the basis of any system of kinship. Chapters I through IV of *The Elementary Structures of Kinship* are devoted to an interpretation of this prohibition. Prior to Lévi-Strauss it was understood as resulting either from a social reflection on a natural phenomenon, or from the projection on the social level of feelings and tendencies that human nature can explain entirely. It has also been explained as a rule which was accidentally expressed in biological terms even though it was wholly social in origin. In each case the "prohibition" of incest was understood exclusively in negative terms, as an interdiction. Lévi-Strauss emphasizes that it is also a positive injunction. The prohibition of incest as well as its social expression, exogamy, is a "rule of reciprocity." The woman who is prohibited to me is by this very fact also offered to somebody else. This other man, following the same rule, renounces a woman who therefore directly or indirectly is offered to me. Thus, concludes Lévi-Strauss, the prohibition of incest is instituted in order to secure and to provide a basis for *exchange*, whether directly or indirectly, whether immediately or mediately.[10] The prohibition of incest is the guarantee of and the basis for exchange. It is not the means of exchange: it is the possibility, the potentiality for exchange, i.e., it manifests a part of a *structure* of a system which permits exchanges: a kinship system.

Now what is the nature of these exchanges? A culture is a network of exchanges which occur at various levels: exchanges of physical goods, but also exchanges of social dignities, charges, and privileges as well as exchanges of more abstract entities such as moral values, ideas, etc. At this abstract level where exchange is

9. Claude Lévi-Strauss, *The Elementary Structures of Kinship* (Boston: Beacon, 1969).
10. Ibid., pp. 29–68.

communication, the possibility, the potentiality for exchange is provided in large part by the structures of language, that is, by the structures of a system of signs. Could it be that the various other systems which permit exchanges at various other cultural levels are also systems of *signs*? In view of the similarity in function an affirmative answer to this question can be proposed. Lévi-Strauss verifies it by analyzing the systems of kinship.

The elements of language, the words, are readily apprehended as signs (that is, as relations between specific signifiers and signifieds). The linguists have to make explicit that these signs belong to *systems* of signs. The anthropologist is confronted by the inverse problem. It is accepted that the elements of kinship refer to a system, a social system with an explicit structure. Yet these elements are not directly apprehended as signs, that is, *as having a signification*. Kinship is viewed as a system, but not as a system of *signs*. By applying the linguistic methodology directly (focusing primarily upon structure) one would elucidate what is well known (the structure of kinship) without making any progress: the *signification* of kinship would remain hidden. The structural methodology would remain useless, because in such a case the sociological system (of kinship) as a mere "system of appellations" would have been simply identified with a linguistic system. In order to be able to apply the structural methodology as used in linguistics, it is necessary to overcome the commonly accepted definition of the kinship system in the same way as the linguist must bracket out the system of speech (*parole*) before being able to consider language as a system of signs. Thus Lévi-Strauss proposed that at the synchronic level the system of kinship be viewed as a "system of attitudes." This trans-mutation involves the passage from the linguistic level to the socio-logical level: a "system of attitudes" is a sociological system. Attitudes are signs, that is, attitudes have a signification which is immediately perceived. But the *values* of the attitudes appear only when one can show how these attitudes are related to each other. This structure needs to be elucidated. With the transposition of the system of kinship from a "system of appellations" to a "system of attitudes" the problem becomes similar to that of language. The linguistic model can now be applied. If such a structure can be elucidated, the hypothesis will be demonstrated. *The Elementary Structures of Kinship* is the demonstration proposed by Lévi-Strauss.

In such a brief sketch we cannot explain how Lévi-Strauss transposed linguistic structural methodology in order to use it in anthropology. Following a part of his argument in *Structural Anthropology*, Chapter II, we aim simply at suggesting the dynamics of this transposition. Structural anthropology became possible when it renounced any (conscious or unconscious) pretension to uncover a linguistic structure. Such uncovering would be a legitimate endeavor on its own: terms of kinship do indeed also belong to a *linguistic* system of signs. Yet the linguistic *model* remains valid in anthropological systems. Although different from language itself, social phenomena are indeed a "language" (as Lévi-Strauss puts it at times). An anthropological system is made up of signs kept together by a structure. This is so, Lévi-Strauss explains, because the model first discovered in linguistics is universal. It is characteristic of the human mind (*l'esprit humain*) and hence also of human nature. Such a model is not cultural.[11] This is why the linguistic model can and must be adopted by the anthropologist.

Let us emphasize that. The first step in any structural analysis is *the identification of a system of signs.* At this point we need to reintroduce the concept of the "unconscious." Some systems are conscious: as such they are readily identifiable as systems—e.g., the system of kinship. In such a case a conscious structure is apparent: it belongs either to the level of the enunciation or to the cultural level, that is, levels where historical investigation is possible. The structuralist, aiming at the deep structures, must dissociate the elements of the system from the somewhat more apparent structures of the enunciation and cultural structures in order to identify anew the system. What at the conscious level appears as a system of appellations is now viewed as a system of attitudes, a system of signs of which the structure provides the possibility for exchanges.

This transposition of the analysis to a system of signs hidden in the depth of the phenomenon is in no way an artificial process. Exchange and communication are possible only when the "things" to be exchanged have been transmuted into signs (which at times Lévi-Strauss also terms "symbols"). As Lévi-Strauss expresses it:

> In fact it is not a matter of translating into symbols extrinsic data but to reduce to their nature, which is symbolic, things which escape it only to become uncommunicable.[12]

For our purposes we do not need to discuss in detail *The Elementary Structures of Kinship.* Our brief comments about Lévi-Strauss' approach to the study of kinship only intend to suggest that the linguistic model indeed applies to cultural phenomena beyond

---

11. Cf. Claude Lévi-Strauss, *Structural Anthropology* (New York: Basic Books, 1963), Chapter II. For the distinction between nature and culture, see *Elementary Structures,* Chapter I.
12. "Introduction à l'oeuvre de Marcel Mauss," in Marcel Mauss, *Sociologie et anthropologie* (Paris: P.U.F., 1959), XXXII (my translation).

language itself. Lévi-Strauss opened a new field of investigation, semiology (a term which is generally used to designate the study of systems of signs other than language). Roland Barthes contributed most significantly to the development of this field.[13] The identification of the various systems of signs is still in process and the precise interrelation of these various systems with each other and with the linguistic system still needs to be formulated. For instance, the linguistic system is related to other systems in that it provides one of their means of expression. Thus language can provide the signifiers for the social system (for instance, the terminology about kinship). In such a case the linguistic signs (words) are elements of the *signifiers* of macro-signs. We term "macro-signs" the elements of communication systems which are larger than the linguistic signs (words). The structures of the systems of macro-signs can be termed semiotic structures.

As a consequence of semiological research we can affirm that in a given text there is a complex network of structures at work, not only the hierarchy of linguistic structures described above, but also a similar hierarchy of structures of systems of macro-signs. Rather than attempting to speak about a large number of these structures we chose to focus our work on two semiotic structures of content. They belong to two semiological systems which have been sufficiently identified so that we can now begin to study them systematically at the level of their structures of content: the narrative system and the mythical system. In view of the fact that the Bible is composed of religious texts and to a great extent of narrative texts (sacred historical texts), we can foresee that narrative and mythical structures are among the structures which produce the meaning effect of the Bible. In other words, the elements of the biblical text presuppose, suggest, evoke these structures and in doing so "made sense" for the readers of that time. These structures characterize man *qua* man. We are also presupposing them in our own discourses. We will now deal with narrative structures and mythical structures, proposing for each an example of structural exegesis.

---

13. Among Roland Barthes' works see especially, *Writing Degree Zero and Elements of Semiology* (Boston: Beacon, 1970); *Critical Essays* (Evanston: Northwestern University, 1972); "Introduction à l'analyse structurale des récits," *Communications* 8, 1966. He published two essays of structural analysis of biblical texts: "L'analyse structurale du récit: a propos d'Actes 10–11," *Exégèse et Herméneutique* (Paris: Seuil, 1971), pp. 181–204; and "La lutte avec l'ange: Analyse textuelle de Genèse 32:23–33," in *Analyse structurale et exégèse biblique* (Neuchâtel: Delachaux et Niestlé, 1971); English translation in *Structural Analysis and Biblical Exegesis* (Pittsburgh: The Pickwick Press, 1974).

III

Narrative Structures and Exegesis

In the preceding chapters we suggested why structural exegesis is needed and the broad scope of this undertaking. It is not a matter of developing one structural exegetical method, but a set of such methods. This work has just begun. The meeting of biblical scholars gathered together at Chantilly (France)[1] in September 1969 can be considered as the starting point of systematic research for the development of these new exegetical tools.

Most structural analyses of biblical texts published so far have been focused on the study of narrative structures (or of some aspects of such structures). Each of these essays on structural exegesis (listed in the bibliography below) contributes in its own way to the development of the method and is as such a platform from which new methodological explorations can be launched. Our discussion of "narrative structure and exegesis" has to be viewed in the context of this fast moving methodological quest. It is not an attempt to retrace the various stages of the development of the method. Rather, on the basis of these various essays in structural biblical exegesis published up to December 1974 and also on the basis of the most recent works in structural literary criticism, we shall offer a model for the narrative structures. In this chapter we shall limit ourselves to a discussion of the narrative structures in themselves. The problem of the relation of these structures to other structures is the object of ongoing research. In the limited scope of this book we cannot discuss this problem. Such a dimension requires that all these structures be more clearly identified: we hope that the following formulation of a model for the narrative structures will contribute to this research. As an illustration of this method we shall propose an interpretation of the parable of the Good Samaritan.

A narrative as a whole is a means of communication. The storyteller through his "expression" of the story communicates a story "content." This already suggests that a narrative can be viewed as

1. The papers and discussions of this conference have been published in the collective volume, *Exégèse et Herméneutique* (Paris: Seuil, 1971).

a macro-sign which belongs to a system of macro-signs, i.e., to a system of narratives which theoretically includes all the narratives of a culture. A narrative is a whole (a sign) which has a "signification": the relation of its expression (signifier) to its content (signified). Yet a narrative as any sign also has a "value," the value "narrativity"; that is, its forms of the expression and of the content which are the ways in which some of the potentialities of the corresponding structures of the system of narrative signs are actualized in this specific narrative.

When confronted with certain texts we identify them as narrative: that is, we acknowledge that they have the value "narrativity." What evokes this value for us? First we can note that the value "narrativity" is communicated by the overall text and not by its isolated elements. For instance, even if a text includes references to a sheriff, Indians, and outlaws, it is not necessarily a narrative. Thus we can even specify that the value, narrativity, is determined by the structure of the *content*. For indeed the same narrative content can be expressed in various natural languages as well as in cinematography, painting, mime, etc. A change of expression (signifier) does not remove the value of narrativity, even though other aspects of the meaning effect are modified. There are indeed distinctions between, e.g., "cinematographic narrativity," and "natural language narrativity," and further between "oral" and "written" natural language narrativity, and still further among Hebrew, Greek, and English written narrativity, etc. But the value "narrativity" remains. It is thus determined by the structure of the content. In studying the narrative structure we shall therefore study the structure which is actualized in the forms of the signifieds of the signs "narratives."

A narrative text actualizes in the form of its content a part of the narrative structure and thus evokes it. This implies that such a narrative structure cannot be established on the ground of the study of any given narrative. Even when a great number of such texts have been analyzed, the model of the narrative structure remains a construct open to modifications. But as soon as a model (however tentative it might be) is established it can be used for the study of other texts: it offers a helpful starting point for the analysis even though one may be led to transform it.

A model for the narrative structure has been proposed by A. J. Greimas on the basis of V. Propp's pioneering study of Russian folk tales and E. Souriau's study of classical plays.[2] For our purpose it

2. V. Propp, *Morphology of the Folktale* (Austin: University of Texas, 1963); V. Propp, "Transformations in Fairy Tales" in *Mythology: Selected Readings,*

is not necessary to discuss how these authors progressively established this model. It is enough to present it and to take an example to show how the structure is actualized in a specific biblical text. The model of the narrative structure proposed by Greimas includes six hierarchically distinct elements which we denote as sequence, syntagm, statement, actantial model, function, and actant. We shall illustrate this theoretical explanation with a brief analysis of the parable of the Good Samaritan. We introduce various technical terms in order to facilitate the reading of works on structural analysis of narrative.

1) *Sequences*
The general framework of the narrative structure is provided by a series of sequences of narrative elements. Sequences can also be termed "narrative programs" (*programmes narratifs*). There are three types of sequences: the *correlated sequences* (the initial and the final sequences), the *topical sequences* (so called because their actualizations form the main "topic" of the narrative), and the *subsequences* (their actualizations complement either the correlated or topical sequences). Thus the broader narrative structure presents the following succession of sequences:

—initial correlated sequence
—one or several topical sequences
—final correlated sequence.

A brief example is the best way to express what these sequences

ed. P. Maranda, (Baltimore, Md.: Penguin, 1972), pp. 139–50; E. Souriau, *Les 200,000 situations dramatiques* (Paris: 1950); A.-J. Greimas, *Sémantique structurale: Recherche de méthode* (Paris, Larousse, 1966); A.-J. Greimas, *Du sens: Essais sémiotiques* (Paris: Seuil, 1970); A.-J. Greimas, ed., *Essais de sémiotique poétique* (Paris, Larousse, 1972); A.-J. Greimas, "The Interpretation of Myth: Theory and Practice," in *Structural Analysis of Oral Tradition*, eds. P. Maranda and E. Köngäs Maranda, (Philadelphia: University of Pennsylvania, 1971), pp. 81–121; A.-J. Greimas, "Les actants, les acteurs et les figures," in *Sémiotique narrative et textuelle*, ed. C. Chabrol, (Paris: Larousse, 1973). For readings on other aspects of the analysis of narrative see: C. Brémond, "Morphology of the French Folktale," *Semiotica* 2 (1970):247–76; C. Brémond, "Le message narratif," *Communications* 4 (1964):4–32; C. Brémond, "La logique des possibles narratifs," *Communications* 8 (1966): 60–76. T. Todorov, "Les catégories du récit litteraire," *Communications* 8 (1966):125–51; T. Todorov, "Structural Analysis of Narrative," *Novel* 3 (1969–70):70–76; T. Todorov, "Les transformations narratives," *Poétique* 1 (1970):322–33. L. Marin used this method for the analysis of biblical texts: "Essais d'analyse structurale d'Actes 10:1–11:18" in *Exégèse et Herméneutique*, pp. 213–38; L. Marin, "Essai d'analyse structurale d'un récit-parabole: Matthieu 13: 1–25," *Etudes théologiques et religieuses* (1971/1):35–75; L. Marin, "Les femmes au tombeau: Essai d'analyse structurale d'un texte évangélique," *Langages* 22 (June 1971):39–50; L. Marin, "Jésus devant Pilate: Essai d'analyse structurale," *Langages* 22 (June 1971):51–74. L. Marin, *Sémiotique de la Passion* (Paris: Bibliotèque de Sciences Religieuses, 1971). L. Marin, *Etudes sémiologiques* (Paris: Klincksieck, 1971).

are. The Russian folk tales studied by Propp (and reinterpreted by Greimas) manifest the following structure.

A) An initial correlated sequence. A social order which had been functioning is disrupted. There is at least a risk that members of this society will not be able to carry out the *contract* (or *mandate*) that they have received as people participating in this social order. A social order disrupted, a contract which for one reason or another cannot be carried out, is presupposed as the initial situation of any narrative. The rest of the narrative expresses the attempts (successful or not) to reestablish the original social order, or, in other words, to reestablish the possibility of carrying out the original contract. How this social order has been disrupted might be expressed in a sub-sequence that Propp termed "the villainy."

B) A series of topical sequences. These sequences express how a hero (or several heroes) is(are) mandated to reestablish the original social order, and eventually carry out this *topical contract* (a secondary contract not to be confused with the contract of the initial sequence). In Russian folk tales how this topical contract is established is usually expressed in a sub-sequence that Propp termed the "qualifying test": it describes how the hero acquires some type of helper (for instance, a magical object). When he has this helper the hero is in a position to carry out the topical contract which requires him to neutralize whatever disrupts (or threatens to disrupt) the original social order. He then attempts to carry it out. This is the topical sequence termed by Propp "main test." When the hero has been successful he receives still another mandate which, once carried out, provides some type of glorification for the hero. This is another sub-sequence termed by Propp "glorifying test."[3] When a topical sequence is unsuccessful another topical sequence might be introduced.

C) Final correlated sequence. The social order (or contract) of the initial sequence is reestablished. The members of this social order can carry out their mandate. The final correlated sequence is actualized only if a topical sequence is successful. Yet it is always hoped for by the reader.

The succession of sequences (an initial correlated sequence, one or several topical sequences, and a final correlated sequence) is the general framework of a deep structure, the narrative structure. Let us emphasize once more that this complete structure is presupposed by

---

3. The "qualifying and glorifying tests" are subsequences of the topical sequence because they express secondary aspects of the hero's story: how the hero obtains the helpers he needs (qualifying test) and how he is clearly manifested as hero (glorifying test). The "main test" is the topical sequence because it expresses what solves the problem brought about by the villainy.

any narrative (as sign of a narrative system), although a specific narrative might be the actualization of only a part of this structure. For example, a narrative may manifest only a part of a topical sequence (how a hero subdues a villain). We recognize such a text as narrative because it evokes and presupposes the rest of the structure.

In the parable of the Good Samaritan the initial correlated sequence is manifested in the first verse (yet note that the order of the text does not necessarily follow the order of the paradigmatic narrative structure): "A man was going down from Jerusalem to Jericho and he fell among robbers, who stripped him and beat him and departed, leaving him half dead" (Luke 10:30). The "man" was in the process of performing an action which presumably had a purpose: he was going to Jericho in order to do something. This sequence of the man, the initial sequence, is interrupted by the robbers. The actions of the robbers are the villainy, a sub-sequence which explains how the sequence of the man has been interrupted. The purpose of the rest of the narrative is to reestablish the possibility of fulfilling this initial sequence.

In the parable we find three topical sequences: the first two abort, the third one is carried out. Both the priest and the Levite refuse the topical contract: they refuse to attempt to help the man. Consequently these two topical sequences abort. By contrast the Samaritan accepts this contract and carries it out. He is therefore the hero who helps the wounded man.

The parable does not tell us if the Samaritan's action is successful or not (this is not the point that the author of this specific narrative wants to make). Yet if the action is successful, i.e., if the man is fully reestablished in his former position, we would then expect him to carry out his initial business in one way or another. This final correlated sequence is not actualized in our text.

2) Narrative Syntagms

Each sequence is made out of a succession of three narrative syntagms. This element of the narrative structure is called syntagm because it is made up of a succession, a chain-like series, of smaller "narrative elements" (it should not be confused with the syntagmatic order of the text).

We term the three narrative syntagms of a sequence: the contract syntagm, the disjunction/conjunction syntagm, and the performance syntagm. The *contract syntagm* expresses the establishment of the contract (for instance, the original contract of an initial sequence or the contract of a topical sequence). The contract syntagm can also be termed "narrative program." The *disjunction/conjunction syntagm* expresses the movements of those who have received a contract. They separate themselves from people, things, places (disjunction), and join other people, things, places (conjunction) in order to fulfill their contract. The *performance syntagm* expresses the carrying out of the contract.

In the topical sequence of the parable in which the Samaritan is present these three syntagms are concisely actualized. The contract syntagm is manifested in the words "when he saw him, he had compassion" (Luke 10:33). Seeing the wounded man the Samaritan felt he was called (mandated) to do something. His acceptance of this contract is expressed by the statement "he had compassion." The disjunction/conjunction syntagm is manifested in the words "and went to him." In order to fulfill the contract which he has accepted he must approach the wounded man. The rest of the Samaritan's actions manifest the performance syntagm: this is the Samaritan's performance of his contract.

3) *Narrative Statements*

Each syntagm is made out of narrative statements which are elements of the narrative structure. As "narrative statement" is used technically, it denotes a *structural* unit in which two basic elements of the narrative structure (the "functions" and the "actants") are combined. At the level of the manifestation, the structural unit "statement" becomes actualized in the description of one action (or a series of actions) of a personage in relation to other personages and things. There are a number of canonical statements, that is, of statements to which any combination of "functions" and "actants" can be reduced. Before explaining further what the narrative statements are we need to deal with "functions" and "actants."

4) *Canonical Narrative Functions*

The canonical functions (i.e., functions as elements of the narrative structure and not functions as found in the manifestation) are actualized in the manifestation by the various verbs of action (the predicates of the class of "doing"). In other words, the following list of functions has been obtained by reducing an infinite set of variables (all the predicates of the class of "doing") to a limited number of structural constants. Most of the canonical functions present themselves in binary oppositions. These functions are listed and briefly explained by Jean Calloud.[4] We cannot do better than translate Calloud's presentation.

4. Jean Calloud, *L'analyse structurale du récit. Elements de méthode. Tentations de Jésus au desert* (Lyon: Profac, 1973), pp. 16–17. English translation by Daniel Patte, *Structural Analysis of Narrative* (Philadelphia: Fortress Press, 1976).

Arrival vs. Departure	
Departure vs. Return:	These functions are interrelated according to the category "movement" or "presence/absence."
Conjunction vs. Disjunction:	Encounter of personages with other personages or their separation. Relation through spatial contiguity.
Mandating vs. Acceptance or vs. Refusal:	An action is implicitly or explicitly proposed to an actor who accepts it or refuses it.
Confrontation: (or Affrontment)	Presented in isolation as it is, this function raises special problems. Two actors confronting each other are exactly in symmetrical positions. It could eventually be viewed as a binary opposition: Confrontation vs. Association (on the basis of the category Exclusion vs. Integration).
Domination vs. Submission:	Victory vs. Defeat as end-product of the preceding function.
Communication vs. Reception:	On the axis of the transmission (or transfer) of any kind of "objects."
Attribution vs. Deprivation:	This is another way to express the preceding function by opposing it to its negative form.

In the manifestation, any predicate of the class of "doing" presupposes, evokes, suggests one or another of these seven canonical functions.

In the topical sequence of the parable several canonical functions are manifested: mandating ("when he saw him"), acceptance ("he had compassion"), conjunction ("and went to him"), disjunction or departure (the Samaritan leaves: Luke 10:35), and confrontation (the Samaritan confronts the effects of the robbers' action). Several actions of the Samaritan should lead to the domination (a successful healing of the wounds) but this function is not actualized. The "attribution" (of health to the wounded man) is not actualized either but is hoped for.

5) *Actants and Actantial Model*

As with the functions, the "actants" have been obtained by reducing an infinite set of variables (the various personages of the various narratives) to a limited number of structural constants—"actantial roles" or "actants" or spheres of action. Actants are therefore structural elements which should not be confused with the actors of the manifestation.

There are six actants which form together the actantial model:

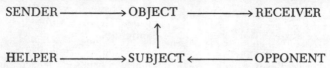

In order to avoid any confusion with other usages the terms designating the actants will be capitalized. It is appropriate to discuss the three axes along which the six actants lie.

The axis of Communication: SENDER *(destinateur)*, OBJECT *(objet)*, RECEIVER *(destinataire)*. Along this axis lie all the phenomena of communication, transference, transmission, and virtual or real reception. The SENDER is the actantial position of the personages who propose to communicate something (OBJECT) to somebody else (RECEIVER). Such a communication can be either fulfilled or frustrated. In this latter case this axis expresses deprivation, lack, quest, etc.

The SENDER is the actantial position of the personages who determine what OBJECT needs to be communicated to which RECEIVER. Thus the SENDER initiates a program of action: a mandate. This mandate is given by the SENDER to a personage who will assume the position of SUBJECT.

Upon this axis the OBJECT is first defined as "what is communicated" by the SENDER or "what is lacking" to the RECEIVER. It receives another definition on the axis of volition.

The axis of Volition: SUBJECT *(sujet)*, OBJECT *(objet)*. This is the axis of the plot, of the project (volition). Through various actions the personage in the position of SUBJECT facilitates the communication by suppressing the obstacles which hinder it. Without the SUBJECT the transference of the OBJECT would not be possible, but the communication does not originate with the SUBJECT. Again the communication is initiated by the SENDER.[5]

The OBJECT is further defined by its relation to the SUBJECT as that which he wills to attribute to the RECEIVER.

The axis of Power: HELPER *(adjuvant)*, SUBJECT *(sujet)*, OPPONENT *(opposant)*. Upon this axis the SUBJECT is further defined in terms of the "power" needed to pass from volition to action. This "power" is provided to the SUBJECT in the form of

5. Cf. Calloud, *op. cit.,* p. 26.

the HELPER. The HELPER can be personages but may also be qualities, information, knowledge, or inanimate objects. The OPPONENT is the negative power (opposing force, negative qualities, villains, or inanimate evil objects). It can be viewed as the ANTI-SUBJECT (which it becomes explicitly when it overcomes the SUBJECT and his HELPER) of an anti-actantial model, that is, of an actantial model actualized with inverse values.

This actantial model is presupposed, evoked, suggested by any personage of the manifestation even though only a part of the model might be actualized. It should be noted that the same personage of the manifestation may actualize several actantial positions.

In the topical sequence of the parable each of the actants is actualized with the exception of the SENDER. This is the case in many narratives: the SENDER often is an abstract entity (e.g., God, destiny, chance, a society as a whole, conscience) which is not directly manifested. The RECEIVER is the wounded man; the OBJECT, health; the SUBJECT, the Samaritan; the HELPER, know-how, oil, wine, donkey, money, and innkeeper; and the OPPONENT, the robbers and the effects of their action. We can represent the investment of the actantial model in this sequence as follows:

SENDER	OBJECT	RECEIVER
?	health	wounded man

HELPER	SUBJECT	OPPONENT
know-how, oil, wine, donkey, money, innkeeper	Samaritan	Robbers and effects of their action

The Syntagms of a Sequence

After this brief description of the elements of the narrative structure (sequences, syntagms, statements, functions, and actants) we can now show how these elements are interrelated in a sequence. In this process the concept "statement" will be further clarified. We shall identify three types of "statements" distinguished according to their place and role in the sequence: *"process statement"*; *"modal statement"*; *"state statement"* or *"qualification."*

The sequence begins with a *contractual syntagm*. It defines and establishes (implicitly in most instances) each of the actantial positions. The communicator of the mandate is the SENDER. The SENDER designates the SUBJECT (the receptor of the mandate). The mandate defines the OBJECT to be transmitted and the RECEIVER who needs this OBJECT. The HELPER which is communicated together with the mandate to the SUBJECT also presupposes the OPPONENT: HELPER and OPPONENT are symmetrical.

The contract syntagm is made out of two *contractual statements*. CS 1 and CS 2 will be used to refer to these statements.

CS 1: The first statement includes two successive and symmetric functions: mandating + acceptance, or mandating + refusal. If the contract (which can be a positive mandate or a prohibition) is refused the sequence aborts and the following steps do not take place. This is the case of the sequences of the priest and Levite. If the contract is accepted by an actor, he is instituted in the actantial position of SUBJECT. In this latter case the SUBJECT is invested with a first *modality, volition*: he has the will to carry out a specific mandate. When imposed from without this modality can be termed *obligation*.[6] CS 1 can be manifested in either a "modal statement of volition" or in a "process statement." When the statement expresses that the SUBJECT *has* "will," as in the sequence of the Samaritan, it is a "modal statement of volition": the Samaritan *has* compassion (cf. diagram p. 49). When the statement expresses the process of communication through which the SUBJECT was convinced to accept the mandate (i.e., was made to have "volition"), it is a "process statement of volition."

CS 2: This statement includes the functions communication + reception. Among the objects communicated are various HELPERS which will enable the SUBJECT to carry out his mandate. If the SUBJECT is prevented from receiving his HELPER either the sequence aborts here or will be unsuccessful later. If he receives it the SUBJECT is invested with the other modalities, *power* and *cognition*: he has now the power and the knowledge (or know-how) necessary for carrying out the mandate. Consequently CS 2 can be either a "modal statement of power and/or cognition" or a "process statement" of communication. In the sequence of the Samaritan CS 2 is not actualized (consequently we leave it blank in the diagram p. 49). Yet it is presupposed: the Samaritan has helpers which are revealed as they are used.

The actualization of the actantial model in the contract syntagm is thus a potential program of action (a potential performance) which is actualized in the following syntagms.

The *disjunction/conjunction syntagm* is the first stage of the

6. As suggested by Michael Rengstorf in the yet unpublished paper on "The Modalities according to A.-J. Greimas and a Semiotic Analysis of Flaubert," presented at the colloquium on Biblical Semiotics, Annecy (France) July 1974. The technical vocabulary of this chapter—translation of Greimas' French terminology—has been established in collaboration with Michael Rengstorf who is preparing a translation of Greimas' work.

realization of the contract. If the contract is accepted the actor who becomes SUBJECT leaves his former network of relations (relations with things, locations, and other actors) and is associated with other things, locations, and actors. A disjunction/conjunction syntagm is made out of one statement (disjunctional statement or DS) which includes the successive functions arrival + departure, or departure + return, thus movements and encounters of actors.

After the completion of the contract we find at times a second DS which is often symmetric to the former (e.g., if the subject arrived in this place, he leaves that place). In fact this narrative statement is a DS of another sequence: the personage performs the movement which will allow him to carry out another contract. The disjunction/conjunction syntagms are easy to recognize in a text and help to delimit the sequences. When a movement takes place a contract has been accepted. Another movement indicates that another sequence is introduced.

The disjunction/conjunction syntagm presupposes the actantial model of the contract. The actor instituted in the actantial position of SUBJECT is both subject and object of the movement: he moves himself in order to take his position as SUBJECT of the actantial model proposed in the contract. The OPPONENT might prevent the disjunction. In such a case the sequence is interrupted at this point: in the parable of the Good Samaritan the sequence of the man is interrupted by the robbers at the disjunction/conjunction syntagm (cf. diagram p. 47). If the movement of the SUBJECT takes place as in the sequence of the Samaritan (cf. diagram p. 49) the performance syntagm is introduced.

The *performance syntagm* expresses how the contract is carried out. It is made out of a succession of three "process statements" characterized by the following functions. The performance statements will be termed PS 1, PS 2, and PS 3.

PS 1. Function: Confrontation. The SUBJECT confronts the "lack" (i.e., the need that the RECEIVER has of the OBJECT) which is directly or indirectly provoked by the OPPONENT. The confrontation can be accepted or refused. If it is refused the sequence is interrupted. If it is accepted the second performance statement is introduced.

PS 2. Function: Domination vs. Submission. If the SUBJECT is submitted to the OPPONENT the sequence is interrupted here. If the SUBJECT dominates the OPPONENT he can then carry out his mandate: the following statement is introduced.

PS 3. Function: Attribution. The OBJECT which fulfills the lack is given to the RECEIVER. This attribution is facilitated by the SUBJECT. PS 3 is the end of the sequence. If the sequence reaches

PS 3 it has succeeded and when the attribution is completed the sequence ends. The subject leaves the network of relations demanded by the contract. He relinquishes the position of SUBJECT. Both PS 1 and PS 2 are actualized in the sequence of the Samaritan, yet we do not know if the object "health" has actually been attributed or not, i.e., if PS 2 is an actual domination of the opponent. Consequently we leave PS 3 blank (cf. diagram p. 49).

The following schema attempts to represent a sequence. It has been devised as a form for recording the actualization of a sequence in a given narrative. Each set of six blocks (labeled CS 1, CS 2, DS 1, PS 1, PS 2, and PS 3) corresponds to a narrative statement within the sequence and represents the actantial model, which might or might not have been actualized either partially or fully.

This form is such that it allows the recording not only of the functions and actants which are actualized in the text but also the locating of this actualization in the textual manifestation. For this purpose the text is divided into "lexies," that is, reading units which actualize one narrative statement. A lexie might be a verse, a part of a verse, or several verses. It is important to record them because as we noted above the textual manifestation does not necessarily follow the order of the structure. This form also allows the recording of the relationship between various sequences. A sub-sequence tells the "story" of one of the actants and in so doing further defines the actualization of this actant. It is therefore important to record exactly at which place in the structure this actant is further defined. The following forms have been filled in so as to record the sequence of the man (sequence #1 in the text, the initial correlated sequence), the sub-sequence of the robbers (sequence #2 in the text, the villainy), and the sequence of the Samaritan (sequence #5 in the text, a topical sequence). The sequences of the priest and of the Levite (sequences #3 and #4 in the text) are interrupted at the level of the contractual statement #1: the contract is refused, i.e., volition is not established. It is enough to provide the actualization of the contractual statement #1 (CS 1) of these two sequences (that we write in a single model).

Lexie no. 31 and 32	CS 1	Mandating
	Health, vigor	Man
	Priest Levite	Robbers and the effects of their actions

Sub-sequence of Qualification ☐
Volition *not* established ☒   *sequence interrupted*
Volition established ☐   to CS 2

Luke
NARRATIVE NO. 10:30-35   TITLE Good Samaritan

SEQUENCE NO. IN THE TEXT 1

CORRELATED
SEQUENCE NO. 1   OR   □ TOPICAL
                              SEQUENCE NO. _____

□□□ SUB-SEQUENCE }
    -OR-   }—OF— _____ ;FROM _____ ; _____
    QUALIFICATION }   (ACTANT)   (SEQUENCE)   (STATEMENT)

CONTRACT SYNTAGM

LEXIE NO. _____   CS1   MANDATING
□ □
□ □

SUB-SEQUENCE OR QUALIFICATION?
□ VOLITION NOT ESTABLISHED   □ SEQUENCE INTERRUPTED
  VOLITION ESTABLISHED   □ TO CS2

LEXIE NO. _____   CS2   COMMUNICATION
□ □
□ □

SUB-SEQUENCE OR QUALIFICATION?
□ POWER AND/OR COGNITION NOT RECEIVED   □ SEQUENCE INTERRUPTED
□ POWER AND/OR COGNITION RECEIVED   □ TO DS

DISJUNCTION/CONJUNCTION SYNTAGM

LEXIE NO. 30a   DS   MOVEMENT

FROM PERSON _____   TO PERSON _____
PLACE Jerusalem   PLACE Jericho
THING _____   THING _____

□ □   Man   X   Robbers
□ □   X

SUB-SEQUENCE OR QUALIFICATION?
X MOVEMENT NOT COMPLETED   □ SEQUENCE INTERRUPTED
□ MOVEMENT COMPLETED   □ TO PS1

PERFORMANCE SYNTAGM

LEXIE NO. _____   PS1   CONFRONTATION
□ □
□ □

SUB-SEQUENCE OR QUALIFICATION?
□ CONFRONTATION REFUSED   □ SEQUENCE INTERRUPTED
□ CONFRONTATION ACCEPTED   □ TO PS2

LEXIE NO. _____   PS2   DOMINATION/SUBMISSION
□ □
□ □

SUB-SEQUENCE OR QUALIFICATION?
□ SUBMISSION   □ SEQUENCE INTERRUPTED
□ DOMINATION   □ TO PS3

LEXIE NO. _____   PS3   ATTRIBUTION
□ □
□ □

SUB-SEQUENCE OR QUALIFICATION?
□ NOT COMPLETED   □ SEQUENCE INTERRUPTED
□ COMPLETED   □ END OF SEQUENCE

47

CORRELATED SEQUENCE NO. ___ OR TOPICAL SEQUENCE NO. ___

SUB-SEQUENCE ⎫
-OR-   ⎬-OF- Opponent ; FROM 1 ; DS
QUALIFICATION ⎭   (ACTANT)   (SEQUENCE) (STATEMENT)

PERFORMANCE SYNTAGM

LEXIE NO. 30b   CS1   CONFRONTATION

| Their number | Belongings of the man | Robbers |
| | Robbers | The man and his vigor |

SUB-SEQUENCE OR QUALIFICATION?

CONFRONTATION REFUSED   SEQUENCE INTERRUPTED
CONFRONTATION ACCEPTED [X] TO PS2

(Man confronted by robbers).....

LEXIE NO. 30c   PS2   DOMINATION/SUBMISSION

| Their number | Belongings of the man | Robbers |
| | Robbers | The man and his vigor |

SUB-SEQUENCE OR QUALIFICATION?

SUBMISSION   SEQUENCE INTERRUPTED
DOMINATION [X] TO PS3

(Beating of the man).......

LEXIE NO. 30c   PS3   ATTRIBUTION

| | Belongings of the man | Robbers |
| | Robbers | |

SUB-SEQUENCE OR QUALIFICATION?

NOT COMPLETED   SEQUENCE INTERRUPTED
COMPLETED [X] END OF SEQUENCE

(Stripping of the man).......

Luke
NARRATIVE NO. 10:30-35 TITLE Good Samaritan
SEQUENCE NO. IN THE TEXT 2

CONTRACT SYNTAGM

LEXIE NO. ___   CS1   MANDATING

SUB-SEQUENCE OR QUALIFICATION?
VOLITION NOT ESTABLISHED   SEQUENCE INTERRUPTED
VOLITION ESTABLISHED   TO CS2

LEXIE NO. ___   CS2   COMMUNICATION

SUB-SEQUENCE OR QUALIFICATION?
POWER AND/OR COGNITION NOT RECEIVED   SEQUENCE INTERRUPTED
POWER AND/OR COGNITION RECEIVED   TO DS

DISJUNCTION/CONJUNCTION SYNTAGM

LEXIE NO. ___   DS   MOVEMENT

FROM PERSON ___   TO PERSON
PLACE ___   PLACE
THING ___   THING

SUB-SEQUENCE OR QUALIFICATION?
MOVEMENT NOT COMPLETED   SEQUENCE INTERRUPTED
MOVEMENT COMPLETED   TO PS1

CORRELATED SEQUENCE NO. _____ OR ☐ TOPICAL SEQUENCE NO. 3

SUB-SEQUENCE ⎰ ⎱
-OR- ⎱-OF- ⎰ ,FROM _____ (SEQUENCE) ; _____
QUALIFICATION (ACTANT) (SEQUENCE) (STATEMENT)

PERFORMANCE SYNTAGM

LEXIE NO. 34b-35   PS1   CONFRONTATION

	Health, vigor		Man
	Samaritan		Robbers and the effects of their actions
Know-how, oil, wine, donkey, money, innkeeper			

SUB-SEQUENCE OR QUALIFICATION?

CONFRONTATION REFUSED ☐   SEQUENCE INTERRUPTED ☐
CONFRONTATION ACCEPTED ☒   TO PS2

LEXIE NO. 34b-35   PS2   DOMINATION/SUBMISSION

	Health, vigor		Man
	Samaritan		Robbers and the effects of their actions
Know-how, oil, wine, donkey, money, innkeeper			

SUB-SEQUENCE OR QUALIFICATION?

SUBMISSION ? ☐   SEQUENCE INTERRUPTED ☐
DOMINATION 2 ☐   TO PS3

LEXIE NO. _____   PS3   ATTRIBUTION

| | | | |
| | | | |

SUB-SEQUENCE OR QUALIFICATION?

NOT COMPLETED ☐   SEQUENCE INTERRUPTED ☐
COMPLETED ☐   END OF SEQUENCE ☐

Luke
NARRATIVE NO. 10:30-35   TITLE Good Samaritan

SEQUENCE NO. IN THE TEXT 5

CONTRACT SYNTAGM

LEXIE NO. 33   CS1   MANDATING

| | Health, vigor | | Man |
| | Samaritan | | Robbers and the effects of their actions |

SUB-SEQUENCE OR QUALIFICATION?

VOLITION NOT ESTABLISHED ☐   SEQUENCE INTERRUPTED ☐
VOLITION ESTABLISHED ☒   TO CS2

LEXIE NO. _____   CS2   COMMUNICATION

| | | | |
| | | | |

SUB-SEQUENCE OR QUALIFICATION?

POWER AND/OR COGNITION NOT RECEIVED ☐   SEQUENCE INTERRUPTED ☐
POWER AND/OR COGNITION RECEIVED ☐   TO DS

DISJUNCTION/CONJUNCTION SYNTAGM

LEXIE NO. 34a   DS   MOVEMENT

FROM PERSON _____   TO PERSON _____ | | Man |

PLACE Road   PLACE _____

THING _____   THING _____ | | Health, vigor | | Man |
                            | | Samaritan; | | Robbers and the effects of their actions |

SUB-SEQUENCE OR QUALIFICATION?

MOVEMENT NOT COMPLETED ☐   SEQUENCE INTERRUPTED ☐
MOVEMENT COMPLETED ☒   TO PS1

(Went to him).........MOVEMENT COMPLETED

For a complete analysis of the parable of the Good Samaritan in terms of the narrative structure see my essay "An Analysis of Narrative Structure and the Good Samaritan." The example shown is simply provided in order to bring some concreteness to our presentation. Note how little of the sequence (and therefore of the narrative structure) is actualized. But this evokes for the reader the whole structure and consequently he can recognize the value "narrativity" in this text.

Correlated and Topical Sequences

Both correlated and topical sequences are constituted according to the model described above. Yet they do not "behave" exactly in the same way because of their role in the overall narrative structure. The occasion of a narrative is an unfulfilled contract. The first correlated sequence (initial sequence) is therefore, by definition, a sequence which was interrupted at one or another point of its development. The purpose of the main body of the narrative (the topical sequence) is to reestablish the possibility that this main contract be carried out. If, for instance, the first correlated sequence *aborted because of lack* of HELPERS (or to put it differently because the OPPONENT is too powerful), the topical sequences function *to provide an adequate* HELPER. When (and if) this is accomplished the second correlated sequence (final sequence) can take place; the original contract is at last carried out successfully.

The contract is the same in both initial and final correlated sequences. Thus the actantial positions of SENDER, OBJECT, RECEIVER have the same actualization. When the initial contract is interrupted the sequence is "suspended" but does not really end. The contract remains as potential contract and the actants mentioned above as potential actants.

The topical sequence which follows presents a different actualization of the actantial model. The goal of the topical contract is the reestablishment of the possibility of the initial contract. More specifically the OBJECT of the topical contract is the fulfillment of the "lack" which caused the initial sequence to be interrupted. For instance, if the initial sequence was interrupted because of the lack of a HELPER the topical sequence presents a new contract in which a SUBJECT (which may or may not be different from the SUBJECT of the initial sequence) is mandated to facilitate the giving of a specific HELPER (which becomes the OBJECT of the topical se-

7. D. Patte, "An Analysis of Narrative Structure and the Good Samaritan," *Semeia* 2 (1974):1–26.

quence) to the actor who was in the position of SUBJECT in the
initial sequence and now becomes the RECEIVER. The actualization of the other actantial positions may or may not have changed.
By contrast, when a topical sequence is interrupted it can end
once and for all. A second topical sequence is introduced: the
OBJECT and RECEIVER remain the same but the SUBJECT and
other actantial positions receive new actualization. In a more complex narrative there might be sub-topical sequences which are
attempts to salvage the aborted topical sequence.

The structure of the simplest narrative can be represented as
follows (unfulfilled and fulfilled situations are often respectively
designated by the linguistic term "non posited" and "posited"):

Contents	inversed content (non posited)			posited content		
	correlated content	Topical content		Topical content		correlated content
Narrative Sequences	Initial sequence (unfulfilled contract)	Topical contract syntagm (potential program)	Topical disjunction/ conjunction syntagm	Topical performance syntagm	End of topical sequence = actualized topical program	Final sequence (fulfilled contract)

At any point of any correlated or topical sequence each of the
actantial positions may be further actualized by means of:

a) A *qualification* (expressed by the verbs to be, to have, and the
predicates of the class of "being") which displays at a specific point
in the manifestation the stage reached in the unfolding of the narrative. It is a kind of recapitulation (often partial) which stops the
flow of the narrative. It can also be termed *"state statement."*

b) A *sub-sequence* (or even a sub-narrative) which tells the
"story" of one or the other of the actors, things, or locations which
occupies in a given sequence one of the actantial positions.

A qualification or a sub-sequence stops the development of the
main narrative. It is an excursus. When it is completed one comes
back to the point where the main narrative had been stopped.

Narrative Structure
and Exegesis

First it should be kept in mind that the model presented above is
a construct which certainly needs improvements. Yet as is, it is a
helpful starting point for the analysis of any narrative and thus also
of biblical narratives. Since this model represents the structure of
the system of narratives (as signs), by definition we cannot expect
it to be fully actualized in any narrative. The purpose of the analy-

sis of specific narratives is therefore twofold: first, to verify the validity of this model and second, to study in which ways these specific narratives actualize the structure.

As has been shown by the analyses already performed one can hope to distinguish various narrative sub-genres by means of this method. Studies are presently underway to examine whether this method could eventually help in distinguishing among evangelical parables, example stories, Jewish parables, and Hellenistic parables. Eventually such a method might also provide one of the new criteria to be used for the study of the history of the synoptic traditions. Only an extensive use of this method will reveal its full potential.

Furthermore, as we shall see, such an analysis is the necessary prelude to the structural analysis of the narrative in terms of the mythical structures and beyond this second analysis, to a semantic analysis. These constraints interact in a text and contribute to the formation of its meaning effect by excluding a series of potential meaning effects. As a result of these three analyses the exegete will have a set of criteria for judging the validity of various interpretations of this text. But, of course, he will not be in a position to apprehend fully what the meaning effect of the text was before analyzing it in terms of all the other structures (other deep structures, cultural structures, and structures of the enunciation). This last remark expresses both the promises and the strict limitations of structural exegesis. By itself the analysis of a single text in terms of the narrative structure yields very limited results. It is only after an analysis in terms of the mythical structure that exegetical results begin to appear, as we shall see in our next chapter when we conclude our analysis of the parable of the Good Samaritan.

IV

Mythical Structures and Exegesis

Another promising field of structural investigation for biblical exegesis is the analysis of mythical structures. Exegetical research on the mythical structures is even less well developed than exegetical research on the narrative structures. Yet a growing number of scholars are beginning to develop this specific method from which, as we shall suggest, we can expect significant exegetical results.

Structural study of myths was first introduced and developed by Claude Lévi-Strauss in an essay published in 1955, and then in the four volumes of his *Mythologiques*[1] in which he analyzed more than eight hundred myths. Since Lévi-Strauss' work has been and is still the basis for any structural study of myths we shall limit our brief discussion to the model which he proposes. We shall attempt to understand this model in terms of the general linguistic model already discussed, thereby suggesting the place of the mythical structures in a broad hierarchy of structures. We shall note especially their relationship to the narrative structures with which they are at times confused. Throughout this discussion we intend to suggest that even though mythical structures can be more directly apprehended in mythological "texts," they are also at work in non-mythological texts and other cultural phenomena. Mythical structures are actually structures of a mythical universe and can have various kinds of expression. Hence they are also at work in the biblical texts even though these texts are not, strictly speaking, mythological. In the second part of this chapter, an analysis of Galatians 1:1–10 is proposed as an illustration of this method of analysis.

---

1. See the following works by Claude Lévi Strauss:
"The Structural Study of Myth," *Structural Anthropology*, pp. 202–28; *Mythologiques I: Le cru et le cuit* (Paris: Plon, 1964 [English trans. *The Raw and the Cooked* (New York: Harper and Row, 1969)]; *Mythologiques II: Du miel aux cendres* (Paris: Plon, 1967); *Mythologiques III: L'origine des manières de table* (Paris: Plon, 1968); *Mythologiques IV: L'homme nu* (Paris: Plon, 1971).

A MODEL FOR THE MYTHICAL STRUCTURES

The term "myth" is used with various connotations by different scholars. In order to avoid any confusion we shall use the term "myth" (and the corresponding adjective, "mythical") in a technical, structural sense. In our discussion, the term "myth" will not denote a "mythological text." We shall use this latter phrase in order to refer to the written or oral mythological stories.

A mythological text confronts the readers or hearers as a fanciful, fantastic story. It is neither realistic nor logical. In other words, at the conscious, logical level, it does not make sense. Yet for the people among whom this mythological story emerged, was told and retold, it was meaningful. On the basis of our discussion of the hierarchy of structures, we can say that a mythological text is characterized by the quasi-absence of constraints from the structures of the enunciation. That is, a mythological text does not have a conscious, logical argument. To put it another way, the structures at work in mythological texts are primarily deep structures. Such texts therefore offer privileged opportunities for the study of deep structures since there is only very limited interference from other structures.

What are the deep structures at work in a mythological text? We can readily assume that in addition to linguistic structures and cultural structures there are narrative structures since a mythological text is a story, a narrative. Thus A. J. Greimas analyzed in terms of narrative structures one of the mythological texts that Lévi-Strauss had studied in his *Mythologiques*.[2] This is to say that a mythological text can be viewed as a sign belonging to the system of sign-narratives. For such an analysis the mythological text is reduced to its "narrative elements." Following the method described above one can then study the actualization of the narrative structure (a deep structure) in this specific text.

Lévi-Strauss suggested and indeed demonstrated that there is another deep structure at work in mythological texts: a mythical structure. If this is true, a mythological text manifests the interaction of constraints from two deep structures which can be expected to interfere partially with each other. Consequently, as we shall see below, the analyst should be able to apprehend the presence of the mythical structure in its interferences with the narrative struc-

2. A.-J. Greimas, "Pour une théorie de l'interprétation du récit mythique," *Du sens*, pp. 185–230; also published in *Communications* 8 (1966). Cf. also A.-J. Greimas, "The Interpretation of Myth: Theory and Practice" in P. Maranda and E. Köngäs Maranda, eds., *Structural Analysis of Oral Tradition* (Philadelphia: University of Pennsylvania, 1970). This is in large part a translation of the preceding essay.

ture. Mythological texts are characterized by redundancies, that is, by elements which are superfluous to a narrative.[3] Yet these redundancies are by no means the only manifestations of the mythical structure which is at work throughout the mythological text. After the presence of the mythical structure is recognized, it must still be identified. In his essay, "The Structural Study of Myth," Lévi-Strauss proposed, from an analysis of Zuni (Pueblo) mythological "texts," that a given mythological text should be studied together with all others which belong to the same "group." This "group" or "set" consists of all the mythological texts of a given culture. Many will be variants of a specific mythological text (that is, variants which have similar contents). But as Lévi-Strauss uses the term "variant," all these mythological texts, whatever might be their contents, are variants of the "myth" for indeed, in the structural perspective, *"a myth is made up of all its variants."*[4]

Thus Lévi-Strauss defines a myth as a system of mythological texts, i.e., a system of mythical signs (macro-signs) in which each mythological text is to be viewed as a sign. The mythical structure is the structure of this system of mythical signs.

In order to discover what this structure is, Lévi-Strauss reduced the mythological texts to "pertinent" units, that is, to those units through which these texts are either correlated with or opposed to each other.

Lévi-Strauss denotes as *mythemes* the basic mythical units which are comparable to phonemes and semes. The mythemes are obtained by reducing the events of the mythological story to sentences which are as short as possible. Each mytheme expresses, in Lévi-Strauss' words,

> that a certain function [French: *prédicat*] is, at a given time, linked to a given subject. Or, to put it otherwise, each gross constituent unit (mytheme) will consist of a relation.[5]

A mytheme can be symbolized as follows:

$$F_x(a)$$

This can be read: a function "x" is linked to a given subject (or state) "a". We shall return to this formulation of the mytheme.

It is clear that Lévi-Strauss does not study the "expression" of the mythological texts but their "contents." Thus it is already im-

3. *Structural Anthropology*, p. 226; *Le cru et le cuit*, pp. 339, 345–46.
4. *Structural Anthropology*, p. 213. (Our italics.) Cf. also pp. 214 ff. This definition of myth is assumed by Lévi-Strauss throughout his work: cf., for instance, *Le cru et le cuit*, p. 22.
5. *Structural Anthropology*, p. 207.

plied that the mythical structure as discussed here is a deep structure of the *content*.

There are other mythical units made up of several mythemes, which Lévi-Strauss denotes simply as "bundles of relations" or what we could call *"bundles of mythemes"* or *"broad mythemes."* While a mytheme is syntagmatic (the relation between a function and a subject being discovered in the syntagmatic order of the mythological text) a "bundle of mythemes" is paradigmatic, that is, it gathers together mythemes which might be scattered throughout the mythological text. For instance, in the Oedipus myth[6] the mythemes "Oedipus marries his mother, Jocasta" and "Antigone buries her brother, Polynices, despite prohibition," belong to the same "bundle of mythemes." As Lévi-Strauss suggests, they have in common that both subjects trespass social laws because blood relations are *overrated*. This "bundle of mythemes" can therefore be reduced to a new, broader mytheme. Thus in this case the two preceding mythemes can be expressed in the broad mytheme: "People overrating blood relations." Similarly the mythemes "Oedipus kills his father, Laios" and "Eteocles kills his brother, Polynices" belong to the same bundle of mythemes because they have in common the *underrating* of blood relations and hence form together the broad mytheme: "People underrating blood relations."

The mythical structure as a whole is the framework which provides for the interrelation of the various bundles of mythemes (or "broad mythemes"). This mythical structure Lévi-Strauss often calls "mythical thought" or "mythical logic." He characterizes it in the following quotations:

> . . . The purpose of myth is to provide a logical model capable of overcoming a contradiction . . .[7]

> . . . Mythical thought always progresses from the awareness of oppositions toward their resolution . . .[8]

These oppositions of which one becomes aware in mythical thought are fundamental oppositions: for instance, Life-Death, Nature-Culture, Heaven-Earth, God-Man. These oppositions cannot be overcome: they are *real* oppositions. Nevertheless the myth transcends them by breaking them up, i.e., by replacing them with secondary oppositions which can be somehow viewed as equivalent to the fundamental opposition. These secondary oppositions can

---

6. It is discussed by Lévi-Strauss in *Structural Anthropology*, pp. 209–215. It is clear that the broad mythemes are themselves made up of a function and of a state. Thus the formula $F_x(a)$ can also symbolize a broad mytheme.

7. *Structural Anthropology*, p. 226.

8. Ibid., p. 221. Cf. also *L'homme nu*, pp. 596–611.

themselves be overcome through some type of mediation. Let us illustrate our discussion by making use of a few elements of Lévi-Strauss' analysis of the Zuni myth. Life and death are the two opposite terms of a fundamental opposition and therefore have no intermediary. In a myth this pair is replaced by a pair of equivalent terms (broad mythemes): for instance, "agriculture" (equivalent to "life") and "warfare" (equivalent to "death"). Agriculture and warfare together form an opposition which admits of a third term as a mediator: hunting. Like agriculture, hunting provides life-giving food. Like warfare, hunting brings death. By means of this first transposition life and death are no longer perceived as being in absolute opposition. For example, death can be viewed as sustaining life. Yet this mediation of the fundamental opposition through a secondary opposition with a mediator is always tenuous. Thus another secondary opposition is introduced by the myth. It is an opposition which is more easily mediated and which is related to the preceding opposition through the equivalence of one or several of its terms.[9] To follow up on the same example (Zuni myth) the new secondary opposition replaces one of the polar terms (e.g., agriculture) and the mediator (hunting) of the preceding secondary opposition by a new triad. Thus "herbivorous animals" can be viewed as equivalent to "agriculture"; "beast of prey" as equivalent to "hunting." The mediator of this new opposition being "the carrion-eating animals": they eat animal food but they do not kill. Other secondary oppositions with their mediations are similarly introduced so that in the manifestation they do not appear to be at all related to the fundamental opposition. And yet they are apprehended as very meaningful oppositions by the people of that culture, who unconsciously perceive them as symbolizing the sacred order which provides wholeness to human experience, because these oppositions suggest and evoke for them the complete mythical structure.

Thus the mythical structure is the progressive mediation of a fundamental opposition through a series of secondary oppositions

9. This relation of equivalence between the two secondary oppositions is expressed by Lévi-Strauss in the formula $F_x(a):F_y(b) \simeq F(b):F_{\bar{a}}(y)$. He explains this formula as follows: "Here, with two terms, a and b, being given as well as two functions, x and y, of these terms, it is assumed that a relation of equivalence exists between two situations defined respectively by an inversion of *terms* and *relations*, under two conditions: 1) that one term be replaced by its opposite (in the above formula, a and $\bar{a}$); 2) that an inversion be made between the *function value* and the *term value* of two elements (above, y and a)," *Structural Anthropology*, p. 225. For further interpretation of this formula and its use in biblical exegesis, see my essay, "Structural Network in Narrative," *Soundings* (June 1975) and below, our discussion of the interrelation of the narrative and mythical structures.

which admit a mediator. The terms which occupy the polar positions as well as the position of mediator are the "bundles of mythemes" that we discussed above.

As in the case of any structure, a given manifestation although presupposing the whole structure actualizes only part of it. Thus a given mythological text might manifest the fundamental opposition and it alone. In such a case the mythological text actualizes the impossibility of overcoming directly the opposition and thus actualizes the need for the rest of the mythical structure. Similarly another mythological text might manifest only one (or a few) of the mediated oppositions, yet it evokes the whole progressive mediation whose other elements are actualized in other mythological texts and, as we shall suggest below, in other aspects of the culture of the given society.

We need indeed to discuss the scope of this mythical structure. It is manifested by all the mythological texts present in a given culture. But are the mythological texts the only mythical signs? Following Lévi-Strauss we have suggested that a myth mediates the fundamental, metaphysical oppositions through "a theoretically infinite number"[10] of secondary oppositions which are amenable to a mediation. Collectively, these secondary oppositions embrace most aspects of the culture of the given society.[11] When this is recognized, a myth must be viewed as involving a whole culture and not simply the set of its mythological texts. In other words the mythical structure is at work throughout a culture. A specific myth as specific actualization of this structure provides an order which transcends the fundamental oppositions and thus overcomes the threat of chaos that these oppositions could have engendered. The myth discloses wholeness in all aspects of human experience in that culture, because all these aspects presuppose, evoke, and suggest the mythical structure as a whole.

Several consequences can be drawn from these remarks. First, since the mythical structure can be manifested in cultural elements other than mythological texts, it is possible to envision a mythical structure actualized in purely secular cultural elements. In other words, the mythical structure can be said to be at work in our modern, scientific culture. This is how we interpret one of Lévi-Strauss' main theses in *The Savage Mind*.[12] The modern, scientific

10. *Op. cit.*, p. 226.
11. Lévi-Strauss has shown this in his *Mythologiques*. Cf. also Lévi-Strauss, "Four Winnebago Myths: A Structural Sketch," in Stanley Diamond ed., *Culture in History* (New York: Columbia University, 1960), p. 356.
12. Lévi-Strauss, *The Savage Mind* (Chicago: University of Chicago, 1966).

way of thinking is not essentially different from the "savage" myth-ological way of thinking.[13] These ways of thinking do nevertheless differ. The first emphasizes the structures of the enunciations (con-scious and logical structures): thus the deep structures remain buried in the depth of the scientific speech. By contrast the myth-ological way of thinking allows deep structures to emerge at the surface of the mythological speech.

A second consequence, more directly relevant for our exegetical endeavor, is that the mythical structure is at work in texts which are not mythological (and thus in the biblical texts). The mythological texts are privileged texts for the study of the mythical structure since they present minimal interferences with it. It was only through the study of mythological texts that a model for the mythical struc-ture could be constructed. But once this model is formulated, we can analyze other texts in an attempt to verify whether the theory proposed above holds true. More specifically, is it true that the mythical structure imposes its constraints upon non-mythological texts and thus upon the biblical texts? If this theory is verified, and we believe it will be (as the examples below show), then we can study the specific actualization of the mythical structure in the biblical texts, i.e., the specificity of the biblical myth.

We shall first consider how the mythical structure is actualized in a theological text; Galatians 1:1–10. In doing so we shall consider the relationship between a structure of the enunciation (a theologi-cal argument) and the mythical structure. In our second example we shall observe how the mythical structure is actualized in a nar-rative text, the parable of the Good Samaritan. In this second case we shall view the interrelation of the narrative and mythical struc-tures. We shall suggest that the analysis in terms of the narrative structure is the basis upon which the analysis in terms of the mythi-cal structure can be performed with the necessary rigor. It is at the level of the analysis in terms of the mythical structure that we shall reach the first significant exegetical results.

AN ANALYSIS OF THE MYTHICAL
STRUCTURES OF GALATIANS 1:1-10

Elements of Method

The discourse of the Epistle to the Galatians is, among other things, theological. A theological argument is a conscious attempt to express in a logical manner religious convictions, that is, "self-

13. Ibid., p. 5.

evident religious truths." These religious truths are "self-evident" because they impose themselves upon the believer. In other words, they are religious "meaning effects" produced by the unconscious interaction of deep structures and especially produced by a specific actualization of the mythical structure. Far from being characterized by redundancies, as are mythological texts, a theological argument is concise. What would be expressed in one or several mythological stories is expressed here in a few phrases (or single terms) incorporated into a logical argument. These phrases and terms represent in most instances "broad mythemes" (or bundles of mythemes) which are in the polar positions of an opposition. These theological phrases often represent elliptically the "broad mythemes." It should be noted that a single mytheme of a bundle of mythemes can stand for the entire bundle. Thus in order to discover the broad mythemes in the letter to the Galatians, instead of proceeding to the two reductions required for the analysis of a mythological text (i.e., to the syntagmatic reduction of each part of the story into a short sentence, a mytheme, and to the paradigmatic reduction of each bundle of mythemes into a broad mytheme), we shall have to expand Paul's text. Each pertinent phrase or term has to be expressed in the form of a short sentence which is a broad mytheme. A second expansion could then be made in order to express the mythemes themselves, which must be viewed as specific manifestations of each broad mytheme. We shall not perform this second step of the analysis, which is necessary for the study of the elementary structures and of the cultural codes. We shall rather propose an analysis of the intermediate mythical structure, that is, of the structure which correlates and opposes broad mythemes.

A theological argument is also characterized by the fact that in it the fundamental opposition is assumed to have been mediated. In a theological argument convictions are viewed as established. In a myth convictions are in the process of being established. Consequently a theological argument (and a ritual, as Lévi-Strauss has shown)[14] manifests the same mythical structure as the corresponding myth but with the opposite "orientation." In a myth a first opposition is mediated by another, more secondary, opposition: the position of mediator in the first opposition occupies one of the poles (that we can term the *positive* pole) of the following opposition. For instance, in the Zuni myth discussed by Lévi-Strauss the relation of the two secondary oppositions can be written as follows:

14. Lévi-Strauss, *L'homme nu, Mythologiques*, vol. IV, (Paris: Plon, 1971), pp. 596–611.

Agriculture

Herbivorous Animal

Hunting   Hunting (Beasts of Prey)

Warfare

Fig. 1

or more abstractly:[15]

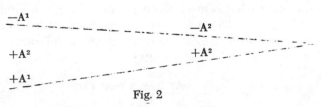

Fig. 2

In a myth the mediating term of a secondary opposition is one of the poles of an *even more secondary* opposition. In other words, the mythical structure is oriented from the weakest secondary opposition toward the fundamental opposition. By contrast a theological argument (as well as a ritual) presents the inverse orientation: from the fundamental opposition towards the secondary oppositions. The mediation of the fundamental opposition is viewed as that which permits the mediation of the secondary oppositions (as will be illustrated below). This inversion of the orientation of the structure is not a major obstacle for the analysis of the mythical structure in a ritual or in a theological argument. Indeed the series of oppositions remains the same despite the fact that the mediations are perceived in two opposite ways. Yet we shall have to keep in mind that the mediating terms proposed in the theological argument result from the constraints of a structure of the enunciation (a theo*logical* structure). Instead of being the "positive" poles of the

15. Using Lévi-Strauss' formula we can write still more abstractly:

Thus we could read: the opposition $+A^1/-A^1$ is in a relation of equivalence with the opposition $+A^2/-A^2$. Although we shall keep this formula in mind, we shall not exhaust its possibilities: its primary function is as a tool for the identification of the elements (which we could term "mythemes") which compose the broad mythemes. Such an identification, the first step of the analysis of the *elementary* structure, is beyond the scope of this short introduction.

more *secondary* oppositions, as for the mythical structure, the mediating terms are the "positive" poles of more *fundamental* oppositions.

In a first stage of the analysis it is convenient to record the mediating terms proposed in the theological argument. This procedure allows the identification of the terms which have to be viewed as the "positive" poles of the successive oppositions. Let us emphasize that we term "positive" pole of an opposition that pole which is also the mediator of another opposition. The positive poles express therefore what is most characteristic of a given myth.

According to Lévi-Strauss' model the positions of broad mythemes in the mythical structure can be schematized as follows:

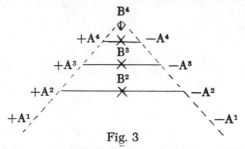

Fig. 3

$+A^1/-A^1$ is the fundamental opposition while $+A^2/-A^2$, $+A^3/-A^3$, and $+A^4/-A^4$ are secondary oppositions which include as mediators the broad mythemes B^2, B^3, and B^4.

In this schema we have denoted the mediating terms B^2, B^3, B^4. In the mythical structure they should be respectively $+A^3$, $+A^4$ (and eventually $+A^5$). In the theological argument, with its inverse orientation, they should be respectively $+A^1$, $+A^2$, $+A^3$.

This schematization suggests that the broad mythemes are related to each other in two ways. First, they are part of specific oppositions. This relation is expressed by the numbers. We shall denote opposition by the symbol /, e.g., $+A^1/-A^1$. Second, each broad mytheme is correlated with the other broad mythemes which occupy similar positions in the structure. Thus all the broad mythemes which belong to the positive side (which we shall represent by the the symbol $+S$) of the structure are correlated with each other. So are the broad mythemes which belong to the negative side (which we shall represent by $-S$) of the structure. We shall denote correlation by the symbol: $\equiv$.

We shall perform our analysis in two steps: a syntagmatic reading and a paradigmatic reading. First, following the text, we shall attempt to identify the broad mythemes and note the relations of opposition and of correlation that each broad mytheme has with other broad mythemes. We shall also identify the mediating terms proposed in the theological argument. Second, in the paradigmatic reading we shall study the structure which is manifested by these broad mythemes. At this stage of our analysis we shall make use of the model proposed by Lévi-Strauss for the mythical structure. Yet we shall keep in mind that it is a *model*, a theory. We shall not attempt to impose it if it does not fit the data. Rather we shall always be ready to adapt and transform it.

One characteristic of our text already suggests that Lévi-Strauss' model is not fully adequate. The Epistle to the Galatians is a polemical text, i.e., it presents the conflict between two myths: the mythical system "Paul's gospel," and the mythical system "anti-gospel" of Paul's opponents. At the structural level we can therefore expect to find two interrelated mythical structures, or, better, a twofold mythical structure. As we shall see there are other mythical systems involved in the text: the Pharisaic mythical system and a Hellenistic mythical system. We shall represent these various mythical systems as follows:

S^1: the mythical system "Paul's gospel."
S^2: the Pharisaic mythical system.
S^3: the Hellenistic mythical system.
S^4: the "anti-gospel" mythical system.

As we can expect if S^2 and S^3 (as whole mythical system or as represented by some of their mythemes) are parts of S^1 they will belong to its negative side. For indeed if, for example, the Pharisaic mythical system belongs to the positive side of Paul's mythical system it would mean that his gospel is nothing else than a form of Pharisaic Judaism. Let us emphasize this: if we must say, and indeed we shall have to, that S^2 and S^3 are on the negative side of S^1, it means that they are indeed parts of S^1: they participate in the mythical system "Paul's gospel." The negative side of the structure is "welded" together with the positive side by the mediations. We shall see that S^4 is not related in this way to S^1.

Syntagmatic Reading of
Galatians 1:1–10
    v. 1a—*"Paul an apostle"*[16]
The two words imply that the identification "Paul-apostle" is not self-evident. Paul was not an apostle (when a Pharisee, 1:13–14), and there is always the possibility that he might forego his apostle-

16. We shall quote the *Revised Standard Version* as long as it does not hide the correlations and oppositions present in the Greek text. In the opposite eventuality we shall modify this translation and quote between parentheses the Greek text.

ship (by preaching another gospel, 1:8). Thus we find the opposition: "Paul as a common man (Pharisee or otherwise)/Paul as apostle." The text expresses that a mediation of this opposition took place: Paul is an apostle.

Because in verse 6 and elsewhere throughout the epistle it is manifested as a mediating term of another opposition, the broad mytheme "Paul as apostle" belongs to the positive side of the gospel mythical structure, while "Paul as a common man" belongs to the negative side of this structure. From the context (Paul's letters) we can suggest that this latter broad mytheme could be formulated as: "people having a Pharisaic way of life" or, better, "people belonging to the Pharisaic mythical system" (S^2). As suggested above, in our text certain other entire mythical systems play the role of broad mythemes. Thus these other systems are viewed as elements of the gospel mythical system in which they function as "broad mythemes."

v. 1b—*"not from men nor through man, but through Jesus Christ and God the Father"*

a) The mediation of the opposition "Paul/apostle" is through Jesus Christ and God the Father. It can be schematized as follows (the middle term represents the mediating term according to the theological argument): "Paul as pharisee/Jesus Christ and God the Father/Paul as apostle." Instead of one, there are two terms in position of mediator: "Jesus Christ" and "God the Father." This is certainly an interference of the theological argument. We cannot decide at this point which one of the two is, at the level of the mythical structure, the actual mediator. Yet we can note that these two broad mythemes are correlated:

$$\text{Jesus Christ} \equiv \text{God the Father.}$$

b) A fundamental opposition is also present:
"God (and Jesus Christ)/man."

v. 1c—*"who raised him from the dead"*

The opposition "Lord[17] Jesus Christ"/"dead Jesus" is mediated according to the theological argument by God's action (raised him).

v. 2—*"and all the brethren who are with me to the churches in Galatia"*

The "brethren" are correlated with Paul-apostle. Thus both broad mythemes belong to the positive side of the structure. There is also an opposition "the Galatians/Paul (and the brethren)," which is mediated by the epistle itself. This opposition refers to the conflict mentioned above. It is the opposition between the Galatians as belonging to the mythical system "anti-gospel" (S^4) versus Paul and the brethren as belonging to the mythical system gospel (S^1).

17. Galatians 1:3.

v. 3—*"Grace to you and peace from God our Father and the Lord Jesus Christ"*

a) "Grace and peace" is correlated with God and Jesus, but also with Paul-apostle who gives the blessing.

b) As a blessing, "Grace to you and peace" is a religious word of authority which establishes a reality. Here it establishes the reality "gospel" for the Galatians: they are included within the gospel mythical system. Verse 6 shows that the Galatians were indeed in need of being reintegrated into the gospel system. The blessing is the mediation of the opposition:

$$\text{Galatians} -S^1 / \text{Galatians} +S^1$$

This can be read: Galatians as belonging to $-S^1$ (the negative side of the gospel structure) versus Galatians as belonging to $+S^1$ (the positive side of the gospel structure).

v. 4a—*"who gave himself for our sins to deliver us from the present evil aeon"*

Two oppositions are mediated by Christ's gift of himself.

a) Men freed from sin (apostle, brethren, Galatians)/sinners.[18]

b) Men freed from sin (apostle, brethren, Galatians)/men under the power of the present evil aeon.

The latter presents a cosmological Hellenistic terminology. From the gospel perspective the Galatians, when involved in their Hellenistic mythical system, were "men under the power of the present evil aeon." The identification of Paul with those under the power of the present evil aeon ("us") expresses the correlation "Paul as belonging to the Pharisaic mythical system ≡ Galatians as belonging to their Hellenistic mythical systems." Both the Hellenistic mythical system (that we call S^3) and the Pharisaic mythical system (that we call S^2) function here as bundles of mythemes.

Both S^2 and S^3 (as entire systems with both their positive and negative sides) belong to the negative side of the mythical structure. The opposition "men freed from the evil aeon/men under the power of the present evil aeon" is equivalent to the opposition "Galatians S^1/Galatians S^3". The first term of the opposition can be read as: Galatians as belonging to S^1 (the gospel mythical system). The positive side of the structure expresses what belongs (positively) to a given mythical system.

By analogy we can suggest that the former opposition "men freed from sin/sinners," expresses a Jewish terminology (the phrase originated in a hermeneutic of the Jewish Scripture as 1 Cor. 15:3 suggests) and that it can be read as the opposition "Men S^1/Men S^2".

18. Rather than "men freed from sin/sins" because of the personal pronoun.

This opposition and its mediation through Christ would then reflect Paul's own experience which is correlated with that of the Galatians (thus "*our* sins"). We can therefore suggest the correlations $S^2 \equiv S^3$.

vv. 4b, 5—"*according to the will of our God and Father; to whom be the glory for ever and ever (eis tous aiōnas tōn aiōnōn). Amen*" Christ's mediation is correlated with God's will. Moreover, despite the theological argument, it is to be noted that the term *aeon* is again used, but this time in correlation with God. The opposition "God/evil aeon," which is implied in the opposition S^1/S^3 is therefore mediated to allow the correlation "God $\equiv$ aeon."

v. 6—"*I am astonished that you are so quickly deserting him who called you in the grace of Christ and turning to a different gospel*" a) The opposition "gospel/other gospel" (S^1/S^4) appears. How it is expressed needs to be noted: "Galatians with the one (Paul) who called them in the grace/Galatians turning to another gospel" or, in brief: Galatians S^1/Galatians S^4. As this opposition is resolved, its second pole predominates. Thus the first pole "Galatians S^1" becomes subordinate to the second pole "Galatians S^4". The Galatians who had belonged to the gospel, now belong to the anti-gospel.

b) The phrase "him who called you in the grace" implies the opposition: "Galatians as pagans/Galatians as Christians," i.e., Galatians S^3/Galatians S^1. The mediation is through "him who called you in the grace." In a diachronic reading one must conclude that the phrase is ambiguous. It can refer either to God the Father or to Paul (so Bligh, Bonnard). In a synchronic reading the ambiguity is seen as resulting from the correlation of Paul-apostle with God in the gospel system. The rest of the epistle makes plain that it is by Paul's missionary activity that the Galatians were converted to the gospel. According to the structure of the theological argument, as we shall see, Paul-apostle is the mediation of the opposition.

v. 7—"*not that there is another gospel, but there are some who trouble you and want to pervert the gospel of Christ*" The opposition S^1/S^4 is expressed in three different ways: "not that there is another gospel," i.e., gospel/non-gospel; "there are some who trouble you," i.e., Galatians/some people (*tines*); "and want to pervert the Gospel of Christ," i.e., gospel/some people. Thus it is suggested that the Galatians belong to S^1 and that "some people" belong to S^4.

v. 8—"*But even if we, or an angel from heaven, should preach to you a gospel contrary to that which we preached to you, let him be anathema (anathema estō)*" In this hypothetical statement it is expressed that Paul (and brethren) belong to S^4 (anti-gospel). Similarly an angel is said to belong to S⁴. By implication we have the correlation "Paul ≡ an angel." These hypotheses are actual possibilities. Paul as man, as sinner, as Pharisee would preach "another gospel." The opposition: "men freed from sin/sinners," that is, Paul S¹/Paul S² could become Paul S¹/Paul S⁴. In other words, Paul as belonging to the gospel is originally opposed by Paul the sinner (i.e., Paul the Pharisee), but in the hypothesis proposed in v. 8 it is opposed by Paul who belongs to the anti-gospel.

S² is therefore correlated with S⁴. By analogy saying that an angel from heaven belongs to S⁴ implies the correlation "angel ≡ present evil aeon." The opposition "men freed from the evil aeon (S¹)/men under the power of the present evil aeon (S³)" could thus read "S¹/ angel S⁴." S³ is therefore correlated with S⁴. These *hypothetical* oppositions are odd in a system which up to this point has presented only actual, real oppositions. This phenomenon begs for an explanation. We can hope that the paradigmatic reading will provide such an explanation.

v. 9—*"As we have said before, so now I say again, if any one is preaching to you a gospel contrary to that which you received, let him be anathema (anathema estō)"*

The opposition "preacher of the gospel/preacher of the anti-gospel" together with the two preceding oppositions (v. 8) is resolved in a radical fashion by Paul-apostle who pronounces a liturgical curse: *anathema estō*. A curse establishes a reality just as does a blessing. Paul's opponents are cursed, that is, separated from God once and for all,[19] and are under a divine condemnation (5:10). Thus the opposition is resolved by the exclusion of one of its polar terms rather than by a dialectic mediation. In all the other cases the oppositions were resolved by the inclusion of both terms in the gospel mythical system. In the present case the opposition is resolved by the radical exclusion of the opponent (or few opponents) from the gospel system.

This brutal inversion of the symmetry needs an explanation. Why are the opponents accursed and the sinners, the pagans, and the Galatians blessed? Again we shall have to wait for the paradigmatic reading for an answer.

v. 10—*"Am I now seeking the favor of men, or of God? Or am I trying to please men? If I were still pleasing men, I would not be a servant of Christ (christou doulos)"*

The opposition "God/man" is again stressed. But this time it is combined with a hypothetical correlation "Paul ≡ man" (rather than

19. For this meaning on *anathema* see Rom. 9:3, and Gal. 4:17.

"Paul ≡ God"). In the last part of the verse, we again find the hypothetical correlation "Paul ≡ man" which is now opposed to the correlation "Paul ≡ Christ." The hypothetical oppositions are therefore important elements of the structure. The explanation of their presence cannot be overlooked.

In the preceding pages we have attempted to summarize the syntagmatic reading through which the pertinent elements of a text can be identified as broad mythemes. It is a process of deconstructing the text into elements of a mythical system. In the syntagmatic reading this deconstruction is tentative: it must be verified by the paradigmatic reading which attempts to discern the structure which governs the interaction of these mythical elements. In practice, the analyst needs to perform this process iteratively: after a first paradigmatic reading, a second syntagmatic reading allows further identification of broad mythemes which leads to a second paradigmatic reading and so on. By successive approximations the analyst (as any scientist) develops the construct which best represents the phenomenon.

Thus by means of the syntagmatic reading we have identified in a first approximation a number of broad mythemes. We found also that certain entire mythical systems had to be viewed as broad mythemes of the gospel mythical system. Our task was complicated by the polemical nature of the text: we had to deal with correlations and oppositions of mythical systems.

Paradigmatic Reading
of Galatians 1:1–10

A paradigmatic reading of the text requires us to consider the various mythical elements in terms of their correlations and oppositions in order to show how they are related in the mythical structure. Using the model proposed by Lévi-Strauss as a guide, let us first consider the elements which in the manifestation are not directly related to the polemic. Such mythical elements should actualize part of the mythical structure so as to form the gospel mythical system (S^1).

The fundamental opposition is clearly the opposition "God/man." Because this opposition is fundamental, it cannot be mediated directly. The very purpose of the progressive mediation is to establish analogically the necessary mediation. We can also specify that the opposition "God/man" is resolved by the passage of man in the divine sphere (e.g., see 1:1). This remark is another way of saying that the broad mytheme "God" must be viewed as the positive pole of the opposition.

The fundamental opposition is assimilated and reduced to a first secondary opposition: "Lord Jesus Christ/dead Jesus." This opposition is mediated in the theological argument by the resurrection, which is an act of God (1:1). The resolution of the opposition is clearly the transformation of the dead Jesus into the Lord Jesus Christ.

The process continues with a second secondary opposition, "Paul-apostle/Paul the Pharisee, sinner." The mediation according to the theological argument is through Jesus Christ (1:4). Yet this mediation is also expressed as being through God the Father (1:1, cf. also 1:16). It appears that this second formulation of the mediation reflects the preceding stage of the structure in which "God" is in the position of mediator. Because of the correlation "Jesus Christ ≡ God" these two terms can be identified in the theological argument (under the constraints of a structure of the enunciation).

Third secondary opposition: the opposition "Galatians as Christians/Galatians as pagans (i.e., under the power of the evil aeon)." Verse 6 can be interpreted to mean that, according to the theological argument, this opposition is mediated by Paul. If this is the case, it constitutes a new step in the progressive mediation. Yet according to 1:4 (and the other possible interpretation of 1:6) the opposition is mediated by Christ's gift of himself, in which case this third secondary opposition is assimilated to the preceding secondary opposition. The explanation of the second presentation of this opposition will be suggested later on.

Fourth secondary opposition: "gospel (as teaching)/other gospel (as teaching)." The Galatians were confronted with this opposition. The symmetry of the system would demand, in the theological argument, a mediation through the Galatians. Yet the text points out an inversed mediation: the Galatians have turned to the other gospel (1:6).

Let us summarize in a diagram the actualization of the mythical structure as it appears at this point of our analysis. For this purpose we will fill in the abstract model presented above (Fig. 3).

The mediations as manifested in the theological argument appear clearly in this diagram. Through the resurrection as mediation, the "dead Jesus" (the cross) is viewed as contributing to the Lordship of Christ. The cross is the "other side" of the Lordship of Christ without which this Lordship would be empty, meaningless. Similarly, Paul the Pharisee is the "other side" of Paul-apostle. Yet Paul's Pharisaism remains an essential component of Paul-apostle. The same is true for the other mediated oppositions. Thus through the mediations the elements "Lord Jesus Christ," "Paul-apostle," "Gala-

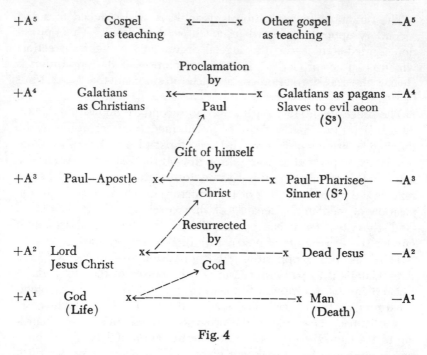

Fig. 4

tians as Christians" are manifested as the positive elements of the gospel mythical structure. Yet their polar opposites are not dismissed: on the contrary, they are incorporated into these positive elements. Thus an essential component of "Paul-apostle" is his former Pharisaism; an essential component of "Galatians as Christians" is their former Hellenism.

The correlations of the various broad mythemes also appear in this diagram. "God," "Lord Jesus Christ," "Paul-apostle," "Galatians as Christians," and "gospel as teaching" are in correlation with each other. Together they form the positive side of the structure. Similarly "man," "dead Jesus," "Paul Pharisee (S²)," "pagan Galatians (S³)," and "other gospel as teaching" are in correlation with each other and together form the negative side of the structure.

When the mediating terms proposed in the theological argument are bracketed out, the mythical structure as progressive mediation appears clearly. The Galatians as Christians are the mediation of the opposition "Paul-apostle/Paul-Pharisee-sinner." These new converts are, so to speak, the proof that Paul is indeed an apostle (new converts are the "seal" of Paul's apostleship: cf. e.g., 1 Cor. 9:2; 2 Cor. 3:2). Paul as apostle is the mediation of the opposition "Lord Jesus/Dead Jesus." In Paul-apostle the crucified Jesus and the resurrected Lord are manifested (Gal. 2:20). Thus Christ is the mediation of the fundamental opposition "God/Man": Christ is the sign of the reconciliation of God with man. Thus it is through faith in Christ that man is set in the right relationship with God (i.e., that one is justified, Gal. 2:16).

It should also be noted that the progressive mediation, as described thus far, could be considered as a complete mythical structure if the opposition "gospel as teaching/other gospel as teaching" were mediated in such a way that the symmetry is respected.[20] If, in the theological argument, the opposition "gospel/other gospel" were mediated by the Galatians in favor of the gospel, the progressive mediation of the opposition "God/man" in favor of God would have been maintained.

By considering that the "other gospel" is the valid teaching, i.e., by giving a positive sign to the "other gospel" and a negative sign to Paul's gospel, the Galatians reverse all the polarities of the gospel mythical system. Since "other gospel" is correlated with "Hellenistic mythical system," "Pharisaic mythical system," "dead Jesus," and "man," all these are now viewed as the positive side of the structure. Through these correlations, it appears that the opposition "Galatians as belonging to S^1/Galatians as belonging to S^4" or in short "Galatians S^1/Galatians S^4" is equivalent to the opposition "Galatians as Christians/Galatians as pagans, slaves to the evil aeon." Both are thus resolved in favor of their second terms. Hence Paul can say that they are again "bewitched" (3:1), and that "they turn back again to the weak and beggarly elemental spirits" (4:9; *stoicheia* can be shown to be structurally correlated with "present evil aeon").

Similarly, from the perspective of the Galatians converted to the other gospel, the following opposition appears: "Paul S^1/Paul S^4." For them this opposition would be satisfactorily resolved if Paul would accept and preach the other gospel (v. 8). Subsequently, from the perspective of "Paul S^4" (i.e., the hypothetical situation in which Paul would belong to the anti-gospel mythical system) the fundamental opposition "God/man" would be resolved in favor of man. Paul would seek to please men rather than God (v. 10).

Including these hypothetical oppositions and their hypothetical mediations the following structure appears. This diagram can be read as the combination of two diagrams presented in Fig. 3 (the second one is upside down). The upside down mythical structure represents the structure of the "other gospel."

---

20. Of course, such a structure would not be closed: a fundamental opposition is never fully mediated and constantly invites further progressive mediations.

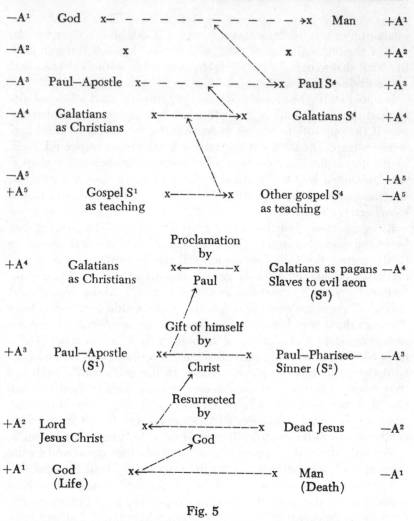

Fig. 5

A glance at this last diagram shows that there is a gap in the symmetrical opposite of the original progressive mediation. The opposition $+A^2/-A^2$ is not actualized: the opposition "Lord Jesus Christ/dead Jesus" and its mediation, according to the theological argument, are lacking. The absence of this opposition with its mediation is expressed in 2:21: "Christ died to no purpose." But this cannot be shown without an exhaustive analysis of the whole letter.

The actualization of the structure by the other gospel defeats the original purpose of the gospel mythical system. The progressive mediation of the fundamental opposition "God/man" is resolved by assigning to man a positive sign and to God a negative sign. Through his hypothetical statements Paul intimates the absurdity of the structure that the Galatians intended to adopt. If Paul would preach this other gospel he would be trying to please men (thus resolving the opposition "God/man" in favor of man) and would not be a servant of Christ (v. 10b). Furthermore, as suggested, the opposition "Lord Jesus Christ/dead Jesus" would be resolved in favor of the dead Jesus. This other gospel is not in fact a gospel (v. 7a).

Then what is S^4? As the diagram shows and as Paul expressed elsewhere (4:9), it is an anti-gospel which disintegrates what the gospel has built. Through the gospel the Galatians were freed from the power of the evil aeon. By accepting the anti-gospel the Galatians forsake their freedom and again become slaves of the evil aeon and of its elemental spirits (4:9).

The opposition S^1/S^4 cannot be assimilated with the oppositions S^1/S^2 and S^1/S^3. It is a radical opposition between gospel and anti-gospel. Gospel and anti-gospel cannot coexist. If the gospel is to be, the anti-gospel must be totally banished. This is what the anathema accomplishes.

The anathema, pronounced against the anti-gospel and its propagators, is the first step taken by Paul to reestablish the integrity of the gospel mythical system. In order to complete this process it is enough that the opposition "Galatians S^1/Galatians S^4" be resolved in favor of "Galatians S^1." In his theological argument Paul proposes himself as mediator. Yet the Galatians will accept him as mediator only if they can acknowledge that the situation in which they presently are (i.e., the situation of having to choose between the gospel and the anti-gospel) is equivalent to their former situation which was characterized by the opposition: "Galatians S^1/Galatians S^3." This is indeed one of the main thrusts of the letter: to convince the Galatians that by accepting the other gospel they have in fact regressed to the situation in which they were before their conversion (4:9). If the Galatians would acknowledge that such is indeed their situation, they would be in a position to receive the grace (and peace) proclaimed by Paul (1:3) as they had done earlier (1:6). For this they would also need to be convinced that Paul is the adequate mediator of the opposition which characterizes their situation. According to the theological argument this would be demonstrated if Paul could show to the Galatians that his own experience is similar to theirs. In other words, Paul needs to convince the Galatians that the opposition "Galatians S^1/Galatians as pagans S³" is equivalent to the opposition "Paul-apostle S¹/Paul as Pharisee S²." This demonstration is indeed an essential part of Paul's argument in the letter (in our text it is expressed in verses 4 and 8).

If, once more, we bracket out the mediating terms proposed in the theological argument, the significance of Paul's letter in terms of the mythical structure appears. If the opposition "Galatians S¹/Galatians as pagans S³" is no longer mediated in such a way that it might be seen as equivalent to the preceding oppositions of the mythical structure, the whole gospel mythical system is threatened.

These remarks suggest one of the ways in which the mythical structure imposes its constraints upon the epistolary-theological argument at the textual surface. On the basis of our analysis of these ten verses we can already draw significant conclusions for the interpretation of the letter as a whole. Paul has to demonstrate the equivalence of four situations. This is accomplished by emphasizing the correlations of their respective terms. These four situations and their correlations can be represented as follows:

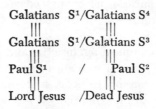

There is no need to emphasize that Paul does express the close correlation of himself and the Galatians. It is a quasi-identification which allows Paul to use the first person plural (e.g., 1:3–4). Similarly Paul identifies himself with Christ (e.g., 2:20), "I have been crucified with Christ; it is no longer I who live, but Christ who lives in me"; see also 3:1, which identifies, in the theological argument, Paul's role as mediator for the Galatians with Christ's crucifixion. Thus in this argument, while speaking of Christ, Paul also speaks of himself, and vice versa. All this has long been recognized by exegetes.

Constraints of the mythical structure also require the following correlations: S⁴ ≡ S³ ≡ S². Thus, according to the structure, Paul should speak of the anti-gospel in terms of the Pharisaic and Hellenistic mythical systems, of the Pharisaic Judaism in terms of the anti-gospel and Hellenistic mythical systems, of the Galatians' former religion in terms of the anti-gospel and Pharisaic mythical systems. Indeed the letter as a whole mixes all three terminologies which, at first reading, is quite confusing. Now, if our structural

analysis is correct, it means that it is illegitimate to draw any conclusions about the specific doctrines of Paul's opponents from the
fact that Paul uses a mixture of Jewish and cosmological terminology
when speaking about the "other gospel." The nature of this "other
gospel" has to be established on different grounds, if at all.

Promise of the Method

The analysis that we proposed has a very limited scope. A complete study of the actualization of the mythical structure in Paul's
gospel would require the analysis of the whole Pauline corpus. We
studied but ten verses! This level of analysis would without any
doubt yield important contributions to the discussion of traditional
exegetical problems. We can foresee that this method will provide
an additional tool to deal with questions both of authorship and of
redaction. When applied to the various New Testament texts, this
method might (and certainly will) reveal quite different actualizations of the mythical structure and thus of several different gospel
mythical systems. In addition, this level of analysis offers new perspectives, which cannot but influence the understanding of the texts
and thus open a number of new hermeneutical possibilities.

Yet this analysis of the mythical structure is also the prelude to the
study of the mythical semantic features and of the cultural codes.
These levels of analysis raise hermeneutical possibilities on an even
wider scale. For instance, an analysis of the mythical semantic
features would permit the specific determination of the respective
places and roles of various elements of the Pharisaic and Hellenistic
mythical systems within the gospel mythical system. This would
require an analysis of the mythical structures of Pharisaism and
Hellenism, since these mythical systems function as bundles of
mythemes. Pharisaic and Hellenistic mythical systems were the
mythical systems to which the early Christians belonged prior to
their conversion. These systems correspond therefore to the mythical system which characterizes our culture (even though it is a
secular culture). Thus a hermeneutic of Paul's letters would, among
other things, ascribe to our modern mythical systems a position in
our faith and life similar to that which the Pharisaic and Hellenistic
mythical systems had in Paul's faith and life. This does not mean
that the Pharisaic and Hellenistic systems should have no role for
us. On the contrary, we can already envision that they would have
a role similar to that which the Pharisaic system had for the
Galatians. These remarks should suffice to suggest the important
hermeneutical possibilities that this method of analysis offers for the
various biblical texts. Yet it is also clear what the scope is of the

task ahead for the exegete. We have taken only the first steps of a long but promising journey.

NARRATIVE AND MYTHICAL STRUCTURES:
THE PARABLE OF THE GOOD SAMARITAN

In our preceding example, dealing with a concise theological text, we have considered a broad actualization of the mythical structure; we were confronted with a fundamental opposition and its resolution through a series of secondary oppositions. As noted above if the same actualization of the mythical structure were to be expressed in a narrative form, it would demand a series of "stories" (cf. the Gospels and the Acts of the Apostles). For indeed, in a single narrative we only find the actualization of a part of the mythical structure. This is why Lévi-Strauss emphasized that "a myth is made up of all its variants," that is, of a series of mythological stories.

A simple narrative (as opposed to a complex narrative which is in fact made up of several narratives) actualizes one opposition (and eventually its mediation). In most instances it is a secondary opposition which is proposed as the metaphoric resolution of a more fundamental opposition which is simply alluded to in the narrative. In studying the actualization of the mythical structure in a narrative we are dealing with a very limited number of "broad mythemes" (or "bundles of mythemes") and are consequently in a position to analyze them more specifically than in a theological text. We can therefore study the semantic features which are selected by the mythical structure. By the very fact that an opposition—e.g., agriculture vs. warfare in Lévi-Strauss' example of the Zuni myth— admits a mediating term—hunting—the mythical structure selects two semantic features (or semes) as the only pertinent ones (i.e., as the only ones which participate in the meaning effect) for each of the terms of the opposition. The mediating terms perform their mediating role because (and only because) they have one semantic feature in common with each of the two poles of the opposition they mediate. "Killing"[21] is the semantic feature common to both "warfare" and "hunting"; "food" is the semantic feature common to both "agriculture" and "hunting." (Note that "killing" is a *function*—an action—and "food" a *state*—a thing.) In the second pair of oppositions the term "hunting" has the same pertinent semantic features ("killing" and "food") even though it is now symbolized by "predator." Since any pole of any opposition can potentially be the mediating term of another opposition, any term has two pertinent semantic features: a function and a state. We can now represent

21. The following interpretation of the Zuni myth is our own.

more abstractly the opposition "warfare/hunting/agriculture" in the following algebraic-like formulation in which "x" and "y" represent functions and "a" and "b" states.

$F_y(b)$ Agriculture
$F_x(b)$ Hunting
$F_x(a)$ Warfare

On the basis of the preceding remarks we can say that the semantic features "x" and "b" are respectively "killing" and "food."

As Lévi-Strauss has shown, the mythical structure also imposes very specific constraints upon the relation of two oppositions. As we have seen, one of the poles (hunting) of the second pair of oppositions is made out of the semantic features of the preceding opposition since this pole, $F_x(b)$, is also the mediating term of the preceding opposition. What about the polar opposite of $F_x(b)$? If the predator is $F_x(b)$, what is the formula for the herbivore in this myth? Lévi-Strauss has shown that it is also defined by the semantic features found in the preceding opposition. In order to understand this we need to analyze further the Zuni myth and determine tentatively the semantic features represented by "y" and "a".[22]

Warfare is killing enemies. Thus "a" is "enemies" (a state). Agriculture is "gathering" food. Thus "y" is "gathering" (a function). What is an herbivore? It is primarily an animal which can be "gathered" as food. In other words, the *function* "y" ("gathering") is present in the herbivore as a *state* "y" ("gathered"). An herbivore is also a friendly animal, an animal which neither attacks man nor acts as an enemy. Thus the *state* "a" ("enemies") is also present in the herbivore as a *function* in a *negative* form ("ā"). Hence the herbivore can be represented as $F_{\bar{a}}(y)$. This formulation of the second pole of the second pair of oppositions was found by Lévi-Strauss to be a constant and not a variable. Thus he could formulate the relation of two pairs of consecutive oppositions in the mythical structure as follows:

$$F_x(a) : F_y(b) : : F_x(b) : F_{\bar{a}}(y)$$

This formula can be read: $F_x(a)$ is to $F_y(b)$ as $F_x(b)$ is to $F_{\bar{a}}(y)$; or in terms of the Zuni myth, warfare is to agriculture as predators are to herbivores.

The mythical structure and the narrative structure filter the

22. The following remarks are intended as an illustration rather than a rigorous analysis. The very complexity of the Zuni myth in its various versions would demand an extensive treatment which cannot be presented within the limits of this work. It should be noted that Lévi-Strauss proposes this formula in order to express the relation between two formulations (two stories) of the same myth (e.g., the Zuni myth). Our interpretation of Lévi-Strauss' formula is justified by the fact that, as discussed below, each story manifests only *one* pair of oppositions.

semantic features in two quite different ways. While the narrative
structure selects the semantic features which produce a meaningful
narrative process, the mythical structure selects those which produce
a meaningful *system of reference* or, in traditional cultures, a meaningful *religious system*. Nevertheless they do not function independently of each other, as is demonstrated by the fact that myths
are also narratives. We can envision their interrelation as the inter-
section of the mythic and narrative planes. It appears that the
personages of the narrative which are defined by their actantial
positions and their narrative functions in various sequences also
function as terms in the mythic oppositions. A given narrative
usually defines only one mythical opposition and its mediation and
merely alludes to the preceding opposition which it mediates.[23]

What are the narrative elements which could be viewed as the
opposing terms of the mythical structure? Some have proposed that
they are the contents of the two correlated sequences—the situation
of lack and the situation of non-lack—the mediating term being the
content of the topical sequence.[24] This *cannot* be the case, for it in
effect reduces the mythical structure to the narrative structure and
thereby confuses two logically distinct categories. The oppositions
of the mythical structure are oppositions of *contraries* comparable
to the opposition "life vs. death" (or "God vs. man"). The opposition "lack vs. non-lack" would be comparable to the opposiiton "life
vs. non-life" (an opposition of *contradictories*).[25] I would like to
propose that the *situation of lack* which is indeed an essential semantic unit in the narrative should rather be opposed to the *semantic
value of the hero*, that is, the subject of the topical sequence as
defined by his relation to the other actantial positions (especially
that of helper) and the functions he performs. The situation of
non-lack (lack overcome) is the mediating term. Further, the hero
appears to function as the mediating term of the preceding opposition. Thus the hero is the pole $F_x(b)$, and the situation of lack the
pole $F_{\bar{a}}(y)$. (I believe this to be a constant, that is, a part of the
deep structure which governs the relationship between mythical and
narrative structures. This part of the structural model is being
verified by the analysis of as many texts as possible.)

23. This is why a series of narrative-mythological texts is needed in order to
invest significantly the mythical structure and the analyst needs to consider
all the variants of each myth. Cf. Lévi-Strauss, *Structural Anthropology*, pp.
213–15.

24. Cf. Louis Marin, *Sémiotique de la Passion* (Paris: Aubier Montaigne and
Cerf, 1971), Ch. I.

25. For a discussion of the difference between contraries and contradictories
see A.-J. Greimas and F. Rastier, "The Interaction of Semiotic Constraints,"
Yale French Studies 41 (1969), 86–105.

We have therefore the following manifestation of the mythical structure in the parable of the Good Samaritan:

$$F_y(b)$$
?

$$F_{\bar{a}}(y)$$
wounded man

healed man

$$F_x(b)$$
Samaritan

$$F_x(b)$$
Samaritan

$$F_x(a)$$
?

What is the opposition $F_x(a)$ vs. $F_y(b)$? I suggested that the narrative *alludes* to it because there does not seem to be any rule pre-selecting narrative elements for these terms. However, by an analysis of the semantic value of "Samaritan" and "wounded man" as defined by the narrative as a whole (and *not* as defined by the cultural codes), we should be able to identify the semantic features represented by "x", "y", "a", and "b" and then to identify $F_x(a)$ and $F_y(b)$. In so doing we are no longer dealing with complex semantic units (the polar oppositions) but with mythical semantic features. We can now consider the oppositions among the semantic features, that is, the oppositions x vs. y, a vs. b.

Let us first consider the semantic value of the function x (i.e., the function of the term "Samaritan"). X represents a "bundle of functions" (in the same way that $F_x(b)$ represents a bundle of mythemes). We find that the Samaritan is compassionate; he approaches a wounded person, he helps, he gives money (to the innkeeper). The opposite attitude (y) is clearly manifested in the text: there are people without feeling (robbers, priest, and Levite) who leave, abandon, pass by without being compassionate, without approaching the wounded man, without helping him. There are also people who take violently and rob: the robbers. Their antisocial actions are contraries to giving money, a socially correct action (being honest). The functions of the robbers (the SUBJECTS of the sub-sequence villainy) alone are in complete opposition to that of the Samaritan. Thus we can list the values of semantic features x and y.

x	y
(Samaritan's function)	(robbers' function)
being compassionate	being without feeling
approaching a person	leaving, abandoning
helping	passing by
giving money	using violence
being honest	taking, robbing

Our identification of the semantic features for the function y can be verified by considering the broad mytheme $F_{\bar{a}}(y)$ which is manifested in our text by the wounded man. The state y (the result of the action y) is the result of violence, the state of being wounded, deprived of one's belongings and abandoned. This is in full agreement with the characteristics of the function y listed above.

We can note also that the priest and the Levite (non-heroes, that is, people who refused to be hero) are characterized by some of the semantic features of the function y (the robbers' function): they abandon the wounded man and are without compassion. Yet they are not violent and they do not rob. We shall see how this aspect of the text contributes to the meaning effect. We must also emphasize that this observation suggests that the functions x and y (and also the states a and b) are not elementary semantic units: they can be sub-divided into semantic features which are organized by another deep structure: the elementary deep structure. We cannot in the limits of this short book discuss the elementary structure and show how an analysis in terms of the elementary structure can be used as a verification of the results of the analysis at the levels of the narrative and mythical structures.[26]

Considering now the states, we should begin with b which characterizes the Samaritan (as hero, $F_x(b)$) and which should also characterize the robbers (if the robbers are $F_y(b)$ as our analysis of the functions suggests). But what have the Samaritan and the robbers in common in the text? The state a (the direct opposite of b) is present in a negative form ($\bar{a}$, "non a") as a function in $F_{\bar{a}}(y)$ (the wounded man). Note that the negative form of a, i.e., $\bar{a}$ belongs with b as opposite of a. The distinction between $\bar{a}$ and b is needed at the level of the elementary structure. What is the function of the wounded man? If we could know that we would have at least one element of the value of the state b. The only clue the text gives us is that he is on the road side, in the ditch. What could be b as a state? "Not being on the road"? What then could be a? "Being on the road"? Looking at the text more closely, we discover that it expresses the direction in which the man, the priest, and the Levite are going. The man was "going down from Jerusalem to Jericho"; the priest "was going down that road." Of the Levite it is said, "So likewise a Levite, when he came to the place," implying

26. On the elementary structure see Daniel Patte, "Structural Network in Narrative," *Soundings* (June 1975), and in *Structuralism: an Interdisciplinary Survey*, Susan Wittig, ed.. (Pittsburgh: The Pickwick Press, 1975); and A.-J. Greimas and F. Rastier "The Interaction of Semiotic Constraints," *Yale French Studies* 41 (1969), 86–105.

a directed travel, in terms of ordered space. By contrast, the Samaritan is "journeying": the verb does not suggest any direction. We do not know which way he is going; his journey is not spatially ordered. The same is true of the robbers: we do not know from which direction they have come or where they are going.

This is all that is manifested in the narrative about the states. This should not surprise us: a narrative primarily describes processes and functions, while the states are qualifications, sometimes expressed in descriptions. The narrative structure does not emphasize the states clearly enough and the mythical structure is no help in the analysis at this point. We shall have to call upon other structural levels, the cultural codes.

a	b
(state of people who are characterized as having)	(state of Samaritan and robbers who are characterized as having)
directed travel	non-directed travel
ordered space	non-ordered space

In order to complete this analysis and to reconstruct the religious meaning effect of this parable we need now to call upon the cultural codes (here, the social and religious codes which ascribe specific values in the Palestinian Jewish culture to various personages). We can use here results of the traditional historical research which provides us with a complex description of the semantic value of Samaritan, priest, Levite, robbers, Jerusalem, Jericho, etc. Yet because of our awareness of the filtering process of the deep structures we can easily identify the pertinent semantic features which were used to produce the meaning effect of the parable.

What is "b"? What state is common to a robber and a Samaritan? They are both rejected by religious people: a robber was irreligious —or better—a-religious; in mythological terms, he was a symbol of chaos. A Samaritan was a heretic, but he was also a symbol of chaos for the Jews of that time, because Samaritans had profaned the temple in Jerusalem. That these are indeed the semantic features which manifest b is confirmed by the fact that in mythological terms "chaos" (b) implies a non-ordered world and thus non-directed travel. (The inn also appears as a figure of this non-ordered world.)

By contrast "a" expresses the directed travel of the man, priest, and Levite. According to the cultural codes the priest and Levite are clearly religious personages. Thus "a" also has the value "religious," or, in mythological terms, non-chaotic. The deep structure suggests that the man is also a religious Jew. Among the many potential semantic features that the word "Jerusalem" could have according to the cultural codes only two are retained: Jerusalem as geographical location which orients travel (as Jericho does) and Jerusalem as symbol of "religion" or more specifically of the Jewish religion.

We can now go back to the broader mythical structure. What is the semantic value of the broad mytheme $F_x(a)$? The characteristics of x and of a are not manifested in any single personage of the text even though the personages of the priest and Levite have some of their semantic features. $F_x(a)$ is therefore an ideal, a truly Jewish religious person. From what we know about Jesus' teaching we could dare to say that the term represents a person who belongs to the kingdom. The mythical structure reads now:

robbers

wounded man
Samaritan

ideal religious
person

That is: the truly religious person is to the robbers as the Samaritan is to the wounded man. The Samaritan is symbolically identified with the truly religious person in the same way that the wounded man is symbolically identified with the robbers (irreligious people).

The Samaritan is symbolically identified with the truly religious person because he provides a valid mediation between the man and the robbers (chaos). The priest and Levite fail to provide such a mediation—even though according to the cultural codes they would be expected to do so. The semantic difference is clear: the Samaritan *acts* as the truly religious person would (the semantic value x) and has the same *state* as the robbers (b: he is in a chaotic, non-ordered world) and therefore does not have the privileged *state* that the truly religious man has (a: a religiously ordered world, ideally, a state like paradise). By contrast the priest and Levite have the *state* of the truly religious person (a) and *act* partly as the robbers do.[27]

The semantic effect of the parable deeply challenges the traditionally religious: as long as they do not venture outside of their religiously ordered world and become irreligious, they cannot be symbolically identified with the truly religious person—they do not belong to the kingdom—and consequently they cannot act as a truly

27. The structuralist method of analysis presented here is explained in detail in my essay, "Structural Analysis and the Parable of the Prodigal Son: Towards a Method," in *Semiology and Parables*, D. Patte, ed., (Pittsburgh: Pickwick Press, 1976).

religious person. As long as they remain priest and Levite (and Jew) they cannot help the wounded man in the ditch. This text does not propose an example which the reader could directly and readily duplicate in his own life. It is not a matter of *acting* as the Samaritan did, but of *becoming* like the Samaritan. Thus, the analysis excludes the possibility that this text is an example story, as many interpreters have proposed.[28] This misinterpretation began with Luke himself: according to him, Jesus exhorted the lawyer to "go and do likewise" (Luke 10:37). Because of the cultural gap which separated the Hellenistic Luke from the Palestinian Jesus, the challenging character of the parable was dismissed: the parable became an example story. A structural analysis of Luke 10:25–37 (i.e., Luke's story of the dialogue between Jesus and a lawyer) would allow us to apprehend the meaning effect of Luke's text, as opposed to Jesus' parable.

If, then, the story of the Good Samaritan is not an example story, but a parable, a metaphor of the kingdom, what was its meaning? And what is its meaning for us? In other words, what are the hermeneutical consequences of our analysis? The only possible answer in the context of the use of Scripture exemplified in the New Testament is that the parable was proposed as a paradigm for discovering the "signs of the kingdom." When one can discover, in the concrete situation in which he lives, a "good Samaritan," one is in the presence of a manifestation of the mysterious kingly activity of God. Yet this identification of the "good Samaritans" must be performed and verified with great care. There are many people performing good deeds who are not "Samaritans" (indeed, the "priests" and "Levites" certainly perform good deeds). In order to fulfill the paradigm of the parable, the "new story" must present a similar actualization of the narrative and mythical structures.

These last remarks are intended as mere suggestions of the promising exegetical and hermeneutical results we can expect from structural analyses of the Bible.

---

28. Among the recent studies which interpret the parable of the Good Samaritan as an example story see Dan O. Via, *The Parables,* (Philadelphia: Fortress Press, 1967), p. 12; Dan O. Via, "Parable and Example Story: A Literary-Structuralist Approach," *Semeia* 1 (1974), 105–133. Rudolf Bultmann, *The History of the Synoptic Tradition* (New York: Harper and Row, 1963), pp. 177–78. (German original 1938).

Conclusion

Our first chapter expressed why, in our view, structural methods are needed among the exegetical methods if we want to carry out the exegetical task to its end, hermeneutic. In so doing we emphasized that structural methods should be viewed as complementing the traditional historico-critical method. The rest of the book provided a first introduction to structural methodology and specific structural methods. Far from claiming that this methodology and these methods are the only valid ones, we would like to emphasize that they must themselves be complemented by other structural methodologies and methods.

The methodology presented above is derived from a linguistic theory: it is presupposed that any cultural phenomenon (and therefore the biblical text) is in the last analysis part of a phenomenon of communication. According to this methodology the analyst first conceives, on the basis of a linguistic model, theoretical models of the structures he wishes to study, then transforms them (more or less radically) and revises them when applying them to texts. This approach involves the danger that the analyst might project upon the text structures which are not at work within it. Yet this danger is greatly alleviated by the fact that the analyst can benefit from the successive refinements of the models brought about by the analyses of other texts. In the case of the deep structures, the analysis of any text from any culture contributes to the refinement of the models which are intended as representations of universal structures.

It is in this way that the models for the narrative and mythical structures presented above have been progressively elaborated. Although they certainly still need refinement, they have been verified by so many scholars on so many texts that they can now be considered as "operational." The models for other deep structures as well as those for the cultural structures and for the structures of the enunciation still need to be established.

Another structural methodological approach is used by many analysts. Each text is analyzed on its own merits so as to discover the constraints, or structures, which contribute to the production of its meaning effect. No model is consciously presupposed by the analyst. In such a case the analyst is led to emphasize the constraints closest to the surface of the text, i.e., the structures of the enunciation and the cultural structures. Without this type of analysis models for the various structures could never be established. They should indeed be multiplied in order to identify the cultural codes and the structures of the enunciation which characterize each biblical text.

We believe that these two structural methodological approaches should be combined in more comprehensive structural analyses. Using the first approach, our models for a few deep structures can be used in order to identify what are the elements of the meaning effect of the text which are produced by these deep structures. In a second stage of the analysis, the second approach could then be used in order to identify the other constraints which contribute to the production of the *other elements* of the meaning effect. We can expect that these other constraints include other deep structures, cultural structures, and structures of the enunciation.

This twofold structural methodology can then be combined with the traditional historico-critical methodology. As noted above, the traditional exegetical methods are used for the study of the enunciation and of the cultural codes (what the author meant to say and his situation in life). The results of traditional exegesis and of structural analysis can then be brought to bear on each other.

The metaphor of the filtering process can help us represent the relationship between the two methodologies. Each structure can be viewed as making a partial selection of the semantic features which participate in the meaning effect of the text. The results of the various structural analyses identify a set of semantic features which are pertinent and also a set of semantic features which are excluded from the meaning effect. The results of traditional exegesis have the same function. If only one kind of result is taken into account the text remains quite ambiguous: the meaning effect is "blurred." But if both kinds of results are included in a comprehensive exegesis most of the ambiguity will be overcome: the meaning effect will be much sharper. The only remaining ambiguity will be that which pertains to the historical gap that separates us from this text and precludes our having a complete knowledge of the cultural codes and of the situation of the enunciation.

Annotated Bibliography

This selected bibliography is designed as a guide for the first steps of the student in the field of structural research beyond this book, which has aimed merely at providing a general understanding of the need for structural exegesis (and of its linguistic paradigm) and a first introduction to two specific structural methods. This bibliography is deliberately limited to a few works in which more complete bibliographies can be found; moreover, the material in languages other than English has been kept to a minimum.

The Linguistic Paradigm

BARTHES, ROLAND. *Writing Degree Zero and Elements of Semiology*. Boston: Beacon, 1970. The second part, *Elements of Semiology* (pp. 89–107), presents the essential transition from linguistics to semiology.

DUCROT, OSWALD, and TODOROV, TZVETAN. *Dictionnaire encyclopédique des sciences du langage*. Paris: Seuil, 1972. This encyclopedia contains essays on each of the various structural linguistic theories, and excellent bibliographies.

HJELMSLEV, LOUIS. *Prolegomena to a Theory of Language*. Madison: University of Wisconsin Press, 1961. This short book presents the linguistic theory briefly discussed above in chapter II.

DE SAUSSURE, FERDINAND. *Course in General Linguistics*. New York: McGraw-Hill, 1966. This pioneer work in the field remains essential.

Structuralism in Literature

CALLOUD, JEAN. *L'analyse structurale du récit. Tentation de Jésus au désert*. Lyon: Profac, 1973. English translation by Daniel Patte, *Structural Analysis of Narrative. Temptation of Jesus in the Wilderness*, forthcoming. A necessary introduction to Greimas' method for the structural analysis of narrative by one of his pupils. This exegetical essay shows how one can proceed in such an analysis.

GREIMAS, ALGIRDAS JULIEN. *Sémantique structurale*. Paris: Larousse, 1966.

―――. *Du Sens*. Paris: Seuil, 1970.
The two books listed above are Greimas' basic works. An English translation by M. Rengstorf is in preparation. Three essays have already been translated.

―――. "The Interaction of Semiotic Constraints." *Yale French Studies* 41 (1969), 86–105.

―――. "The Interpretation of Myth: Theory and Practice." In *Structural Analysis of Oral Tradition*, edited by Pierre Maranda and E. Köngäs Maranda. Philadelphia: Universiy of Pennsylvania Press, 1971.

―――. "Narrative Grammar: Units and Levels," *Modern Language Notes* 86 (1971), 793–806.

PATTE, DANIEL. "An Analysis of Narrative Structure and the Good Samaritan." *Semeia* 2, 1–26. A concise theoretical presentation and a complete analysis of the parable of the Good Samaritan in terms of the narrative structure.

PROPP, VLADIMIR. *Morphology of the Folktale*. Austin: University of Texas Press, 1968. This pioneer work is essential for an understanding of Greimas' work.

———. "Transformations in Fairy Tales." In *Mythology: Selected Readings*, edited by Pierre Maranda, pp. 139–150. Baltimore: Penguin, 1972.

SCHOLES, ROBERT. *Structuralism in Literature: An Introduction.* New Haven: Yale University Press, 1974. A more theoretical presentation of various structural methods used for the study of literature. Its panoramic presentation of various methods is particularly helpful, but cannot go further than general methodological observations. Excellent bibliography.

Further readings should include the works of Roland Barthes, Claude Brémond, Tzvetan Todorov, Claude Chabrol, and Louis Marin. These authors' research presents approaches and theories which are essential for a critical reading of Greimas' work.

Structuralism and the Study of Myth

LÉVI-STRAUSS, CLAUDE. *Structural Anthropology.* Garden City, New York: Basic Books, 1963. This work includes the basic essay "The Structural Study of Myth" (pp. 202–31).

———. "Four Winnebago Myths: A Structural Sketch." In *Culture in History*, edited by Stanley Diamond. New York: Columbia University Press, 1960. An excellent example of the structural treatment of myths. Should be studied before reading the four volumes of the series *Mythologiques* (republished by Columbia University Press in 1964 as *Primitive Views of the World*, edited by Stanley Diamond).

———. *The Raw and the Cooked.* New York: Harper and Row, 1969.

———. *The Savage Mind.* Chicago: University of Chicago Press, 1966. A theoretical book which contains important statements about the relationship of the mythical way of thinking and the modern way of thinking. Its philosophical presuppositions have been much debated.

Further readings should include the works of A. Dundes, W. O. Hendricks, H. Jason, E. Köngäs Maranda, and Pierre Maranda. These authors' research presents approaches and theories which are essential for a critical reading of Lévi-Strauss' work.

Structuralism and New Testament Studies

Structural exegesis was first developed by French scholars. We list here a few important books and special issues of journals.

BOVON, FRANCOIS, ed. *Structural Analysis and Biblical Exegesis*, trans. by A. M. Johnson. Pittsburgh: Pickwick, 1974.

CHABROL, CLAUDE, and MARIN, LOUIS. *Sémiotique narrative: récits bibliques.* Paris: Didier/Larousse, 1971.

Etudes Théologiques et Religieuses, January 1973.

Foi et Vie, June 1974.

LEON-DUFOUR, XAVIER, ed. *Exégèse et herméneutique.* Paris: Seuil, 1971.

MARIN, LOUIS. *Sémiotique de la passion: Topiques et figures.* Paris: Aubier, Cerf, Delachaux et Niestlé, and Desclée de Brouwer, 1971.

In German we mention the journal *Linguistica Biblica* and the works of Erhardt Güttgemanns.

GÜTTGEMANS, ERHARDT. *Offene Fragen zur Formgeschichte des Evangeliums.* Munich: Kaiser, 1970.

———. *Studia Linguistica Neotestamentica.* Munich: Kaiser, 1971.

In English see:

DOTY, WILLIAM G. "Fundamental Questions about Literary-Critical Methodology: A Review Article." *Journal of the American Academy of Religion* 40 (1972), 521–27.

———. "Linguistics and Biblical Criticism." *Journal of the American Academy of Religion* 41 (1973), 114–21.

LAPOINTE, ROGER. "The New Status of Language." *Catholic Biblical Quarterly* 36 (1974), 233–36.

These three English essays deal in their own ways with the questions raised in chapter I. The following essays are New Testament studies which make use of various structural methods.

BUCHER, GLENN R. "Elements for an Analysis of the Gospel Text: The Death of Jesus." *Modern Language Notes* 86 (1971), 835–44.

CROSSAN, JOHN DOMINIC. "Structural Analysis and the Parables of Jesus." *Linguistica Biblica* 29/30 (1973), 41–51.

CULLEY, ROBERT. "Structural Analysis: Is it Done with Mirrors?" *Interpretation* 28 (1974), 165–81.

JACOBSON, RICHARD. "The Structuralists and the Bible." *Interpretation* 28 (1974), 146–64.

PATTE, DANIEL, ed. *Semiology and Parables.* Pittsburgh Monograph Series. Pittsburgh: Pickwick Press, 1975. The proceedings of a conference held at Vanderbilt University in May, 1975. Includes papers by John Dominic Crossan, Louis Marin, Daniel Patte, Dan O. Via, and Susan Wittig. Responses and discussions.

POLZIN, ROBERT. "The Framework of the Book of Job." *Interpretation* 28 (1974), 182–200.

Semeia: An Experimental Journal for Biblical Criticism. This journal, sponsored by the Society of Biblical Literature, is "devoted to the exploration of new and emergent areas and methods of biblical criticism," among which are structural methods. All of the articles in this journal could be listed here. Volume 1 (1974) contains *A Basic Bibliography for Parables Research,* prepared by John Dominic Crossan, which includes a basic bibliography on structuralism (pp. 256–74).

STAROBINSKI, JEAN. "The Struggle with Legion: A Literary Analysis of Mark 5:1–20." Translated by Dan O. Via in *New Literary History* 4 (1973), 331–56.

SPIVEY, ROBERT A. "Structuralism and Biblical Studies. The Uninvited Guest." *Interpretation* 28 (1974), 133–45.

VIA, DAN O. *Kerygma and Comedy in the New Testament: A Structuralist Approach to Hermeneutic.* Philadelphia: Fortress Press, 1975.

————. "Parable and Example Story: A Literary-Structuralist Approach." *Linguistica Biblica* 25/26 (1973), 21–30.

————. "A Structural Approach to Paul's Old Testament Hermeneutic." *Interpretation* 28 (1974), 201–20.

WITTIG, SUSAN, ed. *Structuralism: An Interdisciplinary Survey.* Pittsburgh: Pickwick Press, 1975. A reprint of *Soundings* vol. LVIII, Summer 1975.

Index / Glossary of Technical Terms

A large part of this book is devoted to the explanation of the technical terminology used by structuralist scholars in their description of the various elements of the structural network. For each term we only refer to the passage of the above text in which the term is defined. Brief parenthetical comments suggest the interrelation of the various terms. ("vs.": read here "as opposed to").

641 4